THE CHRISTIAN SCIENCE MONITOR®

Chronicle of the Soviet Coup 1990 - 1992

A Reader in Soviet Politics

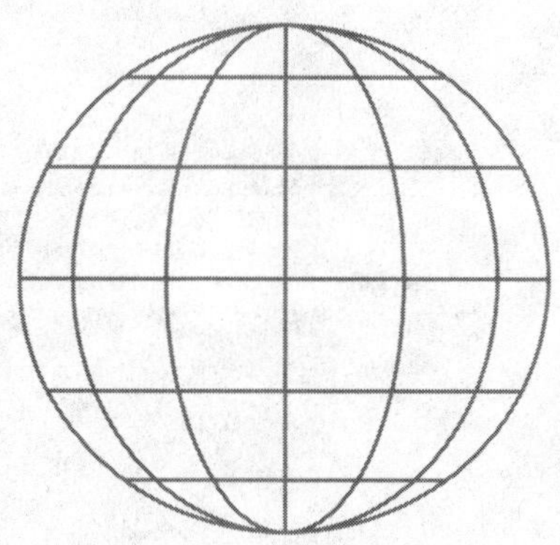

WCB Brown & Benchmark Publishers

Madison, Wisconsin • Dubuque, Iowa • Indianapolis, Indiana
Melbourne, Australia • Oxford, England

Book Team

Editor *Edgar J. Laube*
Developmental Editor *Roger B. Wolkoff*
Production Editor *Ann Fuerste*
Visuals/Design Developmental Consultant *Marilyn A. Phelps*

WCB Brown & Benchmark

A Division of Wm. C. Brown Communications, Inc.

Vice President and General Manager *Thomas E. Doran*
Executive Managing Editor *Ed Bartell*
Executive Editor *Edgar J. Laube*
Director of Marketing *Kathy Law Laube*
National Sales Manager *Eric Ziegler*
Marketing Manager *Carla J. Aspelmeier*
Advertising Manager *Jodi Rymer*
Managing Editor, Production *Colleen A. Yonda*
Manager of Visuals and Design *Faye M. Schilling*
Design Manager *Jac Tilton*
Art Manager *Janice Roerig*
Production Editorial Manager *Vickie Putman Caughron*
Publishing Services Manager *Karen J. Slaght*
Permissions/Records Manager *Connie Allendorf*

Wm. C. Brown Communications, Inc.

Chairman Emeritus *Wm. C. Brown*
Chairman and Chief Executive Officer *Mark C. Falb*
President and Chief Operating Officer *G. Franklin Lewis*
Corporate Vice President, Operations *Beverly Kolz*
Corporate Vice President, President of WCB Manufacturing *Roger Meyer*

Cover design by John R. Rokusek

Library of Congress Catalog Card Number: 92-54394

ISBN 0-697-17434-4

Printed in the United States of America by Wm. C. Brown Communications, Inc., 2460 Kerper Boulevard, Dubuque, IA 52001

10 9 8 7 6 5 4 3 2 1

Contents

Section III:
Post Coup Events 201

Preface

During the fall of 1989 as the iron curtain came tumbling down, it was evident to most of us in the West that a vast change was occurring in the world order. Was it possible that Communism, in place in the Soviet Union since the Bolshevik Revolution of 1917, had failed? Was it likely that a form of democracy might replace the old regime? As we exchanged pieces of the Berlin Wall and caviar as Christmas gifts that year, many of us were filled with a sense of hope (if not euphoria) that political freedoms, private ownership, peace, and Western-style independence had won.

A closer look at the day-to-day events in the USSR, however, revealed problems the Soviets would need to address as they moved toward what Mikhail Gorbachev called "humane democratic socialism." Some of these problems were: the need to find new (or revise old) forms of government, ethnic strife and political unrest, shortages of commodities, the disaffection of Soviet workers, other economic imbalances, and a general sense of uncertainty.

In February of 1990 the Soviets took the first steps toward ending Communism as a political monopoly when the Communist Party Central Committee embraced multiparty politics. Right-wing politicians believed these reforms were too progressive. As part of the established Soviet government, they feared losing jobs and power. For more liberal political groups in the republics, this idea had popular appeal. It paved the way toward nationalism and independence.

Had Gorbachev painted himself into a corner? There was incongruity in his position. He needed to adopt reform measures, such as popular elections, to address social unrest. But the same reform measures had the potential to weaken the Communist government and cost him his job. To retain his position, he became dependent upon popular support as well as a large base of support within the Communist party.

On March 11, 1990, the Republic of Lithuania declared independence from the Soviet Union. To curb this move toward independence, Gorbachev imposed economic sanctions preventing the flow of oil, natural gas, and other commodities to Lithuania, and sent Soviet troops to the region. Two other Baltic States, Latvia and Estonia, followed Lithuania in moves toward independence.

The USSR has a history marked by bloodshed, strife, and many civil wars. Soviet-watchers looked on closely. Would the era of new freedoms end in violence? During earlier years Gorbachev had appeared to be a world-class statesman, doing the unthinkable, transforming the USSR to a new openness. Now many were terrified that his efforts would be lost in a repressive backlash.

The opening of the first McDonald's restaurant in Pushkin Square in February of 1990 provided vivid examples of alternating economic hope and disarray. McDonald's planned to open no less than twenty restaurants in the Soviet Union that year. This signaled the beginning of foreign investment in Soviet capital and labor. Yet 27,000 people applied for 605 jobs at the Pushkin Square restaurant, and in the process of building, McDonald's Corporation repeatedly had difficulties acquiring raw materials from the Soviet Ministries.

Although Western economists believe that capitalism is superior to communism as a means of creating and exchanging goods and services, no prototype existed for converting a centrally planned communist economy to a market system. In summer of 1990, because the Soviet economy was rapidly deteriorating, Boris Yeltsin (President of the Russian Republic), and Mikhail Gorbachev assembled a team of economists to create an economic blueprint for the country. The result was a 500-Day plan, designed to convert the Soviet economy from a centrally planned to a market system.

The 500-Day plan included private ownership of property, taxing powers for local republics, and the public sale of stocks in businesses and factories. The plan also proposed measures that would strengthen the Soviet currency and banking system.

By December of 1990 it was clear that the new blueprint for progress would not spare the Soviets a difficult winter. The fact that the central economy had a defective distribution system meant that sufficient farm crops did not reach the stores. The Soviets were dependent on imports from the Baltic States, but these republics were witholding goods from the market because of Soviet sanctions against them. Cooperation between party bosses and Soviet workers waned. Even though Western countries were willing to send food supplies to the new Federation of Soviet Republics (which replaced the USSR), there was no guarantee the food would reach its destination.

Gorbachev seemed to be dragging his feet, failing to implement significant portions of the 500-day plan. As Soviet historian Yuri Afanasyev said about Gorbachev, "the promoter of perestroikia has become its grave digger."

Boris Yeltsin, President of the Russian Republic (where half of the Soviet population resides) favored reforms far more progressive than those proposed by Gorbachev. In a show of support for Yeltsin and his policies, Soviet workers rallied in the streets of Moscow. In April of 1991 Gorbachev banned such rallies. This was a turnabout for a man who had encouraged workers to demonstrate for economic reform two years earlier. Gorbachev suffered a major setback when the Soviet Parliament failed to support his position of forbidding street demonstrations. His popularity within government and with the Soviet people was ebbing.

The stage was set for change, but none could have foreseen the dramatic events of August 19, 1991. Opposing the direction of the New liberal Soviets, the Soviet hardliners—members of the Old Guard—staged a coup. Forming an eight-man junta, they attempted a military takeover with the intent of arresting democratically elected reformers. This revolutionary group arranged to have Gorbachev detained at his home in the Crimea. Momentarily it seemed like our worst fears were realized, that government would be returned to oppressive powers, backed by the military. However, the August Revolution was so poorly planned that one major American news journalist called the junta the "Keystone Komisars." Due to lack of military planning, and massive resistance by the people, the coup lasted less than seventy-two hours.

The timing of the Revolution was no accident. It came twenty-four hours before the planned signing of a treaty between Gorbachev, Yeltsin, and the republics. The treaty was designed to give nine of the fifteen republics the status of sovereign states. Through this agreement, republics were to gain broad new powers over taxes, natural resources, and elections.

One major result of the coup was the strengthening of the role of Boris N.Yeltsin. Elected President of the Russian Republic by a sixty-percent majority, Yeltsin occupied the Russian parliament during the three-day ordeal, and rallied popular support. Hoards of people gathered outside of the Parliament building and formed a massive blockade against the military. Some of the members of the military joined the masses.

The coup also strengthened the claims for independence in the Baltic states, and seriously weakened the Communist party. Eventually the Communist government would dissolve, leaving Gorbachev without a position.

One uncertainty that remained was who would control nuclear weapons. Former Soviets and Western governments alike were optimistic that the end of the cold war would bring an end to the world's military buildup and result in a welcome "peace dividend." Now, concern for nuclear arms revolves around how the new Republics will govern the use of nuclear power.

With the collapse of the Soviet Union, the new democratic leaders were challenged to fill the void. The old "Soviet" union was replaced with a loose federation of republics called The Commonwealth of Independent States, each with broad powers.

The Revolution also left economic trauma in its wake. The Russian government printed money to cover its mounting debts, which resulted in inflation. People began to hoard commodities. Shortages and distribution problems continued. Yeltsin addressed this problem with a Russia first policy. He began to make moves toward privatizing the Russian economy, hoping that by using a Russia first model, other Republics might follow the lead.

In this book you will find a series of readings covering slightly more than two years of history that indeed changed the world. Readings are grouped into three sections: events that preceded the coup, events that took place during the three-day August Revolution, and post Revolution activities of the Commonwealth countries.

I
Events That Preceded the August Coup

Mikhail Gorbachev, President of the USSR, seemed to the world a political genius during the years of glasnost and perestroika. Gorbachev used his keen ability to compromise to lead two significantly diverse interest groups in the Soviet world. These factions were the new liberal-thinking reformers and the Communist Old Guard.

Events that precede the August 1991 coup in the USSR demonstrate an ever-widening gap between these two groups. For example, when the Baltics asserted their independence, the liberal group backed the movement and the Old Guard encouraged Gorbachev to stem it with military force.

As another example, during the implementation phase of a 500-day plan developed to save the Soviet economy, the liberal faction encouraged Boris Yeltsin to follow the most progressive parts of the plan, whereas Gorbachev was encouraged by the Old Guard to hold back on plans to allow private property and more independence of the republics.

The readings in this section demonstrate the push-pull between these two groups and provide a background for understanding the Revolution.

Gorbachev's Baltic Visit Fails to Curb Threat to National Cohesion

Linda Feldmann

1/16/90

In his five years in power, Mikhail Gorbachev has never faced a greater challenge to the cohesion of the Soviet Union.

The Baltic republic of Lithuania, unconvinced by the Soviet leader's unprecedented three-day visit there last week, is bent on restoring its independence as a nation.

One member of the Lithuanian Communist Party's Central Committee, who asked not to be identified, said it was possible the republic would declare independence on July 12 of this year the 70th anniversary of Lenin's recognition of Lithuanian independence.

To the south, in Azerbaijan and Armenia, the Soviet news media describe a situation they say verges on outright civil war. Rioting over the weekend reportedly left dozens dead.

Suran Arutyunyan, the Communist Party chief of Armenia, declared a state of emergency Sunday. Also yesterday, the nationalist Armenian Popular Front set up an "emergency defense committee," following reports that Azerbaijanis have been arming themselves.

Meanwhile, in the Azerbaijani city of Lenkoran, the local people's front has deposed the Communist Party leadership and has taken over all city services. And in Azerbaijan's predominantly Armenian region of Shaumyan, near the disputed territory of Nagorno-Karabakh, the local party leadership has been kidnapped by Azeri militants.

Top-level delegations have been sent to both Armenia and Azerbaijan. Politburo member Nikolai Slyunkov was shouted down when he attempted to speak to crowds in Yerevan. Yevgeny Primakov, a nonvoting member of the Politburo and one of Gorbachev's closest advisers, was sent to Azerbaijan.

In neighboring Georgia, nationalists are holding nightly rallies in the capital of Tbilisi to demand that members of the Soviet Politburo come to Georgia to discuss how the republic can gain independence.

Lithuania's drive to secede from the Soviet Union differs fundamentally from the unrest in Transcaucasia. In Lithuania, it is a peaceful, democratic action in a Central European nation that enjoyed independence until the Soviet Union annexed it, along with Latvia and Estonia, in 1940. Since the pro-independence movement began to takeoff in 1988, not a drop of blood has been spilled. Despite the profound challenge Lithuania poses to Mr. Gorbachev, he appeared to enjoy the give and take with Lithuanians.

In contrast, the Armenian-Azerbaijani conflict has, in just two years, become as bloody and bogged down as any other centuries-old Middle East conflict. Russians react to it with the same incomprehension and exasperation as Americans did when they watched Iranian students seize their embassy in Tehran in 1979.

But ultimately, Lithuania could pose a greater threat to Gorbachev's position than Azerbaijan. The general secretary hinted as much when he first arrived in the republic's capital of Vilnius last Thursday.

"We must consider our opinion and your opinion," the Soviet leader told a crowd at Lenin Square. "There can be no absolute freedom in this.... We have embarked on this path and I am the one who chose it. My personal fate is linked to this choice."

An outright declaration of independence by Lithuania until recently, considered by analysts to be a vague goal that might be formally acted upon in the distant future would be a devastating blow to the Soviet Union.

It would embolden secessionist movements in other republics. It would deprive the country of part of its European region, an area where Gorbachev's reforms have found more resonance than elsewhere and which he hoped could be the testing ground for radical changes throughout the economy.

Officials from Lithuania's Communist Party whose decision to break away from Moscow last month spawned Gorbachev's visit won't lay out a timetable for secession. But after key elections in February and March to local councils and to the Lithuanian parliament, in which the more radical-minded candidates (both Communist and noncommunist) are expected to dominate, the shape of Lithuania's independence drive will likely be clearer.

Lithuanians reacted skeptically to Gorbachev's announcement that a draft plan was in the works that would provide a mechanism for each republic's constitutionally guaranteed right to secede, wondering how it would work.

In his last hours in Vilnius, Gorbachev himself got a hint that July 12 may be the day. At his final meeting in Lithuania, with a joint session of the independent Communist Party and the small faction that remains loyal to Moscow, a factory official said of July 12: "We think that can become a double holiday."

If a declaration were made then, the Lithuanians would be playing Gorbachev at his own game: removing the vestiges of Joseph Stalin, who incorporated the three Baltic states into the Soviet Union, and returning to the basics of Vladimir Lenin.

This is not to say that Lithuania could possibly be prepared to function as an independent nation by this summer. Rather, such a declaration would be more an indication of the collective emotion of the republic's ethnic Lithuanians, who make up 80 percent of Lithuania's population.

"The Lithuanians' euphoria would crash down if they declared independence and saw how hard life would be," said a Soviet Foreign Ministry official, referring to the republic's dependence on the rest of the Soviet Union for raw materials and other economic support. "The people say they are willing to go through hardship, but will they really be that patient?"

Lithuanian officials themselves admit that their plans for establishing independence remain vague, but they plan on bringing in Western economists to help them make the transition to a market economy as well as to send some of their own top students to the West to business school. Lithuanians, speaking privately, are also counting on economic help from the West.

Are the Lithuanians worried that they could undermine Gorbachev to the point of effectively ending perestroika? They insist not.

"This is the chance we have been waiting almost 50 years for," said Algis, a professor at Vilnius University and Communist Party member. "We have to move while we have the chance."

Soviets Assert Control of Baku to Prevent Further Violence

Linda Feldmann

1/22/90

Soviet leader Mikhail Gorbachev's grim expression and agitated manner said as much as the actual words he used when he addressed the nation Saturday night.

It was an extraordinary day in the 72-year history of the Soviet Union. During the pre-dawn hours Saturday, Soviet troops and tanks smashed their way into the Azerbaijani capital of Baku to assert the government's control of the city and prevent further inter-ethnic violence.

The raid was necessary to counter forces that aimed at "a forceful seizure of power," Mr. Gorbachev said, referring to Azerbaijani nationalists who have grown increasingly bold in the past few weeks.

Sporadic shooting continued yesterday in parts of Baku, Soviet radio said. Outside the capital, nationalist Popular Front forces remained in charge in a number of towns, according to reports emerging from the region, which is closed to foreigners.

The scale of Saturday's use of force by the Soviet military against its own people, in which at least 60 people were killed, was unprecedented in Gorbachev's nearly five years in power. And it spawned a first in Soviet history: an outright declaration of secession by a part of the country, Azerbaijan's autonomous republic of Nakhichevan.

On Saturday, the parliament of this small border territory, separated from the rest of Azerbaijan by a swath of Armenia, declared independence from the Soviet Union, and requested help from Turkey, Iran, and the United Nations. It was in Nakhichevan where, starting Dec. 31, radicals tore down long stretches of the border with Iran. Some analysts say the Soviet border guards' laissez-faire attitude to the destruction helped embolden radicals in other parts of Azerbaijan to take over local governments.

Gorbachev did not mention the Nakhichevan secession in his short Saturday night speech, which was televised nationwide. Focusing instead on the military crackdown in Baku, he seemed apologetic in justifying the military crackdown by saying, essentially, that he had no choice. After two years of efforts by the central authorities to settle through peaceful means the longstanding conflict between Azerbaijan and Armenia, he said, the situation had reached a "dead end."

"Unfortunately the party, state, and government bodies of both republics in these conditions did not display proper responsibility and a balanced approach," he said. "And often, they gave up their principled positions under pressure from nationalist groups."

The Soviet leader referred to decisions over the control of Nagorno-Karabakh, a territory located inside Azerbaijan that is inhabited largely by Armenians and which has been the focal point of almost two years of escalating conflict between Azerbaijan and Armenia.

On Saturday, Abdul-Rakhman Vezirov, the first secretary of the Azerbaijani Communist Party's Central Committee, was fired and replaced by Ayaz Mutalibov, Azerbaijan's prime minister. Later, in Moscow, Gorbachev and other Politburo members met with the new Azerbaijani party leadership.

But analysts here doubt whether a Communist leadership loyal to Moscow can be restored in Azerbaijan. In many areas, the public has lost faith in the local Communist authorities, whom it sees as corrupt and ineffectual, and therefore has accepted the rise to power of the grass-roots Popular Front.

"I would say that the development of events in both republics [Azerbaijan and Armenia] has emerged out from under the control of both party and Soviet organs," says an informed Moscow political analyst, who asked not to be identified.

"In Azerbaijan, they have power only where they do the bidding of the local NFA [Popular Front of Azerbaijan] or can rely on the military power of Soviet soldiers. In fact, you could say that what we're seeing in this republic is a revolution, in which, evidently, the question of Nagorno-Karabakh is only the immediate cause."

In Armenia, the analyst continues, the local nationalist movement is also the real power steering the course of events, although the official organs of power are still nominally in charge. "Here there is a higher degree of national unity, better coordination."

This source and other analysts foresee the extended Soviet military presence in Azerbaijan and Armenia—currently consisting of 24,000 troops from the Army, the Interior Ministry, and the KGB (secret police)—lasting indefinitely.

"It's the Brezhnev Doctrine all over again, only now it is in effect within the Soviet Union itself," says Azerbaijan expert Gassan Gusseinov, referring to Moscow's past practice of keeping reformist East-bloc countries within the Soviet orbit by force.

Soviet mothers were reminded of another legacy of Leonid Brezhnev last Thursday, when the Defense Ministry began calling up Army reserves for duty in Transcaucasia. In a number of cities, women responded by holding rallies and demanding that their boys not be sent to die in "another Afghanistan." The next day, the call-up was rescinded, a clear embarrassment to the armed forces establishment.

Moscow Loses Face Over Azerbaijan

Linda Feldmann

1/31/90

The crisis in the Transcaucasus, now settling into a state of tense equilibrium, has left the Soviet leadership bruised and under continuing attack. When President Mikhail Gorbachev addressed the nation Jan. 20 after troops stormed the Azerbaijani capital of Baku, he showed an uncharacteristic lack of assuredness. Since then, he has made no public statements on the crisis. In the days since the invasion, members of Communist Party Politburo have contradicted each other as they defended the use of force that left more than 100 people dead. Defense Minister Dmitri Yazov said it was necessary to prevent nationalists from seizing power. Foreign Minister Eduard Shevardnadze, however, said it was meant to stop bloodshed between Azerbaijanis and Armenians. The military's short-lived call-up of reserves—canceled after protests by

Russians fearful of "another Afghanistan"—has left the Defense Ministry under fire. Soviet newspapers are publishing pointed headlines such as "Who gave the order?" And the continuing military occupation of Baku has sparked protests by both the Army's reform movement, Shield, and the Russian ultranationalist organization, Pamyat.

The latest indication of the erosion of Soviet credibility is a dialogue, to begin tomorrow in Riga, the capital of Latvia. All parties involved—Armenians, Azerbaijanis, and their Baltic mediators—will represent their respective people's front organizations and not official organs of power. The fact that Balts, and not Russians, will be mediating is also telling. As fellow non-Russians trying to exercise national self-determination, Azerbaijanis and Armenians have watched with admiration as the popular movements in Latvia, Lithuania, and Estonia have gotten concession after concession (such as a law on economic self-sufficiency) from the central authorities. Nationalist activists from Azerbaijan and Armenia say the Baltic popular movements served as models for their own groups. The Baltic mediation effort also reflects the latest stage in the metamorphosis of Russian relations with minorities in the Soviet Union. "In the USSR," write Petr Goncharov and Ksenia Myalo in the liberal weekly New Time, "the function of inter-ethnic mediator has historically been fulfilled by the Russian people. "Though it has suffered no less than others from past social and political experiments, circumstances have changed, and it is now no longer a guarantor—it bears responsibility. Namely [the Russian people] are given all the blame for the crimes and failures of the decades preceding perestroika." Thus for Moscow, say Soviet and foreign analysts, the current impasse in the Transcaucasus represents the culmination of two trends: two years of Kremlin inability to keep rising tensions between Azerbaijan and Armenia from escalating into full-scale civil war, and the accumulated resentment of years of Russian rule—and mismanagement—of non-Russian peoples. But could Moscow, having itself opened the way to greater expression of nationalist feeling, prevented the current crisis in Transcaucasia? The odds were against it, analysts say. "Moscow didn't ignore the problem," says Rufat Novruzov, an Azeri specialist. "It just didn't understand it. It's another political culture."

But the problem goes beyond the ethnically Russian-dominated Politburo's lack of understanding of Azerbaijani and Armenian cultures. It also touches on the Leninist foundation of the Soviet Union. "The fact is the Soviet leadership, conditioned under Marxism-Leninism, is poorly equipped to understand the depth of passions of ethnic disputes," says a senior Western diplomat with long Soviet experience. According to Leninist theory, ethnic differences were to melt away as the "new Soviet man" emerged.

Decades of Soviet rule had submerged centuries of Azeri and Armenian animosity—including the longstanding dispute over Nagorno-Karabakh, a heavily Armenian territory in Azerbaijan. In early 1988, three years into Mr. Gorbachev's policy of greater openness, Armenia revived its claim to Nagorno-Karabakh. At that point, observers say, the stage was already set for an intractable dispute. "Early in '88, the center [Moscow] had to say, 'No! Enough! The Karabakh problem is out of the question,'" says Mr. Novruzov. He and others suggest that it was at that point that Moscow should have deployed a heavy military presence to keep the peace. In July 1988, the Central Committee of the Communist Party and the Presidium of the Supreme Soviet established a special committee to administer Nagorno-Karabakh. But this committee was completely hamstrung. "Arkady Volsky [the committee chairman] had an Azerbaijani gun on one side of his head and an Armenian gun on the other," says Azeri scholar Gassan Gusseinov. "Anytime he did anything, one side or the other would be offended." In September 1989, Mr. Volsky admitted in a newspaper interview that there was little he could do. He recommended that Nagorno-Karabakh be administered by local authorities, while law enforcement would still be controlled by the center. In November, the Supreme Soviet voted to do just that—but the decision angered both Azeris and Armenians. Azerbaijan saw any Armenian role in ruling the territory as the first step toward complete Armenian takeover. The Armenians, irate over the reference in the resolution to "the Nagorno-Karabakh Autonomous Republic of Azerbaijan" took action: In its economic plan adopted Jan. 9, the Armenian parliament incorporated not only Nagorno-Karabakh, but also two other adjacent Azerbaijani districts. For the 150,000-plus Azeri refugees who had fled to Azerbaijan over the past few years from Nagorno-Karabakh and Armenia, this was the latest in a series of indignities visited upon them by the Armenians. In their eyes, the Armenians were now stealing their land, after having forced them off it. All that was needed to turn the Azeris' simmering anger into violence was a spark—and news of Armenia's action provided it. On Jan. 13, Azeri refugees, and others bent on driving Baku's remaining Armenians out, went on a killing spree that horrified the nation.

Soviet Hot Spots

Linda Feldmann

2/1/90

For Soviet leader Mikhail Gorbachev, crisis has overlapped crisis in the first weeks of 1990. On New Year's Eve, the Azeris of the autonomous republic of Nakhichevan began tearing down their border fences with Iran—an act unprecedented in Soviet history. Local chapters of the Azerbaijan Popular Front deposed Communist leaders in several cities. By mid-January, long-brewing tensions between Azerbaijan and the neighboring republic of Armenia escalated to a point of virtual civil war, after Azeris killed dozens of Armenians in Baku, Azerbaijan's capital, and sent thousands fleeing. And when the Kremlin feared that Azerbaijan's nationalist Popular Front was set to take control of Baku, it sent thousands of Army troops to reassert Soviet power. Now Azerbaijan's parliament is talking of secession. As civil war loomed in the Transcaucasus, the Soviet leader and other Politburo members were on a mission to the rebellious Baltic republic of Lithuania, which is in the midst of its own bloodless revolution to reestablish its prewar nationhood. Mr. Gorbachev's visit, sparked by the Lithuanian Communist Party's decision in December to break away from Moscow's control, failed to dampen the Lithuanians' enthusiasm. All around the Soviet Union, local Communist Party leaders are losing their authority. In just the last two weeks, six regional party bosses have been forced to resign. In all three Baltic republics, pro-independence movements look set to take control of local councils in elections to be held in the next two months.

The Soviet leader also faces long-simmering dissatisfaction over the declining standard of living. When popular discontent over food and alcohol shortages has reached a boiling point—such as in Sverdlovsk on New Year's Eve—people have taken to the streets. Labor unrest threatens to reappear, as workers claim that government promises made to negotiate an end to last year's dramatic coal strikes have not been fulfilled.

The issue of official privilege has also ignited passions. For example, there's the tale of the regional executive committee official in Chernigov, Ukraine, whose traffic mishap Jan. 6 led to his firing and expulsion from the party. It seems the townspeople who gathered at Valery Zaika's accident discovered meat and other rarities in the trunk of his car. The angry crowd dragged the car to the front of the regional party committee building and held a spontaneous demonstration. For the people, this was the final outrage. Soon thereafter, a string of party officials, including the first secretary, were fired.

Some analysts suggest that angry masses demanding reform are exactly what Gorbachev needs to push perestroika (restructuring) along. And that the ouster of local Communist Party officials left over from "the years of stagnation" (Leonid Brezhnev's rule) is no great loss.

But as Gorbachev heads into a key meeting of the Communist Party Central Committee Feb. 5 and 6, the question remains whether he'll be able to contain the surge in popular aspirations released by his own reform policies.

Gorbachev Proposes Radical Shift for Party

Linda Feldmann

2/7/90

In an attempt to bolster the plummeting prestige of Soviet communism, Mikhail Gorbachev suggested far-reaching reforms in the party's structure, philosophy, and role.

The Soviet leader, with one eye clearly on the demise of hard-line Communist rulers throughout Eastern Europe, has offered to the Communist Party's policymaking Central Committee the following propositions:

Relinquishing the party's constitutional guarantee of a monopoly on power, enshrined in Article 6.

"The party in a renewing society can exist and play its role as vanguard only as a democratically recognized force," Mr. Gorbachev said. "This means that its status should not be imposed through constitutional endorsement."

Accepting the existence of other legal parties in the Soviet Union. The three Baltic republics already have active multiparty systems. The development of a democratic political culture is lagging in the Russian republic, but noncommunist political parties are beginning to be organized.

At this point, the closest thing the Soviet Union has to a nationwide opposition political party is the newly formed "Democratic Platform within the Communist Party of the Soviet Union."

This group, which combines the forces of the party's radical wing, under such leaders as Boris Yeltsin, Yuri Afanasyev, and Gavril Popov, says it is trying to reform the Communist Party from within. It has taken on what it calls the values of Western social democracy.

Rethinking the party's doctrine of "democratic centralism." Under this practice, which goes back to Vladimir Lenin's rule, party members are required to submit to the decisions of the majority and fulfill them. The idea of consensus-building has always been anathema to this principle. Now, says Gorbachev, "the party's renewal presupposes its thorough, comprehensive democratization," with emphasis on granting power to the party masses.

Cutting the size of the Central Committee and change the nature of its membership. Gorbachev suggested that the committee have 200 members, down from its current collection of 249 (which is already a reduction from previous totals greater than 300).

The composition of the Central Committee would change from being, essentially, a collection of high-level party officials from around the country that meet periodically, to a permanent elected body. Gorbachev also mentioned a proposal to abandon the practice of electing candidate (nonvoting) members to the Central Committee.

This proposal suggests an attempt to wrest power from the Central Committee, which is, on the whole, seen as a braking force on perestroika (restructuring).

Bringing forward the date of the Communist Party Congress from October to late June or early July. This crucial congress, which will have the final decision-making power on the party's new platform, was originally to be held in the spring of 1991, and the decision to bring it up even to October was seen as a concession to the urgency of the need for a perestroika of the party.

According to well-placed Soviet journalists, the congress may even be held in May.

Conservatives and liberals agree that the party is suffering a severe crisis of confidence—"a reflection of the problems in society as a whole," said one Central Committee official—and that the matter must be addressed urgently.

Even during this week's plenum, the news came out that yet another powerful regional party boss—the conservative Leonid Bobykin of Sverdlovsk—had resigned.

The final straw for Mr. Bobykin was a Feb. 5 no-confidence vote at the party conference of one of Sverdlovsk's largest factories. Sverdlovsk has had severe problems with food and alcohol supplies this winter which led to rioting on New Year's Eve.

Since the start of this year, party bosses all over the country have been resigning in disgrace, amid charges of incompetence, and in some cases corruption, and always in conditions of economic decline.

For Western observers analyzing this week's plenum—in many ways the most important of Gorbachev's five years as party leader—the Soviet leader's speech on Monday was remarkable. In just one hour, he overturned many of the fundamental precepts of authoritarian rule put in place by the very man, Lenin, he says he is harkening back to.

But to Soviets, both liberal and conservative, Gorbachev's speech and the draft for a new party platform were a study in vagueness.

He didn't come right out and say that Article 6 should be repealed, despite the fact that a consensus is growing among all political persuasions that this is necessary. And, by saying that he could foresee a day when more than one party was competing for power in the Soviet Union, he seemed to deliberately understate the progress toward a multiparty system already achieved in several republics.

But it is perhaps this very vagueness that allows Gorbachev to walk the tight rope between conservatives and liberals who are exerting pressure from both sides. Neither side is completely happy, but by issuing contradictory statements of what he has in mind, he is giving neither side ammunition against him.

Gorbachev Seen Stronger After Soviet Party Meeting

Linda Feldmann

2/8/90

Even before this week's grueling Communist Party Central Committee gathering had ended and the final verdict on a possible purge of conservatives was known, the meeting was already being dubbed "the hard-liners' last stand."

Clear indication of that came yesterday when the Central Committee ended its three-day session by adopting a platform of radical reform.

"Article 6 will no longer be, there will be a multiparty system. There will be a normal democracy," said delegate Svyatoslav Fyodorov, referring to the part of the Soviet Constitution that guaranteed power to the Communist Party. There was one abstention and one vote against the platform, he said. The vote against came from populist leader Boris Yeltsin.

During the meetings, some conservatives aimed blistering attacks at Soviet leader Mikhail Gorbachev, saying he had run the country and the Communist Party into the ground.

Others were more subtle. One, for example, agreeing with Mr. Gorbachev's suggestion that Article 6 should be dropped, but then, in effect, suggesting ways this "right" could be formally enshrined in other documents.

But Gorbachev's supporters say everything has gone according to script thus far. The Soviet general secretary—solid in his position as leader of the country, no matter what his title—would withstand a verbal onslaught from both the right and the left of the Communist Party elite and then press ahead with a perestroika (restructuring) of the party.

The fact that the plenum ran over into a third day only underscored the high-stakes nature of the policymakers' task: to head the party toward a reform that will regain the faith of the people.

The final plan for reform will be decided at the 28th party congress, now scheduled for late June or early July. The key question about this congress, which will gather party members from around the country, is whether delegates will be selected through direct, secret elections at the grass roots, rather than through the old-style (often rigged) system. If direct elections are held, the chance of fundamental party reform will be greater.

By the second day of the Central Committee plenum, Gorbachev supporters were talking optimistically, discussing the plenum almost as if it were a horse race.

"I'm quite sure Gorbachev will be the winner," Nikolai Shishlin, a Central Committee staff member, told British television on Tuesday.

After Tuesday's session, Estonian Prime Minister Indrek Toome, said to reporters, "The trend is toward radical change."

Other party liberals, however, complained that Gorbachev's opening speech—and the party's draft platform, which by yesterday had not been published—contained no direct assertions of what the party would or should do to renovate itself. Instead, it consisted mainly of principles that could be interpreted in various ways.

Gorbachev wanted it this way, says the deputy director of a Moscow institute who helped write a draft of the platform.

"He is not afraid for his position, it's his ideas he needs to protect," says the official. "Gorbachev's centrism is part of his policy formula. But it's not a passive centrism—it's active, slanted to the left."

As the Soviet Union's economic, political, and moral crises deepen, the Communist Party has polarized to the point of being in danger of splitting, this official and other dedicated party members say. By playing the centrist, Gorbachev aims to keep from alienating the right wing completely.

"At the moment you really start implementing policy," says the institute official, "you want as much support as you can gather. It will require patience. There are no quick fixes. But Gorbachev feels it is necessary to bring along as many conservatives as possible."

Those high-level party officials who cannot change with the times will be removed. In fact, in growing numbers, they are being forced to resign by the party's increasingly disgruntled grass roots.

Though a majority of the Communist Party's 249 Central Committee members support Gorbachev, on the whole the policymaking body is more conservative than the party's rank and file. For many committee members, reform will mean a loss of status and privilege.

According to the latest issue of Arguments and Facts, the 61 percent of the Central Committee members elected four years ago are at least 60 years old or will be by the time their term ends.

At least in public, Central Committee members have tended to favor Gorbachev's proposal for a smaller, permanently functioning Central Committee made up of elected members.

Currently the committee is made up of high-level party bureaucrats who get their positions on the committee automatically. Though it meets only occasionally, its high status allows it to wield influence at crucial periods.

"I agree with the suggested measures about perestroika of the Central Committee of the party," committee member Gennady Yagodin, a high-level education official, said on Soviet television Tuesday night. "Not only just the reduction of the number of members, as Mikhail Sergeyevich Gorbachev suggests, but in reducing the number we activate each one."

Lithuanians Broadcast Freedom

Linda Feldmann

2/15/90

At the stroke of 7 p.m., Rimantas Pleikys flips a switch and leans into the microphone to begin his broadcast.

"Good evening, friends," Mr. Pleikys announces smoothly in his native Lithuanian. "You are listening to Radio M-1 in Vilnius. First, the latest news . . . . "

Just another ordinary radio sign-on, it would seem. But here on the 17th floor of Vilnius's press building, there's still a buzz of anticipation every evening when M-1 goes on the air. It's the "one" in M-1 (the M is for music) that explains why.

This is the Soviet Union's first independent radio station, appropriately located in the capital of the independence-minded republic of Lithuania.

M-1, which took to the airwaves on New Year's Eve, has no censor and gets no government funds. The station consists of two small rooms rented from Lithuania's popular youth newspaper, Lietuvos Rytas (Lithuania's Morning), for 70 rubles ($113) a month. On this particular Saturday evening, young people are scurrying about, getting and delivering things for Pleikys, the station's editorial director. A balding, well-fed young man named Kestas "Halford" Zanevicius—"my friends say I look like the singer Halford from Judas Priest"—gathers compact discs for his heavy-metal rock show.

The setup is standard: a mixing console, three reel-to-reel tape players, a compact-disc player, turntable, and cassette deck, almost all Western-made. Largely empty shelves stand ready to supplement a modest collection of records, tapes, and compact discs. The format is music and information, interspersed with interviews. The six-hour broadcast day ends at 1 a.m.

In short, M-1 has the look and feel of a typical American community radio station—low on funds, long on enthusiasm, and willing to take all comers.

"Anybody can walk in and have their say on the air, as long as they don't advocate violence or racism," explains Pleikys. "Tomorrow we're giving the Hare Krishnas 15 minutes."

For Pleikys and his partner, Hubertas Grushnis, the inauguration of M-1 is the culmination of a two-year dream. The inspiration came from the birth of Lithuania's nationalist movement, Sajudis, which spawned a lively independent press and an array of political parties. Radio and television, meanwhile, remained solely in the government's hands. "We thought this wasn't normal," says Pleikys.

So he and Mr. Grushnis set out to gather the necessary ingredients: official permission to broadcast, equipment, operating funds, and studio space. They also had to prove that they knew what they were doing, and once on the air, that they would behave responsibly.

"At first there were doubts: As soon as you are allowed on the air, you will start to agitate against the Soviet authorities," said a news report in Lietuvos Rytas last month. "Then they shrugged: Where will you get money, resources; plus you need permission . . . . "

One by one, Pleikys and Grushnis cleared all the hurdles. Lithuania's Communist Party—itself now enjoying self-styled independence—issued a resolution Feb. 9, 1989, supporting the idea of independent radio. Then the state-censoring agency, Glavlit, gave written permission to broadcast without censorship. The Ministry of Telecommunications followed with authorization to occupy a frequency—73.34 megahertz (MHz) FM, stereo. (The Soviet FM band is lower on the dial than the American, running from 66 to 74 MHz.)

Money was, and remains, a problem. One compact disc, for example, goes for between 150 and 300 rubles (the range of a typical month's salary) on the black market. The question of start-up funds, at least, was eased last August, when Pleikys linked up with Southwest German Radio. The broadcasters invited him to Stuttgart and helped him raise funds: 15,000 deutsche marks ($9,000) from a West German confectionary company and 2,500 marks ($1,500) from the West German Social Democratic Party.

M-1 hopes to raise additional money by selling on-air advertising. So far, its only ads come under a barter arrangement with Lietuvos Rytas, which in return publishes ads for M-1. By early February, however, the financial situation was dire. Local heavy-metal fans are planning a rock-concert fund-raiser in March.

The station's relationship with Lithuania's youth paper appears close, but the paper's editor, Gedvimas Vainauskas, insists M-1 is not the "radio voice" of Lietuvos Rytas.

"Why did we take in this radio station?" Mr. Vainauskas recalls. "I think our newspaper has always strived to be the first to do something. We were the first to take the medallions off our masthead, the first to remove the slogan 'Proletariat of All Countries, Unite.' We gave our paper a normal [noncommunist] name. Then along came these enthusiasts . . . and we decided to help by giving them a place to operate from."

Pleikys does not belong to any political party, and says he is trying to provide a range of opinions. Recently, for example, the station broadcast a statement by the leader of the radical Lithuanian Liberty League, who criticized the leader of Sajudis. Soon thereafter, Sajudis's leader got equal time. If the leader of Lithuania's minority "loyalist" Communist Party wants to come in and say a few words, he's more than welcome, says Pleikys.

Music programs range from rock to classical to jazz. One recent program focused on the music of Philip Glass. The station has also broadcast evangelical programs from Lithuanian immigrants in the United States and Canada. Soviet rock, however, isn't on the play list, says music director "Halford" Zanevicius—"because it isn't 'something' yet."

Zanevicius's listeners seem to agree. A journalist named Lilia remarks how she got into a cab the other day and was pleasantly shocked to hear the group Fine Young

Cannibals blaring from the radio. Then George Harrison. M-1 had just earned a new fan.

"They're giving us just what we want—Western culture," Lilia says. "State radio and TV have gotten much more creative and independent lately, but in some ways they're still working in the old Soviet style. The guys at M-1 started fresh; they didn't have to do any perestroika. You really feel it."

Over at M-1's cramped quarters, the fan mail is piling up. And with a 12,000-watt signal broadcasting from Vilnius's 250-meter (820-foot) TV tower, Pleikys figures the potential audience approaches 1 million people.

Are they heard abroad? Pleikys smiles: "Well, they're picking us up in Byelorussia."

Will Inertia Slow Economic Bust?

Linda Feldmann

3/1/90

Is the Soviet economy heading for a collapse?

Some radical economists—those who urge a speedy introduction of market-oriented reforms—look at the five-year plan for 1990-95 and predict disaster. Through 1992, the main goal is to stabilize the economy and rebuild popular support for perestroika (restructuring), which has declined as consumer goods have become increasingly scarce.

Only in 1993 will more fundamental reforms, such as in pricing and decentralization, begin to be introduced. By then, the radicals say, it will be too late.

Other specialists foresee a less ominous future. Rair Simonyan, a senior economist at the prestigious Moscow-based Institute of World Economy and International Relations, sees tough times ahead for at least the next two or three years, but not a complete collapse—for ironic reasons.

"The economy has great inertia and can't be altered quickly, neither for the better nor for the worse," says Dr. Simonyan. Within the economy, "there exist stable links and, independent of external factors, the economy somehow continues to work."

Longstanding economic links will keep Eastern Europe and the independence-minded Baltic republics closely tied to the Soviet Union for a long time, despite the evolution in their political relations, he says.

Much, of course, depends on how one defines "collapse." Otto Latsis, an economist at the journal Kommunist, says one sector of the economy—the consumer market—has essentially already fallen apart.

"Out of 1,000 . . . basic consumer goods," Dr. Latsis says, "only about 100 or maybe even less, maybe 50, are freely available. There are no television sets. No cars. No irons. No building materials . . . . By 1989, the consumer market had deteriorated to such a point where, without rationing, it could not function."

But the problem is not in production levels, he says. Production of TV sets, for example, has even increased. The problem is in the money supply, which was dramatically increased over the past few years, in large part to raise the salaries of disgruntled employees.

The result has been inflation, a boom in the budget deficit, and the emptying of store shelves.

As faith in perestroika and in the ruble has declined, consumers with excess cash have sought increasingly to put their money in goods, especially in precious metals. In January, the government moved to profit from the run on gold by raising the price of jewelry by 50 percent.

"What could happen now," says Latsis, "is a mass running away from money, like in Poland in 1982. Everybody withdraws their money, and the shelves are empty. It's a danger that now threatens . . . . If this happens, the market will be broken and there will be no goods left. Trade will vanish."

Rationing has become increasingly common. In Leningrad, for example, the sale of scarce items is now restricted to residents who can show permission to live there. The system was introduced early in January, after Estonians—who now pay higher prices for some items under their economic independence plan—started driving to Leningrad to buy cheaper goods.

Technically, Moscow does not have widespread rationing. But in effect it does. More and more, consumer goods such as clothes, household appliances, cosmetics, and furniture are sold through the workplace and not in stores, the way food has been sold for years. This system has made life especially difficult for those who don't work, such as pensioners, invalids, and students.

Inflation is another source of anxiety in a country unaccustomed to this problem. Around the country, inflation statistics vary according to the supply levels. Officially, overall inflation stood at 2.3 percent in January, but other experts variously measure it at between 7 percent and 20 percent annually.

The biggest factor destroying the consumer market, says Latsis, is the budget deficit, which sky-rocketed from 47 billion rubles in 1986 to 90 billion rubles (US $150 billion) in 1988.

In 1989, the government capped the deficit at 92 billion, and this year plans to slash the deficit to 60 billion rubles. A deficit of 20 billion to 25 billion is acceptable, says Latsis.

Soviet Voters Apathetic On Eve of Key Local Vote

Linda Feldmann

3/2/90

With the Soviet Communist Party in disarray and popular dissatisfaction on the rise, the careers of old-line party leaders are on the line in Sunday's local elections.

A year ago, the Soviet Union's first multicandidate elections dealt a stinging blow to the party's prestige, as a surprising number of high-level party apparatchiks were rejected by voters. Since then, the party has continued to lose authority. In the past two months, a string of party leaders around the country have been forced to resign.

But pro-reform activists are cautious in their predictions about Sunday, when voters in Russia, the Ukraine, and Byelorussia—70 percent of the Soviet population—vote for local councils and republican parliaments.

Activists charge that party bosses in many areas have used "undemocratic means" to keep certain candidates off the ballot or prevent any opposition at all. They also foresee possible irregularities in vote counting.

The labor newspaper Trud reported yesterday, for example, that most of the party leadership of Ivanovo, a city of 475,000 near Moscow, is running unopposed.

And in the resort city of Sochi, yesterday's Komsomolskaya Pravda writes, local radio was shut down Feb. 8 after it allowed a group of candidates to go on the air and call for voters to cross out the names of candidates running unopposed.

"I have never been confident of a victory for democratic forces in these elections," says liberal deputy Sergei Stankevich.

"And so we have called for a tactic of 'liberated regions.' That is, it is possible to win in several regions, mainly in large industrial centers, in large cities. Even if it's not possible to win an entire city, we can win parts of a city."

Victories in large cities like Moscow, he explains, will mean access to the mass media—which in turn can be used to widen their influence into areas where "for now, apparatchiks still rule."

Overall, the mood on election eve is not what it was a year ago. Random interviews with voters showed a disillusionment with the democratic process.

"There are two problems," explained Yulia, a young housewife from Moscow's Cheryomunsky region. "One, there's a feeling of 'Well, we tried this last year, and it didn't work.' In fact, life has gotten tougher. The Supreme Soviet just talks and talks and nothing gets better.

"Two, in some races there are dozens of candidates running and it's hard to find out who they are or what they propose. Then in other races, just one person is running.

"In our election for regional council, I plan on crossing out the name. The only candidate is a factory director. He needs to be under the control of the council, not a part of it!"

For the leaders of the Soviet parliament's liberal Interregional Group, including Mr. Stankevich, Sunday's vote marks the next phase of their push for change. They have been frustrated by what they see as Soviet leader Mikhail Gorbachev's autocratic methods of getting his way—such as in Tuesday's vote for an empowered executive presidency, which liberals worry could open the door to dictatorship.

The liberal leaders' plan is to expand their fight for accelerated economic and political reform to republican parliaments and local councils. Under the law allowing one person to hold two seats, such leaders as Boris Yeltsin, Yuri Afanasyev, Stankevich, and Mikhail Bocharov are running for the Russian parliament. Mr. Yeltsin has designs on the presidency of Russia. Radical economist Gavril Popov is running for Moscow City Council, and has said he would "not object" to a nomination for mayor.

At the same time, the group plans to keep fighting Mr. Gorbachev's plan for the presidency. The bill would allow the president to declare martial law or a state of emergency in parts of the country, declare war in case of attack, and appoint and dismiss officials.

The problem, liberals say, is not in establishing an executive presidency, but in doing so now, before a proper system of checks and balances is in place. Furthermore, the plan calls for the new president—who will be Gorbachev—to be elected by the highest legislative body, the Congress of People's Deputies, for the first four-year term, which liberals decry as undemocratic.

Interregional Group leaders are considering calling for nationwide demonstrations on March 11 to protest the plan. On March 12 and 13, an extraordinary session of the Congress of People's Deputies will gather to consider the bill on the presidency and other constitutional amendments. The Congress is considered more compliant than the smaller Supreme Soviet, which approved the law in principle by a vote of 305 to 65.

Soviet Reformers Gain In First Free Local Vote

Linda Feldmann

3/7/90

The Communist Party is down but not out in the first democratic local elections in Soviet history.

Pro-reform candidates scored well in several major urban centers in Sunday's vote across the Soviet Union's three Slavic republics, according to early returns.

But in other regions, both rural and urban, the old-line Communist Party machine held its position, often without any opposition in balloting for district and city councils and republican parliaments.

The three republics, Russia, Ukraine, and Byelorussia, account for 70 percent of the Soviet population.

In highly politicized cities, such as Moscow, Leningrad, and Kiev, activists viewed the elections as an opportunity to promote from below the changes begun at the top. As expected, gadfly politician Boris Yeltsin, who ran for the Russian parliament from his native Sverdlovsk, won a seat with more than 80 percent of the vote.

"Last year, the vote was for a nationwide parliament that handled large abstract issues, such as land and private property," said Mikhail Zarapin, a candidate for the Russian parliament who ran as part of the so-called "Democratic Russia" bloc.

"But you see that food store across the street?" he adds, pointing from the lobby of the council headquarters of Moscow's Taganski region. "This time, the elections are all about who will have a direct say over who runs stores like that one."

In other regions, such as Krasnodar, a city of 4.5 million people in southwest Russia, opposition to the party apparatus is only just forming and did not make any headway Sunday. "The party machine is very much in control," said a Western observer who spent election day there.

In those places where the roots of multiparty democracy are already taking hold, the races were more between conservatives and liberals than between Communists and noncommunists, since many of the democratic-bloc candidates also hold Communist Party membership.

But the internal factionalization of the Soviet Communist Party will not necessarily save it. The leaders of the party's self-styled democratic wing expect to break out of the party some time in the next several months and join forces with liberal noncommunists, many of whom call themselves social democrats. Whether the formal split takes place before or after the crucial Communist Party Congress this summer remains to be seen.

Meanwhile the radical-reform forces present a double-edged sword for Soviet leader Mikhail Gorbachev, according to aide Fyodor Burlatsky.

"The fact that the democratic bloc is winning is very good," says Mr. Burlatsky in an interview. "But there is apt to be a division of forces within this bloc itself . . . . This will become clear during the session of the Supreme Soviet and local soviets [councils]: who stands for Gorbachev's line, the line of maximum possible reform. The other side is those who are conservative minded and are hoping for the return to older, calmer times with stricter rule."

In politically active cities, the proliferation of candidates has forced runoff votes in most races.

In Moscow, for example, an average of seven candidates vied for each seat in local and republican councils.

In those cases where a candidate won at least 50 percent of the vote in the first round, thereby avoiding a runoff, almost all belonged to the pro-reform Democratic Russia bloc. And in many of the runoffs, in which the top two vote-getters will go head to head, at least one Democratic Russia candidate will take part. Runoffs will be held in two weeks.

In Moscow, only eight of the 65 races for the Russian parliament have been decided—and they're all from the Democratic Russian group. Included in that group is Vladislav Starkov, editor of the popular weekly Argumenti i Fakti, who gained fame last year after a barrage of criticism from Mr. Gorbachev.

Other first-round winners were radical economist Tatyana Koryagina, former political prisoner Sergei Kovalyov, and Alexander Politkovski, from the popular TV program Vzglyad.

In Leningrad, the Democratic Elections '90 bloc said its candidates looked set to win a majority of seats in the city council and were well placed for the runoffs for parliament.

In Kiev, the Ukranian capital, all but one of 22 districts will face runoffs for parliament, but candidates from the nationalist Rukh movement look strong in the second round of voting. In the more politicized western Ukraine, which was incorporated into the Soviet Union under the 1939 Hitler-Stalin pact, Rukh candidates won sizable majorities—such as the movement's president, Ivan Drach, and freed political prisoners Mikhail Horyn and Vyacheslav Chornovil.

Burlatsky is cautionary about the apparent gains by the democratic forces, who seem to be united only in their opposition to the party bureaucracy.

New Opposition Parties Blossom In Soviet Union

Linda Feldmann

3/9/90

At first glance, the lineup of grim faces staring down from most Moscow buildings looked like standard-issue Politburo posters. But on closer inspection, these were not all Politburo-esque faces. Some sported beards. Some were not much older than 30. And beneath some, the resumes were distinctly unorthodox: "World-famous artist," "Served in labor camp for political views," "Organizer of new social movements."

In many of the cities of Russia, the Ukraine, and Byelorussia, such were the campaign posters for last Sunday's elections for local councils and republican parliaments. Although voters faced the usual lack of choice in many regions, the multiparty system had a genuine test in Moscow, Leningrad, Kiev, Lvov, and other politically active cities.

Sunday's vote, in which reformist candidates scored well, represented the latest stage in the evolution of Soviet-style democracy. Over the past three years, a variety of informal clubs and civic organizations have given way to what a Communist Party Central Committee aide called the "fetuses" of political parties.

These groups, which sprang up under Soviet leader Mikhail Gorbachev's campaign to awaken a slumbering populace, provided an outlet for political activism that the Communist Party had long ago ceased to offer.

"Democratic development in the Soviet Union is more than just the creation of parties," says Andrei Fadin, political editor of the independent weekly Commersant. "There are the popular movements, people's fronts, associations." Inside the once-monolithic Communist Party, the spectrum of views ranges from historian Yuri Afanasyev's line of radical reform to Leningrad teacher Nina Andreyeva's push for a return to the old order.

On the outside, tiny groups and larger movements exist to suit almost any taste, from anarcho-syndicalists to social democrats to monarchists.

"Parallel processes are taking place," says Igor Chubais, a leader of the Communist Party faction called Democratic Platform.

With the Communist Party set to recognize opposition parties, some noncommunist groupings are poised to claim legal status. The Ukrainian Social Democratic Party will hold its founding congress on March 25. Early in May, the Social Democratic Party of Russia will do the same. These follow the establishment of Social Democratic parties in Georgia, Byelorussia, Estonia (which has three), Latvia, and Lithuania. A party is also forming in Moldavia. They are all under the umbrella Social Democratic Association.

But in the face of a major transformation of the Soviet state—Lithuania is set to declare independence as early as Sunday—any talk of a "dawn of democracy" in this once-totalitarian nation boils down to a discussion of each individual republic.

Within the vast Russian federation, last Sunday's elections spurred the creation of candidate "blocs": the Democratic Russia bloc, which included social democrats, reform-minded communists, and other pro-reform candidates and the Social-Patriotic Movement of Russia, which linked the United Workers' Front and various other Russian nationalist organizations, including elements of the ultra-rightist Pamyat.

Judging by Sunday's results, Democratic Russia clearly ran a more effective campaign than its right-wing counterpart. On the eve of the vote, Moscow mailboxes were stuffed with computer printouts of the local Democratic Russia slate. Buildings were plastered with lists of endorsements.

The Patriotic bloc blames its second-place showing on a lack of access to the news media, which are "dominated by pro-capitalists," says Igor Malyarov, an unsuccessful United Workers' Front candidate for the Russian parliament. "Our position was constantly misrepresented. We are the radicals, but not from the right wing. We aim to establish true communism, so that makes us left wing."

To Democratic Russia, the other bloc is an illusion. "This election was a choice between pro-reform and antireform," says Oleg Rumyantsev, a co-chairman of the Social Democratic Association. "The apparat and this so-called patriotic alliance were really one and the same."

A battle among moderate reformers, radicals, and entrenched interests is also being waged inside the party. The Afanasyev wing, united under the Democratic Platform, has all but decided to quit the party. The split will likely take place after this summer's crucial Communist Party Congress, affording the radicals' views wide coverage in the party-controlled media.

Just how many rank-and-file communists will follow the breakaway leaders' exodus remains to be seen. The Central Committee staff member predicts a negligible impact. "Without them," he says, "the Communist Party will be able to reach consensus on important matters more easily."

After the breakaway, a new type of battle is likely to emerge—over the identity of the nascent Social Democratic Party. Will it be dominated by former communists, or by avowed anticommunists? Or will there be more than one Social Democratic Party?

"The main idea of the Communist Party is to make a multiparty system of communist parties," Oleg Rumyantsev says. "I think we must intervene into this plan of several post-communist parties.... [Boris] Yeltsin may be a member of a new renovated Communist Party. But Afanasyev, no." He ticks off names of communists whom he feels have opportunistically wrapped themselves in the social democratic mantle to win votes. But not all soon-to-be former communists would be automatically excluded from his party.

Rumyantsev's concern over ideological purity cuts to the heart of a key question hanging over Russia's new party politics: How democratic are these so-called democratic movements?

A recent episode brought this matter to the fore. Radical economist Larisa Piyasheva was kicked out of the Democratic Russia bloc just before Sunday's vote. Her crime: She had written articles sharply critical of the economic ideas of fellow bloc members Ilya Zaslavsky and Gavril Popov.

"In America, you don't have a bloc system in elections, so you can't compare," says Vladimir Bokser, a Democratic Russia organizer. "Every member signed an agreement to support the other bloc candidates, because in the fight against the entrenched powers, unity is crucial. Piyasheva violated that agreement."

Others were ashamed by the incident. "Unfortunately, it reflects the system in which we all grew up," says Mikhail Zarapin, another bloc member. "In our society, we have never been tolerant of opposing views."

Lithuania Risks Economic Ruin for Independence

Linda Feldmann/Esther Schrader

3/12/90

Lithuania is embarking on an unprecedented gamble in its 50 years of Soviet rule.

By declaring independence from the Soviet Union, a move being hurriedly prepared yesterday by the republic's newly elected parliament, the Baltic state is risking economic ruin.

The declaration—a "reaffirmation of nationhood" that rejects the Soviet annexation of Lithuania in 1940—will make the republic independent in name only. Though plans for economic independence have been in the works for months, the republic remains fully integrated into the Soviet economic structure.

Moscow is not expected to use force to keep the Lithuanians in the Soviet fold. But it plans to make them pay for 50 years of capital investment and subsidized production. Moscow has threatened that Lithuania will also be charged for the cost of resettling any residents who wish to leave. Twenty percent of the republic's population is non-Lithuanian, mostly Russian and Polish.

There are already signs, Lithuanian Communist sources say, that deliveries of supplies to the resource-poor Baltic nation are slowing. That's partially due to the overall decline in the Soviet Union's centrally directed economic system, "but some of this is certainly intentional," says Gediminas Kirkilas, a Central Committee aide.

Mr. Kirkilas cited shortages of energy and metal shortages as the most troubling examples. Yuri Maslyukov, chairman of the State Planning Committee (Gosplan), pointedly noted that Lithuania depends on Moscow for 75 percent of its energy needs. His remarks were published Saturday in the government daily Izvestia just as the Lithuanian parliament was convening.

The independence drive is spearheaded by the Lithuanian national movement Sajudis, which won a clear majority of the 141 parliamentary seats in last month's elections. Even with 10 seats not yet filled, Sajudis rushed to convene the republic's parliament before today's start of the extraordinary session of the Soviet higher parliament, the Congress of People's Deputies.

The congress is expected to grant Soviet leader Mikhail Gorbachev sweeping new powers when it ratifies the newly created position of "executive president." Mr. Gorbachev is virtually certain to be elected by the deputies to fill the post. Sajudis feared unilateral actions by a new super-President Gorbachev, such as a state of emergency, would block their independence drive.

Local communists doubt the wisdom of this tactic and accuse Sajudis of deceiving a now-fearful Lithuanian public about the pace of their independence timetable in parliament.

"The vote was against us Communists, not for extreme Sajudis actions," said Mr. Kirkalis. The Lithuanian Communist Party, which broke off from the Communist Party of the Soviet Union last December, also advocates independence, but at a slower pace.

"First, we need to work out the basis of economic self-sufficiency, and then declare legal independence," said Algimantas Zhukas, an aide to Lithuanian Communist Party leader (and republican president) Algirdas Brazauskas.

There were indications that Sajudis was getting cold feet about the speed of its independence moves, but having assembled the Western news media and raised expectations, the ruling council felt obliged to press on.

Sajudis is gambling that Moscow will not risk world condemnation by imposing severe hardship on Lithuania. But the Kremlin's response thus far has been anything but comforting to edgy citizens worried about the price of Lithuanian independence.

Last week, Gorbachev handed Lithuanian leader Brazauskas a bill for Soviet investment that reportedly totaled 21 billion rubles ($33 billion), payable in hard currency. And Gosplan director Maslyukov asserted Saturday that Lithuania has a 1.5 billion-ruble trade deficit with the rest of the Soviet Union.

Sajudis co-chairman Romualdas Ozalas dismisses Moscow's tough talk as scare tactics. "We have survived abundance, we will survive a blockade," he said.

The Kremlin's rhetoric may be aimed as much at other independence-minded Baltic republics, Estonia and Latvia, also annexed under the 1939 Hitler-Stalin pact.

The Lithuanians are also worried that the complex negotiations with Moscow over the financial terms of independence may not be guided by popular leader Brazauskas.

The defeat of the Brazauskas-led Communists at the polls means that the Sajudis majority in parliament is likely to elect their chairman, Vytautas Landsbergis, to the presidency. The prospect of Mr. Landsbergis, who lacks Brazauskas's personal familiarity with the halls of Kremlin power, conducting the most-important negotiations in the republic's history is not comforting to many Lithuanians. But yesterday it appeared possible that Brazauskas would become a deputy to Landsbergis and be put in charge of negotiations with Moscow.

The nationalist movement's economic blueprint for a newly independent Lithuania looks to the Finnish model. Finland, like Lithuania, has few natural resources but has succeeded economically by importing raw materials from the Soviet Union and exporting finished products to both Moscow and the West.

For now, though, Lithuania needs to earn hard currency quickly and plans on doing so by boosting tourism and establishing joint ventures with the West.

Sajudis officials cite the nation's Westernized work ethic, skilled labor pool, and low wage rate as attractive incentives for potential investors. According to Sajudis economist Kazimiera Prunskiene, Lithuania plans to introduce its own convertible currency within six months. But a team of Austrian bankers who visited the republic recently told them to hold off on any currency plans for at least a year.

Strong Soviet Presidency Sparks Debate

Linda Feldmann

3/15/90

By lining himself up to become the Soviet Union's executive president, Mikhail Gorbachev is taking a high-stakes risk that closely links his own abilities and intentions to his country's future.

After his election to the post, expected at the current extraordinary session of the legislative Congress of People's Deputies, Mr. Gorbachev will have broad—some say dictatorial—powers to impose states of emergency, hire and fire top officials, and challenge the parliament.

Few people quarrel with the need for such a post, in principle. It takes the Soviet presidency out of its ceremonial status as speaker of the parliament and places it at the top of an executive branch of government whose role has until now been carried out only by the Communist Party.

But the manner in which the new presidency has been established—and the degree of power Gorbachev will enjoy—has sparked a heated debate that some observers say could even jeopardize Gorbachev's election to the presidency.

But Soviet officials backing Gorbachev cite the gravity of the national crisis as the overriding concern.

"We are in such a difficult situation, that we need urgent action by the president in many directions to promote perestroika—in the economy, in the social sphere, to put in order the legal sphere, to try to smooth over ethnic conflicts," says Georgy Shakhnazarov, an aide to Gorbachev. "He needs his presidential 'first 100 days.'"

According to another party official, those first 100 days will include a "tightening of the screws"—not in the sense of a return to Stalinism, the official says, but rather a return to "elementary order and discipline."

Soviet officials say there is no time to lose. Thus the first executive president is not to be elected by direct popular vote, but rather by the congress. Since the congress was popularly elected, the will of the people will be reflected in a congressional vote for president, they say.

But opponents of Gorbachev's bid for a congressional vote, centered in the congress's left-radical Inter-Regional Group and in the minority republics, insist that a congressional vote will favor the most-populous, Slavic-dominated republics—and drown out the voice of ethnic minorities.

Some observers speculate that Gorbachev, whose popularity at home has declined, was afraid to face the voters directly—before his plan to improve the consumer-goods crisis has shown results.

It was this haste to put the new executive president in place that spurred the Lithuanian parliament on March 11 to declare the republic's independence from the Soviet Union. The Lithuanians feared that Gorbachev would use the enhanced powers of the presidency to block secession.

"You can only suppress with power. You can't put things in order," says Yuri Boyars, a deputy from the neighboring Baltic republic of Latvia.

In a speech to the Congress, Inter-Regional Group leader Yuri Afanasyev explained the group's objections to the new presidency. The law may be introduced, he said, "only if and when it can be incorporated in a whole, single organic text of a new democratic Constitution."

Mr. Afanasyev laid out five conditions for the establishment of a new presidency:

Conclusion of a new union agreement among the Soviet republics, that would redefine the power relationship between Moscow and the republics' governments. There is virtual national consensus that such a new agreement is long overdue.

Formation of a "fully authoritative Supreme Soviet." As long as Gorbachev is able to dominate the parliament to the degree he does now, it cannot serve as a real check on his power. Some Soviet scholars on presidential power are troubled by the new law's provision that will allow the Soviet president to suggest to the Congress of People's Deputies (also compliant to Gorbachev) that it dissolve and reelect the Supreme Soviet when its two chambers cannot settle a dispute.

Establishment of a system of direct presidential election based on a new union agreement.

Development of a multiparty system, in which a presidential race takes place in an arena of "normal political struggle." On March 13 the amendment of Article 6 of the Constitution, which guaranteed the Communist Party's leading role, paved the way for legalization of other parties.

A rule that prevents the president from holding a position of power in a political party.

Afanasyev hurt the Inter-Regional Group's cause when he then criticized Vladimir Lenin directly—still a politically suicidal approach. Afanasyev referred to "the principle of a state policy of mass violence and terror."

But the last point in Afanasyev's argument, forbidding the president to hold a party position, almost received the two-thirds majority of votes need to include it in the Constitution. If it had passed, a newly installed President Gorbachev would have been required to resign as general-secretary of the Communist Party.

This may happen anyway, says Gorbachev aide Shakhnazarov.

Lenders Leery As Debts Mount

Amy Kaslow

3/16/90

Until recently, the Soviet Union boasted a virtually unblemished record for paying its bills on time. Today, financial analysts and international bankers are leery of the country's deteriorating creditworthiness. Perestroika (restructuring) is suffering the consequences.

Put simply, the country cannot generate ample foreign exchange from its exports to satisfy pressing consumer demands, modernize antiquated industry, and engage in a host of costly changes that will revitalize its ailing economy.

The ranking Soviet exports that command hard currency payments are oil and gas, gold, and weapons. CIA estimates put Soviet hard currency income at $26 billion for 1986; another more current estimate is $37 billion per year. Regardless, almost all of these earnings are used to purchase Western imports and serve an increasing debt, now $50 billion to $60 billion.

Gorby fever

"From 1979 to 1984 the Soviets were not borrowing from Western banks," says Judy Shelton, a fellow at Stanford University's Hoover Institution and author of a new book, "The Coming Soviet Crash." In 1985 and 1986, she says, "bankers saw the USSR as a fresh address. And then they were caught up in the excitement of Gorbachev. Today, creditors are scared. A lot of joint ventures, brought out with great fanfare, aren't making it."

Ms. Shelton says the Soviets see joint ventures as "the best way to transfer capital. It's not borrowing, so it doesn't scare the bankers." The Soviets have set up many trade organizations with self-financing systems, she says, and this transition to decentralized accounting is proving difficult for an economy steeped in centralized planning. "A lot of accounts are piling up," Shelton says.

Soviet planners are looking for ways to supplement hard currency holdings. Last November at the COMECON meeting in Sofia, Bulgaria, Soviet leader Mikhail Gorbachev called for the introduction of hard currency payments at world market prices for Soviet energy supplies to Eastern Europe.

The USSR also acts as a creditor, but at considerable cost to its own economy. Soviet defense exports are central, says Roger Robinson, a Washington-based consultant and former National Security Council official. Soviet loans to Third World countries, he says, "range somewhere between $50 to $60 billion . . . . The majority of these loans were arms sales to impoverished client-states like Nicaragua, Vietnam, Ethiopia and Syria." This money is largely non-repayable.

"Weapons exports to the Middle East are the only manufactured goods that reap substantial foreign exchange," says Ms. Shelton. "Before the price of oil dropped, the Soviets were paid in cash by Syria, Libya, and Iraq. After [the Arab oil-producing states] were hit by the drop in oil prices, other means of payment had to be established."

Shelton recounts a hushed discussion with a defector who used to run the foreign accounts desk. "He told me that he asked Iraq [then engaged in a financially debilitating war with Iran] to pay not in dollars, but in gold, which the Soviets could turn around and sell in the world market."

Just as US politicians anticipate a "peace dividend" as a bonus to federal budget programs, the Supreme Soviet is examining prospects for converting defense industries into civil production.

Soviet peace dividend?

The five-year plan is to cut defense expenditures by one-third, according to a report issued by the USSR State Planning Committee. The estimated cost for technical re-equipment, new plants, and employee training is 40 billion rubles (US $66 billion). The top production priorities are: foodstuffs and consumer goods, equipment for the light and food industries, computer technology, communications systems, medical equipment, civilian aircraft, and ships.

Increased domestic production would free some of the country's precious foreign currency holdings that now go for consumer goods. Just as significant is the Soviet intention to export more of this production to reap hard currency.

Ms. Shelton refers to Soviet economist Abel Aganbegyan's view that the transition from defense to civilian production "is going very, very slowly. New capital is needed to build new factories and to retool exisitng ones. The one thing the Soviets do not have in the budget is funds for capital investment."

Estonia Takes Quiet Steps Toward Independence

Linda Feldmann

3/20/90

Estonia will not declare independence—it will simply achieve it.

That was the message from Estonians of various political groupings last weekend as the republic went to the polls to elect a new parliament (Supreme Soviet).

As reports circulated that troops were maneuvering in the sister Baltic republic of Lithuania, Estonians were quietly assuring themselves that their own route to independence might in the end be less fraught with peril than that of the Lithuanians.

The Estonian plan is to negotiate an independence agreement with Moscow that would remove Soviet troops from Estonian soil and hand full control of the republic's affairs, including the economy, to local control. On Sunday evening, senior Estonian leaders headed for Moscow at the request of Soviet President Mikhail Gorbachev for discussions.

Estonian sentiment in favor of full independence has gained intensity—fanned by the formation of a grass-roots alternative parliament called the Congress of Estonia. The new grass-roots parliament does not wield any real power, but carries tremendous moral force as an expression of the will of the Estonia's native population.

The relationship between the Congress, the newly elected Supreme Soviet, and the crumbling Communist Party are changing the political landscape of this tiny republic of 1.5 million. The balance of forces in the new Supreme Soviet, and the makeup of the Estonian government it will elect, will play a pivotal role in determining Estonia's stance on independence.

Political figures once considered on the radical fringe—such as Tunne Kelam, the Estonian National Independence Party leader, and Trivimi Velliste, leader of the Estonian Historical Preservation Society—are now key players as leaders in the Congress.

Estonia's current Communist leaders want to include Mr. Kelam and Mr. Velliste in the team that will negotiate independence with Moscow.

But Congress leaders regard themselves as the legitimate representatives of the Estonian people and plan to hold their own negotiations with the new Estonian Supreme Soviet as a vehicle for establishing contacts with the Kremlin. People like Prime Minister Indrek Toome and Arnold Ruutel, the popular Estonian President, can also play a useful role "initially" in negotiating with Moscow, says Velliste.

Early returns on Monday from Russian-dominated areas showed the Popular Front doing relatively well. In preliminary results for 45 of the 105 seats, the Popular Front won 19. Nine went to the Communist Party and the Free Estonia coalition, a new group formed by several top Estonian Communist Party leaders in an apparent effort to distance themselves from the party.

The Communist Party itself is crumbling, its leaders admit. After the party's congress on March 23, its 100,000 members will regroup—some in a small Communist Party loyal to Moscow, some in a small independent Communist Party, and the rest in other parties.

"I'm sure that a fairly large number will, for a while at least, not belong to any party," Prime Minister Toome, a founder of Free Estonia, said in an interview. "They will want to look around and see what's happening, and define themselves. Today, no one can talk seriously about new political parties. We have personalities and their fans."

Though Congress leaders do not recognize the Supreme Soviet as a legitimate body, they still are trying to use it as a tool for achieving their aims. Thus, 84 members of the Congress are also running for the Supreme Soviet—as a sort of Trojan Horse that will, when the time comes, introduce a motion to disband the Supreme Soviet. The Congress also hopes to make its policies into Supreme Soviet policies via its candidates.

Congress leaders acknowledge the paradox of their approach, but say they need to be pragmatic.

"When you're driving in a car, you must take all the instruments of repair with you along the way," says Estonian writer Lennart Meri. "But we know where we are going. We are restoring the independence of a small nation that has been occupied."

The election of the Congress of Estonia put the Estonian Popular Front in a tough position. At first, the front opposed it, saying it would divide pro-independence forces. But as the drive to register Estonian citizens picked up momentum, many Popular Front leaders joined the bandwagon and ran for the Congress as well.

"The Congress's main effect has been to radicalize Estonia's Communist leadership," says a longtime Western observer of Estonian politics. "But the people must let those experienced in the Kremlin handle negotiations."

Soviets Soften Stance on Use of Force in Baltic Republics

Linda Feldmann

3/22/90

Troop movements and military overflights have ended in Lithuania, calming fears that Moscow might order outright military intervention to block Lithuanian independence.

But analysts here and in the Lithuanian capital, Vilnius, say they don't think Soviet leader Mikhail Gorbachev had seriously planned a full military crackdown on the rebellious Baltic republic—at least for now. Foreign Minister Eduard Shevardnadze underscored this Tuesday in Namibia, when he told reporters, "We are against the use of force in any region and particularly against using force domestically."

Mr. Shevardnadze's statement apparently flies in the face of recent examples of Soviet military use—January's troop invasion into Baku, aimed at reasserting Soviet control there, and the April 1989 use of Army troops and poison gas to break up a demonstration in Tbilisi, Georgia.

But the question of the future of the Baltic republics seems to be a fundamentally different situation. A Soviet parliament commission has already declared illegal the secret 1939 protocol that allowed the Soviet Union to annex the three small nations. Western nations do not formally recognize the Baltics' inclusion in the Soviet Union.

If the Kremlin were to use force to prevent Baltic independence, it would likely spell the end of Mr. Gorbachev's five-year program of economic and political restructuring. But analysts say the Kremlin's approach has been more to use all the available levers—flexing military muscle while maintaining at least low-level contacts with Lithuanian representatives in Moscow.

"Gorbachev wanted to show the Lithuanians who's really in control," says a Western diplomatic observer. "He has done that convincingly, and now he can negotiate with them at his own pace. It's clear that both sides would rather talk than fight."

On Monday, as a three-day Kremlin deadline requiring Lithuania to rescind its March 11 declaration of independence expired, Gorbachev met for 30 minutes with Lithuanian members of the Soviet parliament. The Lithuanians, who say they now attend sessions as nonvoting observers, presented Gorbachev with a statement from Lithuanian President Vytautas Landsbergis rejecting the Soviet parliament's declaration last week that Lithuania had acted illegally.

On Monday, Gorbachev authorized "priority measures" to enforce his stand, later defined as including an increase in guards at the republic's nuclear power plants and other "vital installations of federal property." On Tuesday, Mr. Landsbergis reported that extra guards had appeared outside the Ignalina nuclear power plant. The Lithuanians voted in parliament to set up border posts and customs checkpoints.

Gorbachev's carrot-and-stick approach seems calculated to set a precedent for his handling of other independence-minded republics—Lithuania's Baltic neighbors, Estonia and Latvia, and Georgia to the south.

Earlier this week, the top Communist leaders of Estonia and Latvia came to Moscow for talks with Gorbachev. A report by the Soviet news agency Tass Tuesday described Gorbachev's meeting with Latvian President Anatoly Gorbunovs, party leader Jan Vagris, and Prime Minister Vilnis-Edvins Bresis as aimed at discussing "the development of the Soviet federation and the principles of a future union treaty."

On Monday, Gorbachev spent four hours talking to Estonia's Communist leaders. The main items of discussion were the future of the republic's Communist Party, which has lost its cohesion, and republican sovereignty.

On Sunday, elections in Latvia and Estonia for the republics' parliaments gave decisive victories to the independence-minded popular fronts. In Latvia, Tass said the Popular Front won 109 of the 170 seats decided in the first round of voting. Runoff elections will be held for the remaining 31 seats. In Estonia, Popular Front candidates were also expected to win a majority of seats, initial results indicate.

Gorbachev must also revise his political calculations for the three Slavic republics—Russia, the Ukraine, and Byelorussia—where pro-reform radicals scored major victories in runoff elections Sunday for local councils and republican parliaments. The city councils of Moscow, Leningrad, and Kiev will all be controlled by candidates who ran on radical reform platforms.

In addition, a majority of the republican parliamentary deputies elected in those cities are from the radical camp.

In Minsk, the capital of Byelorussia, both the mayor and the city's party chief were defeated in the election. And in the Arctic Pechora mining region, Mikhail Shchadov, the minister of the Soviet coal industry, was defeated for the Russian parliament by Viktor Yakovlev, a shift foreman from Vorkuta.

Soviet Muscle-Flexing Raises Stakes in Lithuania

Linda Feldmann

3/26/90

Gorbachev-watchers are having a field day as the Soviet president's duel with Lithuanian leader Vytautas Landsbergis unfolds in day-by-day drama.

Why is Mikhail Gorbachev intentionally, as it seems, raising tensions with the breakaway Baltic republic? How far is he willing to go to keep Lithuania in the Soviet fold? How can he emerge without losing face?

In the most striking example of Soviet muscle-flexing, armored personnel carriers rumbled past the Lithuanian parliament building as deputies met inside in the wee hours of Saturday morning.

A week ago, Western diplomatic observers said Moscow's show of force appeared to be designed to demonstrate where the real power lies in this showdown, in advance of negotiations. Some are wondering aloud if Gorbachev is contemplating some form of state of emergency. Moscow also might be trying to provoke interethnic clashes between the 80 percent majority Lithuanians and the minority Russians and Poles, as a pretext for martial law.

But as the level of concern rises among Lithuanians, so does resolve to stand their ground. Some local leaders are calling Moscow's bluff.

"It seems to me that Moscow is completely immobilized by other forces and bound by promises to the United States not to use force," pro-independence editor Algimantas Cekuolis said in Vilnius. "But of course the traditional response of Russia when it's short of arguments is to use military force, and it's short of arguments. But I think eventually reason will prevail."

Western analysts tend to be more surprised than Soviets at the turn of events since Lithuania's parliament declared the republic's independence on March 11. Moscow and Vilnius have traded volleys almost daily, ratcheting tensions upward since the March 12-15 extraordinary Congress of People's Deputies that gave Mr. Gorbachev added powers as "executive president."

On March 15, the congress nullified Lithuania's decision. The next day, Gorbachev sent Mr. Landsbergis a telegram, giving Lithuania three days to rescind its declaration. Lithuania rejected the demand. Over that weekend, Lithuanian leaders complained of military planes flying low over Vilnius and troop maneuvers in the countryside.

Last Monday, the Soviet prime minister had warned against Lithuania's plans to take over control of federal enterprises and establish its own border posts. Two days later, Gorbachev issued a decree ordering the KGB to step up border security; all citizens to hand in firearms within seven days; and tightened control of foreigners' presence in the republic. Two American diplomats were later ordered to leave. On Thursday, Gorbachev ordered Lithuania to halt formation of voluntary border forces and ordered Lithuanian deserters from the Soviet Army to return to their units.

In Moscow, foreign affairs analyst Leonid Mlechin predicted that Gorbachev will use his tactical skills to emerge from the crisis without appearing to have made major concessions. For now, Lithuania's leaders say they will not submit to a republicwide referendum on secession, explaining that the people have already made their choice. But that may be the kind of concession Lithuania will need to make to get its way.

Mr. Mlechin, a writer for the liberal weekly New Times, offered three reasons why Gorbachev has been turning up the pressure on Lithuania.

"First," he said, "Gorbachev is reacting to the population, which is sharply against separation. If he acted against public opinion, it would strengthen feeling against him.

"Second, if he lets [Lithuania] go, then others will start knocking at the door—and we know who they are. He also doesn't want to go down in history as the man who gave this country a push toward its dissolution."

A third factor, Mlechin continued, is that Gorbachev is an emotional person and he is insulted by Lithuania's move. "He is thinking, 'I gave them all these opportunities, and they spit in my face,' " said Mlechin.

The central Soviet press has been largely negative about Lithuania's attempt to restore its prewar independence. One commentary carried by the Soviet news agency Tass—"Lithuanian Deputies: Saints or Thugs?"—highlighted the alleged criminal careers of two members of parliament. Newspapers have also prominently covered the concerns of Lithuania's minority communities and the small faction of the republic's Communist Party that remains loyal to Moscow.

But Sunday, in a front-page article from Lithuania, the national party daily Pravda offered a more tempered analysis: "Today, many people here are living with a divided consciousness—which law to follow, whose will to fulfill? On the one hand, the republic's parliament was elected legally and it should not go unrecognized. But on the other, its legal acts clearly contradict the Constitution of the USSR. People want definition, they await rational actions from politicians."

Lithuanians Meet Kremlin Officials

Linda Feldmann

4/5/90

After three weeks of heated rhetoric and military muscle-flexing, Moscow and the Lithuanians have finally sat down for quiet discussions.

For now, the most important thing is that they are meeting at all. And for the Lithuanian team that came to Moscow the morning of April 2 hoping to gain an audience with someone of at least moderate importance, getting to see Alexander Yakovlev—Politburo member, Presidential Council member, and a close ally of President Mikhail Gorbachev—was a pleasant surprise.

The April 3 discussions, seen by the Lithuanians as a prelude to formal negotiations over independence, did not reach any firm conclusions, say Lithuanian sources. They were scheduled to meet April 4 with Vadim Bakatin, interior minister and a Presidential Council member, but the meeting did not take place. It was not clear why, or whether the meeting would be held later.

The semantics of the April 3 meeting were delicate.

"I would like to clarify," said Lithuanian lawyer Egidius Bickauskas, taking special care that journalists use the right terminology, "that this is not a meeting between an official delegation and a government official. This is something between a consultation and a conversation."

Only hours earlier, Arkady Maslennikov, Mr. Gorbachev's newly appointed press secretary, had said that the Soviet government was not willing to talk to any Soviet delegation that claimed to represent a foreign country.

But Moscow has been insisting all along—despite the heightened Soviet military presence in Lithuania and the building-by-building takeover of Communist Party property there—that it would prefer to settle its clash with Lithuania, which declared independence on March 11, through peaceful dialogue. Both parties seemed to be searching for the right way to frame their approaches to one another.

From Moscow's perspective, says Igor Sedykh, Novosti Press Agency analyst, the Lithuanians who came to Moscow this week are "the first serious delegation" sent by the Baltic republic. At the lead is Deputy Prime Minister

Romualdas Ozolas, a member of the Soviet Congress of People's Deputies and a relative moderate within the leadership of Lithuania's ruling Sajudis movement. Also meeting with Mr. Yakovlev were Romas Gudaitis and Mecislovas Laurinkus, both members of the presidium of the Lithuanian parliament.

In addition, Lithuania has named Mr. Bickauskas as its permanent representative in Moscow. This creates another conflict with Moscow; only the Soviet Council of Ministers has the right to designate republics' Moscow representatives. But Bickauskas is respected here as a talented young lawyer with good diplomatic skills, and as a formerly active member of the standing Soviet parliament, the Supreme Soviet, he knows the Moscow political landscape. "Ozolas and Bickauskas—they are 'figures,'" says Mr. Sedykh.

Some Soviet officials have complained that if Lithuanian President Vytautas Landsbergis had been serious about starting a dialogue sooner, he could have come to Moscow himself.

Nikolai Medvedev, a Russian Lithuanian and another "bridge builder" sent to Moscow by Mr. Landsbergis, says the public mood in Lithuania would not allow the Lithuanian leader to come here now. "They would do this," says Mr. Medvedev, turning his head away.

Another element in the Moscow-Lithuania drama was the Soviet parliament's passage April 3 of a law on secession—another of what Soviet television called the "late laws" being pushed through the legislative process. The law must be approved by a two-thirds vote by the larger parliamentary body, the Congress of People's Deputies, which must approve any proposed changes to the Soviet Constitution.

Formally, the Soviet Constitution allows any republic to secede. The new law is called "late," because it was conceptualized long after the Baltic independence drive started—and at this point, the proverbial horse has left the barn. Furthermore, the three Baltic republics say this law does not apply to them, because they became part of the Soviet Union unwillingly. But Baltic representatives here are nevertheless keenly interested in the law's provisions, which are so stiff that, says Medvedev, "it's not a law on leaving, it's a law on not leaving."

In a meeting with American reporters April 4, Presidential Council member Yuri Osipyan tried to put a positive spin on the new legislation.

"I believe that, under the Soviet Constitution and under our new laws, every republic has the right to secede from the Soviet Union," said Professor Osipyan, a leading physicist.

"Moreover, you know that we are discussing the machinery of secession. So if the Lithuanian leadership will just wait for a while—I don't mean 5 or 10 years, I mean a period of several months—we would be able to discuss the situation within the framework of the emerging laws."

Under the law, a republic may secede after fulfilling the following steps:

At least two-thirds of the citizens of a republic favor secession in a republicwide referendum.

A Congress of People's Deputies sets a transitional period of no more than five years, during which property and financial issues with the republic are settled.

The status of any territories in the republic that did not belong to it at the time it joined the Soviet Union would be reviewed. The status of areas inhabited by nonnative ethnic groups would also be reconsidered.

If a referendum on secession does not pass by two-thirds, a new referendum may be held only after 10 years have passed.

Any autonomous republics or regions within a republic will have separate referendums.

During the transition period, one-tenth of the population—or the republic's government—may decide to hold a new referendum.

The decision to secede will be reversed if the second vote does not pass by two-thirds.

At the end of the transitional period, the Congress of People's Deputies must confirm that all interests have been satisfied before actual secession may take place.

Soviet Conservatives Fight Back Against Liberals in the Party

Linda Feldmann

4/16/90

The fate of this summer's 28th congress of the Soviet Communist Party—seen as crucial as the party continues to lose credibility—may already be sealed.

When the party leadership decided to move forward the date of its next five-year congress from fall to summer, the stated reason was the "urgent need for party renewal."

Translation: Time to get rid of the dead wood in the Central Committee, which is more conservative than the party as a whole.

But the Central Committee's release last week of an "open letter" harshly critical of the party's left-radical bloc, called the Democratic Platform, has launched open warfare within the party and sent a strong signal that the congress is likely to be dominated by conservative delegates.

The timing of the letter, several weeks in formulation, according to party officials, is no accident. The process of electing congress delegates in local party organizations is starting. And local party bosses now have clear marching orders: Supporters of the Democratic Platform, accused in the letter of attempting to destroy the party from within, are beyond the pale of current Communist thought and are not welcome at the congress, which opens July 2.

The platform's leaders—which include Boris Yeltsin, Yuri Afanasyev, and Gavril Popov—say their group has more than 100,000 active supporters in 100 cities.

Igor Chubais, a platform leader who was expelled from the party the day the letter was released, says he doesn't think platform supporters will be completely shut out of the congress.

"Some will be allowed to participate, so the party can show how 'democratic' it has become," says Mr. Chubais. "But the sense is clear. The Democratic Platform is now under control."

There was always a paradoxical aspect to Soviet leader Mikhail Gorbachev's plan for party renewal. In essence, the Central Committee was to approve rules for the democratic selection of delegates, who could then vote them out of their positions. Would the conservatives sit still for this?

In the eyes of Democratic Platform leaders, they haven't. The letter, which was read over central television and published on the front pages of central newspapers, bears the stamp of Politburo conservative Yegor Ligachev—himself thought to have been in danger of losing his Central Committee seat at the congress.

But even if Mr. Ligachev initiated the letter, the whole party leadership—including Gorbachev—would have signed off on it as a consensus document, points out a Central Committee official. This may be a signal that Gorbachev, now executive president of the country, isn't as devoted to preserving the party as he was in the past. In his month as president, Gorbachev has clearly tried to shift the power balance toward his new Presidential Council and away from the party Politburo.

This is not to say that Gorbachev would have wanted to fight to keep the likes of Mr. Afanasyev, a historian who openly denounces Vladimir Lenin, in the party. Afanasyev and Mr. Popov, likely to be Moscow's next mayor, have already indicated plans to leave the party anyway.

The question is more one of image: A party expelling members looks like a party on the defensive.

But the greatest irony is that Gorbachev has consistently adopted the policies of the party's left, while continuing to lash out verbally at its members. Some analysts say the latest maneuver against the Democratic Platform would protect Gorbachev's right flank, as he stands on the threshold of risky reforms toward a market-oriented economy.

For the platform leadership, the attack from the Central Committee has forced the question of tactics toward the party congress—to go or not to go. At a meeting after the letter's release, platform leaders agreed to disagree. Afanasyev, Popov, and Chubais say they have no choice but to leave the party, that it is no longer possible to take constructive action from inside the party.

"The best option would have been to have the party split at the congress, for maximum effect," says Chubais, "but it is no longer possible to wait."

Many of Afanasyev's followers had urged him to stick with the party until the congress, thus allowing his views wide play in the central news media, which will broadcast and print transcripts of the proceedings. Furthermore, some view bowing out of the party now as playing right into the hands of the conservatives.

"I look at things differently," Afanasyev said in an interview. "It seems to me, after that announcement, that to remain involved with the 28th party congress would be a powerful illusion to the party membership, and, more important, to society, regarding the possibility of renewing this party."

"I want to say," he continued, "that that hope is meaningless, and that with this party you need not only to break away, but to gain as much distance from it as possible."

Central Committee member Boris Yeltsin, speaking privately Saturday to a small group of deputies from the new Russian parliament, said he would keep his membership through the party congress and then assess the new Central Committee makeup before deciding what to do.

If elected president of the Russian Republic, a post he was nominated for on Saturday by the Russian parliament's so-called Democratic Bloc, Mr. Yeltsin said he would "suspend" his membership in the Communist Party.

"I will need to represent the partyless and the masses," he said.

Soviet Military Under the Gun In Gorbachev Era

Peter Grier

4/23/90

These are tough times for the Soviet military. Its prestige has been battered by the Afghan war. Its tanks are rumbling home from Eastern Europe as the Warsaw Pact disintegrates. Its influence in Moscow has been diminished by perestroika, while at the same time it pulls police duty in Lithuania and other restive Soviet republics.

Now the generals may be trying to fight back, say military analysts in the United States. With President Gorbachev's programs drawing increasing criticism at home, senior military commanders are beginning to speak out on basic policy. Resurgent military clout might be the reason the Soviets have recently taken a harder line in arms control negotiations.

"There's no doubt that the Soviet military is under a great deal of stress," said Henry Rowan, US assistant defense secretary for international security affairs, at a recent meeting with reporters.

Chief of the Soviet general staff Mikhail Moiseyev has put off a mid-May visit to the United States indefinitely, saying he must help prepare for the May 30 Bush-Gorbachev summit. Though new to his job, General Moiseyev is said to play a much more active role in arms control policy than did his predecessor, Marshal Sergei Akhromeyev.

"The high command seems more predisposed to be drawn into the political fray," says Robert Nurick, a RAND analyst of Soviet defense policy.

In the Brezhnev era, to be a member of the Soviet armed forces was to be part of arguably the most powerful and prestigious institution in the nation. The military had first call on scarce raw materials, and many Soviet weapons were the equal of those produced in the more technologically sophisticated West.

That status began to slip in the late 1970s as the economic weakness of the Soviet Union became apparent, according to US experts. When Gorbachev took over, the slide became a free fall.

Like a shrewd politician consolidating his power Gorbachev moved to take control of the military structure. By 1989, the military high command had been almost completely replaced. The new commanders were on average 10 years younger than their predecessors. Many had served in Afghanistan. According to a RAND Corporation study, they were distinguished not by enthusiasm for perestroika (economic restructuring) but by evident sensitivity to unrest in the ranks of the military itself.

To diminish the military's political clout, Gorbachev and his allies began to attack it in public. In one notable speech Foreign Minister Eduard Shevardnadze criticized military decisionmaking and called the country's chemical weapons program something motivated by "primitive and distorted" notions.

The Kremlin also set policies that cut against the military grain, from unilateral force cuts in Europe, to the Afghan withdrawal, to the many Soviet concessions made in arms talks. While military commanders may have agreed with many of these moves, the speed and unpredictability of Gorbachev's policy was unsettling.

Though the military appears to share many of Gorbachev's broader foreign policy goals, "senior military commanders have been very reluctant to pay the price" in force reductions that Gorbachev wants, according to a RAND study.

And while Gorbachev has been attacking the military from without, it has been beset by troubles within. Low pay and long hours have always been the lot of the largely conscripted rank and file; now officers' lives are apparently worsening as well.

There is no longer enough officer housing to go around. Defense Minister Dmitri Yazov recently told a Soviet reporter there are 7,500 officers without apartments in Moscow alone. The decline in social status of the officer corps has been so rapid that they are now prime targets for crime and murder. Soviet military publications show that 59 officers were killed last year, according to Harriet Fast Scott, a Washington consultant on the Soviet military.

Ethnic tensions rippling through the country as a whole are if anything worse in the armed forces. While officers remain largely ethnic Russian and Slav, an increasing percentage of conscripts are from Central Asia and other far-flung parts of the country and speak Russian poorly, if at all.

The Soviet draft-age cohort is "up to 40 percent Muslim," says Alexander Alexiev, a RAND specialist in Soviet nationalities.

The Soviet practice of sending young draftees far from their home for service has been a spark lighting the nationalist revolt in the Baltics and other separatist republics. Baltic draftees face fierce ethnic hazing, and perhaps worse—in 1986 an Estonian separatist group reported that 12 Estonian draftees were shot during a protest strike against their work cleaning up the Chernobyl nuclear plant. General Moiseyev has said that draft evasion last year was eight times the level of 1985.

Use of regular Army troops as a police force in Azerbaijan and a tool of intimidation in Lithuania has solidified the military's image as conservative and anti-separatist. The military appears ambivalent about its new internal role. In public statements many officers have seemed sensitive to the fact that internal deployments lower their status in the eyes of much of the population and exacerbate the military's own ethnic problems. At the same time, conservative older commanders see themselves as a bastion of the state and see that role as an opportunity.

"They don't like to do it, but they know this is the last leverage they have with the party," says RAND's Mr. Alexiev.

Conservatives Turn Up Heat On Gorbachev

Linda Feldmann

4/27/90

Lithuanians, be grateful. Soviet leader Mikhail Gorbachev could be responding to you more harshly than he has. In fact, the public is demanding it.

That was the message from Prime Minister Nikolai Ryzhkov to Romas Gudaitis in an unscheduled encounter in the foyer of the Soviet parliament Wednesday.

Mr. Gudaitis, part of the four-member Lithuanian delegation sent here to pursue contacts with the Soviet government, spent his half-hour tête-á-tête with Mr. Ryzhkov, hearing the now-worn arguments over Lithuania's March 11 declaration of independence. Yes, under the Soviet Constitution Lithuania has the right to secede. But no, it must follow the procedure outlined in the new law on secession. Lithuania must return to its status of March 10. Then everyone can sit down for talks.

The Kremlin's deadlock with Lithuania is not expected to break for at least a couple of weeks, after the Baltic republic begins to feel the effects of Moscow's drastic reduction of energy supplies, Soviet and Western analysts say. But in the meantime, remarks like Ryzhkov's about the pressure Mr. Gorbachev faces raise questions about the forces at play behind the scenes, not only over Lithuania but also over the economy and German unity.

"We've received lots of telegrams reporting many resolutions of meetings, which ask: 'Why, Gorbachev, haven't you introduced presidential rule?' " Ryzhkov told Gudaitis as reporters pressed in around them.

"You know that Gorbachev is doing his utmost not to take this step. And he is holding back the administration from this step. Why don't you consider this? . . . Do you really not know that the whole union criticizes us for indecisiveness?"

Ryzhkov also warned of the consolidation of right-wing forces and their pressure for "decisive measures." He hastened to add that he personally opposes direct presidential rule in Lithuania.

The line "we have telegrams supporting our position" is a time-honored Kremlin argument, but in the case of Lithuania, there is reason to believe that public sympathy in Russia does not favor the Lithuanians' cause. Early this month, a Moscow demonstration called in support of Lithuania was sparsely attended—fewer than 1,000 people. Unscientific street surveys have revealed a sense of indignation that the Lithuanians aren't "following the rules."

And at a recent meeting of the leadership of the Soviet parliament's pro-reform Interregional Group of Deputies, many spoke harshly of the Lithuanians' behavior. Sergei Stankevich, now also deputy mayor of Moscow, complained that the Lithuanians—who were meant to be comrades-in-arms in the fight for radical economic restructuring—were bailing out at the crucial moment.

Such an attitude may not bode well for Lithuania's plan to approach radical city governments like Moscow's for direct trade ties. (This plan would probably not be workable in any event, since Soviet forces tightly control Lithuania's borders.)

When considering the pressures Gorbachev faces on Lithuania, the broader context must be taken into account, analysts say.

"There is a fairly substantial body of opinion—some military, party apparat, Russian chauvinist—that feels that defending the borders is a basic national issue," a Western ambassador says. "It's clear that a series of developments have become increasingly worrisome to military leaders and military-minded people. The feeling is a little more desperate than it was a couple of years ago."

Aside from Lithuania, the ambassador lists the humiliating Afghan withdrawal, the accelerating Soviet military departure from Eastern Europe, the quickening pace of German reunification, and the rising Soviet crime rate.

When Sergei Akhromeyev, a Gorbachev military adviser, told the British Broadcasting Corporation this week that military force may be needed in Lithuania, Soviet civilian leaders distanced themselves from the remark—especially as Washington considered sanctions against Moscow for its actions.

Still, Marshal Akhromeyev's statement reflected the common view at the Soviet Defense Ministry, where complaints about the Foreign Ministry's "softness" are frequently heard.

But for the military, the issue most threatening to national stability is the impending economic reform measures. After appearing on the verge of announcing reforms in prices, taxes, and property a few weeks ago, the government backed away. Gorbachev's Presidential Council has been locked in debate over how to proceed.

On Wednesday, Ryzhkov said the toughest question remains price reform. Other government figures have said the cost of many everyday items could double or triple, as the state attempts to rationalize its pricing structure.

The risk for Gorbachev is that workers will strike over the sharp rise in the cost of living. In his visit to the industrial city of Sverdlovsk this week, Gorbachev has stressed that the much-anticipated economic reforms will not be "shock therapy" on the lines of Poland's economic reform.

But if Gorbachev is going to begin a real structural reform, he will have to take measures that hurt. And, as many officials have observed, the Soviet Union has not had the years of economic pain—as Poland has had—to prepare it for the changes.

"We may be facing what Poland experienced in the early '80s, when the country became ungovernable," says Vikenty Matveev, a columnist for the newspaper Izvestia.

Latvians Brace for Moscow's Sanctions

Linda Feldmann

5/7/90

With one eye firmly on neighboring Lithuania, Latvia has striven to reach a formula for independence that would at least soften the blow for Moscow.

The Baltic republic's declaration, approved Friday by just over the necessary two-thirds majority in the Latvian parliament, did not proclaim independence outright. Rather, it announced the beginning of a process that would ultimately lead to renewed nationhood.

But Soviet President Mikhail Gorbachev, who now faces a unified Baltic bloc set on breaking away from his country, apparently is not impressed.

The official Soviet news agency Tass said that Mr. Gorbachev has ruled out talks with Latvia until the republic fully restores the Soviet Constitution. Tass quoted Alfred Rubiks, the leader of the pro-Moscow majority of Latvia's Communist Party, as saying that Gorbachev considers Friday's declaration "a breach of constitutional norms which is leading to a breakdown of state ties between the republic and the USSR."

Mr. Rubiks, who said he spoke with the Soviet president by telephone, warned that Gorbachev "reserves the right to take retaliatory political, economic, and administrative measures."

Many pro-independence Latvians had already been expecting sanctions from Moscow, no matter how muted the declaration of independence. Mavriks Vulfsons, a leading Latvian legislator, reacted with equanimity when asked what he thought Moscow might do.

"Nothing in particular, nothing tragic," responded Mr. Vulfsons. "Well, maybe they'll postpone the May 15 negotiations [with Gorbachev aides]."

As Moscow and Lithuania have been slugging it out loudly and publicly, the Kremlin has continued quiet discussions with the other two Baltic republics.

With the example of Lithuania's escalating economic crisis as a present reminder of what could face Latvia and Estonia, Gorbachev advisers, including Politburo and Presidential Council member Alexander Yakovlev, have offered the other two Baltic republics the "special status" of confederation with the Soviet Union.

The term confederation could be interpreted as a loose alliance of independent nations—but many Latvians, remembering that the republic's 1939 "mutual defense pact" with the Soviet Union led to annexation in 1940, are leery of such a deal.

"After seeing Gorbachev's attitude to Russian democrats, I personally disbelieve this man," says Juris Bojars, a parliament deputy, referring to the Soviet Communist Party's attempt to drive some pro-reform radicals out of the party.

"If we really had a proper confederation—why not? But I cannot believe it. After our very strong pressure, they [promised] us economic independence, but they haven't given it to us. The government constantly undermines this independence. If we cannot achieve even economic independence, how can we achieve, in the framework of the Soviet Union, real sovereignty?"

Meanwhile, Latvians are bracing for harsh economic sanctions. The Latvian Popular Front has formed an antiblockade committee. Vegetable gardening has grown in popularity. Already Latvia is feeling the effect of Moscow's wrath, as sanctions against Lithuania reverberate beyond that republic's borders. Much of Latvia's gasoline comes from Lithuania's Mazeikiai oil refinery, now deprived of deliveries.

Still, Latvia is clearly trying to avoid the experience of Lithuania, which declared immediate independence March 11. Moscow's retaliatory cutoff of oil and deep cuts in gas deliveries have immobilized the republic's economy. Deputy Prime Minister Algirdas Brazauskas says Lithuania will be out of oil in the next two weeks unless it finds alternative sources.

Pro-independence Latvians are also mindful of the republic's sizable non-Latvian population, almost half of its citizens. Although many non-Latvians support independence—42 percent, according to a recent poll by the Soviet government daily Izvestia—Latvia's minorities nevertheless want assurances that their rights will be protected.

Unlike Lithuania, Latvia left parts of the Soviet Constitution in force, while reinstating some of the underlying principles of Latvia's 1922 Constitution. Latvia also stressed its desire to maintain a dialogue with Moscow during the unspecified transition period toward independence.

In contrast with Lithuania and Estonia, Latvia said it is willing to compromise on the military. The presence of Soviet military bases in Latvia "should be based on a treaty that would develop from the principles of the Oct. 5, 1939, mutual defense pact," Anatolijs Gorbunovs told the Latvian parliament in his nomination speech for the chairmanship.

One form of compromise could be to have only Latvian troops serving on Latvian soil, and no Latvians serving outside the republic.

Of the three Baltic republics, Latvia has the most Soviet troops, and the Army's Baltic unit has its headquarters here. Latvia also has three ports that are key to the Soviet Union's Baltic military strategy.

But Latvia's biggest asset may be the parliament's reelection of Mr. Gorbunovs as the republic's president.

Gorbunovs, an ethnic Latvian despite his Russian name, has long experience with Moscow as a party functionary who rose through the ranks to become leader of Latvia's parliament in October 1988.

Gorbunovs once denounced pro-independence activists as traitors, but has since evolved in his political thinking. The Popular Front supported him in the recent parliamentary elections as a smooth diplomat who can unify the ethnically divided republic. In fact, he is more popular among the republic's Russians than among Latvians.

Throughout his nomination speech, Gorbunovs struck a tone of pragmatism.

"We sometimes idealize or understand the term independence primitively," Gorbunovs said, warning that Latvia will have to rely only on itself on the tough road ahead. "It would be naive of us to wait for Western 'CARE packages.'"

Kremlin to Put Unpopular Plan On Economy to Popular Vote

Linda Feldmann

5/25/90

With an air of trepidation, the Kremlin has gone public with its long-awaited program for transition to a "regulated market economy"—and will put it to a vote.

The plan calls for the breakup of some state monopolies to encourage internal competition and create incentives for more and better work. Consumers will soon pay more for certain goods, in an effort to bring prices closer to the costs of production.

The price of bread, some varieties of which have not risen in cost since the 1917 revolution, will go up threefold on July 1. And on Jan. 1, 1991, a wide array of consumer items and services—such as meat, milk, clothes, repairs, and transportation—will become more expensive. Citizens will receive either cash payments or a 15 percent rise in salaries to compensate for the higher prices.

Unemployment will be allowed to rise—from 2 million to as many as 8 million, says Gennady Yanaev, the head of the official trade union organization—but there will be accompanying programs to buffer the blow, either in the form of unemployment compensation or a public works program.

A key element of this reform, largely unspoken, for both the government and the populace is anxiety. In short, the Soviet public does not understand the basics of a free-market system, and is highly skeptical of any plan that will deepen economic hardship—even temporarily, as the government assures.

As far as many consumers are concerned, any plan that entails higher prices is no good. Soviet President Mikhail Gorbachev's five years of power have brought a bracing rush of changes, but his reforms have failed to stimulate the declining economy. The public is losing faith and patience.

The Kremlin knows this, and has sought a means to build up a mandate to introduce the changes while minimizing the risk of demonstrations and strikes. Enter the Polish example. Though Mr. Gorbachev and Prime Minister Nikolai Ryzhkov have issued assurances that a Polish-style "shock" turn toward a market economy would not suit the Soviet Union, the Kremlin borrowed a page from Poland: a referendum on economic reform.

"Certainly, a transition as steep as this one is impossible without national accord," Yuri Maslyukov, chairman of the state planning committee, told a press conference Wednesday.

So, he continued, before the end of the year the government would hold a nationwide referendum on its economic reform package. If the population votes "no," he said, "the government should resign."

On the face of it, the Soviet leadership has set itself up for a major defeat. Such a referendum on the economy would quickly become a vote of confidence in the entire government, and ultimately Gorbachev. And the results, if the vote were held today, could well go against him.

But the wording, timing, and procedure of this unprecedented referendum have not been worked out. And some are convinced the leadership will not permit itself to lose.

"We're about to see the propaganda campaign of our lives here," says a Moscow intellectual. "TV, radio, the press, you name it. They will tell us the choice is either their plan or chaos and collapse."

As for the question of possible government resignation, Mr. Maslyukov did not elaborate on who would step down if the referendum failed. But for several weeks already there have been growing whispers that Ryzhkov, a central figure in economic questions, may be on his way out. If Ryzhkov were to lose his post, he could be seen as a scapegoat for the leadership's failure to brake the nation's economic decline.

Ryzhkov is tainted by the ill-fated economic reform plan he introduced only last December—a plan that gave a more conservative hue to one proposed only a month earlier by Gorbachev's top economic adviser, Leonid Abalkin. The now defunct Ryzhkov plan called for the reforms to begin only in 1993.

The new plan is not exactly a return to the Abalkin variant, as it reflects more clearly the considerable concerns that the reforms will cause hardships to low-income citizens and result in massive unemployment. A new law on employment will seek to guarantee a job for anyone who wants one—a right already enshrined in the Soviet Constitution—and provide unemployment compensation if a job is not available.

In his speech to parliament, Ryzhkov outlined the three-stage, five-year approach to the plan:

1. By the end of this year, the legal base will be put in place for the transition.

2. In 1991 and 1992, the groundwork is to be laid for creation of a market system, including price reform, a new tax system, and higher interest rates.

3. From 1993 to 1995, central control is to diminish sharply, and competition among enterprises will be allowed, thus creating a market force that can allow prices to find their natural level.

Gorbachev Beleaguered at Home

Linda Feldmann

5/30/90

Arms control was meant to be the focus of Soviet President Mikhail Gorbachev's long-awaited summit with President Bush.

But when the two leaders begin their talks, a key issue is likely to be the tumultuous Soviet political and economic scene—ranging from yesterday's stunning election of Boris Yeltsin to the presidency of the Russian Federation's Parliament to killings in Armenia to widespread criticism of the government's new economic plan.

Mr. Gorbachev arrives in Washington a beleaguered man. This was underscored yesterday by the victory of his toughest political rival, Mr. Yeltsin, despite Gorbachev's best efforts to deny him the top political post in the Russian Republic. The victory establishes Yeltsin as Gorbachev's only real individual competitor and creates the possibility of an alternative center of power in the country.

Yeltsin has an important soap box from which to whip up popular sentiment against Gorbachev's programs, which he finds too cautious. And with the Soviet Union increasingly breaking down into a collection of separate semi-nations that pass their own laws and ignore Moscow's dictates, Yeltsin in his position as the president of Russia could challenge Gorbachev for control of one of the Soviet leader's few remaining sure constituencies.

This explains why Gorbachev devoted much of his time on the first few days of the Russian Parliament to lobbying in the corridors. But the anti-Yeltsin campaign could not find a candidate who could win more votes than the gadfly populist.

Even so, it took all of Yeltsin's political skills to break a deadlock in the voting until he finally squeaked by with 535 votes, just four more than the minimum 51 percent needed to win.

Gorbachev's troubles were already evident in an uncharacteristically weak televised address he made to the nation Sunday evening. The Soviet leader's usual public relations sense seemed to escape him as he scolded and hectored the populace for not understanding that the government's planned price increases are for their own good.

"We are still the children of our times," he said. "We have lots of complexes, and we are overburdened with old habits. We really like simple solutions to the most complex issues. They are not to be found."

This blame-the-public tone—in American politics, often a sign that a politician is running out of ideas—emerged two weeks ago as Gorbachev worked the halls of the Russian Parliament. Gorbachev told reporters that it was the "conservative mentality of Soviet citizens" that was hindering the planned transition to a market economy.

On the nationalities front, Lithuania has taken a back seat for now to Armenia, where in the capital of Yerevan at least 20 civilians were killed Sunday by Soviet troops. Two soldiers were also reported dead. The clashes were a reminder that these deep-seated Soviet ethnic problems that vanish from the headlines don't really go away—they bubble under the surface until the next crisis comes along.

The killings took place when Soviet soldiers accompanying a passenger train into Yerevan fired on a crowd of people they claimed were trying to seize their weapons. Some eyewitnesses say the crowd was peaceful and had encircled the train to try to persuade the soldiers to leave.

At root lies the continuing dispute over Nagorno-Karabakh, a territory inside neighboring Azerbaijan that is largely inhabited by Armenians but run by Azerbaijan. Armenia defied Moscow last week—and heightened tensions with Azerbaijan—when it decided to include Nagorno-Karabakh in local Armenian elections by allowing Armenian residents of the territory to vote secretly in their homes. Anticipating trouble and claiming a buildup of arsenals by Armenian militants, Moscow stepped up troop presence in the region.

Meanwhile, the more peaceful but also deadlocked situation over Lithuanian independence is likely to get greater play at the summit because of Washington's official policy of nonrecognition of the three Baltic republics' annexation by the Soviet Union.

In the long run, Lithuania is viewed as more threatening to Gorbachev's position than the crisis in the Caucasus, because it poses an immediate challenge to the territorial integrity. But for now Gorbachev looks set on insisting that all three Baltic republics follow the tough law on secession passed by the Soviet parliament in March.

The talk of Moscow remains the long-anticipated—and feared—announcement last week of a plan for eventual shift to a "regulated market economy." Criticism has been legion, from the man on the street who balks at prices that will double or triple in some cases to respected economists like Vasily Selyunin, who sees merits to the program but also weaknesses that would ultimately make it unworkable.

In short, Mr. Selyunin said in a recent speech, the government plan maintains the system of state orders for a number of products, bars leasing and joint-stock arrangements in extractive industries, and retains strict price controls on raw materials like fuel and metals. This means prices for these won't rise to match inflation, which could lead to strikes in these industries. Miners have already stated their opposition to the economic plan. In the Ukrainian mining region of Donbass, miners will vote June 9 whether to go on strike.

In Moscow, a weekend rush to the stores has largely subsided, although for the most part, there never was the type of widespread "panic" and "turmoil" reported. Now that non-Muscovites are blocked from buying most Moscow goods, with the introduction of a passport control system to allow entrance into stores, Muscovites can breathe a little easier.

Still, the locals have mixed emotions. The outsiders, who used to account for 2 to 3 million extra people in Moscow each day, are largely blocked from buying goods out from under them. But introduction of the passport regime has underscored the sense of crisis over the economy.

Arms Control Accords Mark Step Away From Cold War

Peter Grier

6/4/90

The arms control measures signed by President Bush and Soviet President Mikhail Gorbachev in a half-hour long summit ceremony are the culmination of years of tough and sometimes frustrating negotiations between the superpowers.

The START strategic nuclear talks have been going on for eight years, but it was not until this weekend that a United States and Soviet leader put pen to paper and agreed to basic provisions of a landmark START treaty. The protocols on nuclear test verification signed at the same time go with treaties that were negotiated in the mid-1970s, but never ratified.

That so much could be codified so quickly after so long illustrates the old proverb that progress in arms control becomes possible only after warming political relations make it less necessary. But by helping make the improvement in the US-Soviet relationship concrete, and by calling for destruction of many weapons of mass destruction, the arms measures signed last weekend represent an important step on the road away from the cold war.

"As we move forward, our job will be not so much to avoid war as to build peace," said Secretary of State James Baker III at a briefing for reporters.

Not that progress was foreordained. Last-minute snags turned Friday into a slog for Secretary Baker and Soviet Foreign Minister Eduard Shevardnadze as they readied agreements for signing.

For some hours it was questionable whether the long-awaited outline of major START provisions would go forward after all. Besides problems with START itself, negotiators were hung up on phrasing of the statement of goals for follow-on, START 2 negotiations.

Eventually the two sides agreed that any START 2 talks will try to enhance stability by controlling threatening, multi-warhead missiles. Earlier in the week, the US rebuffed an attempt by the Soviets to change present arms talks structure and get strategic defense and space weapons added to the list of things to talk about in START 2.

Finally, an hour late, the START outline was produced for signing along with other agreements. Since Bush and Gorbachev said from the time the summit was announced that shaking hands on nuclear arms was a big reason for the meeting, they would have both been embarrassed if in the end no such document was produced.

Details of summit arms control progress include:

START. In pledging their agreement on major issues concerning a START treaty that will reduce strategic arsenals for the first time in the nuclear age, Bush and Gorbachev said they felt a full treaty could be ready for signing later this year. A US official said START, after eight years was now "97 percent" done.

Under the treaty, both sides will be held to 1,600 nuclear delivery vehicles—missiles and bombers. Though both sides will be held to 6,000 nuclear warheads, about half their current stockpiles, a bomber only counts as one "warhead," no matter how many nuclear weapons it carries—making actual reductions in the 30 percent range.

In last-minute summit progress, negotiators agreed to a sublimit on mobile strategic missiles, including a flat ban on a mobile version of the large Soviet SS-18. Among issues still open is whether the treaty will cover the Soviet Backfire bomber. The Soviets have offered to make a politically binding statement that the plane cannot fly across continents, but "we continue to differ on some other aspects of what would be in that statement," said a US official who spoke on condition his name not be used.

In the US, START is already being criticized from the right for giving away too much; and from the left, for not cutting enough. "It's not an ideal treaty, but for the first time it puts a cap on the structure of these weapons," says Jack Mendelsohn, deputy director of the Arms Control Association. "You're going to have a baseline to which you can add additional constraints over time."

Chemical weapons. Bush and Gorbachev signed a bilateral agreement that calls for destruction of most superpower chemical weapon stocks by 2002. Production will stop when the treaty enters into force. Destruction will begin by 1992.

US officials said the chemical agreement is formal enough that it must be considered by Congress. Both presidents said they hoped this agreement points the way to an eventual worldwide ban on chemical weapons.

Nuclear testing. Bush and Gorbachev signed verification procedures for two existing but unratified treaties which ban nuclear explosions with planned yields greater than 150 kilotons.

Three verification methods were approved, for use in varying situations: Hydrodynamic yield, a US procedure involving measuring shock waves through cables placed near an explosion; on-site inspections, including the taking of rock samples; and seismic monitoring from sites near nuclear test sites.

The superpower leaders also issued a statement reaffirming their interest in finishing a treaty reducing conventional weapons in Europe by the end of the year.

Getting such a pledge was important to the US, which has been increasingly worried that with their allies falling away, the USSR is becoming less and less interested in the conventional force in Europe (CFE) talks between NATO and what is left of the Warsaw Pact.

No substantive progress was made on CFE. But "the Soviets did arrive here at the summit with what seemed to us to be a more forthcoming attitude" on CFE, said one US official.

US, Soviets Turn Summit Snags to Progress

Marshall Ingwerson

6/4/90

If the arms-control accords signed in Washington on Friday represent old business from the age of confrontation and containment, the trade agreement signed the same day sets the framework for a new, different era.

"It's really the first step into the new relationship," says Jim Montgomery, former assistant secretary of state and now executive director of East-West Forum, a Washington thinktank.

"It is perhaps only symbolic economically, but politically it is extremely important," says Stanislav Shatalin, a member of the Soviet President's Council and a top-ranking economic adviser.

The trade pact is among the prizes Mr. Gorbachev carries with him back to the Soviet Union today—after his brief stopovers in Minneapolis and San Francisco.

Once it runs its legislative course, the measure will cut tariffs on Soviet goods by 80 to 90 percent, define property rights, establish channels for repatriating ruble profits and settling international disputes, and otherwise help normalize commerce.

Just hours before the agreement was signed on Friday, it looked increasingly unlikely to emerge from political discord between the two countries over Lithuanian independence.

In the end, President Bush chose his signals. Instead of a signal of concern over Lithuania, he decided on a signal that US-Soviet relations would move forward into the post-containment era.

He handed Gorbachev what appeared to be the top two Soviet priorities at this summit—the outline of a strategic weapons treaty and a trade agreement.

The top American priorities—conventional arms cutbacks in Europe, Soviet acceptance of a united Germany's membership in NATO—little visible progress.

Gorbachev has been quite conscious of the Soviet Union's relative weakness at this summit. Without acknowledging it directly, he has warned the US repeatedly not to try to take advantage of Soviet problems, not to "dictate" or "go fishing in troubled waters."

But he made it clear that American support was important to changing the Soviet economy, and he used Soviet weakness as a prod.

"Does the United States want a Soviet Union which is weak, torn by complexes and problems and turmoil? Or do you want a dynamic Soviet state that is open to the outside world . . . ?" he asked congressional leaders during a meeting Friday morning.

President Bush had answered that question, in effect, a week earlier, when he said that America's chief enemy in post-Cold War Europe had become uncertainty and instability. The signing of a trade agreement is another answer that cultivates stronger ties to the West rather than isolates the Soviets.

For Gorbachev, the agreement should boost confidence in economic reforms that increasingly lack credibility.

The whole range of steps the West can take to help the Soviet Union move to a market economy—easing credit and export controls, for example—depend "psychologically and politically" on a US-Soviet trade agreement, Mr. Montgomery says.

The agreement is by no means a done deal, however. It must pass both houses of Congress with a majority vote.

That lays the groundwork for its most important element, most-favored-nation (MFN) tariff treatment for imports from the Soviet Union.

The president must grant MFN status, and Congress can block it with a resolution.

As with a regular bill, the President can veto and Congress can override the veto.

The obstacles to passing the agreement and winning MFN status for the Soviets have become increasingly clear.

Six months ago at the Malta summit, the trade deal appeared certain. Then Soviet pressure on Lithuania began straining superpower relations.

On May 1, the Senate voted 73 to 24 to urge Bush not to sign a trade agreement until sanctions against Lithuania were lifted and the Kremlin began negotiating Lithuanian independence.

In early May, the White House began signaling through background press briefings that Soviet pressure on Lithuania was endangering the administration's own support of the trade agreement.

For reasons that still aren't clear, the Kremlin pulled a bill to liberalize emigration from its legislative calendar just before the summit.

The emigration law is a condition of granting the Soviets MFN status.

Without the law, and with pressure still on Lithuania, the administration was not interested in signing the trade bill.

On Friday morning, congressional leaders told Gorbachev that the trade bill could not pass without some Soviet softening toward Baltic independence.

The congressmen explained that they were under political pressure from constituents on the issue.

"We're not linking trade to the Baltic problem," Senate Minority Leader Bob Dole (R) of Kansas explained afterward. "We're just trying to explain the political realities."

Nevertheless, Bush signed the bill later that day. He is likely to wait until the Soviets pass the emigration legislation, and perhaps longer, before submitting it to Capitol Hill.

The chief value of the agreement is as a major go-ahead signal for international investment in and commerce with the Soviet Union.

"MFN may bring a dollar and a quarter off the price of a bottle of vodka," says William Butler, a London-based lawyer retained by a Soviet economic commission, "but the real value is the signal that the water is fine" for foreign investors.

Ernst Winter, Vienna-based editor of a new newsletter for Soviets on North American enterprises and a former United Nations development official, says that he believes US trade will begin affecting the Soviet economy in as little as two years—even if the current Soviet leadership tries to slow it down.

"The pressure from below is enormous," he says.

Gorbachev and Yeltsin Square Off

Daniel Sneider

6/6/90

Mikhail Gorbachev leaves the heavens of great-power summitry and cheering American crowds and returns today to the earthly tumult of Soviet politics and a people increasingly mistrustful of his promises for reform.

Despite voluminous coverage of Mr. Gorbachev's visit by Soviet television and newspapers, there is little evidence that he has gained much in popularity from his success abroad.

The relaxation of the threat of war with the West is taken for granted here. The concerns of Soviet people are focused at home, especially on the crisis shortages in the economy. The recently proposed economic reform, which includes planned rises in the prices of most basic commodities, has drawn fire from all sides.

"Americans see Gorbachev from far away, while we see him up close," commented one Moscow housewife when asked about the gap in reactions. "We judge him in the marketplace." And there Soviet shoppers find the worst combination—fewer goods at higher prices.

The sight of Gorbachev and his wife Raisa enjoying adulation amidst the opulence of American life brings mostly sarcastic comparisons by Muscovites with the dreariness of their own lives.

In Gorbachev's absence, the frustrations of the Soviet people gained a new and potent expression in the form of the upset election of populist politician Boris Yeltsin as the president of the Russian Republic, the heartland of the Soviet Union. Despite intense personal lobbying up to the eve of his departure, Gorbachev was unable to persuade a majority of members of the republic's newly elected parliament to back his chosen candidate.

According to a Moscow-based pollster, Gorbachev continues to be No. 1 in popularity. But before, he says, "Gorbachev was like a tree in the grass" compared with other political figures. Now Mr. Yeltsin also has a visible following.

Yeltsin's public popularity owes much to his ability to express quite contradictory feelings in his sometimes vague declarations. On one hand, he heads the Democratic Bloc in the parliament, the liberal faction that criticizes Gorbachev's government for hesitating in pushing through radical reform. At the same time, he enjoys support from ordinary people who are fearful that a market economy will bring inflation, the end of subsidized low prices for basic goods, housing, and other services, and the uncertainties of unemployment and bankruptcy.

The results of a recent poll bear out those analysts who argue that the Soviet population is still widely pro-reform. Some 75 percent of those surveyed thought the pace of reforms was "too slow." But those same people are skeptical of the government's reform plans, with only a third supporting them and 47 percent dismissing them as "only symbolic."

Yeltsin also clearly benefits from a carefully cultivated image of a man who has defied authority.

In the past, Gorbachev was very effective at using Yeltsin's presence to balance out his critics on the right, those conservative communists who oppose significant change. Some observers suggest that even with his greater power, Yeltsin could continue to play that role.

"He is helpful to Gorbachev," argues Rair Simonyan, a senior economist at the government think tank Imemo. "Maybe in this combination, Gorbachev will have more opportunity to be decisive and radical."

The concept of a balancing role is fine, says a senior official of the Communist Party's Central Committee. "If it were a different man with the same slogans, maybe I would support him," he says. "But Yeltsin is a very dangerous enemy to Gorbachev."

Yeltsin has a "totalitarian personality," the Communist official says, comparing him with Joseph Stalin and Adolf Hitler and the situation in the Soviet Union today to 1920s Germany, when the Nazi movement was born.

During his US visit, Gorbachev accused Yeltsin of constantly changing his positions and playing a "destructive" role.

Those statements barely conceal what many Soviet observers characterize as a deep emotional chasm between the two men.

Yeltsin has so far taken a public high road, offering cooperation with Gorbachev and formation of a de facto coalition government in the Russian parliament with the defeated forces of the Communist Party.

Yeltsin supporters say he has become a more sophisticated leader, able to express more complex ideas and to rely less on crude attacks on privilege. He has been particularly effective in presenting the idea of sovereignty for Russia, the largest of the Soviet Union's 15 republics. Echoing the calls for autonomy and independence heard from the non-Russian republics, he proposes that Russia sell its rich resources of coal, oil, gas, and other raw materials at world-level prices and conclude trade pacts with other republics.

The white-haired Siberian challenged Gorbachev on this front almost immediately after his election, suggesting that Russia might break the Soviet government's economic blockade of independence-minded Lithuania and meeting with Lithuanian President Vytautus Landsbergis.

Such appeals to nationalism will only lead to "absolute anarchy," says the Communist official. He acknowledges that Yeltsin has surrounded himself with a circle of "talented, intellectual aides" from the left. "I'm sure they believe they used Yeltsin as a battering ram" against the system, he says, "but they are very naive when they dream they will use him and afterward can go forward without him."

A leading member of the Democratic Platform, the left faction of the Communist Party, rejects that charge. Yeltsin, he retorts, "is a man of morality," and the only one who knows from the inside how to change the Soviet system.

Russians are almost eagerly awaiting the clash that is expected from Gorbachev's return. The drama of this confrontation is likely to occupy center stage in Soviet politics for many months.

Critics Slam Economic Reform Plan

Daniel Sneider

6/8/90

Mikhail Gorbachev is back in town and the first order of business is to save his government's much-assailed economic reform plan.

The widespread view here is that Mr. Gorbachev's ability to stay in power will depend in large part on his ability to gain support for the controversial program for a transition to a "regulated market economy."

Gorbachev is scheduled to address the Soviet parliament next Tuesday, his first major public statement since his return from the United States. The speech will probably be followed quickly by a vote on his economic design.

This weekend, according to press reports, a special meeting of the Communist Party Central Committee will be convened. According to Interfax news agency, the meeting may take up a new version of the plan, responding in some way to the barrage of public criticism it has received.

The plan, unveiled two weeks ago after months of discussion within the government, has been hit from both sides of the Soviet political spectrum.

Party conservatives have attacked the government for failing to protect workers and the poor from the fallout of inflation and unemployment expected to accompany the shift to a market economy. Much of their fire is aimed at plans to double and treble the long-subsidized prices for basic goods such as bread.

The radicals on the left, including many leading economists, charge the government with indecisiveness, with failing clearly to establish a market structure. Instead, they argue, the government has compromised with the right, creating what economist Oleg Bogomolov calls an unworkable "hybrid of a command economy and a quasi-market."

The reaction has forced the government to back away from an earlier promise to hold a referendum on the program and to resign if it lost.

The reform plan, by the government's own account, would have been far easier to put across two or three years ago when Gorbachev enjoyed great popularity and could blame the inevitable pain of transition on the problems left by the previous Soviet regime. But after five years in power, marked by a zigzag path of reform and retreat, the government's credibility has worn thin.

More for political than economic reasons, the Gorbachev government rejected the advice of more-radical economists to follow the path of Poland's "shock therapy." In one stroke, the Poles freed all prices from state control, ended subsidies of state-run industries, and began privatizing those government assets. The popularly elected Polish Solidarity government imposed a wage freeze, despite the higher prices and unemployment that have come with the program.

"If we embarked on the Polish way . . . we wouldn't be able to ride it out for even half a year," Deputy Prime Minister Leonid Abalkin, the architect of the reform strategy, frankly admitted in an interview with Commersant, an independent Soviet economic weekly.

Instead the government, six months after putting forward an even more timid plan, proposes a gradual transition to market conditions. The three-stage, decade-long reform begins in 1991 (moved up two years from the earlier version). The government is first revising prices upward, to reflect the actual costs of production and to curb an estimated $160 billion in annual subsidies for food and some consumer goods.

The government has tried to soften this blow by pairing it with a complex plan to compensate citizens with salary increases and other payments.

"People see only prices going up," comments Rair Simonyan, a senior economist at Imemo, an influential government think tank. "They don't believe in compensation."

In this economist's view, the government erred in beginning price reform before it had first created real market conditions, where enterprises, including private ones, can freely find labor, materials, and financing. Without those conditions, which under the plan will not be fully in place until 1995, he sees no way for producers to respond to the incentive of higher prices.

Economist Otto Latsis expresses another view shared by many economists: that the "shock" is unavoidable, so it is best to free prices completely, thus bringing positive results more quickly.

"In the Soviet Union," he said in a recent interview, "we have always emphasized the negative consequences of shock therapy: soaring prices, unemployment, and inflation. But we miss one point. Indeed, prices will grow, but simultaneously the market will be filled with goods."

Such critics say the government is simply repeating the error of the Communist Polish government of two years ago, which opted for a similarly gradual approach, only to find itself in a crisis that brought the popular Solidarity government to power.

What makes this the most difficult moment to attempt change, however, is the unavoidable fact that the Soviet Union has slid into the first phase of a deep and classical economic recession. According to Planecon Report, an authoritative Washington newsletter, Soviet growth is now negative and may drop by 4 percent to 5 percent this year. Inflation reached 11 percent by the end of last year, reports Commersant, and it may double this year. The Soviet Union is running its first trade deficit in 14 years.

The Soviet consumer sees the crisis most vividly in the form of severe, across-the-board shortages. In an economy where shortage and hoarding are the norm, the past year has seen a noticeable deterioration. Out of 1,100 groups of commodities defined by the government, 95 percent are in short supply, according to Mr. Latsis, an editor of Kommunist, the theoretical journal of the Communist Party.

The final element of the crisis is a massive and growing government budget deficit, which went from 48 billion rubles in 1986 to 92 billion last year. The deficit is supposed to come down to 60 billion this year but the democratically elected Soviet parliament has resisted such cuts.

Warsaw Pact Is Over As a Military Alliance

Eric Bourne

6/12/90

The demise of the Warsaw Pact as a military force in international relations is probably the most momentous sequel to the East European revolution.

To all intents and purposes, the Pact became a spent force the moment Poland initiated the revolution last year. Now it is fact.

The break from the alliance's military past was made by its top governing body, the Consultative Council, in Moscow last week. It was the Council's first meeting in a year. Its composition was an ironic comment from the Soviet viewpoint on all that has happened in Eastern Europe and in East-West relations since then.

Formerly, the Council included heads of state, together with ruling Communist Party, government, and military chiefs and their foreign ministers. All, of course, were communists.

This meeting was a metamorphosis. For the first time in 35 years, the Soviets had to deal with six equals. In addition, the Soviets were virtually the only communists at the Council table: Mr. Gorbachev was the only party chief, and he and Poland's Gen. Wojciech Jaruzelski were the only communist heads of state.

Romania and Bulgaria were represented by quasi-communists, though they presented reformist credentials. The other East Europeans were represented by noncommunists or anticommunists as diverse as Czechoslovakia's President Vaclav Havel and a pacifist East German defense minister.

After this meeting of the Warsaw Pact, its future—if any—must be said mostly to rest with NATO. Immediately after the event, the NATO foreign ministers went some way to offer a helping hand. They not only hailed the moves toward a "transformation" of the Pact. They also made tentative proposals for cooperation between the countries of both alliances in constructing a "new Europe."

In the broad sense, that is very consistent with Gorbachev's ideas. But his former allies showed they have their own views. Some—Hungary, for instance—are in a hurry to quit the alliance before 1992, the year of the West Europeans' single market.

Meantime, Soviet troop withdrawals from Czechoslovakia and Hungary continue. Poland, momentarily, hesitates over similar withdrawals until the security aspects of German reunification—specifically, guarantees for Poland's borders—are settled to its satisfaction. Here again, NATO will be the key factor.

Even so, Poland has already formally laid down a new defense concept: National forces exist to defend the nation, not outside alliances. In other words, the doctrine of mutual "brotherly defense" of "socialism" that Moscow invoked against the Czechs in 1968 is specifically excluded.

In general terms, the East Europeans are ready to give Gorbachev time and support for his "pan-European" ideas. But the East Germans, Poles, and Czechs have already circulated their own draft for a permanent standing council of the Conference on Security and Cooperation in Europe, bringing the nonaligned and neutral Europeans into its existing membership of 35 states.

Some of the East Europeans take the Western view that the best way to ensure against revival of past German ambitions is a unified Germany inside NATO. There is no support for Gorbachev's demand for a neutral Germany.

There is, however, some consensus for not immediately discarding the Pact but first modifying it into a political, consultative body able to negotiate with a similarly restructured NATO in working out the new formulas for all-European security. Proposals for the alliance's reorientation are due by the end of October.

The Bush-Gorbachev summit nudged things in that direction, though the security alignment of a single Germany—thorniest question of all in superpower relations—remained unresolved.

Following his summit success, however, Gorbachev may finally be persuaded that a united Germany within NATO's control is a less fearsome phenomenon than he has so far professed to fear. There will undoubtedly be strong pressures from the East Europeans to help him make up his mind.

Central Asian Crisis Could Overshadow Baltics Issues

Daniel Sneider

6/12/90

Soviet authorities have been forced in the past week to turn their attention south, away from the drive for independence by the Baltic republics and toward ethnic violence in Soviet Central Asia.

The number of people killed after a week of border clashes between the republics of Kirghizia and Uzbekistan has risen to 116, according to Soviet press reports yesterday. A regional state of emergency has been imposed since June 7, including the Kirghizian capital of Frunze.

The violence, only the latest in a string of such incidents, is rooted in the poverty of the region, experts say. The combination of economic crisis, nationalism, and the spreading influence of Islam could portend a secession crisis more far-reaching than the Baltics, they warn.

Soviet authorities in Moscow have paid far less attention to the region compared with their preoccupation with the independence movement in the Baltics. This focus is a "deliberate cultural phenomenon," says Tair Tairov, a Central Asia expert. "The Baltics are part of Europe. But here it is a Muslim area."

The outbreaks of Central Asian violence go back to December 1987 riots in the Kazakh capital of Alma Ata. Last June, at least 110 people died when Uzbeks killed ethnic Turks in 10 days of rioting. Though directed against other Asian groups, such disturbances have taken on an anti-Russian character as well.

The immediate cause of these tensions is "a very high rate of unemployment," Tairov says. In Uzbekistan, the largest of the five Central Asian republics, there are 1 million unemployed out of a population of about 20 million.

The latest violence originates in a conflict between Kirghiz and Uzbeks over land around the Kirghiz city of Osh. The area is at the end of the fertile Fergana Valley, which extends from Uzbekistan into Kirghizia, a mountainous republic inhabited by traditionally nomadic people. The valley within Kirghizia is populated largely by Uzbeks who have for years agitated to be incorporated into Uzbekistan.

Kirghiz radical Kazat Akhmatov told the independent Soviet news agency Postfactum that there were 30,000 homeless in the Osh area alone. Last fall, says Tairov, homeless started occupying the land of Uzbek collective farms. A month and half ago, local authorities started distributing such land.

These moves "triggered the trouble" that began June 4, the expert says. Since the fighting in Osh began, Soviet Interior Ministry troops have been called in to prevent the entry of thousands of Uzbeks who gathered on the border to aid their brethren. Interior Minister Vadim Bakatin describes them as "ready to do battle."

Traditionally the Central Asian republics have been regarded as the most passive and loyal in the Soviet Union. But there are signs of change.

In Uzbekistan, the Soviet Union's third-most-populous republic, Shukrulla Rahmatovich Mirsaidov, the new prime minister, called for "economic independence" in his first speech to the newly elected local parliament in March.

Disaffection is also reflected in the rapid spread of Islamic thought and religious observance. Since last year, Soviet authorities have given greater freedom to officially recognized Muslim clerics, in part, experts say, to combat the spread of more dangerous brands of fundamentalism.

"The influence of such unofficial [Muslim] leaders is very high," says a Soviet expert who does not wish to be identified.

Still, "Central Asians have not yet reached the point where they have challenged the union," Tairov says. "But I think they will come to that."

Gorbachev Bids for a New System

Daniel Sneider

6/15/90

Mikhail Gorbachev's greatest skill has been knowing when it is time to shift gears to find a new way out of a bind.

The Soviet leader displayed that talent once again when he unveiled a proposal earlier this week for creating a new federal structure for the Soviet Union.

The ties between the central government and the republics that make up the Soviet Union could range from the existing federation to a far looser confederation, he told a meeting of heads of the union's 15 republics on Tuesday.

Mr. Gorbachev gave the outlines of his view before the meeting, in an interview with the British Broadcasting Corporation published here on June 10.

"I believe that we will reach a full-blooded federation which will combine the independence and sovereignty of republics with an efficiently acting center," he said.

The central government, he explained, would have only "those rights which the republics themselves cede to it," a striking reversal of the current order in which the republics have only the powers granted by the union.

The concept is a belated attempt to catch up with what is already reality—the growing independence, both political and economic, of the republics. Separatist movements are growing in the south, in the Ukraine, Moldavia, Armenia, Azerbaijan, and elsewhere.

The three Baltic republics of Lithuania, Latvia, and Estonia are the most advanced in this process. Gorbachev acknowledged this by meeting the three Baltic presidents in Moscow separately and beginning what Moscow had been resisting for months—real negotiations on their independence. Gorbachev's new federation concept was offered in part as the framework for those talks.

Gorbachev's government has also come to realize that it can use the more rapid reforms occurring on the local level as a lever to force through controversial plans for transition to a market economy. If those plans are stalled at the center, then popularly elected, more-radical governments in the republics or even in such major cities as Moscow, Leningrad and Kiev, could push them through.

What Gorbachev is talking about today is what Baltic leaders proposed some two years ago—a new treaty of union that would allow them freedom short of full independence. The idea was rejected by the Kremlin then and resisted until earlier this year when the declarations of independence by the Baltic republics forced it on the table.

Still it took another development to bring Gorbachev to this realization—the ascension of radical populist Boris Yeltsin to the president of the giant Russian Federation, the heartland of the Soviet Union. Mr. Yeltsin has gained popularity in part by standing on a platform of Russian sovereignty.

Yeltsin and his backers call for carrying out more radical reforms within Russia. And they want to carry out economic deals directly with the other republics.

Decentralization is Gorbachev's only route to introducing a market reform, says political scientist Igor Klyamkin.

"Today, acting from Moscow you cannot solve any problems in this big empire," he says. Moreover, it allows Gorbachev to place some of the burden of reform on republican governments that have more popular support. "If Yeltsin fails in Russia, it will be his fault."

When the Federation Council meeting of republican presidents took place on Tuesday, "Yeltsin made a very constructive proposal regarding future cooperation among the republics without the center," Latvian president Anatolijs Gorbunovs told reporters.

"Gorbachev agreed with that in general and disagreed with certain points," he added, describing the discussion as "a pleasant, constructive dialogue."

Estonian economist Mikhail Bronstein, a member of the Estonian parliament, proposed the creation of such an "all-union common market," in an article published on June 10 in the Soviet government daily Izvestia. "Within this new structure," he wrote, "the Baltic knot can be untied." He argued that "the process has already begun independent of the center's will."

"The center will just be an onlooker if it stays out," Mr. Bronstein concluded.

Gorbachev, according to his spokesman Arkady Maslennikov, appears to agree.

In explaining his concept at the Federation meeting, Gorbachev said that different versions of perestroika, as the reform process is labeled, are developing from below, sometimes in rather "unorthodox and even painful" forms.

Gorbachev argued that a new union structure would have to accommodate all those forms, suggesting that some republics might enjoy a looser confederal tie to Moscow while others a closer link similar to what exists today. What will keep the Soviet Union together, Gorbachev's spokesman told reporters, is "that the process will develop along with the transfer to a market economy."

According to this view, the benefits of a market will be an incentive for the republics, even the Baltic ones, to stay in the Soviet Union. "This economic factor will be the best cement which will bring union republics closer together and will make them keep together," Maslennikov reported from the discussion at the meeting.

The Gorbachev concept, as explained by senior officials in subsequent days, envisions the central government having authority over foreign policy, defense, and some aspects of national economic policy, particularly control over credit and finance.

Soviet Radicals Lose Faith in Party Reform

Daniel Sneider

6/19/90

No red flags flew and there were no ringing calls for socialism when a group of almost a thousand democratic activists of the Soviet Communist Party met this past weekend in the halls of the October Cinema.

Instead, the talk was of how to end 72 years of rule by the stolid Communist bureaucrats who still occupy the positions of power throughout Soviet society.

The Democratic Platform, as the group is called, unites those who seek to transform the Communist Party of the Soviet Union (CPSU) into a party that supports change to a market economy and political pluralism. But two weeks before the start of a historic 28th Communist Party Congress, the radicals have already given up hope that much will change.

"It is as impossible to reform the CPSU as it is to reform a place of torture," Igor Chubais, a red-bearded leader of the Democratic Platform declared at the start of the two-day conference.

Mr. Chubais, who was ousted from the Communist Party last April, was the most-extreme voice at this meeting, calling for immediate steps to form a new party.

But even though the majority rejected this course, the group endorsed a plan that will likely lead to a walkout from the party congress in July and the formation of a social-democratic party by September.

Those developments, some observers believe, will only strengthen the hand of the conservative forces in the party who have challenged Soviet leader Mikhail Gorbachev's reforms from the right.

The Democratic Platform counts among its supporters many prominant politicians, including Boris Yeltsin, the new president of the Russian Republic, and the radical heads of the governments of Moscow and Leningrad, though these men did not attend this weekend's meeting.

The resolution adopted on Sunday evening presents a series of demands that it calls "the limits of compromise." If those changes are not adopted at the party congress, the document says, "work should be started to form a new political party."

The Democratic Platform calls on the party to renounce communism as its ultimate goal, to rename the party, to give up the monopoly of one ideology within the party, and to "dismantle the organizational foundations of a totalitarian-type party and replace them with a parliamentary-type party." The Communist Party, they say, must put an end to "democratic centralism," which requires party members to follow the will of the majority.

When the Democratic Platform held its first meeting in January, the majority felt that the party could be transformed, group leader Vladimir Lysenko recounted in an interview published last week. But, he added, "the four months that have passed since the conference" show that those who favored a split "might be correct."

According to Mr. Lysenko, all their efforts to hold a dialogue with the party leadership, including with Mr.

Gorbachev and fellow reformers in the Politburo such as Alexander Yakovlev, have been rejected. At a March meeting of the party Central Committee, he said in a speech to open the conference this weekend, "we weren't allowed to speak." On April 11, the Central Committee issued an "open letter" attacking the existence of the group, followed by the expulsion of some 20 members, including Chubais. Some leading activists left to form new parties at that point.

The party bureaucracy manipulated the process of selection of the delegates to the coming congress to block representatives of the Democratic Platform, they charged. They claim the support of some 40 percent of the party members, but out of 5,000 delegates to the Congress, only 100 will be supporters of the Democratic Platform, about 2 percent.

"The CPSU is not only the owner of the buildings but also the owner of the language," Chubais told the conference. The party, though it allowed direct, multi-candidate elections, used its extensive control of the machinery for propaganda to control the election process, he asserted.

It is true that "in many cases party members didn't know who they were voting for," a senior Central Committee official admits. "But the whole picture will reflect well the real situation in the party and in the country." The party breaks down into three main parts, the official says. The extreme left represents 3 to 10 percent and the conservative right 10 to 15 percent. More than 80 percent of the party sits in the center, which he describes as "left centrists," who are "pro-Gorbachev and pro-democratic socialism." These people are against the extremes and "will fight to save the party."

The democratic activists interpret this as an effort to give a reformist gloss to what will be an essentially conservative congress.

"The Central Committee will try to find some middle decisions to show people that it wants reform," said Vladimir Shostakovsky, rector of the Moscow Higher Party School and a Democratic Platform leader. "There can be debates, criticism of the Politburo, votes for documents, but it won't be democratic in reality."

Gorbachev will set the tone for the party congress when he speaks today to open a conference of Russian Communists, the beginning of a process to create a separate Russian Communist Party. Gorbachev, as the Central Committee official indicated, will likely try to stick to the center, while moving the center as a whole to the left. But in interviews published in recent weeks, senior party leaders have rejected the kind of radical reforms sought by the left.

A.S. Kapto, head of the ideology department of the party Central Committee, told the independent Soviet news agency Interfax that the party was not ready to become a parliamentary-type party. If the party fully separated itself from the government roles it plays, "the consequences for the nation may be catastrophic," he said.

That kind of talk is what convinces many democratic activists that the Soviet Communist Party can never be the agent of change in the country. The decision earlier this year to allow a multiparty system has only created a host of what Mr. Shostkovsky calls "dwarf parties." The Democratic Platform radicals envision that they could become the nucleus to unite the disparate anti-Communist Party groups.

But Oleg Rumansyev, a member of the Russian Republic's parliament and a leader of the new Social Democratic Party, says the only value of the Democratic Platform is to stay inside the party as a "destructive force."

"From the moment they step out," he argues, "they will lose their value" and leave control of valuable party property in the hands of the right.

Assaults by Russian Communists Signal Deepening Rifts in Party

Daniel Sneider

6/22/90

For three days, Mikhail Gorbachev has been subjected to an often bitter assault on his reform policies from Marxist conservatives in the Communist Party.

The debate on the conference floor to form a Russian branch of the Communist Party has been dominated by a litany of complaints ranging from attacks on the market economy to accusations from military officers that the Soviet leader has "lost" Eastern Europe to the "imperialists."

At times it has gotten very personal, as men like conservative Politburo member Yegor Ligachev called on Mr. Gorbachev to give up one of his dual posts of party leader and president.

The uncontrolled flood of criticism seems to have gone beyond the leadership's expectations. After the first day, journalists have been barred from the conference site, for what officials said were "technical" reasons.

But after all the socialist revivalist rhetoric has dissipated, Gorbachev is still likely to control the party. As the conference headed into a crucial vote on the leadership of the new group, the Soviet leader had been able to win every vote, every symbolic skirmish, that was meaningful.

The rightist wave at the Russian Communist Party meeting is a preview, though a more conservative-tilted one, of the more vital 28th Congress of the Soviet Communist Party, which begins on July 2. If the conservatives dominate similarly there, the party "could split into a conservative part, a centrist part, and a left part," warned Gennady Koslov, an official of the more-liberal Moscow party organization.

But the tone of the Russian meeting raises what may be a more-relevant question—whether Gorbachev needs a Communist Party dominated by bureaucrats and hard-liners who stand to lose from the reforms he proposes and only work against them.

The meeting these past days has served to revive speculation that Gorbachev might step down as party leader, separating himself from the unpopular party. Gorbachev, the logic goes, would rely instead on the power of the institution of the presidency which he has created and on the elected parliament.

The Soviet leader fed the rumor mills when he angrily responded on Wednesday to an attack on his leadership. "I think some comrades are treating the general secretary [of the party] and president very casually," he retorted. "It's not a question of me [personally]. Tomorrow or in 10 or 12 days, there could be another general secretary."

Party officials were quick to caution against interpreting this as a hint of resignation. Pro-Gorbachev elements of the party particularly expressed this, reflecting a widespread opinion in such circles that Gorbachev simply cannot afford to give up his leadership for fear of losing control of the party, an institution that still commands considerable power in the country.

The prevalence of orthodox Communist views at this meeting is not surprising, because the impetus to form a Russian Communist Party came from the right. There are separate party organizations for the other 14 republics of the Soviet Union, grouped under the umbrella of the Soviet Communist Party. But Russia, as the heart of the Soviet Union, has not had its own grouping.

The Gorbachev leadership resisted the idea, only agreeing to it within the last few months in an attempt to control the process. The pressure from the right was only one element in that decision. The surprise victory of populist politician Boris Yeltsin as president of the Russian parliament, based in part on a program of "sovereignty" for Russia, encouraged those who argued the need for a Russian party as a counterbalance to Mr. Yeltsin and his radical backers.

Some on the left even see the establishment of the Russian party as a clever move by Gorbachev. While Gorbachev is moving to oust the radical left from the party, he will use the party "to push conservative communists into separate national apartments," says Russian parliamentarian Oleg Rumansyev, a leader of the Social Democratic Party.

Gorbachev opened the meeting with a long speech, defending his policies and attempting to situate himself between left and right extremes. He criticized the right for promoting the "absurd" idea "that movement toward the market means a return to capitalism," asking rhetorically whether "the market contradicts socialism if it helps raise the people's standard of living."

Gorbachev described his reforms as the fulfillment of a 30-year process of de-Stalinization. He backed creation of the separate party, but warned against it becoming a vehicle for further separatism in the Soviet Union.

The Soviet leader slapped the left for seeking to turn the party into a "shapeless club," by promoting its transformation into a purely parliamentary party. But he also hit the right for trying to use the Russian party as a vehicle against perestroika (restructuring).

While a leader of the left-wing Democratic Platform faction presented its views, the conference rapidly developed into a forum for the right. A stream of speakers came to the podium to impugn the leadership, as did V. Ladigin, a self-described train driver from Baikal, for bringing "the five ruinous years of perestroika."

Gen. Albert Makashov, head of the Volga military district, drew stormy applause when he named a long list of liberal leading lights as enemies of the military.

Somewhat in response to these criticisms, Gorbachev sought a protective alliance with the left, most evident in the presence of Yeltsin at the dais in the front of the huge hall at the Palace of Congresses. The television cameras pointedly focused on the two men, who were publicly sparring only weeks ago, chatting warmly with each other. Yeltsin, in an interview with the party daily Pravda published Wednesday, defended the leadership against what he called the "one-sided" discussion at the conference.

Some on the left say Yeltsin's new friendship with Gorbachev only heralds his cooption back into the Gorbachev camp. But Yeltsin also told Pravda that he may suspend his party membership after the July party Congress, in order to represent all the people of Russia as president.

After the events of this week, Gorbachev may wish he could follow him down that road.

Party Structure Turned on Its Head

Daniel Sneider

6/29/90

A huge decorative hammer and sickle tops the solid four-story building off the main boulevard of this small Russian city. Identical metal plaques are hammered into the wall on each side of the glass-doored entryway. One proclaims this to be the offices of the Zagorsk Soviet, the city council. The other names it the headquarters of the city committee of the Communist Party of the Soviet Union CPSU).

In every town and city of the Soviet Union this elaborate dual structure exists—the government and, side by side, the party. And for decades the reality of power has been as obvious as the directory in the building lobby—the Soviet occupies the third floor and the party the top floor.

"Before, if you wanted something, it was decided first in principle on the fourth floor," a man from a local factory explains while standing on the steps of the building. "Then the party gave instructions to the Soviet."

But change has begun to come, most of all in the big cities and at the center, where popular elections for the Soviets earlier this year brought many radical governments to power. The CPSU has formally renounced its constitutional monopoly on power, opening the way to a multiparty system which has already begun to operate.

These events are felt even in Zagorsk, a pleasant city of 120,000 about 50 miles north of Moscow. It is known for the ancient Orthodox Church monasteries which draw many tourists. "Now," says the factory official, "I have to go to the third floor."

Party offices quiet

It is quiet up in the party offices. Constantine Starchnko—a garrulous, 85-year-old retired factory worker—has come by to see his "comrade," the first secretary of the party committee. He proudly pulls out a weathered party card showing the date of his entry into the party—1925.

Constantine is not very interested in the 28th Party Congress which begins Monday. "It's all blah, blah—what matters is accomplishments," he says, allowing no room for argument. What the country needs, he eagerly tells anyone who will listen, is "law and order." As for perestroika (restructuring) and the other reforms instituted by Soviet leader Mikhail Gorbachev—"I don't really understand it."

The first secretary is on vacation. Anyway, his secretary tells us, the party has transferred power to the Soviets. "We should go down to talk to someone on the third floor," she suggests.

There sits a clearly beleaguered Nikolai Demin, a heavy-set factory manager who was elected head of the Soviet only a few weeks ago. His anteroom is crowded with petitioners. A steady stream of officials walk in and out, carrying blueprints and piles of documents.

"I rely on my 200 people's deputies for advice," he says, referring to the elected members of the city Soviet. "Like any other political organization, the city [Communist] Party committee works through the deputies, who are party members."

The declaration of a new democratic order is impressive. But reality is more complicated. Mr. Demin is a party member, as are the majority of the deputies. And while some deputies are oppositionists, he admits they are so only "in spirit," because no other political entity yet exists. "The party placed itself in an equal condition with others," he explains, "but it did not give up its vanguard role."

Outside the building, the head of the trade union at the largest factory in town (he declines to give his name) is not too happy about these events. "Now the situation is confusing," he complains, reflecting the conservative views of many in the party apparatus. "Before, the city party committee controlled everything. I don't see anything wrong in that."

Far down the road at the Klimentiev housing complex, the happenings in the Communist Party are of increasingly little import. "Before, it was very important in the country," says Lina, a computer technician. "It was believed that every administrator should be a party member. Now it has outlived itself and everything is going to pieces," she says, refusing like others to reveal her last name.

Lina points for evidence at the local supermarket from which she just emerged. Like markets all over the country, it offers shoppers a pitiful selection—sugar, but only with ration coupons, milk, margarine, cheese and sour cream in the dairy department, browning heads of cabbage, frozen sardines, some lentils, coarse flour, rice from Turkey, lard, and bread. Only some British-made soap, part of huge supplies of imports brought in to correct a horrendous shortage, attracts much interest.

Yvgeni is a party member and a retired railway engine driver who proudly wears a badge on his lapel showing a train engine flying a red flag. He stands watching his granddaughter play in the yard between the yellow-brick apartment blocks, his thick arms crossed, as he talks about his party.

Party not trusted

"People have open eyes on everything happening in the country," he says. "A lot of people don't trust the party. Now that we have a multiparty system, the Communist Party will suggest something specific. And the people will judge."

Dimitri has just left the Soviet Army, in which he served as an officer. He was trained as a Chinese interpreter in a military institute, where he joined the Komsomol, the youth wing of the party, because "if I wasn't a member, I wouldn't graduate." "I don't think there will be any changes until there are no communists in the government," he declares with a slight smile. "If you're not a party member, you can sell vegetables and earn a lot of money but you won't have a good career."

Results questioned

Yuri parks his old yellow Lada in back of the market. He is a party activist, a leader of a cell at his wood-cutting factory. Three years ago he was working hard, meeting people and mobilizing support for Mr. Gorbachev and perestroika. Now, like everyone else, he wonders where the results are of the many promises Gorbachev made.

Yuri's feelings about Gorbachev are mixed. "He would make a great foreign minister," he says—a line heard frequently these days as a sardonic comment on his popularity abroad. Yuri, like virtually everyone else we talk to, favors Boris Yeltsin, the rebellious populist who recently won the presidency of the Russian Federation, the largest republic in the Soviet Union. He still talks wistfully of some kind of socialism, perhaps as in Sweden. But, he says, "People don't care what they live under—socialism or capitalism—what they need is job, vacation, housing and food."

Yuri is disdainful of the voices of party conservatives who claim to be speaking for the rank and file workers in the party. In the last six weeks, he reports, five out of 12 party members in his shop have resigned.

Mr. Yeltsin has said he will leave the party if there is no change, the old railway worker says. Most people agree with him, he adds. "I haven't thought about that for myself," he muses. "My wife says don't do anything until after the congress is over."

Gorbachev Reins In 28th Party Congress

Daniel Sneider

7/5/90

For three days Mikhail Gorbachev has appeared like a man sitting atop a volcano.

The powerful Soviet leader has argued at, cajoled, and imperiously commanded the congress of 4,683 Communists gathered in the Kremlin. His aim at every point is to keep the superheated passions of those who oppose his policies of perestroika, in check.

Mr. Gorbachev has been able, so far, to control the floor of the assembly, but he cannot prevent the break-through of fissures of discontent.

A master of the podium, Gorbachev has used that position to curb debate. In orchestrated fashion, delegates have risen at key moments to issue calls for "unity" and the need to conduct "businesslike" discussions. This is aimed to prevent a repeat of the antileadership feelings which sent a meeting of Russian Communists two weeks ago spinning almost out of control.

Gorbachev appears to have tried to buy peace at this 28th Congress of the Communist Party of the Soviet Union (CPSU), especially from those on the right who have a clear majority among the delegates. He has reached out to the left in the form of language, refusing to retreat from reform ideas in his own speeches.

But when it comes to the structures of power within the party—the organizational issues on which the conservative party men thrive—the right appears to have gained the most.

Gorbachev signaled the compromise with the right in his opening speech, indicating he had abandoned plans to reorganize the leadership bodies of the party. The draft party rules prepared by the leadership call for replacing the Politburo, the all-powerful 20-member group at the top of the party, with a much larger "presidium," including the heads of the constituent Communist parties of each of the 15 republics of the Soviet Union. The post of general secretary of the party, which Gorbachev holds, would become that of chairman of the Presidium.

Conservatives have attacked this idea as an attempt to shift power away from the party to the government. It is viewed as part of Gorbachev's effort to build an alternate power base in the office of the presidency.

Gorbachev told the congress that a pre-meeting on July 1 of the representatives of the delegations insisted on maintaining the current Politburo structure. He did not defend his own idea.

The more crucial outcome of these organizational battles will be the actual composition of the Politburo and of the Central Committee, the 248-man body which rules the party between congresses. Gorbachev, in remarks to Soviet television, indicated that most of the Politburo may be replaced. He announced from the podium that four members had decided to resign, including Nikolai Slyunkov, Vitaly Vorotnikov, Gumer Usmanov, and Alexandra Biryukova.

But the more interesting news came from the speeches of Foreign Minister Eduard Shevardnadze and Alexander Yakovlev, regarded as Gorbachev's closest allies on the Politburo. Both men indicated they, too, would leave that party body, although retaining their government positions. This could be interpreted as a sign that Gorbachev intends to cut the party group off from the policymaking process, something which his conservative opponents say he has already done.

Another hint of Gorbachev's plans to downgrade the party's policy role was buried in the otherwise uninteresting speech of Politburo member Lev Zaikov. He revealed that he headed a previously unmentioned special committee in the Politburo which "coordinated and rigidly controlled" all defense policy decisions, including arms control and military industry. He said that this role should be transferred to the president's Defense Council.

These plans in some sense reflect a reality evident at the congress—that the party organization remains in the hands of the conservatives. Vyacheslav Shostakovsky, one of the leaders of the leftwing Democratic Platform group within the party, predicted to reporters that 90-95 percent of the current Central Committee would be returned.

Gorbachev's own continued leadership of the CPSU seems to have been settled as well. All the leading lights of the right, including new Russian party chief Ivan Polozkov, have publicly stated their support for him.

Meanwhile, the congress has been treated to three days of speeches by the leadership and by a pre-picked list of delegates. Despite the obvious effort to keep the atmosphere cool, there is no way to conceal the huge range of opinion which remains encapsuled in this party. The few voices of the left which dared to speak out were greeted with hisses.

The party faithful, never logical in their feelings, gave rousing applause both to the emotionally moving speech of Alexander Yakovlev, the darling of the liberal left, and to the defiant conservative communist rhetoric of Yegor Ligachev.

In both cases their popularity owes much to the simple honesty with which they presented their views of the future of Communism in this, the first land of Communist Party power.

"The party which some time ago raised the people to revolution in the name of justice and brotherhood has gotten into trouble," Yakovlev told them. "Because the party of ideas has turned into the party of power . . . In these conditions, I believe that only the party which becomes more new, more left and more young, will be able to lead the country further along the path of serious reforms."

"Thoughtless radicalism, improvisation and swinging from side to side have yielded us little good during the past five years of perestroika," Mr. Ligachev retorted the following day. "I believe the party will remain Marxist-Leninist."

Gorbachev's forceful, sometimes even angry, defense of his policies in a more than two-hour speech on the first day of the congress failed to ignite any such fires. "Voices can now be heard," he admitted in the beginning of his address, "claiming that perestroika is to blame for all our present troubles. Excuse me for being blunt, but that is simply nonsense."

The audience responded to his words with chilly silence.

Striking Soviet Miners Press For Radical Change

Linda Feldmann

7/12/90

"The economic situation has only gotten worse," sighs Ivan Bulakh, leaning against a grimy shaft entrance at Donetsk's Panfilovskaya Mine as he waits for his shift to begin. "The government and the party have failed us."

A year after a package of government pledges bought an end to protracted strikes at Soviet coal mines, the workers are disillusioned. Some demands have been met, but overall, say miners in this southeast Ukrainian coal center, the government has not come through for them.

Obsolete work facilities remain. Supplies of food and goods have decreased. Relations with management have not improved.

On the anniversary of the start of last year's costly coal strikes, miners have put their tools down once again. On July 11, at major coal regions around the Soviet Union, workers staged symbolic walkouts of two or 24 hours and held rallies to press for change. But this time the theme is political. The top demand is the resignation of Prime Minister Nikolai Ryzhkov and his government.

And, in a development which goes to heart of how this country has been run for the last 73 years, miners are demanding the ejection of Communist Party officials and organizations from their workplace. They also want the party's removed from the Army, secret police, militia, and the schools—this, as the party discusses "renewal" at its crucial 28th Congress in Moscow.

"My impression about the Congress? Disgusting!" exclaims Vitaly Dubovy, chairman of the workers' labor council at Panfilovskaya Mine, expressing a response typical of most Donetsk workers. "The workers are hardly represented. I'm sure the Congress won't bring any changes. But I know there are progressive forces in the party, so I will keep my membership until it's certain there is no hope."

At a rally in Donetsk's House of Soviets, some of the choicer banners signal the city strike committee's view of the party: "Let the Communist Party live in the Chernobyl nuclear plant!" and "Children in cellars, Communist Party in palaces—let's swap!"

In recent days, workers at several Donetsk mines have voted to remove their official party organizations. One is Yuzhno-Donbasskaya Mine No. 1, where the party committee voted almost unanimously to disband itself. Panfilovskaya Mine appears headed in the same direction. At a meeting of one work collective on July 9, 150 miners voted on how to handle the July 11 job action and what to do about the mine's party committee.

The men, freshly scrubbed and looking weary after their shift, sat quietly at the back of the hall. When Mr. Dubovy offered the floor to anyone who wanted to speak, he was greeted by a long silence. Finally, one miner stood. "What good is a strike really going to do, anyway?" he asked.

"Probably nothing," muttered another miner.

Dubovy countered: "It will help mobilize the population, and it will get the word out to the press."

When a vote was taken, a sprinkling of hands went up in favor of a two-hour strike, more went up for a 24-hour stoppage, and 10 abstained. Then came the vote on the party committee: Immediately, all hands shot up in favor of its abolition.

On the question of walking out, workers explained their reluctance in several ways. Some workers did not want to start another wave of strikes, fearing a further deterioration of the Soviet economy. Coal reserves are down, and another major cutback in production would ripple immediately to the railroads, metallurgical plants, and other industries.

Others explained that Panfilovskaya had not been fulfilling its production targets lately—meaning no premiums for the workers—and they did not want to fall further behind. If they halted work for even a few hours, others say, pits would fill in with dirt, setting back work even more.

But in the end, they understood their symbolic importance to the nation—and the leverage they have as providers of badly needed energy.

"We have the strongest work collective," says Mr. Bulakh, the miner. "We represent all the working people. Everyone will understand us."

Back in the center of town, on the day before the strike, leaders of the Donetsk regional party committee are holding an emergency meeting to discuss strategy. After several hours, the beleaguered group emerges from their session, a resolution in hand on the strike.

The statement expresses sympathy for the workers' demands and applauded their activism. The best approach, it suggests, is to hold rallies, but not to stop working. There must be no "speculation" on the tension of the situation, it says. Greater discipline is needed. Workers must not give in to emotion.

"I believe the workers do have a basis for demanding the government's resignation," says Donetsk ideology chief Yuri Yashchenko. "But then what? Whoever comes next will need time. But there is no time—changes are demanded now."

"And yes, I do understand there is unhappiness with the party," he continues defensively, adding that he's been in his post only two months. "The main reason is that we failed to bring out a system of values—the real transfer of the means of production to the workers . . . . I do know one thing: I personally won't hide. I can leave with a good conscience."

At Panfilovskaya, such words from a comfortable bureaucrat provide little solace. For the miners, the only thing that counts is the situation in their mine. They know that the combines (the machines that break up the coal and lift it out of the ground) date back to the 1950s. They know that human beings are still doing tasks that in the west are now performed by machines.

"Once a French filmmaker visited here who was making a movie about the Soviet Union in the 1930s," says one Panfilovskaya administrator. "He said this would be a perfect place to shoot some scenes."

Soviet Party Shifts to Left After Congress

Daniel Sneider/Linda Feldmann

7/16/90

At the close of the bruising two-week 28th Congress of the Soviet Communist Party, the talk of the town is "who won, right or left?"

Soviet leader Mikhail Gorbachev was quick to declare the Congress a victory for his reform policies, a refutation of the view that the party which has ruled here for more than seven decades is incapable of renovation.

"These apprehensions were not justified," a relaxed Gorbachev said late Friday night. "Those who believed this would be the last Congress and the funeral of the Soviet Communist Party were wrong again. The Soviet Communist Party lives and will live."

Liberal supporters of Mr. Gorbachev, such as Otto Latsis, the editor of the party journal Kommunist, joined in calling the Congress "the defeat of the conservatives." Gorbachev, they declared in numerous commentaries and interviews over the weekend, rallied from the initial right-wing assault to shift the party center decisively to the left.

But these triumphant words were belied by the dramatic departure from the party of the leading lights of the radical left—the populist head of the Russian federation parliament, Boris Yeltsin; the mayor of Moscow, Gavril Popov, and his Leningrad counterpart, Anatoly Sobchak.

Mr. Popov and Mr. Sobchak issued a joint statement decrying the "complete inability of the CPSU [Communist Party of the Soviet Union] to offer the country a real program of transition to the new society." They accused the party of being out of step with the populace by refusing to reject "class strife" and failing to support the transition to a market economy, including the right to private property and the transfer of power to elected legislatures.

All three had indicated their desire to leave before the meeting. All could afford to do so because each has a power base outside the Communist Party. Less certain is the future of other members of the Democratic Platform, the left-wing faction of the party, some of whom also said they intend to break away.

Mr. Yeltsin's departure carries much greater significance than the withdrawal of a handful of top members of the party's Democratic Platform. It means that fully half of the population of the Soviet Union is now governed by a non-Communist.

For Gorbachev, who fought hard to hold the party's divergent political factions together at the Congress, Yeltsin's move is a short-term blow. But in the view of some reformers, Yeltsin's decision could help Gorbachev, because he will show the country that there is life after communism and that the government and party are separate entities.

Indeed some Gorbachev aides acknowledged the validity of some criticisms from the left.

Democratic Platform leaders felt there had been little change in fundamental party rules, particularly the principle of "democratic centralism," which requires party members to follow the will of the majority.

"Inasmuch as these words have been discredited, it would have been better to get rid of them," said Gorbachev adviser Georgy Shakhnazarov. "It would have been a sign that we categorically break away from our past—from disgraces, from repression, suppression of dissent."

Gorbachev's claim of success is best justified by the changes within the party structure. With the election of the final leadership bodies at a Saturday meeting of the new party Central Committee, he has managed an almost total turnover at the top of the party. His most vigorous right-wing opponent, Yegor Ligachev, is left bereft of any party post. The new Politburo and Central Committee are far weaker and more pliable bodies, leaving many key policymaking functions in the hands of Gorbachev's Presidential Council.

The Central Committee has been reorganized, with the bulk of its 412 members entering as proportional representatives of the constituent parties of the 15 Soviet republics and the rest from various organizations such as trade unions or research institutes. The larger, 24-person Politburo includes the 15 republican party chiefs, Gorbachev and his deputy, and seven others with specific organizational duties.

The members of the Communist Party's Politburo were previously considered the most powerful people in the country, the makers of all decisions. But the most glaring fact about this Politburo is that it does not include the most important policymakers such as Alexander Yakovlev, Defense Minister Dimitri Yazov, KGB chief Vladimir Kryuchkov, or Prime Minister Nikolai Ryzhkov. All of them left the Politburo but remain in the Presidential Council and Cabinet.

Gorbachev has "gotten rid of the old guard that has its own anti-Gorbachev position," comments Andrei Fadin, political editor of the independent weekly Commersant. "The new people aren't leftists, but they are more manageable, potentially more ruled by him."

Gorbachev, the analyst believes, "has managed to weaken the top of the party but I don't see that he was strengthened or that the Presidency was strengthened."

Many analysts see a growing vacuum of power, as the Communist Party loses strength, but there are no comparable national institutions which can even hope to replace it. The hopes of the democratic left to create a new party unifying various existing smaller opposition groups, which the departing Democratic Platform leaders say will take place in October, are considered far-fetched.

Many Democratic Platform members interviewed at the Congress felt there is much that can still be achieved from within the party ranks.

"Boris Nikolayevich [Yeltsin] forced many of us to think," says Alexander Karpov, a delegate from the Ukrainian city of Kharkov. "But I know party members who are not delegates here who are counting on us to stay. Remember, the Congress does not reflect the makeup of the party as a whole—it is more left wing."

And for many, membership in the party still provides personal security in their careers, for which the new multiparty system is not yet an alternative.

Soviet Auto Plant Limps Toward Market Economy

Daniel Sneider

8/1/90

The assembly line at the most modern auto factory in the Soviet Union moves like rush-hour traffic in midtown Manhattan.

In one section of the sprawling floor of the Moscow Automobile Works, automatic robots send up showers of sparks as they weld a steady flow of car chassis.

Not far away, the line has simply stopped altogether. Workers take naps in half-assembled cars hanging from overhead rails. Women in the paint section sit around a table to chat and drink tea amidst the acrid fumes.

The workers are waiting for parts. Even the most basic elements of the car—the steel sheets that are pressed to form the body—are in short supply.

Officials at the plant provide telling numbers—a few years ago, the plant used to turn out about 160,000 Moskvich passenger cars a year. Last year, production was down to 78,000, in a factory with the capacity to produce 180,000.

The plant managers offer several explanations for this drop. In part, they say, it is simply teething problems from the introduction last year of a new model, the Moskvich 2141. Along with the model change came an upgrade of plant equipment, including robotization and a redesign of the assembly line, which is still in process. All this has been done with the assistance of the French car company Renault.

But the other part of the story is a now-familiar tale throughout the Soviet economy of shortages and half-baked reforms. The Moskvich plant is caught, like so many others, in a nether world between the old system of command from the center and the promised new world of a market economy.

"We have a problem with a steady supply of parts," Alexi Morozov, director of the plant's foreign relations department, says. "And to keep production running we need inventory."

The plant depends on about 300 suppliers, he explains. Under the old system, the central auto industry ministry and the State Planning Committee set the production quotas for the plant and told it who the suppliers were.

"Then, we made direct contracts with them, indicating the prices and the time limits," Morozov says. "But the system of having one supplier is bad, because they feel like monopolists and can change the price whenever they like."

In the name of ending central control and monopoly, Mikhail Gorbachev's government gave enterprises the theoretical freedom to manage themselves, including making direct contracts. In reality, the official says, "only a few minor things changed." The Moskvich plant now has some contracts with steel plants bypassing the auto ministry. But these are small-scale barter deals: the plant trades its cars to get steel.

Would the plant like to be completely free, the officials are asked. Someday yes, answers Nicholai Kaluga, deputy head of the official trade union that functions as part of the plant management. But "it's unfeasible under the present system of economic relations," he explains. "We still depend on supplies which are controlled by the state."

The attitude of the auto industry ministry toward reform is perhaps best expressed by the response of a senior official to a request for information on the number of cars produced last year in the Soviet Union. It is a "state secret," he told a caller. Over at the Central Statistical Board the secret was revealed, however—1,217,108 cars, some 200,000 less than in 1983.

At best, the government's reforms resemble what novelist Joseph Heller made famous as "Catch-22." For example, about 40 percent of the steel sheets used in the plant were previously imported. The imported steel was centrally bought and distributed to the different auto plants by Gossnab, the central State Committee on Supplies.

"When we became independent, the government ceased to finance imports," says Morozov. But the plant does not earn enough foreign currency to pay for the needed steel imports.

And even if the plant made enough from exports of its cars, they are not allowed to use that money freely, the official continues. All payments made in foreign currency must go through the State Bank for Foreign Economic Relations and "they are keeping it," he says. According to other sources, the bank is using these funds to try to ease a crisis in payments on Soviet foreign debts.

The situation reached such a crisis that the directors of all the motor works in the Soviet Union—there are four major plants—had to go directly to Prime Minister Nikolai Ryzhkov to beg for steel. Now, the Moskvich officials say, supplies are coming but not at the previous level.

On the factory floor, the reality is plain to see. The steel shortage has slowed the line, Mr. Kaluga admits. And the steel they have is of uneven quality. The automated equipment has to be heavily supplemented by manual labor. In one area, workers with hand tools smooth the edges of doors and other parts.

The most skilled craftsmen in the plant work in a branch section of the assembly line where they repair the defects in cars bodies coming off the line. With small hammers, the workers bang away on door frames and body panels, removing bumps and trying to make the parts all fit.

Compared with plants this writer has visited in Japan, the assembly line seems like a maze. It is less a continuous process than a series of subassembly lines whose linkages are difficult to discern. The plant is poorly lit, half concealed in dark shadows. Sparks fly into walkways and there is no apparent attention to safety, even obligatory cautionary signs.

A conversation with a few workers at a halted section of the line quickly gathers a group of rough-faced men in stained T-shirts. Pyotr Turin has been working here for 14 years and makes 350 rubles a month, a good wage by Soviet standards. Asked what changes the workers would like to see here, Pyotr quickly replies. "The shop should be completely redesigned. We need better working conditions, better tools. The parts should be delivered on time."

Do the managers ever ask your opinion? "Never," several workers reply. "We workers know better than the managers what to do," a worker says sharply, to the nodding assent of his comrades.

Trade union official Kaluga returns to join the conversation. "Let's get going," he says. "You're slowing down the line."

Speaking later, Kaluga admits that the views of workers have less weight than they might in a similar plant in the West. "We've been separating workers from management problems for too long," he says. "It's difficult to reverse this."

"All organizations now have to win the trust of workers anew," he says, quickly adding that his union still has that trust. On the floor, where the 23,000 production workers of this plant can be found, the view is again different.

The union is "under the heel of the administration," Turin says flatly. The workers all eagerly voice their support for forming an independent union, something that has already begun at the larger Volga Auto Works.

The managers and the workers share one feeling—no one wants to go back to the old system of the command economy. "Now we have the taste of freedom, and we are not going to give it up," says Kaluga.

Iraqi Move Tests US-Soviet Ties

Daniel Sneider

8/3/90

While US Secretary of State James Baker III and Soviet Foreign Minister Eduard Shevardnadze wrap up a successful meeting in Siberia, the reality of superpower cooperation is being seriously tested by the Iraqi invasion of Kuwait.

Following Mr. Shevardnadze's return to Moscow Thursday afternoon, the Soviet Foreign Ministry issued a statement clearly condemning the Iraqi invasion. It called for the "immediate and unconditional withdrawal of Iraqi troops from Kuwaiti territory. The sovereignty, national independence, and territorial integrity of Kuwait must be fully restored and defended."

The Soviets also have joined a collective effort at the UN Security Council to end the conflict.

The Soviet stance comes despite the existence of a treaty of friendship and cooperation and the Soviet role as Iraq's main weapons supplier.

"This invasion is absolutely unacceptable," comments Viktor Kreminiyuk, a specialist on regional conflict at the influential U.S.A.-Canada Institute, a Moscow think tank. He describes Iraqi leader Saddam Hussein as "a madman on a bicycle," adding that it is "absolutely incredible that he would attack a peaceful state."

The Iraqi invasion, he says, "is a test for the extent of Soviet-American cooperation in keeping peace. Diplomatic means, both through the United Nations and outside it, should be tried first, Kreminiyuk argues, "but if it doesn't work, something has to be done." United States military action against Iraq at that point, "would be tacitly supported" by the Soviet Union, he says.

The emergence of this new crisis in the Middle East comes just as the US and Soviet Union have made breakthroughs in forging joint positions on solving long-standing regional conflicts in Afghanistan and Cambodia. Mr. Baker and Shevardnadze, in a joint press conference yesterday after two days of talks in the Siberian city of Irkutsk, announced significant progress toward settlement of the Afghan war.

The two leaders also opened a new dialogue on the Asia-Pacific region, one which the Soviets hope will lead to broader security talks like those in Europe. The two men reported progress on a wide array of other issues, from German reunification and a new US-Soviet summit later this year to US economic assistance.

The agreement reached on Afghanistan at the Irkutsk meeting opens the door to ending the 12-year-long war in that central Asian nation. At their press conference yesterday, according to wire service reports, Baker and Shevardnadze described a formula for ending the war between the Soviet-backed government of President Najibullah and US-backed rebels. It calls for creation of an interim agency to conduct free elections under United Nations supervision.

"We both recognize the role of the United Nations and some form of monitoring and control of the elections by the United Nations," Shevardnadze said. "There is also mutual recognition of the need for free elections, and there is recognition of that by the Afghan government. There is recognition of the need to create some kind of commission or authority to conduct free and fair elections."

Both officials said there was still some negotiation ahead before this can take place. The formation of an interim authority is likely to pose the greatest challenge. The failure to find an acceptable third party to head such a government, such as the aged, exiled Afghan king, means that it will be a coalition between the Kabul regime and the rebels. The role of Najibullah in that government must still be decided.

The new agreement is a follow-up to the initial Soviet-American deal which led to the withdrawal of Soviet troops from Afghanistan last year. But the Soviets have continued to supply arms to their Afghan allies in Kabul, as has the US to its rebel clients. Soviet analysts believe the agreement at Irkutsk will lead to a mutual reduction of those arms supplies. Beyond the Afghan issue, the two senior officials indicated they were on the same wavelength, following a change in the US position, on promoting a political dialogue in Cambodia.

More broadly, according to Tass, Shevardnadze said they had discussed for the first time "common problems of Asia and the Far East," including stability, security, the end of military confrontation and possibilities for bilateral and multilateral cooperation in the region. The discussion in Siberia included the situation on the Korean peninsula, where the Soviets have been playing an increasing role due to growing ties with South Korea. These developments could mark a shift in the American position, which has resisted holding arms and security talks in Asia and the Pacific. The Soviet Union and the US "do not view each other as adversaries" in Asia or elsewhere, Shevardnadze declared.

Bumper Soviet Crop Rots in Fields

Daniel Sneider

8/6/90

Large blue harvesters move slowly across a field of barley, raising a cloud of dust and chaff as they pass. "Don't try to stop the machines to talk to the drivers," the director of the Shoshanski state farm admonishes his visitors. If they stop the combines, he explains, they may not be able to get them started again.

It is harvest time in this agricultural area some 60 miles northwest of Moscow, as it is all across the Soviet Union. By all accounts, this may be the largest harvest on record. But the bounty is cause for alarm rather than celebration.

In this region of Kalinin a state of emergency has been declared to try to cope with an extreme shortage of labor, machinery, spare parts, and fuel which threatens to leave the crop rotting in the fields.

Last Thursday the Soviet Cabinet met in Moscow and emerged with three decrees effectively spreading those emergency measures to the entire country. All factories and government organizations must assign employees to the harvest, including trucks and drivers. Students are to go for a month of harvest labor. The military is deploying trucks and planes to transport the crops.

"For six months we complained that the weather wouldn't provide for a good harvest, and now that God has provided us with a good harvest we cannot cope with the work," Prime Minister Nikolai Ryzhkov told the Cabinet session.

"Combines are standing idle. There are no batteries. There are no belts. There are no spare parts," Mr. Ryzhkov said. "People are working with three hours sleep. Can we really not find the forces during this period to allow them to work?"

In part, this is a familiar tale of the crisis-ridden Soviet agricultural system. But the urgent, almost panicked, atmosphere surrounding this harvest reflects key differences with previous years.

First, the size of this harvest is well beyond previous levels, posing serious challenges to the ability of the system to cope with storage and processing.

Second, a serious shortage of money is making the Soviet government desperate to bring in the grain in order to reduce its high level of grain imports, the largest in the world.

Third and last, the crisis reflects a breakdown of the old command economy, with Moscow no longer able to order its farms and factories to do its bidding. But a new, market-based economy that could mobilize resources through economic incentives does not exist either.

Vladlen Nikitin, head of the State Commission on Food and Procurement, described the scale of the harvest problems in blunt terms in a stormy Cabinet meeting last week. "There are 300 million tons ripening in the fields," he said, which with normal losses of 30 to 40 million tons could mean a harvest of 260 million tons. This surpasses the previous record harvest, in 1978, of 237 million tons. Last year 211 million tons was produced, and Moscow was forced to buy 44 million tons from abroad. "We cannot buy grain abroad, because the country has no currency," Mr. Nikitin told the meeting, according to an account in the government daily Izvestia.

But, he said, 20 percent of the harvesters are idle due to the lack of drivers, and grain storage facilities are not adequate. There is a shortage of 20,000 grain-carrying railway cars, added Vladimir Ginko, the deputy minister of railways. Even though there is a shortage of vegetables and fruit in the cities, villagers are destroying them because they cannot harvest the produce, Ryzhkov said. According to Nikitin, there are usually 700,000 people mobilized to help with vegetable harvests, but now only 150,000 have been gathered.

"Apparently the central organs have lost control over the situation," the Communist Party daily Pravda said in a front-page commentary yesterday.

Out in Konakovo, state farm director Anatoli Poltorikin agrees. "The system of supply to rural areas has fallen apart," he says. Only 10 percent of his supplies reliably come from the state agencies that are supposed to deliver them. The rest he gets by backdoor barter deals, trading everything from produce to the right to build summer homes on the picturesque banks of the Volga river, which winds through the farm's property.

According to reports in the Soviet press, state and collective farms are also refusing to sell grain to the state above what they are required by quota to supply. This is despite a rise in government procurement prices earlier this year. In the Kharkov region, reports the agricultural daily Selskaya Zhizn, farm officials feel the ruble is worthless and prefer to keep the grain as payment to their workers and to trade for consumer goods and equipment.

The labor shortage reflects this breakdown of order. In the past, factories, schools, and other institutions were ordered by the Communist Party organizations to send their workers and equipment to the farms at harvest time. This often caused losses for factories in their own operations. Due to the economic reforms implemented in the past couple of years, these institutions are theoretically now independent of such controls. And they are also supposed to be self-financing—not dependent on subsidies.

"Now industrial enterprises don't find it profitable to send workers, because they do self-accounting," explains director Poltorikin. "Since there is no extra labor, I have to work overtime," complains farm worker Sergei Permenkov. It leaves him no time to take care of his own five-acre plot which he has privately leased from the state farm under the new reform system of land-leasing.

The state of emergency, the farm director explains, requires the factories to send a certain number of workers, with the losses partially compensated by the state. Some workers have now arrived, though because of the delay, "I will lose some crop," says Mr. Permenkov.

The central government orders call for dispatch of workers, with incentives to them in the form of "payments in kind," namely with food. The enterprises are required to send 15 percent of their trucks with drivers. But, the Pravda article asks provocatively, "Who will give the guarantee that the departments will obey these orders."

Possibly the only reliable force under the government's control is the military, which had already formed 70 truck battalions, with 35,000 trucks, to help. The latest decree assigns another 10,000 trucks, from Aug. 10 to Nov. 1, to the major grain producing areas in Russia and Kazakhstan.

"We will never forgive ourselves if we lose the grain and if we lose the chance nature gave us," the Pravda article concluded.

Armenian Nationalists Extract Concessions From Kremlin

Daniel Sneider

8/10/90

The Soviet government has yielded to a new nationalist government in Armenia, opening yet another breach in the Kremlin's control over the country.

Following meetings between the newly elected nationalist president of the Armenian republic and Soviet government leaders here, the Kremlin backed down from a decree demanding the disarming and disbandment of armed groups. The decree, which was to expire yesterday, was aimed particularly at Armenian nationalist groups who have formed organized militias.

Levon Ter-Petrosian, a former political prisoner who was elected president of Armenia last Saturday, told reporters here yesterday that the Soviet authorities had agreed to entrust the new government with keeping order. All Soviet Army troops, which have been deployed there since early this year following violent clashes between Armenia and neighboring Azerbaijan, have now been removed from the streets of the capital, Yerevan, he said. "I am the new leader of the republic, and I am not responsible for the sins of the former rulers," the linguistic scholar told reporters. "I'm sure I'll get a chance to implement the president's [Mikhail Gorbachev's] order, but we have agreed that this order will be implemented by our own forces without any participation by the Soviet Army. We have reached an agreement that Soviet troops will not be brought into Armenia anymore."

"The opposition forces are in power in Armenia," Galina Starovoytova, an Armenian representative to the Soviet parliament, gleefully declared in opening the new president's press conference. Mr. Ter-Petrosian is a leader of the Armenian National Movement, the largest noncommunist group in the republic. He was arrested twice, most recently in 1988 when he was held along with other nationalists in a Moscow jail for six months.

Ter-Petrosian defeated a candidate of the Communist Party in his election. The party, he told reporters, "still holds a lot of levers" in Armenia. But, he added, "I believe the Armenia Communist Party is demoralized and it will not be able to mount a serious opposition."

The Armenian parliament is expected to pass a declaration of sovereignty within a few days, following in the footsteps of other republics in the Soviet Union. But Ter-Petrosian indicated they intend to take a step further towards full independence, legalizing the militias and forming them into a national army. Armenians "should go through their military service within the territory of the republic," the young president said. "If Armenians serve in the republic, that is a national army though it might be called a Soviet Army."

The Armenian government had openly defied the presidential order, officially suspending it only days after it was issued on July 25. According to reports in the Soviet press, the organized militias, such as the Armenian National Army, simply took off their uniforms and ceased openly carrying weapons.

Soviet Interior Minister Vadim Bakatin issued a statement Wednesday evening acknowledging that the presidential order had been virtually ignored and indefinitely extending the deadline.

"Until recently republican authorities did not take a constructive attitude," he stated, according to a report from the official Tass news agency. "However, there are grounds to maintain that the political situation in the republic is changing. Hope has appeared that the Armenian authorities can resolve, within a short period and on their own, all tasks concerning internal life and the stabilization of the socio-political situation in the republic."

The statement was issued after talks between the new Armenian leader and Mr. Bakatin, Soviet Prime Minister Nikolai Ryzhkov, and a top aide to Mr. Gorbachev, Alexander Yakovlev. Ter-Petrosian said that the talks were the consequence of a telephone call made by President Gorbachev to him following his election.

"He called and congratulated me on my election," Ter-Petrosian recounted. "We had a warm conversation. He expressed readiness to start cooperating with the new leadership, and we accepted that with pleasure."

Gorbachev and his government are clearly hopeful that by making this gesture to the new, noncommunist government they can bring the violent strife that has engulfed Armenia and the neighboring republic of Azerbaijan under control.

Armed groups have been formed in both republics, originally to defend against the alleged assaults of each other. But in recent months in Armenia, attacks have also been directed against Soviet Army and Interior Ministry troops deployed to keep order.

The new Armenian leader took a generally conciliatory tone. He said he was ready to start talks with Azerbaijani authorities at any time to find a compromise solution to the Nagorno-Karabakh dispute.

Gorbachev-Yeltsin Pact Shifts Political Balance

Daniel Sneider

8/14/90

Mikhail Gorbachev is resting in his presidential villa by the Black Sea, preparing for the resumption of the political battle this fall.

Meanwhile, Russian leader Boris Yeltsin is in perpetual motion, spending a brief vacation forging political alliances with the Baltic republics and now barnstorming across the country. Judging by the time devoted to the doings and sayings of the Siberian populist on the evening television news, Mr. Gorbachev need not return to Moscow.

Mr. Yeltsin, who was elected head of the parliament of the Russian Republic last May, is now arguably the most popular politician in the Soviet Union. He enjoys the support and the trust that Gorbachev once possessed and watched fade away during the past year of economic collapse and political disarray.

Now Gorbachev has been forced to seek an alliance with his one-time rival, agreeing to revise his economic reform plans and his response to demands for autonomy within the Soviet Union along the lines of Yeltsin's policies. The political balance of left and right, which Gorbachev has used so well in the past to preserve his power, is now crucially altered.

This political axis was formally set with an agreement at the beginning of August to formulate a joint program for transition to a market economy. The program is to be based on a radical 18-month plan announced earlier by the parliament of the Russian Republic, the largest of the Soviet Union's 15 republics. The economic plan is to become, in turn, part of the basis for a new "union treaty," giving greater freedom to the republics.

The deal is a slap at Gorbachev's central government, supposedly at work on the same task. "The accord came as a complete surprise," wrote the independent weekly Commersant, "taking the normally vigilant staff of the Soviet Council of Ministers [the Cabinet] unawares. This has caused rumors to fly anew that the resignation of Prime Minster [Nikolai] Ryzhkov and the Council of Ministers is imminent."

In an interview with Latvian television, Yeltsin said that he proposed the idea of forming a joint commission in a telephone call to Gorbachev in late July from Latvia, where he was vacationing. The two men, says a seasoned Soviet political analyst, "talk regularly—not as friends, but they have an interest in each other. It's a business connection."

Yeltsin clearly views Gorbachev's agreement as his coup, a view shared by many observers. "It is a personal victory for Yeltsin, since it proves he has secured the center's [represented by Gorbachev] unconditional support for his economic programs," Commersant wrote.

But there are those who see this as equally a case of Gorbachev using Yeltsin to push forward reforms that are blocked by conservative opponents within his government. The particular obstacle is Mr. Ryzhkov, often depicted as the representative of the "military-industrial complex," a product of the vast central industrial ministries who are tied closely to the military and who oppose a diminution of their power.

"If Yeltsin believes he has won, I'm sure it is Gorbachev who has won," says the Soviet analyst, who preferred to remain anonymous. Since last February, Gorbachev made four attempts to get rid of Ryzhkov and failed, he explained. "Now he is using Yeltsin to do this dirty job."

Ryzhkov is politically associated with previous economic reform plans, including the latest presented last spring. That plan offered a three-to-five-year transition to a "regulated market economy," coupled with a highly controversial rise in the subsidized prices of bread, meat, and other consumer goods.

The "price reform," which some economists criticized as merely an effort to reverse the huge budget deficit, triggered a storm of protest. Radicals also attacked the program for being indecisive about setting up the structure for a market economy.

The Ryzhkov plan was voted down by the Supreme Soviet, the Soviet parliament, which asked the government to come back by the beginning of September with a new, more-detailed program. At least two groups, the State Commission on Economic Reform, headed by Deputy Prime Minister Leonid Abalkin, and a special group on alternative plans, headed by radical economist Abel Aganbegyan, have been working along the lines of that directive.

The new commission, which includes Yeltsin deputies, radical economists, and a couple of Gorbachev men, including Mr. Abalkin, is counterpoised to the Ryzhkov effort. The Russian 500-day program was actually drafted last February as part of the work of the economic reform group headed by Abalkin, says economist Grigory Yavlinsky, its main author. The plan was rejected, but got a second life with Yeltsin's new government, in which Mr. Yavlinsky now serves as deputy prime minster and head of their economic reform group.

The Soviet and Russian parliaments are now set to reconvene in the beginning of September.

Gorbachev has already indicated that he will back more-radical approaches. In the past week, the government has unveiled several presidential decrees, including one allowing the formation of small businesses and another setting up a state fund to administer the sale of some 400 state-owned companies.

Both moves reflect growing consensus in favor of moving more quickly toward privatization, the key difference, aside from pace, between the Ryzhkov and Russian plans.

"The soul of the market is competition," said Nikolai Petrakov, the most radical of Gorbachev's economic advisers in an interview just published by the weekly Moscow News.

Leningrad's Aim: A Free Enterprise Citadel

Daniel Sneider

8/16/90

In marbled halls redolent with the pungent odor of mink, Soviet auctioneers sell the fabled furs of Russia to the highest foreign bidder.

For almost 60 years, the annual fur auction in Leningrad's Palace of Fur has been an isolated island of capitalism in the communist sea. The fur market has been "like a country by itself," says New York furrier Ernest Kremnitzer, who has been coming since 1954.

Now the newly installed radical leaders of this former imperial Russian capital propose to make the entire city a citadel of free enterprise. Leningrad, along with five other Russian cities and regions, was declared a "free-enterprise zone" by the Russian Republic's parliament on July 14.

The free-enterprise zones are only one more challenge to the Kremlin's centralized rule over the vast empire known as the Soviet Union. From cities to entire republics, such as the Russian Republic, impatient local governments are no longer waiting for Moscow's promised reforms but are going off on their own. In the tiny offices of the Leningrad Soviet building on St. Isaac's Square, mostly young dreamers and movers are already hard at work on a variety of schemes to make the enterprise-zone goal a reality.

The ideas floating around range from making the city a pacesetter in creating a market economy to what appear to be wild fantasies of separating Leningrad from the rest of the nation.

"We will have our own currency," Alexander Trubachev, a young people's deputy in the Lensoviet, or city council, excitedly tells visitors. "For Leningraders, who will get money in Leningrad rubles, there will be Western goods in shops, goods produced in Leningrad, and goods produced in Russia, but only of the highest quality, paid for in Leningrad currency."

As for those unfortunates from outside the zone, there will be "special shops for 'wooden rubles,' which will have supplies from other parts of Russia or partly from Leningrad," he says.

"The variety of goods will be lower and of lower quality," he adds, with evident disdain.

According to one version of this idea, the Leningrad "currency" will take the form of issuing special Eurocard credit cards to every Leningrader. The cards would be supported by a special regional ruble which is convertible into dollars and other hard currencies. The cards are "substitutes for fencing off the free zone with barbed wire," says Lensoviet deputy Pyotr Filippov, one of the heads of the group formulating reform plans.

More conventionally, the Lensoviet seeks to move more rapidly toward a market economy than the timetable envisioned by the Gorbachev government in Moscow or even by the more radical government of the Russian Republic, headed by populist Boris Yeltsin. There are plans to establish a stock market and a labor exchange, to take over and break up all the state owned enterprises, and to legalize all forms of private property.

The Leningrad city fathers are quite consciously seeking to follow in the footsteps of Peter the Great, the Czar who built the city on marshes along the Baltic Sea as Russia's "window to the West." They, too, are looking in that direction for foreign capital and trade. Foreign investors are welcomed and the city hopes to attract more dollar- and deutche mark-carrying tourists with modern shopping centers and maybe even a Leningrad branch of Disneyland.

The city offers two main attractions for investors, city officials say. It has a concentration of highly skilled workers and scientific researchers, drawn largely by high-technology defense and electronics industries that dominate the local economy.

And the classical Italian-designed architecture of Peter's Leningrad still displays its somewhat-faded charm along the canals and the banks of the River Neva, making it the largest tourist attraction in the country. From the great Hermitage Museum in the former czar's Winter Palace to the Smolny Institute, the boarding school that became the headquarters of the 1917 Bolshevik Revolution, "Leningrad is a museum in itself," says Mr. Filippov.

The city is prepared to offer long term, 25-to-50 year, leases to foreign companies to set up offices and factories here, Filippov explains. An official sitting at the next desk, hearing this, hastily pulls out a portfolio of photos of beautiful but crumbling old Leningrad buildings being offered for lease, repair not included.

At present, the ministry of finance in Moscow must decide on all joint ventures with foreign companies. But, Filippov says defiantly, in the new Leningrad zone, "all international economic relations will be liberated." The city will make those decisions, including on creating convertibility within the zone.

Now, "the republics don't ask for rights—they take them themselves," the burly, bearded former editor of an economic journal says.

Like others here, he looks to the example of the neighboring Baltic republics, with whom Leningrad is discussing forming a common free-market area. The central government has only the power of armed forces to stop them, he argues.

"Do you think the ministry of finance would send such troops to get hold of Leningrad banks," he asks rhetorically.

The radicals came to power following elections in March which brought a two-thirds turnover in the membership of the Lensoviet. Anatoly Sobchak, an attractive and articulate law professor, became the mayor. Along with Gavril Popov, the radical mayor of Moscow who was elected at the same time, and Mr. Yeltsin, he is among the most popular Soviet politicians.

"Three months ago, there were two centers of power in this city," explains Leningrad sociologist Leonid Kesselman. "The main one was in Smolny," where the Communist Party is still headquartered. "Now we can say quite surely that center No. 1 is on St. Isaac's Square."

Here, in the city named after Vladimir Lenin, people are leaving the Communist Party in large numbers, starting with Mayor Sobchak, who is now concluding a tour in the United States. Based on recent polls, Mr. Kesselman predicts that party membership will shrink from 600,000 members to 120,000 members by year-end.

The willingness of Leningraders to accept changes such as private property is six months to a year ahead of the rest of the country, Kesselman says, citing extensive polling results. This willingness stems in part from the deterioration of a city that used to pride itself on its well-preserved beauty and cleanliness.

"The city is half destroyed," Kesselman says. "The main items of food can be found only with difficulties. They are not bought—they are being acquired."

Polls and election results show that Muscovites are also more radicalized than the Soviet heartland, but Leningraders insist they are a breed apart.

"Citizens of Moscow and Leningrad are quite different peoples which by coincidence speak the same language," says Filippov, who frequents Moscow as a member of the Russian parliament.

Moscow, he says, "is a city of cogs, a city of bureaucracy." Leningrad is a city of culture, of science, with a tradition of opposition to state authority.

With a "free" Leningrad, predicts Kesselman, "we will have a situation in this city that the better you work, the better you will live. This is the strongest stimulus for change—not Yeltsin, not Sobchak, not Popov—that people feel everything depends on them."

Soviet State Farmers Slog Through System

Daniel Sneider

8/20/90

Anatoly Poltorikin is young, he is smart, and, for as far as the eye can see, he is all-powerful.

Muscovites in their dachas by the Volga River invite him in for lunch and vodka, pressing packets of foreign cigarettes into his hands as he leaves. At the cow barn, women hauling heavy cans of milk pause to bow slightly when he enters. A young couple renting land from him praise his help but complain about being his "serfs."

Mr. Poltorikin is director of the Shoshanski sovkhoz—or state farm, a 15,000 acre spread of cattle, potatoes, vegetables, and barley fields set among forested hills along the Volga. About 450 people, along with their families, labor there, living in wooden houses or in three-story apartment blocks.

By the standards of Soviet agriculture, Poltorikin is a benevolent and an enlightened despot. The loyal Communist has opened up his state farm to reform, to lease and maybe even sale of land. He wheels and deals to improve farm facilities and conditions.

Wearing a brown suit, sitting behind his desk on the second floor of the farm office, the 36-year-old graduate of an agricultural school eagerly tells of plans to develop his scenic property for vacationers, even for foreigners to rent - dachas (summer homes) here. In another time and another place, Poltorikin would be building shopping malls in California.

Here in the Russian countryside, for all his plans and schemes, his power extends only so far. Despite talk of change, the men up the ladder set the prices for his products and tell him who to sell to and how much. The state bank controls all the farm's earnings. Poltorikin is left with a mere 25 rubles a day to spend on his own discretion for the farm.

"We are all, in some way, victims of the system," Father Sergei, the outspoken young parish priest, says philosophically when asked about the farm director. "He is lord and god here but there are larger lords and gods over him. In contrast to them, he looks like a worm."

State farms such as the Shoshanski sovkhoz control the majority of land in the Soviet Union. The state farm is the twisted outgrowth of a 60-year-long Soviet attempt to put agriculture on the same footing as industry, transforming farmers into wage laborers and putting farms under the aegis of "agro-industrial complexes."

The rest of Soviet farmland is organized into collective farms, or kolkhoz, which differ theoretically in being the joint property of their members.

Down the dirt road from the office, past single-story wooden houses with ornate painted window frames, are rows of drab concrete apartments. Laundry hangs from balcony lines, and Russian pop music drifts down from an open window as women sit on the stoop with their babies.

"You can't buy anything here," complains the wife of a tractor driver. She goes to Moscow a couple of times a month to shop, even for food. The farm's meat and milk go elsewhere.

Talking with Poltorikin about how his farm really works is like peeling an onion. In the past, he explains, the farm was handed a plan by the regional branch of the Agro-Industrial Complex, setting an order for so much milk and so much meat. The state, for its part, provided the fertilizer, machinery, fuel, in short everything they needed.

Now, after agricultural reforms promulgated from Moscow, "we decide the volume of production ourselves," and the government has given incentives for higher production, in the form of higher purchase prices. According to this new system, the local government is supposed to make an agreement to buy all the farm's products and to provide the supplies.

All the proper committees have been set up, Poltorikin tells us. Unfortunately they aren't operating. "We're all still learning democracy and other things," he says, a slight smile creeping across his strong, lean face.

After several questions, it comes out that, after all, "we are still operating according to the old system." The farm has a "contract," for example, with a meat-packing plant in the nearby city of Kalinin. The price is set by the government, varying according not only to quality but to the condition of the farm.

"A farm doing poorly, like this farm," he explains, "is given higher prices to catch up with better performing farms."

Next year, the director assures us though, they have been told they will enter the world of the "regulated market."

But "there's still a lot of confusion about that," the director says. It doesn't mean the farm can rush off to sell its beef for higher prices in Moscow, 80 miles away. As far as the director is concerned, the meat-packing plant in Kalinin gets the beef.

Anyway, the director says firmly, now the farm can sell whatever it produces above the quota. But all the money, along with money from sideline production of bed linen, pillow cases and glassware, goes to the bank where it is "calculated into fulfillment of the plan." He cannot manage this money, cannot decide to spend more for salaries or less on development.

This "noncash," as Soviet bureaucratese so precisely terms it, is used to buy all their supplies, according to the plan. Well, not exactly. Because, it turns out, the farm can get only 10 percent of what they need from the state. The rest, Poltorikin finally admits, comes from "racing around the country" to make back-room barter deals with the producers of their supplies.

What does he trade? "They will never give you anything for your beautiful eyes," Poltorikin says, with a twinkle in his eyes.

"I made a deal with a construction company," he says as he shows off a new concrete cow barn being built. "They got a plot of land and built dachas there, and every year they have to build a half million rubles worth for us."

The dachas spread down along the river banks.

"That's how we're preparing for the market," says Poltorikin. "If tomorrow the state abandons me, I will survive on barter deals, by using our beautiful scenery, the green forests, and the water."

Soviet Sales Of Gold Seen As Sign of Desperation

Amy Kaslow

8/23/90

The Soviet Union has been selling off strategic gold reserves, sparking new concerns about the country's troubled economy.

"Dipping into reserves is the last resort," says Marshall Goldman, head of Harvard University's Russian Research Center.

"It's either a sign of desperation or because the price of gold is unusually high—I think it's a little of both."

Two developments spurred the recent sales, analysts say. First, Moscow's hard-currency crunch is exacerbated by urgently needed consumer imports and pressing repayment demands from Western suppliers. Second, Iraq's invasion into Kuwait spiked gold prices to well over $400 an ounce, signaling a profitable time for Moscow to sell on the international market.

A financial adviser with the Comptroller of the Currency here says that reports of Soviet gold sales—as much as $1 billion over the course of several days, compared with the $2 billion to $3 billion average sale during a single year—are "no surprise." Soviets are "looking to put their payments back on track" and good credit is essential to "their efforts toward convertibility of the ruble," he says.

According to US Central Intelligence Agency estimates, Moscow holds $25 billion to $32 billion in gold reserves. But Roger Robinson, a private consultant who was senior director of international affairs at the National Security Council during the Reagan administration and a former Chase Manhattan banker with Soviet and East European portfolios, puts the range at $15 billion to $22 billion. Since 1986, he says, when Soviet oil revenues plummeted due to lower world oil prices, the Soviets have sold $10 billion of strategic reserves, in addition to selling annual gold production. "They continue to dip into dangerously low reserves to pay for imports," he says.

Before 1986, "the Soviets never sold as much as they mined, which was 200 tons annually," says Judy Shelton, author of "The Coming Soviet Crash." She says Moscow's "credit rating has slipped dramatically" since its payments crisis last fall when Soviet leader Mikhail Gorbachev ordered an emergency $16 billion consumer goods purchase to quell labor unrest.

During 1990, she says, "the Soviets have probably been working the market, selling production and reserves for some quick cash and pledging additional gold as collateral to creditors and suppliers. I know they have been moving a lot of it—Aeroflot flights have landed in London loaded with gold to be used as collateral for new credits with commercial and central banks."

Robinson says the current Soviet objective is to "keep the price of gold reasonably high and stable. They don't want to dump too much on the market, or they'll look desperate and drive the market price lower." He predicts Moscow won't resume gold sales until the precious metal reaches $500 an ounce. "Within two to three weeks after a shooting war in the Persian Gulf, when the Soviet Union isn't there to stabilize the market with sales, gold prices will shoot up. It's classic; they'll watch the demand curve go up while they, the suppliers, hold off."

By Moscow's own accounts, the economy is in a desperate state. The title of the semi-annual report issued earlier this month by the USSR State Committee for Statistics Reports is revealing: "No Economic Improvement as Yet; Crisis Phenomena in Economic Development Intensify." In July, Soviet Prime Minister Nikolai Ryzhkov stated that the Kremlin will not break its current total hard currency foreign debt ceiling of $56.6 billion; but Western estimates put the debt as high as $64 billion. Its trade deficit with the West reached a record $6 billion during the first half of this year. Moscow is now six months in arrears to Western suppliers, owing a debt between $2 billion and $5 billion.

Moscow may partially bridge that gap by reaping gold, oil, and gas windfall profits from the Gulf crisis. Eighty percent of Moscow's foreign exchange earnings are from four principal exports—gold, oil, gas, and arms. Robinson says that Soviet earnings from the Gulf crisis—revenues from oil, gas, and gold—could amount to $7.5 billion over one year.

"With every dollar increase in the world oil price per barrel, Soviet energy export earnings increase by $850 million," says Jan Vanous, director of PlanEcon Inc., a Washington-based firm specializing in East European and Soviet economies. He discounts reports that the Soviets are drawing down heavily on gold reserves, although Soviet gold production for the international market remains steady, he says.

Higher oil prices—if sustained at $25-$30 a barrel—would help reduce Soviet debt, says Mr. Vanous. If Moscow carries out its Jan. 1, 1991, plan to cancel costly preferred trading agreements with Eastern Europe and satellites such as Cuba, Soviet exports from energy to machinery will transform from subsidies to generators of foreign exchange.

At least one Soviet economist questions whether the Soviet Union can actually rely on mineral and energy exports sales. The independence-bound Russian Federation, one of 15 Soviet republics, is rich with raw materials that it now seeks to protect from Soviet exploitation, says Igor Birman, a consultant to the Pentagon's Office of Net Assessment. "In no more than a couple of years, the world will be dealing directly with the republics for such resources, and not the Soviet Union."

Summertime in Soviet Baku, And the Living Is Uneasy

Linda Feldmann

8/28/90

A brisk wind howls across the massive square in front of Azerbaijan's main government building, the obligatory statue of Vladimir Lenin gesturing triumphantly to the empty expanse before him. A mother cat and her five kittens lay about near Lenin's feet as an old man sweeps.

A mile away, the street teems with life at the bazaar, where mountains of onions, tomatoes, and melons—part of this year's plentiful harvest—go for a fraction of the prices at Moscow's farmers' markets. One man hawks produce out of the back of his car. The trunk lid, he explains, keeps the pounding sun off his merchandise.

It's summer in Baku, steamy but windy—the word Baku literally means "city of strong winds"—and the pace is relaxed. Not, certainly, the image of a city in the midst of a state of emergency.

But technically the "emergency" remains, months after January's events: the massacre of Baku Armenians, the perceived threat of an overthrow of Azerbaijan's government, the bloody invasion of Soviet troops into Baku that took scores of innocent lives, the million-strong funeral gathering.

On closer inspection, the normality of Baku life is tinged with reminders that not all is, in fact, normal.

Lenin Square is quiet because it is roped off, with two policemen allowing access as they see fit. Last winter, before the crackdown, the scene here was beginning to resemble Beijing's Tiananmen Square before its own massacre, local residents say. Antigovernment protesters camped out. They built small fires to cook and keep warm. They lacked sanitary facilities.

Now, under the state of emergency, people are not allowed to gather in groups on the street without permission. A nighttime curfew remains in effect, from 1 a.m. to 5 a.m., cut back from the original midnight to 6 a.m. Soviet Army soldiers monitor traffic on the road from the airport to the city, checking passes.

The lack of street activity seems particularly odd in light of next month's elections to the Azerbaijani parliament, the first multi-candidate elections to that body. Campaign posters are nowhere to be seen.

Nor are there any of the free-wheeling street-corner discussion clubs that have sprung up spontaneously in other major Soviet cities. Publication of the Azerbaijani Popular Front newspaper was temporarily suspended by the city's military commandant for reporting that the republic's new parliament chairman had been illegally elected.

The lingering state of emergency has also meant few foreign visitors, depriving "Bakintsy" (as residents are called) of the opportunity to show off their legendary hospitality.

Foreign correspondents technically are not allowed to visit Baku, because of its continuing "closed" status after the January events. But it is possible to gain permission through a not-widely-advertised avenue: Contact the Azerbaijani Foreign Ministry press office and ask for an invitation, which Moscow will likely honor. The Azerbaijanis are happy to schedule one's every waking moment with interviews—an opportunity, as they see it, to counter the pro-Armenian bias they feel pervades the Western press.

On the streets of Baku, no special troop presence is visible. According to Col. Valery Buniyatov, the military commandant, there are now only 1,000 extra Interior Ministry troops in this city of 2 million people—down from more than 10,000 sent in January when the state of emergency was imposed. They back up the police and enforce the curfew, Colonel Buniyatov says.

"A big show of force is not needed now," says Aydin Mamedov, a local political commentator. "It's enough for people to know that the state of emergency still exists. They still have strong memories of what happened in January."

Some residents claim that there are military forces ready "behind the scenes" at all times in case trouble breaks out, a perception that must keep any potential troublemakers—if they are indeed still here—lying low.

Any discussion of the Baku state of emergency gives rise to inevitable, and unanswerable, questions: What would be happening here if the emergency had already been lifted? And what if it were lifted tomorrow?

The people of Baku are divided on the answers. Now that life is more or less back to normal, many Bakintsy are eager to see the remnants of "black January" completely removed. For some, Buniyatov's presence is tangible evidence of Moscow's continued meddling in local affairs. Furthermore, Buniyatov is himself part Azerbaijani (his father is a respected local scholar and World War II hero), but does not speak Azerbaijani, having been raised by his Russian mother. An Azerbaijani phrase book lies on his desk.

According to a family member, Buniyatov has received threats on his life.

Other residents say they feel safer with extra military protection, especially amid statements by officials like Buniyatov that Azerbaijan's hostile neighbor, Armenia, has massed a paramilitary force of 140,000 armed troops—a force that refused to comply with Soviet President Mikhail Gorbachev's July 25 order to disarm.

"Martial law has not been rescinded because there is still danger on the part of extremists. You've heard Gorbachev's order about disarmament . . . ," says Buniyatov, who became Baku's military chief on July 1. There are no illegal armed groups in Azerbaijan, he adds.

A bombing earlier this month on a bus in Azerbaijan, which killed at least 17 people, plays into the fears of extremism. It is not known who planted the bomb, but Azerbaijanis will likely suspect Armenians—especially since the bombing took place near Nagorno-Karabakh, the disputed territory in Azerbaijan that has been the focus of violence in recent years between the two republics.

"Now our main task is to provide security for the elections to the Azerbaijani Supreme Soviet," Buniyatov says. "You see, now we have multiple parties. In the republic we have about 50 different parties, societies, and organizations. Connected with that, there are a variety of opinions, with their own unique circumstances. And therefore, there are contradictions that could destabilize the situation both in the republic and in the city of Baku."

Buniyatov also implies that Baku's 70,000 "Yerazy"—Azerbaijani refugees from Armenia—could also pose a threat to peace. Many of those who rampaged against Baku Armenians last January were Yerazy, and the underlying factors that contributed to their rage are still present: lack of housing, unemployment, and poor overall social conditions.

Democrats Take Over in Lvov

Linda Feldmann

8/28/90

Five months after this region's revolution by ballot box, the winners are crying foul.

The Communists, whom the "Democratic Bloc" defeated soundly in last March's elections for the Lvov regional council, have not relinquished many of the reins of power and are actively sabotaging the new council's decisions, says Ivan Hel, the council's deputy chairman.

"It is a case of authority without authority," says Lubomyr Senyk, vice-chairman of the Lvov chapter of Rukh, the Ukrainian national movement.

Lvov, the capital of the fiercely independence-minded western Ukraine and of a region of 2.8 million people, is an important test case in the Soviet Union's continuing process of withering Communist authority.

Of all the opposition victories in last March's local elections (including Moscow and Leningrad), the Lvov region's was the most stunning: The Democratic Bloc took every seat representing Lvov region in the Ukrainian parliament. In the regional council, Democrats won 186 out of 200 seats. The city council is 85 percent Democratic. Many of the top political figures are former political prisoners, including Mr. Hel.

Speaking from his new office in a building that once housed only Communists, Hel recites a litany of examples to support his charge of insubordination:

The local KGB (secret police), Interior Ministry (which controls the militia), and television do not answer to the new local government, under a decree issued by the former government on the eve of its departure.

Directors of kolkhozy (collective farms) are not offering peasants land to lease, as instructed.

Russian Orthodox Churches are not handing over their property to Ukrainian Greek Catholic congregations, as they have been instructed to do in some villages.

In Lvov's Zolochev region, the old party apparatus "whipped up public sentiment" against the new regional government over use of a water pipeline, causing strikes and other disorders last month, Hel says.

Even the building in which he sits is a point of contention. The regional party committee, under a ruling by the official arbiter of Lvov region, is to turn over the third floor to the regional council. Instead, it has appealed to republican authorities and, for now, remains in place.

Zinon Kotyk, an economic planner on the new council's executive committee, takes issue with Hel's charges.

"In essence, the party doesn't rule here anymore," says Mr. Kotyk, who calls himself politically independent, having just quit the Communist Party but also steering clear of Rukh.

"We're [new] here, and we're still lacking in administrative experience. So the party no longer rules, and we don't completely rule either. That's the complication of the current moment."

Kotyk acknowledges the decree regarding the KGB and militia, but says that in practice most of the militia do carry out local orders. He also cites a "mass exit" from the party, in which thousands of employees of state-run enterprises are turning in their membership cards and dissolving party committees. The same process is happening in some villages, he adds.

But Hel still sees the long reach of the entrenched party structure at work in many of Lvov region's rural areas. As a longtime activist for the legalization of the Ukrainian Greek Catholic, or Uniate, Church—the main religion of the western Ukraine—he is particularly sensitive to the question of church property.

Since coming to power, the Lvov council has decreed the transfer of Russian Orthodox churches for the use of the Uniates in villages where they constitute a majority. But the decrees have not been followed and the militia are not enforcing them, he says.

"As a rule, the local village leadership—chairman of the village council, chairman of the kolkhoz, principal of the school—are all party members," says Hel. "This administrative pyramid from the top obligated them to be Communists—and to be Orthodox."

This was part, he says, of Moscow's Russification plan for the region, which Joseph Stalin took from Poland at the start of World War II. So naturally, the argument follows, these pro-Orthodox village leaders will not, without coercion, hand over property to a church that is technically still banned.

On the question of giving land to peasants, Hel says, kolkhoz chairmen have marched right into his office and demanded to know how they're supposed to fulfill their quotas if they offer lifelong rent of land to peasants, as was decreed by the Lvov regional council.

"We tell them we'll just make adjustments in the quotas," Hel says. "But what they're really afraid of is that the peasants will become independent and won't want to work on kolkhozy."

Hel also complains that, in general, the policies of Moscow are suffocating local efforts to rebuild the economy. Of every 100 rubles earned, only 12 or 13 stay in the local budget.

Earlier this month, the Ukrainian parliament backed up its sovereignty declaration with a law on financial autonomy, which aims to establish the republic's own national bank, budgetary regulation, and customs service.

In the end, Hel tries to show at least some consideration for the Communists of Lvov. Even several months after the people rejected Vladimir Lenin's legacy, a giant statue of him graces the modest lobby of the government-party building where Hel works.

"It will be removed," he says. "We're just trying to figure out how to get it out the door without having to break it into pieces."

Gorbachev and Yeltsin Face Off Over Economy, Role of Republics

Daniel Sneider

8/28/90

Boris Yeltsin has returned to Moscow from a grand tour of his domain, the Russian Republic. Awaiting him is Mikhail Gorbachev.

The two most powerful men in the Soviet Union will have to make decisions this week that will be crucial to the country's future.

Immediately on the agenda is the fate of yet another new plan to move the country to a market-based economy. But the economic program is only a part of the larger issue—the future shape of the nation itself.

Mr. Yeltsin, the Russian Republic's president, is now the acknowledged leader of the movement to devolve power from the center outward to the 15 republics that make up the Soviet Union and downward to the local governments. As the largest and most powerful republic, Russia's declaration of sovereignty has become the standard for all the other republics to follow.

The two men engaged in a public skirmish last week over where to draw the lines of power between republic and center. Mr. Gorbachev, the Soviet president, issued a decree voiding an Aug. 9 Russian resolution that claimed control over all Russian resources. That resolution annulled deals to sell diamonds, gold, and other resources to foreign companies without Russian approval.

"The president's decree does not concern the Russian Supreme Soviet [parliament] decision. He does not have such a right," Yeltsin told reporters while visiting Sakhalin Island in the Soviet Far East. "I would advise [Gorbachev] not to quarrel with Russia, where 150 million people live."

Yeltsin sounded one of his favorite populist themes: Russian resources are being wasted for projects such as foreign aid and defense. "We are helping others at the time when we are hungry ourselves," the Postfactum news agency reported him saying.

The two men have entered "preparation for the decisive battle," observes Andrei Fadin, political editor of the independent weekly Commersant. "Personal relations between them are now better than ever," he says, but a clash of interests puts them on opposite sides.

"If Yeltsin's program is realized, there is no room for Gorbachev's power in the country," Mr. Fadin comments. The other republics will follow Russia's path and "the union leadership will have nothing behind it, nothing to be based on," he says.

The Russian policy effectively deprives the central government of control over foreign trade, even over military aid, because it claims control of all the industries in Russia where the vast majority of defense plants are based.

The main battlefield is the shape of a new union treaty, a constitutional-type agreement that will redefine republic-center relations. Gorbachev offers a federal state, with Moscow still at the center but in looser relationship to its constituent parts. All summer long, the Kremlin has summoned representatives of the republics here to discuss its draft of this new union treaty.

But Yeltsin's insurgent government pronounces another vision—a confederation created amongst the republics themselves, granting to the center whatever powers they decide not to keep. Already Russia is negotiating bilateral treaties with the Baltic republics of Latvia and Estonia. Others are ready to follow.

"The new union treaty can and will arise only from treaties between individual republics," says Fyodor Shelov-Kovedyayev, head of the Russian parliament committee on inter-republican relations, in an interview in Moscow News weekly. If the Kremlin opposes Russia, he warns, the Soviet Union will end up consisting of only the Central Asian republics, Kazakhstan, and Azerbaijan.

In the next days, Yeltsin and Gorbachev will meet, alone and in a larger joint session of the Presidential Council and the Federal Council, the latter bringing together the heads of the republican legislatures. The main agenda item is to decide on a new economic reform plan.

Yeltsin and Gorbachev agreed earlier this month to form a joint group to draft a plan based on the more radical Russian 500-day program. This plan is to become the economic section of the new union treaty. At the same time, Gorbachev's own government, headed by Prime Minister Nikolai Ryzhkov, is drafting a revised version of its reform program.

In theory, the two groups are working together, but there is abundant evidence in the comments from both sides that the two efforts are opposed.

The deputy head of the central State Commission on Economic Reform sniped at the Russian plan for not being "a concrete program but only interesting sketches, concepts, variants of transition," in an interview Friday in the labor newspaper Trud. A. Orlov also accused its authors of seeking "shock therapy," the label for a Polish-style overnight shift to a free market, with free prices and no central planning.

Russia throws the charge back at the Kremlin. Its program pays more attention to protecting the people from the effects of moving to a market economy, Gennady Filshin, deputy chairman of the Russian Cabinet told Sovietskaya Kultura. A "sharp transition" to a market will bring "social catastrophe," he said, including large-scale unemployment.

Despite the harsh rhetoric, there are grounds for compromise. The Ryzhkov group has accepted the need to prepare for the market through more radical privatization of property. Even the use of the word "privatization" is new, replacing "de-statization," an awkward term to avoid that thorny issue.

Both sides also agree to put off free prices, and the inflation that is expected to follow, until safety nets are in place and measures taken to try to absorb the huge volume of rubles without any goods to chase.

Without some agreement, the prospect of chaos is lurking visibly around the corner. The alarm signals could be seen in the Siberian city of Chelyabinsk, where youths rioted for three days following demonstrations against shortages of alcohol and cigarettes. Less violent protests have taken place in many other cities.

And everywhere, nationalism is increasingly the vehicle of expression.

"Centrifugal forces have such speed that the situation is going out of control," Mr. Orlov said. "Just a little more and we'll see either an eruption or super-emergency measures will be taken."

Ukrainian Politics Go Nationalist

Daniel Sneider

8/31/90

A massive shining steel arch stands overlooking the Dnieper River, built more than a decade ago to symbolize the "reunification of the Ukrainian and Russian people."

The natives of this graceful city sneeringly call it the yarmo (yoke), for them only an ugly expression of Russian oppression.

Not far away, on Kreshchatik, the leafy main boulevard, a crowd roiling in constant debate gathers around the flagstaff in front of City Hall. The blue-and-yellow Ukrainian nationalist banner has flown there since mid-July, when it was carried by a massive crowd celebrating the Ukrainian parliament's declaration of sovereignty.

Wreathes of flowers and sheaves of wheat are piled at the base of the flag. A nationalist organizer hands out applications for citizenship in the independent "Republic of the Ukraine."

"The time has come to restore our own things, to build our own national state, to feel like a real people," Ivan Myendik, a young engineer from Lvov says after proudly filling out the form.

Until this spring, Ukrainian nationalism was a political force largely confined to the western part of the republic, the area formerly part of Poland. But here, as elsewhere in the Soviet Union, the demand for separation from the union has won broad support—enough to force the traditionally conservative, and powerful, Ukrainian Communist Party to back sovereignty, at least in name.

Sergei Pravdenko, a liberal Communist deputy in the parliament, comes from Dnepropetrovsk in the southeastern Ukraine. He returned recently to visit voters in a Cossack village in his district. When he was running last March, no one spoke to him about Ukrainian independence.

"On the contrary, it was I who spoke to them about these issues," he recalls. "Now they speak very resolutely about the independence of the Ukraine, without even any of my reservations. I was very surprised."

"Maybe Moscow has some illusions" that the eastern Ukraine will not break from it, he says, "but Moscow had illusions about Lithuania also."

The most visible expression of nationalist strength is the Rukh, the Ukrainian Peoples Movement for Perestroika, the broad front formed last year. Rukh captured 108 seats in the spring elections to the 450-member Supreme Soviet. Rukh organizers say they have since won over about 30 Communists. Mr. Pravdenko puts himself among about 70 Communists who vote "9 out of 10 times" with the Democratic Bloc, as the Rukh-led opposition is called. He puts hard-core party strength at 240 seats.

The Rukh "understands sovereignty as complete secession from the union," explains Communist Party Secretary Anatoly Savchenko. The party sees it as a purely economic issue, "as the more effective use of the resources and potential created in the republic." But, he hastens to add, "both groups criticize the dictatorship of the command economy, the dictatorship of Moscow, and believe that if we had not had these negative things, development would have been more efficient."

In the Rukh headquarters, Sergei Odarich, the 23-year-old former mathematics student who runs the movement's secretariat, speaks in calm, considered tones.

"We believe that without political independence we won't be able to attain economic independence," he says. "That is why we are against joining any unions or blocs until after the Ukraine is really an independent state . . . ."

By Rukh's account, the July 16 Communist vote for the declaration was the result of a combination of popular feeling, clever Rukh tactics, and miscalculation by the Communist leadership.

The shift in public opinion came only after the parliament was convened and people could see, in live TV broadcasts, that Rukh leaders were not the "cannibals the party press represented them as," Mr. Odarich says. "In only one day, the eastern Ukraine became our supporters."

When the parliament convened, then-party leader and parliament chairman Volodymyr Ivashko tried to force a quick discussion of sovereignty. Unlike Volodymyr (Vladimir) Shcherbitsky, his despised predecessor, Mr. Ivashko is a new-style party leader, known for his flexibility and praised by some in Rukh for his openness, although also criticized for his indecisiveness.

Rukh, which wanted to increase support for its more radical views, forced a delay. It controlled the drafting committee, forcing the Communists into the position of offering amendments. While about 60 Communist deputies, including Ivashko and all the leadership, were in Moscow in July for the Communist Party Congress, Rukh put it forward.

The declaration gained backing from the Communist Party's right wing, Odarich says, "which wants sovereignty so democratic ideas emanating from Moscow . . . do not cross the border." The Communists left behind in Kiev were people "used to obeying orders and were angry they were left alone."

Ivashko angered the Communists and Rukh alike when he refused a demand that he return for the debate and instead sent a piqued letter of resignation from both his party and parliamentary post, taking on instead the post of deputy leader of the Soviet party.

The parliament voted overwhelmingly for the declaration with only three amendments—a reference to both Ukrainian and union citizenship; allowing the government the right to issue currency; and declaring that Ukrainian soldiers in the Soviet Army should serve only in the republic, rather than forming a totally separate army.

Liberal Communist Pravdenko argues as well against "emotionalism" in favor of "economic calculation," but he doesn't trust Soviet leader Mikhail Gorbachev's offer of a new union treaty. He envisions the Soviet Union becoming like the European Community, while party leader Savchenko says he thinks it should be a federal system closer to that of the United States.

Since the July vote, the Communist Party has scrambled to redefine the declaration to mean economic self-management, from the enterprise to the republic. Andrei Pecherov, a Communist deputy who heads the parliamentary commission on planning, budget, finance, and prices, argues against the widespread belief that the Ukraine will be better off economically without ties to the union. It doesn't take into account the cost of defense, scientific research, and other indirect benefits, he says. And the artificial price system means the Ukraine's agricultural riches are underpriced, along with the oil it gets from Russia.

But the young Rukh activist handing out applications is confident the Communist Party is "moving much closer to our position." Eventually, "they will reach the idea of the indivisibility of political and economic sovereignty."

The Ukraine's Clash of Faiths

Linda Feldmann

9/5/90

The scene in front of St. George's Cathedral in Lvov couldn't have been more poignant: two clutches of elderly women, screaming at each other in full voice, arguing over whether the cathedral belongs to the Russian Orthodox Church or the Ukrainian Catholics.

"I don't know why they're even bothering," said a young Catholic woman, herself entering the fray with an occasional comment. "No one's going to convince anybody their side is right."

The high-pitched debate, it turns out, was only a taste of things to come.

Within a matter of days, the cathedral grounds became the setting for the latest episode of Ukrainian religious conflict. On Aug. 12, 30,000 Ukrainian Catholics converged to reclaim the church and the neighboring chancery from the Orthodox, who were using the compound as their church's seat in the Lvov region. St. George's had served as the Ukrainian Catholics' headquarters until 1946, when Joseph Stalin orchestrated the liquidation of their church (accusing them of collaborating with the Nazis) and gave its assets to the Russian Orthodox Church.

Armed with decrees issued April 6 by the Lvov city and regional governments granting them this historic hillside compound, the Catholics succeeded in forcing out the resident Orthodox clergy and are celebrating masses there for the first time in 44 years.

This is a "religious war" against the Orthodox, cried Lvov's Orthodox Bishop Andrei Horak at a recent Moscow press conference. He charged that the Catholics smashed windows at the cathedral and took the bishop hostage for four days. The Catholics firmly reject the accusations.

In an interview at St. George's before its takeover, another Orthodox bishop, Andrei Drogobichsky, rejected the "meddling" of Lvov's new non-Communist government. "The church leadership—Orthodox and Uniate—must handle this question," he said, using a term for the Ukrainian Catholics that they find derogatory.

Now, following the takeover, future dialogue between the Russian Orthodox Church and the Vatican has been thrown into doubt, says Metropolitan Juvenaly of Moscow.

For the Ukrainian Catholics, who combine allegiance to Rome with the Eastern Byzantine rite, reestablishing church headquarters at St. George's has been a symbolically important element in their struggle to reclaim confiscated property, including hundreds of churches all over the western Ukraine, and regain full state recognition. (Many Ukrainian Catholics believe that Metropolitan Andrei Shetytsky, considered the father of the contemporary Ukrainian Catholic Church, is buried in the crypt at St. George's.)

The retaking of the cathedral complex culminates a year of rising public activism by the Catholics—emboldened by the Gorbachev-inspired mood of openness, but also fueled by the growing frustration over the government's persistence in withholding formal legalization.

Riding anticommunist wave

In effect, the Ukrainian Greek-Catholics, as they are fully called, have "unbanned" themselves. Riding a wave of growing anticommunist feeling, particularly strong in those western parts of the Ukraine that were seized by Stalin at the start of World War II, the Catholics have regained control of some 400 churches and are now practicing openly without fear of legal persecution. The Ukrainian Catholics say they have 5 million believers, making them the dominant religious group of the western Ukraine.

"To this day," says Metropolitan Volodymyr Sterniuk, the top Ukrainian Catholic hierarch inside the Soviet Union, "our church is not legalized and not rehabilitated. So in fact, we don't have the right to what belongs to us. In reality we do, but from the legal standpoint, we don't. We don't exist at the height that we should."

Ivan Hel, a longtime Ukrainian Catholic lay activist and a top government official in the Lvov region, recalls how last year he was serving a 15-day prison term for organizing "unsanctioned rallies"—that is, mass Ukrainian Catholic Church services.

"Then, last September, there were manifestations in which more than 250,000 people took part," Mr. Hel says. "The authorities understood that the Ukrainian Greek-Catholic Church and the social movement were so strong that they needed to come to grips with it."

The Catholics' struggle took a fateful turn last October, when a priest at another Lvov parish—the Transfiguration Church—unexpectedly invoked the name of the Pope during a Russian Orthodox service, restoring the church's status as Ukrainian Catholic. Scores of other Ukrainian churches followed suit.

On Dec. 1, the state dropped the ban on the church by allowing Ukrainian Catholics to register their communities. But the announcement did not restore control of church property and did not acknowledge the facts of history: that the 1946 gathering in Lvov of Ukrainian Catholic elders in which the church "dissolved itself" was organized by Stalin, as shown in documents revealed last September by the magazine Ogonyok.

Hel says that through March of this year there was an active process of Orthodox churches reverting to Catholic. But it slowed down, because "they," the Communists, started to brake it.

"For example," he says, "a village wants to transfer its church to Greek-Catholic, but the chairman of the village council won't register it. He says, 'There's no such church.'"

"The Russian Orthodox Church was always an instrument of Russification of our people," Hel says. (As of this year, the Russian Orthodox Church in the Ukraine is called the Ukrainian Orthodox Church, though it remains separate from the independent Ukrainian Autocephalous Orthodox Church.)

About 1,500 churches are at stake in the Lvov region. Four hundred are now Ukrainian Catholic; the rest are Orthodox. That means the Ukrainian Catholics, who Hel says account for two-thirds of the population, control only 35 percent of the churches.

In terms of property and revenues, the Russian Orthodox Church stands to lose big if and when the Ukrainian Catholics get back everything they say belongs to them. Of the 10,000 Russian Orthodox parishes registered in the Soviet Union, some 60 percent are located in the Ukraine, according to Radio Liberty research.

In addition, a good portion of Russian Orthodox Churches that are being reopened are in the western Ukraine, raising questions about their actual origins. Further, as many as half of the Ukraine's Russian Orthodox churches are in the western Ukraine, so the Russian Orthodox Church could lose one-third of its churches in the USSR.

Soviet President Mikhail Gorbachev has tried to get around rehabilitating the church by saying that a planned law on freedom of conscience will, in effect, restore the church's status. But the Catholics say that law will not be enough—because it won't return the property.

"It will be a step forward," Hel says. "But how can you call it a law on freedom of conscience when it doesn't give any church—even the Russian Orthodox—the status of a juridical entity . . . . So even with this new law, they [the churches] won't be returned to the Greek-Catholics. They will be called the property of the state which a congregation can only rent."

The dispute has caught Mr. Gorbachev in a tough spot. On the one hand, he wants full diplomatic relations with the Vatican. But he won't get this until he recognizes the Ukrainian Catholics, a point Pope John Paul II made clear in their unprecedented meeting at the Vatican last December. In the eyes of the world, the continued ban of the Catholics stands out as an exception to the Soviet leader's efforts to undo and atone for Stalin's excesses.

On the other hand, Gorbachev wants to maintain the support of the Russian Orthodox Church, which he has found useful in carrying out his policies. The full sanctioning of the western Ukraine's religious identity also raises the specter of even greater nationalist feeling in the Soviet Union's second-largest republic.

Metropolitan Sterniuk explains the continued ban this way: "The authorities fear that free thought will destroy the Soviet system."

Apartment command post

Inside the cramped quarters of Sterniuk's apartment, nestled on a quiet side street in Lvov, nuns and priests shuffle about in hushed tones as they carry out the business of the aging priest and their church.

The feeling is almost that of a deposed regime in exile, poised to reclaim its rightful position. In fact, with the retaking of St. George's, Sterniuk is preparing to live in the cathedral compound.

At age 83, the Metropolitan has seen his church come nearly full circle, from its death in 1946, to its decades of underground activity, to its near rebirth over the past year. In 1947, Sterniuk was sent to prison for five years.

Now, the Metropolitan is taking part in efforts to restore his church's formal status. Last March, Sterniuk signed an agreement with the Orthodox on the status of church property in five Ukrainian towns, but later annulled it. "I did sign a document," he said in an interview, "but when I saw that we were only dealing with the division of churches—and not the return of churches they took in 1946—I broke off the discussions and destroyed what was signed . . . . The Russian Orthodox bishopric didn't want to talk about legalizing our church."

For now, prospects for a settlement of the Ukraine's conflict between Catholics and Orthodox looks dim. But in separate discussions with representatives of both confessions, one theme becomes clear: Nobody wants violence. Both sides have suffered enough in 73 years of officially atheist Soviet Communist rule.

Along Soviet Georgia's Boulevard of Protest

Linda Feldmann

9/6/90

Down with the Communists! Give Georgia back to the Georgians!" a young man declares through a megaphone from the second-floor balcony overlooking the now-Leninless Lenin Square at Tbilisi's Institute for the Study of the Friendship of Peoples.

Two other young men lean over the balcony, shouting through cupped hands at the small crowd below. Periodically, first one, then the other darts back inside the building, evidently for behind-the-scenes consultations.

The onlookers, meanwhile, seem only mildly interested. "Who are these guys? What do they want?" several are asked. All say they don't know, shrugging nonchalantly. Some who had stopped for just a few moments to check out the commotion head on their way.

"It's just another group occupying a building," one bystander finally explains. "Nothing new."

A block down the street, a much larger crowd of several hundred people is milling around in front of the Georgian Republic's government building. Clusters of people argue animatedly. Off to one side, a large olive green tent has been erected to house protesters who plan on spending the night.

Several explanations are offered for what the demonstration is about. One person says it is to protest nasty things written in the official Georgian press about Zviad Gamsakhurdia, Georgia's most popular nationalist. Another says they're there to agitate for an acceptable election law, which would limit the number of participating parties and groups to only the dozen or so largest. Still further down the street, older women dressed all in black sit on benches in the entrance of an art gallery. They are surrounded by large photographs of young adults, their children, who died in circumstances the mothers feel are questionable. The women are demanding that the closed investigations into the deaths be reopened, and they have been occupying the gallery since winter to press their cause.

"We are asking for the help. We are asking for the true [sic]," pleads a banner in English, stretched across one side of the gallery's entrance. A steady flow of passersby stops briefly to talk to the women or just read their placards.

At the end of the street, near Rustaveli Square, the political activism isn't happening in broad daylight. But it's there, at the headquarters of the Georgian Popular Front inside the House of Cinematographers, where men are huddled in a smoke-filled room, chewing over election strategy and the day's gossip.

In the summer of 1990, it's a typical day in the life of Rustaveli Avenue, the grand sycamore-lined thoroughfare of the Georgian capital and the main artery of the republic's lively grass-roots activism.

The scenes of Rustaveli Avenue, named for the revered 12th-century Georgian poet, also present the variety of the activism that has become commonplace—from illegal building occupations to behind-the-scenes political maneuvering.

It's a real-life theater in the round—and sometimes theater of the absurd, where pure emotion, fierce loyalty to clan and family, and penchant for conspiracy-theorizing suggest comparisons to Sicily. It is also, one senses, just the summer warm-up for what promises to be a boisterous campaign for the Supreme Soviet elections on Oct. 28.

There are so many dozens of anti-Communist opposition groups pitted against one another—leaders regularly accuse one another of being KGB (secret police) agents and dupes for the ruling Communists—that they are unwittingly aiding the Communists' election cause, says a local independent journalist.

Furthermore, Givi Gumbaridze, the Communists' new party chief, has adapted his politics just enough toward the pro-independence line that he has been picking up popular support, says the journalist.

Nodar Nathadze, chairman of the Popular Front and a member of the Supreme Soviet, shrugs off concerns about opposition disunity.

"We'll all be together at the critical moment," says Mr. Nathadze, speaking in one of the Popular Front "foxholes," as he calls it, near Rustaveli Avenue.

"One can say that the Communist Party and the government are on a counterattack against the national movement," he adds. "They are working very actively within the movement, sowing conflicts, whipping up feelings in the [30 percent] non-Georgian part of the population."

The Popular Front's strategy for achieving Georgian independence is to work both from within the existing Soviet power structures and outside them, Nathadze says. The Front will contest the Oct. 28 elections, which he says will produce a new parliament that is willing to push harder for "true independence."

But he implies that Georgians will also have to be prepared to fight, literally, for their independence.

"For us to use the parliamentary path is not enough, because we're not like the Balts," Nathadze says. "Russia can strangle us, and no one in the West will listen."

At the other end of Rustaveli Avenue, Mamuka Gorbenadze and his cohorts occupying the institute allow an American reporter into the building for an interview—and are quick to castigate the Popular Front as "very loyal to the existing regime."

Mr. Gorbenadze, deputy chairman of the League of Georgian Citizens, says his group will boycott the elections, because the Supreme Soviet is illegitimate.

The League of Georgian Citizens is patterned after similar groups in the Baltic republics which aim to restrict citizenship to those born in the republic before Soviet incorporation—in Georgia's case, in 1921—and their descendants. But in Georgian fashion, the citizens' league has taken over a building "because we needed a place to work from," says Gorbenadze. (This is the third they've occupied.)

The Georgian league plans to hold elections for a "national congress," a type of shadow parliament, on Sept. 30. Before then, the group hopes to register as many Georgian citizens as possible, collect their Soviet passports for safekeeping, and provide them with Georgian identification cards.

The league has also been mentioned in Soviet news accounts of last week's middle-of-the-night dismantling of the Lenin statue in Lenin Square. One broadcast said league members participated in the action, which took place while police watched.

At No. 11 Rustaveli, the takeover of the art gallery is seen more as a tolerable act of civil disobedience than a criminal deed. It is also a sign of the times when even a group of 45 older women, mostly peasants, can feel enough political empowerment to be willing to camp out in an art gallery for months on end to press their cause. A commission in parliament, headed by the Popular Front's Nodar Nathadze, has taken on the mothers' case.

"Maybe the government will pay attention," says Tamara Mamulashvili, whose 22-year-old son Tamazi died five years ago.

The procurator's office said his shooting was accidental, but Mrs. Mamulashvili did her own investigation and pieced together another version of events: Someone asked Tamazi for his car, he wouldn't relinquish it, and so he was shot. It was the Georgian mafia that wanted his car, and the Georgian mafia that paid off the procurator to declare the death an accident, Mamulashvili says with certainty.

At the procuracy (the attorney general's office), spokesman Aleksei Bochoreshvili can barely tolerate the presence of an American reporter asking about these mothers, and offers no constructive comment. But in an informal chat, another procuracy official sighs at the mention of these cases and says, "No mother is going to be satisfied if someone isn't punished with death for the death of their son or daughter. It's the Georgian moral code."

Soviet Reforms at the Crossroads

Daniel Sneider

9/19/90

Economic plans are nothing new for the Soviet Union. But the two programs put before the Soviet people this past week mark a historic departure.

For the first time, the Soviet Union must choose, not only between plans but between systems.

The choice is at once ideological, economic, and political. The decision could determine the fate of not only the prime minister but the very existence of his ministries.

The debate is propelled by an atmosphere of crisis and systemic breakdown.

"The economic situation in the country is catastrophic," economist Abel Aganbegyan told the Soviet parliament. "And it is much worse than it appears on the surface."

Two different visions of the Soviet Union emerge from the documents and public debate now under way. The government's more moderate plan seeks to modify the state-run socialist economy with the efficiency and bounty of the market. The Soviet Union remains a centralized nation, though distributing greater power and autonomy to the 15 republics.

The radical plan from the Russian Republic is a pragmatic march to capitalism, resembling in concept the United States more than it does even Sweden. The country would become a voluntary union of sovereign republics, somewhat like the 1777 Articles of Confederation, the American states' first attempt at unity.

The radical plan, drawn up by a group of economists organized by Soviet President Mikhail Gorbachev and Russian President Boris Yeltsin, is a document remarkably free of the ideological cant usually found here. In clear, detailed terms, it describes the decades-long process of economic collapse in the Soviet Union and offers a step-by-step, 500-day dismantling of all the basic institutions and their replacement by a relatively unfettered market economy.

There are only three options in this crisis, according to the 500-day program—gradual reform, roll-back, or radical reform. The first option, the government's course, has already been "exhausted," they argue.

A return to a command economy, they say, "is realistic, since it has quite a few supporters both in the power structures and among certain groups of the population, weary of instability in everyday life." But it "cannot be done without mass political repression" and will not solve any economic problems.

The word "socialism" never appears in this document. Such ideological distinctions are meaningless, economist Stanislav Shatalin, the group's leader, told parliament on Monday.

"We choose not between London and Paris but between life and death," he said.

Deputy Prime Minister Leonid Abalkin argued in parliament that the radical 500-day plan is "shock therapy" that the economy and the population are unprepared for. It is unrealistic in its projections of the inflation and unemployment that will be caused during the transition period, he said.

But "one will understand nothing in the current economic dispute if he forgets that a great political game is going on," Mr. Abalkin admitted in an earlier interview with the weekly Economics and Life.

The formal debate in the Soviet parliament is scheduled to end with a vote on Friday. The parliaments of the republics are going through the same process, though the Russian parliament has already moved swiftly to back the radical scheme. The 500-day plan sets Oct. 1 as its starting date and Russian Prime Minister Ivan Silayev told reporters that Russia will go ahead on its own, if necessary, though that path would be more difficult.

Mr. Gorbachev has backed the radical plan, with some evident reluctance. He has lost confidence in his own government's ability to resolve the deepening crisis and appears convinced by its detailed nature of the plan's practicability.

Gorbachev is also bowing to the political logic of the shift of power away from Moscow to the republics.

The key fact, as he has noted in public statements, is that the plan has the backing not only of Russia, the largest republic, but was also drawn up with the participation of all the republics except Estonia.

Gorbachev is clearly discomfited, however, by the ideological and political implications of his decision.

He told the Supreme Soviet on Monday that calls for the resignation of Prime Minister Nikolai Ryzhkov and his Cabinet are "completely unacceptable."

More revealingly, the Soviet leader devoted the bulk of his half-hour speech to refuting the idea that the radical plan "leads to capitalism." By offering multiple forms of property, he argued, they will end "alienation from means of production and property," thereby finding "the solution of the socialist revolution's fundamental concern." He seeks to avoid the charge of betrayal, in part by offering the surprise idea of a referendum solely on the issue of private ownership of land, long defined by Soviet Communists as the key dividing line with capitalism.

Whatever the parliamentary decision, the final political battle over this historic choice has only begun.

Saaremaa

Linda Feldmann

9/21/90

It could be the ferry to Martha's Vineyard. Families relax on the deck, soaking in the end-of-summer sun that has finally emerged victorious over the week's drenching sea-coast rain. Blond children in hand-knit sweaters frolic with dogs. A snack bar dispenses soft drinks.

And aside from the fatigues-clad border guard who examines your passport and special island visa when you drive onshore at the end of the ride, the island looks about as communist as Martha's Vineyard, the popular resort island off the Massachusetts coast.

There isn't a Benetton's (yet) or any cute bed and breakfasts, but Saaremaa—the largest of Estonia's 1,500 islands—has "quaint summer getaway" written all over it. Fishing villages dot the coastline. The occasional windmill, once the island's symbol, punctuates the horizon. Tidy gardens brighten tidy cottages.

Saaremaa hasn't always been so quiet. Over the centuries, the 1,048 square miles of the island have seen a steady stream of foreign invaders and occupants. In the 13th century, it was the Danes and the Germans. In the mid-16th century, Denmark ruled alone. A century later, the Swedes took over. In the 18th century, it was the Russians' turn. During the two world wars, the Germans were here. Late in 1944, Saaremaa was the last bit of Estonia to be "liberated" by the Russians.

Now the people of Saaremaa are bracing for the next invasion: tourists.

Last year, following discussions between the Estonian government and Moscow, access to Saaremaa—a restricted border zone—was eased considerably. Foreigners may now visit the island, after gaining permission from the Estonian Ministry of the Interior. As before, mainland Estonians and other Soviet citizens also must get visas to visit, but they are issued more freely now.

But the most important event paving the way for greater tourism, and for a healthier island economy, came in April: Saaremaa dumped communism. The transfer of power from the party to the local councils has been going on gradually for the past four to six years, officials here say. But the decisive break took place after this spring's Estonian Communist Party congress, when all of the island's top officials quit the party.

"For a long time, the party hasn't played the main role," says Jaan Lember, deputy mayor of Kuressaare, the island's capital. "Now, I can say with finality, the Communist Party plays no role on this island."

The biggest question now regarding the party is what to do with its headquarters, whose ownership is under dispute. The most popular idea is to turn the building into a hotel.

Even for Estonia—the northernmost Baltic republic, which has itself signaled a clear course away from communism and Soviet rule—Saaremaa is radical. It is one of the few places in the republic to dismantle the Soviet structures of government and replace them with the old style of government councils and districts that existed during Estonia's pre-World War II independence. Delegations from Saaremaa have visited nearby Sweden for advice on tourism and how to set up local government.

Kuressaare is one of three towns in the republic to switch to a "self-sufficient" budget. Previously, local revenues went to the Estonian capital, then to Moscow, which would disburse the money as it saw fit. Now the money stays in the town, with only an agreed-upon percentage going to the regional and republic governments. Saaremaa can afford to be in the vanguard of Estonian reform. Ninety-four percent of the 40,000 people here are Estonian, so it has none of the ethnic problems that trouble many regions of mainland Estonia and complicate the republic's drive for independence. (Overall, Estonia is only 60 percent ethnic Estonian; most of the rest are Russian.)

This lack of tension has allowed islanders to do what comes naturally to them: They are starting their own businesses and making profits, a concept far less alien in the Baltics than in Russia. In the last year and a half, more than 200 new enterprises have started on the island, tripling the number of private businesses here. Most of them are small, involving five to 10 people.

"We have practically open business activity for all types of entrepreneurs," says Aivar Sorm, Saaremaa's top economic official. "People come here to start their activity, because there are no limits, in the bad sense, on their business. They do what is profitable."

Exodus of youth halted

For Jaan Lember, the deputy mayor and former head of a fishing collective, the economic changes have saved an important island tradition—and made dining here a more pleasant experience.

With few opportunities in this sleepy island outpost, youths were leaving, villages were emptying, and the fishing industry was dying. That process has now stopped, says Mr. Lember. Fishing cooperatives are forming, with the support of local government, which provides boats, nets, and other materials.

Under the old system, the more fish the fishermen caught, the more money the state would pay them—regardless of whether the catch could be sold or processed before it rotted.

"Now," says Lember, "the primary aim is to put fresh fish on islanders' tables." The amount of fish sold on the island has doubled, he reports. A new cooperative fish store is free to charge whatever the market will bear.

Saaremaa is developing other industries, such as dolomite quarrying (in a joint venture with Canadians), hosiery, and beer. But inevitably, any discussion of the island's economic future winds up with tourism. And the people here know they're sitting on a potential gold mine.

For example, just down the road from Kuressaare's 14th-century castle sits one of the island's few hotels, a brown clapboard house. With a little imagination—and some interior-decoration assistance from the Scandinavians—the place could be transformed into a tasteful country inn with rooms that could go for much more than the 21 rubles a night ($35) that foreign tourists currently pay.

But island leaders speak of tourism in measured tones.

"To get tourists to come here on vacation—not just for a day or two to visit 'exotica' but to spend time here—we'll need to do a lot of work, spend a lot of money, make a capital investment," says Mr. Sorm, the economist. "That could take five to 10 years. And by then, the tourism situation could change dramatically. We don't want tourism to be the main activity of the island. We don't want to depend on tourist income."

Beneath this concern lies a deeper one: a desire to protect the island's special qualities, such as the nature preserve rich in plant species, and the quiet, traditional way of life. The natives are proud of their distinct accent and the island's songs and dances. Sorm, a Saaremaa native, returned to the island two years ago after 12 years on the mainland because "there's no better place to raise kids."

Island children learn history

Only now are the island's children starting to learn the island's history, as Moscow-dictated lessons are dropped for locally designed programs.

"The teachers themselves are studying the materials," says deputy mayor Lember. "There are no printed texts yet, because of the problem with paper. So the teachers are preparing their own lessons and starting to teach."

Historian Olav Pesti recites centuries' worth of foreign occupation, feudal intrigue, and cultural achievement: "In the 13th century," begins the bespectacled Estonian, "Saaremaa was very separate and probably the most developed part of Estonia, because it had close ties with the Swedish islands and the Vikings."

During the Middle Ages, the island historian continues, Saaremaa was divided between two feudal states, though both sides were under the jurisdiction of the Pope. The island was also long an outpost for Estonian nobility.

The lesson ends with Saaremaa's role in World War II, highlighted by its strategic location in the Baltic Sea. In 1941, the Russians launched raids on Berlin from Saaremaa airfields. (The Soviet Union still maintains anti-air defenses on the island.) And in 1944, the last bit of Estonia the Germans were able to hang onto was Saaremaa's Sorve Peninsula—itself strategic because of its proximity to Latvia, only 40 kilometers away across the sea.

The excesses of Hitler and Stalin hit the island hard. Before World War II, Saaremaa's population peaked at 60,000 people. By the end of the 1940s, after mass escapes, the evacuation of the Sorve Peninsula, and deportations to Siberia, the population had shrunk to 33,000. Many Estonians living abroad nowadays are either from Saaremaa or descended from islanders—and some are beginning to trickle back for visits.

But not all visitors are welcome. In fact, it was the islanders themselves who insisted on keeping some restrictions on access to the island, to keep "just anybody" from coming here.

"Yes, they [the border guards] are a sign of Soviet power," says Lember. "But as long as this power does exist, let them stand there. They don't bother us, they're polite, they immediately understand where they've landed . . . . These fellows adopt our culture. They learn how to say 'hello' in Estonian, 'goodbye,' 'thank you.'

"There was a period when they took these guys away. Anyone could come here. Immediately, there was an increase in 'certain' elements here. It's a statistic."

So far, though, the encroachment of outsiders hasn't had much effect on Saaremaa, islanders say. Down at one of the boat yards outside Kuressaare, where black-white-and-blue Estonian flags have recently replaced the Soviet hammer-and-sickle banner, two young blond fishermen shrugged when asked about any changes.

Then one of them, Veljo Heinmets, thought some more.

"Well," he observed drolly, "now foreign correspondents can come and ask questions."

Soviets Swap Blame as Economy Stalls

Daniel Sneider

10/1/90

As the Russian winter approaches, store shelves are empty.

Only talk of catastrophe is in abundance.

Radicals and conservatives daily hurl charges at each other, laying blame for the economic crisis on their opponents and accusing them of plotting to use this time of troubles to launch a coup.

The always-confident Mikhail Gorbachev stands amid the storm, freshly armed with vast powers to legislate and decree changes granted to him last week by a confused and paralyzed parliament.

He used that authority last Thursday to try to will a collapsing economy back to stability, commanding all enterprises to fulfill state-directed contracts through 1991, with penalties on those that fail to do so.

"We must stop the decline," Prime Minister Nikolai Ryzhkov said in a televised address Saturday night. "It is impossible to live without discipline, order, and responsibility."

Radical democrats have responded with angry charges that Mr. Gorbachev is creating one-man rule, undermining democracy, and usurping the powers of the republican governments. In statements issued on Friday, the radical Interregional Group of Deputies, including leaders of the Moscow city government and the Russian government of populist Boris Yeltsin, attacked Gorbachev for retreating from his commitment to a market economy and reverting to command methods.

The group accused Gorbachev of "capitulation . . . before the conservative forces" by failing to make a clear choice between two opposing plans for transition to a market. Gorbachev instead insisted last week on a renewed effort to combine the cautious path proposed by Mr. Ryzhkov's government and the more-rapid shift backed by Mr. Yeltsin.

That decision, the radical statement said, would only lead to "more tensions between the center and the republics, especially Russia, and the breakup of a fledgling center-left coalition that promised a way out of the crisis."

The radicals repeated their demand that the Ryzhkov government resign and called for creation of a parallel parliament of deputies selected by the republican governments.

Yeltsin himself has been silent at this stage of the political battle. His quietude may be partly tactics, waiting to see what Gorbachev does when the new version of the economic plan is presented on Oct. 15. But it may simply be the product of illness—his aides revealed this weekend that Yeltsin was more seriously injured than previously stated in a car crash last week.

Liberal advisers and supporters of Gorbachev argue privately that the Soviet leader is simply maneuvering to avoid a confrontation with Ryzhkov and his backers in the military and the defense industry. In two weeks, they say, Gorbachev will back the radical 500-day economic plan, with a few minor concessions to the government for face-saving.

Stanislav Shatalin, the Gorbachev adviser and economist who headed the group that created the 500-day plan, went on television Saturday and publicly backed Gorbachev's new decree. It does not, he told an interviewer, contradict his program, which also calls for "tough" measures during an initial transition period.

Similar measures are in the 500-day plan, agrees Moscow Mayor Gavril Popov, but only through the first half of next year. By continuing them beyond that, he argued to reporters, the market will never get off the ground. The radicals say the new decree is actually in step with Ryzhkov's views.

Indeed, Ryzhkov has repeatedly argued that the collapse of the economy requires maintaining the control of the system of state-supplied production quotas and supplies through 1991.

"I am very bothered about 1991," he said in a television interview on Sept. 7. "In the thick of all these debates . . . we have totally forgotten that the winter lies ahead . . . . There have to be state orders which must be fulfilled firmly."

In an open letter to the Communist Party daily Pravda the day before, representatives of the defense industry complained that "plan regulation of the economy has been destroyed," endangering national security. They, too, demanded "preservation" of the command system through 1991.

The democratic left sees such statements as evidence of the power of the "military-industrial complex," a term that encompasses the axis of the military, the vast defense-related industry, and the centralized government ministries that run them. These forces, they believe, are the basis of resistance to a market-based economy.

Radical democrats rose in the parliament last week and detailed charges that the military was moving armed troops here in preparation for a coup. The conservative Communist establishment responded with an orchestrated wave of propaganda, quoting from a purported radical document plotting violent revolution.

"The rumors about a military coup are spread by those who themselves go against the people, who risk the people's destiny in order . . . to gain power and to overthrow the existing system," Defense Minister Dimitri Yazov told the conservative daily Sovietskaya Rossiya on Saturday.

A widely printed article from Tass news agency last week cited a "Program of Action—90" of the Russian Democratic Forum as evidence of a radical "countercoup." These charges are now repeated as fact, including by Marshal Yazov.

The party-controlled media are "whipping up rumors" with the aim of creating a "provocation which could be used as a pretext to introduce emergency rule in the country," Moscow Mayor Popov told reporters on Friday. The document and its authors are a fabrication reminiscent of the Stalinist era, added Mikhail Poltoranin, information minister for the Russian government. The Communists almost gleefully use the advent of radical-led governments in cities such as Moscow and Leningrad and the entire Russian Republic to point a finger of blame elsewhere for a change.

The radicals only want "to divert people's attention from bare shelves in vegetable shops or in order to shirk responsibility for ill-preparations for winter in future," Yazov said.

The democrats retort that the difficulties in their cities are being deliberately exacerbated by sabotage from the party apparatus.

"Our business today is to start implementing the 500-day program," Mr. Poltoranin said. "And the apparatus is trying to interfere with this."

Testing Gorbachev's Patience

Linda Feldmann

10/2/90

Leon Trotsky once said there could be no Russia without the Ukraine. Today, Alexander Solzhenitsyn is calling for creation of a Great Russian state made up of the three Soviet Slavic republics—Russia, Byelorussia, and the Ukraine.

Rubbish, says Mykhailo Horyn, who has been saying this his whole life to such suggestions.

The slight, bushy-haired Ukrainian's mission to establish an independent Ukraine has cost him a total of 12 years in prison camps. Most recently, that mission brought him to Washington for meetings at the White House, State Department, Treasury Department, AFL-CIO, and with constitutional lawyers.

Back home, as the Ukrainian movement for full independence gains support, Mr. Horyn's mission increasingly could mean Soviet President Mikhail Gorbachev's worst nationalist nightmare. The Ukraine is the second-largest Soviet republic, with 52 million people, and is crucial to the geographical and economic integrity of the Soviet Union.

In a sense, President Gorbachev brought this upon himself. In 1987, under his policy of liberalization, Horyn was released from prison. Now Horyn is nearing the top of the Ukraine's pro-independence popular movement, Rukh, which controls 147 of 450 seats in the Ukrainian parliament. Currently in charge of Rukh's day-to-day political direction, Horyn is expected to be elected chairman of the movement at its congress this month.

That would itself be a sign of the times. Rukh's current chairman, poet Ivan Drach, was until recently a member of the Communist Party—a point that helped make him an acceptable compromise choice for leader a year ago when Rukh was formed. But that fact "doesn't go down well now in this radicalizing situation," says Adrian Karatnycky, author of a forthcoming book on Soviet nationalities, "The Hidden Nations."

"In six months, Horyn will be forming a new government" in the Ukraine, Mr. Karatnycky predicts. Such statements invite the comparisons to Lech Walesa that have become increasingly common. On first impression, the soft-spoken Horyn doesn't seem like the larger-than-life Polish activist, but in a Monitor interview he displayed the kind of absolute conviction that has won him many supporters—even in the more Russified eastern Ukraine.

Majority favors secession

One of Rukh's biggest challenges is to unify a republic that is divided between the western region, where Ukrainian language and culture dominate, and the larger eastern area, where one hears much more Russian than Ukrainian, at least in the cities.

According to Horyn, of the Ukraine's 52 million people, 11 million are Russian and 5 1/2 million Russian-speaking. Other figures put the ethnic breakdown of the republic at closer to 40 percent non-Ukrainian. Regardless, Horyn dismisses the notion that Ukrainians who don't know their native language or traditions lack the intensity needed to fuel a drive for independence.

"We felt for a long time that national consciousness was dictated by language, but we have realized this is not so," says Horyn, who is from the western Ukrainian city of Lvov.

"I came across this phenomenon speaking in very large factories in Kiev. There I met with the view that we shouldn't rush with this process of 'Ukrainianization,' of bringing in the Ukrainian language. This was already attempted in our history, with Russification. The workers said, 'Let's not repeat the same experience with Ukrainianization.'

"But on the question of creating a national state," Horyn continues, "the workers said, 'We all support you on this.'"

Horyn also cites a July opinion poll of Kiev residents, conducted by the research arm of Lvov's Rukh-controlled government, that shows 57 percent support Ukrainian secession. But, say some Ukrainian-American activists, it is likely that many of these people favor secession largely because they want to escape the collapsing Soviet economy.

Rukh has staged several events this year designed to heighten Ukrainian national awareness and unity. In January, it organized a "human chain" of up to 500,000 people stretching from Lvov and Ivano-Frankovsk to Kiev. This summer Ukrainian youths participated in a month-long "culturological walk" to villages in eastern Ukraine to hold meetings, bonfires, and rallies designed to inform people about Rukh and Ukrainian history and traditions.

In early August, a half million people (half from western Ukraine) gathered in Zaporozhye to celebrate the 500th anniversary of the Ukrainian-Cossack state—a kind of "Ukrainian Woodstock," one observer called it. Horyn calls it "a revelation." [A one-day general strike, centered in Kiev, was scheduled to take place Oct. 1 to protest a new, Gorbachev-proposed union treaty for all the Soviet states.]

"I had thought that national revival would take 10 to 15 years," he says. "Apparently, it will take only 10 months."

Overall, Rukh's priority is the economy. Regardless of the republican parliament's recent declaration of Ukrainian sovereignty and adoption of a law on economic independence, the Ukrainian economy remains tightly woven into the Soviet economy.

At this point, the main aim is to preserve the Ukraine's existing economic connections with the other republics of the Soviet Union, while bypassing the central control mechanisms, says Horyn. The Ukraine has sent delegations to the republics to work out bilateral agreements on economic cooperation.

"For now, our economy will be oriented eastward; but we will eventually reorient toward the West and try to enter the 'common European home,'" says Horyn, using one of Gorbachev's stock phrases.

Critics of Rukh worry that the movement, run by freed dissidents and intellectuals who by definition lack experience in governing, is almost dangerously naive in its hard push for complete independence.

In a meeting with Treasury officials here, Horyn says he encountered a preference there for maintaining the "unitary state" of the USSR to serve as a stabilizing factor in Europe and the world. But at the White House, he says, "there was a certain understanding of what the Ukrainians want."

Case for independence

Horyn rejects the idea that, in the eyes of the US government, the Ukraine has a weaker legal case for independence than the Baltic republics, whose 1940 annexation was never recognized by the US. He argues that the Ukraine is actually in a stronger position than Lithuania, Estonia, and Latvia: Ukraine has its own seat in the United Nations and the Baltic states do not.

Never mind the fact that gaining separate seats in the UN for the Ukraine and Byelorussia was a maneuver by Stalin that had nothing to do with recognizing Ukrainian independence, Horyn says. The fact remains that the US, by going along with Stalin, recognized the Ukraine's separateness as a nation.

Rukh now hopes to make something out of that UN seat, a move that would challenge Gorbachev at his own game of boosting the UN's image and importance. Horyn says the Ukraine wants to replace the Moscow-appointed Ukrainian ambassador and send its own envoy—"someone who will represent the interests of the Ukraine and not those of the empire."

So far, that hasn't happened.

Soviets Gain Freedom of Religion

Daniel Sneider

10/2/90

The Soviet Union has closed the door on a long history of religious persecution by passing a bill that guarantees freedom of worship.

The legislation approved yesterday by the Supreme Soviet provides freedom for each individual to choose a religious belief and practice it openly. It establishes the equality of all religions and creeds under Soviet law and provides for the separation of church and state.

"This bill has been won by our people through much suffering," Mikhail Kulakov, chairman of the Seventh-day Adventist Church told the official news agency Tass. "It will end the persecution of people for their religious convictions."

The Soviet parliament has formalized what is already an accomplished fact—the widespread revival and spread of religious belief and organizations in the Soviet Union. Soviet citizens who once hid their beliefs now proudly wear crosses around their necks and bring their children to church for baptism.

Houses of worship that were closed, turned into "museums of atheism," or used as dusty storerooms are being restored. More than 4,000 buildings have been returned in the last two to three years alone, says the office of the Patriarch of the Russian Orthodox Church, the country's largest faith.

Since Mikhail Gorbachev came to power in 1985, the church has gained a new status in Soviet life. Religious leaders actively participate in both social and political affairs, including as members of parliament from the local level on up. Patriarch Alexsii II, the recently elected head of the Russian Orthodox Church, is himself a member of the Supreme Soviet.

Politicians, even orthodox Communists, feel compelled to seek audiences with church leaders and to speak respectfully of religious belief. Indeed, government officials are increasingly turning to religious groups for aid in resolving violent ethnic conflicts and social problems such as alcoholism and youth crime.

Representatives of all the major religions actively participated in drafting the legislation, including successfully pressing for changes in a first version offered earlier this year. The law ends criminal persecution of belief and bans the official promotion of atheism, long a foundation of the Communist state.

"We must admit the existence of religion and religious faith," Andrei Sebentsov, the parliamentarian who headed the drafting committee, said last week. "Religion was incompatible with barracks socialism," he said, referring to Stalinism, not to today's reformed "socialism."

"The law is important in order for us to live according to democratic principles," Adolf Shayevich, chief rabbi of the Moscow synagogue, told reporters.

The law abolishes the notorious State Committee on Religion, the organization widely viewed by church members as an instrument of KGB (secret police) control over church activities. According to Deputy Sebentsov, it will be replaced by an organization without any administrative authority for the purpose of coordination between the government and religious organizations.

The religious organizations were not entirely satisfied with the bill. One problem is taxation of donations of property and financial donations to religious organizations, which the churches would like to be free from tax.

The Russian Orthodox Church sought the right to teach religion in state schools, though outside the normal curriculum. If the church cannot offer religious instruction to children, Patriach Aleksii II said after his election last June, "they will be deprived of a whole spectrum of culture, without which it is impossible to be an educated man or woman."

Deputies opposed that provision on the grounds it would violate the separation of church and state. Muslim clerics also objected, because their practice allows teaching of religion only in the mosque. The issue will be settled by each republic. The law does legalize religious education, including the creation of church schools. Students at ecclesiastical schools will have the same status as other Soviet students.

The law only allows servicemen the right to engage in religious activity, but a more liberal version of the law passed by the parliament of the Russian Republic earlier this month grants rights to religious services and alternative service for those whose religious belief prohibits using arms.

Soviets Try More Gulf Diplomacy

Daniel Sneider

10/4/90

A top Soviet official and close aide to President Mikhail Gorbachev left Oct. 3 on a peace mission to Iraq.

Yevgeny Primakov, a member of the Presidential Council and an expert on the region, will also travel to Jordan, where he will meet King Hussein and Palestine Liberation Organization leader Yasser Arafat.

In recent days, Soviet officials have been sending out a calculated double message—that the Soviet Union still seeks a peaceful solution to the crisis, but that it is prepared to participate in military action against Iraq, as long as it is under a multinational and United Nations aegis.

The new diplomatic venture may be a last-ditch attempt to find a nonmilitary way out of the conflict. Soviet analysts here increasingly believe that a Gulf war is likely, if not inevitable.

Mr. Primakov's mission has special significance as the first direct effort by Mr. Gorbachev to try to mediate the conflict.

"President Gorbachev is following the crisis very closely and a very intensive exchange of messages is taking place," Soviet Foreign Minister Eduard Shevardnadze told Soviet reporters following his meeting with President Bush on Oct. 2 in New York.

Mr. Shevardnadze revealed that "a personal representative of the [Soviet] president recently visited Iraq," said a dispatch published Oct. 3 in the Communist Party daily Pravda. He did not provide further details.

Soviet officials have made clear that maintenance of a joint United States-Soviet position during the conflict has overriding importance, especially in light of broader arms control and economic links.

"However dangerous the Gulf crisis may be and however important it is to settle it, we should proceed from the fact that it offers a peculiar laboratory, testing our efforts to create a new world order after the end of the cold war," Primakov told the weekly Literaturnaya Gazeta in an interview before leaving.

Shevardnadze signaled the toughening of the Soviet stance toward Iraq during his own speech to the UN last week, when he warned Iraq that the UN was authorized to "suppress acts of aggression." He later told NBC television that Soviet support for UN actions could include "the involvement of Soviet troops under the flag, under the auspices of the United Nations."

The Soviet foreign minister had a different emphasis, however, when he was asked by Soviet newsmen whether Mr. Bush had discussed Soviet military participation in the Gulf.

"The president raised this question," he replied. "But he knows our position very well and is aware of all our approaches."

Shevardnadze praised Bush's speech at the UN for "opening a good perspective . . . of peaceful settlement of the conflict in the Persian Gulf region."

Despite this hopeful talk, Soviet analysts and Soviet press coverage have been taking on a more pessimistic tone. The chance of war in the Gulf is now "maybe 90 percent," says Nodari Simonia, a third-world specialist and deputy director of the influential Institute of World Economy and International Relations.

"Saddam Hussein is not showing any sign that he is even trying to find a way out," Mr. Simonia explains. "Either he is mad or he is not informed at all about what is going on, even inside his own country. If so, he is in no position to make a sensible judgment. And this brings us to the verge of war. The only question is when it starts."

Soviet reporters have begun to send dispatches from Saudi Arabia, including from the official news agency Tass and Soviet television. The Tass correspondent sent a long report on Oct. 1 on his visit to troops dug in along the northern Saudi border. The dispatch pointedly noted that "there are no US forces in the northern district," emphasizing the presence instead of Arab units, including Egyptian forces equipped with Soviet arms. The report ended by quoting a Saudi tank commander welcoming Soviet units to join them there.

At the same time, Soviet officials are privately unequivocal about where the Soviet Union will stand if war breaks out.

"We will support the military activities of the West and their Arab allies in this situation," says a well-informed senior official of the party's Central Committee.

But the official warned that the debate in the Soviet parliament could be difficult.

"Many deputies will vote against any Soviet military activity," he predicted, because of the bad experience of Afghanistan and the cost at a time of economic collapse. But given the unpopularity of Saddam's policies, he added, "I am sure the majority of deputies will support Soviet military action with the West."

The Soviet military will follow the will of Gorbachev and the parliament, the Central Committee official said.

Until now, the military has expressed opposition to such a course. "I am resolutely against using any military means, because war in the Middle East might be unpredictable," Col. Gen. Nikolai Chervov, a senior aide to Chief of General Staff Mikhail Moiseyev, told the Monitor recently. "It might involve millions of victims and will be a heavy blow to everyone, the US included."

The most difficult obstacle to Soviet action is the presence of more than 5,000 Soviets in Iraq, says Simonia. "Practically, they are hostages," the expert says.

The real condition of the Soviets in Iraq has only surfaced in recent days, indicating an effort to prepare Soviet public opinion for the need to "rescue" them. This past weekend, the weekly Argumenty and Fakty, the largest circulation publication in the country, published a letter from a group of 300 Soviet construction workers to the Russian Republic's parliament appealing for help in getting out of Iraq. According to the publication, the workers have almost run out of food and Iraqi stores refuse to sell them any.

The report also criticized the Soviet authorities for abandoning the workers, alleging that all the higher officials at the site including the Communist Party secretary, had already left. The report prompted an admission from the Soviet Foreign Ministry spokesman on Oct. 2 that the Iraqis are blocking the departure of 870 oilmen and 372 construction workers at a power plant.

Clearly on the defensive, the spokesman insisted the Soviet government is taking "energetic measures" to ensure the safety of its citizens and to speed up their "departure," without calling them "hostages."

Soviet Leader Governs by Decree

Daniel Sneider

10/9/90

Law and order. Discipline. Consolidation. Consensus.

These are the words most often found these days in the official Soviet news media. They reflect a growing weariness of chaos and the desire for a "strong hand" to restore stability.

Circles around President Mikhail Gorbachev argue in reasonable tones that an enlightened authoritarianism under Mr. Gorbachev is the only alternative to totalitarianism of the right or left.

"If you want to save your freedom, you must limit your freedom," says a well-placed official of the Communist Party Central Committee.

Some on the left see this as a mere cover for a retreat from democracy. But others, including many liberal intellectuals, endorse the view that democratic institutions are too weak to protect the process of reform at this moment. The combination of economic collapse and the splintering of political power, they say, could lead to disorder followed by a takeover inspired by the military or the KGB (secret police).

Liberal historian Nodari Simonia compares the Soviet Union to countries such as South Korea or Spain, which used strongman rule to modernize and gradually democratize. "In transitional periods, you need authoritarian regimes to carry out the process of democratization," he contends.

Vladimir Sokolov, writing in a recent issue of the liberal weekly Literaturnaya Gazeta, argues that a combination of military and presidential power are needed to put market reforms into effect. He compares this to the role of the United States military occupation of Japan and West Germany after World War II.

This reasoning is being used to justify the recent strengthening of presidential powers. Gorbachev has the authority, given with little dissent by the parliament, to legislate by decree in almost every area of life. Already he has issued two economic decrees. His aides promise many more to come.

"There are signs of the movement toward chaos, toward anarchy," Gorbachev told a recent meeting of intellectuals. He appealed for an end to political confrontation.

"Civic consensus is the alternative to confrontation, the extreme expression of which is civil war. It is also the alternative to a totalitarian barracks system," he said.

The period of change may demand taking "tough administrative measures," he said. "The power should be used but it should be used wisely and responsibly, preserving the main direction of perestroika [restructuring]."

Gorbachev's request for trust in his leadership will likely get support from the party, whose Central Committee began a plenary meeting yesterday to discuss a transition to a market economy. But other political forces see this appeal as nothing but a struggle for power.

Gorbachev is competing for power with Russian leader Boris Yeltsin, some analysts say, hoping to use his new rule by decree to dictate the policies of economic reform. By taking power into his own hands, he is shielding his own unpopular government of Prime Minister Nikolai Ryzhkov from demands that it step down.

The same arguments for an authoritarian path were made last fall, some radical democrats point out, leading to the creation of the presidency with strong powers. But Gorbachev's use of that position has been marked by inconsistency and indecision and his decrees have gone largely unheeded.

"We want to think that Gorbachev is always right and he understands everything," says Irina Bogomtseva, secretary of the Presidium of the radical-led Moscow city government. "But sometimes he makes mistakes, and very bad mistakes."

The suspicion of Gorbachev's motives were heightened when he backed away from full endorsement of a radical plan for economic reform worked out in cooperation with Mr. Yeltsin. A new compromise plan, encompassing elements of the more cautious program advocated by Ryzhkov's government, is to be unveiled on Oct. 15.

Gorbachev aides promise the new version will not deviate from the key aspects of the radical plan and that Gorbachev is already using his new powers to put it in effect. But liberals such as Ms. Bogomtseva say Gorbachev has betrayed his alliance with the left, which is based on sharing power among the central government, the republican governments, and the local authorities.

But even some democratic leftists criticize their own movement for failing to unify itself. Indeed, leaders such as Moscow Mayor Gavril Popov and Leningrad Mayor Anatoly Sobchak rail against the endless parliamentary debates that stymie their governments.

"We criticize Gorbachev for his wariness vis-à-vis the radical democratic wing of perestroika," commentator Len Karpinsky observed in the liberal weekly Moscow News. "But sometimes I can visualize the man taking stock of the democratic forces which he himself brought into being and which he can now rely on. And I don't think that there are many of them."

The Central Committee official compares the present period to the interval between the February and October revolutions of 1917. Ironically, he places Gorbachev in the role of Alexander Kerensky, the liberal socialist leader of the February revolution, and Gorbachev's enemies in the role of the Bolsheviks. Kerensky led a very democratic government, he says, but it was swamped by economic catastrophe, anarchy, and peasant and worker riots. As now, the intelligentsia was also deeply pessimistic after the February revolution, fearing the future.

The problem, then and now, is the weakness of democratic ideas.

"We haven't a democratic tradition in this country," the Communist official argues. "In all periods, Russia was a totalitarian country and had a totalitarian model of governing—and the national psychology is totalitarian too."

That psychology, the official says, limits the possibility of rapid reform. The majority of Soviet peasants do not want to take up private farming. Even before 1917, only 23 percent of land was privately held, he says, citing Kerensky's memoirs. "Collectivization was the reflection of the national psychology."

The party official charges the left with being the Bolsheviks, with wanting, for example, to force privitization of land. And an article by the editors of the party journal Dialog attacked the left for being "White Bolsheviks."

The official charges the opposition, particularly Yeltsin, with an unwillingness to be "tolerant" and to "look for compromise." The confrontation is leading to an uncontrolled situation. There are only three ways out, he says. One is a coup d'état, with a government such as that of President Augusto Pinochet Ugarte in Chile which uses dictatorship to enforce laissez-faire economics. Another is a return to the neo-Stalinist style of former Soviet leader Leonid Brezhnev, based on "nostalgia."

The preferred, and final, alternative is to "place power in the hands of the president." Gorbachev is "a democratic president," whose aversion to totalitarian methods is well tested. After an economic reform plan is finalized, "I hope Yeltsin and Gorbachev will find a new solution," he says.

Soviet Trial Bares Anti-Semitism

Daniel Sneider

10/16/90

By 9:00 a.m., a small crowd had already gathered on the third floor outside the door of the Moscow City courtroom. Young members of the Russian nationalist group Pamyat dressed in black greeted each other with comradely arm clasps.

In the corner, by the window, a retired Army colonel read an anti-Semitic tract in a rushed, wild voice to anyone who would listen.

Pamyat members surreptitiously slipped under their coats bouquets of flowers and rolled up banners passed out by their leaders. As the starting time for the court approached, the tension rose and the crowd pressed in on the door.

Two young men stood by the door, conversing casually.

"If a Jew attacks you, it doesn't make any difference if it is a man or a woman," the slight bearded one said to the nodded assent of his comrade. "It's just an animal and you should shoot it."

Since late July, the raw face of Russian fascism has been on public display in this bare courtroom, which is normally reserved for the transgressions of petty thieves and drunks. Konstantin Smirnov-Ostashvili has occupied the center of this small stage.

The Pamyat leader has gained the distinction of being the first person ever tried under Soviet law for the crime of inciting "inter-ethnic hatred and enmity."

On Friday, in a courtroom packed with raucous Pamyat supporters shouting slogans such as "Jews, Get Out of Here," a judge sentenced Mr. Smirnov-Ostashvili to two years of hard labor.

On Jan. 18, Smirnov-Ostashvili and his black-shirted followers invaded a meeting at the Central Writers' House in Moscow. With megaphone in hand, according to court testimony, he assailed the "Jews" and the "Freemasons." He commanded the "Jews" to go to a room where their names would be taken.

"Your power over us is over," he vowed, as his followers beat attendees.

The incident highlighted the growing public display of anti-Semitism in the Soviet Union, closely linked to the broader spread of Russian nationalism.

The Writers' House attack fueled widespread fears within the Soviet Jewish community of pogroms being readied by groups such as Pamyat. Such rumors, Jewish leaders say, have driven the massive wave of Jewish emigration from the Soviet Union.

PAMYAT is the most prominent extremist movement, itself divided into a number of factions. Several have united in the so-called Orthodox Movement of Russia, including the group headed by Smirnov-Ostashvili.

In an interview in August with Interfax news agency, Alexander Kulakov, head of the National Patriotic Front of Russia, one of the Pamyat groups, described its goal as the "revival of Russia's national identity."

"Russia has no friends," he told Interfax. "The world has already been subordinated by Jewish capital, the very same capital that funded the 1917 revolution and provoked and organized genocide against the Russian people. Internationalism and communism are philosophies of the Jews."

"It's not only anti-Semitism that is growing—its the growth of Russian fascism," says Olla Gerber, a writer and member of the liberal intellectual group April who was in the hall in January when Pamyat arrived. She is critical of Soviet President Mikhail Gorbachev for failing to take a more forthright stand against these forces.

Some liberals have criticized the trial for making a martyr out of what is a tiny group of extremists. In elections held last March, they point out, Pamyat and other Russian nationalist groups did very poorly.

Andrei Makarov, a liberal lawyer who acted as a spokesman for the public in the trial, argued in his closing remarks that although Smirnov-Ostashvili and his group are small, they "have influential sponsors." He pointed a finger at conservative forces in the Communist Party and within the police.

Indeed, Pamyat members, while expressing anticommunist ideas, openly identify with the neo-Stalinist outlook of the party conservatives. Mr. Kulakov supported the newly formed Communist Party of Russia and its head Ivan Polozkov, whom he described to Interfax as "the lesser of existing evils."

The trial, however, confined itself to the narrow facts of the January event, recited in low-key fashion by the judge on Friday morning in a courtroom lined with police and Spetsnaz special forces troops from the military.

The judge's speech was punctuated by Smirnov-Ostashvili's shouted interruptions.

"Why are there only Jews in the list of witnesses," he screamed, thrusting his clenched fist into the air. "They threw out all the Russian names." A bouquet of flowers flew from his admirers. "Long live Russia," he responded.

The judge finally ended his statement, pronouncing his sentence and rushing from the room.

"Court, you serve the laws of Zionism," an unfurled banner proclaimed as Pamyat members jeered.

Eli Livshits, a leader of Irgun Tsioni, a Soviet Zionist group, told the Soviet news agency Postfactum that the trial would not stop "the wave of anti-Semitism which seems to be ripening in the country." He accused the Soviet government of using the case as a superficial show of its opposition to anti-Semitism.

"I feel like I won," Ms. Gerber said in the hallway after the trial concluded. "Ninety percent of my friends who are writers and intellectuals did not believe there would be a trial. And they didn't believe he would be convicted."

Gorbachev Wins Nobel Peace Prize, As Economy Sputters

Daniel Sneider

10/16/90

Soviet President Mikhail Gorbachev's role as the catalyst for reform in Eastern Europe and for ending the cold war won him the Nobel Peace Prize yesterday.

"In the last few years, dramatic changes have taken place in the relationship between East and West," the Nobel committee said. "Confrontation has been replaced by negotiation."

But while Mr. Gorbachev takes his bows in Oslo, his triumphs abroad still provide little relief from his troubles at home. Here attention is focused on empty shelves and on Gorbachev's increasingly tortuous effort to try to cobble together a compromise plan for economic reform.

The president was scheduled to open the session of the Soviet parliament yesterday with a presentation of the new program. Instead, parliament chairman Anatoly Lukyanov announced that the document would be further discussed with parliamentary committees. A presentation will not be made until Thursday, and then by economist Abel Aganbegyan. Discussion in parliament is to continue until Saturday.

The delay followed a weekend of meetings, including a conference on Saturday between Gorbachev and representatives of 11 republics, along with leaders of the Moscow and Leningrad city governments and specialists. The participants were presented with a draft program, drawn up under Mr. Aganbegyan's supervision, which tries to combine two competing plans for transition to a market economy.

The official Tass news agency dispatch on the meeting blandly reported that the republican governments "supported, on the whole, the orientation of the program and made some observations and suggestions."

But a well-informed official of the Communist Party Central Committee suggests that the program ran into a serious attack. "It was not an easy discussion," he says. "It is very hard to combine all the different interests."

Since last month, the Soviet debate on economic reform has revolved around the two rival plans. A radical "500-day plan," based on a program drawn up by the Russian republican government, was produced by a team headed by economist Stanislav Shatalin and organized by Gorbachev and Russian leader Boris Yeltsin. Opposed to that is a program drawn up by Soviet Prime Minister Nikolai Ryzhkov and his deputy Leonid Abalkin, which offers a slower and more limited shift toward a market economy.

The battle is not only over economic policy but political power. The radical plan involves a significant shift of authority to the 15 republican governments which make up the Soviet Union, a cause championed by Mr. Yeltsin. Mr. Ryzhkov and his allies oppose such diminution of central administration. The Russian parliament attempted to pressure the discussion by immediately passing the radical program at the beginning of September and calling for the resignation of the Ryzhkov government.

Gorbachev first declared his preference for the radical plan. But he backed off earlier this month in favor of another try at combining the two programs.

Gorbachev had told the parliament that only political ambition stood in the way of finding a compromise, a view echoed by Communist Party officials and supporters of the government who accused Yeltsin of having only political objectives. But the Central Committee official now admits, the "job of finding a compromise between the two programs is extremely difficult."

"The problem is not only the personal and political ambitions of the authors, but with the plans themselves," the official explains. "The Shatalin plan is too radical, too dangerous to prevent social disorder, but the government's plan is to slow to resolve the social crisis and stop the decline in the economy . . . . Everybody is afraid to make a mistake, because it would be the last chance for the country."

The new version, according to reports, has sidestepped the practical obstacle of combining the two programs. Anatoly Saunin, deputy head of the parliament's planning and budget commission, told Moscow Radio yesterday that it is not a detailed blueprint nor does it set a firm schedule of events, as the 500-day plan does. It outlined the four-stage transfer to a market economy, he said.

After the "guidelines" are adopted, Tass said, the details "will be specified in the process of implementation" by the central government, republican governments, and local administrations.

"The republics should retain broad independence in choosing specific ways and forms of the implementation of the transition to an effective market-oriented economy," Tass said in its report on the Saturday meeting.

But others differ with this account of the new plan. Commersant, an independent weekly business paper, reports that the new outline will be "a repainted version of the government program."

That view was expressed as well by Russian Prime Minister Ivan Silayev in his report to the Russian parliament last week.

"A departure from the principle of radical reform is taking place, the rights of republics are being ignored, and the entire system of economic relations in the union for 1991 is being formed on the old administrative and unitary principles," he said.

He repeated his government's commitment to begin implementing the radical plan on Nov. 1.

Soviets Set to Post Record Harvest

Daniel Sneider

10/17/90

A visitor to one of the most important government economic think tanks found its director preoccupied with the potato harvest.

The director was worrying about where to store the spuds—not those of the nation, just the potatoes gathered by his staff in fields outside Moscow.

As winter approaches, the campaign to gather in the last loads of potatoes and cabbages has taken on a desperate character. In the elevators of the Moscow city government building and elsewhere in the city, officials wear muddy work boots and talk of plans to go dig potatoes.

The potato crisis is only the latest in a string of harvest mobilizations, starting with the grain harvest earlier in the summer. At each point, the Soviet government has issued dire warnings that a bounteous crop was rotting in the fields for lack of labor, fuel, trucks, and storage space. Prime Minister Nikolai Ryzhkov has gone on television to talk of harsh winters to come, even hints of hunger, if people do not add their hands to the cause.

But as the harvest season closes and the data are collated, it is now clear that, despite problems, the Soviet Union has reaped one of the better crops in its history.

The cereal crop is a record one, by some estimates: 240.6 million tons, compared with the 237 million tons of 1978. Western specialists predict Soviet grain imports will drop to 28 million to 30 million tons this year, down from about 40 million tons last year.

The sugar beet harvest is good, Western experts say, near the average of recent years at 83.8 million tons. Even prospects for the potato harvest, which has suffered from constant rains that muddied fields and made machinery unusable, have improved to 79 million tons with recent dry weather around Moscow, Leningrad, and in Byelorussia.

Western experts wonder why Soviet officials publicly predicted an even larger grain harvest in early July, when talk was of 300 million tons, or 260 million after losses from waste. In part, this may have been necessary to get the labor diversion from schools, factories, and the military, which occurred on a scale that "harks back to the mid-'60s and -'70s," notes a Western diplomat.

But as it turns out, weather may have been an equally fortuitous factor. Sunny skies have provided a long harvest period in Kazakhstan, for example, where the grain harvest has jumped from 23 million tons last year to more than 32 million this year.

Some critics accuse the government of deliberately trying to create an atmosphere of crisis to justify resorting to old administrative controls. Whatever the reason, the Ryzhkov government and the Soviet Communist Party have clearly changed their tune.

Deputy party chief Vladimir Ivashko, addressing last week's party Central Committee plenum, spoke about the panic buying and "chaos" among consumers, fed by "talk about an impending famine."

"Such talk is groundless," Mr. Ivashko said. "The harvest of basic crops is higher than in previous years."

Still, Western experts predict periodic shortages, particularly in major cities such as Moscow and Leningrad, where conditions have in some ways become worse than elsewhere in the country.

"It's mostly a distribution problem," says an agricultural specialist at a Western embassy here. The collapse of the centralized command structure particularly affects the large cities, he says, which used to be able to order goods brought in.

"You go outside of Moscow and the situation is better," the expert says. As one gets closer to the agricultural centers, the food situation dramatically improves, an observation borne out by a city-by-city comparison of food conditions recently published by the weekly Literaturnaya Gazeta.

In the Kazakh capital of Alma Ata, the Central Asian breadbasket, shoppers find plentiful and cheap supplies of everything from ducks and mutton to potatoes. The latter cost 30 kopeks a kilogram in state stores (five cents at the tourist exchange rate). In Moscow, only bread and dairy products are readily available at state stores; potatoes in the market cost one to three rubles a kilo.

One factor in the distribution problem is the refusal of collective farms, and sometimes local governments, to sell to the state. Fear of shortage encourages them to hold their grain, for example, as feed for their pigs and cows. Some farms also held back in hopes of higher prices next year.

The Soviet government has been forced to move up the date of new purchase prices and to offer goods for barter to farms. Government purchases of grain as of Sept. 24 were 55 million tons, 65 percent of total state orders, reports the independent Postfactum news agency. Western experts say this is ahead of the pace of purchases of last year, but Postfactum estimates that 75 million to 80 million tons of grain are being withheld.

The shortages are likely to hit hardest in the supply of meat and livestock feed. Imports usually make up the feed-stock shortfall and already contracts have been negotiated for soybean meal to feed chickens.

The key problem for importing food is the lack of cash. The Soviets reportedly are using their huge gold reserves to guarantee credit lines for food imports.

Soviets OK Economic Reform Plan

Daniel Sneider

10/22/90

The Soviet parliament has finally passed a program for taking the country to a market economy. And the politicians are already maneuvering to cast blame for the hard times that everyone agrees lie ahead.

At center stage, squared off against each other, are Soviet President Mikhail Gorbachev and Russian President Boris Yeltsin.

The on-again, off-again rivalry between the two men is definitely on. They had joined hands in August to draft a joint economic program, but Mr. Gorbachev backed off in favor of his own version, the one dutifully passed by an overwhelming vote of the Soviet parliament on Friday.

"Gorbachev and Yeltsin: the honeymoon ends in a divorce," the independently weekly Commersant declared in its front page story on the decision.

Mr. Yeltsin rose from his sick bed last week to fire the first shot, even before the parliament's vote. Gorbachev's plan would bring on "catastrophe," he predicted, with uncontrolled inflation and economic collapse as its first results. He accused the government of concealing a massive budget deficit of 300 billion rubles ($501 billion at the official exchange rate).

The Soviet leader concluded his hour-long address to the parliament on Friday with a return volley. Rather than joining hands to carry out the difficult task of economic reform, Yeltsin is playing "political games," engaging in "confrontation." He dismissed Yeltsin's call for formation of a coalition government, minus Soviet Prime Minister Nikolai Ryzhkov, as an insincere "ultimatum."

"One has the impression that the Russian leadership, to some extent, is afraid of difficulties," Gorbachev said, referring to inflation forecasts. "It wants to make central bodies of power fully responsible for possible negative consequences, which are inevitable during such a major turn, and reserve ways for its retreat."

Mr. Ryzhkov, who has again dodged the political fire aimed at causing his downfall, was even tougher.

"Those who today oppose social concord and who fan up passions are actually gambling with the fate of our people for the sake of their own personal ambitions," he said in his statement to parliament. If they create chaos, he warned, "violence becomes very possible."

Russian political leaders responded by accusing Gorbachev and his deputy of also playing politics, and of spurning offers for compromise and coalition. Gorbachev's remarks were "absolutely devoid of thought about the welfare of the 300 million people of the Soviet Union," Nikolai Travkin, leader of the opposition Democratic Party of Russia, told reporters after the speech. "He is just tugging at the rope, to see who is stronger."

The economic program envisions a period of "stabilization," a euphemism for a policy of severe austerity, including huge budget cuts, rises in prices of state-produced goods, higher interest rates, and cuts in the money supply. All sides agree that such a phase is necessary, but the Russian leaders, who back the more radical 500-day program, accuse the government of concealing the extent of the problem. Russian Deputy Premier Grigory Yavlinsky, the principal author of the radical program, resigned last week charging that deeper austerity was needed because of the central government's moves to raise prices and print money at a huge rate to cover the deficit.

Soviet Deputy Prime Minister Leonid Abalkin retorted with the claim that the budget deficit would be kept to the target of 60 billion rubles for 1990 and reduced by half next year. But most economists believe those estimates are highly understated.

The Soviet statistics committee released results Friday for the first nine months of this year showing a 70 percent growth in the money supply, rising inflation, lowering labor productivity, and a 1.5 percent drop in the gross national product.

"According to the Gorbachev program, the issuance [of money] will be stopped and that means some people will not get their salary," Vladimir Lukin, a leading Russian parliamentarian, predicted to the Monitor. "So they will go on strike. When they go on strike, Gorbachev would like to send them against the republics. We need a very responsible, respected coalition government which could withstand this problem, and of course the Ryzhkov government is incapable."

Indeed, recent poll results confirm that the Ryzhkov government and Gorbachev, are widely unpopular. When it comes to public trust, Yeltsin has a clear advantage.

Commersant cites results of a national poll conducted by prominent sociologist Tatyana Zaslavskaya showing Gorbachev's support dropping from 56 percent in May to 29 percent last month. Yeltsin, in contrast, rose from 29 percent to 58 percent backing during the same period.

That could mean that while the war of words is on now, another deal within the next few months is likely. Although he again rejected calls for Ryzhkov's ouster, Gorbachev opened the door to a coalition with the radicals.

Islam Revival Stirs in Azerbaijan

Linda Feldmann

10/30/90

The young man in the mirrored sunglasses and acid-washed jeans didn't hesitate when asked which candidate he would support in the coming parliamentary elections: "I'll vote for whomever the Sheikh says to."

Hardly the expected response from someone who looked more like a black marketeer than a Muslim believer.

The remark also fuels questions about the level of religious faith in Muslim Azerbaijan, where local leaders—both Communist and anti-Communist, religious and secular—maintain that Islamic fundamentalism is not on the rise. A response like that of the young man, a cab driver, is not typical, said several such leaders.

Still, local leaders affirm that Islam has experienced a renewal of interest here in recent years—much like the revival of the Orthodox Church in Russia and the Eastern-rite Catholic Church in the Ukraine. In the Gorbachev-era mood of openness, mosques are being reopened, the Koran is available, and children are receiving religious education openly. Such rights are now, in theory at least, enshrined in law. And like other ethnic groups around the Soviet Union, Azerbaijanis are turning to religion for solace in hard times and to gain a greater understanding of their ancient cultural heritage.

In an interview, Kazi Sabir Ben Hussein, the deputy chief sheikh of Baku, described how local communities are no longer waiting for permission from Moscow to reopen long-dormant mosques. "People gather at a mosque, take off the lock, and start to pray by themselves," says Sheikh Sabir. "This is perestroika from below."

But don't call it "fundamentalism." Leaders here know that use of the word itself, the same in Russian as in English, sets off alarm bells among the Russian-dominated leadership in Moscow as well as in the West—particularly since the majority of Azerbaijani Muslims practice Shiite Islam, which invites comparisons to Shiite Iran on Azerbaijan's southern border.

Azerbaijanis keenly feel that both Soviet and Western news coverage of the protracted dispute between them and neighboring Armenia already is biased in favor of the Christian Armenians, and the Azerbaijanis are eager not to heighten such feelings.

"Recently, a lot of people have been talking about fundamentalism, about the Islamic factor, and giving a certain nuance to the Islamic movement," says Sabir. "We can't call these people our friends. They are trying to pit other peoples and nations against Azerbaijan."

Nadzhaf Nadzhafov, a moderate political activist and former editor of the Azerbaijani Popular Front newspaper, argues that atheistic Soviet policies have so cut off Azerbaijanis from their Islamic roots that a surge of fundamentalism is simply not possible. Until recently, all but a handful of mosques have been closed. According to experts on Azerbaijan in the West, until a few years ago, the Azerbaijani clergy were so compromised by the Soviet secret police that believers feared attending the mosque lest they be reported.

The Azerbaijani intelligentsia, which does not tend to be religious, has long pushed for a secular society. Even in the late 19th century there was a strong modernist movement among the educated classes.

According to Prof. Tadeusz Swietochowski, a specialist on Azerbaijani history at Monmouth College in West Long Branch, N.J., Azerbaijani secularization emerged as a means of keeping Shiites and Sunnis from clashing. With two-thirds of the population Shiite and one-third Sunni, he says, "radical fundamentalism would equal the split of the nation."

To walk around modern-day Baku, the capital of Azerbaijan, is to experience a mix of cultures, from Azerbaijani and Turkish, which are essentially the same, to Slavic and Western. Despite the bloody strife of last January, Baku residents still point with pride to the ethnic mix of this city of 1.2 million people. Russians who fled have come back. There are even some Armenians still here.

Outwardly, there are no signs of Shiite fundamentalist tendencies. In three days, no women in veils were seen. Except inside the mosque, no one was seen kneeling in prayer toward Mecca. And at the city's main mosque, believers celebrated Ashura, a Muslim fast day, without ritual self-beatings with chains. But Professor Swietochowski cautions that, in fact, there are two nations in Azerbaijan, Baku and non-Baku. He visited rural Azerbaijan in June and saw a marked change from his last visit in 1986. He says he saw religious rituals, such as the killing of sheep. Religious brotherhoods had formed. Portraits of the late Iranian religious leader Ayatollah Khomeini hung in houses. People listened to northern Iran's Radio Tabriz, distinguishable by a special dialect of Azerbaijani, the language of northern Iran.

"In the countryside, people look to Iran and Shiism," Swietochowski says. "Some people talk of Iran as their own." Indeed, Iran's northernmost provinces were once part of the historic region of Azerbaijan, and some Soviet Azerbaijanis dream of reuniting their divided nation. Last New Year's Eve, Soviet Azerbaijanis in the poor region of Nakhichevan tore down border installations and crossed into Iran, some with hopes of finding relatives.

The incident sent chills through the Moscow leadership as it raised old fears of an uncontrollable and, to them, incomprehensible Muslim resurgence in far-flung corners of the country. For Western-oriented Baku intellectuals, the event contained clues that reunification with northern Iran—or "southern Azerbaijan," as some call it—may not be as desirable to some Azerbaijanis as they may have thought. Zardusht Alizade, a leading Azerbaijanis Social Democrat, says he heard reports of pro-fundamentalist Azerbaijanis who went into Iran prepared to embrace Khomeini-ism and came away firmly against it.

Much remains unexplained about the Nakhichevan incident just as, overall in the USSR, understanding of the country's Muslim peoples remains sparse. (In the Soviet Union, whose population is 18 percent Muslim—with a birth rate much higher than that of the Slavs—there is no institute dedicated to training specialists on Islamic affairs.)

IN Azerbaijan, the Sept. 30 elections for the republic's parliament could have provided insights into the role of Islam in local politics. According to David Nissman, a Washington-based Turkologist, there are two known Islamic parties in Azerbaijan. The first, a legal grouping formed in December called Tovbe, could be called "Muslim Social Democrats," Dr. Nissman says. Party leaders are moderate and reformist, and believe that Islam has stagnated.

The other Islamic party is an illegal Khomeini-ist formation that favors, among other things, veiling women. The group's leader, Muhammad Gatami, is an Iranian political refugee who has been arrested several times and was blamed for stirring up disturbances in Azerbaijan in 1988.

In the end, the September campaign and election revealed little about Islam and politics in Azerbaijan. Under Baku's continuing state of emergency, in place since last January's unrest, no one was allowed to run on an Islamic platform. Nor could anyone run who had been imprisoned or detained briefly and freed without any charges.

Azerbaijan's communist rulers are clearly ambivalent about Islam, a feeling reflected in some of their new policies. Earlier this year, it was announced that there would now be flights from Azerbaijan to Mecca, Islam's holiest shrine. But so far, relatively few have made the trip (numbering only in the dozens) and many of the pilgrims have been local Islamic dignitaries.

In Baku, underlying tensions have only been pushed under the surface by military rule. "The Azerbaijani authorities are not ready to cope with the upheaval" that could take place if mass flights to Mecca were offered, says Elizabeth Carlson, a specialist on Transcaucasia at Radio Liberty in Munich. "They're using kid gloves with the Islam issue. The last thing they want is riots."

Rival Demonstrations Hit Moscow

Daniel Sneider

11/8/90

The Soviet Army and the Communist Party used the Revolution Day celebrations on Nov. 7 in Red Square to stage an impressive display of political muscle.

As a light snow fell, the disciplined ranks of the armed forces marched past Vladimir Lenin's mausoleum, followed by columns of tanks, armored personnel carriers, and nuclear missiles. They were followed by a tightly organized demonstration of tens of thousands of Communists, carrying largely conservative banners in defense of "socialism" and critical of both Soviet President Mikhail Gorbachev and of his liberal rival Russian leader Boris Yeltsin. The demonstrators carried portraits of Karl Marx, Lenin—even Joseph Stalin's picture was hoisted by a small group of hard-line Communists.

Mr. Gorbachev, in a brief speech from atop the mausoleum, attempted to portray his perestroika reforms as a "new revolution" that would fulfill the original ideals of the 1917 revolution.

"The past generations are not to blame for the fact that the goals they dreamed of were not achieved or that the ideals which inspired people to assault the old system were subsequently distorted," Gorbachev said.

Gorbachev defended perestroika, but admitted the process was "much more painful and dramatic than could be expected." He acknowledged the signs of crisis: "the scarcity of goods, long lines, high prices, and the slackening of law order. Ethnic discord also causes anguish.

"But," he appealed, "one should not panic, still less call for a reversion to the old ways."

But Gorbachev's reform aims were hardly reflected in the official banners of the Communists who marched in front of him. Almost none mentioned the transition to a "market" economy. Instead the slogans on red cloth declared: "No to Private Property," "We are for Socialism, Not for Capitalism," and "No Unemployment."

Some homemade banners personally assailed Gorbachev. One read: "Gorbachev, You are winning points abroad, but you are losing them in your own country."

The official celebrations of the Bolshevik Revolution were opposed in Moscow, as in many other cities across the nation, by alternative anticommunist demonstrations. A small group of radicals, numbering no more than 20,000, marched into Red Square after the official display was over. They carried pictures of the late dissident democrat Andrei Sakharov and of Mr. Yeltsin, shouting "Resign" and "Down with the Communist Party" as they passed the Kremlin walls.

The competing demonstrations provided a stage for Gorbachev and Yeltsin to play out their political rivalry. The two men stood together atop the mausoleum, along with figures such as Prime Minister Nikolai Ryzhkov, Soviet parliament chairman Anatoly Lukyanov, and radical Moscow Mayor Gavril Popov. Mr. Popov had openly called for citizens to boycott the celebrations.

For the first time, they all stepped down from the podium to symbolically lead the column of Communist demonstrators, and returned to the stand to watch them pass by. The demonstrators carried slogans which repeatedly assailed Yeltsin, Popov, and the other "democrats."

A homemade sign linked Yeltsin to the United States Central Intelligence Agency. Another said his radical economic reform program "is the road to the abyss." The "Democrats" were shown in another poster as a hammer breaking the Soviet Union into pieces.

Yeltsin and Popov pointedly balanced their appearance in such company by joining the radical demonstrators as they marched down Tverskaya Boulevard toward Red Square. As the column came down the hill, the two men pulled up in a car and jumped out, immediately swarmed by hordes of cameramen.

The crowd broke into rhythmic chants of Yeltsin's name. With characteristic populist style, he plunged into the crowd, joining their ranks as they marched on.

The demonstrations passed relatively peacefully, except for several shots fired into the air by an unidentified man from a shotgun near the GUM department store on Red Square, according to the Tass news agency.

More tense confrontations took place in other Soviet cities. In the Ukrainian capital of Kiev, according to the independent Interfax news agency, radical demonstrators tried to block the military parade. Leaders of the opposition Rukh nationalist movement had to intervene to persuade students and other youth to disperse.

In the Lithuanian capital of Vilnius, where the Soviet Army defied the orders of the nationalist republican government not to hold the celebration, clashes took place between paratroopers and students, the Baltic News Service said. Lithuanians lining the parade route shouted anti-Soviet slogans, the agency reported.

Soviet Major Rankles Top Brass

Linda Feldmann

11/13/90

Vladimir Lopatin is only 30 years old and holds only the rank of major, but he has managed to make life rather uncomfortable for the top brass of the Soviet military.

Since his election to the new Soviet parliament last year, Navy Major Lopatin has led the charge of like-minded mid-level-officers-turned-politicians who favor a reform of the military that goes further and faster than anything the four-stars seem to have in mind.

He takes the podium regularly at Supreme Soviet sessions, and his pen is mighty—more than 50 articles published in the Soviet press this year alone. When his military superiors tried to have him expelled from the Communist Party last April, he fought and won. In July, he turned in his party card of his own accord.

Now Lopatin, a dour, stiff boy-man who turns on a toothy politician's grin at the sight of a camera, has turned in his epaulettes and joined an army of a different sort: the Yeltsin Brigade, a growing body of idealists—many of them about half the age of the Russian Republic's president—set to change the Soviet Union from the republic level.

Quit the military

In September, Boris Yeltsin tapped Lopatin to become deputy chairman of Russia's new Committee for National Security and Interaction with the USSR Ministry of Defense and KGB. Lopatin says the position is tantamount to the rank of minister. And so, in keeping with his view that a defense minister should be a civilian, he quit the military.

But his agenda remains the same: a smaller, volunteer Army, removal of party organizations from the military, cuts in military spending, conversion of military production to civilian, and greater say on military issues at the republic level.

Lopatin visited Washington recently on a tour sponsored by Global Outlook, a California-based research institute that focuses on the security aspects of US-Soviet relations. The purpose of his trip, his first to the United States, was to educate and to be educated. Global Outlook also hoped that, by forging international connections, he would be strengthened back home, says research analyst Jennifer Lee.

In interviews, it was not difficult to see how Lopatin could make fast enemies among the power elite of the Soviet defense establishment.

"He is preaching reform with the same vehemence that he taught Marxism-Leninism," says Ms. Lee, referring to his stint as director of the Marxism-Leninism institute in the city of Vologda.

Top Soviet military leaders complain that the likes of Lopatin aren't running the show and therefore can't speak knowledgeably about how to do it better. But regardless, Lopatin claims his point of view is gaining currency among the military's officer corps—even its notoriously conservative upper echelons.

"If, in the beginning of this year, our conception of military reform was supported by a considerable part of the younger officer corps, a part of the middle-level ranks, and only a few in the upper levels," said Lopatin in an interview with The Christian Science Monitor and Radio Liberty, "then now we are supported by an absolute majority in the younger and middle ranks of the officers' corps, and a part of the upper-level—more than just a few." Why?

"I think it's, on the one hand, a result of the growing understanding of the inevitability of these processes, and on the other hand, a result of the formation of a new Russian government," he says.

The first task of Lopatin's committee (it has no chairman) was to assess the current security situation of the Soviet Union. The group concluded that the operative concept equated security only with military aspects, to be provided by three ministries—Defense, KGB, and Interior.

"In our view, such an approach is deeply mistaken and, in and of itself, unsafe . . . ," Lopatin says. "We are widening the sphere of security to include questions of economics, ecology, politics, religious relations, national-ethnic relations, the informational-psychological sphere, the military, etc."

Lopatin's committee is also operating from the premise that the needs of the individual and society take priority over those of the state, another departure from 73 years of Communist rule.

The future Soviet Union will look more like a commonwealth of states, rather than the centrally run arrangement that no longer functions, Lopatin says. He outlines the path to the future in four stages:

Establishment of the republics' sovereignty. With almost all 15 republics having already declared varying degrees of sovereignty, this stage is virtually complete.

Negotiation of bilateral agreements between the republics, on issues that range from the economic to the political. So far, the Russian Republic has reached economic pacts with five republics and is now also negotiating political cooperation agreements, beginning with Georgia. This process looks likely to continue through the end of this year and into the beginning of 1991, Lopatin says.

A definition of common approaches to sovereignty and how to provide for its defense. "In order to defend those common interests, which face a common threat, it is evident that mutual understanding is needed on both defense and security," Lopatin says.

That's why, he continues, the Russian Republic proposes during this transitional period to delegate questions of defense and security—including nuclear weapons—to the central Soviet authority, but with "the control and active participation of the union republics."

Formation of practical structures for coordination and resolution of these common problems. That means the formation of a new type of "center" made of the highest organs of governmental power at the republic level. Lopatin envisions the structure of the new union looking something like that of the European Economic Community.

As the largest of the Soviet Union's 15 republics, and the base for two-thirds of the Soviet "military-industrial complex," according to Lopatin, the Russian Republic has taken it upon itself to try to coordinate this transition to a new type of union.

Lopatin moves through his explanation with the ease of someone who has gone over these premises many times, in meetings with Vice-President Dan Quayle, Defense Secretary Dick Cheney, and others.

But when the talk turns specific, Lopatin backs away from specifics. If there's a shooting war between the US-led multinational force and Iraq, how, if at all, should the Soviet Union be involved? And what if war breaks out between Soviet republics or between local units within republics?

Put in curious position

These are issues that could well come to the fore before a new Soviet military decision-making process could be formulated. But Lopatin responds by sticking to the general outlines of a transition to a "new type of center."

It is also curious that someone who has been so publicly critical of the old-guard security establishment has been put in charge of a committee whose title calls for "interaction with the USSR Ministry of Defense and KGB." But then, Yeltsin—and the young hot-shots he has assembled around him—haven't gotten where they are by being diplomatic.

Gorbachev and Yeltsin Map Future

Daniel Sneider

11/15/90

By all accounts, the meeting this past weekend between Soviet President Mikhail Gorbachev and his Russian rival Boris Yeltsin was no lovefest.

The two men, first alone and then accompanied by their deputies, engaged in five hours of hard bargaining about how to share power, between themselves and their governments. The outcome will determine the shape of a new treaty of union between the Soviet republics.

The Nov. 11 talk was "constructive," Mr. Gorbachev's spokesman said in diplomatic language, but, he admitted, the discussion was also "sharp and polemical" at times.

Despite their apparent dislike of each other, Gorbachev and Mr. Yeltsin are brought together by political necessity. Neither has the power to do without the other.

Gorbachev can issue decrees from behind the walls of the Kremlin, but he cannot hold the Soviet Union together without the agreement of Yeltsin, the more popular leader of the Russian parliament who represents the majority of the Soviet population. Yeltsin, for his part, can speak defiantly of Russian sovereignty and the preeminence of Russian authority, but in reality he does not have the power to act independently.

"I'm not a supporter of Russia's secession from the union," Sergei Stankevich, deputy mayor of Moscow and radical democratic leader, commented after the meeting to Interfax, an independent Soviet news service. "If Russia remains in the union, something its leaders have promised more than once, we are doomed to cooperate by the logic of history."

Such "logic" drove Gorbachev and Yeltsin together last August when they agreed to draw up a new economic reform plan based on a more radical Russian document. The odd man out was Prime Minister Nikolai Ryzhkov, whose own more moderate plan reflects the interests of the still-powerful central ministries and their allies in the Communist Party apparat and the military. Yeltsin openly demanded Mr. Ryzhkov's resignation as part of the price of the coalition.

But that deal collapsed two months later when Gorbachev backed off and, under pressure from the Ryzhkov camp, opted for a vague combination of the two plans. Yeltsin's supporters claim the result, evidenced in the Gorbachev economic plan and in the decrees emanating from his office, is virtually indistinguishable from the conservative path.

The Kremlin's decrees have uniformly asserted the authority of the central government, from claiming control over almost all foreign currency earnings to drawing up the budget for next year. Yeltsin's Russian government has retorted with counterclaims of authority, and even initiated its own radical reform plan on Nov. 1. But on Nov. 13, Yeltsin personally admitted that they had not begun to carry it out, because this could only be done on a country-wide basis.

In the background of this battle is the broader issue of the fate of the entire union, as republics from the Baltics to the Caucasus seek outright independence. Gorbachev's Presidential Council is finalizing a draft union treaty, in essence a new constitution and agreement on union between the 15 republics. It will be published within days, followed by a nationwide debate.

Presidential Council member Grigori Revenko outlined the draft last week, although he did not speak about many crucial details. He described it as a three-part document covering rules for entering the union, and a bill of human rights; defining the union's powers; and defining the structure of the state, including the separation of legislative, executive, and judicial powers.

Mr. Revenko told reporters a republic may decide not to sign the treaty and still have a "special status" within the union. The structure of the national parliament will be reorganized; there would be national direct elections for president and vice president.

Yeltsin told the Russian parliament that he proposed to Gorbachev the formation of a coalition government, with Russia providing the prime minister and defense and finance ministers. He sought a Russian say on foreign and domestic policies, from treaties with Germany to issuance of money and formation of the budget. The division of powers and control over resources between the center and Russia would be decided in talks before the union treaty is finalized.

According to Yeltsin, Gorbachev signed off on all of this, agreeing "in principle" to a new government and to all the rest, with the exception of how to handle taxation.

Neither Gorbachev nor his spokesman would confirm this; they denied plans to reshuffle the government soon. Most observers see such a new government coming only early next year, after the new union treaty is signed, with the change in the formal government structure as the excuse for a shift in personnel. A formal protocol of the Gorbachev-Yeltsin "agreement" is to be drafted and published, a measure Yeltsin says will prevent Gorbachev from backing out again.

Gorbachev presented a partial version of events in a speech on the same day to a meeting of about 1,100 military men who are members of legislatures at all levels. Both he and Yeltsin agreed, he said, "that the present Soviet Union should be changed. It should be transformed into a union of sovereign states but the union should not be dissolved."

Gorbachev's address followed speeches by a string of military men complaining about the diminution of the Army's prestige and authority, and the decay of central order. Col. Pavel Krutikov reminded Gorbachev that in times of crisis, the Army is "the last state institution still maintaining a high degree of organization and combat efficiency."

Gorbachev himself described continued union as an economic necessity which, if ignored, will lead to a blood-bath worse than the Cultural Revolution in China. He staunchly opposed formation of republican armies and called for maintaining a national draft.

Gorbachev was severely criticized Nov. 14 in the Soviet parliament, particularly by military deputies. The parliament voted to hold an emergency discussion, beginning Nov. 16, with a report by Gorbachev on the draft treaty and his meeting with Yeltsin.

Soviet Aims for Paris Talks Deflated by Domestic Woes

Daniel Sneider

11/19/90

The Paris summit meeting on European security opening today should rightly be a moment of triumph for the "new thinking" of Mikhail Gorbachev.

The meeting itself is a Soviet brainchild, the beginning of what Moscow hopes will create a new security order to replace the confrontation between the two blocs. It opens the door for the Soviet Union to enter what Soviets call "the civilized world," linked to the rest of Europe in what Mr. Gorbachev coined "a common home."

But, in what must be a bitter irony for Gorbachev, this success comes at a moment when the issue is no longer whether the Soviets will join Europe but whether there will even be a Soviet Union. Many analysts now believe the greatest threat to European security is not the Soviet Army but the disintegration of the Soviet Union into a horror of warring nuclear-armed mini-states.

Indeed while Gorbachev appears in Paris as the representative of the Soviet Union, he will be dogged by the presence of senior representatives of at least four Soviet republics who are there to claim the status of independent states. The three Baltic republics and Armenia have sent their officials while the Georgian parliament issued an appeal calling on the conference to protect their right to self-determination.

Gorbachev will do his best to persuade the other 33 heads of state present in Paris that he is not an emperor without an empire. He tried to convey the same message to his own countrymen this past weekend when he pushed through the Soviet parliament a bold package of political changes, combining a vast strengthening of his power with an offer to increase the role of the republics in decision-making.

The Soviet aim in Paris had been to make a virtue out of the collapse of the Warsaw Pact alliance with Eastern Europe and the forced withdrawal of its forces from there by creating a new pan-European security structure. This, they hope, would take the sting out of the continued presence and strength of the NATO alliance. Gorbachev also hopes to gain further Western economic aid in the bargain.

But as distinguished foreign policy commentator Alexander Bovin wrote in Izvestia last Friday, this cannot conceal the fact that the Soviet Union has ceased to function as a global power. "We are so bogged down in our internal affairs that we are losing interest in the outside world, in everything that does not directly concern us," Mr. Bovin wrote.

The inward direction of Soviet concerns was manifest during this past week of mounting political crisis, culminating in a stormy Soviet parliament session on Friday. The parliament had demanded the Soviet leader and the leaders of all the 15 republics meet to discuss the deepening economic collapse and the breakdown of authority between the central government and the republics.

The nation's eyes are on empty store shelves, on a wave of shortages that Soviets describe as the worst since World War II. The centralized system of state orders and distribution is being routinely ignored by both republican and local governments and factories. One senior factory official from the Ukraine reports his plant is largely idle because Russian suppliers refuse to deliver unless they receive either meat or dollars in return.

The central government has prepared a new draft treaty of union between the republics. Gorbachev discussed it last Sunday with Boris Yeltsin, the popular head of the Russian federation parliament whose demands for a shift of power to the republics have challenged Gorbachev's waning authority.

Gorbachev's address on Friday tried to assure everyone that food supplies were adequate, while assailing republican leaders for ignoring central orders.

Leaders of all the republics, with the exception of Lithuania, then spoke. Only the five Central Asian republics and Azerbaijan supported the draft union treaty. The Baltics, Georgia and Armenia, all led by nationalist governments, announced they would not sign the treaty.

The Ukraine, Byelorussia, and Russia, together accounting for the vast majority of the union, joined in attacking the central government. Byelorussian Prime Minister Vyacheslav Kebich said the Soviet Union only existed de jure and accused the central government of fostering economic disarray. Mr. Yeltsin reiterated his call for the resignation of Prime Minister Nikolai Ryzhkov's government and creation of a coalition national unity regime formed by the republics.

Gorbachev returned the next day with a 8-point package which clearly was in preparation for some time but which analysts believe he planned to unveil only later, after the union treaty was signed. Clearly his hand was forced by the visible collapse of support for him.

Gorbachev proposed giving the republics a direct hand in governing the center by dissolving his Presidential Council and giving new powers to the Federation Council, which includes the heads of all the republics and the president. An inter-republican committee of experts would act as the working arm of that body.

The central administration will be reorganized, a presidential-style Cabinet with new personnel replacing the current, and widely disliked, Council of Ministers. Reformist leaders, such as Leningrad Mayor Anatoly Sobchak, who supported his plan, may be brought in. Alongside this a Security Council would be created and also a vice presidency.

Much of this is included in the still unpublished draft union treaty, but Gorbachev called for this to be done without waiting for the treaty.

This new regime, he told parliament, will provide tough law and order, combating growing crime including the black market. A special new security service under the president will be created in 10-12 days.

Urgent measures on food supplies will be taken in the same period of time as well as steps to ensure adequate energy supplies for the winter and operation of the railway system. The army was assured its demands for aid to servicemen would be met.

"The common denominator of our approach is to renew and preserve the union," Gorbachev said. "I am resolutely against the division of the state, against the changing of borders, against the destruction of age-long ties between peoples."

He claimed the nationalist governments of many republics did not reflect popular will.

Though the largely pliant Soviet parliament backed him, such words will encourage suspicion among the republics of what Gorbachev's true intentions are. Still it will be hard for Mr. Yeltsin and others not to give Gorbachev some time to prove he is serious.

Gorbachev's New Union Plan Faces Strong Opposition in Republics

Daniel Sneider

11/26/90

Soviet President Mikhail Gorbachev has unveiled his vision of a new pact between the Soviet republics on Saturday, but it is already clear that many republics do not share it.

Lithuanian President Vytautas Landsbergis strongly assailed the published draft treaty of union on republican television, according to press reports. The Lithuanian leader reiterated that the Baltic republic first must be recognized as an independent state, ending the forced occupation by the Soviet Union in 1940.

The new treaty "does not refer to Lithuania from a legal point of view," Mr. Landsbergis said. Estonia and Latvia, the other two Baltic states, have also refused to discuss signing the treaty, a stance taken by the new nationalist government of Georgia.

A combative, even angry Mr. Gorbachev showed little interest in conciliation toward such opposition at a suddenly called press conference Friday evening. Earlier that day the Soviet parliament voted in favor of a resolution giving him vaguely defined new powers to halt economic chaos and restore "law and order."

He lashed out at critics on the democratic left, clearly including Russian leader Boris Yeltsin, who accuse him of wanting to be a dictator. But the Soviet leader saved his toughest remarks for the Baltics, particularly for Latvia which demanded the cessation of Soviet Army activity on its territory.

"If they try to impose [their ideas] and give ultimatums, they will complicate the matter, destablize the situation," Gorbachev retorted to the Latvians. Vowing that he too had his "limits," he threatened to use his powers if there is "a threat to the life of people and security."

Despite the existence of a new proposed union treaty, Gorbachev reiterated his position that republics which wished to leave the Soviet Union must follow a procedure in the existing constitution. That process, which requires a referendum followed by a five-year transition period and another referendum, has been rejected by the Baltics and others as a deliberate obstacle to independence.

"In the Baltic countries, one can exercise the powers given by the Soviet parliament to the President only with the help of brute military force," Landsbergis commented. In this case, he said, "the Baltic countries will defend themselves."

Armenian president Levon Ter-Petrosyan, a nationalist who recently came to power in the Caucasus republic, warned in more careful terms against such a confrontation in an interview with the Communist daily Pravda on Nov. 23.

"Some people believe that if power is strengthened and law and order are secured, everything will be all right," Mr. Ter-Petrosyan said. "It is an illusion. In such a case, the center will face the serious resistance of the republics because sovereignty is a reality for us."

Even more moderate republican leaders such as Mr. Yeltsin who accept the need for a united country have raised fundamental objections to the new draft, focused on the division of powers with the union. The draft, for example, retains union control over key resources such as gold and diamond reserves and energy. While republics own all land and resources, the union reserves that part needed to conduct its responsibilities. (See story below.)

The republics are given a say in common economic policies through an enhanced Federative Council, but the powerful central ministries that run most of the country's factories and enterprises remain.

Much of the operation of that Federative Council remains unclear in the document. Relatively conservative Uzbekistan President Islam Karimov told Pravda as well that the version of the draft treaty "cannot be signed by us." The treaty does not guarantee "the parity and equal rights of all subjects of a future federation."

Mr. Karimov accused the central government of wanting to control the treaty ratification process, including discussing the treaty at the Supreme Soviet and the larger legislative body of the Congress of Peoples Deputies which holds its semiannual meeting starting Dec. 17.

"Today they want to impose the union upon us," Karimov said. "We need the opposite process," in which the republics should work out the treaty and sign it.

Details of Treaty Between Soviet Republics

Daniel Sneider

11/26/90

These are the main points of the new draft union treaty intended to replace the treaty signed on December 1922 that established the Union of Soviet Socialist Republics.

Fundamental principles: The new treaty creates a Union of Sovereign Soviet Republics, dropping the word "socialist." Each republic is a "sovereign state and enjoys full authority over its territory." It calls for protection of human rights, creation of civil society, and democracy based on popular representation and law. All forms of property, including "property of citizens and their associations," are guaranteed.

Division of powers: The republics delegate the following powers to the union government: defense of the union, definition and protection of borders, organization of the armed forces, declaration of war, foreign policy, regulation and coordination of foreign economic activity of republics, and customs. In coordination with republics, the union executes common policy on: finance, credit, and monetary policy based on a single currency; creation and use of gold and diamond reserves; fuel, energy, transportation and communication systems; administration of defense industries, space research, social security.

The republics have the right to own their land and natural resources and collect taxes for their budgets. Republican laws have priority except over areas delegated to the union. A Constitutional Court will settle disputes between republics or between a republic and the union. The delegation of powers cannot be changed without the consent of all the republics.

Structure of government: The president has supreme executive power, heads the Cabinet, represents the union in foreign relations, and is commander in chief. He and a newly established vice president are directly elected by a majority of votes in the union and in most of the republics.

The Federation Council, consisting of the president, vice president, and heads of all republics, determines directions of internal and external policy.

The Supreme Soviet has two houses: one formed by republics; the other, by direct vote.

Bitter Debate Divides Military

Daniel Sneider

12/6/90

Last year on Dec. 8, Maj. Vladimir Lopatin, a 29-year-old political officer, rose to speak from the stage of the Central Soviet Army Theater. Before him, seated in ranks in the columned auditorium, was the cream of the Red Army.

Major Lopatin hoped to present an audacious call for the reform of the Red Army that he and 16 young comrades had penned some days earlier. The country's military forces, they said, should be drastically reduced to match the real level of the threat facing the nation. The Army should be converted into a more qualified professional force.

The Army is falling out of step with the changes in Soviet society, they declared.

"When I was about to speak," the lean-faced Lopatin recalls, "Defense Minister Dmitri Yazov said, 'Comrade Lopatin, sit down. We don't need any military reform. We will adopt a law on defense and it will solve all the problems.'"

This encounter was the opening shot in what has become a bitter debate over the reform of the Soviet military. The battle has divided the ranks of the armed forces themselves, pitting young officers against old and draftees against professionals.

The fight has spilled over into the news media and political life, where the military has become a crucial battleground of Soviet leader Mikhail Gorbachev's perestroika (restructuring).

Liberal reformers demand the Soviet "peace dividend" be freed to save the failing economy and warn of Army coups to defend the old order. Conservatives see the military as a last bastion of order and discipline, even of socialism, and the only force capable of preserving the Union from being splintered by nationalism. People in the middle recognize the need for change but want to protect the proud and strong traditions of their military.

"Since the Army is part of society," Mr. Gorbachev told an Army gathering on Nov. 13, "everything happening inside society affects the Army."

With that thought in mind, The Christian Science Monitor today begins a series of articles on reform in the Red Army. Senior generals and admirals, many of whom have never spoken to the Western press before, provided new insights into the thinking of the Red Army leadership. Young military reformers, academy cadets, seamen aboard ships, and soldiers told of their troubles and concerns.

The origins of military reform arguably date to the evening of April 9, 1989, in the Georgian capital of Tblisi, when Army troops backed by tanks attacked a candlelit gathering of nationalist demonstrators in the city's central square. Twenty people died from poison gas, clubs, and spades, and the event became a cause célèbre for reformers. Liberals attacked the Army for involvement in internal politics and mothers took to the streets protesting against their sons being used for such deeds.

To this day, Col. Gen. Igor Rodionov, who commanded the forces there, bitterly rejects charges of Army brutality as media-invented lies. He accuses the political leadership of misusing the Army by sending it into a domestic conflict better handled by the KGB (the secret police) and the regular police.

Nonetheless, the military leadership saw the need for some change, driven by such problems as the fall in quality of hardware to the poorly trained and badly motivated recruits. Soviet generals wanted to field an Army that emphasized quality not quantity.

The drive for reform came also from Gorbachev, whose bold foreign policy ended the cold war and brought the Soviet Union out of isolation from the West. Gorbachev sought to lessen the burden of the huge military, ultimately declaring large unilateral cuts in forces and their planned withdrawal from Eastern Europe.

Lopatin and his fellow military reformers, backed by liberal scholars, felt they were on the right side of history. In April of this year, after several months of work in a special parliamentary committee, they presented a new draft reform. They sought as well the complete separation of the Army from the Communist Party and installation of a civilian defense minister.

But the Ministry of Defense still resisted. Almost immediately, Red Star, the Army daily, assailed Lopatin for the radicalism of his plan and for undermining the unity of the Army. On April 26, he was expelled from the Communist Party (though later reinstated).

Behind this frontal assault, however, the generals were changing their strategy. "The minister of defense and his followers learned to articulate the word 'reform,'" comments Maj. Gen. Nikita Chaldimov, who heads Army and Society, a pro-reform group.

According to General Chaldimov, the Defense Ministry was under pressure because of growing public support for Lopatin's reform ideas, including the backing of a significant portion of the younger officers.

On June 5, Marshal Yazov unveiled his own highly cautious 10-year plan, but one that incorporated elements of the reformers' ideas. He argued that reform had already begun—spending was being cut and conditions for servicemen improved.

The reform, Yazov said, must update defense hardware, substituting technology for manpower. At the same time, the troops must be better trained and more professional. Although rejecting a fully volunteer force, he offered a limited experiment in the Navy giving recruits the option of a three-year contract at a higher salary; normally draft service is for two years.

More-extreme conservative elements in the military launched their own attack several weeks later, criticizing not only the radicals but also the centrist leadership. Gen. Albert Makashov thundered against Gorbachev at the founding Congress of the Russian Communist Party: "The Army is being driven without combat out of countries which our fathers liberated from fascism."

Lopatin's plan languished in the Supreme Soviet's Committee on Defense and State Security, the majority of whose members hail from the armed services or the defense industry.

"The majority of the committee doesn't respect Major Lopatin," committee member Sergei Tsyplyaev, a Leningrad physicist, says simply.

"In all countries, the military is one of the most conservative structures," Mr. Tsyplyaev explains, "and they like to have everything as it was before."

Gorbachev finally weighed in publicly. In a speech at an Army exercise in Odessa on Aug. 17, he called for serious reform to begin next year. He opened the door, without giving a definitive view, to creating a fully voluntary service and to forming republican military units.

Gorbachev seemed to be leaning toward radical reform. But behind closed doors, the Ministry of Defense was pushing ahead with its own, more limited reform. In August, the ministry finalized its draft reform and in September shepherded it into the parliament with presidential backing to complete it by the end of the year.

Their version argues strongly against a full professional service as too costly, three to four times more than the current force. The ministry rejects republican units and calls for structural changes to be postponed till 1996, when the withdrawal from Eastern Europe and force reductions are set to be completed.

Lopatin grew discouraged. Believing he was blocked at the center, he turned to the Russian Republic government of Boris Yeltsin, which in September appointed him deputy head of a newly formed committee on security. He now sees the republican demands for sovereignty as the new route for military reform. Since the fall, the Russian leadership has held several meetings with the military leadership, trying to woo them to support its more radical economic policies.

Gorbachev, pressed by Mr. Yeltsin and the rebellious republics on one side and the conservative establishment on the other, has not been willing to openly challenge the Army leadership. On Nov. 13, he met with 1,100 Army members of legislatures in the Soviet Army Theater. Yazov, leading off the meeting, barely discussed reform, merely declaring that "reform is being implemented."

Gorbachev rose later to directly attack Lopatin, who had sent Gorbachev a letter the previous day accusing him of ignoring the April reform proposal. Those ideas were heard but not necessarily followed, Gorbachev retorted. Retreating from his earlier position, he backed the ministry's stance, calling for maintaining the present draft system and dismissing the idea of republican forces as "a political game."

Gorbachev, however, indicated shortly afterward at the Supreme Soviet that he might seek a new military leadership more open to reform. He could find support from men like Gen. Vladimir Lobov, the Warsaw Pact commander, who tried to stake out a middle ground in a September article in Kommunist, the official Soviet Communist Party journal.

"More radicalism and action is needed," Lobov wrote. "The Army is steadily losing its authority."

The Army increasingly finds itself in confrontation with nationalist governments in the republics. People in the Baltic republics and Transcaucasia refuse to answer draft calls. Many republics demand that their boys serve only at home, either in the Army or in a republican militia.

In backing his generals, Gorbachev is perhaps mindful that, as retired US Adm. Stanley Fine told a conference here recently, "a large military without a reason for being is not a very safe institution to have for any nation."

Soviet Military Takes New Look at Doctrine

Daniel Sneider

12/7/90

Imagine you are a defense planner at the Soviet Red Army's General Staff, looking out to the West. Over the centuries, a succession of invaders from Polish knights to Adolf Hitler's panzers have thrust into Russia, your homeland.

But for 45 years, your defense lines have been set forward in the center of Europe, a position won through much blood and sacrifice.

Now, within the space of less than a year, the Red Army's defense lines have crumbled along with the Berlin Wall. By next year, all Soviet troops in Hungary and Czechoslovakia and most in Poland will have left; in East Germany by 1994 at the latest.

Although the NATO alliance is virtually untouched, even strengthened by the reunification of Germany, the Warsaw Pact is a dead letter.

That is how the world looks to Maj. Gen. Sergei Bogdanov, the tough 50-year-old head of the sensitive center for operations and strategic research of the General Staff. In his first-ever meeting with a Western correspondent, he gave a military man's view of Soviet security today.

For decades, Soviet military philosophy has been to emphasize the attack, to overwhelm the enemy with massive firepower, on the theory that the best defense is a good offense.

Circumstances are forcing the Army to think again. For the first time, civilians are entering the defense debate. Not unlike critics of the defense establishment in the United States, they question the value of massive defense costs when the country's economy is collapsing. And with the end of the cold war, Soviets are also asking, "Who's the enemy?"

The military leadership is careful not to contradict the broad policies set by President Mikhail Gorbachev. "There are no nations who we could suspect of preparing a war against us," he said during his latest visit to Germany. But a clear difference emerges in the details of their comments.

General Bogdanov stiffly echoes his commander in chief. From arms control agreements to meetings between leaders, including military men, he says, "positive international changes have reduced the tension between the two blocs."

"But," the general adds, with obvious emphasis, "although the direct threat of armed attack against the Soviet Union is disappearing, I personally believe that one cannot boldly say there is no danger, no threat to the Soviet Union at all."

This isn't just one man's notion. That view inspires the Defense Ministry's draft military reform plan. "There is no guarantee against the irreversibility of the positive changes in the world," the draft warns.

A careful analysis, Bogdanov says, yields the conclusion that NATO and the US continue to want to operate "from a position of strength." Despite the "dramatic change" in Soviet forces in Eastern Europe, NATO forces are unchanged, "and it is quite dangerous to us."

Even US-Soviet cooperation in the Persian Gulf crisis has a dark side for the Soviet General Staff.

"The conflict brought the US and Soviet Union closer together," the general notes. "But being a military man, I noticed the US command acquired a sizable experience in mass movement of troops."

Meanwhile, he worries about the leaders of Eastern Europe moving to dissolve the Warsaw Treaty Organization. German Chancellor Helmut Kohl, he says sharply, issues statements to try to "appease the public, but we know a unified Germany will dramatically strengthen NATO."

Although the Soviet Union has adopted a defensive military doctrine, Bogdanov adds, the US continues to "encircle" the Soviet Union with bases. It has not renounced the first use of nuclear weapons, as the Soviet Union has, and the US nuclear attack plan is "still valid."

As proof, the Soviet military points to modernized US submarine-launched Trident II missiles and highly accurate low-flying cruise missiles, which can carry either nuclear or conventional warheads. Bogdanov surprisingly admits that "unfortunately" the Soviet military can not detect the launch of American cruise missiles, making them "most dangerous types of weapons."

Such skepticism finds an eerie echo in the statements of the US Department of Defense, including in the most recent edition of "Soviet Military Power," an annual report. The Soviets, the booklet notes, continue to modernize their land-based nuclear missile systems, which are potential first-strike weapons. Defense Secretary Richard Cheney argues there that, despite the evident changes, "the military might of the Soviet Union is enormous and remains targeted on the United States and our allies."

"It looks like generals are making threats to each other," satirically remarks Maj. Vladimir Lopatin, the leader of a military reform movement among young officers. He is one of a growing group of critics within the Soviet Union who have forced open the first genuine debate on how to define national security.

"The Soviet Union now has more chances of being destroyed as an entity by economic crisis or ecological crisis, or by the total collapse of its domestic structure, than by any threat from abroad," says Alexei Izyumov, a specialist at the USA-Canada Institute.

Although defense spending has been reduced, Mr. Izyumov and his colleagues contend that it still far exceeds the actual threat. Nor, he argues, has the military tried to define what spending level would be appropriate.

Gen. Nikita Chaldimov, a liberal military voice and head of the Army and Society public association, agrees that the direct threat from the West "is now history." But dangers remain, including from a "new Khomeini or another religious fanatic" or from an explosion of nationalism.

Soviet defense officials have spent several years elaborating a new military doctrine, putting the emphasis on defense. Mr. Gorbachev first articulated this in 1986, coining the phrase "reasonable sufficiency" of armed forces. No longer, the doctrine says, should the Soviet Union try to match the West, weapon for weapon.

The doctrine which existed before 1985 "envisioned wars," explains Bogdanov, and sought absolute symmetry between the Warsaw Pact and NATO forces. "As a result of that, we were dragged into the arms race."

"In the early 1960s, we developed a concept which envisioned a preemptive nuclear strike that could be carried out if the aggressive designs of a potential aggressor were detected," he says, revealing aspects of nuclear strategy with unusual frankness. "The new doctrine rejects the possibility of war and it emphasizes prevention of war and preparation to repel aggression."

In a fairly striking contrast to years of Soviet calls for complete elimination of nuclear weapons, Soviet military leaders now unofficially accept the long-reviled concept of nuclear deterrence and mutually assured destruction advocated in the US. Bogdanov says the Soviet Union should have "minimal nuclear means which . . . in case of a nuclear strike by another state could inflict unacceptable damage in response."

General Chaldimov agrees. "There was a time when we proposed eliminating all nuclear weapons with one stroke. Given present circumstances, it's not realistic."

The Ministry of Defense reform plan foresees a 50 percent cut in strategic nuclear weapons by the year 2000, the target of the treaty now being concluded with the US. Later, the treaty's ceiling of 6,000 warheads could be further lowered to 4,000 warheads, says Bogdanov.

The shift toward reliance on a nuclear shield reflects the real decrease in conventional forces, which had always been the backbone of the Soviet armed forces. Total Soviet strength will drop from 3,993,000 to 3,730,000 by mid-1991. By 1995, the Defense Ministry says, it will reach around 3 million. By the end of the reform plan, the year 2000, the Army should be 10 to 12 percent smaller, though more mobile. Air defense units are expected to shrink by 20 percent and the separate Air Force by 8 percent.

Only the Soviet Navy is not slated for cuts. The Soviets insist that the overwhelmingly superior US naval forces be brought closer to parity with them, a goal totally rejected by Washington. The Soviet Union has always been primarily a coastal, defensive naval power, argues Vice Adm. Nikolai Martynyuk, deputy commander of the Soviet Pacific Fleet. The US fleet can float 15 aircraft carriers, he told the Monitor.

Asked about large-deck carriers being built and tested in the Black Sea, the admiral quickly replies, "Even if we deploy the one carrier that took about 10 years to build, it can change nothing . . . . If a miracle comes and we have 15 carriers, our fleet could become an attack fleet. But I don't dream about this."

Decay in the Ranks Pushes Military Brass Toward Reform

Daniel Sneider

12/10/90

In the hills above the Bay of Amur, the men who consider themselves the toughest fighters in the Soviet military stand ready.

Sgt. Valeri Morozov was working in a Moscow factory when his draft call came. Now he stands in his barracks, 4,000 miles away in Vladivostok, his black beret set at an angle, his arms held tautly at his side. Only the fittest recruits have a shot at the Marines, the slight 19-year-old proudly says. He has made eight paratroop jumps already.

But even here, among the elite of the Soviet military, evidence of rot is not hard to detect. On the base's main road, a large billboard shows a fist smashing down upon dedovshchina, the word that describes the widespread physical abuse of new recruits by second-year men.

Soldiers fall back on nationalism if their self-esteem is low, explains Capt. Konstantin Gedman. As is typical in elite forces, the vast majority of Marines, 49 out of 60 in this unit, are Russians or Ukrainians. The men from Central Asia and the Caucuses—the chornii, or blacks, as they are derogatorily called—fill out the ranks of the Army grunts and the construction brigades.

This is only one of the many woes besetting the Soviet Red Army.

Draft calls are being ignored, with recruitment falling 400,000 men short of target already this year. Many of those who do show up, officers complain, are ill or have criminal records. About 15,000 Army men are alleged to have died in the past four years because of harsh noncombat conditions, including ethnic violence among the troops. Living conditions are worsening rapidly, with 173,000 officers and noncommissioned officers waiting for housing, even before troops in Eastern Europe return home.

The decay in the ranks is a key factor in the push for military reform. The most radical reformers want to see the changes that swept the United States military after the Vietnam War. The Soviet Union had its own Vietnam—the 10-year war against Islamic rebels in Afghanistan. The Soviet reformers want to end the draft and create a wholly volunteer professional army. The living conditions and pay of soldiers should be raised, they say, and servicemen should be given legal protection from abuse by superiors.

To do this, the Red Army must change. It was formed in 1918 as the military arm of the Bolshevik Revolution, battling the counterrevolutionary armies during the civil war. To this day, it remains an instrument of the Communist Party: One out of every four Army men is a party member and the party enforces its policies through a vast network of political officers and political propaganda.

The reformers argue that since the Soviet Union is becoming a modern, parliamentary democracy under President Mikhail Gorbachev's policy of perestroika (restructuring), the Army must be placed under neutral civilian control.

All the problems confronting the Soviet military—and the beginnings of change—are visible at this tidy base.

Standing in the soldiers' quarters, Captain Gedman complains of "weak comrades who don't want to work." The recruits cannot master the new technology of weapons. "The boys from the village are strong but it is difficult to teach them intellectual tasks," he says. There is a lack of qualified men to become sergeants, a fellow officer adds.

Down the hall is Lenin's Room, the ubiquitous political education center found in every Soviet military unit. The lean and handsome Maj. Andrei Prokonich is the unit's political officer. In the mid-1980s, he volunteered to fight in Afghanistan, spending two years in combat in the harsh mountains. Now, he delivers lectures twice a week standing next to a bust of Vladimir Lenin and flanked by a poster that proclaims "Always Ready for Battle" and shows a marine, his gun thrusting skyward. Soon, Major Prokonich says, the posters will come down and a recreation room will be created.

"It's better to use a psychological approach than to read a lot of slogans and books," he says dismissively.

The living conditions here are better than average, the men agree. Neat cots stand side by side on carpeted floors in an open room lined with curtained windows. Weight-lifting equipment occupies a corner. A stereo and television hold a prominent spot.

But below the base gates, men with families are crammed into tiny apartment blocks. They fear losing even these if they have to transfer. Soldiers salaries range from 7 to 25 rubles a month ($5 to $16, at the commercial exchange rate), hardly enough for a couple of nights on the town and far below even the minimum average worker's salary of about 200 rubles a month.

The wrenching process of reform within the military can be seen across the Soviet Union.

On the outskirts of Moscow, at the end of a long drive lined with white birch trees, stands the Soviet West Point—or as it is formally known, the General Academy of the Supreme Soviet of the Russian Soviet Federative Socialist Republic.

A group of cadets in their brown wool uniforms, brass buttons shining brightly, stand together in a rare moment of repose. The cadets are loyal sons of the Army; a third of them actually come from families of Army officers. They easily dismiss stories of an Army coup, appearing daily in the liberal Moscow news media.

"It can't happen," answers Yuri Rashkov, to the nods of his comrades. "We are part of the people. We shall not use our guns against our fathers. We trust our commanders—they will never give us such orders."

But if they are confident of their leaders in that arena, the cadets do not hesitate to differ with the generals when it comes to reform. While the Ministry of Defense says a professional army is an expensive betrayal of a citizen force, the cadets shout in an enthusiastic "yes" when asked if they want to command professionals rather than draftees. They know an ordinary GI makes more than a Soviet general.

"There should be a professional army so that every soldier would be motivated by his salary," says Kiril Kuvbatov. "And soldiers should take more care of equipment, and not damage it."

The man responsible for the future of the entire officer corps personnel, Col. Gen. Alexei Mironov, sees it quite differently.

About half of the military, counting commissioned and noncommissioned officers and some servicemen, are already professionals, General Mironov says.

Aside from them, "why would we need a professional in a tank crew loading a gun or in an artillery crew that just carries shells?," he asks rhetorically. "That's a humiliating job . . . This is just selling your body for a tin piece. Two years is enough for a guy to learn this business."

The draft reform of the Ministry of Defense adds an economic argument against a professional army—a volunteer force would cost three to four times more than the present forces do. But the ministry takes initial steps toward a professional army in certain high-technology areas, such as the Navy, nuclear forces, and the Air Force. A naval experiment to begin next year will offer a seaman a choice of a two-year contract at 60 to 70 rubles a month or three years at 200 rubles a month.

Mironov's main concern, though, is to improve the miserable living conditions of the military, particularly officers and men returning from Eastern Europe. Only 40 percent of the returning officers have housing, says Mironov, adding to an annual deficit of 30,000 apartments. He is waiting for promised German aid, and builders, to help meet the demand.

The Army is also considering reforms to help attract qualified officers from a younger generation that, as Mironov puts it, "is more liberal, more freedom loving." The reform will allow officers to leave the service after 10 years rather than the current 25-year contract.

Back in Vladivostok, Comdr. Georgi Rakhmetov is second in command of the Admiral Vinogradov, the most modern antisubmarine warfare cruiser in the Soviet Navy. Commander Rakhmetov is not in charge of torpedo tubes or missile batteries. As the ship's political officer, he is in charge of the minds of his men.

His headquarters is a wood-paneled, carpeted cabin, with a small refrigerator and a television set, where American action films played on the ship's video channel blare away. A photo of Lenin hangs amid bookcases filled with textbooks and pamphlets.

The Admiral Vinogradov has just returned from a friendship visit to San Diego, a first for the Pacific Fleet.

"After the visit, the sailors had a lot of questions. Why do we live so badly now, and why do Americans live so well? And when can we reach the American level of life?"

"I answered them that the idea of socialism is more progressive than the capitalist system. But capitalism now in practice is better than socialism in practice. For 70 years, we made a lot of mistakes. And I tell them perestroika is a good chance for us to live as well as Americans."

Rakhmetov is part of the vast machinery of the Military Political Department, the military arm of the Communist Party Central Committee in Moscow. There Maj. Gen. Alexander Gorbachev (no relation to the Soviet president) is in charge of party work in the Army. Some 38,000 party cells, "more than 1 million Army communists," including three quarters of the officer corps, are under the supervision of this soft-spoken man.

Since April, when the Communist Party abandoned its constitutional monopoly as the only legal party, the demand for "de-politicization" of the Army and KGB (the secret police) has grown. On Sept. 3, President Gorbachev issued a decree ordering a plan for political reform in the armed services to be completed in 3 months.

But the president and the party he heads, plus the Army, have made it clear they will not agree to removing Communist influence from the military.

Instead, explains General Gorbachev, the main political department will be transformed from a party organization to a state body, responsible to the government. "This is not just a mere change of title," he insists. The new body will include specially trained psychologists, sociologists, and lawyers to assist servicemen with their problems.

Parallel to this, however, the network of party cells will remain. "The heads of the military-political organs will be members of the Communist Party," though not under party command. "It is quite a delicate difference," General Gorbachev admits.

Delicate indeed. Other parties are free to try to organize cells, but only "parties favoring the socialist choice will enjoy the support of commanding officers," he says.

Soldiers are free to practice their religious beliefs, but there will be no religious services on base or Bibles in Lenin's Room.

"We uphold communist ideals and our approach is atheist," the general says.

Violence Shakes Soviet Republic

Daniel Sneider

12/11/90

On the evening of Sunday, Dec. 2, in a burst of violence as sudden as it was deadly, five soldiers and at least three townsfolk died in a clash in the quiet Uzbek city of Namangan. Tens more were injured and thousands of demonstrating Uzbek youth and police battled in two days of riots that followed.

The incident has shaken the leadership here in the capital of this Central Asian republic and reverberated back to Moscow. Initial Soviet news-media reports portrayed the event as an unprovoked attack on Soviet soldiers by "militant" youth. The accounts painted dark overtones of anti-Army and anti-Russian acts by fanatic Muslim Central Asians.

The Uzbek government and the democratic nationalist movement reject these views as unfounded lies. They deny any national or religious motive is behind the violence.

Some see the hand of Moscow seeking to blacken the reputation of Uzbeks. Others construct conspiratorial tales of deliberate manipulation by a dying empire that seeks to preserve itself by provoking ethnic conflict as an excuse to deploy its armed forces.

In any case, what happened at Namangan reveals the depth of anger and emotion that lies not far from the apparently tranquil surface of the largest of the four Central Asian republics. The evidence suggests religious feelings played a major role, perhaps for the first time, in prompting a violent clash in this predominantly Islamic part of the Soviet Union.

City is Islamic center

Although all the details are far from clear, a picture does emerge from accounts in the local press and from interviews with government officials and democratic activists who went to Namangan to investigate the incident.

Namangan lies deep in the heartland of Uzbekistan, in the fertile Fergana Valley, where the majority of Uzbeks live. It is by numerous accounts a peaceful town, because of its highly religious population. Namangan is the center of Islamic fundamentalism in Uzbekistan, says Abdul Rashid, representative of the Uzbek Popular movement Birlik, which unites democratic and nationalist activists. Islam's power is attested by the virtual absence of crime and almost no drinking of alcohol, Mr. Rashid says.

Even in June 1989, when riots swept the Fergana Valley as Uzbeks youths fought ethnic Turks from the Caucasus, there was no trouble in Namangan. Since those riots, battalions of special Interior Ministry troops, equipped for riot control, have been stationed throughout the valley, one of them in Namangan.

On Dec. 2 at about 5 p.m. a group of six soldiers—four or five of them ethnic Russians—boarded bus No. 21, purportedly to return to their barracks.

"They were drunk," says Ibrahim Iskanderov, vice president of the Uzbek Academy of Sciences, repeating the findings of a report delivered to the Uzbek Communist Party Central Committee by the head of the government investigating committee.

Col. A. P. Kim, the deputy military prosecutor of the Turkestan military district, in an interview Dec. 6 in Pravda Vostoka, the Uzbek party daily, denied any guilt on the part of the soldiers, but admitted "four of them shared a bottle of vodka."

Soldiers fought with teenagers

All accounts agree that the soldiers got into a fist fight on the bus with local teenage youths. The cause, say various Uzbek sources, was an attempt by the soldiers to molest some women.

"Namangan is a religious town," explains Mahmud Imakov, a Birlik activist who went there to investigate the incident. "Not even Uzbeks dare to touch women. Russians have never been known to do so."

As the fight raged, the bus driver pulled into the town's central square. The driver shouted to a gathering crowd that women had been attacked, their dresses torn. According to Colonel Kim, the crowd grew rapidly to about 1,500 people, mostly youths.

Birlik investigators claim about 50 militiamen (police) were present but did not try to stop the mob, Birlik investigators say. At some point, the bus was set ablaze with at least two of the soldiers burned inside. Five soldiers died and one was rescued by townsfolk, but was badly injured.

By Kim's account, the crowd swelled to 3,500. Armed Interior Ministry troops arrived with four armored personnel carriers bringing the law enforcement strength to 700.

"The soldiers were ordered to fire in the air, but chauvinists among them fired below the waist line," says Mahmud Ali Makmudov, secretary of the Uzbek Writer's Union. He bases his story on a first-hand account told to him by a Namangan resident. Official reports say three people died, but Birlik activists believe at least seven were killed.

Clashes spanned two days

For the next two days, thousands of youths repeatedly clashed with militia and troops. Democratic activists link these events to the violent ethnic clashes in Fergana and those between Uzbeks and Kirghiz in the Kirghiz town of Osh last summer.

"It is a scenario of provocation used by the Moscow mafia," says Mr. Makmudov, referring to conservative Communists and enemies of reform.

Uzbeks also deny charges that anti-Army feelings were behind the violence. Uzbek families are large and many have at least one son in the Army, they point out. But Uzbek activists do express anger over the high number of deaths of Uzbek soldiers in the Soviet Army because of what they say is racist violence.

Such assessments, though in slightly less conspiratorial tones, are even echoed by the Uzbek Communist Party. Though the party is considered one of the Soviet Union's most conservative, it is increasingly reflecting the growth in Uzbek nationalism.

There are those in Moscow who want "to compromise the republic, to paint it black" asserts party Central Committee member Iskanderov. "This republic is more stable. That makes certain people angry. We have no hunger; no strikes."

Mr. Iskanderov and other officials strongly reject the idea that either nationalism or religious fundamentalism was behind the anger in Namangan. Timour Valyev, a thoughtful computer scientist and member of the Uzbek Presidential Council, sees the roots of violence in the potent combination of teenagers and a depressed economy.

For Soviet Reformers, the Peace Dividend Is Slow to Pay Off

Daniel Sneider

12/13/90

On Sept. 6, the men in charge of the Soviet Union's secret nuclear weapons laboratories, its tank factories, and its naval shipyards issued an unusual public appeal in the pages of the Communist Party daily Pravda.

"Esteemed Comrades," it began, "We, the heads of associations, enterprises, and organizations in the defense complex, are worried by the country's grave economic and social situation, whose negative consequences are increasingly taking hold of our enterprises."

This battle cry from the Soviet military-industrial complex was squarely aimed at the liberal economists and promoters of military reform who see the extensive conversion of the defense industry to peaceful uses as an absolute necessity.

"For us, conversion is one of the central problems of transition to a market economy," says Stanislav Shatalin, an adviser to Soviet President Mikhail Gorbachev and the author of a radical economic reform plan.

Unless the enormous intellectual and material resources under the command of the military-industrial complex are freed, Mr. Shatalin and others argue, no market reform can succeed. Moreover, the defense industries are the backbone of the huge industrial ministries and the central planning apparatus which are the core of bureaucratic resistance to a market economy.

Indeed, the Pravda letter openly complained that market reforms had "disrupted" the nation's defense industry. "Plan regulation of the economy has been destroyed;" the defense sector's most skilled employees are leaving to work in more lucrative private business; suppliers are arbitrarily jacking up prices or demanding bribes to fulfill contracts.

At the same time, the Soviet defense industry is being subjected to "destructive criticism." Can the Soviet Union tolerate this when the United States, Britain, and France continue to nurture their defense industry, the letter writers asked.

Resources must keep flowing to them and the "centralized system of management" must be maintained, the defense industry leaders demanded.

The stakes in this confrontation are enormous, not only politically but economically. Estimates of defense spending as a percentage of gross national product range from an official 9 percent to 25 percent, an estimate made by both Soviet and American economists. Officially, about 40 percent of all machinery production is said to be defense-related, but independent Soviet experts put it at 60 percent.

Radicals, including Russian leader Boris Yeltsin, demand a significant reduction in defense spending, by as much as 25 percent to start. While preserving the vital technologies and skills accumulated in the defense industry, rapid conversion should take place, they say, including freeing all but 20 percent to 30 percent of defense factories from state control.

Conversion and reduction of defense spending are official state policy, declared by Mr. Gorbachev in a December 1988 speech to the United Nations.

An initial conversion program was announced and a long-term draft plan presented to a closed meeting of the President Council in late September. According to one of the authors, V.I. Smyslov, vice-chairman of the State Planning Commission (Gosplan), conversion will involve 400 factories under the control of defense-linked ministries and 100 enterprises from other ministries. For reasons unrelated to conversion, the Soviet defense industry has long produced civilian goods inside its defense plants, including all the television sets, radios, video-cassette recorders, cameras, sewing machines, and most of the tape recorders and vacuum cleaners produced in the Soviet Union. Under the draft plan, the total share of production devoted to consumer products will rise from 40 percent in 1988 to 60 percent by 1995.

Defense spending has been officially reduced for the last two years, from 77.9 billion rubles ($48.7 billion at the commercial exchange rate) in 1989, down 8 percent to 71 billion in 1990, and reduced further to 66.5 billion in a proposed 1991 budget. Defense production, under the draft plan, will be reduced 19 percent from 1991-1995.

These plans have been drawn up by the military-industrial complex itself. The conversion plan is the product of the Gosplan, the State Military-Industrial Commission that coordinates the nine defense-linked ministries, and the Ministry of Defense. The only outside body with oversight is the parliament's Committee on National Security, a 43-man group, most of whose members come from the military, the defense industry, or the KGB (Soviet secret police).

"You cannot imagine someone like the chairman of Northrop Corporation or General Dynamics heading a committee on military affairs in the US Congress, but that's our situation," says Alexei Izyumov, a security expert at the prestigious USA-Canada Institute. The committee and the public beyond are deprived of real information on the actual level of defense spending—even what weapons are being produced, the location of defense plants, or the number of their employees is still a secret.

The Committee on Science and Education of the Soviet parliament, drawing on liberal experts, estimates that defense spending is actually close to 200 billion rubles. The published figures are based on nominal ruble prices that significantly underprice military products and overprice the consumer goods made by defense plants, argues Mr. Izyumov.

Moreover, the official budget does not include all nuclear weapons spending, as well as other classified weapons production. The liberal daily Izvestia charged that 1991 defense spending would actually amount to 132 billion rubles once additions were made from other parts of the budget.

Even critics acknowledge, however, that some reductions in defense production have taken place. The most serious is at the big tank plants in the Urals, where almost half the number of tanks are now being built.

But, the critics charge, the draft conversion plan is far too limited in scale and aimed at preserving the control of the military-industrial complex.

"It's not conversion, but simply the creation of new industrial capacity within the structure of military industry," says Sergei Blagovolin, who heads military research at the powerful Imemo think tank. "Military industry wants to control all possible production lines which would be converted into military production in a time of war or war preparation."

Unless the factories are freed from central control to respond to real-market conditions, not to orders from above, there will be no actual transfer of resources to meet civilian needs, these critics say.

The draft plan poses a particular dilemma for Gorbachev, who is publicly committed to serious conversion but who finds the support of the conservative bureaucracy and the military increasingly necessary in his battle with rebellious nationalist movements in the Soviet republics.

When the Presidential Council met in late September, "there was a clear split and fight between those who want real conversion and those who only want the title 'conversion' and nothing more," says an informed source.

Alexander Yakovlev, the leading liberal voice among the president's advisers, attacked the low level of reduction in defense spending in the plan. Mr. Yakovlev told the meeting, the source recounted, "that the real threat to the security of the country is the terrible situation in our economy, our aging industry, our obsolete technology—and not possible military actions from the West." Several others, including Yevgeny Primakov, supported him.

Gorbachev responded in typical compromising fashion.

"Gorbachev said that this plan is a serious step in the right direction, but there was a need to improve some points," the confidant reports. Gosplan officials say they are still working on the document.

But liberal experts believe Gorbachev gave a boost to the military-industrial complex when he opted for a more conservative economic reform plan later in October, rejecting the radical Shatalin plan.

"Gorbachev has ruined this package, because he didn't want to challenge his constituency in the bureaucracy," Izyumov says bitterly.

Gorbachev Fights for Union Treaty

Daniel Sneider

12/20/90

Opposition leader Nikolai Travkin stood at the podium in the vast Kremlin Palace of Congresses and assailed every point of the president's program.

As Mr. Travkin finished, President Mikhail Gorbachev spoke from behind him on the dais.

"You obviously didn't read or listen to my report. Perhaps you don't want to. Here it is," he said dismissively, waving the document. The head of the Democratic Party of Russia, the largest opposition group in the country, submissively took it and walked away.

It was vintage Gorbachev—the Soviet leader at his imperious best, at once both confident and intimidating.

A third of the way through the semiannual gathering of the Congress of Peoples Deputies, it is already clear that Mr. Gorbachev will have little difficulty getting this body to do his bidding, despite public displays of angst and anger. But it is already obvious that more and more, such triumphs are empty victories.

"The time when the Kremlin could command is already past," Russian parliament head Boris Yeltsin told the Congress yesterday. "The republics are no longer afraid of rebukes, and no decree, even the most severe, will function if the interests of the republics have to be sacrificed for it."

Gorbachev is asking the Congress, the country's highest legislative body, to give him vastly expanded presidential powers and to back a new treaty of union that combines a strong federal center with more powers for the republics. He has clearly gained ground when it comes to his call for strong central rule, getting support not only from conservatives but also the democratic left, including figures such as Moscow Mayor Gavril Popov.

Conservatives have enthusiastically backed him in calling for discipline and order to preserve a unified Soviet state. About 50 lawmakers, including the armed forces chief of staff and the patriarch of the Russian Orthodox Church, yesterday urged Gorbachev to combat "separatists" by declaring a state of emergency and rule by decree in areas of nationalist revolt.

Prime Minister Nikolai Ryzhkov, who is expected to step down as premier following reorganization of the Cabinet structure, joined in warning against "political forces" that aim to "destroy" the Soviet state and social system. He was also critical of Gorbachev, saying past steps to strengthen his powers have brought "no significant changes."

The nationalist governments that rule in many Soviet republics have already served notice they will ignore the decisions of the Congress. This was made manifest in the empty seats that had been reserved for the delegations from republics such as Lithuania, Armenia, and Georgia, which refused to come or sent token "observers." The delegation from Moldavia walked out on Tuesday and those from Latvia and Estonia are expected to follow.

Arnold Ruutel, the scholarly president of the Baltic republic of Estonia, addressed the gathering on Tuesday morning as the representative of a foreign state, referring calmly to "relations between the USSR and the Republic of Estonia."

Even the leaders of the Central Asian republics, once thought of as bastions of conservatism, drew their own lines. Islam Karimov, the tough-talking president of Uzbekistan, supported his Kazakh neighbor in demanding that a union treaty be drafted first through agreements among the republics. Power must flow from the republics to the center, not the other way around, as Gorbachev proposes, he said.

The Congress will likely back the union treaty in principle, along with Gorbachev's proposal that the treaty be approved through referendums to be held in each republic and nationwide. Gorbachev describes the referendum as an effort to go around governments that he insists do not represent their people.

Many nationalist governments reject the idea, because they say it allows the Kremlin to win either way—if the population votes against the treaty, the republic is then required to follow an existing law on secession and vote again in five years.

Mr. Yeltsin, backing the idea of a union pact being negotiated first among republics, told the Congress: "This is not a breakup of the union. It is the only means of saving it."

Moscow Weighs Shevardnadze's Resignation

Daniel Sneider

12/24/90

In the aftermath of the dramatic resignation by Soviet Foreign Minister Eduard Shevardnadze, before the assembled Soviet parliament on Friday, this icy capital has been abuzz with troubling questions.

Why did a man considered President Mikhail Gorbachev's closest associate resign in such a public fashion, with a finger of blame clearly pointed in the president's direction? What does Mr. Shevardnadze's departure mean for the future direction of Soviet foreign policy? Is dictatorship really coming, as the white-maned Shevardnadze so eloquently warned?

In the circles around the president, Shevardnadze's action was angrily dismissed as a personal indulgence. "Absolutely disgusting" was the judgment of Arkady Maslennikov, previously the president's spokesman and now the spokesman for the Soviet parliament. "His reasons presented have nothing to do with reality."

The most common explanation for Shevardnadze's behavior is a curiously Russian one, pointing to his nationality.

"He is a Georgian and you know how emotional they are," was a typical comment. Ignoring the content of his speech, many Russians focus on Shevardnadze's angry denunciation of the right-wing colonels who repeatedly attacked him and his foreign policy.

A more sophisticated version of this was offered over dinner Friday by a top official of the State Commission on Economic Reform. Georgia, ruled by nationalists, is heading for independence. Shevardnadze may be seeking to separate himself from the Kremlin so he can grab a leadership role there.

Others reject such conspiratorial explanations in favor of the obvious—Shevardnadze meant what he said. "Shevardnadze said he wanted to resign not because two colonels attacked him," says Vitaly Korotich, editor of the liberal weekly Ogonyok. "He understands that changes are coming in this country which are impossible to fulfill without dictatorship and he doesn't want to serve on an authoritarian team."

In his and others' view, Shevardnadze resigned only one step ahead of the axe. The ouster from prominence of leading liberals such as Interior Minister Vadim Bakatin and Politburo member Alexander Yakovlev meant that Shevardnadze, the most prominent remaining liberal around the president, was next.

The public form of Shevardnadze's exit is seen by many liberals as a telling sign of Mr. Gorbachev's increasing isolation as political and economic stability deteriorate. Shevardnadze felt compelled to talk to his close friend in public, perhaps because he could not do so in private.

Even Prime Minister Nikolai Ryzhkov, considered a conservative voice among the president's men, expressed this view.

"Of all those who started the struggle for perestroika [restructuring] in 1985, after Shevardnadze's resignation, I am the only one who remains at his side now," he told Tass news agency.

And Mr. Ryzhkov, too, is expected to depart if the Congress of People's Deputies approves Gorbachev's proposed reorganization of the presidential system.

Outside of the Soviet Union, the attention has naturally focused on what Shevardnadze's resignation means for Soviet external policy, particularly in the Persian Gulf. The foreign minister spoke about how his Gulf policy of alliance with the West had been attacked, suggesting his absence could bring a policy shift, at least in emphasis.

The Soviet spin controllers have worked overtime to try to counteract such perceptions.

Gorbachev met with his minister late on Friday, an event promoted by the president's spokesman as evidence that, as Tass put it, "Soviet foreign policy will remain the same." Shevardnadze will continue to work on concluding the treaty to control strategic nuclear weapons, it was announced, a gesture clearly aimed at reassuring Washington.

But if that was Gorbachev's intention, then the speech on Saturday by KGB head Vladimir Kryuchkov carried a curiously contradictory message. In a style chillingly reminiscent of pre-glasnost days, he assailed foreign intelligence services for trying to undermine the Soviet economy and promote separatist movements. The West was accused of everything from selling tainted grain to the Soviet Union to prompting a "brain drain" of emigrating Soviet specialists.

The most important question, though, is internal: Whither the polity of the Soviet Union?

The sense of an authoritarian drift is widespread, evidenced in the conservative tone of the president's pronouncements for the past few months. The turning point came in October, when Gorbachev rejected a radical plan for economic reform and sharing power with the 15 republics, drawn up in concert with Russian leader Boris Yeltsin. Instead, he opted for a more cautious path to the market and for a vision of union that preserved a strong federal state at the center.

Gorbachev seeks to enforce this approach through a new union treaty and changes in the power structure which will imbue the president with vast authority. Both changes are before this meeting of the Congress of People's Deputies, the country's highest legislative body, for approval.

But even if the Congress votes dutifully, these measures may be resisted by the nationalist governments ruling now in many non-Russian speaking republics and by the democratic opposition, which nominally leads cities such as Moscow and Leningrad.

"The center is aware that it is impossible to implement its will without the instruments of violence," writes prominent political scientist Andranik Migranyan in the Independent Newspaper, a newly published liberal daily. He compares the present situation to Poland in 1981 when martial law was declared and the Solidarity movement outlawed. But unlike Poland, he argues, the democratic movement in the Soviet Union is very weak.

"I believe the center will be victorious in Russia and in certain other republics, because the democratic power is very fragile and inefficient," Mr. Migranyan says. Indeed, some liberal intellectuals now argue that the democrats were mistaken to take power in Moscow and elsewhere, because they have been discredited by not having real power to make changes. Moscow Mayor Gavril Popov, one of the leading democrats, told a Moscow paper this weekend that he was contemplating his own retirement.

Moscow Deputy Mayor Sergei Stankeivich told the daily Rabochaya Tribuna that the process of reform necessarily advances through alternating waves of democracy, which brings new ideas, and authoritarianism, which implements the ideas practically.

Perhaps such logic is behind the conciliatory posture adopted by Boris Yeltsin toward his rival, Gorbachev, in the last few days. He has distanced himself from Shevardnadze, instead backing "strong presidential power" as "the only thing capable of setting things in order."

If there is resistance to this course, it will likely come from the republics such as the Baltics, Georgia, and Moldavia, which have already declared their de-facto independence. On Saturday, Gorbachev issued a decree ordering the Moldavian government to rescind nationalist laws.

On Saturday, in the Lithuanian capital of Vilnius, President Vytautas Landsbergis called on citizens to prepare for "resistance, self-defense" against anticipated attempts to "impose a union treaty upon Lithuania through threats of bloodshed and use of violence."

Gorbachev Gets His Way—Again

Daniel Sneider

12/27/90

Inside the vast marbled hall of the Kremlin Palace of Congresses, Mikhail Gorbachev reigns supreme.

The deputies of the Soviet parliament, with barely a hitch, have voted dutifully for all that their leader asked. In the past three days, the Congress of People's Deputies has backed Mr. Gorbachev's reorganized and strengthened presidency, his concept of a renewed federal union, and his call for nationwide referendums to decide the issues of union and private property on land.

At press time yesterday, Gorbachev nominated Gennady Yanayev, a former trade union leader, for the post of vice president. Mr. Yanayev is an ethnic Russian and a member of the Communist Party Politburo.

Gorbachev gets powers

On Tuesday and Wednesday, the Congress approved virtually the entire package of constitutional amendments sought by the president. The laws create a powerful presidency with both executive and legislative powers. The Cabinet is now subordinate to him rather than to the parliament. A national security council is formed under the president. And he can now legislate by decree. In a gesture of balance, the laws elevate the Federation Council, on which the heads of the 15 republics sit, into a policymaking body, though with vaguely defined powers.

But outside the hall, these issues are not so easily settled. From the Baltics to Central Asia, the governments of the Soviet republics are making clear they intend to go their own way.

"I am against giving too much power to one person—it is too risky," Russian leader Boris Yeltsin gruffly told reporters on Tuesday. He angrily denounced Gorbachev's push for a referendum on land ownership, after the Russian parliament this month passed a land reform law that allows such privatization. The Russian parliament will take its own decisions, he said.

Gorbachev's approach disregards the popular will expressed in the republican parliaments, which have all issued declarations of sovereignty, Kazakh President Nursultan Nazarbayev told the weekly Literaturnaya Gazeta.

"Of course, we shouldn't let the union fall apart," said Mr. Nazarbayev. "But what kind of union treaty can we talk about in this Congress? It can only happen when the draft is approved in republican parliaments."

The Kazakh leader accused the central government of being unable to provide economic stability, at the same time it refuses to allow republics real sovereign control over their resources.

Gorbachev is eager to overcome the sense of erosion of the center's authority, particularly in the economic sphere. The economy is troubled by a breakdown of respect for the system of state orders and by the refusal to carry out contracted deliveries between republics and regions.

Republics pledge food

This issue was the subject of a Tuesday meeting of the Federation Council.

Gorbachev told the Congress yesterday that the republican leaders agreed to ensure food supplies for 1991 at a level not lower than this year. He said contracts and inter-republican agreements had reached 77 percent of their required level. But, he admitted, the republican leaders could not agree on a 1991 budget, an issue that raises the key question of who actually owns the raw materials and factories that contribute most of the funds for the Soviet budget.

Gorbachev also revealed that Prime Minister Nikolai Ryzhkov was recovering in the hospital after a heart attack. Mr. Ryzhkov has been the target of harsh political criticism over the past year for his conservatism.

The first test of the president's authority and intentions following the conclusion of the Congress, scheduled to end today or Friday morning, seems likely to come in the Baltic republics and in Moldavia. The president and other senior officials have repeatedly singled the leadership of these defiant republics out as obstacles to preserving the union.

The president issued a decree on Moldavia last weekend, giving the government 10 days to act. The decree backed the Moldavian government in its opposition to separatist movements of Russian and Turkish minorities, but called on the Moldavians to rescind nationalist acts, including establishing Romanian as the official language.

For days, reports have issued from the Baltics predicting that presidential rule, enforced through some type of martial law, would be declared shortly. So far the situation has been calm. But Moscow is undoubtedly carrying out an escalating war of nerves.

Gorbachev, according to an account by the Soviet news agency Tass of his conversation Tuesday with reporters and delegates in the hallway, spoke in harsh terms about "destructive elements . . . sponging on separatism."

The republics and the central government must rapidly agree on a division of powers but he insisted, as he has continuously, that the republics now understand the need to live together. The Baltic leaders are pursuing secession more "vigorously" because their support is disappearing, he claimed.

Military applies pressure

More subtle pressure is coming from the military, which held an unusual congress of Army representatives from Baltic-based units in Riga this week. The meeting aired complaints of ill treatment of military personnel, particularly by Latvia's government.

"The situation in Latvia is being further exacerbated by both the political struggle and the ambitions of the leaders of national and nationalistic organizations," Tass wrote on Tuesday in an account of the Riga meeting. "The military are subjected to open persecution. Insults are a currency, acts of provocation and violence, resembling terrorist actions, are increasingly frequent."

Vladimir Kryuchkov, chairman of the KGB (secret police), in a rare press conference on Tuesday, tried to soften the hard-line posture he took before the Congress last Saturday. But the cherubic KGB chief issued a carefully worded warning that if disruptions occur, "extraordinary measures may become necessary."

Such presidential moves do not mean a return to dictatorship, he said, referring to warnings last week by Foreign Minister Eduard Shevardnadze. "It will just mean restoring the order which everyone craves, from the left, from the right, and from the center."

Soviets Confront Stark Choices for Future

Daniel Sneider

1/2/91

For Soviet citizens, and for the world which looks on, the new year looms like a dark abyss. The only surety is that it will be a time of profound change. And that it will bring a reply to many unanswered questions.

After a decade of decay and five years of faltering reform, the economy is sliding into a deep crisis. Virtually all economists, both Soviet and foreign, predict that 1991 will bring an across-the-board decline, from production to trade. Severe shortages will be accompanied by explosive inflation and growing unemployment.

Will the crisis of 1991 force a radical leap to a market economy or a retreat to socialist commands?

The burst of democratic fervor that began with the spring 1989 elections for the Soviet parliament is fading, and disillusionment with democracy itself is spreading. Soviet President Mikhail Gorbachev's popularity has fallen apace with emptying shop shelves and unfulfilled promises. In the midst of a growing political vacuum, the yearning for order and a strong hand grows.

Will the political farewell warning of liberal stalwart Foreign Minister Eduard Shevardnadze that "a dictatorship is on the offensive" be realized in 1991?

Around the periphery of the Soviet Union, where nationalism and the demand for independence has taken deep root, people and their governments view Moscow as a foreign capital. But President Gorbachev is determined to renew a strong federal state, embodied in the ratification of a new treaty of union early this year.

Will 1991 be remembered as the year when the last great multinational empire finally collapsed?

The forces that are at work in the Soviet Union today owe much to the strategy for change that Gorbachev and his allies have pursued since the spring of 1985 in the name of perestroika (restructuring).

Perestroika began as a plan for radical economic reform, to lift the Soviet Union out of economic decay by introducing the use of market relations and advanced technology. Perestroika meant an end to the cold war, stopping the waste of massive resources on defense, and bringing the country out of isolation from the West.

Most of all, Gorbachev held that true economic reform could only rest on political reform—on democratization, on glasnost (openness), which would bring a free flow of information and access to the West. The force of a mobilized population was needed to break the entrenched power of the bureaucracy, embodied in the Communist Party and the vast central ministries, which would naturally resist economic reform.

In this he made a consciously different choice than that of the Chinese Communist leadership, which opened up the economy while keeping a lid on political freedom. The Chinese liberalization produced full stores, but the limits of that approach were brutally demonstrated last summer in Tiananmen Square and the subsequent retreat from economic reform.

The Soviet strategy seems to have come up against its own difficulties. Democratization has unleashed unanticipated forces of nationalism that increasingly seek freedom through independence. Starting with the three Baltic republics, followed by Moldavia, the western Ukraine, Armenia, and Georgia, the Communists have been ousted from power in election contests with openly nationalist movements.

At the same time, by delaying radical economic reform until political conditions were ripe, the government has failed to show tangible results from perestroika. Gradualism has worsened economic conditions as the command economy falls apart without a market structure to replace it. The result, particularly in the Russian-speaking heartland, is the collapse of the government's authority in favor of the kind of radical populism represented by Russian leader Boris Yeltsin. The conservative opponents of change are also strengthened, as they play upon fears of disruption.

No matter which approach to economic reform is followed—a radical "shock" or a cautious gradualism—all economists agree the country must go through a period of "stabilization." That means controlling the huge budget deficit, halting the massive printing of rubles that has been used to cover up economic collapse, lifting controlled prices and ending subsidies to state enterprises.

Only a strong government can carry out this kind of policy, argues Hungarian reform economist Janos Kornai in a recent book. But there are various kinds of "strong governments," he points out.

"A stabilization program accompanied by a great upheaval and a reinforcement of the market economy might be carried out by a repressive authoritarian administration, some military dictatorship of the Chilean or Turkish variety," he writes. But "regardless of the economic results that might be accomplished by a government whose strength lies in repressive measures, I am strongly against paying such a price for stabilization."

"The other possibility," the man considered the father of Hungary's economic reform continues, "is a government whose strength lies in the support of the people, one to which free elections have given a real popular mandate to set the economy right with a firm hand."

These two choices capture Gorbachev's own dilemma. By himself, the Soviet leader does not have the popular support to take the second path. The only way to do so would be to ally with those who do have backing—namely Mr. Yeltsin and the other republican leaders.

"Order is a wonderful thing, and obviously, everybody is yearning for it," says liberal sociologist Tatyana Zaslavskaya. "People are saying, 'There has to be some kind of government of the country!' This is a very positive development, because too many things are slipping out of control.... That's why the Yeltsin-Gorbachev confrontation is beginning to seriously alarm many people. It takes political wisdom to realize they have to work together and bear the burden together."

But to reach such an alliance, Gorbachev would have to yield significant power to the republics, to accept a concept of confederation rather than a centralized federal union. The combination of confederation and radical economic reform was agreed on last August in the "500-day program" drafted by a Gorbachev-Yeltsin team. But in October Gorbachev backed away from that deal, offering in its place a vague package of economic reforms and looser federal union.

Having hesitated to adopt a democratic version of a strong government, Gorbachev seems, at times almost without a clear decision, to have drifted toward the authoritarian option. He has achieved a restructured presidency that has both executive and legislative powers, virtually eclipsing the role of the Soviet parliament. And, as recent weeks have shown, he seems inclined to use those powers to clamp down on nationalist revolts rather than to accommodate them.

But as Swedish economist Anders Aslund predicts in his book on Soviet economic reform, the very effort to curb national unrest can undo the prospects for economic reform. "Such repression would imply centralization and have a negative impact on economic reform as well."

Worst of all, some Soviet reformers fear, by creating an authoritarian structure, Gorbachev may have paved the way for the last radical—himself—to be ousted. Moscow Mayor Gavril Popov, speaking recently on Soviet television, compared Gorbachev to failed reformer Nikita Khrushchev. One by one, Khrushchev's allies were stripped from his side until he was alone and finally ousted.

Mr. Shevardnadze, the man whom Gorbachev said first gave him the idea of perestroika, seemed to point in the same direction when he resigned Dec. 21. Speaking to Gorbachev as much as to the nation, he said: "No one knows what this dictatorship will be like, what kind of dictator will come to power, and what order will be established."

Tensions Rise in Baltics, But Ease in Moscow

Daniel Sneider

1/10/91

Lithuania's Prime Minister Kazimiera Prunskiene has fallen as a casualty in the war between the Kremlin and the Soviet republics.

The popular Lithuanian leader and her Cabinet were suddenly forced to resign on Tuesday when a battering ram of angry protesters, organized by pro-Soviet forces, intimidated the parliament into suspending a controversial economic reform policy.

The departure of the more moderate voice of Ms. Prunskiene is likely to strengthen radical forces on both the nationalist and pro-Soviet side of the political battle, most analysts say. It will lead to further polarization and prospects for confrontation with Moscow, coming on the heels of the announcement that Soviet paratroopers were being dispatched to round up young men in rebellious republics who are refusing to respond to draft calls for Soviet Army duty.

But this rising tide of tension in the Soviet Union was eased somewhat on Tuesday by the announcement that President Mikhail Gorbachev and Russian leader Boris Yeltsin had reached an agreement on financing the 1991 budget. The giant Russian Republic, which provides the majority of funds to the national budget, had earlier declared its intention to sharply reduce its contribution.

The deal has encouraged some who see a Gorbachev-Yeltsin axis as a bar to the visible drift toward right-wing authoritarianism. "Yeltsin understands that now the only way is to support the president against this turn of the tide," comments a well-informed Russian government source. And for Mr. Gorbachev, "maybe an alliance with Yeltsin is the only way to escape being overthrown."

Such thoughts may turn out to be far too optimistic, given the track record of fierce political rivalry already established between the two men. But the economic agreement certainly strengthens Gorbachev's hand, because, as the Russian source puts it, "he saves his face without needing to publicly force the Russian parliament to back down."

At the core of the budget battle is struggle over the division of powers between the central government and the republican governments. Gorbachev is seeking to consolidate a renewed federal union around a strengthened presidency, the policy course he pushed at the meeting of the Congress of People's Deputies that concluded two weeks ago.

But Mr. Yeltsin spoiled the conclusion of the Congress by refusing to sign an economic and budget agreement between the republics and the Kremlin. The Russian parliament had at first said it would allocate only 23 billion rubles ($14.3 billion at the commercial rate of exchange) to central coffers out of the 119 billion rubles expected. Later Yeltsin upped the offer. But it was still significantly short of what the central government said it needed.

The agreement signed on Tuesday now makes it possible for the delayed national budget to be passed and a division of economic powers to be ratified at a meeting of the Federation Council, in which the republics are represented, scheduled for Jan. 12.

The Tass news agency quoted Russian parliament vice-chairman Ruslan Khasbulatov saying that Yeltsin had "upheld" the Russian budget and "fulfilled the will of the Russian Supreme Soviet [parliament]" in the deal.

"The government, the Soviet president and the leaders of the Russian Federation think that a well-considered correlation between the sovereignties and rights of the republics and those of the union as a whole was found," Yuri Maslyukov, head of the State Planning Committee, told the parliament yesterday, according to Tass.

"A compromise was found," says the informed Russian source. "Russia is ready to give up practically the whole sum but the disputed part will be returned to Russia." In principle, he explains, the republic will have a say over how its money is spent on national programs. In addition, Yeltsin won greater control over the energy resources of the republic, including coal, oil, and gas resources.

Such an economic pact, if it is finalized at the Federation Council meeting on Saturday, will allow Gorbachev to increase pressure on the nationalist governments in the Baltics which have balked at joining it. Latvia and Estonia have already adopted their own price policies, massively hiking state-controlled prices as part of a move to a market-based economy. The Lithuanians, who had refused to participate in forming the budget at all, had moved to introduce similar price rises, beginning this week.

The fall of the Prunskiene government over this issue is already being gleefully interpreted by Soviet sources as evidence that independence-oriented policies will fail.

"In exploiting the attractive slogans of independence and national revival, the Lithuanian leadership embarked on a path of open violation of Soviet laws," Tass analyst Andrei Orlov wrote in a commentary on the resignation of the government. "In so doing, it failed to assess correctly the potential of economic reform and the population's preparedness for self-sacrifice."

But the situation in Lithuania is far more complicated than that account suggests. The price hikes had in fact been in preparation for a considerable period of time, discussed and approved by the parliament and anticipated by the population.

Moreover, Lithuanian government sources say, the 5,000 people who gathered in front of the parliament on Tuesday formed a well-organized crowd, pulled together by the right-wing Interfront organization, an umbrella for Russian minorities and orthodox Communists in the Baltics and other non-Russian republics. The demonstrators were exploiting the weakened state of the Prunskiene government, which has been under political attack in the parliament for months by radical elements of the nationalist Sajudis movement.

Prunskiene, a popular economist, has been the key voice arguing in favor of negotiation with Moscow.

"Radicals on both sides confronting each other will provoke incidents, which will provoke the military to intervene," predicted Soviet analyst Igor Seduyk.

Change Comes Slowly to Kirghizia

Daniel Sneider

1/10/91

The Communist Party of Kirghizia rules this Soviet republic from the marble fortress of the House of Soviets in Frunze's central square.

But not 20 minutes drive away, the ugly Soviet apartment blocks disappear. In their place, Kirghiz sheepherders on horseback wearing peaked felt caps guide their flocks across the foothills of the jagged, snow-capped peaks.

Before the revolution, this city was called Pishpek, a tiny outpost of Russian and Ukrainian settlers at the edge of the empire in Inner Asia. They lived amid the nomadic Kirghiz, a Turkic people who have herded across the mighty Tian Shan mountains since at least the second millennium BC.

Although democratization and reform have swept the Soviet Union since 1985, change has come slowly to this Central Asian republic. The combination of Communist Party orthodoxy and deep-rooted culture has earned it the reputation as the most conservative corner of the country.

But perestroika (restructuring) has finally arrived in this mountainous land, personified by the surprising October election of Askar Akayev, a gentle 46-year-old Kirghiz physicist, to the presidency of the republic. Against all odds, and all expectations, he took the job from party leader and government boss Absamat Masaliyev, who had kept Kirghizia as the only republic not to join the wave of nationalism and sovereignty declarations.

"The democrats won over the conservatives," Mr. Akayev says simply, referring to the block of 114 democratic deputies which emerged, seemingly out of nowhere, to spearhead his victory.

Much of the credit for this goes to the fledgling Democratic Movement of Kirghizstan, which was born only this past year, on May 26. It is modeled on the "popular fronts" that have led nationalist revolts in many Soviet republics.

"We were influenced first of all by the Baltic republics, who started to resist the central totalitarian system," says Kazat Akhmatov, the writer and former Communist official who co-chairs the organization.

The movement has its origins in several small groups of activists who began organizing in 1988, Akhmatov explains. The May conference united 22 groups, the most important of which were Ashar, an organization of mostly young people demanding land to build housing; Asaba, a Frunze youth organization; and the Association of Young Historians.

The program set at the May meeting called for a struggle against party rule and the command economy, for complete economic and political sovereignty within a confederation, and for "restoration of national language, history, and culture."

Economic independence, in the view of many Kirghiz, means an end to being virtually a semicolonial dependency of Moscow. In neighboring Uzbekistan, that status means giving over most of agriculture to cotton, which is shipped out raw at fixed low prices. In Kirghizia, cotton, wool, and tobacco are produced, almost none of which is processed here.

"All Central Asian republics are now a source of raw materials," says economist and Deputy Premier Turar Koichuyevich, who heads the commission on economic reform.

Kirghizia, like other Central Asian republics, suffers from a combination of economic backwardness, high population growth, and a shortage of land. The population of 4,260,000 is growing by 100,000 a year, while only 5 to 6 percent of its land is arable, the rest consisting of mountains. According to the latest Soviet census figures, the republic is 52.3 percent Kirghiz, 21.5 percent Russian, 12.9 percent Uzbek, and the rest other nationalities.

These conditions led to the tragic clash between Kirghiz and Uzbeks in the Osh region, where the eastern end of the fertile Fergana Valley extends into Kirghizia. According to Deputy Interior Minister Valeri Balikin, some 250 people died in weeks of fighting from early June last year, which was triggered by the decision of the local Kirghiz party boss to take land from an Uzbek-populated collective farm and give it to homeless Kirghiz.

The Osh events led directly to the party's defeat in October, admits Medetkan Sherimkulov, the party leader just elected as new chairman of the republic's parliament. The population still blames the party leadership for the Osh bloodshed. Beginning on June 6, thousands of mostly young demonstrators besieged the party headquarters in Frunze, demanding the resignation of Mr. Masaliyev and the Osh party boss.

"We were on the brink of an armed clash," recalls democratic leader Akhmatov, averted only by the declaration of emergency rule.

But even after this, the party leadership did not get the message.

At the party congress later that month, only Akayev, then president of the Academy of Sciences, criticized the handling of the Osh events.

The Democratic Movement launched a campaign against Masaliyev, portraying him as a conservative out of touch with Soviet President Mikhail Gorbachev's reforms. "[Masaliyev] helped us a lot," says Akhmatov, by openly aligning himself at the Soviet Communist Party Congress in early July with the most right-wing elements of the party, opposing democratization and market reforms.

When the parliament convened in October for its second session since democratic elections, the democrats surprised the party leadership by announcing that almost a third of the members had aligned themselves in a democratic bloc. The heterogeneous group includes hard-core followers of the Democratic Movement and party opponents of Masaliyev, as well as 30 Russian-speaking deputies who, although not supporting nationalist ideas, support democratization.

At the same time, the movement launched a mass hunger strike. The parliament building was surrounded by demonstrators who covered its walls with verses and jokes against Masaliyev. Inside the building, they outmaneuvered the overconfident Masaliyev, who had agreed to the creation of a new presidential system, with the president elected by the parliament. The democrats threw a wrench into the works by nominating two other party leaders, cleverly exploiting deep regional differences between north and south Kirghiz. Masaliyev failed to get a majority and under the election rules could not run again.

Late at night, the democrats contacted Akayev in Moscow, where he sat in the Soviet parliament, and urged him to run in a second round. He rushed back and faced 11 other candidates, narrowly triumphing in a runoff vote.

"As his first act, he immediately went out to meet the hunger strikers," Akhmatov says. "And they welcomed him with affection."

Since then, the scientist turned politician has moved carefully, pushing reform as far as the still-powerful but shaken party apparatus will allow it. On Dec. 12, the parliament finally passed a sovereignty declaration, dropping the words "Soviet" and "socialist" from its formal name. Land reform, including privatization of the sheep herds, is on its way, with party acquiescence.

Masaliyev yielded his post as head of parliament and the word among political observers here is that his days as party leader are also numbered. Sitting on the top floor of the House of Soviets, overlooking the ever-present bust of Vladimir Lenin, his outstretched arm pointing to some unseen goal, party heir apparent Sherimkulov chooses his words with care.

"We have to get used to living under a multiparty system and with pluralism of opinion."

Soviet Military Takes Charge In Lithuania

Daniel Sneider

1/14/91

Did Soviet democracy die in the early hours of Sunday morning in the streets of Vilnius under a hail of Soviet Army bullets?

The answer to that question depends in large part on whether Soviet President Mikhail Gorbachev ordered the tanks to roll. If he did not, the president has lost control of his own military. If he did, he would seem to have lost faith in the process of democratization he himself set in motion.

Mr. Gorbachev confused the issue Saturday when he agreed, under pressure from Russian leader Boris Yeltsin and other republican leaders, to send a commission to investigate the situation in Lithuania, where the Soviet military is fighting to install a pro-Moscow government. On Sunday, Soviet troops stormed the republic's main TV and radio center, killing at least 13 people and injuring more than 100.

Republican leaders, including representatives of the Baltic republics, left a Saturday night meeting of the Federation Council of the leadership of the Soviet republics assured that no further use of force would take place until this mission was complete. Only hours later, military action began.

"Gorbachev decided to speed it up and finish everything before the delegation arrives in Vilnius," suggests a well-informed Soviet journalist who did not wish to be identified. "Then the delegation will arrive to find 'order' restored."

The commission arrived yesterday and went to the parliament building, where the elected Lithuanian government and tens of thousands of supporters remained behind barricades.

What is clear is that the democratically elected government of Lithuania is being overthrown by the Soviet military. The Army is putting in its place a "Committee for National Salvation," a thin veil for the rump of Soviet Communist Party loyalists.

Both in manner and almost to the precise detail, the events unfolding in the Lithuanian capital follow the pattern of the 1968 Soviet Army ouster of the liberal Czechoslovakian government. Then, as now, the Army actions were portrayed as the response to a group of "patriots."

A similar process appears to be under way in both Latvia and Estonia, the two neighboring Baltic republics where democratic governments are also pursuing independence. According to reports reaching Moscow Sunday morning, Soviet tanks rolled through the streets of Riga, the Latvian capital, late Saturday night. Estonian Radio reports that the roads to Riga are closed by Soviet troops. A mass rally called by the Latvian Popular Front, the nationalist movement, was scheduled to take place yesterday.

At a Saturday evening press conference, Estonian Prime Minister Edgar Savisaar predicted that the events in

Lithuanian would be repeated in Estonia and Latvia. "There is real evidence that they do not even have sufficient support from the Russian population [in those republics], so they are trying to use the force of the Army."

If he made this move, Gorbachev would seem to be unconcerned about the reaction from the West.

"His only will is to preserve his power at any price," the Soviet journalist says bitterly. "Now I understand his own power is much dearer to him even than friendship with Bush and the West. Now their hands are free. There is no more fear of Western reaction because the West is too occupied with the Gulf [crisis]."

United States Secretary of State James Baker III sharply criticized Moscow yesterday for using force in Lithuania, which he said would endanger the US-Soviet partnership.

In Moscow, thousands of democrats rallied yesterday under banners warning: "Today Lithuania, Tomorrow Latvia and Estonia, The Day After Russia." The Democratic Russia faction of the Russian parliament called on Sunday for an emergency session of the parliament to respond to the Lithuania crisis.

Hopes that the conflict could be averted were raised on Saturday night following the Federation Council meeting, whose morning session was devoted entirely to the Lithuanian crisis. Interior Minister Boris Pugo and Defense Minister Dmitri Yazov presented what has become the official version of events—that chaos and anarchy had developed in Lithuania, that the Lithuanian government was no longer in control of the situation, and that the Army was intervening solely to restore legal order.

This account was strongly disputed by Egidius Bickauskas, the Lithuanian representative to Moscow, who attended the meeting as an observer. He was supported by Mr. Yeltsin, whose parliament had issued a strong statement denouncing the use of force in the Baltics. According to Mr. Bickauskas, the leaders of many republics spoke expressing the same position, including the leaders of Byelorussia, Moldavia, Latvia, Estonia, and Uzbekistan, calling for a political solution.

Gorbachev was described as being surprised by the views of the republic leaders.

"He was quite satisfied with the report given by Interior Minister Pugo and he was surprised at the reaction of many republics," Mr. Savisaar told reporters.

"What is obvious for everyone is not obvious for the president," Bickauskas observed.

At one point in the meeting, Savisaar told Gorbachev that the head of the Baltic Military District had informed the Estonian government that about 2,000 paratroopers would be sent to Tallinn yesterday. The decision ran counter to what had been agreed in negotiations between the Estonian government and the Defense Ministry. Both Marshal Yazov and the president, the Estonian prime minister recounted, "said they had heard nothing about it. Yazov said if any paratroopers appear in Tallinn, it must be considered a provocation."

The intervention of the republics compelled Gorbachev to propose sending a commission composed of several republican leaders, including nationalist Armenian President Levan Ter-Petrosyan, to provide an accurate account of what was happening.

"Everyone agreed that this problem can't be settled by force—it can be settled only through political means," Uzbek President Islam Karimov told reporters after the meeting. Even the Lithuanian representative, speaking to reporters later, greeted this as a "positive" development, as did Lithuanian President Vytautas Landsbergis.

"Today's meeting showed the Federation Council is able to act as a collective force," Bickauskas said.

The events of the next hours dashed such hopes in brutal fashion. A Soviet source says Bickauskas tried to call Gorbachev during the night, but was only told the president would be informed in the morning of his call.

Soviets Present Own Version of Baltic Events

Daniel Sneider

1/15/91

The crisis in Lithuania has brought a rebirth of Soviet propaganda methods.

The official news media have portrayed the military crackdown on the democratic government in Lithuania in terms unrecognizable to Western eyewitnesses.

From the start, the Soviet people have been told that Soviet troops intervened to support the demands of the local population for "order," ending conditions of chaos. Here is a chronology of the Soviet media campaign:

Jan. 7: The Defense Ministry announces deployment of paratrooper units to seven republics, including the three Baltic republics, "to help enforce the draft."

Jan. 8: About 5,000 mostly Russian demonstrators organized by the Communist Party assault Lithuania's parliament in a protest against price increases. The nationalist-controlled parliament reverses the price policy, forcing the resignation of the Cabinet. "The crisis of power in Lithuania is intensifying," the Tass news agency reports.

Rafik Nishanov, the chairman of the Soviet parliament's Council on Nationalities, tells parliament that the Lithuanian population demands order to end the "numerous violations of basic human rights, the defilement of Soviet soldiers' graves and monuments, and disregard for the main provisions of the Soviet Constitution."

Jan. 9: Lt. Gen. Franz Markovsky of the Soviet Army General Staff tells Soviet television that paratroopers will not perform "gendarme functions" and that "the military command is not planning a military coup in any of the Soviet republics."

Mr. Nishanov, on the instructions of Soviet President Mikhail Gorbachev, meets a group of unnamed representatives of "Lithuanian public and democratic organizations" who demand "direct presidential rule in Lithuania to protect human rights and ensure security and normal living conditions." Soviet media play up reports of a Communist rally in Vilnius demanding to end the "paralysis of power."

Jan. 10: Mr. Gorbachev sends a message to Lithuania's parliament in which he threatens to respond to demands to impose presidential rule from "numerous" organizations and citizens unless the republic revokes its pro-independence laws and follows the Soviet Constitution.

The Lithuanian Communist Party organizes strikes in enterprises mainly manned by Russian workers to demand dissolution of parliament and presidential rule.

A new prime minister and Cabinet are elected. Lithuanian President Vytautas Landsbergis rejects Gorbachev's ultimatum. Tass reports "the Lithuanian leaders are whipping up tension, using as a pretext the appeal of the Soviet president."

Jan. 11: A previously unknown "Congress of Democratic Forces of Lithuania" led by the Communist Party sends an ultimatum to the government demanding it respond to Gorbachev's appeal by 3 p.m. local time. Otherwise, "a Committee for the National Salvation of Lithuania will be formed to take over the future of the Lithuanian Soviet Socialist Republic."

Soviet troops storm key facilities, including Lithuanian defense department and publishing house, a move Tass describes as a measure "to return property to the legitimate owner—the Communist Party Central Committee."

Jan. 12: The newly created Lithuanian Committee for National Salvation issues a statement: "The republican authorities have lost control over the course of events and are trying to retain their influence through deceit and demagoguery. . . . The National Salvation Committee considers it its duty to take all power and avert the economic crisis and a fratricidal war."

Jan. 13: At 1:00 a.m., Soviet troops assault the television and radio center, leaving at least 13 dead and more than 100 injured. At 9:29 a.m., Tass briefly reports the "incident" saying the clash left two dead, including one serviceman, and about 30 wounded.

Later Tass says: "Since anti-Soviet broadcasts were constantly conducted through the channels of national television and radio and hostile remarks against the leadership of the USSR were voiced, the leadership of the National Salvation Committee decided to bring state television and radio under control."

Tass claims troops fired only after "aggressive behavior by a group of militants." At 3:57 in the afternoon, it cites Lithuanian officials reporting that 13 people were killed and 112 injured.

On the evening TV news, Interior Minister Boris Pugo, repeating Tass's version of events, denies allegations of a military coup as "groundless rumors," and says the steps were taken in response to a violation of the rights of part of Lithuania's population.

Soviets Shift Tactics After Crackdown in Lithuania

Daniel Sneider

1/15/91

As a tense truce took hold yesterday in the Lithuanian capital, the government of President Mikhail Gorbachev is facing a rising tide of anger over the bloody assault early Sunday morning by Army troops on unarmed Lithuanian nationalists.

The strong intervention of leaders of republican governments, led by Russian leader Boris Yeltsin, appears to have halted—for now—the military overthrow of the Lithuanian nationalist government.

Lithuanian President Vytautus Landsbergis told his parliament yesterday that Mr. Gorbachev, in a phone conversation with him, had authorized a delegation of republican leaders which arrived in Vilnius on Sunday to negotiate on his behalf.

Meanwhile, Gorbachev and his ministers arrived at the Soviet parliament yesterday to face a barrage of hostile questions about the legality and authority of their acts. Interior Minister Boris Pugo and Defense Minister Dmitri Yazov offered a contradictory and less than credible explanation for the events that led to the death of at least

13 people when troops seized the Lithuanian television and radio center in a pre-dawn Sunday attack.

In his speech, Gorbachev himself was silent about the affair, confining himself to the announcement of his candidate for the new prime minister and several deputy premiers. He nominated Finance Minister Valentin Pavlov as the premier, signaling continuity with the conservative economic policies of Premier Nikolai Ryzhkov's government.

But in remarks later to reporters, Gorbachev endorsed the version of events offered by his ministers, claiming the government was only responding to "anti-Constitutional" acts by the Lithuanian government. He claimed he heard about the Sunday attack only early that morning. He also played down the impact of the negative reaction from the West, cautioning that the Baltics were a complex situation that should not become the basis for confrontation between the Soviet Union and the West.

Gorbachev's ministers repeated the defense offered throughout the crisis by the official media. The main cause of the crisis "is the policy of the Lithuanian leadership," asserted Marshal Yazov, including "the adoption of a number of hasty anticonstitutional measures which led to widespread infringement of human rights." The Lithuanians, "using democratic slogans, exerted purposeful and concerted efforts to establish a bourgeois-type dictatorship," the military leader said.

The interior minister described a series of events that he claimed led to political chaos and "an extremely dangerous confrontation" between the nationalists and people demanding establishment of presidential rule. Mr. Pugo, who used to head the KGB (secret police) in the Baltic republic of Latvia, contended the security forces has acted to halt provocative "anti-Soviet propaganda" being broadcast by the Lithuanian government at the request of the shadowy Committee for National Salvation, whose leaders he refused even to name.

But while making this elaborate justification for a virtual attempted coup against a democratically elected government, the two senior Kremlin officials claimed that the decisions were made by the officials on the scene. "I can say definitely that there were no orders from the center," Pugo stated, evoking derisive cries of disbelief in the chamber. The defense minister went so far as to pin responsibility on the Vilnius garrison command, which he said acted to enforce law and order in keeping with the regulations of the Soviet Army.

Deputy after deputy rose to challenge this version of events, to question how it is that an unknown organization can order the Army into action against an established government. The only identified members of the Committee on National Salvation are two leaders of the small pro-Soviet Lithuanian Communist Party, deputy Moscow mayor and parliament member Sergei Stankeivich pointed out to reporters during a break.

"It is fantastic how a military commander reacted to the appeals of an underground committee," Mr. Stankeivich, a liberal leader, said. "How can one call it a struggle for power?"

Maj. Vladimir Lopatin, the leader of a reform movement within the military, totally rejected the idea, based on his own military experience, that a garrison commander would make such a decision on his own.

That skepticism was even expressed by staunch Gorbachev ally, dissident historian Roy Medvedev, also a Communist Party Central Committee member. "There may have been no orders from the center but I'm convinced that the center was fully informed," he told reporters in the hall. "The very fact that Yazov did not repeal the order of the Vilnius commander amounts to agreement."

While the Baltic crisis is far from over, Gorbachev has clearly been forced to recalculate his tactics, particularly because of the forceful intervention of the popular Russian leader Boris Yeltsin.

Yeltsin clearly worries that if the Kremlin succeeds in overthrowing the elected democratic governments of the Baltics, his radical Russian government is also in danger.

Soviets Try to Mollify West as Grip Tightens at Home

Daniel Sneider

1/17/91

While the Lithuanian parliament waited nervously behind homemade barricades for the tanks to come, a smiling Mikhail Gorbachev appeared before his parliament on Tuesday to present his new foreign minister.

Alexander Bessmertnykh, hastily flown in from his post as the Soviet ambassador to Washington, wasted no time in assuring a worried world. The Soviet government would pursue a "political solution" to the crisis in the Baltics. And as the world seemed headed for war in the Gulf, Soviet foreign policy, including support for the anti-Iraq coalition, holds firm.

"The policy of new thinking will be preserved, will continue and develop," he told the Supreme Soviet.

Hours later, Mr. Gorbachev appeared again before the parliament. He angrily denounced a string of enemies who have defied him, from Russian President Boris Yeltsin and the democratic press to the leaders of Latvia and Lithuania.

As the Baltic and Gulf crises unfold in parallel, Gorbachev's government increasingly shows two faces—one to the outside world and one at home. The move to the right in domestic affairs, spearheaded by the crackdown on the nationalist governments in the republics, has not yet been mirrored by any retreat from the post-cold war outlook labeled "new thinking."

Some Soviet analysts argue that there is a clear logic to that apparent contradiction. At a time when the Kremlin is struggling to keep control at home, it seeks to avoid any conflict abroad, especially with the West.

"Foreign policy is the area that Gorbachev will try to keep as stable as possible in order not to aggravate the situation," says Alexei Izyumov, an expert at the prestigious USA-Canada Institute. "I don't think that foreign policy will suffer if events don't become just uncontrollable."

Other Soviets put the relationship between external and internal events in more sinister fashion. "Moscow figures that, when in the Gulf war thousands upon thousands of people may perish, the West won't pay attention to one or two dozen people killed in the Baltic states," Mavrik Wolfson, head of the Latvian parliament's foreign affairs committee, told the weekly Kommersant.

Increasingly there is concern, however, that the violence in the Baltics will seriously harm ties to the West. If no adequate accounting is given, warned former Interior Minister Vadim Bakatin, "all our international contacts will be endangered."

The choice of Mr. Bessmertnykh was dictated not by the last week's events in Lithuania, Mr. Izyumov says, but by the need to ease Western concern about a Soviet policy shift following the dramatic resignation of Foreign Minister Eduard Shevardnadze on Dec. 20. The popular Soviet official left with a public warning of coming "dictatorship."

Bessmertnykh is well-liked in Washington and seen as a Shevardnadze man. He is a professional diplomat and a specialist on the United States and, although he is not a political figure, his leanings are considered liberal.

Washington would have been far less pleased with the most likely alternatives being discussed in Moscow—Yevgeni Primakov, a top presidential aide, or Alexander Dzasokhov, chairman of the parliament's foreign affairs committee. Both are senior Communist Party officials, but equally important, both are long associated with the Kremlin's policy of wooing radical third-world regimes.

Mr. Primakov, an Arab specialist, emerged as a key player in Soviet Gulf policy as Gorbachev's special envoy on two missions to Baghdad, where US officials felt he was softening the Soviet stance. But some Soviet analysts say he didn't get the Foreign Ministry job because he didn't want it, preferring to emerge as the head of a new National Security Council where he will continue to exert considerable influence.

In an interview with Komsomolskaya Pravda published on Tuesday, Primakov repeated the demand for unconditional Iraqi withdrawal from Kuwait.

But he also argued on behalf of Iraqi President Saddam Hussein, his acquaintance of 21 years, for accommodating Iraqi concerns on a range of issues, including access to the sea, a share of the Rumallah oil field, protection against attack and removal of the US military presence after withdrawal, and settlement of the Arab-Israeli conflict.

Perhaps the most telling of Primakov's comments was his observation that although Saddam was surprised by the Soviet reaction, he understands the Soviet Union is seeking a peaceful solution, unlike "the other superpowers."

Meanwhile, the Soviets are seeking to quiet Western concerns about retreat on the superpower arms control front. There have been charges that the Soviet military violated the spirit of the treaty reducing conventional forces in Europe by moving massive forces east of the Urals, outside the treaty's range. And the slow pace of negotiations on the strategic nuclear arms pact in Geneva has raised worries that long-sought agreement would not be ready in time for a planned US-Soviet summit in mid-February.

Maj. Gen. Vladimir Kouklev, a senior Soviet negotiator, presented a soothing picture in a Monitor interview, acknowledging possible "mistakes" in the data on conventional forces submitted by the Soviets and predicting the issue would be resolved in coming weeks. Soviet nuclear arms negotiators recently returned from Geneva, he added. "We reviewed all outstanding problems and felt, given the desire for resolution, they can be settled by the known time limit."

Moscow's Power-Grab in Latvia Repeats Lithuania

Daniel Sneider

1/22/91

A violent assault by Soviet special forces on the headquarters of the Latvian Interior Ministry in Riga late Sunday night provides dramatic evidence that the Baltic crisis is far from over.

According to reports from Latvia, at least four people were killed and 10 injured when a unit of "black berets," as the special Soviet Interior Ministry troops are called, made an attempt to seize the Latvian government building just after 9 p.m. local time. In a 90-minute gun battle in the center of the city, the troops seized several floors of the building, despite resistance from a small number of Latvian police inside. They withdrew after five hours of negotiations between Latvian Premier Ivar Godmanis and Soviet Interior Minister Boris Pugo in Moscow.

The reported victims of the attack included a Latvian television journalist and two Latvian policemen killed, and a Finnish television journalist and Soviet TV cameraman injured.

Although the precise circumstances of the attack are disputed, there is little question that the events in Latvia are following the pattern of Moscow- and Communist Party-inspired confrontation that led to the tragic bloodshed in Lithuania only a week before.

As in Lithuania, a Communist-controlled "Salvation Committee" has claimed to seize power, ousting a democratically elected nationalist government. And Soviet military forces have been deployed in a manner calculated to raise tensions and to justify the claims coming from Moscow that "chaos" in the Baltic republic requires the imposition of direct presidential rule.

The escalation of tension in Latvia came only hours after Russian democratic activists organized a massive demonstration in central Moscow, numbering at least 100,000, to protest the "danger of dictatorship" and express solidarity with the Baltic republics. The demonstration backed Russian leader Boris Yeltsin, who has emerged as the champion of all the republican governments against the dictates of the Kremlin.

In a tough speech yesterday to the Russian parliament, which opened a week early because of the Baltic crisis, the popular Russian leader accused the government of President Mikhail Gorbachev of "toppling constitutional bodies" in the Baltics.

Stressing the "critical" nature of the crisis, Mr. Yeltsin pointed to the right-wing turn of the Gorbachev government in recent weeks. Indeed, many of Gorbachev's best known liberal advisers, including former Foreign Minister Eduard Shevardnadze, Alexander Yakovlev, and economists Stanislav Shatalin and Nikolai Petrakov, have left the government. But, Yeltsin argued, "the reactionary turn has not yet reached a stage of no return."

Yeltsin's strategy of combating the right-wing shift is centered on forming an alliance of republican governments, with the Ukraine, Russia, Byelorussia, and Kazakhstan at its core.

The special Interior Ministry forces, called the OMON, have been the spearhead of Kremlin pressure on the nationalist Latvian government, starting on Jan. 2, when they seized the central publishing house. The OMON regiment is directly responsible to Interior Minister Pugo, a former head of the Latvian Communist Party and of the Latvian KGB (secret police).

As tensions rose in Lithuania, the Latvian government, elected by an overwhelming majority last spring, took steps to defend itself, including building barricades around the parliament and other key facilities.

On Saturday, the "All-Latvian Public Salvation Committee," a group whose only known backing comes from the Communist Party, issued a statement claiming the government had brought Latvia to the "brink of a national catastrophe" and was seeking to establish a "bourgeois dictatorship."

The "committee," claiming to act on behalf of "the working people," proclaimed that it was seizing "the whole of state power," dissolving the parliament and the government.

At the same time, the OMON forces were issuing their own dire warnings, claiming that they were threatened by the police forces loyal to the Latvian government. In an article published Saturday in the Soviet Communist Party daily Pravda, the OMON regiment commander Cheslav Mlynnik is quoted as saying, "We are ready to resist the attack if it happens." The article cites undocumented threats to OMON family members. "We warn," the OMON commander said, "if only one hair drops from the head of our relatives, we will answer."

These developments now seem to have been part of the preparation for the assault that took place on Sunday night. The account being circulated by pro-Moscow sources, including the Tass news agency, claims that the troops were responding to the kidnap and rape of an officer's wife, followed by threats to harm others unless Latvian nationalists detained during the seizure of the printing house were released. When the special forces came to "negotiate" with the Latvian Interior Ministry, the account continues, they were fired on without warning. "The detail was forced to return fire and capture the republican Interior Ministry," Tass said.

But Western journalists present in Riga dispute this version. According to a report from the British Broadcasting Corporation, two busloads and two carloads of troops arrived and opened fire without provocation.

The Latvian parliament, meeting in emergency session, decided to form special militia units to defend the government following the attack.

Soviet Power Struggle Looms

Daniel Sneider

1/25/91

The central axis of political conflict in the Soviet Union has moved from the Baltic republics to Moscow. The future of Soviet politics will rest on the outcome of the struggle for power between Mikhail Gorbachev and Boris Yeltsin.

The crackling tension between the two most powerful figures in Soviet politics has risen to a high pitch. The hopes that they might unite in a pragmatic center-left alliance to advance radical reform has faded, virtually without trace.

Mr. Gorbachev, the Soviet president, has firmly placed himself in the ranks of those who assert that only strong central rule can keep the Soviet Union intact, even when it means the use of force. Mr. Yeltsin, the Russian president, has chosen to champion an alliance of nationalist governments among the Soviet republics as a means of preserving some union and as a virtual alternative power structure.

Both men are positioning themselves for the next clash, within days, when the Federation Council meets to discuss the Baltic events. It is not clear who holds the balance of power among the 14 other republican leaders who make up the Council. Nor does anyone know whether the Council, which Gorbachev promised would have enhanced powers, can emerge as a powerful institutional counterbalance to the Soviet president.

"The political confrontation has reached a critical stage," Anatoly Karpuchev wrote Wednesday in an anti-Yeltsin commentary in the Communist Party daily Pravda. Yeltsin's backers "want the Federation Council to take power in the union and Boris Yeltsin will play a major role in it."

Gorbachev made his feelings clear on Tuesday night when he appeared before the Soviet and foreign press in an attempt to persuade the world that there was no change in the direction of his policies. At first, he spoke in seemingly conciliatory terms about the need to prevent "an escalation of antagonism" in the Baltics and to "secure civil accord and cooperation."

But moments later the Soviet leader directed angry words at Yeltsin, though not by name, for his actions in support of the Baltic republics and for his call on Russian soldiers not to turn their arms against democratically elected governments. "Such irresponsible statements are fraught with serious dangers, especially when they come from the Russian leadership," he said.

Yeltsin, speaking the previous day to the Russian Republic's parliament, which he heads, had warned that the Baltic events are only one manifestation of a "reactionary changeover." But "if the republics find a common and agreed political line, they will be able to thwart such attempts."

The Yeltsin strategy, which he has been pursuing for months, rests on ignoring the central government as much as possible and creating a network of horizontal ties between republics. Economic pacts have now been signed with most republics and key political treaties with the Baltic republics of Estonia and Latvia. A final agreement with Lithuania is being negotiated. Instead of a union treaty imposed from the Kremlin, Yeltsin proposes to conclude an agreement first among the three Slavic republics (Russia, Byelorussia, and the Ukraine), along with heavily Russian-populated Kazakhstan. Later, republics such as Uzbekistan, the largest in Central Asia, could join in.

"Of course, it leads to the weakening of the center," political scientist Andranik Migranyan commented in a major article published on Wednesday in the liberal daily Komsomolskaya Pravda. "But from both moral and rational points of view, it's preferable to the restoration of control through force."

For Yeltsin, supporting the Baltics is a matter of personal political survival, argues Mr. Migranyan, because "the next target is the Russian leadership and he himself." Indeed, Yeltsin is the target of a well-orchestrated and growing propaganda campaign in the conservative Communist press and on central television. A letter campaign, a classic tactic, has opened up in the pages of the party-controlled press.

"We are shocked by your political cynicism, Boris Nikolaievich," wrote a group of mostly Russian historians from Moldavia in Sovietskaya Rossiya on Jan 18. "Your support of totalitarian chauvinist regimes in the Baltic republics is an act of treachery against Russians, Poles,

Byelorussians, and other national minorities of this and other regions."

Although Yeltsin can still draw on a deep well of personal popularity, he is far from immune to such assaults, particularly appeals to Russian nationalism. Within the Russian parliament, the Communist bloc has sufficient strength to make Yeltsin move cautiously on pushing through a resolution backing his Baltic policy. A group of Communist deputies is offering its own resolution, censuring Yeltsin for committing "a number of unlawful and hasty actions and exceeding his powers," specifically citing the treaties with Estonia and Latvia.

Moreover, Russian efforts to introduce a more radical economic reform policy on their own, or even in collaboration with the other republics, has been largely without result. "The move toward growing independence and sovereignty is not based on reality," says Rair Simonyan, an economist with the Institute of World Economy and International Relations. "They have neither the specialists, the channels, nor the means to put any independent policy into effect."

That has been graphically demonstrated by the reaction to the shock monetary reform announced on Tuesday night by the Soviet government, pulling all 50 and 100 ruble notes out of circulation. Although the reform is supposedly aimed at controlling inflation during a transition to a market economy, economists such as Mr. Simonyan assail it for its "confiscatory character." In effect, it freezes the accounts of households and enterprises, hitting particularly hard at people on low, fixed incomes.

But despite the manifestly unpopular nature of the move, not to mention its dubious economic effectiveness, the Russian government on Wednesday backed it. Russian Premier Ivan Silayev announced only that it would prolong the three-day period for turning in old money and would increase the amount of old notes that pensioners can exchange.

Soviets Face Muslim Activists

Daniel Sneider

2/5/91

As the clock nears 2 on a Friday afternoon, the bustling streets of Tashkent's Old City fall strangely silent. The men selling watermelons stop and turn to face the low brick walls of Tilah Sheik mosque.

An imam sings out "Allah Akbar," the traditional Islamic call to prayer. Inside the packed courtyard, men young and old, wearing Islamic tubeteikas—black, square, embroidered caps—touch their heads to the ground.

The scene here in the capital of the Soviet republic of Uzbekistan occurs all across Soviet Central Asia, where three quarters of the Soviet Union's estimated 45 million Muslims live.

After decades of official repression, Islam has emerged as a powerful and visible force across this inner Asian zone of the Soviet empire. Increasingly, the local Communist leadership seeks to coopt Islam, as well as nationalism, to preserve its authority.

Across the street from the mosque is the headquarters of the Muslim Religious Board for Central Asia and Kazakhstan, the official religious organization headed by Mukhamadsadyk Mamayusupov, a mufti. He is treated as a respected public figure, appearing on television and called on by the Communist officialdom as a force for moral and social order.

The Communists and the mufti have a common enemy—the small but growing movement of Islamic fundamentalists. Mostly young, inspired by fundamentalist movements elsewhere in the Islamic world, they are emerging from a broad, underground movement of unofficial Islamic worship, to begin to form political organizations. They preach a doctrine of purified religious life and of Pan-Islamic brotherhood that is aimed against the Communist state and what they view as its allies in a corrupt official Islamic establishment.

Behind the whitewashed clay walls of the Old City, through a narrow wooden door into a packed earth courtyard, some of the leaders of this fundamentalist movement gather to talk to a Western reporter. These are the people the mufti and the communists have labeled Wahhabis, referring to the Sunni fundamentalist movement based in Saudi Arabia. Sitting around a low table in a carpeted room, they speak of their cause.

"We started our party because the mufti did not work on behalf of the Muslims in Uzbekistan," says Tulkan Irgashov, leader of the Hizbullah Party. "Our mufti called us Wahhabis, but we never called ourselves that. Wahhabism emerged because there were people who wanted to live solely according to the Koran. There were many people who only wanted material things and luxury and betrayed the Koran. The same thing is happening in Uzbekistan and the mufti has done nothing to fight this.

"I have four children and I don't live in luxury," he said, thrusting his short-bearded face forward. "But there are many people who have money which they did not get by sweat and labor. And this is wrong."

His voice raises in anger and his gold teeth flash. "The Muslims are united," he says. "We are one people. There should be no national borders. The mufti is a puppet in the hands of the KGB [the secret police] and he does not help Muslims to have free contact with the rest of the world."

"We don't want our soldiers to be used against Iraq," Mr. Irgashov says, slamming his fist on the table, speaking about a month before the start of the Gulf war. "We don't want a second Afghanistan. The Soviet Communists sent Muslim soldiers to Afghanistan where they were killed and had to kill fellow Muslims."

Sadeksalevich Sharafuddinhajaev speaks more softly about the issues that the movement is pressing. Arabic must be taught in the schools, he says, so that the people can read the Koran.

"Today, although people are performing namaz [the daily prayers], they do not read the Koran and do not understand it properly," he explains. "When an individual knows Koran and Sunna well, he prays in a state of cleanliness."

Religious law, the sharia, should be enforced, including ending the separation of church and state and allowing polygamy, he adds.

The fundamentalists call for reviving the pre-revolutionary entity known as Turkestan, reuniting what Vladimir Lenin and Joseph Stalin broke into Uzbekistan, Kirghizia, Tajikistan, Turkmenistan, and Kazakhstan.

"Now we have one military district and one mufti but five presidents," Mr. Sharafuddinhajaev says. "There should be one president. We are the people of Islam . . . . We are not different nationalities."

The fundamentalists echo the calls for economic independence and complaints of colonial dependency that are now standard even for the Communist leaderships in Central Asia.

"We need capitalist technology and Islamic ideology," Sharafuddinhajaev argues.

The fundamentalists recount charges of corruption against the mufti, accusations that he sells Korans donated by the Saudi government for money, which is a violation of the Koran. Unaccounted-for funds are being siphoned into his private business, they say, reeling off figures from documents.

The mufti and the Religious Board, the angry Islamic activists continue, work closely with the authorities.

About 7,000 Muslims gathered at the Tilah Sheik mosque late last August to protest the alleged corruption of the mufti and demand an investigation. The authorities persuaded the demonstrators to disperse with promises of action.

But a later gathering in mid-September, timed to coincide with an "international Islamic conference" in Tashkent, an official showcase of new liberal policies toward religion in Central Asia, was dispersed by Interior Ministry special forces, the activists say.

The term Wahhabi first emerged in February 1989, when a Muslim political demonstration led to the removal of the previous mufti, according to Abdur Rashid, a nationalist activist and former writer for Muslims of the Soviet East, the official journal of the Religious Board.

But the roots of the movement go back to the unofficial Islamic movement, which carried out religious services in secret. They were strongly opposed to the official, recognized imams, who are widely viewed as under the control of the KGB and the Communist Party.

The fundamentalists are particularly strong in the rural areas of Uzbekistan, in the fertile but impoverished Fergana Valley, where most of the people live.

Unofficial religious leaders "stayed in provincial places where the authorities didn't pay much attention, unlike cities such as Samarkand, Tashkent, and Bukhara, where the tourists go," Mr. Rashid explains.

A wave of official repression was unleashed against the movement in the late 1970s. But through contacts with Muslim students from abroad and in recent years from Saudi and other missionaries, Rashid recounts, "the idea of Muslim revolution, of Islamic renaissance, got in here despite the official ideology."

The Iranian revolution had particular impact in Tajikistan, which shares a Persian culture, and in Turkmenistan, which borders Iran. Together with Uzbekistan, these are the strongholds of the fundamentalists.

The Westernized intellectuals who lead the Uzbek nationalist movement Birlik (Unity) are uncomfortable with the growing political role of the Islamic movement.

"For us, the No. 1 priority is motherland and unity," says Mahmud Ali Makmudov, secretary of the Uzbek Writers Union and an advocate of an independent, united Turkestan. "Religion comes next."

"We sometimes argue with [the fundamentalists] and say you are just another form of communism," says poet Mirza Tura, a nationalist activist.

Sometime after 1 p.m., Irgashov stops his fierce lecture and glances at his watch.

"It is time for prayer," he says, rising abruptly and disappearing quickly out into the street with his brothers behind him.

Soviet Critics Say Rift With US Over Gulf War Aims Is Likely

Daniel Sneider

2/21/91

Whatever the Iraqi response to Soviet President Mikhail Gorbachev's plan to end the Gulf war, his diplomatic effort has already yielded one result. It has revealed the existence of a clear divergence of interests between the Soviet Union and the United States.

Soviet officials deny a split with the US over Gulf policy. They back unconditional Iraqi withdrawal from Kuwait, but unlike the US, seek to ensure the survival of Saddam Hussein's regime.

The gap that has opened up between the two superpowers, which began the Gulf conflict last August in an unprecedented posture of unity, has raised the question here of whether the broader US-Soviet entente is endangered.

"For five or six years, the goal of our foreign policy has been friendly relations with the United States and other Western nations," comments Sergei Blagovolin, a senior analyst at the influential Institute of World Economy and International Relations. "But now I'm not sure that it is so." Mr. Blagovolin has been a leading advocate of partnership with the West, even including military cooperation.

Commentary in Red Star, the daily paper of the Soviet Defense Ministry, was even more pointed. "The interests of the USSR and the USA do not coincide at all," wrote Red Star commentator Y. Budkov, referring to Blagovolin and others by name. "That is why the formation of a united front for us would mean nothing but serving the interests of the USA."

Such comments are by no means hard to find these days in the Soviet press. The tone of the Communist Party daily Pravda is uniformly critical of American policy, as is Red Star. But even more liberal dailies, such as the government daily Izvestia, sometimes reflect such views.

Izvestia foreign affairs commentator Stanislav Kondrashov argued last week, for example, that the Soviet Union was a "Eurasian nation" whose views "cannot fuse with those of the West, as it was erroneously supposed." The Gulf war, he says, is "the first experience of cooperation with the US in the post-cold-war epoch." But the results prove that the US pursues its own aims, "and from us they want only the confirmation of our loyalty . . . which they interpret as they please."

Liberals such as Blagovolin find disturbing evidence in the Soviet peace initiative of a return to the pro-third-world tilt that was characteristic of Soviet cold war foreign policy. The appearance of Yevgeni Primakov, Mr. Gorbachev's Gulf envoy, in a Soviet television interview Tuesday revealed views "much closer to Saddam than to the coalition," Blagovolin said.

Indeed, speaking confidently of a positive outcome to the Gorbachev peace plan, Mr. Primakov at times sounded like a lawyer for the Iraqi regime. He warned sharply against launching a ground attack at this moment. Such a decision would only be made, he said, by those who want to destroy Saddam's regime and damage Iraq as a nation.

In short, the Soviet initiative aims to find a solution that will allow Saddam and Iraq to remain intact as a force in the region. Although the details of the Soviet plan remain unrevealed at this writing, knowledgeable Soviet experts deny that it involves clear linkage of Iraqi withdrawal from Kuwait to other conditions.

"The Soviet idea is not linkage, but an invisible package," says Vitaly Naumkin, deputy director of the Institute of Oriental Studies, the think tank formerly headed by Primakov. "We are not speaking about conditions but what will happen after withdrawal. Saddam Hussein has a right to know what will be."

Mr. Naumkin, speaking Wednesday, before the expected return of Iraqi Foreign Minister Tariq Aziz with a reply to the Soviet plan, claimed to be undisturbed by the apparent US rejection of the terms of the plan. He referred to "unexpected things" that may emerge in the hours ahead. But, he admits, "the problem is whether we accept [Saddam] or not," though this difference should not lead to a split.

Like many Soviet officials, the Mideast expert sharply denied the existence of a split with the United States. "Here everybody understands that Soviet-American relations is bigger than this," he said.

That same insistence dominated the appearance of Soviet Foreign Minster Alexander Bessmertnykh before the Soviet parliament on Tuesday. He fairly staunchly defended the US conduct of the Gulf war in the face of a barrage of almost universally anti-American questions from members of parliament. He replied to accusations that the US bombing attacks were exceeding the bounds of the UN resolutions, which Moscow has supported.

"As for civilians, comrades, don't forget about the Kuwaitis," he retorted. "There have been lots of civilian casualties—women, old people. They are also suffering and we must try to protect them as well. I think having stood up for the protection of a small Islamic people against aggression, we have made the right choice."

Still the hostile tone of the parliament's response accurately reflects the pressure on the Gorbachev government from a right-wing complex of forces, led by the Soyuz ("Unity") parliamentary group, behind which stands the military and conservative wing of the Communist Party.

From the Baltics crisis to internal economic policies, the right-wing pressure has been reflected in anti-Western statements by Gorbachev government officials. To some degree, the West is used as a scapegoat for those internal difficulties, accused of everything from promoting separatism to flooding the country with illegally gained rubles.

With Tough Talk, Yeltsin Fights to Bolster Support

Daniel Sneider

2/22/91

While the Gulf war captures attention here, the Soviet Union's war at home is far from over.

Russian leader Boris Yeltsin's televised call Tuesday for the resignation of President Mikhail Gorbachev and the transfer of power to a council of republican leaders was dramatic evidence that the struggle for power continues. The Yeltsin-Gorbachev battle is merely the core of a broader conflict between the Kremlin's version of central-directed rule and the republican bid for a decentralized division of power.

The key issues in that fight center on the harsh economic stabilization policies of Soviet Prime Minister Valentin Pavlov and Mr. Gorbachev's effort to gain support for a new treaty of union in a controversial March 17 national referendum.

Mr. Yeltsin, appearing at times nervous, staked out a tough stance of opposition to the government's economic policies, particularly a planned several-fold increase in retail prices. He suggested that a better concept of union could emerge from the alliance of the leaders of the five largest republics—Russia, Byelorussia, the Ukraine, Kazakhstan, and Uzbekistan.

But Yeltsin's harshest words were reserved for Gorbachev, his one-time friend turned rival, whom he accused of abandoning reform for the sake of personal power.

That Yeltsin holds such views is not surprising. But up till now he has avoided such a frontal confrontation. The decision to go onto open attack may be a reflection of weakness rather than strength, however.

Particularly since he intervened in January in support of the pro-independence Baltic governments, Yeltsin has been the target of a harsh polemical campaign, spearheaded by the conservative Communist press.

Within the Russian parliament, Yeltsin has also been under attack from the faction of Russian Communists. A group of parliamentary leaders issued a statement yesterday, proposing convening an extraordinary Congress of Russian Peoples Deputies at which they hope to oust Yeltsin as parliament head. Yeltsin's support in that body, the ultimate legislative authority, is weak.

The move is an attempt to preempt Yeltsin's strategy to create a directly elected presidency that would give Yeltsin a popular mandate and free him from the threat of a no-confidence vote. Yeltsin expects to hold a direct election in July or August, followed by parliamentary elections that could produce a more radically minded legislature, says Yeltsin aide Pavel Voshanov.

Yeltsin has depended on his huge popular following, but even that is slipping, in part because of the fierce orchestrated media assault on him. A Russian parliament poll of Muscovites, considered a stronghold of pro-Yeltsin sentiment, showed a sharp drop in support for Yeltsin, though not a corresponding gain for Gorbachev. From November to January, Yeltsin dropped from 33 percent backing to 19 percent, while Gorbachev went from 26 percent to 19 as well. About 53 percent polled could not name a political leader worthy to be president.

But the key crack in Yeltsin's strength is his failure to construct a strong alliance of the core republics. According to his earlier plan, the group of four republics (Uzbekistan was added later) would draft its own union treaty. This would be a bottom-up approach, based on the network of bilateral, horizontal economic and political pacts signed between the republics. After the Baltic crisis, Yeltsin tried to organize a summit in Minsk of the republican leaders to announce this, but the meeting failed to materialize.

Yeltsin aides suspect Kremlin pressure played a role, reflected in public criticism that the republican leaders were seeking to form a "parallel central authority" and destabilize the country.

Yeltsin was forced to settle for a meeting of the four leaders, joined by Uzbekistan, following the meeting last Saturday of the Federation Council, which groups the heads of all 15 republics. They agreed to set up a body to control the implementation of the bilateral economic pacts between them, to ensure a flow of supplies to enterprises in their republics. They also agreed to oppose the price-reform policy and proposals for the formation of a new Soviet cabinet presented at the Council meeting.

But at a joint press conference on Wednesday at least two of those leaders—Kazakh President Nursultan Nazarbayev and Ukrainian President Leonid Kravchuk—disassociated themselves from Yeltsin's call for Gorbachev to step aside. "At this turning point, when we are experiencing economic crisis, Yeltsin actually is organizing a political crisis," Mr. Nazarbayev said.

Both men also were careful to make clear they opposed Gorbachev's policies as well, particularly on the sharing of power with the republics. Mr. Kravchuk echoed Yeltsin's view that Gorbachev "began to veer from his own [earlier] statements."

The republics, or at least eight who are still committed to a renewed union, are focusing their efforts on a working group that is charged with finalizing the draft of the new union treaty, based on the Gorbachev proposal. Those negotiations have become increasingly heated, particularly on the vital issue of division of powers between the central government and the republics.

The other republics refused to participate, many of them publicly opting for the path to independence. The three Baltic republics, Moldavia, and the Caucasus republics of Georgia, Armenia, and Azerbaijan have not joined the talks. All except Azerbaijan have also either refused to hold the March 17 vote or will conduct, as Lithuania did already, a vote asking whether the population favors independence rather than continued union.

Soviets Vent Differences With US on Gulf Policy

Daniel Sneider

2/28/91

Soviet officials from President Mikhail Gorbachev on down are not concealing their unhappiness with the coalition decision to launch and continue the ground war against Iraq. But Moscow is also making it clear that it is not ready to press its differences with Washington to the point of an open break.

Since receiving the Iraqi withdrawal statement late Monday night, the Soviet Union has been pushing for the UN Security Council to agree on a cease-fire proposal. [The Council agreed Tuesday there would be no move on the cease-fire until Iraq sent a precise, written acceptance of all 12 UN resolutions.]

But so far the Soviets are not prepared to call an open Security Council meeting against the wishes of the United States, a meeting that would certainly result in the two countries voting on different sides of the Gulf issue for the first time since the Iraqi invasion of Kuwait last August.

"We will not exert any pressure," Soviet spokesman Vitaly Ignatenko told reporters Tuesday. "That period in our relations is past."

Still, a sense of irritation has crept into Soviet official attitudes toward the US. Speaking at a Minsk tractor factory on Tuesday, Mr. Gorbachev commented that, despite the progress in US-Soviet ties, those relations are still very "fragile." According to the official Tass news agency account, Gorbachev went on to call on the US to show "a great sense of responsibility" not to destroy what has been achieved.

Veteran Arabist Yevgeny Primakov, Gorbachev's personal envoy during the Persian Gulf crisis, began an account—and a defense—yesterday of the Soviet Gulf diplomacy from the beginning of the crisis. Mr. Primakov's stand is clearly expressed in the title of the first in a series begun yesterday in the Communist Party daily Pravda—"The War That Should Not Have Been."

Primakov made numerous trips to Iraq during the crisis, the latest two weeks ago, where he used his more than 20-year friendship with Iraqi leader Saddam Hussein to try to negotiate an end to the conflict. The first part of his account covers the period from the Iraqi invasion through his first trip to Baghdad on Oct. 4. He provides evidence for the argument that the door for a political solution was open virtually from the start, provided the West was willing to deal with broader Middle East issues, particularly the Arab-Israeli conflict.

Primakov begins his account with the statement made by Saddam on Aug. 12, in which he linked withdrawal from Kuwait to Israeli withdrawal from the occupied territories and the withdrawal of Syrian troops from Lebanon. The West rejected such linkage as an unacceptable attempt to seek political justification for aggression. But Primakov suggests it should have been taken seriously. Wasn't it possible, he asks, "to use political settlement of the Kuwait crisis as an impulse towards solution of . . . the Arab-Israeli problem?"

The Soviet presidential adviser says that the Soviets pushed this view in early September at the Helsinki summit between the two presidents. Although the US would not agree, he says, the summit had a positive outcome in that President Bush agreed he "was going to resolve the Kuwait problem by peaceful means."

Primakov's account of his first meeting with Saddam in October largely supports his contention, which he has made previously, that the Iraqi leader needed a face-saving way out of the conflict. Primakov describes himself telling Saddam that there is no way out other than withdrawal.

Saddam, he recalls, replied: "If I face such a dilemma—to kneel, to surrender, or to struggle—then I would choose the latter." But, Saddam continued, "being a realist, I understand that in certain circumstances, it is possible to withdraw the troops, but I can only do this if such a withdrawal is conditioned by solution of other problems of the region."

At the airport, Primakov recounts, Foreign Minister Tariq Aziz told him that they awaited "concrete proposals."

The Primakov account in Pravda stops there, but in a separate interview published yesterday in the weekly Literaturnaya Gazeta, Primakov talks about his final visit two weeks ago and says Saddam was ready to consider unconditional pullout then. He criticizes Mr. Bush for the decision to begin the ground war, contending they should have given "at least a couple of days for the politicians to work it out."

Although the Soviet peace plan to which Iraq finally agreed contained no reference to other problems in the region, the Soviets have indicated they may have made different assurances privately to Iraq.

Gorbachev said on Tuesday that the UN must take up the effort to solve the Arab-Israeli conflict when the Kuwait conflict is settled.

"Without solving it," Tass quotes him as saying, "we shall preserve the powder keg there which can blow up the world. What has happened in the Middle East shows how pressing the issue is."

Gorbachev Seeks New Mandate

Daniel Sneider

3/1/91

Mikhail Gorbachev has returned to address a seemingly forgotten constituency—the Soviet people. After more than a year filled with foreign visits and diplomacy, economic collapse and rising political tension, the Soviet leader made his first official trip within the country, to the republic of Byelorussia.

The televised scenes from tractor factories in Minsk or radiation-poisoned towns near the Chernobyl reactor in the Ukraine were familiar ones from the past—Mr. Gorbachev mixing it up with ordinary people, fielding their complaints, sometimes with a joke, but at times with irritation.

But Gorbachev has studiously avoided such politicking for 13 months, a period during which his popularity has dropped to near rock-bottom levels. What brought the Soviet president back to the campaign trail?

The immediate aim of Gorbachev's efforts is to gain a clear positive vote in a March 17 referendum. The referendum asks voters to say yes or no to a vaguely worded question about whether they think it is necessary to preserve the Soviet Union as a "renovated federation."

Gorbachev seeks mandate

Yet Gorbachev left little doubt that he sees this as a vote on his own rule, one that he hopes will give him a renewed mandate for power. "This referendum is a decisive one," he told the workers.

Many Soviets are asking, however, what Gorbachev intends to do with such a mandate. Would this be a vote for change or a blank check for a shift toward more authoritarian rule, for new crackdowns on nationalist-led republican governments of the type seen in the Baltics in January?

At times during this three-day campaign swing, Gorbachev has offered solace to those who see him still as the only effective leader able to bring democratic and market reforms to the Soviet Union. But the overriding theme of this visit has been a conservative one, a rousing call to keep the Soviet Union intact, to maintain stability, and to adopt a version of economic reform that remains totally within the framework of Soviet communism.

Byelorussia was chosen as the site to deliver this conservative message because, as the daily Komsomolskaya Pravda put it, "of all the republics it is the closest to the center." Seven republics have refused to hold the March 17 vote. Others, including the Ukraine and Russia, have added questions designed to weaken the endorsement of the center's view.

In his two major speeches in Byelorussia, the Soviet leader has sharply drawn a line for the first time between himself and the radical democrats, particularly Russian leader Boris Yeltsin and his backers. The democrats, once the allies of perestroika (restructuring), are now described as its opponents, even as the agents of chaos and civil war.

When it comes to Mr. Yeltsin, "what is at issue is two political lines and associated strategic goals," not a personality clash, Gorbachev said at the Lenin Tractor Factory on Tuesday.

The factory speech was the most reformist, referring to the necessity to "move faster to the market," to conclude a new union treaty that would redistribute powers to the republics from the center, and to have democracy "based upon the law." But even this was tempered by cautionary conditions.

A renewed federation does not mean division, Gorbachev said.

"Partition will cause an escalation of confrontation which will lead to great clashes," he said, warning those who seek independence from the union.

Political struggle through elections is acceptable, Gorbachev said, but not "anticonstitutional activity," a phrase used repeatedly by the Kremlin to describe the actions of the nationalist governments in the Baltic republics.

The move to the market must be made in accordance with Soviet conditions, not based on foreign models, Gorbachev told the workers. "If somebody thinks that the market will solve all our problems, it is a blunder."

Leader offers harsh vision

Later that day, speaking before what was described as Byelorussian scientists and intellectuals, the Soviet leader offered his most conservative vision to date, accompanied by a harsh assault on his democratic opponents.

Though acknowledging the deterioration of life lately, Gorbachev seeks to shift blame for these troubles onto the shoulders of the democrats and the nationalist forces in the republics.

"Over the past 12 to 18 months, our efforts have been largely blocked by the most intense struggle for power," Gorbachev said. The struggle by his opponents goes beyond the bounds of law. "All this threatens to push us off the road of reforms onto the path of confrontation, right up to a civil war."

Gorbachev accused democrats such as Moscow Mayor Gavril Popov by name of seeking to disrupt the March 17 referendum, referring indirectly to the decision by the Democratic Russia faction in the Russian parliament to urge a "no" vote.

"There is no need to wonder that these 'democrats' enter a political alliance with separatists and nationalist groups," he said angrily. "They have one aim in common: to weaken and, if possible, to dismantle the union."

The president also had some words of warning for those in the West who have been critical of the crackdown in the Baltics and of the shift in Soviet internal policies. "There have been attempts to act as a teacher, to look down upon us. This is unacceptable."

Perhaps the most striking aspect of this speech was that Gorbachev spoke more in his capacity as Communist Party general secretary than as president. The democrats should not be called "leftists," he said at one point. Rather they should be seen from the classical communist viewpoint as rightists, since they "reject the socialist idea and favor the capitalization of society." As for himself, "I will go to the other world as a communist," he vowed defiantly.

Gorbachev's loyalty cited

"Mikhail Sergeyevich confirmed his loyalty to the socialist choice," commented Komsomolskaya Pravda. "Many people, especially the older generation for whom [communist] ideology replaced religion, will be satisfied. But today it is difficult to persuade the people to calm down by promising them a better life in the next century with the socialist idea."

Even in this relatively safe area, Gorbachev was confronted with the reality that the Soviet population is more concerned about sausages than socialism.

At one point during his factory tour, Gorbachev was engaged by a group of workers. Only one thing was on their minds—the several-fold price rises that the government plans to introduce shortly. Would the government compensate them, the workers demanded to know. Gorbachev, under pressure, said they would be compensated "100 percent," a promise that his own prime minister explicitly refused to make in front of the parliament recently.

Economic reality remains the essential weakness of Gorbachev's strategy. He may be able to win the March 17 vote, he may weaken or even remove Yeltsin and his other rivals, but he has not yet been able to turn the economy around. Gorbachev's increasing reliance on the Communist Party for his political base clearly rules out any attempt to solve the economic collapse through a radical shift to market relations. But the past months have so far provided evidence that the attempt to use a curtailed market to revitalize a state-run economy is also a failure.

What Moscow and Washington Learned About Each Other in Iraq

Scott Armstrong

3/6/91

Nowhere will the stunning success of the United States military in the Persian Gulf have bigger repercussions than in the massive Soviet defense establishment. The war provided the Soviets with an unprecedented look at US military tactics and a new generation of high-tech weaponry. US-based analysts on Soviet military affairs say the knowledge Moscow gleaned could have a big impact on future Soviet military planning, manpower decisions, and perhaps on the direction of the Soviet economy. "There must be tremendous resentment in having seen coalition forces perform so well after the Soviets did so poorly in Afghanistan," says Benjamin Lambeth, a Soviet military expert at the RAND Corporation. The US may have learned a few things about the Soviets, too, since the Iraqis fielded a largely Soviet-trained and Soviet-equipped army. But analysts say the knowledge to be gained here is far less substantial, since an Iraqi in Russian clothing does not a Russian make. "The technological performance of our weapons systems clearly has had a devastating impact on their pysche," says retired Lt. Gen. William Odom, former head of the National Security Agency. They must improve their industrial base, he says, or "they are not going to be in the race." In an era of diminished East-West tensions, it might seem odd for the two countries to be so interested in each other's military capabilities, particularly in a war in which they were on the same side. It might also seem unusual because one of the scenarios the information would be most useful for—a conventional East-West war in Europe—now seems remote. Yet the United States and the Soviet Union can still obliterate each other in less than 30 minutes. Both sides continue to base their military planning on the other's intentions and arsenals. US analysts say the Soviets picked up as much information as they could through spy satellites, electronic eavesdropping, the Western press, and informants in the Iraqi military, an institution they have long had a close relationship with. Among the things that likely impressed—or horrified—them:

Technology

The Soviets got their first look at some US weapons developed since the Vietnam War and a good look at others that have been around awhile. The result, experts say, can only be sobering to the Soviet military. In the air, Tomahawk cruise missiles, which can carry nuclear warheads, operated with seeing-eye-dog accuracy. F-117 Stealth fighters penetrated Soviet-built air defenses with impunity. "Smart" bombs, electronic jamming equipment, and Patriot missiles seemed to wow even some US officials. On the ground, the test of US versus Soviet technology was less telling, since coalition forces had complete air superiority and the ground war did not last long. Even so, US troops got combat experience with some weapons whose performance has been doubtful, such as the M-1A1 tank and Apache helicopter.

Manpower

Stephen Meyer, a Soviet defense expert at the Massachusetts Institute of Technology, says the one thing Soviet military officials visiting this country are always impressed with is the training and proficiency of US soldiers and noncommissioned officers. The all-volunteer force sent overseas was older, more educated, and better motivated than the draft armies of Vietnam. Their performance is one reason the technological side of the war went so well. This could cause the Soviet to debate whether to continue with a national conscript army or move toward a smaller, more professional force.

"What the Gulf war shows them is that the training competency required for soldiers and field-grade officers is not easy to obtain—and, when you have it, it's awesome," says General Odom. "You are not going to deal with" an army of this kind with "two-year draftees."

Strategy

Although the Soviets have long been familiar with the US's air-land strategy, the war, as one analyst puts it, "put some substance behind it." Moscow has to be impressed with the way coalition forces coordinated air-ground attacks. "I think this war will play into the hands of reformers: If you want a modern military, you better get a modern economy," says Dr. Meyer. Still, if the Soviets are impressed, they won't say so too loudly. Moscow has pooh-poohed the idea that the Gulf conflict was a US-Soviet proxy war or a test of the two countries' weaponry. Beneath these denunciations, however, residues of concern have surfaced. A recent article in the Soviet defense newspaper Krasnaya Zvezda questioned the wisdom of Soviet military doctrine that concentrates primarily on defensive actions. Whether this was spurred by the Iraqi debacle in the war is not known, but one US defense-industry newsletter notes that the Soviets "may even determine that it needs to reevaluate its approach to warfare." The Pentagon probably did not learn much about the Soviets. Maybe a little more about Soviet T-72 tanks, air defenses, and top-down command. But, for the most part, Iraqi military tactics are their own, developed during the Iran-Iraq war. Analysts, in fact, caution either side against drawing broad conclusions about a US-Soviet clash from the war. The Iraqis are not the Russians in might, manpower, or almost any other way. Nor is Kuwait Europe.

China Offers Food Aid to Soviets

James L. Tyson

3/8/91

In a veiled act of political triumph, diplomats say, China's leaders begin talks Sunday with a Soviet deputy premier over food aid for Moscow, China's unspoken rival in socialism. A scheduled visit to Beijing by Soviet Deputy Premier Yuri Maslukov marks a stunning role reversal for the world's two socialist giants. For decades China accepted huge amounts of aid from its Soviet patron before the two countries fell out over ideology in the early 1960s. The food aid, worth at least $700 million, signals how the two countries have recently drawn closer, in part because of fears that the United States will parlay its victory in the Gulf into world hegemony, the diplomats say. The loan package, aimed at appeasing restive Soviet citizens, vindicates Beijing's claim that economic reform must precede all other sweeping changes in a socialist system, the diplomats say, on condition of anonymity. China's leaders achieved unprecedented prosperity by unleashing market forces on the economy beginning in the late 1970s. They privately criticized Moscow for easing political controls in the mid-1980s and neglecting economic reform. Beijing "is rubbing the Soviets' noses in the aid a bit," a Western diplomat notes. The "commodity loan" of between $700 million and $800 million will be made up of canned goods, pork, wheat, and other foodstuffs, says an East European diplomat. This weekend, leaders of the two countries will discuss the interest rate, length of repayment, and other terms of the loan. The Soviets will pay back a portion of the loan through barter, according to the diplomat. Moscow has prepared Beijing for Mr. Maslukov's visit with flattering official commentaries in the press, which China has quickly and prominently featured in its own newspapers. "China's experience in economic reform is very valuable," Pravda said on Feb. 14, according to Cankao Xiaoxi (For Your Reference), China's official bulletin. "There is no fundamental dispute between the USSR and China on many major issues, and this proves that the further development of Sino-Soviet relations has great potential," Pravda said. Since officially ending three decades of hostility in May 1989, the two countries have steadily improved their relations on virtually every front:

Defense. Beijing is negotiating the purchase of several top-of-the-line jet fighters and other weaponry while advising Moscow on how to retool military factories for producing civilian goods. The two sides are also nearing an agreement on the details for large-scale troop reductions along their common border, diplomats say.

Trade. The two countries have promoted cross-border commerce and agreed on large barter deals. For instance, China plans to acquire two Soviet nuclear reactors in exchange for light industrial goods.

Communist Party affairs. Party leader Jiang Zemin plans to visit the Soviet Union in mid-May in the first such tour in more than three decades.

Foreign affairs. Moscow and Beijing called for a negotiated settlement of the Gulf conflict and opposed a United States-led ground offensive after consultations on the issue. Both have expressed concern that the US will emerge from the war as the world's predominant power. "China and the Soviet Union have been gradually making deeper contacts and improving their relations for nearly two years, but admittedly the Gulf war has sped up this trend," says the East European diplomat. The Soviets have sought the loan from China in part because the West has cooled relations with Moscow since the crackdown on secessionist movements in the Baltics and the comeback of conservative influence in the Kremlin, the diplomat says. The West need not fear the steady improvement in Sino-Soviet relations, according to Western diplomats. The two countries are too preoccupied with economic and political problems at home to pose a threat beyond their borders. And while both powers must uproot the legacy left from centuries of mutual distrust, Beijing apparently has further reason to feel hostile toward its northern neighbor. China's leadership has privately condemned Soviet leader Mikhail Gorbachev as a traitor to communism and held him responsible for the downfall of communism in Eastern Europe, Chinese sources say.

Byelorussia Backs Gorbachev Plan

Daniel Sneider

3/14/91

Inside the faceless apartment blocks and along the neat boulevards of the Byelorussian capital, people are pondering how to respond to the nationwide referendum this coming Sunday asking whether they wish "to preserve the USSR." "Yes, of course," snaps back Zoya Norkina, as if the question hardly needed to be asked. "What are we without a union," the 36-year-old surgeon continues, peering from under her fur hat. But isn't that a vote for President Mikhail Gorbachev, she is asked. "Is Gorbachev so bad?" she retorts. Such replies are frequent in the streets of Minsk, far more so than a similar random poll might find among the residents of the Soviet capital. From the streets to the halls of the government, the country's fifth-largest republic seems ready to deliver Mr. Gorbachev a firm majority in favor of his vision of the union. "The more we delay the establishment of a new union, the more we depart from it," Prime Minister Vyacheslav Kebich says firmly. "Now everyone is waiting for the results of the referendum." A "yes" vote is an endorsement of the draft treaty of union currently being prepared under Gorbachev's auspices, even if the republican negotiators and their parliaments don't agree on the final text before the vote takes place, the brusque former economic planner argues. "People are voting for an idea—whether or not there will be a union .... I would like to look into the eyes of any [republican] parliament after the people vote 'yes,'" Mr. Kebich says, with a slight threatening undertone. Some 6 of the 15 Soviet republics have refused to even hold the March 17 vote, and others have altered the question or added others. But in this Slavic republic of Byelorussia ("White Russia"), a placid conservatism prevails. It is for this reason, White Russians say, that Gorbachev suddenly appeared here two weeks ago for his only campaign swing before the referendum. "This is the only republic he can go to quite freely," says a bearded deputy to a local Soviet (council) who refused to give his name. "Even in the Ukraine he wouldn't get the supportive reception he got here." Byelorussia stands firm A joke widely told here acidly asserts there are only two socialist republics left in the world—Byelorussia and Cuba. Indeed, from the Kremlin's embattled ramparts, Byelorussia must seem like a Communist Camelot. Alone among the non-Russian republics, nationalism is a weak force here. The Communist Party remains firmly in power, with the republic led by moderate Communists of a reformist bent. The state-run economy functions well enough to keep stores filled with meat, milk, and cheese, items not easily found on Moscow shelves. Historically, White Russia has never existed as a separate nation-state. The area now defined by the republic's borders was ruled for long periods of time, however, by neighboring Lithuania and Poland, giving the people and their language a clear cultural distinction from their Great Russian brothers to the east. More than seven decades of Communist rule have further dulled nationalist consciousness, argues Zinon Pozdniak, the tall, balding historian who heads the pro-independence Byelorussian National Front (BNF). The Communist Party followed a philosophy of "national negation," he says, symbolized by the virtual elimination of the Byelorussian language in schools. The BNF, which was founded in 1988 and advocates independence, democracy, and anticommunism, has failed to generate the kind of mass movement seen in the Baltics and other republics. Opposition is vibrant. Still, the BNF is the core of a vibrant opposition faction in the 345-member parliament. It leads the Byelorussian Popular Front, a group of 37 deputies which also includes the Social Democratic Party, Christian Democratic Party, and others. Along with the loose Democratic Club of liberal Communists numbering 80 to 100 deputies, the democratic movement has been able to wield considerable influence on the Communist government. The BNF's greatest support comes from its role in forcing the disclosure of government data showing the full extent of the damage done by the Chernobyl nuclear disaster in 1986. About 20 percent of the republic's 10.2 million people live on land contaminated by the radioactive fallout which drifted north into Byelorussia from the reactor site in northern Ukraine, Mr. Pozdniak says. No one can escape Chernobyl's lingering pall, from the reports of growing illness among children to signs at the central market warning shoppers not to buy food unchecked for radiation levels. Gorbachev's visit to the most contaminated areas and promises of aid did little to alleviate deep feelings of neglect. "Gorbachev should have come here in April 1986," engineer Alexander Stashevski says sharply. "When you are in trouble, help should be offered immediately, not five years later. And we have to see what kind of assistance it will be—he knows how to talk." Such feelings of resentment make the referendum a dilemma for many Byelorussians who favor union but feel the vague referendum formula of "a renovated federation of equal sovereign republics" leaves much unanswered. "The formulation is not correct, because the basic principles of the new union haven't been developed yet," says Mr. Stashevski, who identifies himself as a liberal Communist. "The dictatorship of the center and the mere proclamation of equality should be discarded." He says he favors a European Community-style association. Such sentiments are reflected in the stance of the republican leadership, which wants a union in which the republics control most aspects of day-to-day administration. All taxes should be collected by republican governments, argues Kebich, with only enough funds passed on to the central government to pay for specific programs such as defense, space, and all-union energy, rail, and communications systems. The republics should develop their own ties to foreign countries and companies, adds Kebich, who just returned from a trip to Japan.

Support for Yeltsin. The Byelorussian leadership of Kebich and President Nikolai Dementei moved cautiously a couple of months ago to back Russian President Boris Yeltsin's concept of forming a new union on the basis of a horizontal compact of the three Slavic republics of Russia, Ukraine, and Byelorussia, along with the heavily

Russian-populated republic of Kazakhstan. At one point, the leaders of the four were to meet here in Minsk to sign an agreement. But pressure from the Kremlin and distrust of Mr. Yeltsin's aims put the plans on the shelf. And now they deny any intent to oppose Gorbachev. "This is not a parallel union," says Kebich, whom many say was a key backer of the idea. "It is a desire to establish a new union," he adds, dismissing the meeting proposal as "just the design of certain political circles," a clear reference to Yeltsin. BNF leader Pozdniak has a sympathetic view of their situation. Perhaps not unlike many other White Russians, "Kebich is the kind of leader who knows and understands more than he can accomplish."

Soviets Dispute Meaning of Vote On Union Treaty

Daniel Sneider

3/15/91

As the Sunday referendum for a union treaty approaches, the Soviet government is unleashing a rising crescendo of propaganda aimed at persuading voters that their ballot could determine the fate of the Soviet Union as a united country. But in reality this is a referendum with many questions but one likely to produce few answers. Only four of the country's 15 republics are simply offering the official question that asks voters if they wish to "preserve the USSR as a renovated federation." The six most nationalistic republics are refusing outright to hold the vote. And the other five republics have either altered the wording or added their own questions, allowing their citizens to vote for a different notion of union. Even the outcome of the vote on the official query has no juridical consequence. Soviet government officials such as parliament chairman Anatoly Lukyanov have unequivocally stated that even if a republic votes "no" to the union, "it will stay within the USSR." The republic must still go through a complex procedure for exit, including at least one more vote, which many republics see as an impossible barrier. And if voters say "yes," it is far from obvious what they are giving their approval to. The central government interprets this as endorsement of a new union treaty which has been under discussion for months. But even the eight republics that are participating in the drafting have not yet agreed to a final version, nor have their parliaments discussed it. That process could take a month or more, admitted Grigory Revenko, the Gorbachev adviser responsible for the issue. In Russia, where more than half the population lives, the vote is shaping up into a surrogate contest between Soviet President Mikhail Gorbachev and Russian leader Boris Yeltsin, his arch rival. Yeltsin supporters, who gathered in impressive rallies across Russia last Sunday, call for a "no" to the union query but a "yes" to an added question proposing creation of a Russian presidency. The Soviet Communist Party leadership is uncomfortable with that definition of the contest. People will be voting "not for Gorbachev or Yeltsin but for the future of their country," Moscow party chief Yuri Prokofiev insisted to reporters this week. Mr. Yeltsin hastened to agree, in his own way. "Today the issue is not relations between Gorbachev and Yeltsin," he told readers of Komsomolskaya Pravda yesterday. "What matters is the existence of the system, the protection of Russian sovereignty. If Russia is without any rights, as it used to be, it will never come out of its dilapidated state." Many among the anticommunist democrats and nationalists say the Kremlin could use a "yes" vote to justify forceful interventions of the kind seen in the Baltics in January. The Gorbachev government has retorted by linking those forces to an effort to destroy the country. "There are movements which call themselves parties," Mr. Revenko told reporters Tuesday, referring to the democrats and to nationalists in the republics. "They say no to the referendum, no to the Union, then back to 1917, to civil war. That's what I call them—civil war people." Yeltsin rejects such scare talk. "A civil war is unthinkable in this country," he said in the published interview. For the Russian leader, the issue is the rights of the republics versus those of the center and whether Russia and other republics will be free to pursue a more reformist agenda than the increasingly conservative path the Kremlin has chosen. Yeltsin's tactics are largely a response to a fierce Communist Party-led assault on him, aimed at trying to engineer a vote ousting him as head of the parliament. The Communists succeeded in forcing the convening of an emergency meeting on March 28 of the Congress of Peoples Deputies, the highest legislative body, for this purpose. Yeltsin is countering with the creation of a presidency, which he hopes would free him from the interference of the strong Communist presence in the parliament. The Russian government is also preparing a two-year economic program to present to the Congress, entitled "Russia's Special Road," which offers a better deal than the Kremlin's economic program. The official Tass news agency and the independent Interfax agency say the program will provide automatic indexation of incomes to compensate for price hikes planned by the Gorbachev government from early April. It offers tax exemptions for food and other consumer industries and free market conditions in the bu lk of the economy. Most important, the program asks for a treaty that clearly limits the jurisdiction of the central government, including full division of all property and Russia's share of export earnings. If the center refuses, Russia will tax centrally controlled agencies and enterprises and control food exports. Many republics share the Russian view that the latest draft treaty, published Saturday, falls short. The Ukrainian parliament added a question to the Sunday ballot stating that the Ukraine would participate in a union only on the basis of its own declaration of sovereignty. Uzbekistan and Azerbaijan have placed similar questions before their voters. Kazakhstan replaced the words in the official question defining the union as "a renewed federation of equal sovereign republics in which human rights and liberties will be fully guaranteed for all nationalities" with simply "union of sovereign states." The nationalist-controlled governments of the Baltic republics of Estonia, Latvia, and Lithuania have already held their own polls in which voters overwhelmingly backed independence. Georgia intends to vote on March 31, as does Armenia on Sept. 21. The Kremlin does not consider these past votes legally binding and plans to hold its own referendums within those republics as well as in Moldavia, with Soviet Army bases and factories run by the central government as the polling places. The Russian-speaking population and other national minorities in those republics are being encouraged to vote. Soviet officials have hinted their votes could be used to justify post-referendum interventions to protect their "rights." "The goal of the referendum is to strengthen law and order in the country, to secure the rights of a citizen irrespective of where he lives," Mr. Lukyanov told Komsomolskaya Pravda on March 13.

Soviets Approve Gorbachev Plan To Save Union

Daniel Sneider

3/19/91

Early returns from Sunday's nationwide referendum on the future of the Soviet Union show a majority voting in favor of continued union.

But the "yes" vote is far from a clear mandate for Soviet President Mikhail Gorbachev. At best, many parts of the country voted narrowly for his union, including Moscow, the capital of the USSR. In others voters found ways to say that the union they want is not the same as the one that Mr. Gorbachev wants.

The turnout was generally high. But in many areas, voters complained about the question posed by the central government. And in others, voters used the presence of altered or additional questions to send their mixed message to the Kremlin.

In the Ukraine, the country's second most-populous republic, voters cast ballots more strongly in favor of a concept of union backed by nationalists. According to preliminary estimates made by the Ukrainian nationalist movement Rukh, more than 50 percent voted "yes" in response to the central government question asking if they favor "preservation of the Union of Soviet Socialist Republics as a renewed federation." But about 85 percent voted "yes" to a question offered by the Ukrainian parliament which called for remaining in the union only on the basis of their own declaration of sovereignty.

In some areas of the Ukraine, the anti-Moscow feelings ran even higher. In the capital, Kiev, Rukh estimates a 55 percent "no" vote against the central government's union formula. And in the western Ukraine, where nationalist sentiments run strong, about 90 percent backed a question supporting independence.

The results show "most Ukrainians want to keep the republic part of the union but with a higher degree of independence and sovereignty than before," comments Yuri Lukyanov, deputy head of Rukh's information department in a telephone interview from Kiev.

The people of the Russian Federation, the largest republic with about 150 million population, also had the opportunity to say two things in this referendum. Aside from the question on the union, Russians also voted on whether they favored creation of a Russian presidency directly elected by the voters. For many this was a surrogate vote between Gorbachev and his rival, Russian leader Boris Yeltsin.

In a radio address Friday, Mr. Yeltsin made clear that he favored a negative answer to the union query, not to oppose a union as such but "as a signal to the union leadership that their policy needs serious changes."

Gorbachev, speaking to reporters after voting on Sunday, opposed the Russian presidency, while insisting this was not a contest between himself and Yeltsin.

The early Russian results reported by the independent news agency Interfax, mainly from the Soviet Far East, where polls closed earlier because of the time difference, seem to indicate that Russians gave an edge to Yeltsin. Although majorities said "yes" to the union, the pro-Yeltsin vote was generally higher. For example, in the Far Eastern area of Magadan, 64 percent said "yes" to the union while 71 percent said "yes" to Yeltsin's presidency.

In other areas, the results seemed less clear. The official Tass news agency reported that in the oil-producing Tyumen region in western Siberia, the same bare 53 percent majority voted both for the union and for the Russian presidency. In the Siberian region of Chita, Tass says 85 percent said "yes" to union but a little over 50 to the presidency.

Moscow itself proved to be a bastion of anti-Gorbachev sentiment. According to Interfax, citing Moscow city government officials, the union received an estimated 50 percent backing. Yeltsin's query got 78 percent backing, however.

In Moscow, as elsewhere, many people felt the question was the problem. It asked: "Do you think it is necessary to preserve the Union of Soviet Socialist Republics as a renewed federation of equal sovereign republics in which the rights and freedoms of individuals of all nationalities will be fully guaranteed?"

"Too much is combined in one question, and I can't say yes to all the parts of that long question," said carpenter Victor Zakarovas as he left voting station No. 47 in the working-class Moscow district of Sevastopol.

In Kazakhstan, the government simply changed the question, asking only if people backed a "union of sovereign states." According to Interfax, that formula garnered higher backing, with 94 percent giving their support.

The only places where the Kremlin got unambiguous support for its union question seemed to be in more conservative Central Asian republics and among the Russian-speaking minorities in the six nationalist-led republics that refused to officially carry out the vote. In the Central Asian republic of Turkmenia, considered perhaps the nation's most conservative, Radio Moscow reports, 95 percent voted "yes."

Similar majorities were reported from areas of Moldavia and the Baltic republics of Latvia and Estonia, where Russians and Army members voted on military bases or at central-government controlled factories. In Moldavia, clashes were reported with nationalist pickets opposing the vote. The same type of voting took place in Lithuania, Armenia, and Georgia, the other republics boycotting the referendum.

Baltic leaders and others expressed concern that the referendum could be used as a prelude to new crackdowns on nationalist governments. On Monday, Soviet Interior Ministry special troops arrested the head of the Lithuanian defense force, a move Lithuanian officials see as ominous.

Gorbachev Feels Heat on Economy

Daniel Sneider

3/21/91

From the grimy coal pits of Russia and the Ukraine, Soviet miners are sending President Mikhail Gorbachev an unpleasant message.

"The president does not represent the interests of the people," Victor Yakovlev, a miner from Vorkuta and a member of the Russian parliament declares. "He has to resign."

This demand was issued at a press conference Tuesday announcing the formation of a national committee to lead a strike movement that has been growing slowly since the beginning of March. Coming two days after the nationwide referendum, the miners were serving notice that Mr. Gorbachev may have won a solid majority for the preservation of the Soviet Union, but he did not gain a popular mandate.

In part, Gorbachev's problems have been complicated by his failure to win an overwhelming victory at the polls. Though officials claim a 77 percent "yes" vote for preservation of the union, this figure is inflated by the 90 percent-plus majorities racked up in the conservative Communist-ruled Central Asian republics.

In the politically more crucial areas of the Ukraine, the major Russian cities, and the industrial regions of the Urals, as much as half the population voted "no" in a clear antigovernment protest. And Gorbachev's archrival, Russian Republic leader Boris Yeltsin, appeared to have won resounding backing for his proposal to create a Russian presidency, for which he is more than ready to run.

But the prospects for trouble come less from Mr. Yeltsin than from the economic collapse. Indeed, Gorbachev adviser Grigory Revenko laid blame for the "no" vote in cities such as Moscow, Leningrad, and Sverdlovsk on the empty store shelves there. Long lines of people are hardly limited to those cities, however, though conditions may be worse there than elsewhere.

Gorbachev laid out that reality in a speech to a meeting of economists last weekend. Industrial production is down 4.5 percent already this year, meat production by 13 percent. And production of oil for export, the main currency earner, is down from 125 million to 60 million tons.

And now Gorbachev's backing will face an even more severe test in the form of a long-awaited across-the-board hike in retail prices, which was decreed on Tuesday night, to begin on April 2. Prices are due to rise an average of 60 percent, but some will double or triple. The government promises to use part of the new revenue for compensation measures starting this week, including wage increases, but these will not cover the full amount.

The price reform is a key element of broader reforms, ending the government-subsidized gap between low prices and far higher costs of production. In theory, as prices are freed, it can lead to fuller store shelves. But many economists say without other reforms such as privatization, including land, the state-run economy is unable to respond to the price reform.

In the short-term, many goods absent for months may suddenly appear because they have been hoarded by distributors and enterprises awaiting the price hikes. But most observers expect this to be a short-lived phenomenon.

"The reform won't rid us of shortages," wrote the trade union daily Trud yesterday, "because there won't be more production. Thus the price reform won't resolve our sharpest economic problem. On the contrary there is a threat of hyperinflation."

All of this sets the stage for a wave of industrial strikes, led by the miners. Two years ago the miners went on an unprecedented strike seeking higher wages, better working conditions, and a better price for their coal. After what the miners describe as two years of broken promises, their demands have become political as well as economic. The government has refused to respond to what it calls diktat, but now the strike has grown to include 280,000 miners in 165 mines, the strike leaders say.

After the referendum, there are signs that Gorbachev intends to take a softer and more reformist tack than he has in recent months. "The referendum lays the foundation for further democratic reforms in this country," Gorbachev adviser Revenko told reporters Tuesday. He placed long-delayed economic reform measures, such as privatization of small business and land ownership, at the top of the list.

The Gorbachev aide also talked about moving rapidly to conclude the draft union treaty. He took a more conciliatory tone toward Yeltsin and other republican leaders, calling for "calm" and cooperation in solving economic troubles. But for some, including the embittered miners, such talk comes far too late.

Yeltsin Pits Power of People Against His Foes

Daniel Sneider

3/27/91

This week Russian leader Boris Yeltsin begins a fight for his political life.

An emergency session of the Congress of People's Deputies, the Russian republic's highest legislative body, opens March 28. It is a meeting called by Mr. Yeltsin's opponents with the clear intention of ousting him as parliament head. The Communist Party bloc that is spearheading the anti-Yeltsin drive has a large part of the delegates under its control.

But Yeltsin has what may prove to be a far more potent, if dangerous, weapon—the support of angry people. The Russian leader is marching into the Kremlin meeting hall with the power of hundreds of thousands of striking coal miners behind him.

With the Soviet government about to implement an unpopular rise in retail prices beginning on April 2, potentially millions of industrial workers wait to join the miners. And on the opening day of the Congress, Yeltsin's liberal allies in the Democratic Russia bloc intend to mobilize a massive rally of Muscovites to support him.

Yeltsin is also coming off the March 17 referendum, which delivered him a political victory in the form of 70 percent support for the creation of a Russian presidency, for which he intends to run. All this has caused his opponents to have second thoughts. The anti-Yeltsin bloc in the Russian parliament is no longer talking clearly about using the Congress to hold a no-confidence vote on Yeltsin. Instead, they may try to block his plans to create the post of president.

Indeed, Vladimir Isakov, one of the six Russian parliament leaders who pushed for the convening of the Congress, admitted in an interview last week that they might have to resign instead. The opponents of Yeltsin "are retreating because so obviously they cannot challenge public opinion," comments Igor Sedikh, editor in chief of Russia's independent information agency. "The Communist aim to dethrone Yeltsin is no longer valid."

Yeltsin chose pointedly to demonstrate his strength March 22 at the Kirov industrial plant in Leningrad, a site visited only a week before by Soviet Prime Minister Valentin Pavlov.

"The Communist Party has left the trenches and is on the offensive, pursuing its aim to take over power in Russia, to stage a constitutional coup," Yeltsin said in a fiery speech to thousands of cheering workers. "Today we need to save the country not from the enemy without, but from the enemy within."

Yeltsin directly backed the miners, whose strike has shut down a quarter of the country's 600 mines. "They accuse me of supporting the strikers, but what could I do? The strikers have political demands, the resignation of Gorbachev."

The Kirov workers responded with chants of "Down with Gorbachev" and "Resign, Resign."

Yeltsin offers more than simple confrontation, however. He and his government plan to put their own Russian economic program, a kind of Russia-only version of a 500-day radical reform plan discarded by both Russia and the Soviet Union, on the Congress agenda.

Yeltsin told the Kirov workers, for example, that they should transfer their plant, a major defense-industry facility, to the jurisdiction of the Russian government. That did not mean going from one set of ministerial bosses to another, he assured. The plant would be independent, with Russia's only involvement in the form of collecting taxes. The Russian prime minister delivered a similar message to striking coal miners.

Soviet President Mikhail Gorbachev's government is clearly worried by these developments. Since the miners' strike began on March 1, Mr. Pavlov and the president have refused to meet the strikers, until they return to work and drop political demands.

On Monday, Pavlov sent a letter to the Russian parliament blaming it for refusing to deal with the economic issues of the miners and attacking Yeltsin for encouraging "anticonstitutional and political demands." But shortly after that, Soviet Justice Minister Sergei Lushikov told the Soviet parliament that Pavlov decided to meet the miners on March 29, though only to discuss "economic questions."

The government showed its concern in another form by instructing the Moscow city government to ban all rallies, pickets, and marches in Moscow from March 26 to April 15. Security forces were ordered to ensure compliance with the resolution, but the Moscow city government, which is controlled by democrats, has already given permission for a March 28 rally.

All this is likely to amplify the atmosphere of confrontation inside the meeting of the Congress of People's Deputies. The balance of power between Yeltsin and his opponents is very delicate within the Congress, which only narrowly elected him as parliament head last June. The Communists have been strong enough since then to block or water down important reformist legislation sought by the Yeltsin leadership. They did so earlier this week when the regular parliament session threw back a draft bill to privatize housing.

The agenda for the Congress session has three items on it—a report from Yeltsin and discussion of the draft new treaty of union and a new treaty for the Russian Republic. The first item was intended to be a platform for attack on Yeltsin, but he intends to turn it around, presenting his new economic program instead.

Yeltsin also hopes to use the referendum vote to push through the constitutional shift to a presidential system. The referendum question was phrased in general terms, and there still must be a Congress vote on the specific changes in the Constitution. By being directly elected president, Yeltsin hopes to undermine Communist strength in parliament, moving finally to call new parliamentary elections.

On the presidential issue, "it will be a real battle," says Mr. Sedikh. The Communists are seeking allies among deputies from the 16 autonomous republics within the Russian Federation. These republics, created out of smaller national groupings such as Tatars, have been wooed by the Communists with the promise that they would gain greater independence.

Yeltsin, trying to hold their support, told a rally last weekend in the autonomous republic of North Ossetia that residents would have a better life through support for a "united and sovereign Russia."

Uzbek Communists Embrace Nationalism

Daniel Sneider

3/28/91

Ibrahim Iskanderov's office as the vice president of the Uzbek Academy of Sciences is decorated in the style of a successful Communist official. Brocade drapes hang in the picture windows. A long dark hardwood conference table stands to one side. A dozen telephones crowd alongside his broad desk.

Above the desk, an oil portrait of Vladimir Lenin fills an entire wall. The former head of the state planning agency and ex-deputy premier of Uzbekistan peppers his conversation with references to Karl Marx's "Das Kapital."

But Mr. Iskanderov uses Marxism to make an argument no Uzbek Communist would even have whispered to his closest friends a few years ago. Uzbekistan suffers from a "colonial relationship with the Soviet Union," he says.

According to Marx's labor theory of value, he carefully explains, Uzbek cotton is sold for a mere fifth of its worth.

"We have remained a source of raw materials," Iskanderov says. "Today 90 percent of our cotton is exported to the center and the profit stays in the center."

New type of party emerges

Iskanderov is no dissident. He faithfully reflects the views of Islam Karimov, who became Uzbekistan's party boss in June 1989 and then republican president in March 1990. The former economic planner represents a new brand of Communist in this stronghold of party power—the "national Communist."

Here and in other parts of the Soviet Union, Communists are finding that to survive they must shed the rhetoric of "proletarian internationalism" and embrace the cause of nationalism. In the Baltic republics, not unlike in Eastern Europe, the national Communists have formally broken from the Soviet Communist Party, even adopting a new identity as social democrats. Others, such as Uzbekistan's Mr. Karimov or the Ukraine's Leonid Kravchuk, have more cautiously endorsed the ideas of nationalist movements while avoiding an open split with Moscow.

Anticommunists first

The nationalist cause was first championed in Uzbekistan by Birlik ("Unity"), an anticommunist movement for democratization founded in November 1988. Birlik advocated a broad program, including democratization, providing land to peasants, ending military service outside the republic, and solving severe ecological problems. But it hit hardest by exposing the systematic distortion of the Uzbek economy through the cotton monoculture.

Until recently, about 90 percent of Uzbek farmland was devoted to cotton cultivation. Under the Soviet central planning system, cheap raw cotton is shipped to mills in other republics, forcing Uzbekistan to buy clothing from outside at greater cost.

"They were telling us that the motherland should be self-sufficient in cotton," recalls Academician Tashmukhammedov, the director of the Institute of Plant Physiology and a Birlik leader. "But we lost bread and meat independence."

With a touch of bitterness, Birlik leaders say Karimov has snatched many of their ideas. Karimov has opened the door to greater private use of land, on a lease basis. Most important, he has reduced cotton cultivation by about 20 percent in the last two years and got Moscow to pay a higher price for it. And among republican leaders, Karimov has emerged as one of the most forceful advocates of republican control over resources and internal affairs, within a Soviet federation.

Yet Karimov's role divides the ranks of the democratic and nationalist movement. Some democrats say he is a Communist wolf in nationalist clothing, one who suppresses the democratic movement to retain a Communist monopoly of power.

"Karimov is a Stalinist," the bearded Birlik co-chairman Abdur Makat Pulatov says angrily, replying in part to the less harsh views of his colleagues in the poster-festooned Birlik headquarters. "He is an advocate of the command-administered system, against privatization, for the kolkhoz [collective farms]. He wants the press to be controlled."

Mr. Tashmukhammedov sees Karimov more positively. "Karimov is like [Soviet leader Mikhail] Gorbachev: One can push him left. But we can't push the [party] apparatus left. They are our main target." And is Karimov truly a nationalist? "He would like to secede, without democratization," answers Tashmukhammedov.

"He is merely playing with the national feelings of the people," disagrees Mr. Pulatov. When the new treaty of union is ready, "he'll be the first to sign it."

Wherever the truth may lie, there is no denying that Karimov's national communism has been successful in gaining popular support, including from the Uzbek intelligentsia.

"Today [Karimov] would even win direct elections," says Timour Valyev, a cybernetics professor and former Birlik leader. He formally left the movement last fall when he became a member of Karimov's Presidential Council.

Karimov is an "honest person," says Mr. Valyev. "He is trying, using his own ways, to improve living conditions for the people of Uzbekistan. He may be mistaken on certain points but he is capable of learning and drawing lessons." In part, he says, Karimov is limited by the power of the party and state bureaucracy, particularly on the distribution of land for private farming.

Real reforms blocked?

The party bosses block real agricultural reform, agrees agronomist Mirza-Ali Muhammedjanov. He served as agriculture minister about 30 years ago, but was ousted for his opposition to the cotton monoculture. Agricultural land should be given to peasants on a permanent lease with the right to pass it on to their children, he says. At least 80 percent of state and collective farms are inefficient and should be disbanded, he explains. Collectivization is closely tied to the cotton monoculture and the severe agricultural crisis, he concludes. Full privatization is difficult in Uzbekistan because of the high ratio of population to land, he argues.

The Karimov leadership offers a moderate version of this view. The party has proposed long-term leasing of land but without inheritance. It wants to retain the collective farms that are its power base in the rural areas where about 80 percent of the Uzbek population lives. And while Karimov talks sharply about the need to gain control of Uzbek destiny, he steers far clear of any talk of independence.

"We gave it a thought," says Iskanderov. "But the economic connections with other republics are so deep-rooted that we cannot cut them today."

Economists such as Iskanderov want to reform the distortions that sprang from the myth that the Soviet economy is an integrated structure in which each republic has its specializations.

"In this republic, we should have been developing light industry and cotton mills," explains Iskanderov. "Instead they built jumbo factories with 37,000 workers, and built them in cities while there was no industrial development in rural areas."

Though independence is rejected, there are nascent moves to form an economic bloc of the four Central Asian republics and Kazakhstan, all of which share similar complaints of colonial exploitation by the center. Iskanderov chairs a study group that is developing plans for such a grouping.

Muhammedjanov, who proudly shows visitors his medal for 50 years of Communist Party membership, finds Karimov a refreshing change from the earlier leaders. "He can resist Moscow. He has his own opinion. Maybe he overplays it sometimes. Many say he has a dictatorial nature. Some elements of that are there. If he develops those, it will be too bad."

Pragmatic Leader Guides Ukraine

Daniel Sneider

4/2/91

The biggest political mystery in the Ukraine today is the identity of its leader, parliament head Leonid Kravchuk. Is he the Leonid Kravchuk who patiently worked his way up the apparatus of the orthodox Ukrainian Communist Party to become its ideology chief? Or is he a hidden Ukrainian nationalist whose true feelings are now emerging into the open? Mr. Kravchuk suggests a third possibility—that he is an example of a new phenomenon in the Soviet Union, a politician who tries to represent his constituents. "I have not come from being a communist to being a nationalist, but to be more precise, from being a communist to a democrat," he told the Monitor in an exclusive interview. "I express the interests of not only Ukrainians but also the interests of Russians, of Jews, of Bulgarians, Hungarians, and Romanians who live in the land of the Ukraine." More than any other Soviet republic, the Ukraine will determine the fate of the Soviet Union as a united country. With a population of 51.5 million, it is the largest and richest republic after Russia. The entire range of Soviet opinion can be found within its borders. In the west, the cry for independence dominates; in the east, where most of the more than 11 million Russians live, the Union still holds sway.

Leader prefers compromise

Since he was elected head of the Ukrainian parliament last July, Kravchuk has emerged as a leader who prefers pragmatic compromise to ideological conflict. His advocacy of Ukrainian sovereignty has brought him into occasional alliance with Rukh, the Popular Movement of the Ukraine uniting democrats and nationalists. And it has sparked an open split with the conservative Communist Party leadership. But Kravchuk is also an outspoken critic of what he calls "narrow nationalism." He has pursued Ukraine's interests with a moderation and caution that often irritates and sometimes worries the more radical forces in and around Rukh. "Kravchuk would like to be president of the Ukraine and would like to have control of the Ukrainian economy," says Mykhailo Horyn, one of the more fiery nationalists among Rukh's leadership. "But he also doesn't want conflict with [Soviet President Mikhail] Gorbachev. In the villages, they say Kravchuk would want heated ice." Yet Mr. Horyn and others are carefully solicitous of Kravchuk, making deals with him and always seeking to widen the wedge between the silver-haired son of a Ukrainian peasant and his comrades in the Communist Party. Rukh and its allies are a minority in the Ukrainian Supreme Soviet, where the Communists still hold power. They can only succeed in getting their way, as they have at several key moments, by winning a portion of the Communist vote. That combination worked last summer when the parliament passed a relatively radical declaration of sovereignty. And it worked again with the March 17 Gorbachev-sponsored referendum asking support for a "renewed federation" to preserve the union. Rukh wanted a second question seeking support for an association of independent states.

Communists retreat

Kravchuk offered a compromise that asked whether the Ukraine should be part of a "union of sovereign states on the basis of the declaration of sovereignty." The Communist Party leadership openly opposed Kravchuk's proposal, but a combination of more than a third of the Communist deputies plus the democratic minority was enough to pass it. The Communists had to backpedal, telling people to vote yes on both questions. Voters gave a yes to both questions, but with a significant edge to the Ukrainian oposition. Rukh leader Horyn says the Ukrainian people have voted for confederation of independent states, while the Communists argue they voted for a single, unitary nation.

New union sought

"The Ukrainian people expressed the desire to live not just in the union but in a new union," Kravchuk says with typical care. "This union should be called the Union of Sovereign States in which each republic will be an independent state with its own rights; will have the right of free entry and exit from the union; will bear the full responsibility for the circumstances of its own people; and will protect the interests of its people, but not to the detriment of others." The Ukrainian leader does not conceal that on this point his view diverges from that of the Communist Party leadership, including Mr. Gorbachev. The Soviet leader insists the referendum is an endorsement of a draft union treaty that he claims the republics have already basically agreed to. Kravchuk calls this "serious political exaggeration." Only the parliaments of the republics have the power to adopt the union treaty, not the president or even the Soviet parliament, Kravchuk insists. And when it comes to the current draft, "the basic clauses of this document do not confirm the principle of sovereignty of states," he asserts, a view shared by Rukh. Kravchuk points to several examples where the powers of the republics are not clearly established. "Property should belong to the republic, which may delegate it for temporary use [to the central government] but not lose the right to it. But the draft says this in a way that can be interpreted in different ways." The same is true for taxes, he says, which should be collected solely by republics which in turn give money to the center only to pay for the powers they delegate to it. Joint powers are supposedly exercised through the Soviet Federation Council, which includes heads of all the republics, but "in such a form, it has neither powers nor jurisdiction." Without absolute legal clarity, "this document can be changed any time or just crossed out, as happened with the first union treaty signed in 1922," he asserts. The Ukrainian parliament will begin its discussion of its own draft in May, Kravchuk says and when that is completed, they will meet with the representatives of other republics. Compromises can be made at that point, he continues, but not "on matters of principle."

Clamor Grows For Gorbachev To Step Down

Daniel Sneider

4/8/91

The roomful of miners was handpicked, but Mikhail Gorbachev was still forced more than once to answer a question that militant striking miners have turned into a demand: Will the president resign?

"Whatever tramping of feet and sneering, whatever slogans, whatever jeering from the squares, it won't knock me off the rails," he angrily vowed in last week's encounter.

Tough words aside, discussion of President Gorbachev's fall from power has moved from political parlors to the halls of parliaments and public squares. It was on the lips of tens of thousands of Minsk factory workers who filled the central square last Thursday. The miners in the coal pits have disdained offers of money until Gorbachev is gone.

The possibility of Mr. Gorbachev's departure gained the most currency when his arch rival, Russian leader Boris Yeltsin, scored a stunning political victory at the close of the emergency session of the highest Russian legislature Friday. After more than a week of deadlock in the battle between Mr. Yeltsin and his democratic allies and their foes in the Russian Communist Party, the silver-haired politician won a strong endorsement of his plans to create a Russian presidency. He was even granted interim expanded "extraordinary powers" as head of the Russian parliament.

If all goes as planned, an open, direct election will be held on June 12 and Yeltsin will emerge as the first leader in the history of Russia to be selected by his own people. It is a claim that Gorbachev, who chose the safe route of indirect election by a largely controlled parliament, cannot make. That contrast alone makes Gorbachev's position eminently precarious.

The president's vulnerability is reflected in increasing calls for his resignation from those within the ranks of the Communist Party—not only from its most conservative elements—who want to distance themselves from a losing cause. At the Russian Congress, moderate Communist Vladimir Isakov, head of one of the two houses of the Russian parliament, spoke on behalf of the anti-Yeltsin forces. Surprisingly, he not only attacked Yeltsin but suggested as well that "maybe Mikhail Sergeiyevich [Gorbachev] should really think about passing the wheel into other hands."

Indeed some on the democratic left who have led the anti-Gorbachev drive are backing off those calls out of concern that the Communists may simply cast Gorbachev aside in favor of another Communist figure.

"We categorically reject the attempts to oust President Gorbachev from his post without changing the current structure of power," read a joint statement issued Friday by the leftist Social Democratic and Republic parties together with a newly formed "Communists for Democracy" group. They called for immediate negotiations and consultations to form a "coalition interrepublican government."

Yeltsin also took a more conciliatory stance following his triumph at the Congress, which ended Friday. "The president and the Soviet leadership must know that no differences can be an obstacle for businesslike cooperation between the Union and the Russian leadership," he told reporters on Friday.

But Yeltsin also began to set his terms. "The basis for this cooperation must be resolute movement toward a normal market economy and the strengthening of Russian sovereignty." Those are the same conditions that Gorbachev rejected last fall, when he dumped a program for radical economic reform that had been jointly drawn up with Yeltsin.

Gorbachev may again reject such offers, particularly because they include a massive shift of power from the central government to the governments of the republics. But last week's spontaneous strike in normally placid Minsk should serve as a warning that the Soviet government may face a wave of mass strikes of unprecedented proportions.

The source of Gorbachev's difficulties is not hard to discern. Despite his manifest leadership in dismantling the totalitarian state, faltering economic reforms have only worsened conditions. He has compounded his problem by introducing a harsh economic austerity program, including large price increases on most goods. In any country, only a very popular government could hope to carry out such a program and survive.

But the virtual absence of trust in Gorbachev's government has been vividly demonstrated by the striking miners. They have rejected offers of wage and pension increases. After two years of broken promises, they say, they don't believe anything this government says. Only a new government will win their agreement to stop striking, strike leaders say.

"Everybody understands, whether they like it or not, that today Boris Yeltsin is the only man in the USSR whom the miners would trust," a commentary in the liberal daily Komsomolskaya Pravda said on Saturday.

But Yeltsin will not tell the miners to stop if he does not have the power to solve their problems. He told the press on Friday that he had agreed with the miners to set up a joint commission with all republican governments to look into their demands.

Ironically, the conservative ranks of the Communist Party may have read the labor unrest far sooner than the Kremlin, which seems so removed from down-to-earth reality these days. Some observers believe that behind Yeltsin's triumph at the end of the Congress lies a reconciliation with the Russian Communist Party, the most conservative element of the Soviet party.

The Communists had initially called the emergency meeting of the Congress of People's Deputies in hopes of ousting Yeltsin. But after days of deadlock, on April 2, Russian Communist leader Ivan Polozkov declared that "the situation in Russia is bad. And it is our duty to stop the decline in all spheres of life." That is why, he continued, now is not the time "to change the leadership."

News of Mr. Polozkov's public surrender rippled immediately through the party ranks. Shortly afterward, the Communists for Democracy, a liberal faction, declared its formation.

By Thursday, when Yeltsin surprised the hall by asking for interim powers until a presidency is created, a significant chunk of votes had slipped over to Yeltsin's column.

"The people have won," liberal Soviet parliament member Galina Starovoitova told the daily Nezavisimaya Gazeta. "It means the possibility of peaceful transfer of power, of peaceful revolution, is looming ahead."

A Day At Komsomolskaya Pravda

Daniel Sneider

4/10/91

At precisely 11 a.m., a bell rings, doors open, and the lively chatter of men and women fills the carpeted corridor on the 6th floor of the drab building on Pravda street. The crowd bustles into the blue-paneled room at the end of the hall, where the morning editorial meeting of Komsomolskaya Pravda is about to begin. Editor Yadviga Uferova sits at the center of a long horseshoe table, the ubiquitous portrait of Vladimir Lenin to her right, and various editors arrayed to either side.

This is how the day begins at the Soviet daily newspaper which, with some 18.2 million readers, proudly claims the title of the world's largest circulation daily. Komsomolka, as it is known, owes much of its popularity to its lively and innovative style. From muck-raking exposés to spirited political commentary, Komsomolka has been at the cutting edge of the era of glasnost or openness which began under President Mikhail Gorbachev in 1986. Today the four-page broadsheet is in the front lines of defending press freedom as glasnost comes under fire from conservative Communists. The morning meeting begins as usual with a review of the previous day's paper. "It is one of the few issues which came out on time," Ms. Uferova says in a slightly disapproving tone. The tall, businesslike editor moves briskly through the layout of the next paper, from the front page to a feature on the nation's first private detective agency. An editor requests space for a report on an emergency meeting of private businessmen. Uferova agrees without hesitating. Right after the meeting closes, a working team of mostly young people gathers in Uferova's office to discuss story ideas. One suggests using a Voice of America report that Leningrad Mayor Anatoli Sobchak is seeking strong executive powers as a front-page item. Confirm it first, says Uferova. She tells them to develop a Tass story about the pilfering of European food aid by adding their own reporting. Komsomolka is a pioneer of that kind of independent reporting, something rarely found in the Soviet press even under glasnost. Half of its 350-person staff are writers, including 40 correspondents spread across the Soviet Union and in seven foreign bureaus. Although it is the official newspaper of the Komsomol, the Soviet Communist Party youth organization, the paper is sympathetic to the democratic movement. During the crackdown in the Baltics last January, Komsomolka stood out as one of the few sources of accurate reporting. For a time, the paper was banned from Army barracks.

Influential voice

Still Komsomolka's reach is so vast that it is also a preferred platform for senior government and party officials to express their opinions. Similarly it was exiled Russian writer Alexander Solzhenitsyn's choice as the publisher of a lengthy political treatise on the future of Russia, printed last fall as a special insert. "It is a democratic paper with elements of radicalism—but controversial because they print right and left," says Pavel Voshanov, one of the paper's most reknowned political writers, who has taken leave to serve as press aide to Russian leader Boris Yeltsin. The paper offers not only tough independence but spicy stories that keep readers coming back for more. Vladimir Filin is a 33-year old Moscow State University history graduate who sports James Dean looks and combines investigative reporting with a police beat. Mr. Filin's investigations recently caught worldwide attention with a revelation of a booming illegal arms business in the Soviet Union. By publicly offering to buy illegal arms, Filin arranged clandestine meetings with gun dealers ready to sell machine guns and rocket launchers, as well as nationalist militants offering to buy what he collected. "I like adventures," says Filin, a twice-decorated Afghan war veteran. He distinguishes his style from the "classical" Soviet journalism that consists of long, didactic essays. "Today what we need are reporters who are capable of reporting," Filin says. Even in the pre-glasnost days, the paper had a reputation for liveliness in contrast to the party daily Pravda, its officious elder brother in the next building. In 1984, for example, Vitaly Ignatenko broke new ground with an article entitled "Duty" that gave Soviet readers their first glimpse of the toll of the Afghan war. Mr. Ignatenko is now spokesman for President Mikhail Gorbachev. Komsomolka's inventiveness makes it a target for conservative Communists. The paper was the first to substitute its own reports for the official Tass news agency dispatches. Political writer Voshanov wrote the path-breaking articles, which he says garnered phone calls from the Party Central Committee and criticism from Mr. Gorbachev.

Pressure from the Party

Uferova remembers the reaction to their reporting of the dramatic first meeting of the freely elected Soviet legislature in 1989. The party secretary in charge of ideology demanded that the Komsomol rein in the paper. "We were told that Komsomolskaya Pravda only writes about the black side and the time has come to sack its leaders," she recalls. The paper held a meeting where Voshanov, speaking for the writers, vowed to strike if the changes were made. But when the editors were called before the Komsomol leadership, the paper was praised for creating a new genre of journalism. "They disobeyed the orders from the Central Committee," Uferova says. Nonetheless, everyone at the paper is aware that they are still highly vulnerable to pressure. The paper is printed by the Central Committee publishing house, which also controls its bank accounts. With its enormous circulation, "they will have no other place to print," says Voshanov. "So editors have to be flexible enough to report what they want and still not spoil relations with the Central Committee." The paper has felt the chill of the recent shift to the right in the official media and the government's threat to curb press freedom. Independent voices on central television have been systematically eliminated since December and replaced by a drone of old-style propaganda. The government daily Izvestia (a relatively critical voice) has been pressured to oust a top liberal editor. But the Komsomolka editors show a decidedly defiant spirit. Uferova was the editor on duty recently when the liberal film director Elim Klimov called at 8 p.m. and asked them to print a statement of 63 artists protesting the rightward shift of the central television agency. "I said, 'Let's do it immediately.' And in one hour we had it printed," she says. But the crackdown on the press has made them wary. "We realize that glasnost is something which may shrink before our eyes," Uferova says. For today, the paper must be finished. In the late afternoon, proof pages are spread on the table, headlines written, pictures chosen. Changes go on until late at night, when Uferova signs off on the copy. Then, at 11:30 p.m., the whole staff boards the office bus to go home.

Soviet Budget Crisis, Strike Wave Reveal Limits of Gorbachev's Power

Daniel Sneider/Justin Burke

4/12/91

On Tuesday, Soviet President Mikhail Gorbachev unveiled an "anticrisis" program, calling for an end to strikes and demonstrations and promising further economic reform.

The next day, the central Lenin Square in Minsk was filled with about 75,000 striking workers calling for the ouster of Mr. Gorbachev and his government.

"Gorbachev has lost touch with the people," strike leader Georgi Mukhin told reporters before the rally, which continued yesterday.

The general strike in the capital of the Byelorussian republic comes on top of the ongoing strike that is seriously disrupting the Soviet coal industry. In the republic of Georgia, which declared its independence Tuesday, the nationalist government has called for a general strike to protest the presence of troops in a troubled region of the republic.

Increasingly, Gorbachev seems like an emperor without an empire. At the Tuesday meeting of the Federation Council, which groups the leaders of the 15 republics, Soviet officials complained about the failure of republics to pay their promised tax receipts into the central coffers. At the same time, the republican leaders are far from ready to sign the new union treaty that Gorbachev hopes will bring order.

The central government places much of the blame for the growing economic crisis at the feet of the rebellious republics whom it claims are disrupting economic plans.

"The president stressed that the economy is in serious danger," presidential adviser Georgi Shakhnazarov told reporters during a briefing. "If we do not establish some order, we might face anything, even hunger."

So far, Gorbachev's call for a ban on strikes and demonstrations remains a warning. But he "does not exclude the possibility of using his powers to the full extent," Mr. Shakhnazarov added.

This clearly would mean deploying the military and the paramilitary militia in a "state of emergency," perhaps to open the coal mines.

The president is under pressure to do exactly that by the conservative wing of the Communist Party, led by the Soyuz (Union) group of parliamentary deputies, whose leaders met Gorbachev on Monday. They have been threatening to call an emergency meeting of the Congress of People's Deputies, the highest parliamentary body, and to oust the president in a vote there.

"We told the president that emergency measures to establish order and stop anarchy and chaos at all managing levels are a necessary condition for further reforms," Soyuz leader Yuri Blokhin told the Tass news agency. The group agreed to stop organizing the emergency meeting until the "anticrisis program" and the draft union treaty are discussed in the standing Soviet parliament.

The anticrisis program is a mixture of a call for order and discipline with promises to introduce long-discussed market reforms. On the reform side, the one-year plan would privatize small business and retail trade, open stock and commodity markets, encourage foreign investment, decentralize foreign trade, and complete a shift to free market prices by Oct. 1, 1992.

But these measures, none of which are new, are paired with a harsh austerity program and a bid to curb republican powers. Aside from a moratorium on "political strikes," the plan threatens to cut off subsidies to republics that refuse to join the new union treaty or to contribute to the central budget. The Soviet central bank would get new powers to control the flow of credit to republics. And centralized control of grain and other food supplies would be established.

Gorbachev is seeking quick approval of this program, within the next few days, by the republican governments. But the budget crisis reveals the limits of his power over the republics.

At the Federation Council meeting, the Ukrainian and Russian republics, who account for the bulk of the missing funds, explained they have "financial difficulties." The flow of tax money from the republics has slowed, creating a budget deficit of 31.1 billion rubles ($17.3 billion) in the first quarter of this year, more than the projected yearly deficit of 26.7 billion ($14.8 billion). At the same time, however, the republics continue to demand and receive money from the center.

"Being afraid of pushing the republics toward the introduction of their own currencies, the State Bank of the USSR is satisfying their demands," Alexander Orlov, deputy head of the parliament's budget committee, told the daily Rabochaya Tribuna on Wednesday. They are doing this by simply cranking up the printing presses, he revealed, increasing the money supply in the first two months of this year by 88 billion rubles, compared to 11 billion in a comparable period last year.

Strikers Step Up Demand For Gorbachev's Ouster

Daniel Sneider

4/19/91

Mikhail Gorbachev has been wined and dined in Tokyo, but a different sort of reception awaits the Soviet leader when he returns home this weekend.

Labor unrest is spreading across the Soviet Union, this week among industrial workers in the Ukraine, next week perhaps in a general strike across Russia. Political demands, including the resignation of the government, are prominent in every strike action.

At the same time, anti-Gorbachev rumblings inside the Communist Party are growing. Party organizations around the country are planning to turn the planned plenary meeting of the party Central Committee on April 24 into a forum for attack on Mr. Gorbachev, who is party leader.

The strike wave continues to be led by the militant miners, about 300,000 of whom have stopped work since the beginning of March, demanding the ouster of the government. The government claims that huge losses, including of steel and energy production, are rippling through the economy as a result of the strike.

Despite a report Wednesday that one large mine returned to work, the strike is holding. The independent daily Kuranty reports 82 mines and 14 mine-related enterprises in the Ukrainian Donbas region are on strike. In the Russian Kuzbass, in the northern Urals, and on Sakhalin Island, 131 mines and related enterprises are shut down. The Raspadskaya pit in Siberia resumed work only after the mine was shifted from central government control to the jurisdiction of the Russian government, led by Boris Yeltsin.

In Kiev in the Ukraine, miners and other workers protested last Sunday. A number of active-duty soldiers attended, the Soviet government daily Izvestia said.

At a larger rally on April 16, miners from all over the Ukraine set up a republican strike committee. They demanded dissolution of the Soviet and Ukrainian parliaments and dissolution of Communist Party cells in factories and in all military, KGB (secret police), and police units. They called for nationalizing party property.

On the same day, "warning" strikes took place across Kiev, led by municipal transport workers. A senior executive at a major Kiev industrial plant said antigovernment feelings became deeply entrenched after price hikes were introduced this month. Demands to oust Gorbachev are voiced not only by workers, he reports, but also by party apparatus officials at the district and regional level.

In Byelorussia, where workers staged a general strike last week, tense talks are taking place between the strike committee and the republican government. The committee is planning to resume strikes on April 23 if its basic demands, which include new parliamentary elections, are not met. Students are organizing strike committees to join the workers.

In Russia, the leadership of the federation of Russian independent trade unions has called for a warning strike on April 26 to press economic demands and back the miners. On April 16, representatives of workers at the giant Kirov factory in Leningrad met to draft a list of political demands similar to those of the miners and to plan a strike. Miners representatives attended, said the Postfactum news agency report.

The Soviet parliament, meanwhile, is considering an amendment to the labor law which would ban "political strikes." It is expected to be adopted next week. But without massive use of armed force, it is difficult to see how that law could be enforced. At this point, only Mr. Yeltsin has the authority to call workers back to work. Speaking at a Wednesday press conference in Paris, he said he opposed strike bans.

The Communist Party daily Pravda attacked the strike committees in a front-page editorial Wednesday, calling them "unconstitutional." But the party ranks seem to have little taste for taking on the workers. Instead, they are focusing on Gorbachev. Party leaders from major cities, meeting in Smolensk on April 15, issued an appeal that accused Gorbachev of "undermining the authority of the party and the peoples' confidence in it." They demanded that the party leadership be called to account at the coming plenum for its mistakes.

Similar calls have been issued by the Kiev party committee, by the Leningrad party committee, by the

Byelorussian Communist Party, and others, sparking rumors that a move to oust Gorbachev as party leader is under way.

Failing Economy Pushes Gorbachev Near the Edge

Daniel Sneider

4/23/91

Tired and empty-handed, Mikhail Gorbachev has returned from his journey to the Far East to face darkening skies at home.

As the Soviet economy does a disappearing act, Mr. Gorbachev's enemies on the right and left are closing in. Gatherings of conservatives and democrats joined in pushing for the fall of Gorbachev's government this past weekend, though with quite different aims in mind.

The proposed solutions to the nation's crisis range from conservative demands for a state of emergency to democrats' calls for formation of a "round table" coalition government.

Yesterday Soviet Prime Minister Valentin Pavlov presented the final version of the government's own "anti-crisis" program to the Soviet parliament. The program promises to stop an economic slide that, according to just-released government data, resulted in a whopping 10 percent drop in the gross national product in the first three months of the year.

"We have to work," Mr. Pavlov said. "We have to understand the nation is in danger." The portly, crew-cut premier says the economy can be turned around by the last quarter of this year through a combination of market reforms, austerity, and strict resubordination of the rebellious republican governments to the authority of the central administration.

"The sociopolitical situation should be stabilized," Pavlov told the Russian Information Agency after a Cabinet meeting this past Saturday. "If there is no discipline, responsibility, and order, it is senseless to speak about the country coming out of the crisis."

Pavlov's problem—and Gorbachev's—is that the population is being asked to endure hardship by a government that it neither trusts nor supports.

"Only a government trusted by the people can carry out strict measures to form the basis for a market economy," economist Stanislav Shatalin, author of a radical 500-day reform plan, told a conference this past weekend.

The government's anti-crisis program contains little that is likely to garner support, particularly from the republics' governments. It does offer some long-awaited reform steps, such as freeing prices, giving state-run enterprises freedom of action, privatizing state property, and lifting controls on wage levels. Some of these measures are similar to the 500-day reform plan.

But the government plan also combines the market steps with an attempt to restore central direction and curb republican autonomy. For example, it proposes a special management regime for the power, communication, and transport industries, hinting at moves to halt all strikes in those industries. All decisions by republican and local officials that contradict the center's policies would be frozen, and officials failing to carry out the orders of "superiors" would be punished. It also proposes banning political strikes for the rest of the year, a move aimed at muting the growing labor movement led by the nearly two-month-long miners' strike that demands the government's resignation.

Radical economist Nikolai Petrakov, who left his post as an economic adviser to Gorbachev early this year, condemned the program as based on "principles of imperial thinking." Speaking at a conference to assess the Soviet crisis, Mr. Petrakov said the call to restore a strict hierarchical power structure would return the country to the situation before perestroika (restructuring). "In fact," Petrakov said, "violence is the only method for implementing the Cabinet's program."

The Pavlov program does not have much backing from the right either. The Soyuz (Unity) faction of conservative Communists, which met this past weekend, presented its own program. They want to decrease prices rather than free them, and to abolish the government's 5 percent sales tax. But they echo the government plan in calling for introduction of a six-month state of emergency, including suspension of organized political activity and reestablishment of centralized economic management.

The Soyuz program is directly aimed at Gorbachev, whom program advocates accuse of indecisiveness. The conservatives called for an emergency meeting of the country's highest legislature, the Congress of People's Deputies, to call Gorbachev to account. "I am personally for Gorbachev's resignation," Soyuz co-chairman Viktor Alksnis told reporters.

Hard-liners are also preparing to assail Gorbachev tomorrow when a plenary meeting of the Soviet Communist Party's Central Committee is convened. Rumors of Gorbachev's pending ouster as Party general secretary abound, fueled by calls from local party organizations across the country to disassociate the party from the government's economic policies.

"The Communist Party should be led by another man," said Col. Nikolai Petrushenko, one of Soyuz's more flamboyant leaders. "It would make it possible for the party to bluntly state that the policy pursued by the president is the program of the opposition and not the program and goals of the CPSU [Communist Party of the Soviet Union]."

A gathering of democratic factions from republic parliaments across the Soviet Union met Sunday and yesterday in Moscow as well. The democrats called for a transfer of power from central government structures to the republics and formation of a "government of popular trust."

Increasingly, however, the democrats are quieting attacks on Gorbachev, in part because of right-wing moves against him. Instead they are offering to form a coalition bloc. Russian parliament deputy chairman Ruslan Khasbulatov, deputy to Russian leader Boris Yeltsin, told the conference last weekend that he did not support miners' demands for Gorbachev's resignation. "However," Mr. Khasbulatov continued, "the president should consider formation of a national reconciliation government with the participation of the republics."

The prominent Polish intellectual Adam Michnik, a leader of the Solidarity movement, compared Gorbachev's situation to that of Poland's former President, Gen. Wojciech Jaruzelski. After a visit here, Mr. Michnik wrote in the liberal weekly Moscow News:

"Jaruzelski was in a similar predicament twice before: on the verge of the introduction of the state of emergency, and in December 1988, before deciding to legalize Solidarity and embark on the Round Table policy. The general had to accept the idea of this Round Table, because military rule hadn't solved the country's problems. What will Gorbachev's choice be?"

Armenia Strives for Independence

Daniel Sneider

5/1/91

Young Armenian boys now climb up to drink their sodas and gab on the empty gray pedestal that stands in the central square of this ancient city. The glowering bronze statue of Lenin is gone.

The red flag, too, is nowhere to be seen, replaced by the tricolor of the short-lived but revered Armenian Republic, whose two-year existence was snuffed out by the Soviets in 1920. Far from Moscow, in its mountain fastness, Armenia is well on its way to independence. Without the bloody drama of Lithuania or the bombast of neighboring Georgia, Armenia's nationalist government is moving at a deliberate pace to restore its lost freedom.

"The Armenian nation is now convinced that the Soviet empire is a disintegrating empire," Armenian leader Levon Ter-Petrosyan says, with barely any expression on his long, serious face.

Since he was elected as head of the Armenian parliament last August, following parliamentary elections, Mr. Ter-Petrosyan has given Armenia skillful leadership. He speaks with the calm precision befitting a scholar of ancient Middle Eastern languages, but also with the determination of a veteran of the underground independence movement that emerged to lead mass demonstrations in early 1988.

Alone among the six Soviet republics that have proclaimed their desire to leave the union, the Armenian government has decided to do so strictly according to the Soviet law on secession. That law requires a two-thirds majority for independence, followed by a five-year transition period, capped by a Soviet parliament vote. In accordance with that law, Armenia will hold a vote on Sept. 21, after which it is prepared to follow the required transition period.

"Our government is in favor of pursuing a serious, quiet strategy that avoids confrontation in the process of achieving self-determination," Ter-Petrosyan says.

It is a strategy well-suited to the conditions born of Armenia's historical legacy. Armenia is by far the most homogeneous republic in the Soviet Union, with Armenians making up more than 93 percent of its 3.3 million people. There are no national minorities, especially Russians, for Moscow to use as an internal lever against independence. Armenia can also look for help from the almost 2 million Armenians of the diaspora, most of whom fled the Turkish massacres of 1915, which depopulated most of historical Armenia.

But Soviet Armenia's geographic and economic position is hardly enviable. The land is small and mountainous, suited to growing grapes and fruit and raising sheep, but poor in grain and dairy products. Armenia's only international border crossing is with Turkey, its historic enemy. And the transportation lines from Russia run through Georgia and Azerbaijan and have been frequently cut by blockade.

The yearning for independence has been activated by the loss of trust in Russia as Christian Armenia's historic protector against its Muslim, Turkic neighbors. Since 1988, Armenia has been embroiled in a violent dispute with neighboring Azerbaijan. The center of that dispute is the autonomous region of Nagorno-Karabakh, an Armenian-populated area within Azerbaijan, which seeks to rejoin the Armenian republic. That conflict led to attacks on Armenians resident in Azerbaijan, in Sumgait in 1988, in Baku in 1989, with constant battles along the border continuing till today. "The Armenian nation had rooted in itself a psychology that participation in the Soviet Union was a guarantee of its security and development," Ter-Petrosyan says. "Today the Armenian nation is convinced that the Soviet Union no longer represents that guarantee."

A long transition is useful to set in place what the Armenian leader calls his republic's "own guarantees." One is the creation of an Armenian defense force, already visible in the special units of militia who serve on the border. The Armenian government has also asked that all conscripts to the Soviet Army be allowed to serve on their own territory, a request Armenian officials say has been granted de facto.

The government is also intent on increasing the small percentage of the Armenian economy—about 10 to 15 percent—that is not linked to the Soviet economy. Their main means is a campaign of privatization, unprecedented in the Soviet Union for its speed and scale. About 60 percent of all land has been distributed to private owners, breaking up most of the collective farms in Armenia. Beginning last week, retail stores and small businesses are being auctioned off.

Threats from the central government that Armenia will be cut off from budget subsidies and goods are dismissed by officials here. Ultimately, Armenia is looking overseas to developing an independent foreign policy. Perhaps the most controversial aspect of Armenia's transition strategy is its effort to develop cordial ties with Turkey, including commercial links. Ter-Petrosyan's recent meeting with the Turkish ambassador to Moscow was greeted by demonstrators who accused him of betraying the cause of restoring Armenia's lost territory and gaining recognition of the Armenian genocide.

"But to be realistic compels us to conclude that we have no other path," Ter-Petrosyan says. "Independent of our own wishes, Russian or Soviet forces may leave this region."

This path is not without its critics. On the more radical side, Armenian nationalist Paruyr Hayrikyan accuses his former comrades of "looking to Moscow." The longtime activist, who served some 17 years in Soviet prisons, calls for immediate independence, ignoring Soviet law.

The Armenian Communist Party, which holds a large chunk of seats in the parliament, accuses the government of moving too fast toward independence. It seeks to blame deteriorating economic conditions and the failure to solve the Karabakh problem on the break with Moscow. But the party is a disappearing force, spending its time now fending off a recent parliament decision to nationalize the party's property.

Ter-Petrosyan brushes off a decree by Soviet President Mikhail Gorbachev voiding the nationalization, calmly observing that Moscow has more serious problems on its plate. "That means," he says with a rare smile, "that tactically we chose the right time."

Yeltsin's Deal With Strikers Tests Pact With Gorbachev

Daniel Sneider

5/3/91

Russian leader Boris Yeltsin has returned from the coal fields of Siberia with a deal that promises to end the two-month strike that has hurt Soviet industry and fueled a political crisis.

Mr. Yeltsin announced to a May Day rally of miners in Novokuznetsk that the coal mines would be transferred from the central government to the Russian Federation government he heads. But Russia isn't "going to create its own bureaucratic structures," Yeltsin told reporters. He vowed that the miners would own the mines, be free to sell the coal and keep the earnings, including almost all of the precious foreign currency.

Yeltsin, at some political risk to himself, has offered the miners a graceful exit from a bitter political strike that demanded the resignation of the government of Soviet President Mikhail Gorbachev. Yeltsin spent three days in the coal fields defending his own truce reached last week with Mr. Gorbachev.

"Yeltsin is working as a fireman," explains Pavel Voshanov, a senior Yeltsin aide. "He has to put out the fire, because the fire can cause destabilizing processes that neither Russia nor the center can put an end to."

The strike committee leaders have accepted the deal, but with the skepticism of those who have seen many past promises go unfulfilled. "We don't have any confidence in the [Soviet] Union government," strike leader Vyacheslav Golikov told the Russian Information Agency. The strike leaders say the walkout will continue until a written agreement is signed between the Russian and central governments, promised for May 5.

The consummation of this agreement will be the first test of a broader pact reached last week between Gorbachev, Yeltsin, and the leaders of eight other Soviet republics. The joint declaration issued following that nine-hour gathering, called at Gorbachev's initiative, ended—at least for now—the political war between the two major Soviet political figures.

In principle, Gorbachev acknowledged the republican demand for a shift of power away from the center, embodied in a new treaty of union. Once that treaty is signed, a new constitution will be passed and elections, including for president, will follow. But at its core, the declaration was an attempt to halt the strike wave that spread from the mines to industrial enterprises in the Ukraine, Byelorussia, and Russia.

The miners' backing was key to Yeltsin's own recent political victory over conservative Communist forces that tried to oust him as head of the Russian parliament. He rode the strike movement to win approval of creation of a strong Russian presidency, which he seems certain to win in elections scheduled for June 12.

Now Yeltsin has run into fierce criticism from some among the radical wing of the democratic movement for aborting a challenge that many hoped would lead to real change in the Soviet political and economic system.

But the Yeltsin camp argues that the strike wave was as much a threat to them as to the central government.

"This wave of strikes cannot give birth to any normal political system," retorts Mr. Voshanov, who is also known as one the most astute political writers in Russia. The workers are motivated only by their instinctive reaction to having been "robbed and deceived," he argues.

"The situation is very dangerous because any demagogue, any political adventurer, can mislead the people. There will be no question of democracy. Under such conditions, the most severe dictatorship can emerge . . . . Under present conditions, the most reactionary forces derived the most pleasure from this situation. It is very good that leaders, even those who opposed each other, understood the danger in time."

Yeltsin and his associates defend the deal with Gorbachev as having satisfied the main demands of the miners, including calls for the government to resign. The document calls for the new constitution to be prepared within six months of the signing of the union treaty, followed by elections of all "power bodies," a phrase that Yeltsin understands to include the presidency.

Gorbachev pushed for the union treaty to be signed by this month, but the republics won agreement to their insistence that the document be redrafted to accommodate their changes, to be signed in midsummmer.

The shift of the mines to republican jurisdiction is also offered by the Yeltsin government as evidence of real change. The miners made this demand last year, along with the demand that they be free to sell their coal as they want, without the interference of the system of centrally administered state orders.

This change ultimately has profound implications, striking at the core issue of who controls the economy. The breakup of the massive central industrial ministries, freeing enterprises to act independently, is a key part of market economic reforms. But the Gorbachev Cabinet has resisted such changes, arguing it would further the chaotic conditions in the economy.

The central government has also insisted on control of hard-currency earnings, saying the money is needed to pay foreign debts. About 40 percent of such money is now taken by the center; the rest goes to republics, but only to pay their share of the debt, leaving 6 percent for the enterprise. The Yeltsin coal deal offers the mines 80 percent, the rest taken by republican taxes.

"The miners have turned out to be the initiators of the destruction of the old command-administrative system and creators of a new system of economic management," Yeltsin reportedly told the miners rally on Wednesday. He presented the deal as a precedent for other industries.

But the document reached at the Gorbachev-republic meeting does not state anything about this issue. Gorbachev agreed to this verbally in order to settle the mine strike, says Yeltsin aide Voshanov. "There is no guarantee this will be spread to other industries," he admits. Some things are stated concretely in the document, "but in other cases, Yeltsin is seeing some gaps and trying to use them," Voshanov adds.

As a number of Soviet observers have pointed out, the document is ambiguous on some key points.

For example, the acknowledgment of republican rights rests entirely on a reference to "sovereign states," rather than "republics." But as a Tass commentary on Tuesday pointed out, this formula was contained in the draft union treaty published in early March, a draft rejected by almost all the republican leaders,

Behind their claims of a minor breakthrough, there is palpable fear in Yeltsin circles that the deal with Gorbachev could collapse.

"All the years of perestroika [restructuring] taught us the president can agree to something and then go back on his words," says Voshanov.

Gorbachev Woos and Assails West

Daniel Sneider

5/9/91

On Monday night, Soviet President Mikhail Gorbachev held his first formal press conference since the aftermath of the bloody military crackdown against Lithuanian nationalists in January.

Mr. Gorbachev is eager to capitalize on the political stability, however temporary, won by the deal reached two weeks ago with the heads of 9 of the 15 Soviet republics. He has sent envoys abroad in search of Western aid suspended after the Baltic crackdown, while there are hints that obstacles to a United States-Soviet summit could be removed soon.

Yet the Soviet President's replies bore the same combination of defensiveness and a testy counterattack against critics, particularly those in the West, that has marked his appearances since those dark January days. Gorbachev insists he has been misunderstood by those who see a turn to the right. And he demands the undivided support of the West, seeing anything less as a retreat to the "cold war."

When a Western reporter asked Gorbachev to describe how Western countries should conduct relations with the republics, he shot back: "We should all proceed from the premise that first, the Soviet Union does exist. Second, it will continue to exist. Third, it is a powerful state. And fourth, it is going to stay that way."

In the five minute ramble that followed, Gorbachev referred to a new federalism that would give republics more power, but at no time did he provide a clue as to what ties with Soviet republics were permissible in his eyes.

What is clearly not OK is the meeting held yesterday in the White House between President George Bush and the leaders of the three Baltic republics—Latvia, Lithuania, and Estonia—which are seeking independence from the Soviet Union. On April 30, a Tass commentary assailed reports that the Bush administration was pursuing a "dual policy" toward the Soviet Union of having direct contacts with republics while clearly supporting Gorbachev.

"Ill-timed" contacts

Such contacts, Tass said, were "ill-timed," and undermine the accord reached with republics. This interpretation of the pact with the republics is hardly shared by the republican leaders. Indeed, the Gorbachev-approved draft of a new treaty of union states clearly that the republics "are entitled to establish direct diplomatic, consular, trade and other ties with foreign states."

The Bush 'dual' policy, Tass says, encourages instability at a time when "contrary to prophecies by some analysts," Gorbachev's role as a leader is "confirmed . . . rather than diminished."

Gorbachev laid part of the blame for this on the Western press, which he accused of reaching "hasty conclusions, thus casting doubt on everything that's been achieved."

This was by no means a one-time outburst. Only the day before the Soviet leader devoted an entire meeting with media baron Rupert Murdoch to the theme of the Western failure to understand Soviet reality. According to a lengthy Tass account, Gorbachev emphasized what he sees as "emerging signs that the US is readjusting its attitude to the Soviet Union."

The US is subjecting the relationship to "unnecessary tests" that threaten to "plunge the world into a 'cold' or 'semicold' war," Gorbachev said.

Economic test

At least one major 'test' is Western economic aid which has been slowed since the Baltic events. Western investors are also scared off by both instability and economic chaos, as well as the anti-Western outbursts of Soviet leaders.

Soviet Prime Minister Valentin Pavlov, who last February accused Western banks of conspiring to carry out economic sabotage, went to Brussels last week to plead for aid from the European Community. In Washington earlier this week, Eduard Shevardnadze, the liberal former Soviet foreign minister, urged approval of a $1.5 billion food credit in order to preserve reforms in the Soviet Union.

Gorbachev clearly feels the urgency for aid, but he also finds Western pressure hard to swallow. At his Monday press conference, he testily dismissed advice-givers from the West who think "that 300 million [people] cannot settle their own problems and offer them ready-made recipes."

Still there are signs that Gorbachev is trying to ease the path to aid. On Sunday the Soviet parliament is scheduled to vote on a long-delayed law easing restrictions on emigration. Passage of that legislation is necessary to make the Soviet Union eligible under US law for most-favored-nation trade status and government credits.

And there are tantalizing hints that the disputes over implementing the treaty to reduce conventional forces in Europe may be solved, opening the door to concluding a treaty on nuclear forces and to holding a delayed US-Soviet summit. On Tuesday Gorbachev met with US Ambassador Jack Matlock, where according to a Tass account, "mindful of Bush's wishes, they agreed on urgent measures related to the conventional forces treaty."

Soviet Military Cautions Against Breakup of Union

Daniel Sneider

5/10/91

Soviet military leaders yesterday marked the anniversary of the victory over Nazi Germany with stern warnings against any attempt by rebellious republics to leave the Soviet Union.

"Today the ambitious, nationalist and separatist forces are doing their utmost to ruin the union," Defense Minister Dmitri Yazov wrote in the Communist Party daily Pravda.

"Only a strong and single union of sovereign Soviet republics can act on the world arena as a superpower," Marshal Yazov declared. "That is exactly what the war proved to the world."

Yazov's statements were echoed by other military leaders whose remarks were carried in the official and Communist Party-controlled news media. Retired Air force commander Marshal Ivan Kozhedub linked the nationalist political leaders to the fascists defeated in World War II. The military was once again prepared to fulfill its responsibilities, he wrote in Rabochaya Tribuna, to block "the ambitious leaders who are playing the role of undertakers of the superpower."

Yazov also called on the Soviet people to remain on guard against the West. Military parity should be maintained because "there is no guarantee that positive processes . . . are irreversible," he wrote. With the dissolution of the Warsaw Pact, he continued, "the military-political situation in Europe is changing radically, but not in our favor."

One lesson of the Nazi invasion of the Soviet Union, Yazov said, is that "we shouldn't, even for the sake of peace, disarm ourselves irresponsibly, lose vigilance." He pointed to the Gulf war as evidence that "the military threat, the attempts to set up a new world order relying on force, is an objective reality."

These warnings occur against a backdrop of heightening tensions in the Caucasus between the nationalist government of Armenia and Soviet security forces. For the first time, Soviet Army troops are directly involved in operations against what they claim are armed and illegal Armenian groups. The conflict is the outgrowth of a dispute between Armenia and neighboring Azerbaijan over the Armenian-populated territory of Nagorno-Karabakh, which lies within Azerbaijan.

Yuri Shatalin, the commander of the Soviet Interior Ministry troops, told the government daily Izvestia on Wednesday that the Army had taken responsibility for control of the border between Azerbaijan and Armenia.

General Shatalin claimed that this "redeployment" had "alarmed some people," and had triggered firing on military units. In the past, the military tried to avoid involvement in conflicts with the population, but now, Shatalin said, they have been ordered to return fire.

Reports from the Armenian government and Western correspondents on the scene, however, tell a different tale. Armenian officials charge the Soviet government with "declaring war" on their republic for its decision to seek independence from the Soviet Union. Azerbaijan is being backed, they charge, as a reward for its decision to stay in the union.

A Reuters dispatch from the border region yesterday described an Army assault in which 200 troops, in helicopters and armored vehicles, swept into the mountain village of Shurnukh and seized 25 prisoners. The account said the troops opened fire, taking aim at Armenian policemen.

Soviet Security Council member Vadim Bakatin, commenting on the war anniversary in an interview in the Army daily Red Star, struck a more balanced tone on these events.

"The union is necessary, we can even say it is inevitable," said Mr. Bakatin, one of the few remaining prominent liberals among President Mikhail Gorbachev's advisers. "But in the modern world, union is possible only by voluntary union."

Bakatin warned that "all the attempts, even with the best intentions, to forcefully preserve the union, only destroy it." Bakatin was forced out as interior minister last December.

Soviet Armenia Frees Farm Sector

Daniel Sneider

5/16/91

In the shadow of Mt. Ararat, Ishkan Melkunian stands on his own piece of historic ground—a private farm.

A broad smile crinkles the sun-bronzed face of the Armenian farmer as he points to his wife and children carefully tending newly planted rows of melons.

"This is my land," he proclaims. "Now we will get everything that we work for."

Mr. Melkunian is no anomaly, no showpiece island of privatization in a collectivized sea. The kolkhoz collective farm) that ran this village of Poker Vedi since 1939 simply no longer exists. The petty bureaucrats who sat in the offices, the orders from Moscow on what to plant and when to plant it, are gone. The land has been distributed to all the 940 households in the village.

Farms privatized

In the rich Ararat Valley, every kolkhoz and sovkhoz (state farm) has been similarly broken up. Of about 1,000 such collective farms in the Soviet republic of Armenia, only about 120 remain, most only in part. By the end of April, about 60 percent of Armenian farmland had returned to private hands.

Talk of land reform has been a hallmark of perestroika (restructuring) since Mikhail Gorbachev came to power in 1985. But so far it has been only talk, with the exception of small experiments in leasing of land. Even the Russian Republic's more radical government has managed only pronouncements of the theoretical legality of private farms.

Only in this mountainous Caucasian land has the nightmare of Joseph Stalin's forced collectivization of agriculture, begun in the late 1920s, finally come to an end. And it was done with a speed and deliberation that belie the persistent protestations of Soviet officials that land privatization is unrealistic.

Moreover, the Armenian case lends credence to the belief that the impetus for reform in the Soviet Union now lies with the republican governments. The Communist central government in Moscow appears to play a role only as an obstacle to reform.

The road to reform began last August when the Armenian nationalist movement ousted the Communist Party from power following the first free parliamentary elections. Following its declaration of sovereignty, the Armenian parliament moved quickly to pass market-reform laws, starting with a law on private property in October, leading up to adoption of a land code on Jan. 30.

"Land reform comes first, because private ownership of land will naturally lead to private ownership in other areas," says Hrant Bagradian, the deputy premier in charge of economic affairs. Land reform provides employment, increases personal incomes, and creates goods and resources. The next stage, which began in late April, is to privatize small business, particularly services such as food stores, which will sell the produce of the farms. The large firms, which are least prepared to function in a market economy, will come last, he explains.

The land law gave the equal right to ownership of land to all residents of a village, whether members of the collective farm or not. After distribution, the owners have two years to pay a relatively small amount, depending on the quality of land, and then are free to sell it to anyone. The only restriction is that land must be used for agricultural purposes.

Many Soviet economists have argued that the same path should have been followed for the entire country. Instead the Soviet leadership, including Mr. Gorbachev, has opposed private ownership of land. The Armenians have been told they are violating Soviet law, particularly by giving the farmer the right of resale. Even the more liberal Russian law, which has hardly been used, allows resale only to the government.

Mr. Bagradian sees evidence of Moscow's "intent to ensure the reform's failure" in the cutback of deliveries of seed, fertilizers, and other inputs to a third of previous levels. But he is confident they will see increased production this year, simply because farmers are inspired to work.

Across the Soviet Union, initial steps to land reform have faltered because the kolkhoz bureaucracy, which is the Communist Party's power base, refuses to introduce reforms. The Armenians solved that problem by transferring ownership from the kolkhoz to the village council, where the nationalists could control the process.

Poker Vedi is proof that the Armenian land reform, despite problems, is working remarkably smoothly. The entire process took less than two months. After passage of the law, Poker Vedi got detailed instructions on how to carry it out. Those came a little after Feb. 20, recalls Misha Yeragosian, the deputy head of the village council. On Feb. 27, a new election to the council was held, ousting most of the old members.

Party loses support

The Communist Party organization in the village was already in collapse, its committee dissolved, and its offices turned over for other use. Mr. Yeragosian admits to being a party member for 17 years, but hastens to add that "I never believed." Everyone has left the party, he says simply.

Shortly after the election, the council organized survey teams, which went out and mapped and divided the land into 4,000 square-meter plots.

Yeragosian pulls down the weathered, creased survey map and spreads it on the table. The village land is carefully divided into numbered plots, each graded by the quality of the soil into five levels. The price ranged from 4,800 rubles ($3,000 at the commercial rate of exchange) a hectare (10,000 square meters) for the best to 250 rubles ($156) for the worst. A household of up to three people was entitled to 4,000 square meters, of four to five persons, 8,000 square meters, and above six, 12,000 square meters.

Households could opt to work their land on their own or to form groups, which many did, based on their old work brigades in the collective farm. In theory, they could also opt to stay in the collective farm but no one did so.

On March 4, the entire village gathered for a lottery drawing of pieces of paper marked with the plot numbers. In that one fell swoop, the collective farm ceased to exist, with even the kolkhoz chairman taking his private plot. The village council retained the ownership of all the equipment—the tractors and trucks—which they now rent out to the farmers. Fertilizer, pesticides, and so on are being sold by the government from depots that service several villages. The farmers are free to sell their produce wherever they want, with only one exception—that it be within Armenia.

Vahan and Zaruvi Serozibadalian, together with their three children and Vahan's mother and sister, received one hectare of land. The land was graded as third-level quality, for which they will pay 4,670 rubles ($2,920). Vahan and his wife stand by the blue tractor, which he has driven for 10 years in his job as a tractor driver at a nearby state farm. Besides working his own land, Vahan will get paid for plowing his friends' fields.

Not everyone in the village is happy. Samson Myrdtichia is a 45-year-old ironworker who has lived in Poker Vedi since 1950. He and his family live in a house they built themselves, its cool plaster walls covered with calendars and pictures of his sons in military uniform. His wife works their parcel as part of a 40-to-50-hectare spread, farmed by a group of 30 people who had worked together on the collective farm.

"They wouldn't have been able to take care of it alone, so they stayed in a group," he explains over a cup of tea at a bare wooden table. But things are not better, he complains. "There's no technology. And they're working for nothing until they reap a harvest. The kolkhoz was very good the way it was before. The old way. You worked, and at the end of the month you received your salary."

Verab Zadoyan is the village agronomist, the only kolkhoz official to keep his job. Mr. Zadoyan stands and talks in the fields that he still patrols, checking the crops and the work as he has always done. He does not yearn for the "good old days."

"People used to work all day for one or two or three rubles a day. Before, I would plead with people. There would be 300 tons of tomatoes sitting in the fields and people would say, 'Forget it, why should I go out there?' The land was wasted."

A tale of two fields

Zadoyan points to two fields, one carefully planted, the other overgrown with weeds. The first, he says, will be worked by a family; the second, by one of the large groups, which he says don't work well. They chose to stay in groups because their members were afraid to work alone or had husbands working in the city, he says.

In contrast, "the individuals work from sunup to sundown," Zadoyan observes. "By the end of the year, even the collective groups will be splitting into smaller units," he predicts. Gradually the farms will consolidate, becoming more efficient.

The key problem in the village now is water. The smaller parcels make it difficult to divide up and distribute water. A tractor fitted with a plow moves down through the fields, digging new irrigation canals to reach the fields. But farmers complain that their fields are planted and ready but no water has arrived. The village council has set up a priority system, sending water first to land planted with wheat, then with livestock feed, and finally to the fruit and vegetable fields.

After a day at Poker Vedi, there seems little doubt that within a year or two these problems of transition will be sorted out. Those who don't want to farm will move on to other work. Those who remain, will produce and make money.

Why shouldn't this work in Russia, we ask Zadoyan. "Our people are industrious people—the Russian people are not," he responds. "Those that don't drink and work hard, they can make the land work for them."

Soviet Union's Era of Good Feeling

Daniel Sneider

5/20/91

The Soviet Union may be entering its own era of good feelings, a time when arch rivals Russian leader Boris Yeltsin and Soviet President Mikhail Gorbachev exchange declarations of trust and even cooperation.

Many who have been through the rise and fall of several Gorbachev-Yeltsin deals, and watched reform plans falter with them, reserve judgment. But it is difficult to deny that the atmosphere in Moscow has markedly changed in the last three weeks.

This shift began with the April 23 meeting between Mr. Gorbachev and the leaders of nine republics, followed by Gorbachev's defiance of conservative Communists, leading up to apparent agreement last week between 13 of the republican governments and the Kremlin on an "anticrisis" program.

On top of this comes Moscow's latest political titillation—an appeal to the Group of Seven leading industrial nations penned by Yevgeny Primakov, a Gorbachev aide, and Grigory Yavlinsky, a radical economist and one-time Yeltsin aide. The document proposes that a radical reform plan be formulated by the republics and the Kremlin, with the aid of experts from the "seven."

In return for implementing the plan, the Group of Seven would carry out an aid program. This would include debt relief, long-term credits, admittance into the International Monetary Fund and other international organizations, trade privileges, and foreign investment.

Mr. Yavlinsky has credibility as the key author of the "500-day" radical reform plan that was backed and then dumped by Gorbachev last fall. Soviet officials played down Yavlinksy's latest role as "unofficial," but confirmed the substance of his effort.

Deputy Premier Vladimir Shcherbakov said he would accompany Mr. Primakov to Washington soon to discuss economic cooperation. Gorbachev is said to wish to be invited to the Group of Seven's annual summit this July. He has already raised this with United States President Bush, French President Francois Mitterrand, and Japanese leaders.

Yavlinsky's ideas closely follow those of Harvard economist Jeffrey Sachs, the adviser to the Polish government on reforms. The two men appeared side by side at a Harvard University-sponsored conference here last week. Professor Sachs called for the West to put a commitment to about $30 billion in annual aid on the table, but tie it to introduction of a comprehensive reform package and to creation of a popularly-elected government.

"Only a democratic government will win the time and the support to carry out such a program," Sachs suggested, pointing to the example of Poland where Communist-authored reform programs failed for lack of trust. Sachs sees the June 12 election of a Russian president, in which Mr. Yeltsin is considered a sure winner, as "the most decisive event for economic reform that I could possibly imagine."

According to this scenario, the fulfillment of a pledge at the April 23 meeting to hold new parliamentary and presidential elections would complete the stage.

The government of Prime Minister Valentin Pavlov must go, Sachs says, and be replaced by a coalition between the democrats and pro-reform Communists.

Yavlinsky told the liberal weekly Moscow News that he had written his own plan to negotiate an end to the republican unrest and other conflicts. He claimed that Gorbachev encouraged him to merge this with an economic reform plan.

Reform had faltered before for two reasons, Yavlinsky told the conference—the lack of social preparedness and the resistance from the military-industrial complex, the military, and other "antimarket" forces. He claimed to have evidence that "now the situation has changed completely." The popular mood has swung in favor of reforms, evidenced in the actions of striking miners and others, he argued.

More illusively, Yavlinsky referred to changes in the attitude of military industry and its allies, a growing conviction that they can weather the transition to a market economy. Other Soviet analysts point to the emergence of a force of "modernizers," as historian L. Shevsova described it in an article in the government daily Izvestia on May 15.

The new force is based on pragmatic industrial managers and technocrats who favor the market but also want a strong executive.

They look to Korea, Japan, or Singapore as their models. The name most often linked to this grouping is Arkady Volsky, president of the League of Scientific and Industrial Associations and a possible prime minister.

Yavlinsky seems to be close to such views, warning at the conference about "the danger of populism," putting that label on both the Pavlov government and Yeltsin for budget-busting policies.

The image of a stable transition out of the deep Soviet crisis is tantalizing. But Moscow Deputy Mayor Sergei Stankeivich expressed the view of many here when he told the Harvard conference that "it is too early to say whether dialogue or a reversion to power politics will occur."

Soviet Reformers Find There's More to Democracy Than Winning Elections

Daniel Sneider

5/23/91

Last spring Irina Bogomsteva was elected to the Moscow city Soviet, or Mossoviet, as it is called, amid a wave of enthusiasm for democratic reforms. The democratic opposition took power in major cities, such as Moscow, Leningrad, and Kiev, and elected Boris Yeltsin to head the Russian republican parliament.

The democrats promised to create islands of the free market in the communist sea, leading the way for the whole country by their example. By October, Ms. Bogomsteva, who serves on the presidium of the council, was feeling frustrated and powerless.

Ambitious plans for privatization of everything from housing to retail stores had gone nowhere. Though the democrats had taken over the council and elected radical economist Gavril Popov as their chairman, the actual administration of the city was in the hands of the existing executive committee.

"We can't replace the executive committee because they know the old system," Bogomsteva explained. "We don't want that system, but we don't have a new system to replace it with."

The reformers have found that winning elections is not all there is to democracy. The reformers are "very bright but in terms of technical professionalism, they are starting from nothing," says Elizabeth Reveal, the director of finance for the city of Philadelphia.

Ms. Reveal is a participant in a novel effort to provide practical advice to the leaders of the Mossoviet and Moscow Executive. Harvard University's Kennedy School of Government has been cooperating with Mossoviet in a "Strengthening Democratic Institutions Project." The project has included small seminars and, most recently, from May 16-18, a series of seminars modeled on the executive training program the school runs for government officials in the United States.

The program covered topics such as how to make Moscow attractive to foreign investors, practical steps to privatization, the structure of municipal government, and municipal finance. Reveal also participated in a similar series on municipal finance held in Moscow and Leningrad, with participants from all over the Soviet Union, held from May 12-15. These sessions were sponsored by the National Democratic Institute for International Affairs, an arm of the Democratic Party.

"There is an incredible body of knowledge and experience out there in the world," says Reveal. "Here you have a society that has no body of that knowledge extant. They can't afford to reinvent the wheel. They simply haven't got the time."

Kemer Norkin, a member of the budget committee of Mossoviet, had down-to-earth questions to ask Ned Regan, New York State's comptroller. "What information about private companies is closed to you on the pretext of commercial secrets? Are companies that use the property of the state obliged to give additional information? Is your personal fortune accessible to the public? Does your post oblige you to reveal your personal fortune?"

The last question reflects the widespread corruption of public officials as well as Communist charges against the democrats that privatization will only put state property in the hands of the mafia and speculators, with payoffs in the bargain.

At the municipal finance gathering, a local Soviet official asked what an American city council would do if it discovered there were too few barbers in a city. Others peppered municipal officials from the US and Western Europe with queries on how many pages in a budget document, does the mayor prepare the budget or the legislature, or what an accounting system is.

Financial issues are most difficult to translate from the capitalist West. "It's pretty hard to have double-entry bookkeeping if you have no assets and no property," says Reveal.

But this is what the reformers need to know if they want to privatize city services or gain control of the government from the Communist bureaucrats who still run it. Indeed, the reformers at Mossoviet have very little idea of where their money comes from and where it goes. Most of the income of the city is derived not from taxes but from its ownership of state enterprises, such as the network of shops.

But as a study on the Moscow government undertaken for the Harvard project revealed, even those are not clearly Moscow's. All of them are actually registered on the balance sheets of two authorities—the Russian Republic's Ministry of Trade (which is in turn under the central ministry) and either the city or one of the 32 districts into which the city is divided.

The division of authority has not been made nor is it clear how to enforce it. "The concept of law is nonexistent in the way we understand it," comments Reveal.

Nor is there even the same understanding of what democracy is. "When I think of democracy I think of a cacophony of interests, skills . . . all competing raucously," she says. "They think of it as a more monolithic thing."

In the end, the very idea that democracy depends on the open flow of information may have had the most powerful impact on conference participants. "I never thought about why you'd want to share information," one Mossoviet deputy reflected. "I only thought about keeping it for my own use."

A Moscow Teen's Changing World

Daniel Sneider

5/28/91

Pavel Bogachko covers his walls with the same garish posters found in any Soviet teenager's room—Michael Jackson in black leather and studs, Sly Stallone with his muscles bulging, Arnold Schwarzenegger glaring menacingly as the Terminator.

But Pavel waves his hand in embarrassed dismissal. "I'm not interested in them anymore," he says. They have gone the way of the detective novels and science fiction that used to fill his book shelves.

These days Pavel spends several hours of the day absorbed in philosophy and literature. The slight, dark-haired teen eagerly consumes the German philosopher Friedrich Nietzsche and the American psychoanalyst Erich Fromm. He enjoys the novels of Mikhail Bulgakov and Vladimir Nabokov.

Changes at this age are sometimes painful. "I had to leave my old friends because I wasn't interested in what they were anymore," Pavel says. "They got together, played guitars, sang songs, listened to Soviet pop music I don't like, and discussed stupid things—just cursing and talking about girls."

Pavel found two close friends at school. They like to go the Central House of Artists and listen to lectures on ancient Greece or Shakespeare or perhaps mathematics. But Pavel's real love is psychology.

"I want to be a psychologist," the teenager says. "I like to communicate with people very much." Pavel claims inspiration from what may seem an unusual source for the Soviet Union—Dale Carnegie's "How to Win Friends and Influence People." Some suggest it was the contrast between the heavy ideological drumbeat of Soviet life and Carnegie's down-to-earth advice that made a Russian translation of the postwar American classic a best seller here for the past seven years.

But Pavel's role model may also be closer to home—his mother, Olga. She is a psychiatrist working in a factory clinic, treating the contemporary ills of Soviet life from overweight to alcoholism. Pavel's parents divorced when he was 3. He lived for two years with his grandparents in the Central Asian city of Dushanbe after his mother moved to Moscow to work.

Since he was 8, the two of them have lived together in Moscow. "Sometimes I had to work the evening shift," his mother recalls. "When Pavel came back from school, I had already left. And he was asleep when I came back from work. We didn't see each other for days on end. . . . Life made him self-reliant."

Four years ago his mother married Alexander Gushin, an electronics repairman who now works for a cooperative, the Soviet Union's only legal form of private business. And recently his beloved grandparents moved from Tadzhikstan, fearful of ethnic riots. The five of them share an average-size three-room apartment in the center of Moscow—along with Black, a rambunctious cocker spaniel.

The visit by a foreigner to their home is a first—a foreigner is like a lion to the family, Olga comments. The apartment's high ceilings are an echo of a rich past when this was only a piece of a huge apartment built before the Bolshevik Revolution of 1917. Now the kitchen is filled with the round table where the family gathers for its meals and tea.

As is common in cramped Soviet apartments, Pavel's parents sleep on a foldout couch in what doubles as the living room, now shared with his grandparents.

Soviet parents dote on their children. Pavel has his own room, cabinets lined with the books he acquires on his constant searches through nearby bookstores, a scratched wooden desk where he dutifully does his homework each evening. A Soviet-made cassette tape player on which he plays rock music sits on a chair. These days he is into British rocker Sting's music but Pavel also ranks Dire Straits, Pink Floyd, and Queen among his favorites.

A typical schoolday begins, if Pavel doesn't oversleep from staying up late reading, at 7 a.m. After a shower and breakfast, he is out the door before his parents are awake. It is a short walk down back alleys and streets to School No. 204, a school attached to the Pedagogical Institute of the Soviet Academy of Sciences, which Pavel has attended since the fourth grade.

Children entering the lobby of the four-story brick building are greeted by a red banner proclaiming that "To learn self-management is to learn democracy." In the center of the lobby stands a white plaster statue of the school's namesake, Maxim Gorky, the revolutionary writer known as the father of socialist realism. Except in the lower grades, school uniforms were junked this year as part of the reforms of Soviet education. In the hall, two girls do a flirtatious dance around a boy sporting long hair and jeans sewn with the patches of heavy-metal rock groups.

Pavel's 10th-grade curriculum is heavily science-oriented, including physics, chemistry, Russian language and literature, and German. After school, at 3 in the afternoon, Pavel sometimes plays soccer with his friends. But usually it's home for a large snack and maybe a nap before settling down to do a couple of hours of homework. After dinner, the rest of the family sits down in front of the evening news program Vremya, an event observed throughout the Soviet Union.

But neither television nor current events hold much of Pavel's attention. At nine o'clock, when the news comes on, he has his own ritual—an hour's walk with his best friend, Black. "We don't know who is taking whom out," he says with a rare smile. "I need those walks as much the dog does."

Pavel finishes the night with a favorite book. He admits only to occasionally watching some music videos on television—a new phenomenon of Soviet life—or the popular quiz show "Field of Dreams," an unabashed ripoff of America's "Wheel of Fortune."

Pavel may not be a typical teen in some ways, but his disinterest in politics is widely shared among Soviet youth. While the older generation is consumed by politics and the constant crisis of Soviet life, the young are profoundly skeptical.

When his parents and grandparents argue passionately around the dinner table about the merits of Boris Yeltsin or Mikhail Gorbachev, Pavel stands aside. "I say they shouldn't believe any of the politicians," a sentiment that he says irritates his parents.

Pavel seldom picks up a daily paper. When pressed for his views on the profound changes that have swept the Soviet Union, Pavel offers this: "My personal opinion about perestroika [restructuring] is that at a certain point it bore its fruit because it led to the liberation of the mind. But now the train Gorbachev put in motion is sliding back. But," Pavel concludes with a shrug, "I am just an observer."

Why this reverse generation gap on politics? Pavel explains: "Politics is more important for the older generation because they have broken from their ideological prison. They didn't have the chance to discuss their views before and now they are using it. As for the younger generation, we skipped that ideological oppression."

Now the kids make fun of what were life-and-death issues for previous generations. In school, "we argue with our history teacher because she gives us quotes from Lenin without giving any alternatives. No one believes in the ideals of communism."

At home, "we used to have family discussions about the personality of Lenin, and my grandfather was the only one to defend him." Grandpa worked all his life in a factory, except for the years of the war when he fought to defend the Soviet Union against the Nazi invader. "But now even Grandpa doesn't speak up for Lenin anymore."

Pavel's mother sees the generational difference similarly. "What I like most in this generation," she says, looking over at her son, "is their freedom of behavior. They don't feel humiliated as we do. People are always walking around with their shoulders drooping and their heads down, like slaves."

Olga does have one complaint about her boy, though. "Girls call him up all the time but he isn't interested," she says with a worried glance. "Maybe the time hasn't come."

Gorbachev's Rescue Plans Under Fire From Right

Daniel Sneider

6/27/91

Mikhail Gorbachev is busily working on his own agenda for the future. In meetings this week with visiting foreigners, the Soviet leader has optimistically predicted that the next month will bring two sea changes—a new structure of cooperation between the Soviet Union and the West and a new treaty among the Soviet republics to renew the country's federative unity.

But both conservative Communist opponents and nationalist forces in the republics are already serving notice that they intend to make Mr. Gorbachev's path a rocky one.

The London summit of the Group of Seven industrial nations in mid-July is clearly at the center of Gorbachev's plans. Gorbachev is working on a renewed economic reform program which he will carry to London and offer as the basis for Western economic help.

I'll make my own program," Gorbachev told Russian economist Grigory Yavlinsky and his American collaborator Graham Allison of Harvard University, authors of a joint US-Soviet plan for radical reform.

"[Gorbachev] seemed to be seized on a level of detail that was beyond giving it to someone else to do," Mr. Allison remarked to reporters after the meeting. Mr. Yavlinsky had been invited for an earlier one-on-one meeting last Saturday, which turned into a three-hour discussion with Gorbachev of their proposals.

For those seeking clues to his intentions, Gorbachev offered warm words about the Yavlinsky-Harvard approach, but also continued ambiguity.

"He said he appreciated 90 percent of it," Yavlinsky reported. "I did not ask what the other 10 percent was."

On the same day, Gorbachev discussed the other major plank in his political platform with visiting Finnish President Mauno Koivisto—a new treaty of union among the republics that make up the Soviet Union. Mr. Koivisto said Gorbachev told him that "the union treaty will evidently be ready next month."

The orthodox Communists and their allies continue to assail both legs of the Gorbachev program. After being rebuffed last week in a bid to shift government power to favored Prime Minister Valentin Pavlov, leaders of the parliamentary group Soyuz (Union) went back on the offensive in public statements this week.

Soyuz leaders echoed the remarks of Vladimir Kryuchkov, chairman of the KGB (the secret police), in a closed parliament session last week, when he warned Western aid was a chimera and pointed to evidence of US Central Intelligence Agency plots to destablize the nation.

"We do not see any particularly real help or investment from abroad," Soyuz leader Yuri Blokhin told reporters Monday.

The conservatives accuse the West of seeking political conditions for aid while maintaining its own strength.

"In the West, they are perfecting military equipment very rapidly," Soyuz co-chairman Anatoly Chikhoiev told the conservative daily Sovietskaya Rossiya on Tuesday. "The results of the Persian Gulf war show it will be a great blunder to convert all our defense industry and science into production of reapers."

The right wing attacks have an increasingly xenophobic tone. Sovietskaya Rossiya trotted out Arnold Lokshin, an American emigre who is a darling of Communist circles, to assail the Yavlinsky-Harvard plan.

"The future of the Soviet people is being discussed in Harvard University with George Bush's administration having a final say," he wrote yesterday.

Soyuz leader Blokhin said the group will oppose the union treaty, which is scheduled for discussion in the Supreme Soviet (the parliament) during the first half of July. "It is clearly seen from the text of the draft treaty that the USSR will be built on a confederative basis, not a federal one," he insisted.

But the more serious challenge to Gorbachev's schedule for ratifying the union treaty comes from the republics, which criticize the document for continuing to maintain a strong central government. In the Ukraine, the democratic opposition led by the nationalist Rukh movement and the Ukrainian Republic Party are opposing signing of the treaty.

"Despite the new beautified phraseology, this version is worse than the previous one," Vladimir Yavorivsky, a leading opposition parliamentarian, told the independent news agency Interfax. "We have been deprived of all—our foreign policy is controlled by the center, our foreign trade is monitored by the center, and our power engineering is in its hands."

The Ukrainian opposition insists that the government stand by a parliamentary resolution passed last year, which states that the Ukraine must first adopt a new constitution and establish its full sovereignty before signing a union treaty.

In an interview yesterday with the labor newspaper Trud, Ukrainian leader Leonid Kravchuk, a moderate Communist, appeared to back that view: "If we sign the treaty, which is still a one-sided document . . . which encroaches upon the sovereign rights of the peoples of the republic, and nothing changes for the better as is promised, it will be a great deception of the hopes of the people."

Mr. Kravchuk said he favors a more confederative structure in which sovereign republics form a union, with the central government acting only to implement areas of joint jurisdiction among republics. For example, he backs formation of a national bank and currency for the Ukraine and opposes any role of the Soviet parliament in signing the treaty. The Ukrainian parliament Tuesday also voted to oppose any federal taxes, a position shared by the Russian Federation parliament.

The parliament of Kazakhstan gave tentative backing to the treaty Tuesday, but raised three major objections to its content, including the need for a more clear-cut division of jurisdiction with the central government.

All this suggests Gorbachev's hopes for a quick approval of the union treaty are overly optimistic.

Baltic Leaders Set Out Terms For Gorbachev

Daniel Sneider

7/2/91

While civil war has erupted in nearby Yugoslavia, the nationalist leaders of the three Baltic republics are offering the Soviet Union a civilized divorce.

Today the Baltic governments plan to present Soviet President Mikhail Gorbachev with a document outlining an ongoing economic association with the Soviet Union. Baltic leaders, who met at this Latvian seaside resort last Friday to draw up the proposal, remain determined, however, to move rapidly toward independence. They express some optimism that, as one senior Baltic official put it, "Gorbachev is ready to let the Balts go."

The Baltic republics cannot sign the new draft of a treaty of union drawn up by 9 of the 15 Soviet republics, Baltic leaders told the Monitor in exclusive interviews here.

"This draft treaty is similar to what we offered two-and-a-half years ago," says Latvian President Anatolijs Gorbunovs, but is no longer acceptable. "Today it is too late," explains Latvian Foreign Minister Janis Jurkans.

The Baltic leaders also reject forming an economic union, an alternate structure which some Soviet officials have suggested could include the republics that do not sign the union treaty.

"Such a formal union which would embrace the Baltic republics is out of the question because we are separate, independent states," says Estonian President Arnold Ruutel.

"If this union were to be joined by some Western states, it would be another thing," says Lithuanian Premier Gediminas Vagnoris.

Instead, the Baltic republics offer Mr. Gorbachev basic principles for "economic cooperation . . . during the transition period" to independence, as their document states. The seven-point outline proposes the following:

* Foreign trade would be regulated by the Baltic states but Soviet goods transported through their territory would be subject to Soviet customs laws.
* Goods would be bartered, using a clearing system to meet an agreed trade balance.
* Baltic states would provide finance to the Soviet government for participation in joint programs, such as energy systems.
* The ruble would be the currency used during the transition.
* The Baltic states would guarantee social security payments for all their inhabitants.
* All the enterprises will be subject to Baltic authority, but financial and property disputes will be settled by special commissions set up by both sides.
* Baltic representatives will take part, as they wish, in the work of Soviet economic authorities.

The final point opens the door to Baltic governments joining the republics that sign the union treaty in forming and carrying out joint economic policies.

"We can send our representatives to different union bodies in order to organize economic relations," says Mr. Ruutel. "But they won't be representatives of a 'union republic, he cautions. "They will have the status of an observer or something similar."

The leaders share the view that after more than a year of stalled talks, Gorbachev will finally come to grips with the Baltic problem after the union treaty is signed.

"I am very confident that as soon as the treaty is signed, the approach to the Balts will be a very civilized one," Mr. Jurkans says.

Even the more hard-line Lithuanians express some guarded optimism that Gorbachev may respond more positively than in the past. While there is "no serious change" in Gorbachev's view of Baltic independence yet, says Mr. Vagnoris, "I believe that [Russian President Boris] Yeltsin's election fosters a change in Gorbachev's position."

The recent wave of renewed attacks by Soviet Interior Ministry commando units on Baltic customs posts and other government sites have raised concerns that conservative Communist forces may seek to block a peaceful solution. For this reason, Baltic leaders urge that the signing of the union treaty by the nine republics take place as soon as possible.

"I am very scared that prolonging the signing might lead to serious instability in the country," says Jurkans. "The military, KGB [secret service], and Communist Party are trying to provoke the situation, trying to make things difficult for Gorbachev. I think this holdout may damage this peaceful transition."

When Estonian President Ruutel met Gorbachev last week at the former's request, "I warned him that if such barbarous attacks continue any real dialogue is out of the question," Ruutel recounts. He was less than satisfied with Gorbachev's response that Moscow was not behind the incidents and that the procurator's office is investigating them.

"This is the same answer as after the Vilnius events," Ruutel says, referring to the Army crackdown that left 13 dead in Lithuania's capital in January. A procurator's report cleared the Army and blamed the nationalist government.

Still, Baltic leaders see Gorbachev as an honest if vacillating negotiating partner. In the past, Mr. Gorbunovs says, "the Soviet Union took our suggestions into consideration only after a great delay. That is why we will urge the president to consider our proposals as soon as possible."

According to the independent Interfax news agency, Gorbachev will be meeting today with all the republican leaders to discuss the economic situation after the first half of the year. It is likely that the meeting will also discuss an economic reform plan which is being drafted for Gorbachev to take to the London summit of Western industrial leaders in mid-July in his search for economic assistance.

In the past, Baltic leaders have called on the West to press the Soviet Union to grant them independence as a price for such aid. "We would like the West to tell Gorbachev that there is an urgent need to resolve this conflict because it is unprofitable both to the Baltic states and to the USSR," says Vagnoris.

But others also endorse the view that Western aid to Gorbachev is in the Baltic interest. Gorbachev's survival depends on it, says Jurkans, and "for us, the success of democratic changes in the Soviet Union is crucial. If the democratization process is stopped, we may forget our independence."

Shevardnadze Heads New Soviet Reform Movement

Daniel Sneider

7/3/91

After weeks of preparation, a group of prominent Soviet liberals led by former Foreign Minister Eduard Shevardnadze announced on July 1 the formation of a new reform movement to rival the ruling Communist Party.

The organizers fell short of their goal to unite the existing, fractured democratic opposition parties into one organization. They settled instead for the formation of a "Democratic Reform Movement," which will hold a founding conference in mid-September to decide its plans. Mr. Shevardnadze told reporters that he hoped to transform the movement into a new parliamentary-type party at that point.

The liberal founders include a number of prominent reform-minded Communists who say they will not leave the party. Their aim is to split the party, dividing those who support the reform policies of Soviet President Mikhail Gorbachev from conservative opponents of such change.

"We count on the support of the reformist wing of the Communist Party of the Soviet Union [CPSU]," the declaration of the new group stated.

Mr. Gorbachev sent a positive resonse to the announcement. "It is clear the movement does not have a confrontational character and invites the cooperation of all parties and movements that support perestroika and wish success to it," presidential spokesman Vitaly Ignatenko told reporters on July 2. "If it coincides with declared objectives, we can do nothing but welcome it."

In recent days, divisions within the party have been evident, with statements from conservatives in Siberia openly calling for Gorbachev's ouster as party general secretary. The party's Central Control Commission met last week to warn mostly conservative factions that their anti-Gorbachev activity violates party rules. A meeting of the party Central Committee is planned for later this month and promises to be a stormy affair.

"The party is not a monolith any longer," acknowledged deputy party leader Vladimir Ivashko to reporters on Monday. "There are cracks in the party."

The party leader appeared to be bidding to keep the Communist reformers within the party's ranks, disassociating the party leadership from a move to expel Shevardnadze for his activity in forming the new movement.

The movement advertises itself as the actual bearers of Gorbachev's policies of perestroika (restructuring) and glasnost (openness) which began in 1985. Their statement of principles includes protection of individual rights, parliamentary politics, radical transformation of the economy into a market-based system including private property, demilitarization of the society and economy, opposition to extreme nationalism, and support for a looser but united Soviet federation.

Among the nine signees are some prominent former or current advisers to Gorbachev. Aside from Shevardnadze, who resigned his post in dramatic fashion last December warning of the threat of "dictatorship," the list includes Alexander Yakovlev, considered the father of glasnost; economists Nikolai Petrakov and Stanislav Shatalin, Gorbachev's advisers until early this year; and Arkady Volsky, a Gorbachev confident who heads the power Scientific and Industrial Association, which groups pro-reform senior managers of Soviet state-run enterprises.

Russian President Boris Yeltsin is not among the backers, but he has long insisted that he wants to be "above" party. A number of his closest political supporters, however, are among the founders, including Russian Prime Minister Ivan Silayev, Russian Vice-President Alexander Rutskoi, who heads a reform Communist faction in the Russian parliament, and Gavril Popov and Anatoly Sobchak, the radical mayors of Moscow and Leningrad.

In recent interviews, Shevardnadze has argued for a new political organization.

"What I stand for . . . is to build a well-balanced, two-party system in our society," Shevardnadze told the independent news agency Interfax. "Whether the CPSU splits or not, we need a constructive opposition that would exist parallel to it . . . . They would criticize the state and cooperate with it, offering the country their solutions."

Shevardnadze explained that the decision to hold off on forming a party was motivated in large part by a desire to bring liberal Communists into their fold.

"If we set up an alliance, not a party, that would enable all the democratically minded people to take part in the movement . . . . If we set the condition of leaving the Communist Party or any other party, we'd face people with a choice and probably scare away some democratic people."

The reaction of existing opposition parties has been less than enthusiastic to the new formation. The left-wing Social Democratic Party and Republican Party of Russia, which met over the past weekend, balked at the idea of dissolving themselves into a new "super-party" in which they would become "factions."

"The political spectrum of the opposition is too wide to be fitted into one tight party," Republican Party leaders stated, according to press reports.

They also object to forming the party as an all-Soviet party, saying this will alienate democratic movements in the republics which prefer republic-based parties.

The Democratic Party of Russia, the largest existing opposition party led by Nikolai Travkin, was one of the sponsors of the move to form a new broad party. But at the last minute, according to reports here, Mr. Travkin backed off from signing the declaration.

Travkin favors creation of a strong, well-organized party to take on the powerful organization of the Communists.

How Treaty Would Divide Powers in the Soviet Union

Daniel Sneider

7/5/91

These are the main points of the third draft of a new draft union treaty intended to replace the December 1922 treaty that established the Union of Soviet Socialist Republics.

Basic principles: A Union of Sovereign Soviet Republics is created, in which each republic "party to the treaty is a sovereign state." Each is "entitled to establish direct diplomatic, consular, trade, and other ties with foreign states," so long as such ties do not violate the country's international commitments.

Division of powers: Powers are divided between a union sphere of jurisdiction and a sphere of joint jurisdiction. The union deals with protection of the sovereignty and territory of the country, including organizing defense; carrying out unionwide foreign policy; coordination of foreign economic activity; approval and execution of a union budget; issuance of money; adoption of a constitution; preservation of gold, diamond, and currency stocks; coordination of law and order activities.

The republics and union jointly protect the constitution; define policy for security, foreign affairs, socioeconomic development; control the execution of the budget, monetary policy, energy policy, and fundamental scientific research; ensure observance of union laws, presidential decrees, and resolutions.

All powers not delegated to either sphere remain under the jurisdiction of the republics and are carried out by them independently or on the basis of bilateral or multilateral agreements.

The treaty says that, as the market economy develops and the direct state role diminishes, the powers of republican and union governments may be altered accordingly by mutual agreement.

Property ownership: "The land, subsoil, water, and other natural resources, flora, and fauna are the property of the republics . . . . The states that form the union give to it the objects of property which are necessary for the implementation of the powers vested in the union."

Taxes: Republics levy taxes to finance their budgets. Federal union taxes are also set by agreement with the republics. Republics also make proportional contributions to unionwide programs, taking into account their level of development.

Structure of the union government: Legislative power is exercised by the Supreme Soviet (parliament), which has two chambers: a Soviet of the Republics and a Soviet of the Union. The former is formed by representatives of republics delegated by their legislatures; the latter, by direct, proportional vote.

The executive consists of a president and vice president elected by direct vote for no more than two five-year terms. The president has authority over the Cabinet, represents the union in foreign relations, and is commander in chief.

A constitutional court examines questions of constitutionality of laws of the union and republics and resolves disputes between them as well as among republics.

Soviets Move Toward New Confederation

Daniel Sneider

7/5/91

Today the Soviet Union is in the final stages of making a historic choice of a structure to bind its constituent republics into one nation. After three drafts, a new treaty of union of the republics is virtually ready for signing, though not without the resolution of some remaining disputes.

What kind of system have the Soviets chosen?

A close look at the new document reveals a curious—and at times, contradictory—blend of federation and confederation. It invests the republics with sovereignty, but it also maintains a strong central government with considerable powers.

The mixture reflects the complex history that led up to this moment and the intense political struggle that has surrounded the drafting process.

The new treaty replaces the 1922 treaty, the product of the Bolshevik Revolution of 1917 and the civil war that followed.

That document enshrined Bolshevik leader Vladimir Lenin's rejection of the imperialism of Russia in favor of national self-determination.

In theory, the republics are organized along national lines, with each nation voluntarily joining the Communist union. In reality, particularly under Joseph Stalin's dictatorship, the republican divisions were convenient tools to divide and rule. And the Soviet Union was a ruthlessly centralized dictatorship.

Now the revived nationalist movements that have taken power in many republics demand that power be given to them, in effect fulfilling the original Leninist idea in a loose confederation.

The succession of three drafts—the first last November, the second in March, and the latest in mid-June—have steadily moved from centralized federation to a more confederal arrangment. The republics, led by the most powerful, such as the Russian Federation, the Ukraine, and Kazakhstan, have chipped away at central authority.

But they have also settled for an ambiguity, where agreement was absent, that augers for troubles to come.

There are three key issues that reveal the fuzzy deal embodied in the treaty—the division of jurisdiction between union and republics; taxation and property; the structure of the federal government.

The treaty defines areas of union jurisdiction and of joint jurisdiction that are far from clearly separated.

The federal government, for example, has the power to carry out foreign policy and defense. But the republics are given authority to define those policies. The union approves and executes the federal budget as well as monetary policy, but the republics "control" this process.

The draft gives republics control over property, but says the union government receives the property it needs to carry out its powers. This could suggest, for example, that all defense industries are union property, an interpretation that some republican leaders already dispute.

The property issue is closely linked to taxes. The draft creates a two-channel tax system, with both republican and federal taxes. In practice, taxes are mostly paid by state-owned enterprises in the form of paying most of their profits to the state. So ownership of the enterprise amounts to the right to tax.

Both the Russian and the Ukrainian governments have already stated they oppose any federal tax and view all enterprises on their soil as their property. They argue for contributing funds to the federal government for those union programs to which they agree. Already, retorts Soviet Premier Valentin Pavlov, the refusal of these two governments to give agreed sums to the federal budget has caused a huge deficit.

Soviet leader Mikhail Gorbachev and some republics also argue that dividing enterprises amounts to maintaining a state-controlled economy rather than moving to a market system. Kazakhstan President Nursultan Nazarbayev calls this demand for republican jurisdiction "populism."

"What is jurisdiction?" he asks. "The enterprises should follow the laws of a particular territory. That is all."

Perhaps most troubling the draft provides no executive mechanism for implementing joint powers. A previous draft created a Federation Council, which grouped republican leaders with the union president in a decisionmaking body. Now the only integrative structure is a two-chamber legislature: a Soviet of Republics and a Soviet of the Union.

The Soviet of the Republics is formed along the same lines as the current Soviet of Nationalities, with a fixed, equal number of representatives for each republic and for each of the smaller autonomous republics and regions, national units within republics. That house, like the United States Senate, passes treaties and votes on Cabinet and high court nominations. The other house, whose members are elected like US representatives, can pass laws over the objection of the republican body but only with a two-thirds majority.

Otherwise, all joint decisionmaking will take place in special committees or by separate agreement, none of which is actually spelled out in the current draft treaty.

It is not difficult to anticipate that the Soviet leadership will find itself in a short time confronted with the need to significantly alter this historic document.

Yeltsin Inauguration Marks New Soviet Era

Daniel Sneider

7/11/91

"Russia is reborn."

With those words, Boris Yeltsin concluded his inaugural address as the first freely elected president of Russia. The silver-haired Siberian politician took office in a ceremony full of blaring trumpets and political choreography but virtually without the symbols of Communist rule. It was a moment to recognize the change in Soviet politics wrought by this indefatigable political fighter.

"The president is not a god, not a new monarch, not a miracle worker," Mr. Yeltsin declared in his short speech. "He is an ordinary citizen, but with enormous responsibility for the destiny of Russia."

The former Siberian mining engineer and Communist Party boss referred frequently to the need to restore Russia's historical identity. "Russia is ready to get out of the crisis. Great Russia is rising from its knees and will become a prosperous, law-governed, democratic, peaceful, and sovereign state."

The hour-long morning televised event, held in the Kremlin Palace of Congresses, was attended by leaders of most of the republics of the Soviet Union, including leaders of those republics, such as the Baltics, which seek independence. Their presence reflects the importance of the Russian Federation, the largest of the 15 republics with a population of 150 million.

But attention was naturally focused on the appearance of Soviet President Mikhail Gorbachev, who delivered an address greeting the election of the man who has been at different times his ally and his foe.

"Someone might say: 'So what, one more president in this country, joked Mr. Gorbachev as he opened his speech. "But," he quickly went on, "my belief is that this is a very important event, not only for Russia but . . . for all our multinational motherland."

Greeting from Gorbachev

Indeed, the sight of the two men clasping hands at the center of the stage fairly captures the current mood of Soviet politics. Gorbachev has yielded significant power to Yeltsin and the other republican leaders, formalized in a new draft treaty of union. But in return, Gorbachev is getting the support of these leaders, who enjoy far greater political legitimacy and popularity than the Soviet president.

On Monday, Gorbachev met with the leaders of the nine republics who have agreed to sign the union treaty and got their support for the program and stance the Soviet leader will take with him to London next week for a meeting with the leaders of the Western industrial nations. But Yeltsin added something more the next day, when he told reporters that he would back Gorbachev for election to the Soviet presidency as long as he continued on his present policy course.

Not everyone is happy with this course of events. On the right, conservative Communists rail against Gorbachev for betraying the socialist cause and yielding to the disintegration of the nation. And among more radical elements of the democratic left, there is a fear that Yeltsin is making unnecessary concessions that will only maintain the Communist Party in power, albeit in a more benign form.

"It is a mistake of Boris Yeltsin," says Russian parliamentary deputy Oleg Rumantsyev, a leader of the Social Democratic Party. "The temporary peaceful interval which was achieved in April was a good decision, because this helped us to elect a Russian president. But if we sign an agreement between democratic republics and the Communist center, all the results of our democratic revolution will come to zero."

From rebel to statesman

Yeltsin is clearly happy, however, to enjoy his transformation from a populist rebel into a pragmatic statesman. And no matter what alliances political expediency may dictate, Yeltsin's inauguration ceremony was imbued with an effort to draw a clear line between this "reborn" Russia and its Communist past. The traditional portrait of Vladimir Lenin that hangs on a curtain behind the stage was gone, replaced by the Russian Federation flag and an outline of the huge republic, which stretches from the Baltic Sea to the Pacific Ocean.

Perhaps nothing marked the change of era more clearly than the appearance of Alexi II, the patriarch of the Russian Orthodox Church, on the stage of the Kremlin Palace of Congresses. In a long and openly political address, the Russian religious leader decried the "seven decades of destruction of [Russia's] spiritual order" under Communist rule.

"You have taken responsibility for a country that is seriously ill," the bearded patriarch said, looking over at Yeltsin. "Three generations have been brought up under conditions which killed any wish and ability to work. First the people were made to forget the labor of prayer. Then they were made to forget the labor of thought, the desire to search for truth."

The patriarch called on the new president to redeem his pledges to return churches taken away under Communist rule and to restore the names of Russia's holy cities. And he called on Yeltsin to show "tolerance and wisdom," including toward his enemies.

"An ill society and people who have endured so much need understanding, love, and tolerance," the patriarch preached.

Gorbachev Readies Party Reform

Daniel Sneider

7/12/91

Many times in the past six years, Mikhail Gorbachev has faced challenges to his reform policies from within the giant Soviet Communist Party he heads. Each time, including last April, Mr. Gorbachev has blunted the assault.

Now the Soviet president is preparing to turn the tables on his attackers. When the plenum of the party's Central Committee meets on July 25, Gorbachev and his allies will show the door to his most hard-line opponents.

Party insiders play down talk of a formal division emerging at the plenary session.

"All our officials will try to organize to prevent a crisis of the party, a party split," says Alexander Buzgalin, a radical Marxist and Central Committee member.

But party leaders have already clearly indicated they will seek to isolate elements of the conservative right who might then leave on their own. Those people "will have to determine their own fate, their party allegiance," party deputy leader Vladimir Ivashko said earlier this week. "Naturally people who detest each other due to ideological considerations cannot be members of one party."

Some conservatives already are moving in this direction.

"If the Communist Party becomes a social democratic party, including in name," Alexander Lapin, a leader of the "Unity" group headed by neo-Stalinist Nina Andreyeva, told the Postfactum news agency, then "we will be free to declare [ourselves] heir to the . . . Communist Party."

Leaders decide to act

The decision of Gorbachev and the centrist party leadership finally to move strongly against the right is a direct consequence of two important developments. First, there was the so-called nine-plus-one agreement on April 23, between Gorbachev and the leaders of nine Soviet republics, at the core of which is the conciliation between Gorbachev and Russian President Boris Yeltsin.

Then, at the end of June, nine prominent political figures, led by former Foreign Minister Eduard Shevardnadze and including key liberal Communists, announced the creation of a new broad Movement for Democratic Reform. Their aim, the organizers say, is to ensure the ultimate success of Gorbachev's perestroika (restructuring), a goal that won them Gorbachev's backing. The movement will decide whether to become a party in September, but its founders clearly intend it to be a vehicle for parliamentary elections expected in the near future.

Both events have significantly shored up Gorbachev's political position and given him important allies on the democratic left. The movement offers the Soviet leader a far more credible platform for his own reelection as well. Mr. Yeltsin and others have already stated they would back him under such conditions.

A struggle has erupted in the Central Committee since the movement was announced, says Mr. Buzgalin. The "fundamentalists," as he calls the hard-liners, "will try to torpedo Gorbachev's support for this movement. But it is impossible now to change the balance of forces within the Central Committee. The majority will support the leader."

Buzgalin, a leading intellectual associated with the group Marxism in the 21st Century, sees Mr. Shevardnadze's movement as an attempt to organize a compromise between "the reformist part of our bureaucracy, those who support Gorbachev, and part of the democratic, liberal movement, that part which is now in power."

Reformers boost new group

He refers to movement leaders such as Leningrad Mayor Anatoly Sobchak and Moscow Mayor Gavril Popov, as well as Yeltsin who, while he is not a member, is closely linked to the group.

Critics on the democratic left see this not as a move to destroy the Communist Party but rather to save it. Movement leaders such as party theoretician Alexander Yakovlev and Arkady Volsky, who heads a movement of managers of state-run enterprises, "would like somehow to preserve the CPSU," says Vitaly Tretiakov, editor of the liberal Nezavisimaya Gazeta. (CPSU stands for Communist Party of the Soviet Union.)

"These are people of the older generation," Mr. Tretiakov continues. "The party might be good or bad but all their life has belonged to the party. At the beginning of perestroika, Gorbachev thought it was possible to improve the old system. The CPSU at that time was the only party. Now we are at the brink of party perestroika and again there is the same idea—just make the party better without changing it."

The aim of Mr. Yakovlev and others—though not perhaps of those who have left the party, such as Mr. Popov, Mr. Sobchak, and Shevardnadze—is to divide the party into a hard-line Communist group and a reformist party closer in spirit to the social democratic parties of Europe. The former want "to make two parties of bad Communists and good Communists," says Tretiakov. "The bad Communists are for [the late Soviet dictator Joseph] Stalin, for Communism in 20 years, against the market. And the good Communists are for socialism with a human face, the regulated market, and so on."

Party is fragmented

Yakovlev, the man credited with creating the policy of glasnost (openness) and a close Gorbachev adviser, virtually said as much in an interview in Izvestia on July 2 explaining the aim of the new movement.

"A single CPSU has not existed for a long time," he said. "The CPSU is pregnant with a multiparty system."

In recent remarks, Gorbachev has hinted he shares this view. The plenum will adopt a new party program that will change the image of the party, he told reporters at a press conference this week. "This will be a process of consolidation and renovation of the party, a process of establishing a new party of socialist orientation."

Some critics see this as a part of a sophisticated effort by the bureaucratic elite (the nomenklatura) to preserve its power and influence in a market-based society. "Nomenklatura capitalism," as it has been called, is typified by the rapid movement of the party into business activities and by the move to transform the state-run enterprises into "joint stock companies" in which the current managers retain their control through stock ownership.

Radical democrats say this attempt to reinvigorate the Communist Party could derail democratic and economic reform.

Oleg Rumyantsev, a Russian parliamentarian and leader of the Social Democratic Party, points to the example of Eastern Europe. "No democratic reform in Eastern Europe was finished with the old Communist center remaining," he warns.

Gorbachev Bids For Investment And G-7 Backing

Daniel Sneider

7/15/91

Soviet President Mikhail Gorbachev will travel to London this week, not to ask for aid, but to offer the West a new structure for economic cooperation, his senior aides say.

"We aren't going to ask for charity," deputy premier Vladimir Shcherbakov said in an interview here before his departure to London. "We offer mutually beneficial cooperation."

But while they do not seek "aid," the senior official made it clear that the Soviet Union will insist that it is the extent of Western assistance that will dictate the pace of economic reform.

Mr. Gorbachev has already dispatched a lengthy letter detailing his proposals and providing evidence of commitment to radical economic reforms. The proposals have not been made public, but Mr. Shcherbakov, who has played a significant role in this process, revealed key points in an interview with the Monitor and two European publications:

Investment, not aid. The Soviets will offer a list of investment projects for Western companies to join. In turn, the Soviets will ask for a "political decision by leaders of the Group of Seven (G-7) industrialized nations at their London meeting this week to push their companies to invest.

International Monetary Fund membership. The Soviets will seek full membership in the IMF and World Bank, arguing that this is essential for them to join the global economy.

Radical reform. The Soviets will contend that Western attitudes will determine how fast the ruble becomes convertible, prices are liberalized, and state-run industry is made private.

Political unity. Gorbachev will emphasize that the political situation has stabilized, that he speaks on behalf not only of his own government, but also of the republics, including Boris Yeltsin's Russia.

The London proposals integrate several economic programs, including the government's "anticrisis program" endorsed by the republics, as well as the radical plan of Soviet economist Grigory Yavlinsky, assisted by Harvard scholars and the suggestions of international financial institutions.

"We are unanimous in our strategy," Shcherbakov said, referring to Yavlinsky. "But we differ in approach to tactics."

Yavlinsky and Harvard Professor Jeffrey Sachs, principal authors of the radical plan, say it is impossible to combine their approach with the government's more conservative program. The blunt deputy premier accused the Yavlinsky program of advocating "shock therapy" unacceptable to the Soviet population.

Gorbachev, in his public remarks, has emphasized foreign investment as the main form of cooperation he seeks, distinguishing it from Western government aid. The priority for investment, Shcherbakov says, is the oil and gas industry, where foreign companies can upgrade equipment and get their investment back in the form of oil. Next in importance, he said, is conversion of defense industries to civilian uses, the processing of waste and raw materials, consumer-good production (particularly food processing and medicines), and environmental protection.

Ordering investment

But Shcherbakov made it clear the Soviet government rejects the idea that investment is determined by whether a company thinks it can make a profit. Rather, Gorbachev is coming to London with the belief that Western governments can tell companies in their countries what to do.

"If the Japanese government does not favor cooperation with a country, Japanese capital will never invest in that country," Shcherbakov explains. "It is the same for other countries. If the IMF invests $1 million, at once $10 million will be invested by private capital. The policies of the IMF are determined by the Group of Seven. That is why we say, first of all, you [the G-7] should decide to politically support this policy and tell your companies you politically support it."

The deputy premier, who traveled to Washington last month to explain Soviet reform policies, also indicated that the Soviets would not be happy with an "associate status" in the IMF. Western leaders are prepared to offer this, which gives the Soviets IMF advice but not money as their main concession in London. "Full membership gives lots of privileges," Shcherbakov said. "It's not very clear what associated membership means."

The Soviets, the senior official hinted, will link the speed of reform on key issues to Western actions. In particular, plans to make the ruble internally convertible into foreign currencies by Jan. 1 of next year will depend on whether the West offers a stabilization fund that could be used to bolster the value of the ruble.

"If there is no aid," Shcherbakov said, "the exchange rate [of the ruble] will be very low. Too low. Then we will have to limit the activity of Western companies . . . so that by using this unrealistic exchange rate, they don't buy up all our property."

Shcherbakov also rejected the idea of a rapid move to free prices advocated by Yavlinsky and the IMF. Prices of basic food products, a basket of other consumer goods, and fuel and energy will remain under control. Also, under their program, the system of state orders and control of supplies will still determine as much as 50 percent of all industrial production and 70 percent of energy and food production through 1992.

Republic dissent

Finally, the degree to which republican central governments have agreed on the anticrisis program is far less than Gorbachev is presenting to the West in London. There is no agreement, for example, on the central issue of taxation, with the Ukraine and Russia refusing to allow federal taxes.

In the midst of our interview, Shcherbakov received a call from Gorbachev asking about the response of republican governments to draft agreements on six unresolved issues. With reporters present, Shcherbakov told Gorbachev that the republics and the central government would meet after the London meeting to resolve basic problems, including the republics' contribution to the federal budget; a common method of determining the production costs of enterprises so that they do not escape taxation; the prices that are to remain controlled—and at what level—and those that are to be freed; the division of property between central and republican governments; the nationalization of state enterprises; and the division of Soviet foreign debt among the republics.

Although the program is supposed to begin July 1, Shcherbakov told Gorbachev, "If we cannot begin in July, we will begin it in August."

Gorbachev Returns Home To Tough Tests

Daniel Sneider

7/19/91

Mikhail Gorbachev sat down on Wednesday with the leaders of the seven richest capitalist nations and reached for a bottle of juice. He fumbled with the unfamiliar product of Western consumer society, unable to open it, finally putting it down with a slightly frustrated smile.

It was an unintended metaphor for this historic moment. Mr. Gorbachev was invited to an unprecedented seat at the table of the world's capitalist system. But he cannot yet enjoy its fruits.

British Prime Minister John Major, the meeting's host, summed up the symbolic meaning later: "This has been a day that history may see as a landmark, a first step toward helping the Soviet Union become a member of the world economic community."

Gorbachev largely struck the same positive note in his remarks. He could not, however, conceal his disappointment at the lack of concrete action coming out of the meeting. He referred repeatedly to the "need to remove roadblocks . . . piled up over those years of confrontation."

Indeed the day's most tangible result was not Mr. Major's "first step" but a last step—the announcement of the conclusion of the decade-long negotiation on a strategic nuclear arms reduction treaty between the United States and the Soviet Union.

Since the Khruschev era of the late 1950s, the East-West relationship has been primarily mediated through arms control negotiations. Two nuclear-armed superpowers locked in confrontation have sought, through treaty and talk, to reduce the risk of war.

That era is clearly over. There are no major arms control tasks that either side is eager to promote. And the dialogue is now focused on economics, on the shift to a market economy in the East and how the West will engage that process.

As US President Bush told reporters on Wednesday evening, "Because reform is not just an internal reform, it's democracy that they're moving toward and have really manifested a real interest in . . . . And as that develops, I am just convinced that any things that have been in our way of friendship before, such as arms and our worries about each other, will diminish."

Gorbachev came to London, where the Group of Seven (G-7) major industrial powers were holding their annual economic summit, with a complex and contradictory agenda. On one hand, he repeatedly declared that the Soviet Union came not as a supplicant for Western aid but as a great power, offering to open a new field of cooperation.

But there was another message contained in a 54-page document that preceded Gorbachev to London. It contained numerous proposals for cooperation, but also for assistance ranging from the restructuring of the Soviet Union's $65 billion debt to Western creation of a fund to support the value of the Soviet ruble as it is made convertible into other currencies.

The letter was a reminder that the Soviet leader heads a deeply unpopular government and is presiding over a profound economic crisis as it carries out a faltering attempt to bring market methods to a bureaucratic, state-run economy. In the midst of this, Gorbachev is trying to negotiate a sharing of power between the federal center and the 15 republics that make up the Soviet Union—six of which want to be independent and the rest of which seek a high degree of autonomy.

The West offered a combination of engagement and caution, the latter a response to Gorbachev's letter which disappointed many in failing to present a coherent reform plan with a clear timetable for action.

The Soviets will get a special associate status at the International Monetary Fund and World Bank, allowing the experts from those organizations to help shape reform plans but not yet giving access to their ample financial resources.

Western governments will pitch in with "technical assistance" in areas such as energy, conversion of military production to civilian purposes, food distribution, nuclear power safety, and transportation.

Perhaps the most important decision was the creation of a mechanism for an ongoing link between the Western leaders and Moscow, a "7 plus 1" as Gorbachev put it. The G-7 chairmen—Major this fall and German Chancellor Helmut Kohl next year—will visit the Soviet Union and monitor the reform process. Finance ministers will also visit Moscow for more focused discussions.

This amounts to a promissory note. If the Soviets are ready to accept the IMF's advice, and market reforms, such as liberalizing prices, are implemented, then, as Mr. Bush put it, "we can be helpful to assist flushing it out."

This is clearly not all that Gorbachev hoped for. But he will lose no time in cashing in this note in Moscow. That means first beating back a conservative Communist challenge that is expected to be mounted at a plenary meeting of the Soviet Communist Party that takes place July 25-26.

More important, Gorbachev wants to use the London summit to strengthen his bargaining position with the Soviet republics. A draft treaty of union is still under negotiation, with basic questions such as taxation, division of property, and how to form the budget remaining unresolved.

In his meeting with the G-7, Gorbachev spent a good deal of time discussing his relations with the republics. Bush told reporters that finalization of the union treaty is the necessary precondition to the large-scale foreign investment Gorbachev seeks.

Gorbachev is likely to return to Moscow arguing that he has a mandate from the West to form a stronger federal state, and that without such a system no republic will get the Western capital it seeks. His spokesman hinted at this approach when he pointedly told reporters that "today at the meeting with the G-7 the Soviet Union was treated as a single entity."

But Gorbachev's London capital is hardly limitless. In today's Soviet Union it could disappear in a month. Then the West will be pressed to show that its "first step" will be followed by a second one.

Gorbachev Squares Off With Party Hard-Liners

Daniel Sneider

7/25/91

Today the Soviet Communist Party opens a meeting of its top leadership that figures to be a crucial turning point in its history.

The party's policymaking Central Committee gathers for two days to vote on a draft program, its first since the early 1960s.

The program, according to a version published this week, repudiates Marxist-Leninist ideology and the party's clandestine, revolutionary traditions. Instead it offers an image and platform virtually indistinguishable from the parliamentary social democratic parties of Western Europe.

In no uncertain terms, the draft program, reportedly prepared under President Mikhail Gorbachev's direction, rejects class struggle and the dictatorship of the proletariat. The goal of a communist society is replaced by a vision of a "new civilization" that "does not fit into the customary ideas of classic industrial society, with its sharp division into antagonistic classes."

The program will be the trigger for a sharp debate between the pro-reform and orthodox Communist wings of the ruling party, with much of the conservative fire aimed at Mr. Gorbachev himself. The battle at the Central Committee plenum has been widely advertised as the opening step toward a formal split of the massive Communist Party into two or maybe three parts.

Gorbachev has won every past encounter with his party opponents, including one only last April when the conservatives made an abortive bid to oust him from the party leadership. He seems poised to win again, but in recent days the prospects for a far tougher struggle than earlier expected have risen.

The most vocal opposition to Gorbachev comes from extremist elements who grouped themselves into the self-named Bolshevik Platform in mid-July. Led by neo-Stalinist Nina Andreeva, they oppose what she calls "the transfer of the Communist Party of the Soviet Union [CPSU] onto the rails of right-wing bourgeois democracy."

A more serious expression of hard-line views was published on Tuesday in the daily Sovietskaya Rossiya by 12 conservatives including Deputy Defense Minister Valentin Varennikov and Deputy Interior Minister and Army hero Boris Gromov. With a direct appeal to the armed forces to join them, they call for creation of a "popular patriotic movement" for "the salvation of the Motherland."

"How did it happen that we . . . put in power those who do not love this country, who enslave themselves to foreign patrons and seek advice and blessing across the seas?" they ask, referring to Gorbachev's recent meeting in London with Western leaders.

More troubling for Gorbachev are signs that he can no longer depend on the loyalty of the party center. Leningrad party leader Boris Gidaspov, while distancing himself from hard-liners, told reporters last week that Gorbachev's reforms amounted to "a replacement of Marxism by pure Darwinism, when the rich devour the poor."

Moscow party boss Yuri Prokofiev, considered a moderate and a Gorbachev backer, called last week for Gorbachev to step down as party leader, and take a post as honorary chairman.

Gorbachev can count only on the liberal wing of the party, which by most accounts includes about 100 out of the 412 members of the Central Committee. Many of the leaders of this group, such as industrialist Arkady Volsky, are members of the Movement for Democratic Reforms formed last month by former Foreign Minister Eduard Shevardnadze and eight other prominent liberals. The Communist right has assailed this move, which it views as a stalking horse for Gorbachev and the possible nucleus of a new social democratic party.

Gorbachev will also depend on indirect backing from the leaders of the republics, such as Russia's Boris Yeltsin and Kazakhstan's Nursultan Nazarbeyev. Last April Gorbachev preempted a similar challenge from the right at a Central Committee meeting with the now famous April 23 "nine plus one" agreement with the heads of nine of the 15 republics on a the outlines of a new treaty of union.

Gorbachev appears to be attempting the same thing now, with a meeting that began on Tuesday aimed at finalizing the treaty for ratification by republican parliaments. By press time yesterday with the meeting still continuing, the republics had reportedly settled all the issues except the nettlesome question of taxation. Russia and the Ukraine still oppose a federal tax.

The Gorbachev-republic axis took a blow last weekend when Mr. Yeltsin banned all party organizations in government bodies and industrial enterprises, a move clearly aimed at the Communist Party and denounced by it as antidemocratic and a violation of existing laws.

The decree will undoubtedly be a focus of the plenum, with conservatives citing it as evidence of the hostile nature of the democratic opposition.

Gorbachev's spokesman took a somewhat careful tone, saying the decree disrupts the move toward accord, "causes anxiety, and introduces tension and confrontation."

Yeltsin, trying to defuse its impact, told the Russian Information Agency that "my relations with President Gorbachev remain normal and there is no confrontation."

START Could End US-Soviet Arms Talks

Daniel Sneider

7/26/91

Next week Presidents Bush and Gorbachev will stand in an ornate Kremlin room and put their pens to what some here believe will be the last Soviet-American arms control treaty.

The Strategic Arms Reduction Treaty (START) culminates more than nine years of negotiations. But taking the failed SALT II pact into account, the two superpowers have been trying to reach an agreement on strategic nuclear weapons since 1974. While both sides have spoken of a follow-up treaty, most Soviet analysts discount this as an unrealistic proposition.

"It is clear that the two countries are exhausted by the current START negotiations," comments Sergei Blagovolin, who heads military studies at the prestigious Institute of World Economy and International Relations. "I don't think another treaty negotiation now is really very important for the future of our relations."

Instead, liberals like Mr. Blagovolin envision a shift away from the cold war preoccupation with preserving a balance of power to joint action, even including military cooperation.

"The main idea," the expert predicts, "will be establishing a real cooperative security structure between the Soviet Union and the West." The two sides will focus more on threats to their mutual security from other sources, including "the dramatic rise of new threats from the south," as well as instability in Europe, as seen in Yugoslavia, he explains.

Such Soviet policymakers want to extend the kind of initial steps away from the cold war taken during the Gulf war when the Soviet Union gave tacit support to the Western war against Iraq. The new agenda, says Vladik Zubok, an expert on United States-Soviet relations at the USA-Canada Institute, includes cooperating to limit arms transfers to third-world nations, barring the proliferation of nuclear weapons and conversion of defense industries to civilian use.

"It's too early to bury arms-control summits," Mr. Zubok believes. But these discussions will no longer be a purely US-Soviet affair. Broader meetings such as the one in London last week between the Group of Seven Western leaders and Soviet President Mikhail Gorbachev will gradually replace bilateral summits, he asserts.

This does not mean military issues will disappear from the table. From the post-cold-war point of view, the two sides might begin a discussion of a "mutually acceptable restructuring of military forces," suggests Blagovolin. Such talks could even extend to creating a future military division of labor between the NATO alliance and the Soviet Union, he adds.

Such ideas are by no means confined to Soviet think tanks. Concrete proposals along these lines were contained within the detailed annex which Mr. Gorbachev attached to the letter he dispatched to the London summit. The annex provided detailed proposals for cooperation in a number of fields, of which first place was given to defense conversion.

Alongside proposals for Western firms to develop civilian aircraft and other commercial products, Gorbachev suggests a number of joint military projects, all of a carefully "defensive" nature. The most striking is the idea of joint development of early warning systems "to prevent unauthorized or terrorist operated launches of ballistic missiles." The proposal is aimed at potential nuclear powers such as Iraq and echoes the idea, proposed by Blagovolin and others, of joint development of Star Wars-type, space-based warning systems.

The Gorbachev package also suggests development of technologies to safely eliminate chemical, nuclear, and conventional weapons and to process nuclear waste, including from nuclear submarines.

As part of this London package, the Soviets are looking for the US to remove the long-standing COCOM (Coordinating Committee on Export Controls) restrictions on the flow of high technology to the Soviet Union. "The COCOM limitations continue to be a serious obstacle to economic cooperation between Soviet enterprises and foreign companies," Gorbachev wrote.

Observers here expect some of these ideas, particularly for defense conversion, to be on the summit agenda next week.

Quite a different challenge to classical arms control comes from the other end of the political spectrum, from those conservatives who argue that the process has benefited only the West. Sources close to senior government officials predict that as soon as the START treaty is signed, a concerted campaign will begin to block ratification by the Soviet parliament of both START and the treaty to reduce conventional forces in Europe (CFE).

Signs of that effort are already present. An article written by a Foreign Ministry official and published in the conservative daily Sovietskaya Rossiya July 13 has provoked considerable comment among officials. The article attacks former Foreign Minister Eduard Shevardnadze and the three treaties negotiated largely under his direction—the 1987 pact to eliminate intermediate nuclear forces, the CFE treaty signed last November, and START. The military was betrayed by Mr. Shevardnadze and his fellow liberals, the official says.

"Now for many of our reactionaries in the [Armed Forces] General Staff, in the [Communist] Party structure, in military industry, it is quite clear the implementation of these treaties will mark a turning point," comments Blagovolin. It will mean a major reduction and reorganization of the military, moves which will ultimately "shatter the military-industrial complex." For these circles, "it is not a question of the security of the nation, but their own security."

But the Soviet military is not uniform in its views. The final stages of START were negotiated directly by the Chief of the General Staff, Mikhail Moiseyev, whose views are considered more flexible than those of Defense Minister Dmitri Yazov and Gorbachev's military adviser and former chief of staff, Marshal Sergei Akhromeyev. Soviet sources say some influential officers at the level of deputy military district commanders back Mr. Moiseyev and favor far more concerted military reform.

These pro-reform circles have their counterparts in the defense industry. Managers in some of the most high-technology sectors, such as the aircraft industry, are eagerly pursuing joint ventures with Western firms. They recognize the need both for opening up to the West and for sharp reductions in defense spending.

Whether by necessity or craft, Gorbachev made what some think is a clever move by getting Moiseyev's imprimatur for the START agreement. By involving Moiseyev and others like him, says Zubok, "you show them they're in the loop. Sometimes that's enough."

Conciliatory Steps Mask Divisions Among Soviets on Eve of Summit

Daniel Sneider

7/29/91

When President Bush arrives tonight in Moscow he will find an apparently rejuvenated Mikhail Gorbachev.

Only a few months ago, the Soviet president seemed on the edge of political demise. The restive republics, led by Russia and its populist leader Boris Yeltsin, were threatening to dismember the federal state. At the same time conservative ideologues were demanding Mr. Gorbachev's removal as head of the ruling Communist Party of the Soviet Union (CPSU).

Now Gorbachev has an agreement on a new treaty of union with the republics virtually signed and sealed. And the Communist Party Central Committee voted on Friday, after a relatively calm meeting, to accept a new program that repudiates Marxist-Leninist ideology in favor of social-democratic reformism.

But to a considerable degree, Soviet observers say, these perceptions are illusory. The agreement with the republics is still not complete. And there is very little consensus in the CPSU other than the desire not to lose power.

The all-day attempt to complete the negotiations on the draft treaty of union last Tuesday fell short of the mark. The Russian and Ukrainian governments, which between them contribute the lion's share of Soviet taxes, refuse to have any direct federal tax collection. They will contribute the money they feel is needed to finance federal programs, but at their own determination.

According to Ivan Laptev, head of the Soviet of the Union, one of the two houses of the Soviet parliament, a compromise has been worked out in which a joint center-republican body will determine what the money is used for, and on that basis republics will pay a fixed percentage. But no Russian or Ukrainian official has confirmed such a deal.

Moreover, such a compromise signals that Gorbachev survives as the leader of the Soviet Union only by ceding a tremendous amount of power to the republics. The day Mr. Bush arrives, Russia will sign its own treaty with the Baltic republic of Lithuania, a republic that refuses to sign the union treaty.

"The timing of this event," wrote Izvestia commentator Stanislav Kondrashov last Friday, "testifies to the desire to demonstrate to the President of the United States . . . that his major interlocutor in Moscow does not control completely the schedule of events nor even the events themselves."

Bush will carefully weave his way around this reality. His schedule calls for him to spend most of his time with Gorbachev, a man he clearly feels comfortable dealing with. But he will also see Yeltsin and, perhaps more importantly, will spend a day in the Ukrainian capital of Kiev.

The events at the party meeting may be even more difficult for Bush to comprehend. Gorbachev presented what is unquestionably a radical departure from even the version of perestroika (restructuring) agreed to at past party gatherings. The draft party program explicitly abandons the doctrine that divided the communist movement founded by Lenin from the mild socialism of the German Social Democratic Party and similar European movements.

"The model that has been imposed on the party and society for decades has suffered a strategic defeat," Gorbachev said in his closing speech on Friday. "It follows from this conclusion that we have come to face the necessity of a new drastic change of our entire viewpoint on socialism."

But almost all the speakers who rose during the two-day gathering shared the views of men like Leningrad party boss Boris Gidaspov, who assailed the draft program as "another step, and a big one, to the ideological and organizational weakening of the communist movement." Yet the party leadership voted overwhelmingly to accept the draft, though it will be amended somewhat in the next two weeks before being presented to the party membership and to a party congress at the end of the year for final approval.

How does one explain why the largely conservative party bureaucracy voted this way?

"Because their armchair is more important than the program," answered Alexander Yakovlev, former ideology chief of the party and one of the chief architects of Gorbachev's reforms, speaking to a small group of journalists Saturday. Mr. Yakovlev, who stepped down Saturday from his last official post as adviser to Gorbachev, is a leader of the new liberal Movement for Democratic Reforms.

Yakovlev dismisses the idea of a right-wing move to split the party. "The right-wingers will accept everything because they are losing ground," he says. But on another level, Yakovlev suggests that this agreement was a tactical move. He points to the fate of the policies adopted last summer at the 28th Party Congress.

"There were a lot of democratic and progressive things, but nobody was going to implement these resolutions. The same thing will happen to the program. They will vote for it, but they will pursue a different policy."

Yakovlev says it is too late to reform the party. "It doesn't matter anymore," he says. "The train has left the station."

But the party retains power over the KGB, the Army, and other security organizations, Moscow News analyst Lyudmila Telen wrote last week. "The CPSU remains a state structure rather than a party and gives orders to a powerful apparat of coercion."

II
The August Revolution

Social unrest in the Soviet Union led to reforms too liberal and too forward thinking for a group of eight top ranking Communist party hard-liners. In an effort to stem the tide of reform these eight men planned and implemented a coups on August 19, 1991 designed to strengthen the role of the Communist Party in the process of change. Their unsuccessful bid to claim power lasted merely 72 hours.

As readings in this section demonstrate, reaction to the coups was massive. Western nations suspended aid to the U.S.S.R. amidst great political uncertainty. Gorbachev resigned as General Secretary of the Communist party. Liberal Soviets gained legitimacy as representatives of Government. Communist Icons were demolished, and new programs were unveiled to help the ailing Soviet Economy.

Gorbachev Ouster Casts Shadow Over US-Soviet Rapprochement

George D. Moffett III / Marshall Ingwerson

8/20/91

The Soviet coup early yesterday morning strikes a dangerous blow to the deepening American relationship with the Soviet Union.

That relationship had become strongly centered on President Mikhail Gorbachev who, although no longer the banner-carrier for reform, succeeded until yesterday in holding the Soviet Union's tumultuous factions together.

Although fully aware that Soviet leader Mikhail Gorbachev was walking a precarious tightrope between conservatives and liberals who criticized the pace of his economic and political reforms, Bush administration officials were caught completely off-guard by news of Gorbachev's ouster.

President Bush was awakened and informed of the coup at his summer house in Kennebunkport, Maine, just before midnight Sunday. In the morning, he called it a "disturbing development" that could have "serious consequences" for relations with the US. Bush announced all US aid to the Soviet Union was on hold.

Bush has frequently insisted that US relations with the Soviet Union do not depend on Gorbachev. Even so, US officials have credited the former Soviet leader with unusual skill in following a middle line between liberal revolution and the kind of conservative reaction that swept him from power yesterday.

Gorbachev's departure occurs at a high point in US-Soviet relations. Just last month Bush and Gorbachev met in Moscow where they concluded a strategic arms reduction treaty. Days earlier, Bush and the leaders of six other industrial democracies pledged further efforts to speed free market reforms in the Soviet Union.

The personal chemistry and trust that has developed between the two leaders over the past couple of years was apparent at the Moscow summit. In Moscow, Bush underscored Gorbachev's importance as the Soviet Union's strongest link to the West and its economic resources by offering the Soviets everything he could, without spending American money. Most significantly, Bush finally offered the Soviets most-favored-nation trading status.

In the early hours after Gorbachev's ouster one concern here is that such reforms, halting as they have been, could be reversed. A more pressing concern is that opposition to the takeover could produce violence and political instability, especially in several restive republics which have been seeking to break away from the Soviet Union.

The risk that the hard-liners now in power will return to a cold-war confrontation that threatens Europe and the West is not rated high. The Soviet Union still has over 10,000 nuclear warheads mounted on intercontinental ballistic missiles capable of reaching the United States. Its ground forces, however, have largely withdrawn from non-Soviet Europe.

Further, most American analysts predict that the hard-line right will be too consumed with the task of consolidating its power within the Soviet Union to try to expand its sphere of influence abroad. The Soviet economy, also, is in too much of a shambles to support military adventures.

Yesterday's coup occurred just as a new union treaty designed to redistribute power within the country was about to be signed by Gorbachev. That treaty, which would grant more autonomy to the republics, is almost certain to be scrapped amid threats by the new leadership to suspend the parliament of any republic pressing for secession.

Any massive Soviet intervention to block secession, for example in the three Baltic republics, could present the US with the difficult choice of whether to intervene.

In addition to the strategic arms treaty, now awaiting Senate ratification, Sunday's coup also places a treaty on conventional forces in Europe, signed in November, in doubt.

Gorbachev's departure also threatens joint initiatives which could help bring peace to regions of the world that were once theaters of intense superpower competition.

A major question mark now looms over plans to convene a comprehensive Middle East peace conference under joint US and Soviet auspices. Israel may be less inclined to participate with a hard-line Soviet sponsor. Analysts will be watching, meanwhile, to see if Syria is influenced by the changes in Moscow to revert to its traditional hard-line policy towards Israel and to eschew US-led peace efforts.

While in the Ukraine just over two weeks ago, President Bush stressed that American policy was not focused on personalities, namely Gorbachev. But rather it supported the principles of democracy and reform, whether they came from Moscow or the restless republics.

But the program Bush promoted was clearly that of Gorbachev, as the man in the middle of Soviet politics.

With the loss of Gorbachev to a hard-line coup, Bush policy may be proven right even as it fails. Bush's critics accused the President of holding back stronger support for the independence movements in the republics. The greater threat to stability—if the early course of this coup is borne out—remained on the Soviet right.

Soviet Coup Long Time in Making

Daniel Sneider

8/21/91

Moscow's midnight coup was an act by desperate men in desperate times. The axis of Communist Party stalwarts, the military, the secret police, and their allies in the state bureaucracy that seized power on Aug. 18 clearly felt their long-held power slipping from their grasp.

At least three factors compelled the coup: The imminent signing of a new union treaty shifting power to the republics was primary, along with the prospect of a splintering of the Communist Party. Behind this was a precipitous economic collapse.

Putch leaders and their tanks are moving rapidly to dismantle the opposing structures of power created by six years of reform. One key obstacle stands in their way: the democratically elected government of Russian Federation President Boris Yeltsin.

In this battle, Mr. Yeltsin must rely on two forces. One is his fellow leaders of the Soviet republics, men such as Kazakhstan's Nursultan Nazarbayev and the Ukraine's Leonid Kravchuk, and the nationalist movements behind them. The second is the determinations of a mobilized Russian populace to stave off what the gutsy Russian leader Aug. 19 called the "eternal night."

Right-wing offensive

This political war, with these battle lines, was already well-formed last year. The right-wing coalition behind the coup is the same alliance that succeeded last fall in pressing Soviet President Mikhail Gorbachev to move away from his reform course.

In early December former Latvian KGB chief Boris Pugo became interior minister and Communist bureaucrat Gennady Yanayev became vice president. Both now sit on Moscow's ruling eight-man State of Emergency Committee.

The eight include the KGB chief, Vladimir Kryuchkov, and Defense Minister Dmitri Yazov who engineered the bloody crackdown on Baltic independence movements last January. Also among them are the prime minister and economic czar, Valentin Pavlov, and the communist official running the defense industry complex, Oleg Baklanov.

The beleaguered forces for reform were divided and weakened. In late December, Foreign Minister Eduard

Shevardnadze tried to rally the democrats with his dramatic resignation, warning of impending "dictatorship."

By April, the political tide had begun to turn against the grey-faced soldiers of the state. The soot-coated miners of Russia and the Ukraine began the shift with their mass political strike in March. Riding that wave, Yeltsin smashed a Communist attempt to oust him in late March.

Mr. Gorbachev sensed the shifting winds and turned with them. On April 23, at the famous nine-plus-one gathering with leaders of nine republics led by Yeltsin, Gorbachev made a historic compromise. A new union treaty would shift enormous power from the Kremlin to the republics, he agreed, and a new constitution and national elections would follow shortly.

Opposition rallies

As the union treaty took shape in tough bargaining sessions over the summer, the democratic opposition also rallied. Yeltsin's June 12 election to the newly created Russian presidency was followed by a July announcement of a new Movement for Democratic Reforms headed by Mr. Shevardnadze and eight other prominent liberals. The Communist Party appeared on the verge of a split, isolating hard-line elements. Just before the convening of a key party Central Committee plenum on July 25, Yeltsin delivered a hammer blow in the form of a ban on Communist Party cells in government offices and enterprises in Russia.

Underlying this political struggle was the unraveling Soviet economy. The Pavlov government and its military-industry allies proposed an "anti-crisis" program that relied on using the familiar levers of state control to "stabilize" the economy. But by mid-July, Gorbachev, at the urging of the Western leaders he met in London, appeared more ready to opt instead for radical reforms.

Soviet experts on both sides predicted that reforms would be too late to avert deep food shortages and hyperinflation. The democrats feared this could be used to justify a rightist takeover, while their Communist opponents worried about losing their last levers of control over the economy in chaos.

The timing for the coup was clearly determined by the Aug. 20 date set for the signing of the union treaty. The movement of armed force and KGB units bears all the earmarks of careful preparation.

But the coup events also betray the weakness of the junta, the virtual absence of popular support for its members, and their fear of the backing Yeltsin commands. That may explain the elaborate steps the junta has taken to assert its constitutional legitimacy, including its claim that Gorbachev has been replaced for reasons of health and might return.

The coup leaders are also eager to ease Western reaction, if only to concentrate on winning the battle on the home front. They insist that they are not abandoning Gorbachev's domestic reforms or his new foreign policy.

In evaluating the coup's strength, the full loyalty of the military's officer corps is also in doubt. The units deployed in Moscow, according to reports, are elite forces. But one knows how the young officers and draftees would respond to an order to fire on fellow Russians or Ukranians.

Nothing to lose

The less than commanding position of the new leadership may account for its curious decision not to round up Yeltsin in the first hours of the coup, leaving him to lead a resistance. But it would be premature to predict their defeat. If anything, suggests one Soviet analyst reached by telephone in Moscow, their desperation makes them more aggressive.

"They are people who have nothing to lose, the observer says of the putch bosses. "They won't withdraw. They'll go to the end. This makes the situation very dangerous."

Resistance Builds to Hard-Line Soviet Regime: West Suspends Aid; Concern Grows About the Intent of New Leadership in Kremlin

Amy Kaslow

8/21/91

The stunning seizure of power from Soviet President Mikhail Gorbachev on Aug. 19 targeted a man who carefully wooed the West for political support and financial help.

Western economic leaders, who just weeks ago agreed to jointly assist Moscow through painful economic reforms, are now confounded by the Kremlin's new inhabitants, a collective leadership of Communist loyalists who say they're saving the Soviets from economic breakdown. Mr. Gorbachev's American, European, and Asian supporters have responded by suspending aid, from food to finances. It is unclear whether the coup means a complete abandonment of the limited economic and democratic reforms or whether the road is blocked for further liberalization.

The Group of Seven (G-7) world economic leaders, whose meetings in London last month were dominated by the prospect of an all-out Soviet political and economic crisis, are concerned that the current situation will lead to chaos. The new Soviet regime, coordinated by an eight-man committee that includes the head of the Red Army and the KGB, may represent the West's worst fears.

British Prime Minister John Major, chairman of the G-7, calls the Soviet government change "ominous." The new leadership seems to favor an incongruous mixture of communist perks and production quotas with the benefits of a robust economy, including modern technology and access to world financing.

If the new regime endures and reasserts central control over the economy, "it will roll back reforms and cost the country its economic stature and international aid," says Jay Mitchell, an economist with PlanEcon Inc., a group of Washington-based Soviet and East European economic analysts. The West has long-regarded a political settlement between Moscow center and the republics as essential to reforms. Mr. Mitchell says a return of Soviet hard-line rule will counter new autonomous developments, such as the republics' agitation for control over natural resources, the Ukraine's formation of its own currency, and the Baltics' erection of customs posts.

"The regime's Stalinist-type leaders will, at gunpoint, make sure goods are in the stores and prevent the new capitalist cooperatives from 'price gouging,' " Mitchell says. "They'll make things more 'fair' so that nobody can get rich and everybody is poorer." Soviet Prime Minister Valentin Pavlov "isn't even skillful with his xenophobia," Mitchell quips. "He says, 'We want to have business with Western firms' as he accuses them of 'CIA plots' to control the Soviet economy."

Washington-based businessman Jonathan Halperin, president of FYI Information Resources, with Soviet affiliates and partners throughout the Soviet Union, says his colleagues are now very troubled. The roughly 2,000 registered Soviet independent joint-ventures and 500,000 privately managed businesses are under Mr. Pavlov's watchful eye.

Aid from the World Bank and the International Monetary Fund is clearly in jeopardy. The G-7 offered Moscow special associate status with these lending institutions as an initiation into the international community.

"We'll have to sort things out to see if it's possible to move ahead on any level," World Bank President Barber Conable said in an interview. "There has to be a consensus of our members behind anything we do for a non-member. . . . There's a real limit on what we can do." On Aug. 20, the World Bank Board of Governors was to consider the creation of a special three-year $25 million to $30 million Soviet trust fund, co-financed by other donor/lenders, to help Moscow pay for World Bank technical assistance.

The fund was scratched from the board's agenda after the Aug. 19 forced ouster of Gorbachev.

A United States Treasury official says the Export-Import Bank's consideration of lifting its $300 million cap on financing US exports to Moscow is also derailed, like all other US bilateral aid, such as grain credits and preferred trading status.

Germany, Moscow's primary source of financial and economic aid, has committed roughly $30 billion to the Soviet Union's reform process. Much of the money is for the removal and relocation of the 270,000 troops still stationed in eastern Germany, an area that was, until two years ago, a Soviet satellite country. The soldiers are not eager to return to their dismal homeland, where they face unemployment, food lines, and housing shortages. Germans, however, are very anxious that the soldiers will not leave, given the return of Soviet hard-line rule.

German Finance Ministry spokesman Christian Kastrop says, "Our bilateral treaties [stipulating Soviet troop withdrawal] are our first concern." He rules out increased German financial transfers as a means of ensuring troop removal. "There is no possibility for the Soviet Union to have more wishes granted by us," Mr. Kastrop says. The Soviets' "very severe economic problems" contributed to the removal of Gorbachev, Kastrop says. "But new leadership will only keep the old economic system" at the country's expense, he warns.

"We have made it quite clear that we are connecting our economic help with political and economic reforms. If the democratic process is endangered, we have to rethink our approach very clearly," Kastrop says, referring to Bonn's multibillion-dollar commitment to the Soviets.

All of the other Soviet fledgling Western financial relationships will be tested on this basis, he says, including those with the 12-nation European Community, the World Bank, the IMF and G-7.

EC Moved Strongly To Back Gorbachev

Howard LaFranchi

8/22/91

European leaders took advantage of signs of disarray and confusion within the Soviet Union's newly declared leadership to strengthen their support for reformist forces resisting Monday's coup against Soviet leader Mikhail Gorbachev. The hardening of tone was reflected at Tuesday's emergency meeting of European Community foreign ministers, where the EC's aid program to the Soviet Union was suspended.

Leaders of the European Community's 12 member countries are expected at an emergency EC summit tomorrow at The Hague to reinforce pressure in favor of continued economic and democratic reforms. This includes pushing for the Soviets to respect international agreements such as arms control and promised Soviet troop withdrawals in Europe.

The summit is also likely to take up measures aimed at reassuring the Soviet Union's former satellites countries in Eastern Europe that the Community views as irreversible their attachment to a democratic and free-market Europe.

After what was initially a surprisingly moderate response to Mr. Gorbachev's ouster by several European capitals, European leaders markedly hardened their tone.

The change reflected at least two factors: One was an apparent reassessment of the West's ability to influence a still-fluid situation in the Soviet Union. The feeling was growing that a firm stand from the West can still sway Soviet events, and that Western support for the reformist resistance, including Russian President Boris Yeltsin and his backers, is crucial.

On the economic front, the EC tomorrow could freeze progress towards a European energy pact, which was to open Soviet energy potential to European investment. It is a further attempt to influence Soviet action, this time through the purse.

The change also reflects a willingness by Paris and Bonn to fall in line with the swifter, stronger reaction of Washington and London against Monday's coup. French President Francois Mitterrand said in a televised speech Monday night that economic sanctions were "premature," but by Tuesday French Foreign Minister Roland Dumas was saying, "The hour has come to pass judgment on events in the Soviet Union."

Nervous German leaders, who Monday appeared to adopt a wait-and-see attitude, by Tuesday were calling for Mr. Gorbachev's return to power. At the emergency meeting of EC foreign ministers, $400 million in emergency food aid alone was exempted as the rest of the $1.15 billion assistance package, agreed last December for the Soviets, was put on hold.

Saying the return to power of Gorbachev would be "the best proof of a return to legality," Dutch Foreign Minister Hans van den Broeck, the EC president, explained his colleagues' call for Gorbachev's reinstatement and the right to visit him.

Viewing warily the seizure of power in Moscow by forces that blame Gorbachev for the "loss" of Eastern Europe, EC leaders appeared abruptly awakened to a need to more strongly assist Central and Eastern European countries seeking to join the West. German Foreign Minister Hans-Dietrich Genscher called for accelerating the process through which Eastern European countries may gain EC associate status.

Even EC Commission President Jacques Delors, until now an implacable supporter of "deepening" Community political and economic integration before "widening" beyond the current 12 members, this week indicated a change of position.

Referring to the difficult negotiations that have followed Com-munity leaders' strong rhetorical commitment to Eastern Europe, Mr. Delors promised "reasonable and realistic" EC concessions in agriculture, coal, steel, and textiles. The Community can no longer "make fine speeches on Sunday" only to later in the week "oppose the trade concessions enabling those countries to sell their goods and improve their standards of living," he said.

Assessing West's Role in Soviet Hard-Liners' Bid

Daniel Sneider

8/22/91

Even before the apparent collapse of the Moscow putsch, the question was already being asked: Did the West pave the way for the coup?

The charge is being made that by not giving Soviet President Mikhail Gorbachev the economic aid he was seeking, most recently at the mid-July summit of Western leaders in London, the West paved the way for his overthrow.

Other critics see the aborted coup attempt as proof that the West had overly focused its policies on Mr. Gorbachev, ignoring the shift of political power to figures such as Russia's Boris Yeltsin. Gorbachev, it is argued, was an easy victim of the hard-liners he harbored within his own government, while Mr. Yeltsin has emerged as the sole and most solid obstacle to the coup leaders.

The economic aid issue is not new. It came up last fall when Gorbachev was deciding on a new plan for economic reform in the Soviet Union. He had apparently decided in favor of a radical so-called 500 days program, backed by Yeltsin. But under pressure from the conservatives—the same people behind Sunday night's coup—he backed off in October.

The Western leaders, meeting at the annual Group of Seven industrial nations summit in July 1990 in Houston, had opted for a cautious approach to helping Moscow. Limited direct aid was offered and a study of the Soviet economy was commissioned. Many observers, both in the Soviet Union and outside, felt the West's failure to state its readiness to supply large amounts of financial credits and other assistance was a key factor behind Gorbachev's October decision to opt for a slower approach.

The same choice, though under far more stark political conditions and economic chaos, was on the agenda when the Western leaders met in London. This time Gorbachev came in person to make his appeal for fresh economic aid.

The London summit gave Gorbachev little in the way of tangible economic aid, opting instead to offer associate membership in the International Monetary Fund and the IMF's assistance in developing reform policies. The Western leadership found Gorbachev's plans far too vague and indecisive. In effect they gave him political backing and an undefined promise of help when his plans showed more commitment to clear, radical change.

While Gorbachev put the best face on the London results, his demeanor betrayed his disappointment at not coming back with more to show. The leaders of the Moscow junta did not conceal their sneering attitude toward his failure, using it to partly justify their actions.

"Only irresponsible people can bank on some aid from abroad," the State Committee for the State of Emergency declared. "No handouts can solve our problems; our rescue is in our own hands."

Western leaders also seemed to have missed the change which accompanied Gorbachev's political weakening—the shift of power and of the impetus for reform to the leaders of the 15 republics which make up the union. That shift means a growing role for Boris Yeltsin, leader of the Russian republic where half the population lives, and Ukrainian leader Leonid Kravchuk, Kazakhstan's Nursultan Nazarbayev and others.

When it appeared that Gorbachev's days of political manuever had ended, Western leaders had only Yeltsin to talk to on the other end of the telephone line. For Yeltsin, it is probably a case of better late than never.

Coup Failure Reveals Deep Split Within Soviet Military

Daniel Sneider

8/23/91

The 10 T-72 battle tanks that stood in front of the Russian Republic's parliament building to defend it from attack by fellow units of the Red Army were visible proof of the split in the Soviet Armed Forces exacerbated by the attempted coup.

From the first hours of the coup, there was evidence that the putsch plotters did not command the allegiance of a large portion of the 3.8 million-man Army. A very small number of units were actually involved in the coup actions, which were confined to Moscow, Leningrad, and the three Baltic republics. This suggests that the junta could not control broader forces.

Moreover, the units that joined the coup—such as the Tamanskaya Motor Rifle Division and the Paratroop Division from Ryazan which were deployed in Moscow—were elite, virtually all-professional forces. The former is a showpiece unit, turned out for visiting foreign military officials. They were backed by the Interior Ministry's own elite, "black beret" special forces.

The conscript-formed motorized infantry divisions that are the mainstay of the Soviet Army remained in their barracks. And according to Pentagon intelligence reports, there was an eerie absence of activity within those forces. They were not placed on alert, nor was there evidence of the heightened communications between Defense Ministry headquarters and the military district commands that many experts expected to see in such a military-backed coup.

There were also hints that a significant portion of the Soviet Armed Forces General Staff were, at most, passive bystanders to the coup. The only military figure publicly with the coup was Defense Minister Dmitri Yazov. It has been presumed, given his position and known political views, that Lt. Gen. Boris Gromov was also a participant. General Gromov is an Afghan War hero who was appointed Deputy Interior Minister late last year, a move widely seen as an attempt to tie the military more closely to enforcing political order within the country.

But the man who, most interestingly, has been absent during these past days was Chief of the General Staff Mikhail Moiseyev, who has emerged after the coup as the acting Minister of Defense. That fact would not surprise some Soviet observers, because General Moiseyev had signaled he was at odds with General Yazov and Deputy Defense Minister Valentin Varennikov, both considered extreme conservatives.

Moiseyev's break with them was most evident in July, when he helped to negotiate a conclusion to the START treaty limiting nuclear arms, and to resolve differences over implementing the treaty to limit conventional forces in Europe. Both treaties were targets of conservatives, who saw them as unequal and part of the retreat of Soviet power under Mikhail Gorbachev.

A well-informed Soviet military expert closely tied to reform circles gave further evidence of a deep split developing in the military. In a July interview, he revealed that a group of senior military officers at the level of deputy commanders of military districts had secretly joined to promote a serious new effort at military reform. The official version of military reform backed by Yazov and others was already widely discredited as a largely paper affair. These officers, the source said, were convinced of the need for serious cuts in defense spending, for conversion of the defense industry to civilian production, and for a new security relationship with the West. According to the expert, the group sought Mr. Gorbachev's support to organize a study team to draft a new reform plan. Gorbachev urged the group to move quickly, far more rapidly than they had planned, to complete their work. He told them, the source said, to get the work done by August.

Did Gorbachev know something even then about the dangers awaiting them? There is no clear evidence of that, but he was at least aware, at that point, that the military was divided at the highest level on basic policy issues. That split may ultimately be what saved Gorbachev's life and his government.

Soviet Power Locus Shifts to Yeltsin

Daniel Sneider

8/23/91

Mikhail Gorbachev is back in the Kremlin again. But during his forced absence, the seat of power has moved down the Moscow River to Boris Yeltsin's "White House."

The stunning hard-liner coup in Moscow and its equally dramatic collapse have already indelibly altered the Soviet political map. Mr. Gorbachev returns as a man betrayed by his own ministers and generals—the very men he put in place—who first covertly and finally overtly opposed his reforms. Mr. Yeltsin now stands as the uncompromised and unquestioned leader of democratic and economic reform in the Soviet Union, lauded around the world for his courage.

By losing, the conservative Communists and their military and secret police allies may have sped up the prospects for change. The democratic forces, led by Yeltsin, now gain momentum. Gorbachev's practice of maneuvering between reformers and conservatives has lost all context as well as credibility.

It remains to be seen what kind of Gorbachev the Soviet people will now see. Will, for example, Gorbachev move resolutely to sweep out the institutions, such as the KGB and the Interior Ministry, which spearheaded the coup? How will he reorganize his own cabinet, whose leadership formed the core of the eight-man junta? And will Gorbachev remain the head of the Soviet Communist Party—the organizational base of the coup plotters?

In the days ahead the Soviet people will be watching carefully for the first signs of answers to these questions. They will also be watching how Gorbachev and Yeltsin reshape their relationship, both in private and in public. But Gorbachev's stance is less relevant now than before. It is Yeltsin, not Gorbachev, who stands as the guarantor of democratic reform in the Soviet Union.

Yeltsin seems content to have Gorbachev sit in the post of Soviet president, seeing far more future in being the president of the vast Russian Federation. But it is uncertain whether he will move to assert his newly won power in more open fashion.

While there are certainly surprises yet to come in the aftermath of the attempted coup, there is little question of where Yeltsin is likely to try to lead the Soviet Union. The failed coup seems certain to strengthen the shift of governmental authority away from the central administration and into the hands of the governments of the republics.

The desperate effort to seize power was prompted by the imminent signing, planned for Aug. 20, of a new treaty of union which would have formalized a considerable republican role. The coup leaders made it clear they considered the treaty tantamount to a dismemberment of the Soviet Union.

Ironically, their own actions may lead to the realization of those fears. The treaty was already imbued with a great deal of ambiguity about the precise division of power between center and republic, combining both elements of confederation and federation. There also was no clear agreement on how to handle six of the 15 republics, including the three Baltic republics, who had declared they would not sign the treaty.

Gorbachev had indicated in numerous statements that he would seek to interpret the treaty as an agreement to maintain a strong military policy. While he hinted that Baltic and other demands for independence might be dealt with more sympathetically, he also continued to voice hopes that those breakaway republics would see the light and return to the fold.

Yeltsin's view, which now seems certain to dominate, was quite different. His vision of the union is confederal, with republics retaining the power to tax and control over their property and resources, and giving to the central government only what they determine it needs to run essential programs. Moreover, Yeltsin has repeatedly stated his willingness to let the Baltics and others go free without a fuss, a view he already embodied in separate Russian treaties with each of the Baltic republics.

Some Soviet analysts believe the republics may even seek to redraw the treaty after the coup, strengthening their control over defense and security policy.

US Perspective on Coup Failure: Gorbachev Must Grab Chance for Reform

Linda Feldmann

8/23/91

The failed coup attempt against Soviet President Mikhail Gorbachev presents opportunities as well as challenges for United States policy toward the Soviet Union.

In the short term, administration officials—including President Bush—and Soviet specialists see a boost to relations.

With the removal of the top conservatives in Gorbachev's leadership, his hand has been freed to take a more radical approach on reform.

"The fears that some of us have had—many of us, actually—about right-wing take-overs will no longer be as extant," Mr. Bush told reporters Wednesday. "I expect the relationship to be, if anything, even better."

A key question is how Gorbachev will handle the new lease on his political life. Before his detention, his popularity had plummeted to less than 10 percent in opinion polls.

But if he follows the cue given him by the Soviet people—that they back reformist, democratically elected rulers like Russian Republic President Boris Yeltsin—he could build back a mandate.

"It's immensely easier now" for Gorbachev to supply the missing national program, says Tyrus W. Cobb, a Soviet specialist at the Center for Strategic and International Studies in Washington. "There could not have been a better script to remove Gorbachev from his precipice."

Some analysts also suggest Gorbachev may decide he needs to hold direct popular elections, perhaps as early as this fall, for the presidency of the Soviet Union. "If anything," says a senior administration official, "the coup attempt has shown the value of being elected now in the USSR."

If Gorbachev does manage to turn the coup to his political advantage, then the US's main interlocutor would be operating with more authority than he would have possessed otherwise, at least in the near term, says Peter Reddaway, a professor of political science at George Washington University. The leadership crisis also makes it possible for Yeltsin to extend his tactical alliance with Gorbachev, which was waning before the coup and which US policymakers believe is central to any forward movement on the key issues of economic and political reform. "Gorbachev will have to commit himself more strongly than before to the reformists and that will make it easier for the West to help," says Dr. Reddaway. "In the short term, the situation will be improved all around."

Gabriel Schoenfeld, also of the Center for Strategic and International Studies, predicts the West will be willing to take more of a gamble in giving the Soviets tangible aid, now that there is less worry over hard-liners undoing reform. "The West has seen what's at stake if reform isn't successful," says Mr. Schoenfeld. "The coup has paved the way for economic reform. The people will have to make sacrifices, but now they, too, realize where the alternative lies."

The senior administration official, speaking on background, suggests that, in the wake of the coup, there will be a desire in the West to make a gesture of support for the Soviet people. One way to do that, he says, would be to give the country a modicum of humanitarian aid as a taste of the larger-scale aid that may follow if the Moscow does take the plunge into radical market reforms.

Over the long term, the coup could complicate US policymaking. Undoing the coup will do nothing to retrieve the Soviet Union from economic chaos. Moreover, with the power of the center substantially weakened, political stability could be taxed as never before.

"More will depend on local factors," says Reddaway. "Every republic is different, and those differences are going to be far more important now than ever in the past. Every question you would ask about the Soviet Union before the coup you now have to ask 15 times."

The new union treaty will play a key role in how the US is able to relate to the different power centers in the republics. It devolves considerable decisionmaking power to the 15 republics—for example, granting them control over their economic resources. But many provisions of the treaty, which is expected to be signed eventually by nine or ten of the republics, are vague, and the US will not be able to work within its new structures until it sees how it is implemented.

For now, the Bush administration plans to continue diversifying its contacts with democratic forces throughout the USSR, while dealing with the center on areas where it has jurisdiction, such as arms control. This dual-track framework for relations, which has been developing over time, paid dividends during the coup. Bush has met with Yeltsin several times and appeared comfortable throwing his full support behind him during the crisis.

Yeltsin's new elite status shakes the old order of US-Soviet relations, in which the US openly backed Gorbachev. If tensions flare up again between Yeltsin and Gorbachev after a while, as some analysts predict, the US could be put in an awkward position. "There's now a kingmaker who is much more powerful than the king," says William Zimmerman, director of the Center for Russian and East European Studies at the University of Michigan. "Yeltsin will seize the moment to press Gorbachev to move forward into real marketization and to give power to the republics."

The US itself may want to seize the moment with Gorbachev in certain long-troublesome foreign policy areas, such as Cuba and Afghanistan. If Gorbachev has been thwarted in a desire to cut back on aid to those countries by hard liners, now could be his chance for a shift in policy.

Technology Thwarted Coup Leaders' Success

Laurent Belsie

8/26/91

Everette Dennis, an American journalism specialist in Moscow for a short trip, woke up to a coup last Monday morning.

As scheduled that day, he met with Moscow University students, who talked of little else. Some had seen tanks; others found out about the takeover through the Kremlin's pronouncements.

But one student learned the news when he got a call from his mother in central Asia. Another heard it from a American friend who called from Nashville, Tenn.

If the leaders of the coup were bent on leading a revolt, they failed utterly to grasp the revolution in telecommunications. Even in the Soviet Union faxes, electronic mail, computer bulletin boards, and cable television have opened the floodgates of information. Would-be dictators ignore this technology at their peril.

"The availability of these alternative channels proved to be very important," says Owen Johnson, a journalism professor and director of the Indiana University Russian and East European Institute.

"People had this sense that they knew what was going on," explains Mr. Dennis, executive director of the Freedom Forum Media Studies Center at Columbia University. That led to greater certainty among the demonstrators and, he believes, a quicker end to the takeover. (Dennis left the USSR Tuesday and reached The Monitor by telephone in Prague.) Although the coup leaders did crack down on the press, they did nothing to control a basic technology like the telephone. This failure, analysts say, allowed their opponents to organize.

The Soviet Union's earlier dictators were more astute.

"Education is a weapon," Stalin once said, "whose effects depend on who holds it in his hands and at whom it is aimed." Lenin understood the more subtle point about information as an organizing tool: "The press should be not only a collective propagandist and a collective agitator, but also a collective organizer of the masses."

In this case, continued phone service allowed Soviets from Russian Republic leader Boris Yeltsin on down to organize, put out statements, and relay and receive news. During the height of the crisis, for example, Mr. Yeltsin received calls from President Bush and Britain's Prime Minister John Major, who later came out with strong messages of support for the opposition.

By not controlling the telephone, the coup leaders allowed a whole range of newer communications technologies to flourish.

"The really strange thing about this coup is that communication is no real problem," wrote Bob Clough to users of CompuServe, a US-based computer information service. Mr. Clough, an American working in Moscow selling software, was able to hook into the service by direct dialing to Finland. According to him, a whole range of similar computer bulletin boards within the Soviet Union continued to operate during the crisis.

Even on a normal day, AT&T's allotted 67 circuits can't handle the volume of US calls to the Soviet Union. (Much smaller European countries have hundreds of such circuits.) When news of the coup hit the US late Sunday night, the call volume soared a hundredfold, says Jim Messenger, an AT&T spokesman.

So, people found ingenious methods to get through.

William Hogan, director of Harvard University's Project on Economic Reform in Ukraine, called his colleagues in Kiev through a friend in Poland, who has very modern telephone equipment. Mr. Hogan also made extensive use of electronic mail through two services with Soviet links—Internet and SovAm Teleport (a US-Soviet joint venture).

News also flowed in both directions with apparent ease. Hogan relayed western wire service reports to his colleagues in Kiev. A joint venture, called Interfax, distributed news from the Soviet Union to the outside world (see related story).

And traditional sources of western news, such as the BBC and Voice of America, were supplemented by Atlanta-based Cable News Network. Although its broadcasts are limited to such places as hotels within the Soviet Union, CNN is nevertheless picked up by regular Muscovites who stick antennas out their windows and aim them at a huge broadcasting tower in Moscow.

Everybody does it," says Diane Schatz, an American who lives in Moscow. In February, she and her husband bought several eight-ruble antennas and gave them to their Russian friends. The antennas don't work on Soviet TV sets, she says, but Muscovites are buying Western sets.

Ms. Schatz is director of special projects for SovAm Teleport USA. This US-Soviet joint venture started in 1989 to provide electronic-mail through a satellite link between teleports in Staten Island, N.Y., and Moscow. The organization is now completing its second joint venture to hook up Soviet hotels with the West. The system, due to open in the fall, will bypass the Soviet's international gateway switch with a satellite-linked switch of its own.

As these links proliferate, regimes will find it much harder to cut off the flow of information.

Certainly, the leaders of the coup could have done a better job of controlling the flow of information, these analysts say. China's leaders cut off Western broadcasts as well as their own before sending tanks into Tiananmen Square.

Iraq pulled the plug on Kuwait's telephone system after it invaded and, apparently, closed down its own international links when the allies started bombing.

"It's not necessarily technology that has made this increased flow of information possible," Mr. Johnson says. Political leaders decide that. "If they still want to use force they still can shut down much of this technological information flow."

But that decision incurs tremendous costs because the same lines that relay news also facilitate commerce.

"No modern industrial state can have a sound economy and a totalitarian government," says Dean Mills, a former Moscow correspondent and dean of the journalism school at the University of Missouri at Columbia. "You can't operate an economy that closes off information."

Yeltsin Spearheads Soviet 'Revolution From Below'

Daniel Sneider

8/26/91

An anticommunist revolution as shattering and profound as the 1917 Bolshevik takeover is sweeping across the Soviet Union.

"Until recently, we were speaking about a revolution from above," former Foreign Minister Eduard Shevardnadze told reporters on Saturday.

"But today we must speak about a revolution from below, and it is a genuine revolution."

Since the statue of the founder of the Soviet secret police was toppled late Thursday night in Moscow, the leaders of the revolution, with Russia's Boris Yeltsin at their head, have moved rapidly to dismantle the Bolshevik state. From the sealed doors of the Soviet Communist Party headquarters on the "Old Square" in Moscow to the graffiti-smeared walls of the KGB around the corner, the instruments of Soviet power are being forcefully shut down.

At the same time, the Soviet Union is coming apart. On Saturday the Ukrainian parliament voted overwhelmingly to declare independence, following in the footsteps of the Baltic states of Estonia and Latvia. In turn, Russia recognized the Baltic independence. In Russia itself, the revolution is now clearly fed by an upsurge of national pride whose symbols openly harken back to the pre-Bolshevik era.

As the revolutionary wave advances, Soviet President Mikhail Gorbachev has had to run quickly to prevent being left behind and totally isolated from the popular mood. Since his rescue from the hard-line coup plotters on Wednesday, Gorbachev's stance has shifted under pressure from Yeltsin and his government.

At his initial press conference on Thursday, the Soviet president was still defending the Communist Party. By the next day, after meeting Yeltsin and other republican leaders and after being publicly called to account in front of the Russian parliament, Gorbachev scrapped his initial replacements of coup plotters in the Cabinet and started formation of a new governing coalition.

Late on Saturday night, Gorbachev took the step that Yeltsin, Shevardnadze, and others had taken months, even years before—he resigned from his post as head of the Communist Party; ordered the seizure of the party's extensive property; banned its cells from the Army, police, and all state institutions; and called on the party leadership to disband itself. These announcements followed a series of moves by Yeltsin's government and others which amount, in their totality, to a political revolution. The breathtaking sequence since Thursday follows:

On Friday:

* The Communist Party daily Pravda publishes what may be its last issue after Yeltsin suspends the paper and five other party newspapers that had supported the coup.

* Yeltsin issues a decree suspending the hard-line Russian Communist Party, despite Gorbachev's initial objections.

* Gorbachev announces before Russian parliament that the entire Cabinet has been asked to resign. New ministers, replacing interim appointments of the day before, are announced, including Defense Minister and former Air Force chief Yevgeny Shaposhnikov, Interior Minister Viktor Barannikov, KGB chief Vadim Bakatin.

On Saturday:

* Yeltsin announces Russia's formal recognition of independence of Latvia and Estonia and calls on Gorbachev to follow suit.

* Gorbachev resigns from party leadership, assailing the party leaders for failing to mobilize members against the coup. He bans party cells in all state organizations and orders local governments to take control of all party property.

* The Russian government seizes the archives of the KGB and the Communist Party to prevent "illegal destruction of documents."

* Gorbachev announces formation of the core of a new government, setting up a committee headed by Russian Prime Minister Ivan Silayev to manage the economy. It includes reformist industrialist Arkady Volsky, Moscow Deputy Mayor Yuri Luzhkov, and radical economist Grigory Yavlinsky, the author of the 500-day economic reform plan and widely believed to be the choice for the new Soviet prime minister.

* With the support of 346 out of 450 deputies, the Ukrainian parliament votes to declare independence, with ratification by a Dec. 1 referendum. The parliament votes to create a Ukrainian currency and defense ministry and to take control of all Soviet military units on its territory. Ukrainian parliament head Leonid Kravchuk announces his resignation from the Soviet Communist Party Politburo and Central Committee.

* Leningrad authorities seize and seal the Communist Party headquarters in the Smolny Institute, headquarters of the Bolshevik revolution of 1917.

On Sunday:

* The parliament in the republic of Moldavia announces it will declare independence today.

Following these steps, the revolution is likely to sweep away the last of the institutions in which the old guard still holds power—the Supreme Soviet of the Soviet Union, the national parliament. A special session of the body has been called for this morning, with republican leaders reportedly to attend. The immediate target will be parliament chairman Anatoly Lukyanov, a long-time Gorbachev associate who is accused of being involved in the coup. But the democratic forces are also likely to seek a quick dissolution of the body and new elections.

A meeting of deputies from the northwest region of Russia, called by Leningrad Mayor Anatoly Sobchak, called Saturday for an emergency meeting of the Congress of Peoples' Deputies, the parent legislative body, to appoint a new vice president and parliament head.

The political revolution is poised to lead toward an economic revolution as the obstacles to radical moves to a market economy fall away. With the collapse of the Communist Party, which has been the main instrument for economic decisionmaking for decades, a market economy is a virtual necessity. The state bureaucracy is unable to exercise even the lessened level of control it has up to today.

Indeed the collapse of existing institutions is so rapid that democratic leaders are warning of chaos and the need to ensure economic order, fearing that such conditions could give the conservatives another chance to seize power.

"Now we have a sort of euphoria," Mr. Shevardnadze said. "But tomorrow, the day after tomorrow, in a week, in 10 days, the people will begin judging the leaders including the democrats by the way they cope with real problems . . . . The harvest is very bad, a slump in production is going on . . . . If we are not able to resolve the most urgent social and economic problems in a short . . . time, the people may take to the streets, and then the question will arise: Who will be at the head of this movement."

Western Countries Hasten to Recognize Baltic Republics

Francine S. Kiefer

8/27/91

The number of Western countries setting up diplomatic relations with the Baltic republics is snowballing.

"We hope that by the close of business [today], all the members of the European Community (EC) will have established diplomatic relations" with Lithuania, Latvia, and Estonia, says a Foreign Ministry official in Denmark. The Danes, yesterday, sent an ambassador to the Baltics—the first from a Western country.

In Brussels today, EC foreign ministers will discuss establishing diplomatic relations with the Baltic states. They will also consider EC associate membership for the Baltics and EC foreign policy as more Soviet republics declare their independence.

"The whole world of countries must newly shape its relations to the Soviet Union because it is obvious that a series of republics are seeking independence," said German Foreign Minister Hans-Dietrich Genscher in a radio interview yesterday. The Ukraine and Byelorussia both declared independence over the weekend, and Moldavia's legislature will debate the subject today.

Germany and Denmark are both pushing for EC associate status for the Baltics. Similar agreements are being negotiated with Poland, Czechoslovakia, and Hungary, but these talks have dragged because EC members are reluctant to open up their markets to East European agricultural and textile exports.

But economists say the Baltics should not, in the near term, threaten the West European market—they are not export oriented and they are not mass producers of agriculture. So it may not be as difficult to get the Community into high gear on associate status for the Baltics as it has been for Eastern Europe.

The European Commission, meanwhile, released a study yesterday saying the Baltics would need $3 billion in short-term economic aid.

Most Western countries never legally accepted the 1940 Soviet annexation of the three republics, which was based on a secret pact between Hitler and Stalin in 1939. The West maintains that the Baltics are a unique case, and that starting up diplomatic relations with them does not necessitate the same for other Soviet republics, or, even further afield, for Slovenia and Croatia in strife-torn Yugoslavia—which will also be on today's EC agenda.

Generally, Europe is inclined to build ties on the republic level without undercutting ties with the central government in Moscow. It was fear of endangering those relations that held many countries back from official recognition of the Baltics last week, even though the three had declared their independence and banned the Communist Party, says Roland Freudenstein, a Soviet specialist with the German Society for Foreign Affairs in Bonn.

The turning point, says Mr. Freudenstein, was when Boris Yeltsin, as president of Russia, extended recognition to the Baltic states on Saturday. That amounted to official sanction from the most popular and powerful politician in the Soviet Union, and a guarantee that outstanding issues, such as military and economic relations between Russia and the Baltics, would be resolved.

Soviets Assess Future of Union

Daniel Sneider

8/27/91

Appearing before the packed chamber of the Soviet parliament yesterday, a subdued but determined President Mikhail Gorbachev laid out a concise and radical reform program.

After last week's aborted hard-line coup, Mr. Gorbachev appeared ready to move rapidly to implement the reforms which he admitted he had failed to carry out earlier. Gorbachev's seven-point agenda includes new national elections, de-facto recognition of those republics which seek independence from the union, reorganization of the KGB and transformation of the military into a professional force under civilian control, full privatization—including of land—and a rapid shift to a market economy.

Gorbachev soberly held himself partly responsible for the coup, for failing to fundamentally change the intertwined structure of Communist Party and state power.

"Because of compromise," he admitted, "no decisive economic reforms were carried out. There was no coordination and no accord with the democratic forces. The reactionary forces managed to draw us sometimes, though we had the same goals, to different sides of the barricades."

"On my part," Gorbachev vowed, "there will no longer be any hesitation in carrying out decisive reforms, as long as I . . . am president of the country. From now on, there will be no compromise with those with whom compromise is impossible."

Gorbachev called for the signing of the new treaty of union between the republics as soon as possible but said that he agreed with republican leaders who are now seeking amendments to the existing draft. Given the new realities, including the declaration of independence by the Ukraine, the Soviet Union can no longer be a federation, but only a loose confederation, Kazakhstan President Nursultan Nazarbayev told the parliament.

Gorbachev indicated for the first time that he was ready to accept the independence of those republics, including the three Baltics, which don't wish to sign the treaty. As soon as the treaty is signed, he said, they can begin negotiations with those republics to settle issues such as the protection of the rights of minorities, settlement of those who wish to return to the union, and the status of military facilities on their territory.

Gorbachev called for signing an economic treaty as soon as possible which would encompass all 15 current republics, providing a basis for future economic ties between the union and the newly independent republics.

A new constitution is to be drafted after the union treaty is signed, but Gorbachev moved to reorganize the national government, based on agreement with the republican leaders, even before that happens. An emergency session of the Congress of Peoples Deputies, the senior legislative body, will convene Sept. 2, the parliament voted yesterday. At that meeting a new vice-president will be chosen and steps taken to dissolve the existing parliament, whose passivity in the face of the coup has tainted it.

Liberals in government

The existing Security Council, an advisory body to the president, will take on a new role running the country. Its membership will be expanded to include republican leaders and prominent liberals such as former presidential aide Alexander Yakovlev, Leningrad Mayor Anatoly Sobchak, and Moscow Mayor Gavriil Popov. They will work with a new economic committee headed by Russian Prime Minister Ivan Silayev which will manage the economy.

The parliament session was dominated by attacks on the body itself. Many charged the parliament with backing the coup and called for its dissolution. Gorbachev indirectly supported charges that party chairman Anatoli Lukyanov, a long-time associate, was behind the coup. When the parliament opened Monday, Mr. Lukyanov was not in his chair. But speaking to reporters outside in the hall, he continued to deny his involvement in the coup.

"The coup would have been impossible if the Supreme Soviet of the Soviet Union and its chairman would have decisively opposed it immediately as the Supreme Soviet of Russia did," Gorbachev said.

Reforming the military

The Soviet leader called for constitutional control to be established over all activity of the armed forces and law enforcement bodies. Military reform should be accelerated and emphasis should be put on professionalism in the Army, he added. The KGB should be reorganized, including transferring the KGB's considerable armed forces to the control of the Defense Ministry.

Gorbachev outlined a brief program of rapid economic reform, calling for all previous decisions to be reviewed. The program includes cutting the budget deficit, providing social protection for the unemployed during the transition to a market economy, getting food and energy supplies stabilized, rapidly establishing a convertible currency, and privatization. For the first time, Gorbachev declared that "land should be given to everyone who wants to work it."

Finally Gorbachev proposed that preparations for new elections to all bodies, including the parliament and the presidency, begin immediately.

In a last sober note, the Soviet leader declared that "everyone who took part in organizing and carrying out the coup has to get what he deserves. But we should not allow a witchhunt."

Republican leaders' views

A stream of republican leaders followed him to the podium, begun by Russian parliament chairman Ruslan Khasbulatov. He warned there should be no euphoria, that "reactionary forces have not been crushed. Only their headquarters have been smashed. But the coup had a well-organized and deep structure. Now the reactionary forces are in a state of disorganization. While they are in this state, we should carry on decisive reforms."

The Russian politician, speaking for the newly powerful government of Russian President Boris Yeltsin, proposed privatization of agriculture, private property without any restrictions, freeing enterprises from all government direction, controlling them only through taxes. Mr. Khasbulatov demanded a sharp cut in defense spending, at least 50 billion rubles this year (about a quarter of the official budget).

Soviets Question Breakup of Empire

Daniel Sneider

8/28/91

As Western ambassadors begin arriving in the Baltic states, what was once a far-out scenario has become a reality—the breakup of the Soviet empire.

The Romanian-populated republic of Moldavia joined the three Baltic states of Estonia, Latvia, and Lithuania Aug. 27 in declaring its independence from the Soviet Union. Even the staid republic of Byelorussia, where nationalist sentiments are not strongly entrenched, has rushed to declare its sovereignty.

In the halls of the Soviet parliament, which began an emergency session on Aug. 26, the talk is whether the Soviet Union will survive as a unified state. "The center is dead," Armenian President Levon Ter-Petrosyan happily proclaimed. (Interview, Page 3.) Asked by the news agency Interfax about a proposal that he resume his post as Soviet foreign minister, Eduard Shevardnadze retorted: "When there is no USSR, what do you need a minister for?"

In response to Soviet President Mikhail Gorbachev's call for new Soviet elections, Leningrad deputy Sergei Tsyplyaev said, "Of course we must organize new elections, but the question is in what country to organize them . . . . In a few months, we will have fully destroyed the previous union and have 15 independent republics, or more."

These developments are hailed by some as a logical outcome of the fall of the Communist state since the failed hard-line coup last week. But increasingly, even among supporters of the democratic movement, these events are greeted with apprehension.

On the part of the non-Russian republics, voices are rising against Russian domination of any future union. On the part of Russia and among a section of the democrats, there is the concern that the Communists in such places as the Central Asian republics, the Ukraine, and Byelorussia, are now using nationalism to preserve the old system there.

Russian domination is already a political reality. What remains of the Soviet central government is being taken over by the Russian Federation government of Boris Yeltsin, with Russian Premier Ivan Silayev now functioning as Soviet premier and appointing members of his Cabinet to take over all major Soviet ministries.

Kazakhstan President Nursultan Nazarbayev showed these anti-Russian sentiments when he spoke to reporters at the Soviet parliament Aug. 26. "The president and prime minister are Russian, and now we hear that they may agree that the vice president be from Central Asia," he said, adding sarcastically, "Well, thank you very much."

Both Mr. Nazarbayev and Ukrainian deputy Yuri Shcherbak presented a vision of a new union as a far looser confederation than previously envisaged. Nazarbayev wants to relegate a union government to protecting borders, but with defense, including nuclear-weapons control, jointly run by republics. Each republic would have its own army, delegating some men to a joint force.

Mr. Shcherbak called for scrapping the proposed new treaty of union entirely, putting in its place a "Euro-Asian economic community" and a military-political structure similar to NATO.

The tensions between Russia and these two large neighbors, both of which have considerable Russian minorities, took an additional leap when Yeltsin's spokesman issued a statement Aug. 26, warning that if the republics pull out of the union, "the Russian Federation retains the right to raise the question of revising borders." The statement exempted the Baltic states, with whom Russia has signed treaties.

But the spokesman explained that the statement referred mainly to northern Kazakhstan and to the Donbass region and the Crimea in Ukraine, all Russian-populated areas. "If these republics enter the [renewed] union with Russia it is not a problem," spokesman Pavel Voshchanov told reporters. "But if they go, we must take care of the population that lives there and not forget that these lands were settled by Russians."

Russian deputy Oleg Rumantsyev, a liberal leader, echoes these sentiments. "If we are provoked toward civil war by irresponsible leaders of the republics," he says, "then we will respond from a position of force and self-confidence."

Russian Vice President Alexander Rutskoi called for the union to be preserved for both economic and military reasons. In a press conference, he warned the breakup of the union could encourage "the rebirth of the Russian empire" by leaving all the strategic nuclear weapons and major military forces in Russia.

Behind such talk, some Soviet observers say, is the fear Russia will be left in a union solely of itself and the Muslim republics of Central Asia. For this reason, the stance of the Ukraine is considered the key to the future of any union. Without the Ukraine, comments Soviet analyst Sergei Blagovolin, "it will be a terrible cocktail of Russia and the Central Asian republics. In this case, it will be better for us to be alone."

Leading democrats such as Leningrad Mayor Anatoli Sobchak and Moscow Mayor Gavriil Popov have emerged as strong advocates of maintaining the union and central administration. They warn that the Communist Party governments that remain in power in Central Asia, Byelorussia, and the Ukraine are now using "national communism" to survive.

These democrats "proceed from the apprehension that secession of certain republics from the USSR will lead to the preservation of Communist regimes," Vera Kuznitzsova commented in the independent newspaper Nezavisimaya Gazeta Aug. 27.

Such concerns are shared by non-Communists in those republics.

"The Communists need an independent Byelorussia not for the interests of Byelorussia itself," liberal Byelorussian deputy Aleksander Adamovich told the Monitor. "They need it to preserve their own and the party's power." He raised the specter of a Communist Byelorussia that would have nuclear capacity and enter into a territorial, ideological confrontation with Russia.

The rapid decision of the Ukrainian parliament, where the Communists still dominate, to declare independence last week is also questioned by Rukh, the coalition of democratic and nationalist forces in the republic.

Rukh leader Ivan Drach dismissed this in Nezavisimaya Aug. 27, as a "cunning maneuver of the [regime] to preserve itself and the local party structures." But as a result, "the Ukrainian supporters of independence face a rather dramatic option: either to join the democratic empire or to begin with national Communist independence," he said.

The only alternative to breakup seems to be a revision of the draft treaty of union, which would make the Soviet Union a full confederation, with an economic union at its core.

Soviet Defense Minister Pushes for Rapid Reform

Daniel Sneider

8/28/91

The newly appointed Soviet defense minister, Air Force Comdr. Yevgeny Shaposhnikov, has moved quickly to align himself with those advocating serious military reform.

"We are ready to make a transition to a professional army," he said Aug. 26, hours before he was promoted to the rank of Marshal. The call to transform the largely conscript Soviet Army into a professional force has been a key demand of military reformers.

"But it will take some time," the new senior defense official quickly added. "Such decisions cannot be implemented overnight. Sociological research should be conducted among young men from 18 to 30 years old in order to determine how many of them are willing to serve in a professional army. We should determine our financial means, but it is not for me but for the parliament to decide."

Marshal Shaposhnikov's remarks followed an interview Aug. 25, in which he pledged to carry out a wholesale replacement of senior military commanders, many of whom were implicated in last week's attempted coup. "Eighty percent of the command will be renewed," he told Soviet television. Their replacements will be younger, he added.

The new minister, who replaced Marshal Dmitri Yazov after Marshal Yazov's arrest for his part in the coup, backed moves to remove all political structures from the military. Loyalty to the constitution will be the new principle for personnel selection, he said. "Personal loyalties will not be taken into consideration. They should be people of the highest moral qualities and professionalism."

Shaposhnikov drew praise from Maj. Vladimir Lopatin, a young air force officer who led the movement for reform and serves as a deputy head of the Russian republican government's defense organization.

Maj. Lopatin told the Monitor the organization had received calls from military officers across the country. "They said the Air Forces were up to the mark, and we can count on the new minister to bring the whole armed forces up to the same mark. My attitude is the same. Military reform has already started with the resignation of the old military leadership and departyization of the armed forces."

Soviet President Mikhail Gorbachev, in his speech to the parliament on Aug. 26, called for establishing stricter controls over the armed forces' activities. Such controls "will become a major part of the new law on military reform," which he urged the parliament to pass quickly. Mr. Gorbachev backed the need to "increase the professional makeup of the Army."

Military reform expert Sergei Blagovolin, of the prestigious Institute for World Economy and International Relations, praised the new minister as a "good professional soldier and an honest person." He also backed the appointment of former Warsaw Pact commander Vladimir Lobov to replace coup-tainted General Mikhail Moiseyev as Chief of the General Staff. Mr. Lobov, "is quite conservative, but he is an honest soldier," he said.

But Mr. Blagovolin warned that Shaposhnikov is "not very popular throughout the military." He is the first Air Force general to be named defense minister, a post reserved virtually exclusively for the powerful ground forces.

Sergei Tsyplyaev, a liberal member of the parliament's defense and security committee, cautioned the appointment should be viewed as an interim one. The need to put the military under the control of the constitutional authorities means that "it is necessary to have a civilian minister," he told the Monitor.

'Where Were You on August 19?'

Daniel Sneider

8/28/91

Little more than a week ago, Vladimir Shcherbakov was one of the most powerful men in the Soviet Union. The deputy premier in charge of economic planning was widely respected as a plain-talking economic administrator. He strode confidently at President Mikhail Gorbachev's side during the London summit with Western leaders as a principal economic aide.

On the morning of Aug. 26, Mr. Shcherbakov stood in the hallway of the Soviet parliament a broken man. Deep circles were carved below his normally sparkling eyes. His wit and ease had been replaced by the repeated phrases of a man yearning to be understood, if not forgiven.

The red-haired senior government official is only one of hundreds, perhaps thousands, like him who are now being called to account across the Soviet Union for their involvement in last week's failed hard-line coup. The criteria for judgment of guilt go well beyond those who openly identified themselves as coup leaders or supporters. It includes those in positions of authority who acquiesced through their silence.

The standard was set by Boris Yeltsin and his Russian government: Those who did not actively oppose the coup, as they did, are now suspect. As Mr. Gorbachev put it bluntly to the entire parliament on Aug. 26: "The Supreme Soviet failed to move, and members of the Cabinet of Ministers panicked and failed to take action."

Some of the denials of guilt have taken a tragicomic form, like the videotaped confession of Premier Valentin Pavlov, one of the eight coup leaders, taken at the time of his arrest and shown on Russian television Aug. 24. Asked why they had failed in their coup, Mr. Pavlov replied that "the majority of the Emergency Committee [as the coup leadership called itself] didn't know what was going on."

Blame the others

As is becoming typical, Pavlov tried to blame his co-conspirators. Vice President Gennady Yanayev told them Gorbachev was sick but "no one could explain properly what was wrong with him." Then, he continued, "everyone started wondering whether we should go to the Supreme Soviet [parliament]." But unfortunately parliament chairman Anatoly Lukyanov told the coup committee that the earliest a session could be convened would be Aug. 26, a week later.

Mr. Lukyanov, who was dismissed from his post that day, denied any involvement to reporters. But as to why he hadn't called the parliament into session to oppose the coup, as the Russian parliament leadership did immediately, Lukyanov weakly responded that parliamentary procedure requires a vote of two-thirds of the deputies to convene an emergency session.

"For me, it is totally clear that Lukyanov was one of the most important people preparing the coup," says Sergei Tsypyaev, a deputy from Leningrad. "He was just waiting to see the result."

Shcherbakov offers his own tortured explanation for his behavior, which included participating in a Cabinet meeting which backed the adventure on the evening of the first day of the coup.

"We had been told that it was the radical democrats, the extremists, who meant to seize power and the emergency situation was necessary to prevent them from doing it," he says. The Emergency Committee went to Gorbachev with this version of events but "Gorbachev refused to declare a state of emergency, saying that he didn't believe the democrats were moving to seize power, that it was [the committee members] who were provoking the situation. Then they told Gorbachev: 'Look, how much longer are you going to believe [the democrats]? Can't you see that every single agreement with them has been violated . . . . They are already concentrating their forces . . . . It is a question of hours. Either you make this decision or we are going to make it without you and then explain everything to others.'

'He could've been taken ill'

At the same time, Shcherbakov argues that he had no reason to disbelieve the coup leaders when they claimed the vice president was taking over for an ill and incapacitated president.

"Yanayev's coming to power would have been legal if there was proof of Gorbachev's illness. I demanded such proof all the time . . . . I spoke with the president on Aug. 18 [the day before the coup] but he could have been taken ill, anything could have happened, he could have fallen down, injured himself, had a heart attack."

In the manner of those Nazis who stood trial for war crimes at Nuremberg, the economic planner says he was only "following orders. As a person, I am against any use of force or suppression . . . . But I am a government official as well. The government is headed by those who have legal power. If I did not obey them, then I would have been committing an anti-constitutional deed."

But the rotund bureaucrat does most of his squirming when forced to explain the recently revealed minutes of the Cabinet meeting where Premier Pavlov won backing for the takeover. "[Pavlov] signed the statement; let him answer for it," he says.

As for his stated readiness to run the economy under the state of emergency, "I was responsible for Gosplan [the State Planning Commission], which is at present the only organ that still has some control over the economy. If I left then, work would be paralyzed."

When Gorbachev returned to Moscow, Shcherbakov says the president called and forgave him, an account that is not confirmed from Gorbachev's side.

But the finger of guilt has not moved away so easily from his brow.

Shcherbakov concludes his defense by vowing that "as long as my name is not cleared of suspicion, I will not go on working."

Moscow Witnesses An Information Revolution

John Hughes

8/29/91

When Voice of America (VOA) correspondents reporting the crowd scenes around the Russian parliament in Moscow during the recent coup attempt were trapped on the barricades, they pulled out their Finnish-made cellular phones and called in their reports to their Moscow bureau. The bureau transmitted the reports live to VOA headquarters in Washington, which broadcast them almost instantly by shortwave back to millions of listeners across the Soviet Union.

Meanwhile, inside the parliament building, correspondents for Radio Liberty, another American government-financed radio station, were filing reports to headquarters in Munich. Radio Liberty beamed them back to the Soviet Union in Russian and 11 other Soviet languages. Its sister station, Radio Free Europe, broadcast what was happening in Moscow to the Baltic republics, to Eastern European countries, and to 115,000 Soviet citizens trapped in Poland following the Pope's visit there.

Also inside parliament, Boris Yeltsin was busy sending fax messages to a friend in Washington, which were speedily made available to the international media. Meanwhile, Mikhail Gorbachev, under house arrest in the Crimea and supposedly out of touch after plotters removed his communications equipment, found some old shortwave radios in the guest rooms of his villa and followed events by listening to the VOA, Radio Liberty, and the British Broadcasting Corporation. Mr. Gorbachev reportedly used another new means of communication—video tape—to smuggle out a message proving he was in good health.

One of the plotters' most serious miscalculations was their belief that they could throttle the information flow to the Soviet people and cause them to hear only the inane version of events ("Gorbachev is sick and needs rest") that they put out. The plotters did what dictators everywhere do first. They seized TV stations and tried to close down opposition radio stations and newspapers in an attempt to neutralize a press that had become increasingly independent under Gorbachev.

What they failed to realize is that the world is undergoing an information revolution. New and innovative techniques already developed, along with others coming down the line, make it impossible to close off whole countries to the flow of news. It was this opportunity that the American government-operated radios seized, boosting their broadcasting hours and blasting news reports round-the-clock into the Soviet homeland and around the world. In addition to eyewitness reports, the radios interviewed experts, aired Mr. Yeltsin's speeches that the plotters tried to stifle, and broadcast verbatim President Bush's press conferences.

Coincidentally, a task force appointed by Mr. Bush is looking into the future of these radio operations. As chairman of that task force, nothing I say in this column is designed to prejudge the recommendations we may make to the president. But from the events of recent days one fact emerges uncontested: In restoring the Soviet Union to a constructive course, the VOA, Radio Liberty, and Radio Free Europe played a significant role. It was one of their finest moments.

This is not to underestimate the courage of the Russian people, whose behavior is another lesson for would-be dictators who seek to set the clock back: Give the people a taste of the freedom they yearn for and it will be difficult to take it back. With facts readily available over shortwave radios and other means of communication, Soviet citizens simply did not buy the unsophisticated propaganda the plotters put out. They resisted, and they triumphed.

Nor, despite some twists and turns in implementing glasnost, should we underestimate Gorbachev's contribution in opening up the Soviet press. When there were repressive actions in the Baltic republics, the state-owned Soviet media were made to toe the line, but overall, a new generation of inquiring journalists and more freedom are being tolerated. Ironically, one of the reasons the plotters could not jam American and British broadcasts was because Gorbachev had sold much of the jamming equipment to new independent radio stations for their own use.

EC Speeds Up Moves To Include Eastern Europe

Howard LaFranchi

8/29/91

European Community foreign ministers took action this week that will likely lead the Community to include more than its 12 Western European members much sooner than expected.

Most notably, the EC decided unanimously Tuesday to recognize the independence of the three Baltic republics, and to establish individual diplomatic relations with them.

In addition to recognizing the sovereignty of Estonia, Latvia, and Lithuania, the EC agreed to "support the Baltic States in their economic and political development," and to "explore all avenues for economic cooperation."

That emphasis on political and economic cooperation, along with a decision to accelerate the conclusion of economic accords with Eastern Europe, is part of a snowball effect that, in the wake of a whirlwind decomposition of the Soviet Union, may now lead to a powerhouse EC of 20 members or more before the year 2000.

Faster EC expansion

"A number of actions on seemingly different topics were taken [by the ministers]," says one long-time British observer of the EC, "but when you boil it all down it implies movement towards an enlargement of the Community much sooner than anyone up to now had thought."

Not too long ago French President Francois Mitterrand said it would be "dozens and dozens of years" before any of the Eastern European countries would be ready economically to join the EC. The prospect of an unstable and splintering Soviet giant to the east is causing the EC to open its arms a little faster.

The ministers decided to move up their next meeting from Sept. 30 to Sept. 4, to discuss proposals from the European Commission, the EC's executive branch, and to hasten association negotiations with Poland, Hungary, and Czechoslovakia.

The proposals will include deeper economic concessions to open the EC to goods from these countries, a step that will in effect begin binding their economies to the EC.

Other assistance to Bulgaria, Romania, and Albania will also be on the table. The foreign ministers of the Baltic states will be invited to attend the meeting, where first steps towards closer EC ties will be considered.

The EC's growing preoccupation with Eastern Europe has led to building speculation that the Community will be forced to slow its own drive to bind its 12 members in closer economic and political union. But Commission President Jacques Delors says this should not be allowed to happen.

"History is accelerating, so we must accelerate with it," he said Tuesday, adding, "We must reinforce our capacity to act . . . and to carry our full weight in the world and notably in Greater Europe."

Dutch Foreign Minister Hans van den Broeck, whose country currently holds the EC's revolving six-month presidency, said the Community would also call a summit of its 12 heads of state for mid-September to focus on changes in Eastern Europe, including how Western Europe should respond to rapid changes in the Soviet Union.

A French proposal to invite Soviet President Mikhail Gorbachev and Russian President Boris Yeltsin to the summit garnered some support, but also caused one Dutch spokesman to quip, "Does anyone really think either one of them is about to leave their country right now?"

While there were no grandiose calls from the ministers for huge new aid programs to the Soviet Union, the general tenor was that reforms now taking place merited a stronger Western response.

Easing Soviet winter

French Foreign Minister Roland Dumas said the EC and other international organizations must now find a more "dynamic" approach for working with both the Soviet central government and the republics on economic aid.

Mr. Delors said the first priority will be to "fill the stores" in the Soviet Union in order to head off catastrophic winter food shortages. Modernization of the country's distribution system is a key, he said.

First, however, the question of "Who is responsible for what?" will have to be answered, Delors noted. He said that virtually all the Soviet officials with whom the commission agreed on allocating $500 million in technical assistance no longer hold their positions.

Obviously worried by the potential ramifications of a period of instability or anarchy in the Soviet Union, Mr. van den Broeck said the Community would "seek in the future to promote a coherent voice" to speak for Soviet interests in foreign policy, defense, and financial relations.

Soviets Rush Economic Plan, as Chaos Threatens

Daniel Sneider

8/29/91

Amid fear of the Soviet Union's breakup, the new authorities in Moscow are desperately trying to prop up the collapsing Soviet economy and launch radical market reforms.

A four-man committee headed by Russian Premier Ivan Silayev is now the only effective authority running the Soviet economy. The first priority of the committee is "to prevent an emergency situation in the country arising out of complete economic breakup," says committee member Arkady Volsky, the head of the Scientific and Industrial League.

At the same time, the group, formed after last week's failed coup, is working on proposals to create "a new structure of economic management," Mr. Volsky told reporters yesterday. A group headed by committee member Grigory Yavlinsky, the radical economist who wrote the aborted 500-day reform plan last year, is now drawing up plans for shifting quickly to a market economy. Mr. Yavlinsky is also drafting proposals for Western aid to the new government's program.

Volsky expressed optimism about the eventual success of the committee's efforts, revealing that representatives of all 15 Soviet republics are active in its work, including observers from the three Baltic republics that have declared independence.

Still, the fledgling democrat-controlled central government and its backers in Russian President Boris Yeltsin's Russian government are working against a tide of republican nationalism.

"Strong emotions have swept everybody," admits Alexander Vladislavlev, deputy head of the Industrial League and, like Volsky, a leader of the Movement for Democratic Reforms.

The Soviet and Russian leaderships have moved to contain the explosion of nationalist sentiments in the wake of the political revolution that has swept Russia. After a series of meetings between Soviet President Mikhail Gorbachev and republican leaders on Tuesday, a delegation from the Soviet parliament headed by Leningrad Mayor Anatoly Sobchak and a Russian delegation headed by Vice President Alexander Rutskoi were dispatched to the Ukraine yesterday.

Ukrainian-Russian tensions have now emerged as the central focus of concern over the breakup of the Soviet Union. After the Ukrainian parliament voted late last week to declare independence, the Russian government issued a statement earlier this week saying that in the event of secession, it would seek to redraw its borders with the Ukraine. In that event, Russian leaders have called for the return of the Crimea, a largely Russian-populated area granted to the Ukraine by former Soviet leader Nikita Khrushchev.

Economic warfare between the republics is now a "very serious danger," says Hungarian-American financier George Soros, a backer of Soviet economic reform and an adviser to the Ukrainian government. "Looking further ahead, the warfare may be more than just economic," he said yesterday at a press conference with Volsky. Agreement with the Ukraine, the second largest republic after Russia and a major producer of grain, raw materials, and industrial goods, is urgent "if economic chaos is to be avoided," Mr. Soros said.

The most urgent economic problem is likely to be food, especially as the Soviet Union heads into the winter. Volsky revealed that out of an estimated 80 million to 85 million tons of grain needed to feed Soviet urban areas, only 24 million to 25 million tons have been acquired by the government. Most of what is needed is available within the country, he said, but "our agricultural producers are holding back on their grain."

The Ukraine and Kazakhstan are the two largest surplus grain producers. Both are republics whose governments have expressed strong opposition in recent days to Russian domination of the new post-coup government. Volsky said that the grain shortfall could be filled only by offering new economic incentives, which the government was preparing, to collective and individual farms, and through imports. Soviet reform economist Nikolai Petrakov, a former adviser to Mr. Gorbachev, suggested yesterday that cities may have to barter manufactured goods to get food.

Soviet Democrats Move To Make New KGB Safe For Democracy

Daniel Sneider

8/30/91

The new democratic order in the Soviet Union is moving rapidly to bring perhaps its most feared opponent to heel—the dreaded KGB secret police.

In decrees issued the past few days, Soviet President Mikhail Gorbachev has sacked the entire senior leadership of the KGB, transferred control of hundreds of thousands of KGB troops, and set up a commission to investigate the agency and prepare proposals for its reorganization.

The anti-KGB operation is a direct response to the prominent role played by its director, Vladimir Krychkov, in the leadership of the junta which attempted to seize power last week. As more details emerge of the coup plot, it is increasingly clear that the KGB was the center of the planning for the operation. Senior KGB officials were directly involved in leading the deployment of KGB units, including commando groups designated to storm the Russian parliament of Boris Yeltsin and teams sent out to arrest prominent democrats.

Immediately after the failure of the coup and the arrest of its leaders, Mr. Gorbachev installed prominent liberal Vadim Bakatin as the new KGB chairman. He also transferred KGB military troops, which number several hundred thousand, including border forces and units for internal control, to the Defense Ministry. This includes two elite Army divisions which had been put under KGB authority last winter.

The handling of the KGB has been distinctly harsher than that meted out to the Army, some of whose senior leaders and troops also participated in the coup. But the refusal of many of Army units and officers to join the coup was key to its failure. Gorbachev told the Soviet military daily Krasnaya Zvezda on Wednesday that "one of the major reasons for the coup failure is that those who usurped power failed to turn the Army against the people. The Army lived up to its expectations."

Some KGB officers have insisted that they, too, resisted the coup. The commanders of the special "Alpha" anti-terror squad told the Tass news agency that they had refused to follow orders to storm the Russian parliament building late on the first night of the coup. "We believe that our refusal to obey the unlawful order has saved the country from civil war," they told Tass.

The head of the Russian republic's KGB branch, Viktor Ivanenko, expressed similar views to Tass, insisting that Mr. Kryuchkov was isolated and had little support from the "overwhelming majority of KGB officers."

Still, the judgment on the KGB seems to be that only a virtual dissolution and reorganization will suffice. On Aug. 28, Gorbachev dissolved the KGB Collegium, the senior leadership body of the organization. One member of that group, deputy KGB chief Col. Gen. Viktor Grushko, was also arrested and charged with treason. The following day, two more KGB deputy chiefs including the head of the personnel department, Lt. Gen. Vitaly Ponomarev, were sacked.

At the same time, a commission of inquiry was created under the chairmanship of Sergei Stepashin, the head of Russian parliament's security committee. Before Oct. 26, the group is to draw up a report on the role of the KGB in the failed coup and formulate proposals to restructure the KGB and amend the appropriate legislation.

Former KGB general Oleg Kalugin, who was a celebrated defector to the side of the democrats last year and is now a member of parliament, foresees a complete transformation of the agency. He told reporters that it should become "a regular police force concerned with the protection of the constitution, with counterintelligence activities, intelligence—and that's all.

"No political functions, no troops, no secret laboratories where they manufacture poison and special weapons. Interception of communications will be taken from them, protection of the president will be taken from them. We shall make it a safe organization for a democratic society."

Baltics Poised to Unleash Market Potential

Linda Feldmann

8/30/91

In the eyes of the world, three tiny countries have just been reborn: Latvia, Lithuania, and Estonia. How can these resource-poor Baltic nations, for 51 years subsumed by the mammoth centrally commanded Soviet economy, make a go of it in the world?

The challenge is daunting, say Western economists, businessmen, and government experts, but the potential is enormous.

The people are educated, Western-oriented, and eager for change. But most important, the location and geography of these states—on the western edge of the Soviet Union, with major ports along the Baltic Sea—have positioned the three as the "gatekeeper" to and from the

East. It is a historical role the Baltic nations are poised to resume.

Riga, the capital of Latvia and the largest port in the Baltics, will be "the Hong Kong of Europe," says a United States government specialist on the Baltics. In the past year, representatives of Hong Kong and Singapore have visited the Baltics and vice versa.

In the postwar era, Finland has prospered by importing Soviet raw materials and exporting finished products as well as marketing its connections in the Soviet bureaucracy. In time, with low wages and a skilled work force, the Baltic states can become the "maquiladoras" of Scandinavia, just as Mexican border factories provide cheap labor for US companies.

And with the upheavals in the central Soviet bureaucracy since Soviet President Mikhail Gorbachev's rise to power, the Finns have lost some of their insider's edge. For the Baltics, one consolation for their 51 years of incorporation into the Soviet economy is that they know that system intimately and can profit financially from their ties, especially to those regions that don't already have the foreign presence that Moscow and Leningrad have.

According to Jenik Radon, a New York lawyer with business and government connections in the Baltics, the Estonian capital of Tallinn has consulting firms advising the Soviet Pacific island of Sakhalin on how to develop its timber industry. In Riga, a consultancy is advising the Siberian peninsula of Kamchatka on its own timber industry.

The Baltic Sea ports will provide revenue for these nations, though the Russian Republic plans to build a bulk cargo port 150 kilometers west of Leningrad that is meant to replace the Latvian ports of Venspils and Klaipeda. Currently, more than 50 percent of Soviet exports go through Latvian ports.

Another advantage for the Baltic peoples is that, literally, they speak the Russians' language.

Numerous experts on the Baltic economies say that in five to 10 years the Baltic states will be well on their way toward a market economy and will enjoy a much higher standard of living than the Soviet republics.

But getting from here to there won't be easy.

The Baltic nations still lack the basic financial structures and culture of a market economy. There are no money markets, no mobile labor force, no stock markets.

"There is a lack of public acceptance of the middleman function as such, and there is no tradition of paying for know-how," write Swedish development experts Leif Grahm and Lennart Konigson in a survey on Baltic industry.

"Until the facilitating, brokering functions gain acceptance and industry realizes that it has to pay a price for know-how—whether it is a matter of advertising, engineering, or management consultants—[the Baltics'] possibilities for realizing [their] potential will remain constrained."

In short, after 50 years of a centrally planned economy commanded from Moscow, the Baltic states have to relearn the basics of capitalism. And they need to unlearn the communist notion that making money as a middle man is immoral.

"Building a new culture will take time," said Mr. Grahm in an interview.

Even though the Baltic republics have little in the way of hard currency, they do have industrial structures that are valuable. Some of these can be sold off to Western business and the proceeds used to make investments in the West. Only through active involvement in the Western economy will Baltic businessmen learn how market economies work, Grahm says. "These people are very smart, they're just ignorant—high IQ, bad training," says the US official.

The issue of selling off state industries remains to be ironed out in the Baltics. There has been some discussion of distributing properties to pre-annexation landowners. In Latvia, there has been discussion of a voucher system, in which each citizen can sell his points to someone else or pool his with others' to buy a factory or other state enterprise.

One of the problems, says Grahm, is that there has been no discussion of the relationship between entrepreneurship and responsible management. He also raises concerns about a growing "mafia" in the Baltics that has arisen out of the decline of fear in the country.

One of the public misperceptions about the breakup of the Soviet Union—including the breakaway of the Baltic republics—is that political independence equals economic self-sufficiency. In fact, the vast network of bilateral republican agreements that have been forged of late within the USSR can serve as the economic foundation of a future confederation of former Soviet republics. Even more germane than inter-republic agreements is enterprise to enterprise accords.

"In reality, a bilateral agreement between Vilnius [the Lithuanian capital] and Kiev [the Ukrainian capital], for example, isn't relevant, except that it legalizes negotiations between enterprises," says Matthew Sagers, an economist at PlanEcon consulting firm. "The key is when you have an agreement between a carburetor manufacturer in Vilnius and a Kharkov [in the Ukraine] tractor plant."

In the spring of 1990, when Moscow cut energy supplies to Lithuania over its pro-independence policies, Lithuania was forced to forge independent economic relationships—an experience that showed the republic that it could be done and helped prepare it for real independence.

US, Britain Emphasize 'Balanced' Soviet Aid

Alexander MacLeod

9/3/91

The world's leading industrial nations will let their hearts help to determine the scope of the short-term relief they supply to the Soviet Union in the aftermath of the anti-Gorbachev coup.

But hard-headed assessments of Moscow's plans to reform the Soviet economy will decide the extent of longer-term Western aid.

This careful balancing of the demands of compassion and the imperatives of political realism was struck Friday at two key meetings that Western political leaders say will help to set future guidelines for the capitalist world's response to the Soviet crisis.

In Kennebunkport, Maine, United States President George Bush and British Prime Minister John Major, current chairman of the Group of Seven (G-7) industrialized nations, agreed on a six-point plan of action for the coming months.

Also on Friday, sherpas (senior officials) of the G-7 countries met in London and began detailing short- and longer-term responses to the Soviet crisis.

On Sunday, Major flew to Moscow for separate talks with Soviet President Mikhail Gorbachev and Russian Federation president Boris Yeltsin.

The six-point plan Mr. Bush and Mr. Major agreed on calls for implementing existing food credits; assessing the need for aid during the winter; providing teams to help with food production and distribution; increasing "know-how" programs; speeding up the Soviet Union's association with the IMF, and for the IMF and World Bank to work out structural reform plans.

Window of opportunity

Bush and Major said the upheavals in Moscow presented the West with a "window of opportunity" to advance the reform program in the Soviet Union. But although they agreed to act "compassionately and urgently" to prevent starvation this winter, they found common ground in stressing that economic aid must be linked to what Major called "a clear, comprehensive reform program."

The G-7 officials agreed in London to reflect this balanced approach in preparing a report that Major took with him to Moscow. Major's chief concern, his officials said, was to ensure that food and other commodities do not fall into the hands of black-marketeers. Downing Street officials said Major would remind Mr. Gorbachev and Mr. Yeltsin that the Soviet republics are rich in raw materials but need to drastically reform their economies if they are to recover.

This week British supermarket chiefs were holding meetings with John Gummer, the agriculture minister, to thrash out a detailed food-aid plan. Some large British grocery chains are reported to be considering sending relief supplies directly to the Soviet Union.

Thursday's London G-7 meeting was a follow-up to the July summit in the British capital at which the broad outlines of a policy toward the Soviet crisis were drawn up.

Horst Koehler, Germany's sherpa, says a new situation now exists in the Soviet Union, requiring the provision of more economic aid. But when he urged the meeting to recommend an upgraded program of direct economic aid, he was voted down by the other delegates.

An Italian official said afterwards that there was "a huge problem in deciding who to negotiate with in the Soviet Union." Until the situation becomes clearer it is "wise to be cautious" and focus on short-term relief, the official added.

Sir Ronald Mackintosh a senior food aid adviser to the British prime minister said the Soviet Union could produce enough food for its own people, but had big problems in getting it to them.

"One of the big differences between their system and ours is that there's virtually no preservation or packaging as we know them," Sir Ronald said. "There's no long-life milk or fruit juice, no frozen vegetables, no vacuum-packed biscuits. They don't have sophisticated cold stores where meat and fruit are kept in peak condition until they are needed, and they have no home freezers. So, if food isn't eaten quickly, it's simply thrown away or fed to animals."

Reform a priority

The London meeting of G-7 officials decided that the chief priority in the Soviet Union had to be for the people managing the economy to produce a convincing economic and political reform program.

It decided also that all members of the group should begin forging or improving their bilateral links with the

Soviet republics, particularly the Russian Republic and the Ukraine.

Bush and Major said they would continue to consult each other throughout September on the need for food aid and medical assistance. British officials say they expect the onset of the Soviet winter in early October.

It was reported in London that Britain's foreign secretary Douglas Hurd is advocating that the European Community should buy up surplus wheat from former East Bloc countries and make it available to the Soviet Union through food credits.

Lev Voronin, the Soviet ambassador to the EC, took up this theme Friday. He says the fate of the Soviet Union depends to a large extent on the position taken by the EC.

"The priority is an increase in humanitarian food assistance to combat food shortages caused by declining productivity and technical advice to help with the introduction of a market economy," Mr. Voronin said.

The EC's existing food aid program to the Soviet Union includes about $300 million in emergency food aid, and about $600 million in food credits.

Western officials say distribution of the aid has been greatly hampered by inexperience and corruption on the part of Soviet officials.

Divergent Views Persist Over Future Soviet Army

Daniel Sneider

9/4/91

As the Soviet Union disintegrates, both Soviet and Western leaders are haunted by the breakup of a huge, nuclear-armed Soviet military.

Russian President Boris Yeltsin, addressing the Congress of People's Deputies Sept. 3, tried to calm fears that the Soviet nuclear arsenal would get out of control. "Russia will guarantee that the nuclear potential does not fall into the hands of either hawks or extremists," he said, adding that structures to do this were being formed now.

The leaders of the Soviet republics, who now collectively run the country, have been quick to declare their agreement that a united Army with control over nuclear weapons should continue to exist. But beyond that commitment in principle, little consensus has been reached on what this may mean in practice.

The proposal for organization of a transitional Soviet administration, presented Sept. 2 by the republics and President Mikhail Gorbachev, calls for signing an agreement "to preserve united armed forces and . . . to carry out radical military reforms in the armed forces . . . taking into account republican interests."

"We shall have a joint, military-strategic space and the strategic [nuclear] forces shall operate in all the corners of this space," Yvgeny Primakov, Gorbachev's national security advisor, told the Monitor. "But at the same time, . . . some actions should be discussed with [the] republics."

"Every Soviet citizen, as well as every American citizen, is worried about the unity of the Army," said Air Force Maj. Gen. Pyotr Klimuk, a cosmonaut and People's Deputy. "If the Army is torn apart by the republics, it is difficult to predict where that might lead."

But military leaders are unclear as to what the republics mean when they refer to keeping a single Army. "They are saying that the Army we have now has to be preserved," said General of the Army Stanislav Postnikov, commander of the Western Theater. "There are some hints that some sort of a [republican] national guard will be created, but that is still in the air," he said.

Even the idea of a national guard is far from clear. For some, it suggests a several-thousand-man force, devoted mostly to internal security and protecting frontiers. But Ukrainian President Leonid Kravchuk, in a Sept. 2 press conference suggested it would work as a full-scale army.

That idea is unacceptable to the Soviet armed forces leadership. "The Army basically should be united and should be subordinated to one, central command, because it implies certain consequences, primarily for the command of strategic nuclear weapons," Col. Gen. Bronislav Omelichev, first deputy head of the General Staff and a People's Deputy, told the Monitor. "If there is a strong desire to create republican armies, this has to be solved in the framework of a single, union Army, with republican armies performing certain tasks necessary to defend these sovereign republics."

Other ideas are circulating. Gen. Vladimir Lobov, the newly appointed Chief of the General Staff, suggested in a Sept. 2 newspaper interview, that the national guard would consist of the Soviet troops based on the territory of a republic, wearing both the national insignia and republican emblems. He proposed that 60 percent of all conscripts serve in their own republic, making up most of the troops stationed there.

The content of proposed "radical reform" is equally fuzzy. According to Maj. Gen. Klimuk, the new defense minister, Air Marshal Yevgeny Shaposhnikov discussed his reform ideas with the military deputies at a closed meeting Sept. 2.

While not revealing the content of that discussion, General Klimuk said the ideas include proposals that "each republic should have a partial say in financing the Army. We should clearly define what kind of Army we need—we need an Army not to attack but to defend the borders of the country." The unresolved issues include the scale of conscription and the years of service, Klimuk said.

"Reform should be carried out boldly, resolutely, and swiftly, but not recklessly," General Lobov told the Nezavisimaya Gazeta.

General Lobov proposed that the minister of defense be a civilian and that the armed forces be jointly run by the commander-in-chief, the Soviet President, and by the General Staff. The civilian minister would deal with military supply problems and infrastructure, he explained, while the general staff would be responsible for training and operation of armed forces. "I hope the new structure of the Army will to a significant degree suit everybody and all the republics will participate in it," Lobov said. "The single economic space should be protected by a single defense space."

Republics Ill-Prepared for Solo Economies

Amy Kaslow

9/5/91

Ambitious in their political aspirations for independence, the breakaway Soviet republics are reluctantly recognizing the economic limitations to full autonomy.

As the once all-powerful Soviet center dissolves, local leaders have been trying to literally capitalize on the long-repressed republic pride. Soviet President Mikhail Gorbachev's desperate pleas for some semblance of an economic union have been met by local leaders' calls for their own national currencies.

Management over every aspect of the economy once held by the tight-fisted central government in Moscow—including budgets, money supply, trade, production and natural resources—is up for grabs by leaders in all 15 republics.

Both Soviet and Western economists warn that a total break now from the giant, if tottering, Soviet economy would only leave individual republics scrambling for survival. Decades of Moscow's central planning have ensured that the republics are interdependent in every economic sphere: energy, food, consumer goods, light and heavy industry.

The ailing Soviet economy would collapse without at least a central clearinghouse for production and distribution by republics, says Leonid Grigoriev, Soviet economist at Moscow's Institute of World Economy and International Relations. Mr. Grigoriev has spent the past several years doing economic plans for local republic leaders as well as for Mr. Gorbachev. He was a co-author of the controversial 500-day plan for Soviet economic reform announced last fall.

Not one of the individual republics, no matter how mineral-rich or industrialized, can afford such a collapse of the larger economy as it embarks on its own, he says. The collapse of the Council for Mutual Economic Assistance (Comecon), which coordinated trade with former Soviet satellites in Eastern Europe, has made inter-republic barter trade even more crucial.

Because Soviet agricultural and industrial production has been largely region-specific, individual republics are poorly diversified. With the exception of the food industry and machine-building and metalworking sectors—each present in almost all geographical areas—regions tend to be dominated by clusters of specialized manufacturing plants geared to the national market.

Regional interdependence

Uzbekistan, for example, is the principal supplier of cotton to the Soviet Union. This so-called "cotton monoculture" leaves the republic vulnerable to blight and incapable of feeding, clothing, or housing itself.

Opportunities for entering the global marketplace are few. Aside from certain raw materials, such as oil and natural gas, there is little that republics can now export internationally. Soviet manufactured goods are mostly sub-standard and probable losers in the highly competitive world market. Except for natural gas, the energy sector is degenerating.

Severing links now means that the republics would be cut off from their automatic markets and suppliers. This would exacerbate economic troubles, says Matthew Sagers, senior economist at PlanEcon Inc. in Washington.

Dr. Sagers says political changes in recent weeks will give economic restructuring a jump-start on the local republic level, but republics will need each other. Local leaders recognize the folly in now venturing out on their own and abandoning all former Soviet commercial ties.

Highly indebted and cash-poor, these republics are now incapable of sustained self-sufficiency or financing economic reforms by themselves.

"No one has any choice but to join an economic union of some sort," Mr. Grigoriev says.

Last week there was an ironic twist in the union's disintegration. As the richest republics were busy forging new relationships with each other, the poorest declared their independence. Russia and the Ukraine, the two most populous and productive Soviet republics, agreed to establish new ties. Kazakhstan and Russia, the two largest republics in terms of territory, also pressed for a new economic union. The heavily subsidized Central Asian republics of Uzbekistan and Kirghizia announced their secession as a way of jockeying for a better economic position with the economically dominant Russian republic, Grigoriev says.

"Republics, totally unprepared for economic independence, are taking advantage of the collapse of the center," agrees Jonathan Halperin, president of FYI Information Resources, based in Washington. Mr. Halperin's advisory firm is involved in the community of 500,000 independently operated businesses (not state-run) in the Soviet Union.

Nationalist divisions

But links that bond the republics may be very difficult to forge, Grigoriev says. Political obstacles remain, including mistrust along ethnic and nationalist lines. "They remember who ate whose cow 500 years ago," he says.

Grigoriev warns of strife in republics that have sizable Russian populations. "The Russians will go from being first-class citizens in a huge country to second-class status in a small country. They will not take that well."

Among the first to suffer from the union's ongoing political breakdown will be the Central Asian republics, says Grigoriev. The predominantly Muslim and rural region, including Kazakhstan, Turkmenia, Uzbekistan, Kirghizia, and Tadzhikistan, received subsidies from Moscow-center at the expense of wealthier republics.

Moscow's role as collector of national earnings and distributor of incomes has abruptly ended. Russia, the Ukraine, Georgia, Armenia, the Baltics, and other relatively well-heeled republics whose incomes were partly distributed to the nation's fund for Central Asian subsidies have ceased to be a ready source. "There will be a huge economic crisis for republics who received subsidies," Grigoriev says.

If the breakaway republics defy economic cooperation, large portions of the Soviet landscape will turn from poorly diversified to dangerously deprived. Northern Russia and Siberia boast heavy industry, for example, but are almost wholly dependent on imports of consumer goods from other parts of the vast Russian territory and from other republics. If trade agreements are abrogated and the already unreliable transportation and communication links are weakened by the breakup, economic calamity will ensue, Grigoriev says.

Who'll pay the debts?

Should the republics' separatists ultimately reject a union bound by a financial center, the collective liabilities of the 15 republics remain. In recent days Gorbachev pledged to calculate each republic's portion of the national budget in order to transfer the sums to the local level.

Meanwhile, republics are demanding their fair share of the center's gold reserves. The amount of reserves—long a state secret—will soon be told.

As important as doling out assets is the far more difficult task of apportioning the national hard-currency debt, estimated at $65 billion. "The distribution will be very complicated," Grigoriev says. The country's debts are spread among many kinds of creditors. "One country [republic] will owe debts to France and own assets in Ethiopia."

The dire straits of the Soviet economy point to the republics' need to bond together. According to PlanEcon estimates, the Soviet gross national product fell by one tenth during the first half of this year, and foreign trade plummeted by 37 percent. Soviet oil and coal mining industries are atrophying due to the high cost and inefficiency of extracting oil and coal. The country's grain harvest is down by more than half.

Ukraine battered

The most robust republics are in peril. The Ukraine, once called "the breadbasket of Europe," and "an economic powerhouse" has been reduced to a third-rate producer due to low worker incentive, agricultural inefficiencies, inadequate storage facilities, and poor transportation.

Even without economic restructuring, high unemployment will soon occur, says Jay Mitchell, a PlanEcon economist. Inefficient factories will not survive without subsidies. Local political opposition can slow down the closure of the major employer in a town, he says, and delay reform. "The state-owned enterprises won't die so quickly because they have a lot of resources. Many giants live longer than they should because they have supplies, equipment, and money stashed away."

If there is no safety net prepared for the unemployed, tensions will ignite, says Adrian Karatnycky of the AFL-CIO's international department in Washington.

The Federation of Russian Independent Trade Unions, representing roughly 90 percent of the work force, or some 60 million workers, has long been in the communist grip. Hardliners will try to appeal to disenchanted workers, says Mr. Karatnycky, whose organization supports the independent Federation of Free Trade Union workers, with 60,000 members in the Soviet Union. The latter, he says "totally distrusts the center."

In terms of wresting control from Moscow over local natural resources, the Russian and Ukrainian coal miners are the bedrock of the worker's reform movement. After a wave of carefully orchestrated and economically debilitating strikes, the coal miners won the transfer of mines from the center to the republics. The AFL-CIO promotes democratization of unionized labor there.

Workers have found important common ground with independently operated enterprises, say Karatnycky and Halperin. Karatnycky says the unions have received financial contributions from the business community.

"Historically, trade unions have been the mechanisms of control, not the voice of the workers," says Halperin. "The miners' strikes were an effective means of making a political statement—for more local control, freedom and rights, and management of local affairs. These are the same objectives of independent businesses—greater economic autonomy instead of politically dictated goals." As large manufacturing facilities go private, often at the urging of the workers, the two groups could form a powerful merger, Halperin says.

Banking system needed

Before much more can develop on the local level, there need to be banks where "people can go for mortgages and companies for funds," Mr. Mitchell says. Without a viable banking system, "you almost put a noose around economic restructuring."

Halperin says banking and other goals and instruments of reform will ultimately be coordinated among republics.

"After a period of trial and error, the republics will cede back power to a central body which can better coordinate" the intricate trade and financial relationships, he says.

The Old 'New' Media Is New Again, and Powerful

Daniel Sneider

9/5/91

When a Soviet turns on the television or picks up his morning papers these days, he probably can't help feeling as if his world has been turned upside down.

The central television is populated by the faces of those who disappeared from its screens during the months of right-wing drift since last fall. The frisky democratic papers which used to peck away at the citadels of power are now the favorites of the new officialdom.

Meanwhile the staid mouthpieces of the Communist Party press, banned in the early days after the failed hard-line coup, have reappeared, but only in the form of independent products of their staffs. And the once-powerful propaganda bosses whine about their unfair treatment at the hands of the new victors.

In the media, as elsewhere in Soviet life, the division is now sharply drawn between those who collaborated by publicizing the orders of the would-be junta and those who resisted.

In the newspaper world, the junta itself drew that line. It banned all papers but a handful of official Communist Party organs. Some 11 banned independent and liberal newspapers responded by pooling resources to publish an underground sheet, Obshchaya Gazeta (literally "joint newspaper").

"This coup or any other coup would have been a failure in any case," observes Vitaly Tretiakov, editor of Nezavisimaya Gazeta, one of the leading independent papers. "But . . . a huge role belongs to the independent press."

While they could not crush the papers completely, the junta did have effective control over the television, taking the Russian republic's television station off the air and using the central television to broadcast propaganda.

"We had absolutely no information," says Tolya, a doctor from the Ukrainian capital of Kiev. "They showed us the ballet, Swan Lake three times a day."

Within hours of the coup's failure, Russian President Boris Yeltsin, wiped out the powerful official media. The Communist Party press was suspended; the head of the state television and radio corporation, Leonid Kravchenko, was sacked; the official Novosti news agency placed under Russian government control; and shortly after, the director-general of the official Tass news agency, Lev Spiridonov, was also fired.

The victims of the democratic revolution have rushed to defend themselves, though not convincingly to many who have watched them serve the interests of Communist officialdom for years.

"Yes, we broadcast those documents," Mr. Kravchenko told reporters at the Soviet parliament this week. "I had only one choice at that time. No one could understand what was going on . . . . What could we do? Armed people, including civilians, were everywhere."

But such excuses have not stopped the media upheaval. Mr. Gorbachev's press spokesman, Vitaly Ignatenko, has taken over at Tass, which he intends to make independent. The new television head is Yegor Yakovlev, the editor of Moscow News, arguably the most liberal weekly in the Soviet Union.

The change has been most visible on the evening news show Vremya ("time"), the most watched and most influential program on Soviet television. The new leadership has opened up a competition between two news teams: one of Vremya reporters who were non-collaborators, and another from the popular late-night "Television News Service," which Kravchenko took off the air in the aftermath of the January military crackdown in the Baltics.

In the newspaper world, the Communist press, including the conservative flagships Pravda and Sovietskaya Rossiya, which reappeared during the past week, without Communist symbols, as independent journals owned by their staffs. The key issue now is the fate of the huge Communist Party-owned publishing houses, now seized by the Russian government, where all the papers are published.

Editors such as Tretiakov worry that the once-communist papers that are now independent might still enjoy an advantage from access to this press. Alternately one of the larger democratic papers, such as the former government daily Izvestia, might try to take control of it. Those papers "want to have the best pieces of this press for themselves," he worries. "And then intense competition will begin."

Soviet Reformers Seek Mantle Of Legitimacy

Daniel Sneider

9/5/91

After three days of sometimes dramatic debate, the emergency session of the Soviet Congress of People's Deputies, the country's highest legislative authority, was ready to render judgment on creating a new political order for the country.

The Congress has grappled with an unusual dilemma—how to have a political revolution and constitutional continuity at the same time.

The aftermath of the failed putsch of Aug. 19-21 has amounted to nothing less than a revolution. Powerful institutions of Soviet life, including the Communist Party and the central Cabinet, have been disbanded by decree of the new authorities.

All this has been done in the name of protecting constitutional legitimacy. The opposition to the coup, led by Russian President Boris Yeltsin, insisted it was the true defender of constitutional order and was seeking to restore the rightful Soviet president to office. In the name of the Constitution, Mr. Yeltsin issued a decree that removed people from posts, suspended newspapers from publication, and halted the political activity of Communists and others.

But at the Congress of People's Deputies the democratic steamroller driven by Yeltsin and Soviet President Mikhail Gorbachev has come under criticism for rolling over the Constitution. That has forced democratic reformers to back off a bit. Initially the democrats sought to circumvent and dissolve the parliament and Congress. But they have now found they will have to work with the elected deputies—at least for a little while.

At press time, the Congress was poised to vote on three major documents which together would reshape the Soviet political system. One is a revised version of the plan, presented Monday by Mr. Gorbachev and 11 republican leaders, for revamping the structure of the Soviet Union itself, changing it from a federation into a loose confederation. The second guarantees human rights and freedoms. The third is a bill of constitutional amendments which alter the central government institutions during the transition to a new treaty of union and a new constitution.

The draft resolution on the new shape of the union, as published by Reuters, calls for establishing a transitional power structure. The Russian government sought some changes, but the final version was not clear at press time.

The draft recognizes republican declarations of sovereignty and calls for the signing of a new union treaty "by all republics wishing to do so."

In the meantime, the resolution says, new inter-republican treaties on economic and financial cooperation, ecology, human rights, religious freedom, and other subjects should be concluded. It calls for creation of an economic common market, "in the framework of which free movement of goods, people, and capital can be ensured." Independent states such as the Baltics or even former Soviet satellites of Eastern Europe, could join this economic treaty, it suggests.

The new "union of sovereign states" should reach an agreement on a unified security structure and foreign policy, the document states. The basis of that should be observance of all Soviet treaty obligations, including treaties on arms control and foreign debts. United armed forces will be maintained, but will be radically reformed. Military spending will be reduced and defense doctrines jointly agreed upon.

The Congress, according to this resolution, "confirms the responsibility of the union as a nuclear power" and pledges to take "special measures for establishment of the most reliable guarantees ruling out unsanctioned deployment of nuclear weapons." It adds a call for further agreements on reducing strategic nuclear weapons and for negotiations to completely eliminate shorter-range nuclear weapons.

The structure of the central government during the transition period is defined in a separate draft law, made available to the Monitor by the Russian Information Agency.

This creates a State Council composed of the Soviet president and the leaders of the republics to make decisions on basic domestic and foreign policy, as proposed on Monday.

The Cabinet and ministerial structure is replaced by an interrepublican economic committee formed by the republics on an equal basis.

The key compromise to the original Gorbachev-Yeltsin plan is a decision to retain the present Supreme Soviet, the standing legislature whose members are elected from the larger Congress of People's Deputies. The republican leaders initially sought to get rid of the entire parliamentary structure, replacing it with a council of representatives, 20 from each republic. Now they will retain the lower chamber of the Supreme Soviet, the Council of the Union. But they will reorganize the upper Council of the Republics, with a new membership chosen by the republican parliaments and new powers.

The new, more powerful republican chamber is clearly formed as a check on the conservative union legislature where members of the now-suspended Communist Party still dominate its ranks. The republican chamber is given the power to legislate activity of all union bodies, on interrepublican matters, and to ratify international treaties. All other legislation must be passed by both chambers. This draft closely follows the structure called for in the draft union treaty which was due to be signed on Aug. 20, the day after the attempted coup began.

The decision to retain the Supreme Soviet in some form is a clear concession to attacks from conservatives, who insist it is the only source of constitutional legitimacy remaining after the coup.

"Both the Supreme Soviet and the congress are incapable of acting and should be dissolved," Col. Viktor Alksnis, leader of the conservative Soyuz (Unity) faction, told the weekly "Argumenti i Facti. The trouble is that today it's the only legitimate body that can secure the transfer to the new power structures. Thus, it's very sad, it should be preserved."

Gorbachev Looks to Western Aid After Political Overhaul

Daniel Sneider

9/6/91

After a night and a morning of wrangling and arm-twisting, Soviet President Mikhail Gorbachev and the republican leaders standing behind him emerged triumphant.

The emergency session of the Congress of People's Deputies, the country's supreme legislature, finally approved sweeping political changes. Virtually undoing the edifice erected by the Bolshevik revolution of 1917, the Congress agreed to the republican plan to convert the Soviet Union into a loose confederation, with the republics holding a veto over central policymaking.

"The Congress rose to the occasion at this crucial and, without any exaggeration, historic moment," President Gorbachev said in his closing address yesterday. The Soviet leader expressed hope that the country could gain stability after the tumultuous events since the attempted putsch of Aug. 19-21. "We hope these great decisions will enable us to get out of our crisis," he said.

The new Soviet leadership clearly expects that its efforts to shape a political consensus will lead rapidly to an influx of Western economic assistance. United States Secretary of State James Baker III arrives here next week on a visit in which Western aid is likely to be the primary subject on the agenda.

The victory of Mr. Gorbachev, Russian President Boris Yeltsin, and the 10 other republican governments, in presenting a joint political plan at the beginning of the Congress session on Monday, was far from easy.

The Congress was presented with two key documents: a resolution that described the basic principles of a transitional administration; and a bill of amendments to the Soviet Constitution reorganizing the central government in conformity with the confederate principles.

On Wednesday evening, when the Congress was scheduled to conclude, Gorbachev failed to get the two-thirds majority approval needed for the constitutional changes. Gorbachev and the republican leaders worked through the night to make changes and reconvened the Congress yesterday morning to try again.

Several factors blocked passage: Many conservative deputies refused to agree to a change that amounts to the dissolution of the Congress; the Russians had to appease smaller nationalities within the larger Russian Federation.

When the delegates reconvened yesterday morning, Gorbachev threatened to disband the Congress if they failed to get approval.

"The situation dictates that we should use more dynamic action or we may face a situation of starvation and maybe freezing during the winter," Gorbachev advisor Georgi Shaknazarov explained to the Monitor. "Unfortunately, some deputies do not want to sacrifice their ambitions and privileges."

Some changes made to the documents overnight made them more palatable. The broad resolution was largely intact, but a key clause recognizing the independence of republics, opening the door to accepting Baltic independence, was amended.

In order to gain independence, it added, those republics must negotiate with the Soviet Union "to solve the entire range of issues related to secession," likely to include guarantees of the rights of minorities, particularly Russians, living in those republics as well as the status of Soviet military bases.

The resistance to the bill on government restructuring was focused on the effective dissolution of the Congress and the standing parliament elected from its midst, the Supreme Soviet, and their replacement with a two-chamber body including an upper Council of the Republics and a lower Council of the Union.

The republican chamber was originally to be formed with 20 representatives from each republic, chosen by their legislatures. The revised version gives Russia 52 delegates, to allow for representing the "autonomous republics" within it. But each republic still has the equivalent of only one vote in the body.

In the newer draft, the lower chamber was made even more subordinate to the republics with its members drawn from the existing Congress of Deputies but only in coordination with republican governments. The upper republican chamber has to approve all laws and the draft also gives republics the right to void any union law which contradicts their own legislation.

With a firm-handed Gorbachev in the chair, the republican leadership moved to ram these changes through, but they ran into resistance in the vote on the new parliament.

Three times the Congress fell short of the two-thirds majority needed. Gorbachev, warned the delegates: "Either we take a decision and follow the path we have agreed to or we stop here," ending the Congress. The next time, Gorbachev had his way by a safe margin.

The new Supreme Soviet is to be convened by Oct. 2, giving the republican governments time to pick their representatives.

Executive power in the Soviet Union, under the new law, now rests with a State Council formed by Gorbachev and the republican leaders (the post of vice president was eliminated after Vice President Gennady Yanayev joined the coup leadership).

The Cabinet is replaced by an interrepublican economic committee to manage the economy. The only other all-union bodies which are explicitly retained are those dealing with defense, internal security, and foreign policy.

Yeltsin Charts Steady Course for Democracy

Daniel Sneider

9/9/91

Boris Yeltsin is a man who makes many people anxious. In the United States where Bush administration officials continue to express apprehension about where Mr. Yeltsin is taking Russia and the Soviet Union.

The charismatic Russian leader's emergence at the head of the democratic revolution sweeping the Soviet Union seemed at first to calm fears that he was nothing more than a power-hungry demagogue. But in the aftermath of the failed Aug. 19-21 coup, with talk of a new Russian imperialism in the air here, criticism of Yeltsin picked up again.

"Yeltsin is basically power hungry," the New York Times quoted one American official saying. "He has no program of his own."

This perception of Yeltsin is not new. But it reveals a flawed understanding of the events of the past year and half in the Soviet Union. During that period, which began with Yeltsin's surprise election as the chairman of the Supreme Soviet (parliament) of the Russian Federation on May 29, 1990, the Russian leader has followed a remarkably consistent course. He has pursued a coherent program with determination and, at times, tactical wisdom.

The Soviet Union that is emerging from the wreckage of the Communist state is almost precisely the one that Yeltsin has been seeking. From his first day in office, Yeltsin has articulated a view of the Soviet Union as a confederation, formed from the bottom up by sovereign republics without a commanding center. He has sought radical economic reform, a quick move to a market economy, and democratization of political life. And he has called on Soviet President Mikhail Gorbachev to oust the conservatives around him and to form a coalition government with the democrats and republican leaders.

Understanding Yeltsin

To understand the swirl of images of Boris Yeltsin—populist, nationalist, demagogue—it is useful to listen to what the Siberian politician has been saying.

From the moment Mr. Gorbachev failed to block his election, Yeltsin advocated a new concept of the relationship between the republics and the central government. He moved quickly, for example, to declare the sovereignty of Russia, following the path taken by the Baltic republics.

"We must hold out against the dictates of the center," Yeltsin said in his first press conference on May 30 last year. "Our state, country, union will be strong only through strong republics, and the stronger and more independent the union republics are, the stronger the center, the stronger our union will be, conversely."

After meeting with Gorbachev, Yeltsin spoke to the Russian parliament on June 13, where he expanded his concept of a new union. "Each state will determine its place along a path ranging . . . from a federation to a confederation," he said. "The level of independence will be determined by each one of the sovereign states that will belong to the union on the basis of a union treaty. In places it will be a process differentiated between a federation and confederation . . . . It is a process that includes democratization . . . and indeed a reform of the state set-up of our union."

New economic plan

Gorbachev, speaking to the Congress earlier this week, described the plan drawn up by himself and 10 republican leaders as a "voluntary" union. "Let it be possible to have a federative membership on some questions, confederative on others, and associative on a third. I think that the formula 'the Union of Sovereign States' enables us to take all that into consideration."

Later, in June 1990, Yeltsin began to push a new 500-day program for radical economic reform, drawn up by economist Grigory Yavlinsky. He moved it simultaneously to conclude bilateral economic and political treaties with other republics. This would create "a kind of horizontal complex without a vertical structure, without a state planning committee and so on," he told a press conference June 26.

In early July last year, the Soviet Communist Party convened its 28th Party Congress. Speculation was widespread that Gorbachev would step down from the Party leadership, freeing himself from that political millstone. He did not, but Yeltsin rose dramatically at the end of the Party Congress on July 6, to resign from the party. More than a year before the Party conservative leadership tried its August putsch, Yeltsin distanced himself from them.

Terse warning

"The last years have shown that it has not proved possible to neutralize the activity of the party's conservative forces. On the contrary, we have spoken too much about us all being in the same boat, on the same side of the barricades, that we are fighting shoulder to shoulder with identical thinking . . . . This position has created a regime of security for the conservative forces in the CPSU [Communist Party of the Soviet Union] and has strengthened their conviction that it is possible to gain revenge."

Early that August, Gorbachev agreed to form a joint group with Yeltsin to draft a radical reform plan, based on the 500-day program. But later that month, Gorbachev moved to compromise with a more conservative plan offered by his government.

"People are tired of waiting," Yeltsin warned in a Sept. 1 press conference. "For two years now we have been talking about this program for the transition to market economy, yet nothing is being done. There must be one single program. You cannot cross a hedgehog with a snake . . . ."

Yeltsin offered the first of what would be many versions of a proposal to form a new government structure, uniting republican leaders and the Soviet president, to carry out reform. "It ought to be a council of the presidents of union and sovereign states," he said, describing the State Council finally created Thursday by the Congress of People's Deputies.

But by October, Gorbachev had backed off from the radical reform plan, opting for a vague combined program. This is doomed to failure, Yeltsin told the Russian parliament Oct. 16. There are now three options, he continued: for Russia to go on its own; to form a "real coalition," a cabinet in which some ministers are proposed by Russia and some by Gorbachev; or to bide their time for six months, he suggested, until it becomes clear that the Soviet plan was mistaken "and again propose sensible economic steps."

Events followed the third course. Gorbachev moved steadily to the right. A bloody military crackdown on Baltic nationalist governments followed in January, which Yeltsin openly opposed. On Feb. 19, 1991, Yeltsin made a rare appearance on Soviet television where he countered charges that he was seeking to dismember the Soviet Union.

Yeltsin also struck back, blaming Gorbachev for throwing away the chance for the 500-day plan.

"What is now taking place is a rolling-back in the opposite direction . . . . After such cooperation I think that my personal mistake was excessive trust in the president. . . . I distance myself from the position and policy of the president and advocate his immediate resignation, the handing over of power to a collective body, the Federation Council of the republics."

Support from miners

Yeltsin, backed by a nationwide miners' strike supporting his political demands, resisted Communist attempts to remove him from office in March. On April 23, Gorbachev held a historic meeting with nine republican leaders and agreed to a new version of the union treaty which would give significant power to the republics. Yeltsin consolidated his position by holding free, direct elections for the Russian presidency on June 12.

In his major campaign speech, in Moscow June 1, Yeltsin stressed that the events of previous months had proven that "the country and its citizens are not prepared to turn back." The democratic and workers movement, organized in a wave of mass meetings in Russia during those months, "made the president also understand, after all, that if he will not lean on the 'left shoulder' he will be left with no chance at all."

"It is not just in Russia that changes are taking place," Yeltsin noted, "the situation is developing in the same direction in other republics." The concept of a union of sovereign states "is not an abstraction or a model, but a definition of a real process."

He warned that "any attempt to retreat . . . back to a unitary state will result in large losses for Russia and the Union," a specter almost realized by the coup plotters just two months later.

New Soviet Leadership Presses Economic Plan

Daniel Sneider

9/9/91

The Baltic republics are officially free after more than a half-century of Soviet occupation. The city Czar Peter the Great built as his window on the West has shed the image of the birthplace of the Bolshevik revolution and restored its historic name of St. Petersburg.

These decisions, made last Friday, are symbolic markers of the great historical drama unfolding in what is now called the "former Soviet Union." But these are relatively easy steps, impelled by the collapse of the old regime.

Now the men who make up the new Soviet leadership are buckling down to a far more trying task—how to keep what remains of the Soviet Union together and avert economic catastrophe.

The Soviet leadership met on Friday to begin implementing the decisions of the emergency meeting of the Soviet legislature last week on forming a transitional administration. Until the republican governments make their decisions on whom to send to a new union parliament and to a new interrepublican economic committee, the country is being managed by the interim team set up in the days after the failed coup.

At the top is the State Council, the new collective leadership of the Soviet confederation, grouping Soviet President Mikhail Gorbachev and the heads of the 10 republics who have opted, for now, to remain in the union.

The State Council met early Friday, where the decision to recognize the independence of the Baltic states was finally formally adopted. Following the meeting, Mr. Gorbachev issued a decree stating that until the interrepublican group was established, the committee for management of the national economy, formed after the coup and headed by Russian republican Premier Ivan Silayev, will act in place of the former Cabinet.

The immediate priority of the interim government is to conclude an agreement on economic union, one that could embrace all 15 former Soviet republics, including the three Baltics, and potentially even their former allies in Eastern Europe. At the State Council meeting, the deputy head of the economic management committee, radical economist Grigory Yavlinsky, reported on progress toward that goal.

Mr. Yavlinsky told the State Council, according to the Tass news agency, that a draft treaty of economic union is finished and that all the republics have agreed to send representatives to Moscow to finalize the text. According to reports, the treaty includes agreements on a range of issues including monetary policy, financial relations, trade, and foreign debt and credits.

Yavlinsky has repeatedly expressed his belief that there must be a unified Soviet economic space, with common monetary and financial policies, if there is to be any hope for reform or for restoring economic stability. He also stresses that without this, it will be difficult to receive Western aid.

"We have to ask the question of whether the republics are going to do something together or not," Yavlinsky told a meeting of the Geneva-based World Economic Forum in Moscow last week. "Only in answering this can we start negotiations with the G-7 [the Group of Seven leading industrial nations]."

"There are a lot of things possible to do," Yavlinsky continued. "Privatization measures can be implemented at all levels: such things as independent banks, a reserve system, a federal reserve system, liberalization of prices." Yavlinsky is the principal author of the aborted 500-day radical reform plan offered last year and coauthor, along with a Harvard University team, of the "Grand Bargain" plan for Western cooperation and radical reform.

One of the more difficult issues is the question of a single currency. The Baltic states have already expressed their intention to issue their own currencies, as has the Ukraine.

Deputy head of the economic management committee, Arkady Volsky, told the Economic Forum meeting that he "would insist on a common currency" for the new union. But Yavlinsky indicated his draft treaty will allow every republic to have its own currency.

Republican currencies don't make economic sense, reform economist Nikolai Petrakov, a former adviser to Gorbachev, told the trade union daily Trud last week. "It is a step backward, but the reality is such that disintegration of the former Soviet Union is inevitable. That is why it is necessary to at least preserve the single economic space, to separate and then unite on a new basis."

If separate currencies are introduced, Mr. Petrakov suggests it will be necessary to reach an agreement on a common monetary policy and interaction of banking systems, with the value of the ruble floating freely in relation to the republican currencies. The banking system is likely to be modeled on the United States Federal Reserve system, in which all 50 states have representation.

According to various reports, the treaty also includes an agreement on division of the Soviet foreign debt, and it reserves funds of hard currency, gold, and diamonds. Thomas Alibegov, deputy head of the Soviet Foreign Economic Bank, told the independent Interfax news agency that the Soviet foreign debt, estimated at $60 billion to $65 billion, would be distributed among the republics.

A Latvian official told a press conference on Sept. 5 that the republican officials had agreed on criteria for this division. Latvia's share of both the debt and the reserves, for example, was calculated at 0.9 percent.

USSR Breakup Defies History

Peter Grier

9/11/91

The disintegration of the Soviet empire will surely rank as a turning point of our time. It is one of those rare events that make clear the distinction between what is history and what is merely news.

The suddenness of the collapse and the scope of political and economic changes underway throughout the former Soviet Union and Eastern Europe are almost unprecedented, according to historians. The problem now will be making the changes work while avoiding the recriminations and violence which have marked past periods of revolutionary political transition.

"There have been very few peaceful breakups of empires," says John Lewis Gaddis, director of Ohio University's Contemporary History Institute.

In historical terms, it is already remarkable that so much change has occurred with so little fighting. In September 1989, who would have believed that within two years the world would see the Berlin Wall torn down, Germany reunited, former Warsaw Pact nations clamoring to join NATO, and the Soviet Union itself disbanded—all without any concerted resistance?

The situation in Yugoslavia stands as a warning of what the Soviet breakup has avoided, or may yet become. Previous European political upheavals of this century invariably followed the bloodshed of wars. The Russian Revolution of 1917 came near the end of World War I; construction of the Iron Curtain across Eastern Europe was a political consequence of the position of Allied armies at the end of World War II.

"It is close to unprecedented to have this shift taking place without war," says Dr. Gaddis.

One analogous period in recent history might well be the 1890s to the beginning of World War I. During that time the post-Waterloo structure of European power that had survived throughout the 19th century began to break up for good, notes Walter LaFeber, a professor of history at Cornell University. Feelings of nationalism and ethnicism exploded throughout the Balkans and other areas of Eastern and Central Europe. The world order turned upside down, with old power Britain declining in importance and upstarts Germany, Japan, and the United States rising. The fragmentation of power and empires was similar to what is sweeping Europe today. In that sense the fall of communism "is an interesting movement back into history," says Dr. LaFeber.

The French Revolution of 1789 also provides striking similarities with today's events in the Soviet Union. Both involved ossified regimes stretched too far abroad, while not providing adequate consumer comfort at home, says Simon Schama, a professor of history at Harvard and author of "Citizens," a history of the French Revolution.

Both revolutions involved rulers (Gorbachev, Louis XVI) who waffled about introducing reforms. At their height both involved huge crowds physically storming symbols of their overseers: the Bastille in France and the square in front of KGB headquarters in Moscow.

This comparison gives one pause, considering the terror that later enveloped France, but Dr. Schama cautions that historical analogies shouldn't be taken too literally. He says there are two key problems illustrated by the French Revolution that Soviet citizens now face: "How to make economic changes and political reform work in tandem . . . and how to make a big state effective while securing freedom and justice."

Americans forget, he points out, that their nation's relatively smooth transition from the violence of revolution to the debate of constructing new political institutions is, in historical terms, unique. The US was helped in that transition by an already deeply rooted sense of self-government created by the Virginia House of Burgesses and other colonial political institutions. The Soviet Union, however, has no such history and is still learning true democracy from scratch.

In the Russian past there have been popular rebellions, and there has been some experience with urban self-government, says William McNeill, professor of history emeritus at the University of Chicago. But until this century the vast majority of the population consisted of peasants who worked the land.

"What is different about the Russian past is that they never had the practice of majority vote," he says. "They had the feeling that unless everybody agreed, it wasn't right."

Dr. McNeill says that he thinks such a frame of mind may well persist in the Soviet Union, making possible the return of dictatorship in some form. The great remaining question, he says, is whether the economic troubles almost certainly looming on the horizon will lead to further upheaval. Future stability in the region is a major Western concern. Another historical analogy may shed light on this problem: the breakup of the Austro-Hungarian Empire at the end of World War I. The Austro-Hungarian dissolution resulted in whole new states, such as Czechoslovakia and Yugoslavia, and radically changed the borders of older nations such as Poland and Romania.

In geopolitical terms, the major problem was that these changes left "small, ineffective, and rather tempting states," says Charles Gati, an Eastern European expert at Union College. It should have been clear in 1920 that a larger power would inevitably move into this vacuum, he says. Hitler's Germany finally did, sparking World War II. With Yugoslavia now potentially dividing into microstates, plus the independence of the Baltics and the looser Soviet republic, such a situation might reoccur.

Russians Urge More Unified Economic Plan

Daniel Sneider

9/12/91

As winter approaches and economic crisis deepens, the Soviet leadership is rushing to find an economic plan acceptable to most of the now-independent republics.

Some variations of a proposed economic agreement are circulating among the central administration and the republican governments. Proposals range from a loose convention among independent republican economies to a relatively centralized system with a single currency, monetary, tax, and customs structure.

The current team managing the Soviet economy, headed by Russian Premier Ivan Silayev, is leaning toward the more unified approach. Mr. Silayev's deputy, radical economist Grigory Yavlinsky, has drawn up a draft treaty of economic union that was submitted last week to Soviet President Mikhail Gorbachev and leaders of 10 republics grouped in the new State Council.

"We have major economic difficulties," Mr. Yavlinsky told reporters yesterday. "Inflation is rampant. Production is going down. The goal of this document is to lead the country out of the crisis."

Yavlinsky admitted that there would be difficulties in getting the republics to agree to this draft treaty, but he added, "Economic union is not a choice. It is a necessity. This much is clear to everybody." He said if republics delay in signing the treaty, Russia is prepared to move forward alone.

Representatives of all the Soviet republics, including the Baltics, participated in the discussions leading to this draft treaty. But the treaty will still have to be approved by each republican government. The Ukraine, the second richest Soviet republic after Russia, will likely not make its decision until after a Dec. 1 referendum on independence.

Yavlinsky predicted the process of finalizing the treaty will be lengthy. "It will be difficult to reconcile this document with the political ambitions of various leaders."

Yavlinsky refused to give specific figures for Western aid needed to help the Soviet Union through this crisis. But he said that "transition to a market in this country without interaction and integration with Western countries is simply impossible." He said the West would not be ready to give aid until a treaty on union is signed.

The draft treaty of economic union is a voluntary association, allowing for an associative status for republics ready to assume only parts of the joint obligations. The republics that do not want to join will be treated as foreign countries, the document states.

The economic union will jointly form policy on a range of areas including monetary and credit policy, finances, taxes, customs, currency, legal regulation, and the movement of goods, services, and labor, according to a summary of the text yesterday in the daily newspaper Izvestia. Policy will be made at the highest level by the State Council. Below that will be an interstate economic committee, a banking union, and an arbitration body.

The draft treaty states that private property will be given priority in the new economic union and freedom of entrepreneurship guaranteed. Goods and services would move freely throughout the union, as well as the labor force, without any restrictions by individual republics.

One of the more controversial aspects of the Yavlinsky plan is its suggestion that the ruble be preserved as a single currency in the union and that steps be taken to strengthen its value during the next two years. That would include stringent curbs in government spending and tightening credit to bring down the massive inflation that makes the ruble virtually worthless. On this basis, the treaty says, partial convertibility of the ruble to allow foreigners to buy and sell rubles, for example, will be instituted more quickly.

Many republics, including the powerful Ukraine, have already indicated their desire to establish their own currencies, however. The Yavlinsky draft, bowing to that reality slightly, says an introduction of national currencies is permitted but only "under condition that they do not undermine the viability of the ruble," presumably by having their value tied to that of the ruble.

The proposed new banking system is also a mixture of central administration and republican sovereignty. The current State Bank of the USSR would be abolished and replaced by a union of republican central banks, similar to the US Federal Reserve system. The banking union, independent of the executive power, would regulate the ruble rate, control the use of gold and currency reserves, regulate commercial banks, and control the money supply. The other thorny issue is that of budgets and taxes. Even before the failed coup, the Russian republic and the Ukraine had refused to have any federal taxes. The draft treaty reflects that view, calling instead for republics to give a fixed percentage of their national income (or a similar index) to fund common programs of the union.

Finally there is the problem of foreign debt and credits. Many foreign governments have said that they cannot give aid and loans unless they know to whom they are giving them. The draft treaty says the union can receive loans only if all the members agree. Otherwise individual republics can get credits but are fully responsible for them. The draft apparently drops an earlier idea to divide the responsibility for the Soviet Union's huge estimated $60 billion debt among the republics.

Soviet-Cuban Military, Economic Ties Seem Set To Unravel

David Clark Scott

9/13/91

Three decades of Soviet-Cuban military cooperation appear to be drawing to a close, and the Soviets seem set to further revise close economic ties as well.

In the wake of the failed hard-line coup, analysts say Soviet relations with Cuba—its longtime Cold-War ally parked 90 miles off the Florida coast—are shifting to a purely political and economic footing. The results of the Soviet action could loosen Cuban leader Fidal Castro's long hold on power.

On Wednesday, President Mikhail Gorbachev announced the withdrawal of some of the 11,000 Soviet troops that he says are stationed on the Caribbean Island. His comments were also interpreted in some quarters as indicating that the roughly $2 billion Cuba receives in economic subsidies on Soviet oil would be eliminated in favor of a shift to a free-market relationship.

"We intend to transform our relations with Cuba to a plane of mutually beneficial trade and economic ties, and we will remove other elements from that relationship that were born in a different time and a different era," Mr. Gorbachev said.

The Bush administration in recent weeks has indicated the Soviet Union's ongoing relationship with Communist hold-out Fidel Castro is an impediment to US economic aid. US Secretary of State James Baker III, in Moscow on a five-day visit, praised the decision as a "positive step" and a "very substantial gesture."

"This withdrawal is very important symbolically," says Gillian Gunn, a Cuba specialist with the Carnegie Endowment for International Peace. "The Cuban relationship is being redefined, and redefined very quickly."

The troop pullout is seen as another sign of the ascendancy of Soviet reformists, embodied by Russian Federation President Boris Yeltsin, and an indication of mounting Soviet desperation for economic aid. The troop pullout also portends the end of an era of cooperation marked by the 1962 Cuban missile crisis and Cuban involvement in Angola and Ethiopia.

The reaction from Cuba was unusually swift and angry. In a statement, the Cuban Ministry of Foreign Affairs blasted the lack of prior consultation as "inappropriate behavior." It complained about the failure of Gorbachev to speak out about the "illegal occupation" of Guantanamo Bay, which the US rents for a naval base. And in an unusual public correction, the ministry said the "essentially symbolic" Soviet troop total in Cuba was wrong.

"Gorbachev has used Cuba as a bargaining chip with Baker," says Ms. Gunn. If he's annoyed enough, Castro may kick the Soviet troops out [before the withdrawal] to preserve pride and dignity."

If so, would Mr. Castro boot out the estimated 2,100 Soviet signals intelligence technicians running Lourdes, one of the largest Soviet electronic eavesdropping facilities? US analysts say the sophisticated equipment is largely off-limits to Cubans and may be of little initial value. But Cuba might be able to rent the listening post to China, or the highest bidder, for hard currency.

Although the military strategic value of the Lourdes facility to the Soviets is arguably diminishing, they have shown no signs of wanting to abandon it. Indeed, Soviet republics embracing free enterprise may find it of growing value. One Western expert on Soviet signals intelligence says Soviet electronic surveillance centers worldwide are increasingly used for industrial espionage.

"Castro can't afford to burn any bridges," says Jose Cardenas, director of research for the Cuban American National Foundation, a Miami-based conservative lobby group. Mr. Cardenas says that Cuba's economic problems are so bad that Castro cannot afford to risk severing what ties remain to the Soviet Union with a vitriolic response to the troop withdrawal.

But he predicts Castro must respond to the "devastating psychological impact on the Cuban people of the Soviets packing up and leaving them." It increases the likelihood of economic and minor political reforms being announced at the Fourth Party Congress next month, Cardenas says. "I don't see how Castro can go to the Congress without offering some semblance of hope."

Call to Move Lenin From Mausoleum Signals End To a Communist Icon

Daniel Sneider

9/16/91

The failed coup and the whirlwind of political upheaval that has followed have spun off a small eddy of activity in the cobblestoned expanse of Red Square. Suddenly, growing numbers of people from Moscow and afar are making pilgrimages to the boxy granite edifice that houses the embalmed remains of the founder of the Bolshevik state, Vladimir Lenin.

Like Antonina Stepanovna and her husband, they have heard the news that Lenin may soon be removed from the mausoleum. "Today with tears in our eyes," she says, "we came to see him off because we heard he would be taken away. He was a good man. He was the best man. We have lived well because of him."

Leninism falling

One by one, the symbols of Soviet Communism are being whisked aside. Last week, St. Petersburg (formerly Leningrad) Mayor Anatoli Sobchak proposed burying Lenin in the city where his revolution occured, only recently restored to its czarist name. This week, the defense minister almost casually canceled the traditional Nov. 7 parade on the anniversary of the Bolshevik revolution.

The solemn visitors to Lenin's mausoleum seem cast adrift by these momentous changes. "We are going nowhere and nobody knows what is ahead of us," said Volodya Grachov, a Russian student from the Ukraine.

The gathering at the tomb is the lingering expression of a dying faith in what many consider to have been a secular religion. Some historians see construction of Lenin's mausoleum as a deliberate attempt to transfer traditional Russian religious imagery to the new gods. The winding steps down into the crypt are reminiscent of the tomb of an Egyptian god-pharoah. The people file past the waxy body lain in a funereal pose, and in the dimly lit silence a guard motions urgently to a visitor to remove his hat. The feeling is of a shrine.

For many Soviet analysts, the recent dramatic events have not been so much an assault on the communist faith as a revelation of its long process of decay.

"Communism and the Communist Party . . . were dead even before the coup and even before perestroika." says Andranik Migranian, a prominent Soviet political scientist.

"They were dead in an ideological sense. Nobody took them seriously as ideological institutions or structures.

"Long ago, maybe after [former Soviet leader Nikita] Khrushchev, they were demystified. They became pure power structures in a country where the rest of the population was completely alienated from power. These power structures used to use the rhetoric of communism, the old words, without the essence."

"I was a member of the Communist Party for 33 years, until the coup," says Nodari Simonia, deputy director of the Institute for World Economy and International Relations and a well-known political theorist. "When I saw the press conference of those guys," he says, recalling the appearance of the junta on the first day of the putsch, "I decided it is the last day I would be a member of this party."

Mr. Simonia counts himself among "100 or 150 people who had a chance to read the real Marx, the real Lenin in this country." He dismisses Soviet Communism as a "totally falsified ideology . . . . People were just reading and not understanding anything. I know thousands of people who started reading the simplified version of Russian Marxism by Stalin, . . . and they all stopped reading after chapter four. It was just abracadabra for them."

Simonia is an intellectual Marxist, one who sees socialism as an outgrowth of the Western enlightenment. What emerged as Soviet Communism, particularly under Joseph Stalin, bears no relationship to that tradition of thought, he argues. "Russia was least prepared for socialism in 1917, but it happened that the Bolsheviks came to power. For five or six years under Lenin, we pretended we were building communism. But it was never possible in such a backward, peasant country to build socialism, not to mention communism."

Mr. Migranian expresses the view, held by many historians, that Soviet Communism was a peculiarly Russian phenomenon. "Great Russian nationalism traditionally had deeply rooted in Russian consciousness some elements of socialism and communism," he says. "Stalin combined Bolshevik messianism with Russian messianism."

Stalin was most effective in fusing Russian patriotism with communist religious symbology during the war and the struggle against the Nazis. Nikolai Giorgievich, a war veteran, sees no contradiction between his regular visits to Lenin's tomb and his faith in the Russian Orthodox Church. "Communism has nothing to do with us," he says. "We were happy we were victorious during the war. We had to put up with rationing, but everything was done to win the war."

The belief in Communism "was stronger and more sincere in the 1930s, '40s and '50s," says Simonia. "Already in the '60s there was an erosion of this belief. But from the '70s, from the time of [Leonid] Brezhnev, this belief was like Russian religion by the time of the revolution. Some still believed they were going to church, but they were making jokes about the priest."

Today, Simonia continues, "I am sure not more than 35-40 percent still believe in this religion." As for the men who made the coup, "they never believed themselves. They are cynical people. But they hoped that a substantial minority, if not a majority, still believed in this." But such believers as do exist, Simonia says, are not to be found in the big cities such as Moscow and St. Petersburg where the putsch had to be won.

New religious belief

If the secular god of Lenin has failed, what will supplant it? Simonia believes the answer lies in the visible growth of traditional religions of all kinds, from Eastern mysticism to the Russian Orthodox Church.

The mass movements for national independence in the republics is another reflection of the shift in the allegiance of the Soviet population.

"Nationalism and a kind of belief in the miracle of the market economy . . . has replaced the communist idea," Migranian says. "The only exception is Russia where . . . extreme nationalist ideology is not transformed into a mass movement . . . so far."

After the overthrow of the Communist Party, "after the collapse of the central institutions and [Soviet President Mikhail] Gorbachev, everything is open now in Russia for a real nationalist movement."

Behind the New Soviet Agenda

Daniel Sneider

9/16/91

United States Secretary of State James Baker III left the Soviet Union yesterday proudly displaying some important trophies of his visit. In a series of announcements since last Thursday, the Soviet Union agreed to downgrade ties to Cuba and to end arms supplies to the Afghan government it has long backed.

Along with Moscow's recognition of the independence of the three Baltic republics, "this removes three of the most contentious 'old-agenda' issues that have impeded and obstructed progress," Mr. Baker declared happily.

But Soviet analysts and officials question the suggestion that these moves by Moscow are evidence of a change in Soviet foreign policy, a further liberalizing in the wake of the failed coup of last month. Rather, some suggest, it reflects the collapse in the last weeks of a Soviet central government strong enough to pursue a foreign policy of any kind.

"Today it is evident that the Soviet Union, as a superpower possessed by messianic ideas, is finished," wrote Alexander Goltz in the Army daily Red Star last Friday. "We not only lack the means to support our ideas all over the world, we even lack the ideas themselves."

The joint statement on Afghanistan had the appearance of mutuality, with the US also agreeing to cut off supplies to Afghan rebels and to encourage the formation of a new government through United Nations-supervised elections. When it came to Cuba, the Soviets called for reciprocity in the form of a US move to close its naval base at Guantanamo, Cuba. The Cuban government, which has denounced the Soviet decision, dismissed this as a meaningless gesture, and the Pentagon has already stated it has no intention of closing the base.

Mr. Goltz, long a relatively conservative voice in a paper that traditionally upheld the might of the Soviet Union, questions whether what he dismisses as a "former state" can even have a foreign policy. "Foreign policy is being transferred to where there is power," he notes, namely the republics. When it comes to aid to Cuba or Afghanistan, for example, "I am sure that no sovereign republic will spend money in support of such regimes."

As for a Soviet role in regional conflicts, such as Cambodia or the Middle East, "Let's be frank, in a situation of semi-decay, our participation in settling of these conflicts has only a nominal character," Red Star's commentator writes. The Soviet role in the past largely consisted of being a major military power, especially a supplier of weapons, Goltz points out, "but I seriously doubt that Russia or the Ukraine will finance such participation in the future."

On the surface, a new structure of cooperation is being created between the republics and the Soviet Foreign Ministry, now headed newspaper-editor-turned-diplomat Boris Pankin, the only Soviet ambassador to openly oppose the attempted putsch.

Last Friday, Mr. Pankin held a meeting with the foreign ministers or their deputies from nine republics, including the four Central Asian republics, Kazakhstan, Azerbaijan, Armenia, Moldavia, and Russia. Byelorussia's minister missed the meeting for what he called technical reasons. Aside from the three Baltic republics and Georgia, the noticeable absentee was the Ukraine.

According to Soviet press reports, the ministers agreed to form a Council of Foreign Ministers, which will direct the entire Soviet diplomatic service. The republics demanded that their personnel partially replace existing trade and diplomatic representatives in embassies around the world and demanded a share of the hard-currency funds now controlled by the Foreign Ministry.

As for who represents the country, Pankin told the Soviet news agency Interfax that all the republics should be seated in the UN but that the Soviet Union will act as a single state in institutions such as the UN Security Council and the International Monetary Fund. But how this might work in practice is far from clear.

All the republics supposedly agree, for example, that there should be centralized control of nuclear weapons. When Baker proposed talks on getting rid of short-range nuclear weapons—artillery and rockets—he did so in a meeting with the Soviet Armed Forces Chief of Staff Vladimir Lobov. But Russian President Boris Yeltsin had already made a proposal to remove all these weapons earlier last week.

A subtle competition is also developing between the Russian republic and the nominal central government over access to foreign aid. Gorbachev envoy Vadim Medvedev flew off to South Korea yesterday. The main topic on his agenda is to resecure a South Korean pledge to provide $3 billion in credits over the next few years. But Russian leader Yeltsin sent a letter to Korean President Roh Tae Woo last Thursday seeking direct ties between Russia and South Korea and stating his desire to visit Korea.

A much better indication of the reality of who runs foreign policy came during the visit last week to Japan of Ruslan Khasbulatov, the acting chairman of the Russian republic's Parliament.

Soviet-Japanese relations have been deadlocked for at least 20 years over the dispute over ownership of islands in the Southern Kuriles, which the Soviet Union seized from Japan at the close of World War II. Without return of those islands, Japan refuses to sign a formal peace treaty ending the war or to provide large-scale economic assistance. A visit to Japan last April by Soviet President Mikhail Gorbachev, the first ever by a Soviet leader, failed to make a breakthrough on this issue.

Mr. Khasbulatov, who carried with him a letter from Mr. Yeltsin to Japanese Premier Toshiki Kaifu, bluntly told the Japanese that if they want the islands back, they had to come to the Russian government. "The new situation is such that all relations with Japan can be forged only on the basis of talks with Russia," Khasbulatov told Soviet reporters in Tokyo at the close of his visit. "This is not a claim, this is a reality."

The Russian politician also made it clear that Russia expects the return for its cooperation to be massive economic aid—$8 billion to $15 billion he told the Soviet journalists—coming to Russia itself. With such a show of Japanese sincerity, he indicated the Russian government was ready to move quickly to negotiate an end to the island dispute along the lines of a five-stage plan proposed by Yeltsin during a trip to Japan last year—and ignored by Tokyo authorities at the time.

Khasbulatov found the Japanese, like many Western governments, slow to understand the new reality. "I realized that Japan still looks to the Soviet Union, at Gorbachev," he said, according to a Tass report. "They display some inertia, visualizing the world as it was before the coup attempt in Moscow."

Khasubulatov also had some words of warning for those in Moscow who do not themselves understand that Russia will now be making foreign policy with Japan. According to a report in the daily Izvestia, he told a Tokyo press conference that if the new foreign minister doesn't understand this, "we will replace him." Later, speaking privately to the Soviet Embassy staff, he recounted telling the Soviet Ambassador to Japan "that he will stay as long as he is personally loyal to the president, Parliament, and leadership of Russia."

Soviets Prepare Defense For Alleged Coup Plotters

Daniel Sneider

9/17/91

Soviet investigators and prosecutors are busy preparing the most important Soviet trial since the show trials of Stalin's purge victims in the late 1930s.

The investigation of those alleged to have plotted the attempted August coup will be completed in two or three months, Russian Prosecutor General Valentin Stepankov told reporters recently.

The case against these men would seem to be open and shut. All except parliament head Anatoly Lukyanov were openly involved in the putsch. But controversy over the hearing is already brewing and disputes are sure to grow as the event approaches.

Defense lawyers say the charges of "treason against the motherland" do not apply to their clients, who were acting to their knowledge in defense of the "motherland." The defendants' rights to see the evidence on which charges are based have been abridged, they say. And in the latest turn of events, one of the lawyers has accused prosecutors of trying to close the trial to the public on grounds that state secrets will be disclosed.

A team of 75 prosecution investigators from Russia and other republics is gathering evidence. Criminal cases against 20 people are under way and 14 people have been arrested, including seven of the eight men who formed the so-called "emergency committee" that led the coup (one of them, former Interior Minister Boris Pugo, killed himself before arrest). The others include Communist Party officials, Soviet President Mikhail Gorbachev's chief of staff, a senior Army commander, parliament head Lukyanov, andthree top KGB officers.

Defending coup leaders

Arrayed against this powerful state prosecution is a group of lawyers, most of whom have spent their professional lives defending the victims of the men they are now representing.

Ghenri Reznik is the proud descendent of the chief rabbi of Odessa and the less-than-proud relative of a man whom he will only describe as a "key figure of Bolshevism," killed by Stalin in the late 1930s. He is widely known as a human-rights activist, and a leader of Helsinki Watch, many of whose members were arrested by the KGB secret police.

Mr. Reznik takes it as a matter of professional pride that the family of KGB Gen. Yuri Plekhanov, head of the presidential guard, called to seek his services. When he went to the isolation jail where Mr. Plekhanov is held, he brought a letter from the family stating they had employed him. "Plekhanov said he had heard of me," Reznik says, adding with a smile that he didn't know "whether he knew about me in his capacity as a member of the KGB."

The silver-haired Reznik, like other lawyers on the case, refuses to talk about the details of the coup. But he describes his client as a "courageous person, a person who has his convictions—let's not judge them—and a person who has no wish to hide behind the backs of other people." The KGB general has his own ideas about where the country should go, the liberal lawyer continues, "but in no way is he a communist fanatic."

Reznik spent much of his career as a law professor, training the investigators and prosecutors he now faces. Perhaps this is why he was the first to formulate a basis for defense that other lawyers are now echoing. All 14 defendants are charged under Article 64 of the criminal code of the Russian republic, which details crimes of "treason against the motherland," including various forms of espionage. Among this list is the crime of "conspiracy with the goal of seizing power."

Betraying the 'motherland'

Reznik argues this formula cannot be applied to his client. "Betrayal of Gorbachev—does that mean betrayal of the motherland?" he asks. "The Bolsheviks wrote this article in this way . . . because they did not anticipate something like this would happen. We don't have an article dedicated to betrayal of the president." Indeed Article 64 does not even refer to the Constitution, or its violation.

"This article is very ideological," says Alexander Kligman, lawyer for KGB Col. Gen. Viktor Gurshko. "What is the legal sense of the word 'motherland?' " Besides, he asks, "Can powers be seized by people already endowed with a huge amount of power?"

Mr. Kligman has spent his career defending big-time Soviet mafia criminals and the emerging Soviet private businessmen who were the targets of the very KGB division headed by General Grushko. Perhaps, he hints, that is how he got his job.

Like the other lawyers, Kligman has no complaints so far about access to his client. He has met him twice privately and sat in on the interrogations conducted by the investigators in a small room with a barred window in Isolation Facility No. 4. The lawyer is not allowed to interrupt, but can ask his own questions afterward for the record. The defendant also has the right to refuse to answer, a right employed by Mr. Lukyanov, whose arrest was conducted illegally, says his lawyer, Genrik Padva.

Mr. Padva, Kligman, and others complain that, due to a conflict between Soviet and Russian criminal procedures, they are not given access to evidence on which the charges are based. The prosecutors are following a Soviet law, ironically introduced last year by the KGB, which bars access to the evidence until the investigation is complete.

Keeping trials open

But by far the most serious charge about the conduct of the case has been raised by Reznik. He told the Monitor on Sunday that a Russian investigator came to him the previous day and said Reznik had to obtain a special permit to act as defender. "This institution of permits was begun in the beginning of the 1970s in cases involving political dissidents," he explains. The permit is issued by the KGB and the aim has been to block certain lawyers on the grounds that the case involved state secrets.

Reznik sees this as the first step to closing the trial. "It is a grave violation of human rights and of the rights of defense," he says, adding that he is "at a loss" why the democrat-led Russian government would do such a thing. A spokesman for the prosecutor's office did not deny the allegation but refused to comment on it. Asked at his Sept. 6 press conference whether the trial would be open, the prosecutor general replied the issue would be decided by the court, adding secret materials are associated with the case.

Kligman believes the trial will be open in the end. "It has acquired a great public and political importance," he argues.

Though the trial is sure to be extraordinary, the lawyers say they will defend these clients as they would any other. "I will defend General Plekhanov in the same professional and uncompromising way I defended the human rights activists," Reznik says.

Top US Officials In USSR To Help Bolster Economy

Amy Kaslow

9/18/91

The Bush administration is softening its tough stand on financial assistance to the Soviet Union.

US Treasury Secretary Nicholas Brady and Federal Reserve Board Chairman Alan Greenspan are in Moscow this week to assess economic needs of the rapidly deteriorating Soviet Union. They are offering new ways to assist in Soviet economic reforms and to accelerate Soviet membership in the International Monetary Fund and the World Bank.

Soviet President Mikhail Gorbachev, Russian President Boris Yeltsin, Soviet economic officials, and representatives from the republics—all meeting with Mr. Brady and Mr. Greenspan—want United States assistance in the tedious economic and legal negotiations between Moscow center and the republics.

But though relatively forthcoming with humanitarian aid, Washington has steadfastly refused greater commitments until stalled Soviet economic reforms are actually under way. Top US officials recognize that, aside from short-term Western supplies of food and medicine to carry the Soviets through the winter, immediate financial support is needed to help ensure the long-term survival of the Soviet economy.

The Overseas Private Investment Corporation (OPIC), a US government agency that facilitates American investment abroad by providing insurance and financing, will soon open for business with the Soviets. OPIC will target US investments on food production, transportation, communications and energy—all crucial to improving shoring up the Soviet economy.

James Berg, executive vice president of OPIC, says his agency won't wait until Moscow center and interested republics pound out legal and commercial agreements. "We don't need an entire constitution," says Mr. Berg. "Our needs [legal and commercial] can be worked out within a bilateral agreement that is very operational in nature."

OPIC plans to offer up to $1 billion—roughly one-tenth of OPIC's global $10 billion portfolio—in US loans and guarantees for American investors in Soviet projects. "The figure understates dramatically what kind of investment it generates," says Berg. Many American investors have already requested OPIC insurance for Soviet deals, he says. "We assume the risk, so we make it as safe for Americans to invest in Moscow as it is to invest in Iowa," he says, "but not enough people know about us."

Next month in the Soviet Union, OPIC will begin the process of negotiating and signing operating agreements with the Baltics, with the center and the remaining 12 republics. "We want to move quickly," says Berg.

US support is also stronger on the international level. As the largest shareholder in the World Bank and the International Monetary Fund (IMF), Washington has dominated with its go-slow approach to Soviet requests for help. President Bush has consistently conditioned aid on Soviet reforms.

Revolution, rather than reform in the Soviet Union, seems to have forced Washington's hand. Both Brady and Greenspan, in Moscow discussing the planned acceleration, are mindful of breakaway republics' interest in becoming members on their own. Estonia and Lithuania have already applied for separate membership in the global institutions.

Concerned that Russia and other republics with larger economies will follow suit, the US is expected to push for Soviet membership by the end of 1991. An IMF economic reform program for the Soviet Union—including financial aid and expert guidance—would help bind the country, say US officials.

A new development bank, the London-based European Bank for Reconstruction and Development (EBRD) is fighting for more spending power in the Soviet Union. Washington, the EBRD's largest single shareholder, has strongly opposed lifting the regional institution's $70 million annual cap on Soviet financing.

That, too, may change says Ronald Freeman, EBRD's first vice president, once the US "sees how quickly the $70 million pipeline is filled." Mr. Freeman, who oversees 60 percent of the bank's lending, says the Soviet fund is practically exhausted.

The EBRD promotes systemic change by matching basic Soviet needs with Western investors. Its programs function without a Soviet federal constitution in place or any comprehensive agreements between Moscow center and the republics. Freeman told the Monitor recently that EBRD priorities are simple: Negotiate fair deals to win the trust of suspicious Soviets and money from often reluctant foreign investors, principally commercial banks.

Freeman discovers on a deal-by-deal basis who on the Soviet side is authorized to sign contracts and assume risks. "On every level there's a vested interest—from the factories to the ministries to the local municipalities," he says. "It's more like a political campaign where you're trying to get votes from everybody at each level." Freeman says the EBRD is increasingly looked upon by wary Soviets as a seal of approval. He points to EBRD mandates from Moscow and St. Petersburg to privatize industries and help establish city cultural centers—all large projects. He says investing in Soviet energy production, and enhancing Soviet export earnings as a result, is the "most exciting prospect in the world."

Key Choices in the Ukraine Set Pace for Soviets

Daniel Sneider

9/20/91

The future of the Soviet Union will be decided here in the Ukraine, amid its vast wheat fields, down in the grimy coal pits, and along the broad avenues of this capital city.

On Dec. 1, the second most populous and second wealthiest republic after Russia will hold a referendum on independence and choose a president. The elections will decide whether any hope remains of a political union to replace the existing Soviet Union. As nationalist leader Vyacheslav Chernovil, one of the leading candidates for president, bluntly puts it: "A union without the Ukraine is not possible."

The pro-independence mood following last month's failed Soviet coup is so strong that most observers feel a vote for independence is inevitable. But what that will mean depends more on the presidential vote.

At this point, the president is likely to be one of two men: Mr. Chernovil, the radical mayor of the western Ukrainian town of Lvov and a leader of the Rukh independence movement, or Leonid Kravchuk, the former Communist Party ideology chief turned pragmatic politician who now serves as chairman of the Ukrainian parliament.

As Chernovil admits, little differentiates the programs of the two men on the surface. Both envision an independent Ukraine with its own army and currency, and full control over its internal economy. While they support a nuclear-free Ukraine, the two leaders insist that nuclear weapons based here remain until their destruction through international agreement. And both acknowledge the need for some kind of transitional economic association of the former Soviet republics.

But in interviews with both men this week, it is clear that Chernovil offers an uncompromising path to full independence. Mr. Kravchuk, displaying a flexibility that has served him well before, leaves the door open a crack to some form of union.

"A future for the union as we saw it earlier does not exist," Kravchuk told a small group of American reporters before his departure at the end of this week to Canada, the United States, and the United Nations. But, he added, "I can envision a union of republics as an inter-republican structure . . . . It would mean the republics agree as independent states on the creation of some kind of unification, either a council, or a community or commonwealth."

Kravchuk rejects what he calls the idea of confederation backed by Russia, Kazakhstan, and a few other republics. "We support the idea of collective security, collective defense of borders, and collective solution of a number of economic, ecological, space and other problems." Everything else, including finances, credit, taxation, economic management, and so on, is purely a Ukrainian affair, he said.

Kravchuk has, however, publicly stated his support for a draft treaty of economic union drawn up by Soviet economist Gregory Yavlinsky, a document which seeks common financial, monetary, trade, and other economic policies. But in his interview on Wednesday, Kravchuk insisted he saw this as only a transitional arrangement, lasting for this year and maybe next year.

He defends this on practical grounds. "Today we have no Ukrainian currency," he says. "We don't even have a chance to get credits, because . . . the banks of the great powers declare that they prefer to do business with the center." Moreover, the Ukrainian economy—its energy and defense industries particularly—remains linked to the "former union."

Chernovil agrees that it is not useful to break economic ties that have been established over many years. But, he told the Monitor, "The transitional economic structures are needed only for division of certain things—to divide the Army, to divide gold and currency stocks, and to divide the debt. As for other things, we need only bilateral economic ties."

On military questions, the two leaders strike different tones. Kravchuk sees a Ukrainian army, but it would include forces subordinate to "the common center," though with a Ukrainian say over their use. Chernovil sees no need for a common military after the transition period. Kravchuk calls for an agreement with Russia and Kazakhstan on the future of intercontinental ballistic missiles based on the three republics' territories. Both men reject Russian President Boris Yeltsin's proposal to move the missiles to Russia.

"What state hands over its nuclear weapons to another state?" Chernovil asks rhetorically. He reiterated his commitment to a nuclear-free Ukraine. "Of course, it is rather sad that Yeltsin didn't declare that Russia will be a nuclear-free zone."

"I don't know whom we should fear," Chernovil grins, "the US or some of our neighbors."

Beyond practical issues, the two Ukrainian politicians are divided by their pasts. Chernovil does not hesitate to point to his opponent's Communist roots. The mustachioed former journalist also trumpets his dissident past. "The ideas of anti-Communism being implemented now are the same ones for which I spent 15 years in the prison camps. I am not yesterday's or today's democrat. I've been a democrat all my life."

Chernovil also criticizes Kravchuk for his hesitation during the first day of the attempted August coup, when he did not openly condemn it. Chernovil eagerly tells the contrasting tale of his own immediate moves to oppose the coup. At the Parliament that first day, he recounts, "I said to him, 'Leonid Makarovich [Kravchuk], you shouldn't think you will win by being too flexible. The putschists won't like this either. They will probably put me in jail, but you will be the next.' "

Such barbs are not new for Kravchuk, who has long maneuvered between Rukh and more radical groups on one side and the orthodox bosses of the Ukrainian Communist Party on the other. Kravchuk's centrism is particularly important in the eastern and southern parts of the Ukraine, where the 11.5 million Russian-speaking members of the 52 million population could be the key to winning the election.

Kravchuk, asked to describe his differences with Chernovil, paints himself as a realist and his opponent as an extremist. He opposes moves to carry out post-coup purges. "It's not necessary to frighten everyone with the enemy being just around the corner, to sow suspicion between the peoples of east and west [Ukraine]," he explains.

The World From . . . Kiev, Ukraine

Daniel Sneider

9/24/91

From the bullet-pocked walls of Croatian villages to the wooded shores of the Crimean peninsula, the eastern half of Europe is struggling under the weight of history's unanswered questions.

After centuries of war, the empires of western Europe seem to have settled into a more modest definition of their national identities. But in the east, the remains of the Austro-Hungarian Empire were buried under the edifice of the last great empire of Europe, the Russian Empire, albeit in its modern, Soviet form. Unfinished battles over borders and the unfulfilled yearnings of divided peoples were concealed after World War II under the weight of the Red Army and hidden by the rhetoric of Communist internationalism.

The first crumbling of the Soviet Empire took place in central and eastern Europe, as the vassal states of Poland, Czechoslovakia, Hungary, Bulgaria, and Romania freed themselves from its weakened grasp. Now Czechs and Slovaks have resumed debate over the future of their federation. Hungarians look longingly at their brethren and lost lands across the border in Romania. Poland begins to exert its influence in the lands wrested from it in Lithuania, Byelorussia, and the Ukraine, where many Poles still live and their churches still stand.

Here on the western frontier of the Soviet Empire, the talk is of independence, of the restoration of a Ukrainian nationhood only dimly remembered and highly embellished in Ukrainians' eyes. Barely had the doors of the Communist Party Central Committee been shut in Moscow and the slogans of proletarian internationalism stilled when Ukrainians and their Russian brothers set to resume their own unfinished historical battles.

Within days of the Ukrainian declaration of independence Aug. 24, the Russian republican government of Boris Yeltsin issued a statement to the effect that the present borders were valid only so long as the Ukraine remained in the Soviet Union. Should it leave, a Yeltsin spokesman suggested, the fate of Russian-populated areas of the Ukraine, including the east and the Crimean peninsula, is up for grabs.

And as he was quick to remind, in the boundaries of the national republics of the Soviet Union formed after the Bolshevik revolution, the Crimea was made part of the Russian Federation. In 1954, shortly after Joseph Stalin's death, Nikita Khrushchev gave the Crimea to the Ukraine to mark the 300th anniversary of the unification of the Ukraine and Russia. "I don't see why a gift like that should be permanent in a situation of secession," one of Moscow's new leaders, Arkady Volsky pronounced.

Here in Kiev such talk sparks its own response. Outside the headquarters of Rukh, the nationalist, democratic political movement, a political cartoon shows Yeltsin, a Napoleonic cap perched on his head, pointing across the border of the Ukraine and proclaiming that wherever "our people are, is ours."

But Mr. Volsky launched into a vigorous defense of the Russian statement. After all, "Crimea was won by Russian warriors in wars with Tatar Khans," he said defiantly. "It is Russian territory originally."

Rukh leader Vyacheslav Chernovil rejects Volsky's claims. Crimea was the land of Tatars, protected by Turkey until the end of the 18th century. "Crimea was captured not by Russia, but by the Russian Empire, and the Ukraine was a part of this [empire]," he asserted. "Economically and historically, Crimea is bound with the Ukraine."

His argument shows that the work of scholars in dusty historical archives is now the stuff of many political wars to come.

New Role for Russians

Daniel Sneider

9/25/91

After 12 hours of often heated negotiations at a southern Russian spa, the republics of Armenia and Azerbaijan signed an agreement Sept. 23 to take steps to end their conflict for control of the enclave of Nagorno-Karabakh.

For the first time in nearly four years, there is hope of resolving the most bitter of the Soviet Union's ethnic problems, one that has killed hundreds.

Credit for the breakthrough lies with Russian President Boris Yeltsin and President Nursultan Nazarbayev of the Kazakhstan Republic, who acted as mediators and signed the agreement to guarantee it would be implemented.

"This document is signed. It's a historic act and a historic document," a triumphant Mr. Yeltsin told reporters waiting at the sanitarium in Zheleznovodsk. Simply getting the two sides to sit down for direct talks was itself unprecedented.

The Armenia-Azerbaijan talks mark the emergence of Russia, with the support of other republics, as the new effective center of power in the Soviet Union. It also demonstrates the eclipse of Soviet President Mikhail

Gorbachev, who pointedly failed to make even nominal progress in halting the fighting.

"The document should have been completed earlier," Armenian leader Levon Ter-Petrosyan told reporters, "but it didn't happen because the central authorities claimed the role of mediator."

Even a last minute attempt by Mr. Gorbachev to solve the problem proved ineffective. The Soviet leader was preparing his own decree, discussed at a meeting of the State Council—the new leadership body of Gorbachev and republican leaders—on Sept. 16. But the next day, according to reports, Yeltsin and Mr. Nazarbayev decided to act more directly to try to solve the problem.

"Yeltsin and Nazarbayev showed that Gorbachev is nobody now in this current situation," says Andranik Migranian, a Soviet political scientist. The huge Armenian crowd that gathered Sept. 22 in the central square of the Nagorno-Karabakh capital of Stepanakert to greet the two men agreed with this assessment. They carried banners proclaiming, "Boris, you are the hope of Karabakh," and chanted "Russia, Russia."

"The appearance of Yeltsin and Nazarbayev in Nagorno-Karabakh, besides everything else, means that new superpowers are born which have grabbed this status from the Soviet Empire," wrote the correspondent for Nezavisimaya Gazeta (Independent Newspaper).

Yeltsin's strong performance in this crisis contrasts sharply with Gorbachev's virtual passivity during the entire escalation of the Nagorno-Karabakh problem. Karabakh came to symbolize the inability and unwillingness of Gorbachev to deal with the nationalist movements that emerged as the principal rivals to the Communist Party in recent years.

"This is the fourth year since the center, including Gorbachev, has been making no moves after it made a gross mistake in 1988," Yeltsin said in his speech to the Karabakh crowd.

"Moreover, attempts to solve interethnic problems by force have never been successful. We use our political authority. We realize the complexity of the problem and know it cannot be solved at one stroke . . . . It should be a peaceful process . . . of settlements and negotiations by various sides."

The mountainous Karabakh region is a largely Christian, Armenian-populated enclave that was placed within the borders of neighboring Azerbaijan, a Turkic-populated republic, by the Bolsheviks in 1923. Complaining of repression, the enclave's government tried in 1988 to rejoin itself to Armenia, a move supported by the Armenians and opposed by Azerbaijan. Ethnic violence against Armenians in Azerbaijan in 1989 and anti-Azeri violence in response prompted a flood of hundreds of thousands of refugees from both sides.

From the beginning, Gorbachev's government refused to entertain any discussion of a change in the status of Nagorno-Karabakh. In practice, the central government tended to favor the Azeris, who proclaimed their loyalty to the union. They backed the Azeri dissolution of the local Karabakh government two years ago. Soviet armed forces, both Interior Ministry and regular Army units, were sent to keep order, but rapidly join in the conflict.

"The center wanted to keep the integrity of the empire," says Mr. Migranian. "The center couldn't be a mediator between two practically independent republics because it didn't want to recognize their independence."

Morever, the political expert adds, the center was able to use the Nagorno-Karabakh problem as a tool to keep both within the union. For Azerbaijan, the central government was an ally in the name of preserving the borders intact, while Armenia was faced with the possibility of leaving the union without resolving this.

The agreement reached Monday night by no means resolves the Karabakh issue. But it provides ground for serious negotiations based on real concessions from both sides.

The key points of the document, according to various reports of its yet unpublished contents, are: agreement to return to the legal status of the territory before the conflict began in 1988; disarming of the armed groups of both sides by Jan. 1 of next year; holding new elections for the local government and restoring its authority; and steps to resettle Armenians deported from villages in and around Karabakh.

The initial and crucial concession was Armenia's decision to renounce its claim to the territory in favor of restoring the constitutional authority of the local government that had been dissolved by Azerbaijan and the Kremlin.

An important reflection of Yeltsin's new authority was participation in the talks by Soviet Defense Minister Yvgeny Shaposhnikov and Interior Minister Viktor Barannikov. Their troops will now help enforce the agreement.

At one key moment in the talks, the Russian Information Agency reports, there was a threat that if a real process of settlement has not begun by the beginning of next year, Soviet armed forces would pull out.

Yeltsin's new authority also carries responsibility.

"Now he cannot act as a man who is challenging the center," observes Migranian. "Now he is the center."

Soviets Face Sharp Food Shortages

Amy Kaslow

9/30/91

As negotiators here struggle to assemble a legal and economic framework loosely binding the breakaway republics, severe food shortages threaten to thwart agreement.

Prominent Soviet economist Grigory Yavlinksy, now drafting the plan for economic union, says negotiations for an economic union are "very difficult." The problems, he says, are that republics are acting in their self-interest and not moving toward inter-republican cooperation. The most pressing issue facing negotiators is the lack of adequate food supplies. Both central and republican authorities have failed to gain control over the broken-down distribution system.

Food stocks depleted

The Economic Management Committee—the caretaker of the Soviet economy, of which Mr. Yavlinksy is a member—has delivered bad news to the State Council, a body composed of the republics' leaders and chaired by Soviet President Mikhail Gorbachev. Food stocks throughout the nation are quickly being depleted, committee reports say.

The State Council responded by agreeing to preserve existing inter-republican links and to share foreign aid in the form of credits and foodstuffs. But these pledges have registered little impact, as poor management and inter-republican strife prevent deliveries and leave store shelves bare.

Moscow, once supplied by food producers in the Russian republic and all over the Soviet Union, is particularly hard hit. A shattered distribution system has practically choked the country's largest city of commodities and processed goods. What does arrive is rapidly stripped from the shelves by hoarders and black-market profiteers.

In every part of this city, long lines form when coveted foods become available. All types of meat, eggs, butter, and vegetables are in short supply in the state stores that service the 9 million metropolitan residents. The situation is steadily deteriorating. In Moscow's posh Sokol district, ground floor stores located in a grand building that houses the most senior Red Army officers are virtually barren. Display cases in the fish, meat, and dairy sections are empty. Only baby formula, tea, and spices are for sale. At one counter, the last drops of sour cream are poured into an old woman's thermos. Others waiting in the long line for cream are turned away.

"We have plenty of missiles, but no sausage," says one grim Moscow consumer. "Eggs have disappeared," adds another. "I haven't bought them for at least one month."

While food is relatively abundant in shops and cooperatives that rely on a private network outside the state supply system, prices are too high for the average Muscovite.

Nationalist moves on the republic level only make things worse. The Ukrainian Council of Ministers, for example, has forbidden the export, even on a barter basis, of Ukrainian goods, due to concerns about sufficient supplies for the Ukrainian internal market.

The decision has sparked an economic war with neighboring Russia, where a large percentage of the republic's 150 million people rely heavily on Ukrainian grain and other foodstuffs. In response, Russia is withholding energy supplies to the Ukraine. According to the Soviet daily Komsomolskaya Pravda, 22 out of 30 Ukrainian airports are closed and flights in and out of the republics have been drastically reduced because of a fuel shortage.

Republics dole out ration coupons, but people cannot even redeem the amount of goods to which they're entitled. In the vast Russian republic alone, the shortages are rampant.

In Chelyabinsk, a city of over 1 million people in the southern Urals, flour is in severely short supply because the government in the neighboring republic of Kazakhstan has sealed its borders even for barter transactions. Trucks bound for the Southern Urals with grain from Kazakhstan are being stopped and unloaded on Kazakh territory, where the local government fears shortages in its own republic.

In Perm, a city of roughly 1 million people in the middle Urals, basics such as sugar and flour are dwindling. In St. Petersburg, the second largest city in the crumbling Soviet Union, almost all foodstuffs—including sunflower oil, flour, butter, meat and sausage—are rationed. In Kemerovo, in southern Siberia, where a bitter winter is fast-approaching, staples are increasingly scarce. And in Irkutsk, in southeastern Siberia, sugar, butter, grain and flour products, and soap are in short supply.

Leaders in Georgia seeking to cut all ties with the Soviet Union have isolated their republic's economy. Milk, butter, and meat once supplied by neighboring republics are now rarities.

In the disputed province of Nagorno-Karabakh, an Azeri-imposed blockade has caused food shortages. There are repeated reports of hardship among children. The raging conflict continues despite recent efforts by Russian President Boris Yeltsin and Kazakhstan President Nursultan Nazarbayev to mediate.

As communications and transportation collapse, the wholly import-dependent regions of the country, including remote areas such as northern Russia, Siberia, and the poor Central Asian republics, face especially severe shortages.

Threat from the right

Anti-democratic forces will capitalize on such deprivation, warns former Foreign Minister Eduard Shevardnadze, who now co-chairs the Democratic Reform Movement. "The menace has not been removed. It is mounting. There is danger that the positions of the right-wing, reactionary forces will strengthen." He says the dangers of this unrest prompted him to join the consultative group formed by Mr. Gorbachev to help stabilize the situation in the country.

As long as republics fail to muster the most essential cooperation in food supplies, prospects for a broader inter-republic economic network are dim. An influx of international food aid from Europe, North America, and Japan is expected to carry the country through the rough winter ahead, but more formidable foreign financial aid is contingent upon the ability of the center and the republics to work out an economic agreement.

III
Post Coup Events

The aftermath of the August Revolution was sweeping. Foreign nations wanted to know who in the Soviet Union had responsibility for foreign policy and if the Soviet Union was still viable. A move toward nationalism in the Republics was strengthened as they continued to claim independence. Maps of the Soviet Union were changing on a daily basis. The Union was eventually replaced by the Commonwealth of Independent States and during the Christmas season of 1992, two years after the tumbling of the Berlin Wall, Gorbachev resigned as President of the Soviet Union.

In this group of readings you will learn about the events that led to the dissolving of the Soviet Union, and the social, economic, and political challenge the new Commonwealth faces.

Western Doubts on Soviet Reform Stall Aid Effort

Amy Kaslow

10/1/91

International donors, meeting over the next two weeks to respond to desperate Soviet pleas for help, are looking for a ready and reliable set of partners on the receiving end.

But a coherent Soviet leadership—with a mix of central government officials and representatives from the breakaway republics—is as tall an order in this disintegrating union as are the huge sums of foreign aid being sought from the West.

A host of United States, European, and Japanese officials are now visiting Moscow to assess Soviet need and explore ways of distributing foreign assistance. They are seeking evidence of Soviet commitment to economic reforms before they dole out even a portion of the tens of billions of dollars in requested aid.

But central and local leaders here are having difficulty cooperating, much less reaching an agreement, and the jurisdiction between the republics and the union remains undefined.

Soviet President Mikhail Gorbachev had indicated optimistically that the republican leaders and central authorities could sign an economic agreement by this Thursday. But many republics, citing conflicting national interests, have been reluctant to coordinate policies covering debt, currency, trade, banking, and customs.

Mr. Gorbachev has amended his earlier expectation, saying over the weekend that an economic agreement will be signed by mid-October. Observers doubt that even that date can be met. Kirghizia and Armenia have so far withheld their support, and the Ukraine has reserved its participation in an all-union economic treaty until its Dec. 2 presidential election is held.

Even the relative economic powerhouse, Russia, is at odds with the Economic Management Committee of the State Council charged with managing the planned inter-republic economy. Committee chairman Ivan Silayev, whose resignation as prime minister of the Russian Republic took effect Friday, is accused by former Russian colleagues of trying to work out an economic agreement that would in effect undermine Russian sovereignty.

While the Soviets are mired in domestic squabbles, US Treasury Secretary Nicholas Brady is pushing for an early meeting of the Group of Seven to coordinate international policy toward the Soviet Union.

The G-7—economic policy makers from the world's richest countries, including the US, Britain, Canada, France, Germany, Italy, and Japan—will meet in advance of the annual meeting of the World Bank and the International Monetary Fund scheduled later this month in Bangkok.

High on the G-7 agenda is the mammoth $70 billion Soviet debt, which the cash-strapped Soviets are increasingly unable to pay. US and European officials say that in the coming six months, the Soviets need more than $5 billion to service their debt and pay for essential imports.

Soviet prospects for reaping foreign exchange through exports to pay for imports remain dim. Soviet oil, the biggest dollar earner, is needed domestically. Oil production has slipped dramatically this year because of mismanagement, technical problems, and poor equipment. A leading world producer, the Soviet Union may become a net oil importer, if conditions continue to deteriorate.

At issue for international creditors examining ways to bridge this financing gap and to delay or forgive Soviet debt payments, is just who on the Soviet side will assume financial responsibility.

Meanwhile, World Bank President Lewis Preston has dispatched a team to Moscow to explore means to extend technical assistance.

The bank's first step will be to set up a $30 million trust fund, which will be augmented by other public and private lending institutions.

Asked when the bank will have an agreement with the Soviets, Mr. Preston responded, "We have sent people on the spot, but there is no [Soviet] authority to sign." He expects an agreement to be finalized over the next three months.

In the next few days, the IMF is expected to give the Soviets special associate status to provide the Soviets with IMF advice. Full IMF membership remains elusive, says a top Fund official, as long as the Soviets cannot muster agreement over basic leadership.

European officials are perplexed by recent Soviet requests for aid. Mr. Silayev has stunned the European Community with a request for over $14 billion in emergency food assistance over the next six months. Just a week earlier, the Committee's deputy visited Brussels and issued a request for $7 billion in aid.

EC Commissioner Jacques Delors puts Soviet food needs at roughly $4 billion. Soviet officials say they now expect the EC to supply just $7 billion of the total requested.

European officials are wary of Soviet requests. Last winter central and local authorities manipulated $250 million in EC aid, but apparently only part of it reached its intended destination, and months late.

Republic leaders have cautioned that any Western-supplied aid must go to new leadership and not through the old, familiar channels. The West, in turn, is asking whether new systems are adequate to accept and direct the aid.

Norbert Walter, chief economist of Germany's Deutsche Bank, perhaps the strongest commercial banking presence in the Soviet Union, says "for the time being, [commercial] funds won't flow."

Mr. Walter, who has visited the country several times since the coup, says, "It's more and more difficult to meet people who consider themselves in charge."

Germany has been the largest single source of Soviet assistance. Existing German outlays could total $30 billion if a Soviet default on German trade debts and other commercial transactions turns into a government guaranteed gift from Bonn.

"We will not do anything more beyond our duty as an EC and G-7 member," says Elmar Brok, a German member of the European Parliament who chaired the parliament's German unification committee and now sits on the social and foreign affairs committees. "We are financially exhausted," he says, referring to Germany's enormous bill for German unification.

On the Soviet request for billions of dollars, Deustche Bank's Mr. Walter says, "All those numbers are made up to argue for more help. I just throw them out. They're all absolutely crazy numbers. The discussion with the Soviets is anything but over; nobody accepts those numbers as a basis for discussion."

Mayor and City Council Clash in St. Petersburg

George D. Moffett III

10/3/91

In a drab government office, 10 members of St. Petersburg's city council, or "soviet," are hunched over a document they hope will help catapult this elegant but tired city to a brighter future.

Known simply as the "status law," it is designed to give the former Russian capital a measure of autonomy needed to create a prosperous free-market economy.

But a more mundane section of the law, now in draft form, provokes the liveliest discussion: a proposed system of checks and balances designed to ease growing tensions between the council and St. Petersburg's popular new mayor, Anatoly Sobchak.

Under normal circumstances this would be a matter of purely local interest. In fact, St. Petersburg has become a case study in the competition for political power that is taking place at all levels of government following the simultaneous collapse of the Soviet Union and the Communist Party.

"In the past we had only one power—the party—and the council and the mayor were window dressing," says Russian writer Daniil Granin. "Now the executive and legislature are searching for their own places. The most difficult problem is how to divide the power they have now inherited."

"This is not just a St. Petersburg problem," adds Elena Zelinskaya, director of the Northwest Information Agency, a Russian news service. "It's a problem in all the countries that were once under totalitarian rule."

At one level the problem is a contest over political turf. But, as elsewhere in the Soviet Union, the confrontation here between the executive and legislature also has ideological and even generational dimensions.

In city council elections held here last year, dozens of young radicals, many still in their 30s, were swept into power on a platform of rapid democratization. By contrast, Mr. Sobchak—like his counterpart in Moscow, Mayor Gavriil Popov—belongs to a more conservative generation that came to political maturity during the 1960s. Though clearly committed to political and economic reform, Sobchak has sometimes adopted a more cautious approach.

One example has been Sobchak's preference for a top-down approach to economic reform that has focused on converting large, state-run enterprises into joint stock companies. Many members of the city council, on the other hand, say the real catalyst for change must be the city's small entrepreneurs who are capable of creating a market economy from the bottom up.

Move to relocate

Questions have also been raised about the significance of Sobchak's decision to relocate his office and staff from the downtown building it now shares with the council to the Smolny Institute. It is here that Lenin's Bolsheviks planned the October revolution of 1917, and it has been the headquarters of the once-dominant Leningrad Communist Party ever since.

"It means he cannot imagine that power can be in another place," says Ms. Zelinskaya.

The lines of confrontation between Sobchak and the city council have been drawn more sharply in recent weeks. The city's first popularly elected mayor, Sobchak has announced plans to reduce the council from 400—many of whom, one council deputy concedes, are "dead souls to a more manageable 50."

"It's just not possible in a city of 5 million people to have every neighborhood represented," says the city's deputy mayor, Vyacheslav Shcherbakov. "There needs to be serious reform."

Determined to keep Sobchak from becoming a "democratic dictator," one council source says, the council is flexing its muscles and tightening the status law to circumscribe the mayor's extensive powers. The current draft defines the council as the city's "highest authority" and gives it more power over the budget, taxes, and prices.

"We want a balance because [Sobchak] has too much power," says Mikhail Gorney, co-chairman of the council committee reviewing the draft. "He's a brilliant figure, but he wants to decide everything independently."

High public rating

In the competition for influence, it is Sobchak—whose popularity rating is nearly four times higher than the council's, according to a recent opinion poll—who has had the upper hand. The mayor burst onto the international scene when he defied St. Petersburg's military commander in a dramatic showdown during last August's attempted coup and prevented federal troops from entering the city.

Inside Russia, it was the latest achievement for a man many had already come to see as one of the nation's brightest political stars and a possible successor to Russian President Boris Yeltsin. A former law professor, the mayor broke into politics when he was elected to the Congress of People's Deputies, where his telegenic qualities made him a national figure.

After joining the Communist Party, then quitting two years later, he ran for mayor as an independent.

"I want to be a candidate to prove that an ordinary Soviet professor can beat the candidate endorsed by the Communist Party," a former academic colleague recalls Sobchak saying.

The "ordinary" professor won by a whopping 70 percent, out-polling Mr. Yeltsin, who won the Russian presidency the same day. Admirers describe the mayor as a stirring orator who is at once decisive and adaptable. "Just as Yeltsin has grown with events, so has Sobchak," says the former colleague.

Take-charge style

Critics say Sobchak's abrasive, take-charge style is an asset in dealing with coup attempts but a liability in day-to-day politics where compromise is required.

"Sobchak is a very authoritarian man," says St. Petersburg city councilman Alexander Sungurov. "He is sure he knows the answer to every question.

Another view, voiced frequently since the coup, is that while Sobchak is an ideal figure to lead away from communism, his vision may be too limited by his past experience to prevent him from being overtaken by the movement for political and economic reform, as critics say Soviet President Mikhail Gorbachev has been.

"Every person has a role in history," says the former colleague. "Sobchak's is to lead us through the transition. Others will lead us into the future."

Tight Election Ahead for Ukraine

Daniel Sneider

10/3/91

Sergei Odarich's office is a constant whirl of activity. People come rushing in every few minutes with urgent requests. The telephone rings incessantly. At least one person is always waiting outside his door.

Mr. Odarich, a young, bearded organizer, heads up the secretariat of Rukh, the "People's Movement of the Ukraine," the main umbrella organization of the democratic and nationalist movement in this republic. His office is the center of Rukh's preparation for the most important election here in decades.

On Dec. 1, the eligible voters among the 52-million-strong Ukrainian population will go to the polls to cast two crucial ballots—to decide whether the Ukraine should be independent from the Soviet Union and to select the republic's first president. Rukh's organizers feel relatively confident the referendum on independence will pass. But the presidential election is a different matter.

The field for the presidential election is already crowded with 39 registered candidates. Among these, however, only about 10 are known figures. And of these 10, only four are considered politicians of some standing and support. The best known is Leonid Kravchuk, chairman of the Ukrainian parliament and the republic's de facto chief executive. Mr. Kravchuk is a former senior official of the Ukrainian Communist Party who, since being elected head of the parliament last year, has carved out a role for himself as a moderate nationalist with ties to both democratic and communist camps.

Alliance divided

The democratic alliance that has played a crucial role in pushing the Ukraine toward independence is divided in this election campaign. Rukh's governing board chose between three men: Vyacheslav Chernovil, the radical mayor of the Western Ukrainian city of Lvov; Igor Yukhnovsky, the head of the parliamentary opposition; and Levko Lukyanenko, the head of the Ukrainian Republican party. The man who Rukh organizers say would have been their choice, nationalist leader Mikhail Horyn, has been hospitalized for the past few months.

The Rukh board chose Mr. Chernovil as its candidate. But the Republican Party, which represents the more extreme nationalist wing of the movement, decided to mount its own separate campaign. And Mr. Yukhnovsky, whom Odarich admits would garner more votes than Chernovil if the election were held today, is also a registered candidate. Though he will not actively campaign, Odarich worries he may have to back Kravchuk instead of the Rukh candidate.

Despite the pro-independence mood in the Ukraine, Rukh organizers admit they face an uphill battle in the presidential campaign. If the election were held today, Odarich predicts Kravchuk would garner 50 percent to 60 percent of the vote, with Chernovil getting about 25 percent.

The support for Kravchuk comes despite the fact that he lacks overwhelming popularity among Ukrainians, according to most observers. Kravchuk is a consummate pragmatist, but is viewed with suspicion by many who question how far he has really stepped away from his communist past.

Those concerns were amplified during the early days of the August coup attempt when Kravchuk equivocated for a day or two before openly condemning the putsch. He also hesitated when Rukh pushed for suspension of the Ukrainian Communist Party. Rukh leaders say he only agreed with this step when they produced an internal party document seized in Lvov by Chernovil's government, which proved party support for the coup.

But Kravchuk has two crucial factors operating in his favor, Rukh organizers acknowledge. One is the continuing strength of the Communist Party apparatus. The other is geography and ethnicity—the battle for the votes of the eastern and southern Ukraine, where almost all the 11.5 million ethnic Russians live and where the appeal of Ukrainian nationalism is weakest.

Despite the fact that the Communist Party is formally shut down, "the party structures . . . live on, but it is difficult to tell how strong their influence is," Odarich says. According to Igor Sedykh, a veteran Russian journalist just returned from a week's tour through the Ukraine, the party committees, particularly in the east and south, are operating as before. "The party committees have just changed from the ObKom [the regional party committee] to the OblSoviet [the regional soviets]," he says.

Support for Kravchuk

The party does not openly speak against Ukrainian independence, but Rukh organizers believe it will mobilize its still considerable resources to support Kravchuk. They dismiss the split between Kravchuk and the conservative party leadership, though more independent observers see a clear difference between Kravchuk's pro-independence stance and the pro-Union loyalties of party hard-liners.

Ultimately, the most crucial factor will be which way the heavily industrialized eastern Ukraine goes. "We can't win without winning in the east," Odarich says.

Even Kravchuk supporters concede that Chernovil will take almost all the votes in his home ground of the three oblasts (the county-like divisions of the republic) of the western Ukraine: Ivano-Frankovsk, Ternopol, and Lvov. But taken together these account for only 10 percent of the voters, an amount equaled by just one eastern oblast, Donetsk, the center of the Donbass coal mining region. The industrial areas of Kharkov and Lugansk in the east, Zaporozhye in the southeast, and Dniepropetrovsk in the southeast together account for about 8.9 million voters out of a total of 37.7 million.

For this reason, Chernovil is already concentrating his efforts in this area, traveling to Lugansk oblast Sept. 16 for his first campaign swing and talking to miners and to audiences of thousands in the city of Lugansk. In an interview in Kiev, Chernovil claimed to have made visible progress in easing the widespread fear among the largely Russian-speaking population that he favors "Ukrainization," including elimination of the Russian language.

"Those fears are artificially fanned by Communists and by chauvinists," Chernovil said. "I was explaining I am a consistent democrat and support a federative structure in the Ukraine. My world view completely excludes any kind of violence. The process of Ukrainization should be rational."

Economic concern

In the industrial east and south, the other main concern is economic because most of the factories there are closely linked to Russia's economy. Since the Ukrainian government introduced an internal customs control blocking the flow of mainly agricultural goods to Russia, the Russians have retaliated by halting gasoline supplies to the Ukraine. As a result, there is no gas for automobiles in a large part of the east, Mr. Sedykh says. Several factories in the industrial center of Zaporozhye are shut down because of lack of supplies from Russia.

"People are afraid of the severance of economic ties and personal, family ties [to Russia]," admits Chernovil. He believes that "if they are guaranteed that this society will be open, and only during a transition period [to independence], we need to protect our market, the people will understand this."

Chernovil counts on the strong anticommunist feelings, particularly among the coal miners and other industrial workers who have carried out mass strikes in the past two years. Kravchuk's communist past is a liability he will try to avoid by stressing his personality, Chernovil predicts. Rukh organizer Odarich admits Kravchuk has much higher recognition than Chernovil, outside the western Ukraine.

"They will vote for Kravchuk because they know only Kravchuk and others are much less known," Odarich says.

Still the election is two months away—enough time, Rukh's organizers hope, to get their message across and mount a serious challenge.

Soviet Republics Look for Ways To Ease Soaring Unemployment

Amy Kaslow

10/4/91

Natalia Ivanova, a Soviet technical engineer at one of Moscow's huge military industrial complexes, says she will soon be in the unemployment line.

She spends her evenings at the Moscow Employment Center and Labor Exchange, poring over lists of thousands of job opportunities. Ms. Ivanova is still working, but on Sept. 1, she was given two-months notice of her termination.

The massive Soviet defense apparatus, employing millions of workers across the country, will be dramatically downsized over the next several years, says First Deputy Defense Minister Pavel Grachevas. Ivanova is among its first casualties. She says she lacks the political connections necessary to secure a new job in her field. And because she is of childbearing age, employers would prefer an "unburdened man to do the job."

Up to 25,000 people registered at the unemployment office during July and August, according to General Manager Igor Zaslavsky. The center opened July 1. Between 4 million and 5 million of Moscow's 9-million-plus residents work, but some 20 percent of that number will be jobless as economic reforms take hold, government cuts back staff, and industries close inefficient operations, he says. Five hundred new unemployed arrive at the office each day.

Unemployment will be most severe in the country's industrial centers, including Moscow, St. Petersburg, and the Ural mountains, Mr. Zaslavsky says. In Siberia's Tyumen region, where oil is virtually the only industry, production is sliding and workers are being laid off. To prevent worse unemployment in the mostly rural Central Asian republics and in Transcaucasia, sweeping land reform is necessary, he says. "Everyone needs a plot of land to work to support a family."

"For 60 years, we had no unemployment offices," he says. "During [Joseph] Stalin's reign of terror, people were forced to work. So everyone had a job, and Stalin declared there was no unemployment." Zaslavsky, who proudly calls himself a communist, says the work ethic is still integral to the Soviet Constitution. "Two articles, the right to work and the obligation to work, are in the Constitution."

But Ivanova and other women who represent almost 80 percent of the country's unemployed, would like to see constitutional rights that prevent job discrimination against women.

Moscow's Labor Exchange Information Bank lists 70,000 jobs for drivers, metal workers, stone-masons, and carpenters. A graduate of Moscow's Institute of Radio Electronics and Automation, Ivanova typifies the growing unemployed population in this city and around the country: She is well-educated, but will require retraining if she is to find a new job.

"It is not at all simple to find suitable work for these trained people," says Zaslavsky. "There always [used to be] specialists with a diploma, just in case they were needed. But now they don't keep unnecessary workers any longer simply for the sake of full employment."

Employers who can now choose from a large pool of job-seekers, won't take women, says Nadezhda Semenovyh, a job placement specialist at the center. "They prefer men and those who are already capable of doing the work. Retraining new workers costs time and money," she says. "But men alone cannot support the family. Because of price hikes and worsening economic conditions, it's essential for women to work."

The Moscow unemployment office is anxious to encourage small enterprises to create new jobs, says Zaslavsky's deputy, Boris Andreev.

But according to the Soviet business weekly, Commersant, many obstacles stand in the way. Moscow businessmen are in an uproar over Russian President Boris Yeltsin's Aug. 28 decree granting broad powers to Moscow Mayor Gavriil Popov, including the right to limit prices and to impose additional taxes, fines, and duties on independent enterprises. Those hiding profits and evading taxes will be more vigorously pursued, according to Commersant. "The Moscow Convention of Businessmen threatens to turn the capital into an economic desert by moving its firms to other cities," the paper reports.

Zaslavsky's office doles out unemployment money to the jobless three months after they have lost their jobs. Former employers are responsible for paying three months' wages after layoffs. Twelve months of benefits cover only a portion of lost earnings.

If the state takes dramatic measures to free up the economy, "unemployment will be massive," Zaslavsky warns. The state has neither the resources, the infrastructure, nor the political strength to withstand massive joblessness, he says.

"It would have been better to go faster [to a market economy] two years ago, when the country's economic, political, and ethnic problems were not so pronounced. But now, such fast action will only lead to chaos." And the last thing this fragile Soviet society needs, he adds "is a political upheaval."

International aid is expected to help the Soviets create a strong social safety net to avert a national crisis. A recent assessment of the Soviet economy by the International Monetary Fund, World Bank, and others, which will be the blueprint for that assistance, says, "Over a longer period, arrangements should be made to finance the unemployment compensation program through contributions from both employers and employees."

EC Warns Soviets on Aid Conditions

Amy Kaslow

10/7/91

Europe's top diplomat in Moscow, speaking for the 12-nation European Community, has issued a stern warning to the Soviet Union.

Unless the Soviet center and republics resolve differences that now prevent them from embarking on reforms in even a loosely affiliated economy, major financial help from the Community is out of the question.

"Our message is clear," European Community (EC) Ambassador Michael Emerson says. "We're saying to them, 'Don't think that if you all go off in a fanciful [separatist] way and inflict great economic damage upon yourselves that you can come back and pass the tab to us.' "

Beyond stopgap food assistance, the Soviets have requested huge sums of financial aid from the EC, assumed by Soviet leaders to be more forthcoming than reluctant American and Japanese sources. In addition to humanitarian help, the EC has also financed 80 percent of all the globally supplied technical assistance to the Soviets. EC programs range from food distribution and energy projects to financial services and management training.

But feuding among the republics threatens to cut off the crumbling Soviet economy from more substantial help. "They are inextricably linked in terms of production, trade, and finance," says Ambassador Emerson. "Of course we think economic coordination can work. However, we aren't telling them what to do; but simply to choose to do something. They have to be serious if they expect large-scale credits."

Last week in Alma-Ata, capital of the Central Asian republic of Kazakhstan, the 12 remaining republics initialed an agreement loosely linking their economies. Ivan Silayev, interim Soviet prime minister and chairman of the Inter-Republican Economic Committee, hailed the results as "very impressive. And I believe for many people, the results have exceeded all initial expectations."

But for Emerson and his European partners, the Alma-Ata agreement fell far short. "It's a very weak document. It's a very soft use of the word 'coordination,' says Emerson. "We've had some experience with this in the EC. When you can't do anything together, you say you'll coordinate. What was signed in Alma-Ata clearly shows a failure to agree on the fundamentals."

With or without an economic agreement, the Soviets face a tough winter. Addressing immediate needs, the EC is forging ahead on food aid to the Soviets. Meeting in London last week, EC Commission President Jacques Delors, EC President and Dutch Prime Minister Ruud Lubbers, and British Prime Minister John Major agreed on a food and humanitarian aid package worth billions of dollars.

Mr. Major, chairman of the powerful Group of Seven—Britain, Canada, France, Germany, Italy, Japan, and the United States—will likely double the amount committed by EC members when he secures expected additional contributions from non-European G-7 partners later this week.

US and European officials rebuffed an earlier Soviet request for almost $15 billion in aid to carry the country through the harsh winter months. They calculate Soviet needs for the next six months between $2 billion and $5 billion, enough to finance up to 40 million tons of food. The assistance may also help the Soviet Union pay off part of its trade-related debt. If the Soviet Union is forced to default on debt payments, its prospects for borrowing more money to pay for necessary imports will be greatly reduced.

"After we started sniffing around, we realized what happened," says Emerson. "It wasn't too clear that the republics were consulted in all of this."

After the initial $14.7 billion Soviet request was rejected, Soviet leaders returned with a lower, $10.2 billion request. Roughly half, or $5 billion, was expected from the European Community.

"The Soviet style, a product of their history, is to say 'OK, we want $5 billion please', says Emerson. "They supply no paper, no documentation. Their approach is 'Let's not waste time on technical details. Let's get down to business. Are you our friends or not?' They're accustomed to arbitrary dealings, with sledgehammer dictates, and it shows."

European officials told the Soviets to work with the republics and to structure the request "more seriously," Emerson says. EC officials also went to various republics inquiring about local needs and assessing the distribution network.

Emerson says the picture is bleak. While the Soviets "cried wolf over food shortages last year, and have exaggerated their needs this year," international help is now essential to avert a crisis during the coming winter, he says. "Even during this last year, the dietary level of large chunks of the population was appalling. Forty percent of the population has a dietary deficiency."

Echoing the comments of other donors, Emerson says "the difficult trick now is to get the stuff to the right consumers." The world community has been wary of doling out credits, food, and humanitarian aid, given reports of rampant corruption among the recipients. Last year, Soviet critics charged their local leaders with politically manipulating donations and allowing food to be sold on the black market.

US Agriculture Secretary Edward Madigan, on a nine-day tour of the Soviet Union to assess the country's food import needs, says most of the country will have adequate food supplies this winter. Some areas will need humanitarian aid over the coming months, he says. Last Friday, the US Department of Agriculture gave Moscow $400 million in food credits for livestock feed and wheat purchases.

Russian City Aims to Become A Haven for Free Enterprise

George D. Moffett III
10/8/91

An open letter published in a recent issue of a St. Petersburg daily newspaper provides a revealing glimpse of the problems that beset this city's dreams of becoming a bastion of free enterprise.

Addressed to members of the small-business community, it is a spirited protest against the city's decision to entrust economic planning to St. Petersburg's economic old guard.

"We protected democracy during the coup," say the writers, who are also small entrepreneurs. Will power really "return to the hands of people whose time has already passed?" they ask.

Their demand for economic empowerment is the latest indication that significant tactical disagreements lurk behind the strong consensus here for rapid economic liberalization. It has left many worried that free-market reforms—and the prosperity they are expected to bring—may not happen rapidly enough.

"What is going on in St. Petersburg is a quiet fight between newcomers and the former Communists, who are still the most active and experienced part of the society," says Mari Tarlova, an agent for foreign films seeking to do business here. "Nothing can be resolved until this is settled."

Since taking office a year ago, Mayor Anatoly Sobchak has been in the forefront of efforts to turn St. Petersburg into a haven of free enterprise and a magnet for foreign trade, investment, and tourism.

"Peter the Great wanted to open a window on Europe," says city council member Alexander Sungurov, referring to the Russian czar who founded the city. "We want to open a door."

With 75 percent of the Russian Republic's industrial base, 10 percent of its scientists, and most of its high-tech and electronics firms, St. Petersburg has the plant capacity, infrastructure, and skilled labor force to provide the raw material for economic growth.

With the Baltic states independent, St. Petersburg is also Russia's only port with well-established links to European markets. But these advantages may not be enough to offset 75 years of communism.

Economists here divide the city's business community into three categories: managers of formerly state-owned enterprises; black marketeers with strong entrepreneurial skills but, in Ms. Tarlova's words, "no business culture and a criminal mentality;" and small entrepreneurs operating within the law. There are potentially thousands of others who lack the resources to get started, they note.

So far, Mr. Sobchak has relied almost entirely on the first group, including such figures as electronics magnate Georgi Khiya, who was recently chosen to head the city's economic planning commission.

Until recently members of the Communist establishment, these figures have long been the dominant economic force here. The mayor's top-down plan for economic reform has the virtue of drawing on the most senior business talent, supporters say.

But critics worry that the mayor's allies are people of limited vision who are more interested in preserving their positions of influence than in launching sweeping free-market reforms.

If the mayor is serious about reform, his critics say, he will find ways to harness the energies of the aggressive small entrepreneurs who, because they are more responsible to the market, will be the most effective agents of economic change.

"They're right on the border between the producers and the consumers," says city council staff member Tatyana Bogachova. "They understand better than anybody else what the free market is and what the real needs of the people are."

This includes the business-wise black marketeers, who are economically "today's ugly ducklings but tomorrow's golden swans," Ms. Bogachova says.

"The democratic way is to give property to new ventures and put everything on equal terms," says Pyotr Filippov, a member of the city council who is one of the city's leading advocates of economic reform. "You've got to take [small entrepreneurs] into account and unshackle them." Which is just what the city council, where the small business community's views are represented, plans to do.

Two weeks ago, the council authorized a 5.5 million ruble loan fund to help small entrepreneurs get started. It also recommended that the mayor include small business on the city's economic planning boards.

The centerpiece of the city's reform plans is a "free enterprise zone" designated by the Russian parliament last July.

Thanks mostly to Russia's decision to extend long-term leases, various tax advantages, and rights for full ownership of subsidiaries, outside investment has increased somewhat, especially in the tourism and service sectors.

But beyond aggressively promoting itself, the city has done little to restructure the business environment.

"They can announce the zone, but they are changing the rules slowly," acknowledges Mikhail Gorney, a member of the city council's executive committee.

Here, as elsewhere in the Soviet Union, there is still no real concept of private ownership that includes legal entitlement and the right to dispose of property.

Potential investors have also been scared off by the absence of a functioning banking system or a convertible currency that would make it possible to sell for a reasonable profit.

Just as problematic is a city bureaucracy that has often frustrated the most interested suitors. With no central clearinghouse, potential investors are left to their own devices to track down the officials needed to grant operating authority. Once they do, they are frequently asked to pay bribes before permits are granted.

"It's a matter of stripping away the layers [of bureaucracy]," says Matthew Murray, a New York-based consultant on East-West trade and investment. "Each sector of the economy has its own rules and its own people. The key is finding people who combine decisionmaking authority with operational authority."

Under the circumstances, says Mr. Murray, the only reasonable strategy for potential investors is work for long-term market share, not short-term profits.

Arms Control Again Central US-Soviet Issue

Peter Grier

10/9/91

Just this summer it seemed big arms control negotiations were a thing of the past. The START treaty on long-range weaponry had taken nine years and hundreds of pages to complete.

The conventional wisdom was that both superpowers were too tired of haggling to bring up major new arms deals, at least for a while.

What a difference 12 days make. In barely more time than it takes to turn on TV lights, Presidents Bush and Gorbachev have between them decreed the virtual extinction of short-range tactical nuclear weaponry.

What's more, they've opened wide the door to talks on some of their most intractable nuclear differences, including the question of "star wars" strategic defenses.

Arms negotiators are not yet brushing off their pinstripes and making plane reservations for Geneva. But it's clear that for the near future arms control is once again playing a central role in the relationship between the United States and Soviet Union.

After a US delegation headed by Undersecretary of State Reginald Bartholomew returns Oct. 9 from its trip to Moscow, "expect a flurry of activity" in the halls of the Pentagon and State Department in preparation for new kinds of talks, says a knowledgeable US official.

Whether President Bush intended to set off such a chain of events when he announced his unilateral arms proposals on Sept. 27 isn't clear.

Gorbachev has embraced Bush's approach with enthusiasm, however. Undoubtedly one reason for the response is that Gorbachev knows that, like Bush, foreign affairs is an area in which he does best. And considering the political situation in Moscow, anything he can do to look forceful will be of immense help.

"One of the consequences of the Bush initiative is that it tends to elevate the status of Mr. Gorbachev and tends to elevate the status of the central government," says Max Kampleman, a chief US arms negotiator from 1985 to 1989.

Gorbachev's detailed response to Bush's proposals contains much agreement on the central question of tactical nuclear weapons. The Soviet leader pledged to unilaterally eliminate nuclear artillery and short-range rockets, as Bush had. This is no surprise, as the Soviets have long called for pulling tactical nuclear arms out of Europe.

But in the first of what might be called the "see you, and raise your bid" aspects of Gorbachev's outline, the Soviet leader also called on the US to negotiate a withdrawal of the last remaining kinds of tactical nukes: atom bombs for tactical fighter-bombers.

In his own speech Bush had made a point of emphasizing that NATO wanted to retain these weapons.

Until now tactical nuclear bombs have been a part of the NATO deterrent that was relatively uncontroversial with European publics.

"Now they're certain to take a lot of heat," says David Shorr, associate director of the British American Security Information Council, an arms control group.

A second part of Gorbachev's proposal that raises the arms control ante deals with the centerpiece of nuclear arsenals: long-range, or strategic, weapons.

In his speech, President Bush had called for a ban on long-range multiwarhead land-based missiles.

Since this is a type of weapon in which the Soviets are superior to the US, the Bush proposal was widely seen as a negotiating gambit.

Gorbachev simply ignored it. Instead, he called for "intensive negotiations" on all strategic weapons with a goal "approximately to halve them" from the levels called for in the just-signed START agreement.

Gorbachev coupled this with, among other things, the news that the Soviet Union would give up the longstanding superpower need to match each other warhead for warhead.

The Soviet military instead will unilaterally keep its strategic arsenal at 5,000 warheads, rather than the approximate 6,000 warheads allowed by the START pact.

It remains to be seen whether Bush will agree to what would in essence be fast-track START 2 negotiations. But it seems likely that serious follow-on talks will occur in a third major category: defense in space.

The Bush administration has long called for some kind of mutual US-Soviet deployment of strategic defenses. The president repeated that call in his latest proposals, saying the defenses should focus on guarding against rogue launch or third-world threats.

Somewhat surprisingly, Gorbachev agreed to consider nonnuclear defense-system proposals. That means the moribund Defense and space talks in Geneva will gather new energy.

Gorbachev "essentially said he is willing to listen and that is a change," says a US official.

One area the US is still studying its reply is nuclear testing. A test ban has been one of Gorbachev's pet projects almost since he assumed power, and in his arms speech he announced a one-year testing moratorium.

The US has not responded in kind to past Soviet testing pauses and has given little hint what it will do this time.

Mr. Kampleman, for one, believes that some kind of testing limits are "much more feasible" today because of the improved political climate.

All in all, two weeks of unilateral arms proposals have made striking progress in a number of areas. But it seems in many important areas the work may just be beginning.

"It does look like they will need traditional arms control negotiations," says Mr. Shorr.

Soviet Economic Leaders Court Western Investors

Amy Kaslow

10/10/91

The Exhibition of Economic Achievements of the USSR, a 500-acre park along Moscow's Peace Avenue, represents everything Soviet leaders are now struggling against.

Some 400 pavilions, exhibition halls, and massive monuments were built over the past 40 years to pay tribute to Soviet economic and industrial strength. Once an obligatory stop for every Moscow visitor, the complex is now run-down; many of the halls are closed. What remains is a legacy of poor quality, high quantity production, robbed of its potential because of the great emphasis on defense spending.

The electronics pavilion, once an organized display of Soviet engineering products, has been converted into a video hall. A loudspeaker, crackling and distorted, calls in visitors to see Hollywood-made movies. The country now imports most of its electronics equipment, usually second-rate clones of leading Western brands.

"We have been very deficient in quality production," says Ivan Silayev, chairman of the Inter-Republican Economic Committee, and top manager of the Soviet economy. "The emphasis has only been on quantity."

The former Soviet Foreign Minister Eduard Shevardnadze, now a member of President Mikhail Gorbachev's advisory council, warned "The whole economy will collapse," if today's 20 percent decline in production reaches 25 percent. "I'm afraid that people will take to the streets in anger." The influence of the radical right, he says, is growing every day.

Mr. Silayev says his bankrupt country is "counting on Western banks and businesses . . . to establish a totally new economy."

Silayev, Mr. Shevardnadze, and Mr. Gorbachev, are pressing for help this week from a group of businessmen and financiers visiting from the United States—state treasurers, pension fund managers, and investors—whose collective portfolio is valued at roughly $500 billion.

Most of the Americans, who came for a conference on Soviet economic issues and investment opportunities, say they are wary of civil unrest in the remaining 12 republics and unresolved jurisdictional matters between the republics and the center.

Dean LeBaron is undaunted. He is working with Soviet officials to solicit US pension fund investments in Soviet technology firms undergoing privatization. "This market holds the greatest promise of all the emerging markets in the world," he says.

Many of the US investors interviewed here are not convinced. They say they will wait until the political and economic situation is more stable before they will consider investing over the next several years.

Newly arrived US Ambassador Robert Strauss underscores the uncertainty: "It's a time for the average American entrepreneur to peek around . . . . For a long time there will be tremendous perils."

Trying to allay Western fears, Silayev says he's confident that a provisional inter-republican economic agreement initialed last week in Kazakhstan's capital, Alma-Ata, will take hold. Nevertheless, only three republics have committed to signing the final document. "The fact that three have signed it makes it into a union of sovereign republics," Silayev says.

Silayev's top priority is to convert the Soviet economy—now heavily defense-oriented—into one that services the consumer. Pointing to the West as a model, he says, "There, 75 percent of industrial production is for the consumer, and only 25 percent is for heavy industry and defense." By contrast, military and heavy machinery account for 75 percent of Soviet industrial output. "We must reverse this ratio," he says.

Many of the Americans, including private and public sector financial managers, openly balked at helping the Soviets de-militarize a machine that was constructed to confront the West. "As long as they have 27,000 nuclear warheads pointed at the United States, I won't consider putting a dime here," says a West Coast manager of a $12 billion pension fund.

The best candidates for Western investment are sectors of the Soviet economy ready to compete internationally and reap precious foreign exchange.

"We have enormous amounts of wealth to be extracted in oil, wood, gas, and coal," says Silayev, beckoning US investors. "It's possible to cooperate at the local level. We want you to work directly with producers of the oil and coal mines." But, he conceded, "we haven't gotten rid of laws prohibiting this." Silayev says such issues are part of the draft Alma-Ata treaty. "I use this word 'draft' because I want to be careful," he says, stepping back from his earlier, bold declaration that the treaty was a given.

In the past, the Soviets guarded their raw materials as national treasures, spurning foreign involvement. But while the republics are anxious to protect their deposits from the center's exploits, they need foreign investment in this sector.

Rachad Itani, head of merchant banking at Riggs Bank in Washington, says he's bullish. He signed a six-year, $4.5 billion deal in August designed to finance food production, processing, and distribution here with revenues from local mineral sales.

"The Russian Council of Ministers issued us a special decree, enacting a law that gives our joint-stock company—composed of two US firms and 10 Soviet state and local organizations—the right to extract coal, oil, and timber," he says.

Hard currency revenues from these raw material sales will fund the construction of more than 500 food processing plants and the creation of 100,000 jobs over the next six years, Mr. Itani says. "It's a decree, it can't be abrogated."

But there's a hitch in Itani's plan, just like the complications endemic to all international deals here.

Last week, the Supreme Soviet of the Russian Republic attacked the decree issued by the Russian Council of Ministers and declared it illegal. It seems the legislative body only learned of the deal incidentally and that the "law" providing for extraction of the republic's raw materials hit a raw nerve. The Supreme Soviet, charging that the proper decision-making channels were ignored, last week declared the law null and void.

Ukraine Defies Attempts at Soviet Unity

Daniel Sneider

10/11/91

The other day US Ambassador Robert Strauss sat down with Ukrainian leader Leonid Kravchuk to settle what seemed a minor issue—finding a building for the recently opened US consulate in the Ukrainian capital of Kiev. "His answer to me was, 'We're looking very soon for a building for our own embassy in Washington,' " Strauss recounted to a conference of American businessmen earlier this week.

The straight-talking American envoy was irritated by the implied demand for recognition of Ukrainian independence. That feeling is shared in the Russian capital where the increasingly unbending Ukrainian drive for full independence is blocking even the initial attempts to create some form of unity among the republics of the Soviet Union.

Examples of Ukrainian stubbornness are not hard to find. When representatives of the republics met for two days at the beginning of this week to discuss joint defense policy and the creation of a joint defense structure, only the Ukraine, and the three Baltic states, were absent. Mr. Kravchuk told reporters Saturday that the Ukraine insists on control of nuclear weapons based on its territory.

Today, the leaders of the remaining 12 Soviet republics and Soviet President Mikhail Gorbachev will hold a meeting of their joint State Council to discuss economic cooperation. A draft treaty to create an economic community is on the table, as well as a draft treaty of political union.

More urgently, the Committee for Operational Management of the National Economy—the cumbersome title for the interim Soviet government—will present a draft agreement on food supplies for next year. This agreement forms a basis for Soviet requests for emergency food aid from the West and Japan, providing concrete data on the amounts needed of each commodity and how these will be distributed throughout the union. It also specifies the contribution of each republic to an inter-republican food fund.

The food agreement has been drawn up assuming that the Ukraine, the second largest grain producer in the Soviet Union, will participate. But committee chief Ivan Silayev admitted the Ukrainians have not yet signed on. According to the Interfax news agency, the Ukrainians say they will not sign until the economic union treaty is concluded.

But when it comes to that key economic document, the Ukrainian attitude is also far from clear. Ukrainian Prime Minister Vitold Fokin was present at the meeting in Alma-Ata, capital of Kazakh- stan, Oct. 1 when the newest draft was discussed, and signed a statement of intent to conclude the treaty. That act drew fire in the Ukrainian parliament where nationalist forces led by the Rukh popular movement increasingly hold sway.

And when Kravchuk returned Oct. 5 from a long trip to the United States, Canada, and France, he said nothing about such an economic union. He referred only to the need for economic treaties between the independent republics. "As for political union, I am against it," Kravchuk told reporters at a press conference in Kiev. "It can only be in a form which does not deprive the Ukraine of a single drop of its statehood."

Kravchuk's attitude, and that of his government, have much to do with the referendum on Ukrainian independence scheduled for Dec. 1 and a simultaneous election for the new post of president. Kravchuk faces a field led by Rukh candidate Vyacheslav Chernovil. Until that vote is taken, Ukrainians are unlikely to make any substantial moves to join even loose union structures.

Kravchuk returned from his visit abroad proclaiming that the US, Canada, and France were ready to recognize Ukrainian independence after the December vote. When he met with visiting US Agriculture Secretary Edward Madigan Tuesday, Kravchuk said the Ukrainians want no part of a package of American agricultural credits to the Soviet Union. According to an Interfax report, he told Mr. Madigan if that happened, the Ukraine "would automatically become a debtor" and "would not know what share of the food aid it would receive."

"He expects the Ukraine to become a sovereign state and wants to have direct economic ties with the US and other nations of the world," Madigan told reporters at a press conference concluding his Soviet visit Wednesday. When President Bush met Kravchuk in Washington, Madigan continued, the US leader expressed a willingness to have some direct ties such as providing Export-Import Bank credits or sending Peace Corp volunteers.

"But, on the question of independence, that is an internal union matter in which the US will not take sides," Madigan said.

Soviet Union and West Set Out On Unprecedented Financial Path

Sheila Tefft

10/15/91

Despite their budding economic partnership with the Soviet Union, the world's seven industrial powers remain skeptical about rescuing their beleaguered capitalist convert.

Meeting during the weekend in Bangkok, the finance ministers and central bank governors from the major industrial nations agreed to accelerate efforts to salvage their free-falling former rival.

But the financiers, gathered for the annual meeting of the World Bank and the International Monetary Fund, avoided immediate commitments to new loans, debt-payment deferrals, or a huge capital infusion to transform the Soviet economy.

They agreed to send a team of deputies to work out a bailout with Moscow and the republics but underscored their stern conditions for rescue. The Group of Seven (G-7) includes Britain, Canada, France, Germany, Italy, Japan, and the United States.

The G-7 wants to see an economic reform program and a clear delineation of financial responsibilities to be borne by the disintegrating Soviet center and the republics. The industrialized countries also want to know how the Soviets will repay $70 billion in foreign debt, and they want better statistical information about the Soviet economy.

"What we are seeing here," said Alan Greenspan, chairman of the US Federal Reserve Board, "is really for the first time the Soviet Union engaging the West in a level of detail which is unprecedented." US Treasury Secretary Nicholas Brady labeled the plan "a prescription for progress."

"October will be a very famous month in the history of the Soviet Union," said Viktor Gerashchenko, chief of the Soviet central bank.

Behind the rhetoric of summitry, however, deep doubts remained over prospects for resolving differences between Moscow and the Soviet republics, maintaining debt payments, transforming the ruble into a convertible currency, and holding the Soviet Union to reforms that can keep ahead of the country's deepening divide.

In the meeting with officials of the industrialized countries, Grigory Yavlinsky, the top Soviet economic planner and head of the Soviet team here, painted a bleak picture of rapidly falling gold reserves and a limited capacity to make debt payments during the next two months. "The situation from a social and political point of view will become harder and harder," he added at a seminar yesterday on the Soviet economy.

The Soviet Union is seeking more than $10 billion to avoid bankruptcy into early 1992, and experts estimate the country will need as much as $200 billion to overhaul the economy.

But before that level of assistance materializes, "we need ratification and implementation of the economic treaty," said Canadian finance minister Donald Mazankowski. "That's pretty fundamental so we can see who we're going to be dealing with."

Ongoing debate over the pace and size of economic assistance also resurfaced among the industrialized countries. Already committed to bailing out the Soviet Union this winter, the European Community pushed the US, Canada, and Japan to step up assistance. The US offered instead to allow the Soviets to stop paying off the principal on its foreign debt, but private and central bankers objected to this step.

Many Western and Soviet analysts wonder how the Soviets will divide up responsibility for paying off overseas debt. Oleksandr Savchenko, chairman of the Ukraine economic board, said the republics were ready to shoulder their share of the debt but said it should be linked to the distribution of gold reserves, foreign exchange, and overseas property.

Oleg Bogomolov, economic adviser to Russian President Boris Yeltsin, was more pessimistic. Soviet President Mikhail Gorbachev "is connecting his hopes on the new union treaty," he said. "But I'm not sure if it will be accepted by the republics and the parliaments of the republics. And if it is accepted, it is very likely it will not be implemented."

The Soviet lock on the top of the world's political agenda dismays some in Eastern Europe who are grappling with year-old market economies and third- world countries scrambling to retain their share of overstretched international resources.

A group of ministers from developing countries urged that they not be penalized after bearing heavy debt burdens and avoiding rescheduling. "The fear of the developing countries and Eastern Europe is that we would be victims of the prodigal son syndrome," said Rudolf Hommes, Colombia's finance minister and head of a committee of 24 developing countries.

"I really do not see a clear vision in the Soviet Union," said Vaclav Klaus, the Czech finance minister. "You have to be able to start and continue reform. You have to be able to orchestrate it."

Mr. Brady, the US Treasury secretary, also took exception to an International Monetary Fund forecast of a brisk upswing in economic growth among industrialized countries. The IMF predicted that world growth will accelerate to 2.8 percent next year from 1.3 percent this year. Saying that "the US economy appears to be recovering," he nevertheless admitted to weaknesses in certain regions and industries.

The G-7 officials also endorsed a stronger yen in a move to counter a recent swell in Japan's current account surplus. Earlier, US officials said they were concerned about the growing surplus with Europe and the possibility of a surging surplus with the US.

Soviet Republics Claim Assets, But Balk on Debt

Amy Kaslow

10/15/91

While the world's leading bankers debate how to ease the Soviet debt burden, central and local leaders here disagree over just what that burden is.

The disintegration of the central Soviet power base has created a controversy over who is responsible for the country's $70 billion debt—a sum the Soviets are increasingly unable to pay.

"We know many of our partners are concerned about how the new union, the new community will honor its debt to foreign creditors," Ivan Silayev, chairman of the all-union inter-republican economic committee told visiting Western businessmen here last week. "It will be repaid through structures that are successors to the previous government," he assured them.

Soviet President Mikhail Gorbachev is desperately trying to win Western confidence with an all-union economic treaty, which he says will be signed today. But that accord, like its unsuccessful predecessors, fails to specifically assess each republic's role in repaying the Soviet Union's foreign debt.

Republic leaders are anxious to assume their share of financial, gold, and diamond reserves, but they have retreated from similar responsibility for debt.

Grigory Yavlinsky, the architect of the economic treaty, argues that the republics should pool their responsibilities rather than divide the debt among themselves. It would "violate creditors' trust" and "commonly accepted norms," he warns. "Money was loaned in a centralized manner, and should be repaid in a centralized manner."

Leonid Grigoriev, coauthor with Mr. Yavlinsky of an earlier plan to restructure the Soviet economy, stresses that the West supports this centrist approach.

"A common economic space is rational and important for our continued relations externally. But it doesn't take into account political realities," he says.

The current grim reality, comments Commersant, the Soviet business weekly, includes republics that subordinate central economic management to their own immediate interests.

Armenia is one example among many. The republic passed a law in September stipulating that, as an autonomous nation, it is entitled to its share of the former Soviet Union's gold, diamond, and monetary reserves, regardless of the location of these assets. Armenia avoided mentioning its portion of the debt.

Several republic leaders oppose transferring part of their export earnings to the Soviet foreign trade bank so that the central institution can service the collective foreign debt.

These expressions of autonomy threaten interrepublican cooperation on many levels. But if republics do not pool at least some of their resources, they will destroy the widely held hope among foreign creditors that, although the Soviets are cash-poor in the short term, they are asset rich in the long run. Earnings from energy, minerals, and other export sales will be generated faster if production and transportation are coordinated. Creditors recognize that without this foreign exchange, prospects for debt repayments are slim.

Germany, the biggest Soviet creditor, is strongly supporting this view. With more than $20 billion extended, German financiers are worried about the breakdown of their debtor. German Finance Minister Theo Waigel repeatedly points to the need to preserve a central Soviet foreign trade bank to monitor and streamline republics' transactions with international creditors.

"We've seen a sequence of economic plans and they're all inactionable," says Norbert Walter, chief economist of Deutschebank, Germany's largest commercial bank. "Some politicians in the country do not understand how dangerous it would be to repudiate their debt, and until the Soviets settle old, trade-related debts, commercial banks won't extend new money."

Viktor Gerashchenko, head of Gosbank, the Soviet central Bank, faults international lenders such as Germany for exacerbating Soviet credit problems. He says during the past year and a half, the Soviets have lost more than $15 billion in needed credits because Western banks have pulled back from the Soviet market. Political instability in the disintegrating union coupled with the failure of some Soviet companies to repay debts to foreign suppliers has sharply reduced foreign lending.

At a minimum, Mr. Gerashchenko says, $3 billion is needed to bridge the gap. This request is not new to the world's bankers.

"Gorbachev served notice at the London Economic Summit in July that he wanted debt restructuring," says Robert Hormats, vice chairman of Goldman Sachs International. "Banks are unwilling to extend credit in this environment. They don't even know who the debtor really is."

Mr. Hormats, an investment banker, says he would advise would-be creditors "to wait until there is an underlying economic and legal framework." At the very least, he adds, "the republics themselves must figure out who bears responsibility for the debt."

Moscow, Republics Reach Accord

Daniel Sneider

10/15/91

Once again the Soviet Union has stepped to the brink of self-destruction, only to pull back at the last moment.

Plans to form an economic union among the republics of the Soviet Union seemed headed for the rocks last week because of opposition from the governments of Russia and the Ukraine, the two largest and richest republics. But the republican leaders emerged from a meeting last Friday with an agreement to sign a treaty creating an economic community, perhaps as early as today.

The republics also reached consensus on Saturday over food supplies for 1992. In addition, the republics will take up a draft treaty on political union circulated on Friday by Soviet President Mikhail Gorbachev.

The key to this turnabout, observers agree, was the clear backing given to the economic community pact by Russian President Boris Yeltsin who returned from a two-week vacation last Thursday night. In addition, the Ukrainian government eased off its insistence that it would take no steps toward union until after a Dec. 1 referendum on independence.

West discusses aid

The consensus came as a Soviet delegation was heading to Bangkok for meetings with Western financial leaders gathered for the annual meeting of the International Monetary Fund and the World Bank. Following the talks in Bangkok, the Group of Seven leading industrial nations indicated they would not provide further financial aid until a clear definition was given of who among the central government and the republics would be responsible for repaying the debts.

Mr. Gorbachev made a plea to republican leaders at the State Council meeting on Friday to set aside their differences if they were to have any hope of getting Western aid. "People's patience is at a breaking point," the Tass news agency quoted him warning. "Attempts are being made to set members of the State Council against each other, to sow mutual suspicion, to hamper in every way the adoption of the documents." Foreign partners have not failed to notice this, Gorbachev added.

The Soviet leader was followed by economist Grigory Yavlinsky, deputy head of the Committee on Economic Management, the interim body running what remains of the Soviet central government. He assailed republican isolationism, saying it would bring deeper economic recession, the collapse of the monetary system, and a sharp rise in unemployment. Mr. Yavlinsky, who headed the delegation in talks with Western financiers, argued for adoption of the draft economic treaty of which he is the principal author.

It is unlikely that Gorbachev and Yavlinsky's appeals would have been enough to sway the meeting. The more crucial voice was that of Mr. Yeltsin whose attitude toward the economic treaty had been in question. Russian deputy premier Yevgeny Saburov had signed a draft version of the treaty earlier in the month at a meeting of the remaining 12 republics in the Kazakh capital of Alma Ata. But his signature had been repudiated by the Russian cabinet and Russian Vice President Alexander Rutskoi.

Last Thursday the Russian government issued a document severely criticizing the treaty for infringing on Russian interests and preserving too much central control. They specifically called for dropping proposals to form a new central bank to control the money supply, for ensuring that Russia would not finance the bulk of common expenditures, and for clearly distributing the Soviet debt among the republics.

Mr. Saburov attacked the Russian cabinet in a letter of resignation and interviews with Soviet newspapers. "Russia can survive alone but only through hunger, famine and decades of deprivation," he told the independent Nezavisimaya Gazeta. He insisted that without a strong central banking system, the economy would deteriorate, and ties with the West would be totally disrupted. He claimed his signature on the treaty was given with Yeltsin's knowledge and support.

Yeltsin was silent until the Friday meeting when he backed the treaty. Russian Premier Ivan Silayev, who now heads the Inter-Republican Economic Committee, told Russian television on Saturday that Yeltsin had refused to accept Saburov's resignation and that Saburov "had the authority for the talks in Alma Ata and the initialling."

Kazakhstan President Nursultan Nazarbayev praised Yeltsin after the accord last week. "I can tell you that he is a man who sticks to his word," he said of the Russian leader.

But Yeltsin was ambiguous on the crucial banking issue. According to a Tass account of his speech in the State Council meeting, he called for a revision of the document to allow for a more flexible link between republican banks and a central bank.

Even if the treaty is signed on Oct. 15 as planned, 17 separate agreements will need to be reached to detail its implementation—including the creation of a new banking structure. This could take until the end of the year, many observers say.

Prospects for a political union seem even more distant. Gorbachev, speaking on Soviet television in an interview aired Saturday, expressed hope that the republics would back a revised union treaty. He argued that a solely economic union, without political ties, would not work. "That means that someone [a republic] who wants access to the resources of Russia, Kazakhstan, or the Ukraine would be totally free, with no political obligations," he said.

Ukraine's reservations

Mr. Nazarbayev said that the proposed political pact had the backing of Russia, Byelorussia, Kazakhstan, and the four Central Asian republics. But as Gorbachev himself acknowledged, "I cannot think of a union without the Ukraine; I cannot imagine it." He indirectly appealed for a vote against independence but most observers foresee approval in the December referendum.

Ukrainian leader Leonid Kravchuk, who is the leading candidate to become President in an election to be held simultaneously with the referendum, has repeatedly opposed political union. But last Thursday his premier, Vitold Fokin, did back the need for an economic treaty, a stance he reiterated the following day at the State Council meeting. The Ukrainians also agreed to coordinate food policy.

Democratic Spirit Sweeps Armenia

Daniel Sneider

10/17/91

Aganush Gasparyan, wearing a simple black dress with her silver hair pulled tight into a bun, emerged from polling place 201 in a school on the outskirts of this capital city with a slight smile of satisfaction.

"Now they ask the opinion of the people," the grandmother declared. "Many years ago they didn't ask us. They said, this one is going to be the leader and you go vote for him. Now we have the opportunity to choose."

Yesterday the people of this mountainous republic exercised this basic democratic right for the first time in their history. Six candidates, along with vice presidential running mates, are competing for the newly created post of president. About 2.2 million eligible voters entered booths in schools, hospitals, and even geology institutes to mark paper ballots with their choice.

The calm and relatively ordered scenes of democracy here contrast with the tumult in the republic of Georgia just to the north. There, opponents call the recently elected government a budding dictatorship, leading many to question whether democracy will survive in the republics seeking independence from the Soviet Union.

The Armenian election has not been without controversy, however. It took a supreme court decision to reinstate a candidate barred by the central election commission for errors in collecting signatures required to support his candidacy. And some candidates charge the election process has been rigged to favor Levon Ter-Petrosyan, the chairman of the parliament and the leader of the ruling Armenian National Movement.

Bitter campaign debate

The campaign, which officially began on Sept. 28, has been marked as well by often bitter debate over the moderate policies of Mr. Ter-Petrosyan's nationalist government which ousted the Communists from power last year.

While pursuing independence, Ter-Petrosyan is avoiding open confrontation with the Moscow leadership. Tomorrow, for example, he will join other republican leaders in signing a treaty to form a new economic community. Last month he backed a mediation effort by Russian President Boris Yeltsin to try to resolve the bloody dispute with the neighboring Azerbaijan over the fate of the Armenian-populated enclave of Nagorno-Karabakh.

Presidential candidate Paruyr Hayrikyan, a well-known radical nationalist, assails Ter-Petrosyan for betraying the results of a Sept. 21 referendum when about 95 percent of the population voted for independence.

The decision to join talks on an economic pact is "immoral and illegal," he says. The bearded former dissident sees no benefit in economic ties with other Soviet republics. "We are getting the crumbs of what they don't have, what they are going to ask the West for," Mr. Hayrikyan says.

The Nagorno-Karabakh conflict raises even sharper emotions. Hundreds have been killed and hundreds of thousands made homeless in the Armenian-Azeri battle over the fate of this territory which began in 1988. Last month Yeltsin, along with Kazakhstan President Nursultan Nazarbayev, arranged the first face-to-face meeting of the leaders from both sides and brokered an agreement to begin talks under their joint guarantee of security.

This agreement "is capitulation on the part of Armenia," says vice presidential candidate Vahan Hovannessian, who shares the ticket of the Armenian Revolutionary Federation with actor Sos Sarkisyan.

"In order to have a political solution, we must have our own army and defense system," insists Parliament member and presidential candidate Rafael Kazaryan. "Only after that will the Azerbaijanis be willing to talk to us."

Ter-Petrosyan, who spoke exclusively to the Monitor in an interview on the eve of the election, defends his policies with the precision born of his many years as a scholar of ancient languages.

"I want to stress that I never deceived the people, because I expressed my desire to participate in the economic treaty as well as in inter-republican structures before the [independence] referendum," he says. The overwhelming "yes" vote, he believes, was an endorsement of "a peaceful way to complete political independence."

Regional disputes

As for the difficult Nagorno-Karabakh conflict, "such questions are solved either by war or by negotiation," says Ter-Petrosyan, who was one of the leaders of the movement to restore Armenian control over Nagorno-Karabakh. He defends his backing for the Yeltsin mediation effort as a means to guarantee an end to fighting until talks can take place.

"Since neither we nor the Azerbaijanis want this war; since neither the central government nor the two sides are ready to solve the question in a civilized way through political negotiations . . . our objective is to put an end to violations [of human rights] in this region, to establish constitutional law in Nagorno-Karabakh, to restore local government there, and to create a multilateral guarantee of security," he says. (A meeting with the Azeri leader under Gorbachev's sponsorship is planned for tomorrow in Moscow.)

To the charge of "capitulation," the Armenian parliament head retorts: "The people who say this have no policy to offer in opposition to mine."

Ter-Petrosyan's understated leadership apparently finds favor among the Armenian populace who, according to various polls, were ready to vote overwhelmingly for him. "Levon Ter-Petrosyan is the smartest one, the most educated one," says Greta Torossian, a housewife living in a settlement of brick homes with sheet-metal roofs perched on a Yerevan hillside. Along with Gorbachev and Yeltsin, she says proudly, "he is one of the three most clever men in the Soviet Union."

Opposition charges

Hayrikyan sees Ter-Petrosyan differently. He calls Ter-Petrosyan a "totalitarian" who used "government terror" against his opposition, citing an incident where Armenian National Movement supporters attacked Hayrikyan's campaigners.

He says the Armenian leader used his government position to get exposure beyond the one-time official television campaign appearance allowed all candidates. Hayrikyan declares the election result is illegal the day before the vote.

With a smile, Ter-Petrosyan dismisses such talk as a "post-election campaign," saying his opponents are trying to "justify their future defeat."

Other candidates share some of Hayrikyan's complaints and worry that local officials are resorting to old-style tactics of intimidation of voters. But they do not endorse his characterization of the entire election process. "Despite the violations of election rules, we think that the president who will be elected will be the legitimate president of the country," says Mr. Hovannessian.

Indeed, at the polls, democracy seems alive and well. Samvel Gabrielian's wife is in shock when she discovers that her husband voted for Hayrikyan. "Really!" the mechanic's pregnant wife shouts. "Then don't come home."

Samvel shrugs. "We have different points of view."

Soviet Gold Reserves Fall Far Below Estimates

Amy Kaslow
10/18/91

In a stunning display of just how dire the Soviet economic condition has become, Soviet officials this week released figures on the country's perilously low gold reserves.

A top Soviet gold analyst visiting Stockholm's prestigious Institute of Soviet and East European Economics confirms that Soviet reserves stand at 240 tons, worth roughly $2.5 billion.

The number is one-tenth that of United States Central Intelligence Agency estimates.

Analyst Grigory Khanin says the government has sold 135 tons of gold since Jan. 1 to pay for essential imports and to make timely foreign-debt payments. The sales are easy to detect because of the transparent Swiss gold market, which registers sales and purchases. Mr. Khanin says the precipitous drop in Soviet reserves is part of a continuing decline since 1986, "as it is with the entire economy," he says.

Gold, whose price is determined by the international commodities market, is an important barometer of Soviet finances. The crumbling empire's currency, the ruble, cannot be converted, thus its value cannot be assessed by international standards.

Soviet leaders warn that the cash-strapped central government, struggling to service its $70 billion foreign debt, faces a hard-currency shortfall of more than $7 billion for the rest of this year.

Viktor Gerashchencko, head of Gosbank, the Soviet central bank, told finance ministers from the world's richest countries, who met in Bangkok this week, that government coffers are practically empty; they hold only enough to cover only two months of imports and loan payments. Long a closely held state secret, the amount of gold reserves is now publicly profiled as Mr. Gerashchencko and other Soviet economic managers desperately seek international financial help.

"The Soviets said their credit standing would fall if they released the gold level before," says Anders Aslund, director of the Stockholm Institute of Soviet and East European Economics.

Creditors such as Germany have tried to play down Soviet credit problems by pointing repeatedly to the country's vast energy and mineral reserves. They have opposed forgiving any of the former union's debts, stressing that with a wealth of resources to sell for foreign currency, Moscow can and must service its debts. More than one-third of the Soviets' $60 billion debt to the West is due Germany.

The US has lobbied to reschedule some Soviet debt, suggesting that if the heavily exposed Germans do their part by easing the Soviet debt burden today, Washington will be more forthcoming with fresh credits tomorrow.

But a senior US treasury official charged with assessing Soviet credit risk is skeptical. "The only shred of evidence concerning Soviet creditworthiness is the amount of gold or oil it has."

This basis, he says, "is absurd. Especially when I think back to Iraq, a country which promoted itself and was perceived to be a good credit risk because of its huge oil deposits. Baghdad then turned around and repudiated its foreign debts."

In the midst of political and economic chaos, the Soviet internal payments structure is collapsing. Republics have refused to remit foreign-exchange earnings from a variety of exports to Vneshekonombank, the Soviet Bank for Foreign Economic Affairs, responsible for international payments.

Whether Moscow can rely on gold reserves as collateral for new Western credits has much to do with the mining sector's current disarray and the political dynamics between the Moscow center and independent republics.

Khanin says 180,000 people work in the Soviet gold industry, producing some 180 to 200 tons a year. While much of Soviet territory has not been prospected, 60 percent of known mines are in the Russian republic; the rest are in Uzbekistan, Kazakhstan, and Armenia.

Most of the gold is mined by 120,000 state employees, the rest is delivered to central authorities by some 60,000 quasi-private workers. The latter produce twice as much, says Khanin, but they steal much of the gold.

Still, this pilfering is marginal compared to the amount of gold that could be withheld from central accounts by local republic leaders. As import costs soar and credit becomes tighter, local leaders could choose to store much of the gold for local use.

A Sept. 26 bulletin from Tass, the Soviet news agency with close ties to central authorities, offers one of countless conflicting gold reports. "Ten percent of the Soviet gold reserve, worth $4 billion, was secretly transported from the USSR to the West on the instruction of a small group of people from the State Emergency Committee," which governed during the August coup, it says.

Yet the amount of reserves, says the US Treasury official, is immaterial: "It's an illusion to think that Vneshekonombank brings in all revenues, makes all payments, and will meet international responsibilities. The place is falling apart."

Soviet Parliament Goes Warily About Its Business

Daniel Sneider

10/22/91

A newly formed Soviet parliament, uncertain of its role or powers and half-formed in its membership, convened yesterday in the Kremlin.

Soviet President Mikhail Gorbachev sat in his usual spot to the right of the chairman's dais, leaning forward to peer at the largely new set of faces in the chamber. The old parliament had dissolved itself in September following the failed coup. The new body is formed entirely of members sent by the republics.

Mr. Gorbachev tried his best to imbue this parliament, one of the few institutions where he has a role left to play, with some new meaning. In a brief, businesslike speech, the Soviet leader called on the parliament to preserve the union and laid out tasks before it.

"Will we go forward together, or will every republic try to find its own way?" Gorbachev asked rhetorically. "Until we clear up this point, all programs will remain just wishful thinking. We'll remain stuck while the tension in society will continue to grow."

Gorbachev's view was clear.

"Some are for maintaining the old super-centralized totalitarian state, others for an economic union without a political union. There is the opinion that the union no longer exists and we should go to the end in separating and disintegration. I'm convinced that if any one of these points of view prevails, the consequences will be catastrophic for all peoples and republics."

But a simple count of republics represented at this opening session signaled more than the speech about the problems besetting a union of any kind in this country. Of 12 republics still considered part of the Soviet Union, only seven sent representatives to the new body. Russia, Byelorussia, Kazakhstan, Turkmenia, Kirghizia, Uzbekistan, and Tadzhikistan attended, but one-third of the delegates from those republics did not even bother to attend yesterday's session.

The powerful Ukraine opted out entirely, along with the three Caucasus republics of Georgia, Armenia, and Azerbaijan, as well as Moldavia. Asked why the Ukraine was not participating, the permanent Ukrainian representative in Moscow, Vladimir Krizhinovsky replied: "Why isn't the French delegation here? We are an independent country."

Even those who did come to the new Supreme Soviet, as the parliament is still called, were far from certain of its purpose.

"That is the most enigmatic question—nobody knows [the answer]," responded Vladimir Lukin, who heads the foreign affairs committee of the Russian republic parliament and is a member of the new Soviet parliament.

"Juridically speaking, this is a rather questionable assembly," commented economist Nikolai Petrakov, a deputy from Russia and an adviser to President Gorbachev. "But," he added, "we should still have some body in which we can discuss things, just like the European parliament."

The comparison to the European parliament, the elected but largely powerless legislature of the European Community (EC), was made by several delegates in hallway conversations.

At least eight republics—the seven attending the parliament plus Armenia—have agreed to form an economic community, signing a treaty to that effect on Friday. The treaty gives legitimacy to the State Council, which includes the republican leaders and Gorbachev, and to the inter-republican economic committee.

Gorbachev, in his address, supported moves toward market reform pushed by the inter-republican committee. He called for parliament to back economic reform that includes: halting the breakup of the Soviet monetary system; stabilizing the ruble; moving rapidly toward privatization and free-market pricing; and encouraging private entrepreneurship. He also called for business tax breaks, land reform, and reorganization of the Soviet international trade system.

The Soviet president drew little reaction—and no applause—except when he sharply attacked republics for trying to set up their own national armies and for trying to "nationalize" Soviet Army units and equipment on their territory. Such attempts "should be considered ridiculous, irresponsible, even illegal," Gorbachev said, threatening to take "constitutional measures" against such moves, a statement that provoked a ripple through the hall.

But his plea for political union seems likely to fall on deaf ears though the economic community will undoubtedly take some political form. As Mr. Lukin put it, "It is impossible to completely divide economic and political things because economic ties presume coordination."

Armenian Calls for Shift in West

Daniel Sneider

10/24/91

On the eve of his landslide election as Armenia's first president, Levon Ter-Petrosyan displayed confidence in the path toward independence that his mountainous republic has chosen. "I have shown a peaceful way to complete political independence," the then-chairman of the Armenian parliament asserted.

But beneath the surety, Mr. Ter-Petrosyan betrays signs of uncertainty, even more of irritation. He hoped to be rewarded by both Moscow and the West for having avoided confrontation in his country's careful course toward independence. Armenia expected that the recognition of the independence of the Baltic republics after August's failed coup would lead in turn to acceptance of their full freedom from the Soviet Union.

Instead, Ter-Petrosyan accuses the West of repeating its error of refusing to recognize Baltic independence. And by doing so, he worries, it is again encouraging the illusion that a political union can be restored, a theme promoted by Soviet President Mikhail Gorbachev.

"After recognition of the Baltic countries, there is an opinion in the West that the Baltic countries must not serve as a precedent for other republics," Ter-Petrosyan observed in an interview with the Monitor. "And Gorbachev was fast to take up this opinion.... I think it is a very dangerous position because it is opposed to the objective processes which are going on in the USSR now. It can lead to a new aggravation of the situation."

"The West must change its position completely now. It must give a boost to the complete independence of the republics, and simultaneously it must spare neither effort nor expense to help those republics get their independence peacefully."

Ter-Petrosyan's words are by no means those of an extremist. The former scholar of ancient languages has won a reputation as the most pragmatic of the nationalists who have come to power in many former Soviet republics. He has eschewed the bombastic rhetoric of Georgian President Zviad Gamsakhurdia and the tough nonparticipation in all union functions adopted by Moldavia. Alone among those seeking full political independence, on Oct. 18, Armenia signed the treaty advocated by Mr. Gorbachev to form an economic community.

Ter-Petrosyan sees this moderate approach, which has been heavily criticized here by more radical nationalists for being too soft towards Moscow, as a way to meet Western concerns about the breakup of the Soviet Union.

"The West is afraid of confrontation and collision. It is afraid that republics seceding from the federation will cause great problems for the USSR and for the West. From this point of view, the West feels that it must not support republics that are radical in their ideas and that are going to cut all their ties. Armenia serves as an example for the West of how to reach independence peacefully, without this confrontation and collision."

Since taking power from the Communists last year, Ter-Petrosyan's Armenian National Movement has pursued a carefully crafted path toward independence, asserting control over Armenian life while avoiding an open break with Moscow.

This stance comes in part from Armenia's vulnerable geographic and political position. Christian Armenia has traditionally looked to Russia as a protector against its historical Muslim Turkic adversaries in neighboring Turkey and Azerbaijan. Armenia has been embroiled in recent years in a bitter and bloody conflict over the fate of the Armenian-populated enclave of Nagorno-Karabakh which lies within Azerbaijan.

Alone among republics seeking independence, Armenia also agreed to follow the complex procedure for secession called for in Soviet law. The Sept. 21 referendum on independence was scheduled six months earlier, according to the law's requirements. Gorbachev has frequently cited this law, demanding the Baltics follow it to gain their freedom. The Baltics steadfastly refused.

The Baltics insisted that their forced incorporation into the Soviet Union was illegal, based on the secret 1939 Ribbentrop-Molotov pact between Nazi Germany and the Soviet Union preceding the invasion and division of Poland. But in Ter-Petrosyan's view, because Armenia's referendum was held in keeping with the Soviet law, their claim to independence has at least the same juridical basis as the Baltics'.

The Armenian decision to join the recently formed economic community was consistent with this pragmatic approach. As Ter-Petrosyan explained to Armenia's parliament after signing the treaty, Armenia will pursue "complete political independence," while at the same time, "the maximum participation in all constructive processes" going on in the former Soviet Union.

"Levon Ter-Petrosyan's policy is realistic," comments Hovig Eordekian, deputy editor of the newspaper Azg (Nation). "Participation in the interrepublican process is normal because the Armenian economy is so integrated into the Soviet Union."

But Ter-Petrosyan admits concern that Gorbachev is trying to use the need for economic cooperation to push for a renewed political union. Indeed, Gorbachev has circulated a draft treaty of political union and has spoken often of his desire to push it through quickly.

"Gorbachev is insisting on repeating his mistake that brought this country to catastrophe," says Ter-Petrosyan. "Once again the economy is being sacrificed to political aims." He refers to the attempt earlier this spring to forge a new union treaty which ultimately was blocked by the attempted coup in August.

The hopes of Armenia and other republics seeking to leave the union are pinned more on Russian leader Boris Yeltsin. But even Mr. Yeltsin is vulnerable to political opinion, Ter-Petrosyan observes. "On one hand, Yeltsin is a realist in policy. That's why he understands that priority must be given to economic questions. Unfortunately he has to yield to public pressure in Russia."

But Ter-Petrosyan is above all a patient man. In his coming visits to Moscow and abroad, he says, "I will try to persuade" Gorbachev, Yeltsin, and the West that ultimately Armenian independence can coexist with a new structure of cooperation among the former Soviet republics.

Unstated Issue at Today's Summit: Is the Soviet Union Still Viable?

Daniel Sneider

10/29/91

Soviet President Mikhail Gorbachev and United States President Bush will meet today for the first time since August, when a failed coup led to a sweeping anti-Communist revolution in the Soviet Union.

The agenda for their brief meeting in Madrid, before the two men open the jointly sponsored Middle East peace conference tomorrow, is a crowded one. Aside from the Middle East conference, the two leaders are expected to talk about economic assistance to the Soviet Union and about controls on nuclear weapons.

During the past month, the two presidents have exchanged groundbreaking proposals to eliminate tactical nuclear weapons, to stand down from a nuclear alert status, and to move toward a new era of strategic nuclear-weapons stability.

But beneath all these issues lies an unstated question that will dominate all others: the future of the Soviet Union itself—whether it will remain a united nation with a major role to play in world affairs.

Mr. Gorbachev has already been confronted with those questions, outlined in a brief interview published yesterday in the Arab newspaper Al-Sharq Al-Aswat.

"Of course, our country is now experiencing great difficulties, which are inevitable at the stage of such immense and radical transformations," Gorbachev responded. "But all talk about a decline of our role in world politics contradicts facts, including the fact that our country is co-chairman at the Middle East peace conference."

The old Soviet Union may no longer exist, Gorbachev added, but "a new union, the union of sovereign states, is in the throes of being born."

Despite such confidence, it is valid to ask what role, if any, will the Soviet Union play in world affairs. Until his departure yesterday, Gorbachev's trip attracted little attention here, with barely a mention in the Soviet media.

"Everybody is preoccupied with the domestic situation, too preoccupied," comments Vitali Naumkin, deputy director of the Institute of Oriental Studies. "But for Gorbachev it is important—it is an event that proves that in this crucial period, a union foreign policy does exist."

Still, the preparations for the Middle East conference have been entirely the province of the Soviet Foreign Ministry.

"[Foreign Minister Boris] Pankin and his team of experts are traveling around as if we are living in the good old days," says Mr. Naumkin, a leading Soviet Middle East specialist.

While giving credit to US Secretary of State James Baker III for getting the conference off the ground, Soviet experts argue that the conference is the result of the joint activity of both countries over a long period of time, beginning with the original Soviet proposal for the gathering.

In that sense, "both presidents deserve the ceremonial co-chairmanship," says Vladimir Lukin, head of the Russian republic's parliament foreign affairs committee and a member of the Soviet delegation.

The issue of whether or not a Soviet Union exists also plagues prospects for economic aid from the West. On Saturday, senior officials from the 12 republics of the former Soviet Union met with the chairman of the committee managing the Soviet economy, Ivan Silayev, and his deputy, radical economist Grigory Yavlinsky.

Just back from the International Monetary Fund meeting in Bangkok, Mr. Yavlinsky told republic leaders that Western governments were not prepared to throw new funds into the Soviet Union until the republics agreed to honor the Soviet Union's almost $70 billion foreign debt. He argued against the idea, widely promoted by the Ukraine and others, of dividing Soviet debt and reserves of currency and gold.

Those participating in what remains of the Soviet central government clearly hope to use foreign pressure to force the republics into greater economic cooperation as called for in the treaty of economic union signed by eight of the 12 republics in mid-October. On Sunday, republican representatives began meetings here to discuss financial aid with representatives of the Group of Seven leading industrial nations.

Gorbachev may be looking for Bush to apply some indirect pressure on the republics in another crucial area as well: control over nuclear weapons. The Ukrainian announcement last week of plans to form a 400,000- to 500,000-man army has underscored fears that the Soviet nuclear arsenal could be divided among several republics, although the Ukrainian parliament pledged support for central control of those weapons.

The US and Soviet leaderships now share a common interest in the centralized command of nuclear weapons, argues Sergei Rogov, the senior military specialist at the USA-Canada Institute. According to the expert, the Ukrainians not only have missiles deployed on their territory, they also manufacture SS-18 and SS-24 intercontinental ballistic missiles in factories located there. If it wanted to, he says, the Ukraine would be capable in a few years of producing nuclear warheads as well as missiles to deliver them.

"In this situation, it is not the Russian-American nuclear balance but the Russian-Ukrainian balance which becomes the dominant issue," says Mr. Rogov. The Bush arms initiative, along with the Gorbachev response, provides an opening to eliminate the republican-based nuclear weapons as part of steps to eliminate multiple-warhead missiles, he says.

In effect, Bush and Gorbachev "could cook a deal to allow the two countries to say that all the weapons on your territory belong to a category fully eliminated," Rogov says.

New Russian Leaders Threaten Curbs on Independent Press

Daniel Sneider

10/31/91

The Russian government has warned two newspapers, including the country's leading independent journal, for violating the press law and threatened them with closure.

Vitaly Tretiakov, the editor of Nezavisimaya Gazeta (Independent Newspaper) sees this as a clear effort by the Russian government of Boris Yeltsin to curb the freedom of the press. Within two months of the failed Communist coup and the ensuing political revolution, the new authorities are showing signs of following in the footsteps of the old, he charges.

"The democrats very quickly start to manifest the same intolerance of any kind of criticism as their predecessors the Communists did," he told the Monitor yesterday. "The democrats loved us when we criticized the Communists, but they can't stand it when we go after them."

The controversy involves not only press freedom but the growing tension between the Russian republic and its neighbor, the Ukraine. Nezavisimaya and the liberal weekly Moscow News are being warned for printing articles reporting discussions within the Russian government over the possibility of nuclear conflict between the two republics.

In its Oct. 24 report, Nezavisimaya ran an interview with Ukrainian Vice Premier Konstantin Masik, who reported the replies of both Mr. Yeltsin and Soviet President Mikhail Gorbachev to this discussion. Mr. Masik said that Gorbachev dismissed the threat as groundless but that "Yeltsin said he did discuss this possibility with the military, but there is no military capability for it."

The day following the publication of the article, Nezavisimaya received a call from the Russian Ministry of Press and Mass Media telling them the ministry was going to issue an official warning, though not explaining for what.

The following day, the paper Kuranty published the text of the warning (which also mentions Moscow News) stating that the publication of this article violates Article 5 of the Soviet Law on Press which prohibits propagandizing war and inter-ethnic conflict.

According to that law, Mr. Tretiakov wrote in a front page editorial on Oct. 29, the paper can be shut down if it receives a second warning. The charges against the paper were repeated several times over the next days on television news programs, including those by the minister, Mikhail Poltaranin, a former liberal journalist.

Tretiakov dismisses the accusations as "absurd" and without any legal basis. The paper cannot be held responsible for the words of a Ukrainian official, he says.

"There is nothing special or horrible" about the warning, insists Andrei Rylsky, the minister's aide for external relations. He accuses Tretiakov of being wrong when he says the paper can be closed down under the law. "On the contrary, the paper is protected by the ministry," he says.

But an official of the ministry's legal department, who declined to reveal his name, says that "the paper can be closed after receiving a second warning."

Although Mr. Poltaranin publicly issued the warning, the official document "was prepared but it wasn't signed," he explained.

"It is the old trick of passing around a warning in order to intimidate somebody," responds Tretiakov, who founded Nezavisimaya earlier this year. The paper has quickly won a reputation as the most innovative paper in the country. It has set itself apart by not holding back from publishing articles critical of the Yeltsin government and the democratic reform movement and by regularly scooping other papers and publishing investigative articles.

Tretiakov offers two explanations for the move against his paper. "Either the Russian democrats are fed up with Nezavisimaya and are looking for a pretext to pacify it, or the more dangerous conclusion, we hit the bull's-eye [with our report] . . . and they are upset that it was made public. The fury, the absurdity, and the illogical way they are charging us with these crimes unfortunately indicates the second conclusion."

Russia Picks Up the Pieces

Daniel Sneider

11/4/91

The leaders of the former Soviet republics meet today to nail down details of an economic community which they agreed to form last month.

But these moves are tempered by reminders of the perilous fragility of this attempt to preserve some form of union. Only last week, Russian President Boris Yeltsin threatened to dissolve the Soviet central bank and to issue a Russian currency. The Russian message increasingly is a dual one: We are willing to have a union, but we are also ready to go it alone at any moment.

For those who see the glass of union as half-full, as Soviet President Mikhail Gorbachev does, some developments are encouraging. The republics are to meet Nov. 9 in Kiev to finalize an agreement to take collective responsibility for Soviet foreign debt. The chairman of the Ukrainian Parliament, Leonid Kravchuk, told local newspapers over the weekend, that the Ukraine, which had refused to sign the economic treaty, would join today or tomorrow.

The republican representatives agreed last week on the structure of a new Interstate Economic Committee (IEC), which will act as the common market's central government.

Mr. Gorbachev and the heads of 12 republics are expected to ratify their plans, including a drastic reduction in the number of central ministries and agencies, at a meeting of the State Council today.

According to various reports, the former Soviet republics propose to dissolve some 36 central ministries on Nov. 15, along with 37 other agencies such as the Committee for Lenin Prizes and the Council for Religious Affairs. Virtually all the huge industrial ministries are to be scrapped. Those left intact include the Defense, Energy, Interior, Railway, Nuclear Energy, and Foreign Ministries, the customs service, and the aerospace agency. They also decided to maintain the Communications Ministry, the Foreign Exchange committee, Pension Fund, and some other agencies.

These concrete steps are somewhat deceiving however. In many cases, the process is less one of forming a common economic structure than one of dissolution, with Russia picking up the pieces of the former union.

In an interview with the Government Herald last week, Ivan Silayev, the former Russian prime minister who will head the IEC, said that most of 36,000 employees in the dissolved central ministries would find jobs in the comparable Russian ministries.

Indeed, a draft Russian presidential decree on Russian industry reportedly sets out the same kind of production plans that the central ministries previously prepared for the state-run enterprises under their control.

According to the independent Interfax news agency, the Russian Cabinet will set a system of state orders for 1992 in which the state will take up to 70 percent of industrial production and 35 percent of mining production in exchange for supplying raw materials. The draft decree also requires exporters to hand over 80 percent of the foreign currency they earn to the state, an even more onerous share than the Soviet central government previously took.

The ambiguity of the Russian backing for economic union was evident in the tiff last week over the central bank. The issue emerged when Gorbachev asked the Soviet Parliament to approve the printing of 30 billion rubles ($17.6 billion) by the Soviet State Bank (Gosbank) to cover a yawning budget gap. According to a report supplied to the Parliament, the budget deficit for 1991 will be 153.3 billion rubles, with two-thirds of the defense budget left unpaid. The report also said that three-quarters of the Soviet debt payments due this year are unpaid, a shortfall of some $4 billion, the Gosbank chairman told a Japanese newspaper.

Mr. Yeltsin, angered by the request to print more rubles without republican approval, called last week for the Gosbank assets to be divided proportionally among the republican central banks, with Gosbank itself to become the state bank of Russia.

On Friday, Mr. Silayev told the Tass news agency, Yeltsin "changed his mind."

Russia supports formation of a "normal, healthy banking union among the former republics of the USSR," Yeltsin's closest personal aide, Gennady Burbulis, told reporters that same day. However, he attacked the Gosbank as a "monopoly" and said Russia in particular was burdened by the existence of "two presidents" and "two governments . . . on our territory."

"It would be interesting to ask the republics what they prefer—either the Bank of Russia that acts as successor to the USSR Bank or to continue to preserve this monster," Mr. Burbulis added.

Burbulis made it clear the Russian leadership has no interest in the kind of continued political union favored by Gorbachev, contrasting his stance to Yeltsin's far looser vision.

"We'll intensify our relations with the republics on a bilateral basis," he explained. "The deeper these relations are, the sooner there will be a desire to have a community of sovereign states."

Last week, for example, Russian foreign and defense ministers met with their Ukrainian counterparts to begin talks on a bilateral treaty.

The same spirit imbued the Yeltsin economic reform package announced last week. The program of price liberalization, privatization, and other free market measures, particularly planned rises in the prices of Russian oil and gas, will strongly affect other republics. But the decisions were taken independently.

Yet Yeltsin also continues to backing economic and political union.

"He's stuck between two positions," says Sergei Mikhailov, deputy head of the Russian parliament's Foreign Affairs Committee. "On the one hand, he realizes that no one would benefit from the breakup of the union. But on the other hand, he wants to be the president of a great, independent country."

Soviet Swords Into Plowshares? Not Quite Yet

Daniel Sneider

11/7/91

Fresh from an eight-day tour of Soviet defense factories and research labs in Moscow, St. Petersburg, and Kiev, United States Deputy Defense Secretary Donald Atwood struck an upbeat note.

The vast Soviet defense complex is ready to transform itself into civilian production, he told reporters on Tuesday. "The message was that there is a sincere interest on the part of industrialists, ministers, and workers that there can be an orderly transition in many key industries," Mr. Atwood said.

The US government is ready to act as a catalyst for such a transformation, the senior official pledged, though the main job lies with American private investment. To emphasize that, a group of seven American industrialists accompanied him, including senior executives from companies such as Boeing, General Electric, Ford, General Motors, and the Kellogg Company.

But such official optimism runs up against considerable evidence that the Soviet defense industry leaders and the current political leadership are reluctant to push too rapidly for conversion. And American executives say privately that conditions are far from ripe.

"The Russians have to understand how a market economy works," said one executive on the tour. "They have to offer products that are salable. They don't even know what their costs are because they never had to," he said. Foreign investors are "holding back," he said, in part because of the uncertain political future of the Soviet Union. "Who do you do business with?" he asked rhetorically.

Soviet leaders have touted joint ventures with Western firms as a means of easing the pain of conversion. They point out that conversion of the huge Soviet defense complex will be costly, especially dealing with the social consequences. Arkady Volsky, head of the Scientific Industrial League and current deputy chairman of the interim committee managing the Soviet economy, estimates that unemployment in the defense sector could easily hit 2 million people.

While the talk is mostly about shifting from defense to consumer goods production, the Soviets also are increasingly raising what not so long ago would have been the astounding idea that Soviet and American defense firms could jointly develop weapons.

"I was surprised when one Soviet cruise-missile developer proposed joint weapons development with the US and declassifying defense information," recounts Mr. Volsky, who hosted the American defense industry visit. "Soviet defense specialists believe their products are competitive."

Even Soviet President Mikhail Gorbachev, in a meeting with Atwood on Tuesday, proposed cooperation in developing the technology to dispose of chemical weapons and in joint research on new products between Soviet and American defense firms.

Russian President Boris Yeltsin has put an even more curious idea on the table, suggesting that the US and Russia work together to carve up the world arms market. According to a Tass news agency account, he unveiled this proposal at a meeting last week with the heads of large Russian state-run industry, many of which are part of the defense industry complex. Clearly trying to assuage fears of a large-scale cut in defense spending, Mr. Yeltsin told them that no moves toward conversion would be made until defense needs were assessed. Moreover, he said, the Soviets can still make profits by selling arms overseas. "We shall not trade... in nuclear weapons," Yeltsin told the industry executives. "But we can well trade in tanks and Kalashnikov submachine guns." Yeltsin told the meeting that he had recently discussed with US President Bush "the question of whether the arms market should be divided between the two countries," Tass said. "But the US president deemed that inadvisable," the report continued.

Many defense industry leaders here argue against rapid conversion, warning it will throw away huge investments in technology and manpower built up by the defense firms. "The Soviet engine industry can be destroyed overnight, but its reconstruction will take a minimum of 25 to 30 years," said Alexander Sarkisov, chief designer of engines for Soviet fighters and helicopters for the Klimov Association, told the New Times.

Mr. Sarkisov dismissed the current conversion effort, which focuses on defense plants turning out civilian goods. "Look, in the world market a kilo of a modern fighter plane costs over $2,000, and a kilo of saucepans, $1," he contended. "Isn't it more rational to sell engines and spend a proportion of the income on Western-made goods of the kind we are compelled to make as part of reconversion?"

The Soviet aircraft industry has been promoted, particularly by some Western observers, as a prime candidate for Western cooperation for conversion. With Western technology, it is argued, Soviet passenger jets could be sold on world markets. Boeing Senior Vice President Lawrence Clarkson, a member of the touring group, politely calls that prospect "unrealistic."

"Even with Western avionics and engines, they won't meet Western standards of safety," Clarkson says. He says Soviet design capability is quite good but describes the level of their production methods as "very low."

"In the long term, they have a possibility of designing and co-producing aircraft that do meet those standards," Mr. Clarkson says. In the meantime, it is more realistic, he says, for the Soviets to produce parts for Boeing and other Western aircraft.

Soviet industry proposals for joint ventures, however, are based on unrealistic estimates of their abilities, the US industry executive says. "They want to start running the 100-yard dash in 9 seconds. Boeing feels we have to learn to crawl together before we walk together, before we run together, before we run the 100 yard dash together."

An Independent Latvia Chooses Its Citizens

Linda Feldmann

11/7/91

When Lt. Vladimir Zaitsev was transferred to Riga in 1954 to serve at the Soviet military's Baltic headquarters, he thought he was set for life.

He married a local Russian-Polish woman, had two daughters, and eventually retired here like many of his military comrades. It was a relatively comfortable existence: Food was more plentiful than in his native Russia, and in the summer he could relax in a spacious beachfront dacha rented from the Soviet Writers Union by his son-in-law, a well-known Russian satirist.

Now Lieutenant Zaitsev is an alien in a foreign land. Under newly-independent Latvia's citizenship decree, current or retired Soviet military posted here may not vote, own property, or become citizens. The dacha is also history: Two Latvian brothers from Canada recently turned up with the deed to the house, and by law it is now theirs.

"I wouldn't even take Latvian citizenship if they offered it," scowls Zaitsev, which is not his real name. "Latvia doesn't want me, and I have no place to go in Russia," he says. And he is worried that he will lose his pension.

Thousands of Zaitsevs live in Latvia, and they are but a fraction of the people caught in the citizenship dilemma that has consumed this nation since the Soviet coup allowed a sudden renewal of independence in August. Zaitsev's fate has already been settled. He will not become a citizen.

According to an Oct. 15 parliament resolution, only those who were Latvian citizens on June 17, 1940—when the Soviets invaded—and their descendants will automatically be granted citizenship.

Officially, only 52 percent of Latvian residents are ethnic Latvian, the result of five decades of Russification, though many local officials privately admit that figure is likely below 50 percent. Russians account for 34 percent; the rest are Byelorussian, Ukrainian, Polish, or of other origin.

The citizenship question has immobilized the Latvian parliament, which can pass little other legislation until this issue is solved. Privatization and other market reforms are virtually paralyzed, since property ownership is tied to citizenship.

"I fear Western businessmen won't be willing to invest their capital here until stability is guaranteed," says Vladimir Steshenko, chief of the government's nationalities department.

The problem is also exacerbated by a leadership vacuum, say Latvian and Western analysts. Leaders have created their own personal fiefdoms and shown no willingness to form a badly needed centrist political party that could offer some direction on the citizenship problem, these analysts say. None of the top five leaders participated in parliament's Oct. 15 resolution. All were either out of the country or abstained from voting, calling none of the options satisfactory.

"They know they have an explosive situation on their hands and they're trying to protect themselves," says a Western diplomat.

In the past, Latvian parliament chairman Anatolijs Gorbunovs has supported something close to the so-called "zero option," in which all people living in Latvia on the day it restored independence—Aug. 23, 1991—would automatically become citizens. At one time, the Popular Front, the broad anticommunist citizens' movement, also supported this option, but since independence, Latvian politics have radicalized. The Popular Front's stand looks increasingly like that of the Citizens' Congress, which holds that only those who were citizens of pre-Soviet Latvia and their descendants have the right to vote on a naturalization process.

The issue remains far from solved, and could drag on for several months, says Aivars Endzins, chairman of the parliament's legislative committee.

The Oct. 15 resolution constitutes only a framework for resolving the question. One point of debate is over the length of time a non-citizen must have lived in Latvia before he or she is eligible for citizenship. The resolution states 16 years, but Mr. Endzins says the parliament will likely settle on five or 10 years.

But since much of Latvia's foreign population has been here a long time, that won't be the toughest requirement for applicants to fulfill. Much more trouble for some will be the language requirement: A "conversational level" is required by the Oct. 15 resolution. Only 21 percent of the nation's Russians speak Latvian, and a May 1989 law requiring the teaching of Latvian to non-speakers has been poorly implemented.

As Latvia incorporates itself into Western organizations, non-citizens hope Western pressure will force the Latvians to deal "reasonably" with this problem. Western diplomats, however, have little sympathy for the non-Latvians who moved here under the Soviet occupation—especially the military. As long as they have citizenship somewhere, be it Russia or the Ukraine or wherever, their human rights are not being violated, says one diplomat.

"Of course, politically speaking, it's not smart to disenfranchise a large portion of your population," the diplomat cautions.

Latvia's demographic dilemma is complicated by the fact that its cities are overwhelmingly Russian. Riga, the capital, is only one-third Latvian. Daugavpils, the second largest city, is only 13 percent Latvian.

And more than 80 percent of Latvia's private capital is controlled by non-Latvians, says Mr. Steshenko of the Nationalities department. Latvians are more involved in agricultural and professional work, while much of Latvia's skilled laborers are Russian. If a large portion of them decide to leave, it would be a blow to the Latvian economy, he says.

"Those who are coming to my department saying they want to leave are engineer PhD candidates," Steshenko adds. "In that case, I'm not so much a government worker but a priest. I try to calm people down, tell them to wait for a decision."

Yeltsin Runs Into Test of Authority Over Insurgency

Daniel Sneider

11/12/91

The armed rebellion of an ethnic minority in the Caucasus mountains of southern Russia is severely testing the authority of Russian President Boris Yeltsin.

Mr. Yeltsin's decree of a state of emergency in the Chechen-Ingush autonomous republic on Friday—and the subsequent dispatch of special Interior Ministry troops to attempt to enforce it—have triggered a broad political crisis. The militia of the insurgent movement seeking independence for Chechen-Ingush is openly defying the decree.

After two days of intense debate, the Russian parliament refused to back the decree and called instead for political negotiations to be held under parliamentary auspices. And the Democratic Rossiya movement, a key source of political support for Yeltsin, openly split over the weekend, in part over this issue.

Some in the democratic movement warn that Yeltsin is following in the dangerous footsteps of Soviet President Mikhail Gorbachev, trying to solve complex ethnic and national disputes by force. They compare it to Mr. Gorbachev's handling of the Baltic demands for independence from the Soviet Union and of the conflict between Armenia and Azerbaijan over control of the territory of Nagorno-Karabakh.

"The decree is hasty and thoughtless," Russian deputy Vasily Travnikov told the Russian Information Agency (RIA). "Its realization may lead toward civil war . . . . We have our experience—the Baltics, Karabakh—and now we are making the same mistake."

But others see this as a crucial juncture in which Yeltsin must assert his authority more aggressively than Gorbachev.

"This is a test of Yeltsin's decisiveness and his consistency," argues political scientist Adranik Migranyan. "In order not to repeat Gorbachev he has to use force and use it decisively. Either Yeltsin does this or he faces a situation where Russia itself will disintegrate."

Under the structure created by the Bolshevik Revolution, the Russian republic is a federation including some 16 autonomous republics representing large national minorities and at least 15 other smaller, ethnically defined regions. The wave of nationalism among the republics has reached into those areas, such as Tatarstan, home of the Tatar minority, and it has influenced various Muslim peoples in the Caucasus, including the Chechen.

The challenge to Yeltsin's authority comes at a moment when the Russian government is poised to implement radical and unpopular economic reforms. A plan to free state-controlled prices and pursue rapid privatization will trigger 200 to 300 percent inflation rates, Russian officials admit.

Last week Yeltsin announced a reorganization of his government, naming economist Yegor Gaider, principal author of the reform plan, as deputy prime minister in charge of economy.

Mr. Gaider, speaking to the conference of the Democratic Rossiya movement over the weekend, said, "We are facing extremely complicated socioeconomic processes and we have already lost control over them."

Under these circumstances, Yeltsin's ability to consolidate his political power is crucial, comments Mr. Migranyan, who also attended the Democratic Rossiya meeting.

"In order to implement reforms, he must get governability," he says. "But to get governability, he must crush the irredentist movements at the level of republics and even regions."

The Chechen-Ingush case will not be an easy one to resolve. The independence movement is led by a former Air Force reserve general, Djakhan Dudayev, who won presidential elections last month organized by his own group.

The Russian parliament and government refused to accept the legitimacy of the vote, and an attempt at talks led by Russian Vice-President Alexander Rutskoi, an Army major-general, went nowhere. Russian officials such as parliament chairman Ruslan Khasbulatov, himself a Chechen, dismiss the movement as a "bunch of bandits."

General Dudayev's followers are armed with automatic weapons and claim to be able to mobilize a force of 60,000. The Chechen are famous for their guerrilla resistance to Russian rule in the early 19th century.

While the democratic movement has gingerly supported Yeltsin's reforms and even his request for greater executive authority, they are openly opposing the emergency decree.

"Everything should be done to exclude the use of force," Gen. Dmitry Volkogonov, a military historian and adviser to Yeltsin, told RIA, advocating instead further negotiations involving Dudayev and the local Chechen-Ingush administration. General Volkogonov echoed the feeling of many Russian parliamentarians in blaming Vice President Rutskoi, who drafted the emergency decree, for placing Yeltsin "in an awkward situation."

The Russian parliament resolution says the parliament will form a delegation to try to settle the conflict. It calls for moves to control the flow of weapons into the region. And it mandates a parliamentary investigation to determine the individuals responsible for making a decision they say was both politically and militarily unwise.

The resolution may give Yeltsin an opportunity to back away from the decree without losing too much face.

Former Communists Turn to Nationalism

Daniel Sneider

11/13/91

Before the aborted August putsch, the masthead of Pravda proudly carried the communist exhortation: "Workers of the world, unite!"

The slogan has been removed and the space left blank. But if it were replaced, it might read instead: "Russians unite!"

Russian nationalism, once condemned as the enemy of proletarian internationalism, is finding a comfortable home in the pages of the former Communist Party press these days. Both in print and in the activities of the communist faction in the Russian parliament, the remnants of the Soviet Communist Party are rapidly shedding the globalist revolutionary pretensions of Leninism in favor of an openly anti-Western, Russian nationalism.

Pravda, the paper founded by Vladimir Lenin in 1912, has taken a particularly nationalist tack in the last couple of weeks. The strongest signal of this shift was a front page article on Nov. 2 by Igor Shafarevich, a reknowned mathematician who caused a stir in early 1990 with the publication of a Russian nationalist—and some say, anti-Semitic—pamphlet entitled "Russophobia."

The collapse of the Soviet Union, which Pravda once regularly lamented, is no great tragedy, Mr. Shafarevich writes. "Coming to our senses after the first shock, we see that Russia in its new borders may become a more viable country, may stand more firmly on its feet than the former USSR," he argues. Russia's viability comes in large part from its ethnic homogeneity, he continues. Its population is 81 percent Russian. "Russia is now more ethnically homogeneous than Czechoslovakia, Belgium, Spain or Great Britain," he says.

"We have liberated ourselves from the yoke of 'internationalism,' and have returned to the normal existence of a national Russian state which traditionally includes many national minorities," Shafarevich writes. The problem now is to rid Russia of a narrow ruling elite of 'former' communists—he notes Soviet President Mikhail Gorbachev and Russian President Boris Yeltsin—who continue to "think in international terms."

After the country is liberated from these rulers and a new leadership with a nationalist orientation established, "one of the first acts should be the secession of Russia from the nonexistent USSR," Shafarevich concludes. He rejects even economic union as "a means of pumping resources out of a bleeding Russia."

The desire to restore "Great Russia" is not hidden in this tract. The article assails those who have abandoned the Russian minority in the Baltic states or want to "hand over the Kurile Islands" to Japan. Referring in passing to the Soviet-American alliance in promoting Middle East peace and in the Gulf war, Shafarevich attacks the current leadership for "attaching us to the American chariot and ruining our friendly relations with the Islamic world."

Svetlana Goryacheva, a Russian communist and former deputy chairman of the Russian parliament, expressed that anti-Western sentiment strongly in an interview published in the weekly Glasnost, formerly the publication of the Communist Party Central Committee. Mr. Yeltsin is surrounded by "people who idolize the capitalist way of development, who are sure there is a necessity for the Americanization of our state." The Americans are now dictating Russia's future and determining who "will be head of the union," she says.

But sooner or later the people will awake, Goryacheva predicts. "Genuine citizens and patriots will soon unite and save their multinational fatherland," she says in the interview published Nov. 7.

A clearly anti-Western vision of Russia also appeared in Pravda on Nov. 7 in an open letter from popular film director Nikita Mikhalkov, son of a famous Russian writer. Talk of Russia becoming a part of the "common European home," a favorite theme of Mr. Gorbachev's and Yeltsin's is "yet another enthusiastic delusion of our intelligensia," he writes.

"The Russian people, the people of the Russian world, are neither Europeans nor Asians," Mikhalkov says. "We had, we have, and I believe we will have, our own path—that of Eurasianism . . . . We are the people who remember their history, who love their land and for whom the Russian Orthodox Church was always a pillar."

"There is nothing strange in this combination of Russian nationalism and Russian communism," says political scientist Andranik Migranyan. The fall of the "central imperial structures" and the disappearance of "communist rhetoric" since the failed coup has removed the barriers between Russian communists and the rest of the nationalist movement, he says.

Indeed, since the coup the communist faction in the Russian parliament has been a strong backer of those of Yeltsin's policies which lead toward a strengthening of an independent Russian state. They supported Yeltsin's moves to strengthen the powers of the presidency in order to implement radical reforms.

But many see a cynical motive in the national communists' support: that they anticipate the failure of the economic reforms, the population's alienation from pro-market liberals, and the opportunity to inherit the structure of a strong state. This resurgence, some observers worry, could be accompanied by a Russian version of fascism.

"The emergence of a wide and strong block of Russian nationalist forces can help Yeltsin consolidate his power," says Migranyan. "But in the long run this can create a national socialist regime."

Rifts in Russia

Daniel Sneider

11/18/91

The Chechen and Ingush peoples of the northern Caucasus region of Russia learned by watching the larger republics that have broken away from the Soviet Union. In late October, they elected their own president—a fiery nationalist and ex-general named Djokhar Dudayev—and asserted their own independence.

Russian President Boris Yeltsin at first tried to crack down. He declared a state of emergency and dispatched a few thousand KGB troops toward the tiny breakaway "autonomous republic." That repulsed Mr. Yeltsin's liberal supporters in the Russian Parliament. They accused him of using the same heavy-handed tactics that caused so much trouble in the Baltics and in Georgia.

Their concerns were justified. Military action against the Chechen—a people known for tenacity in battle—could, as one member of Parliament put it, become "another Afghanistan." Beyond that, negotiations are much more in line with Yeltsin's professed principles. He recently attempted to mediate the snarled dispute between Armenia and Azerbaijan. Chechen-Ingush gives him a chance to apply diplomacy within his own huge, polyglot republic.

It's not clear, however, that Mr. Dudayev is open to talk. Still, an arrangement that would keep the little republic within the Russian federation while granting it expanded self-rule is logical. An independent Chechen-Ingush, with its 7,450 square miles (about the size of New Jersey) and 1.3 million people, has doubtful viability.

Russians are concerned that bigger, more centrally located chunks of their republic—notably

Tatarstan—might push for independence too. A negotiated political resolution to the Chechen-Ingush problem could be a warm-up for greater challenges just down the road.

All this arises as the Russian leader is attempting to implement radical economic reforms in the face of growing public discontent and the arrival of winter. Somehow the argument for free-market reform—that it holds the only hope of long-term prosperity—has to be effectively joined with the argument for continued federation.

This task could be a make-or-break test for Yeltsin and his reformist colleagues.

Individual Soviet Republics Wrangle With West Over Aid

Daniel Sneider

11/20/91

The Soviet Union is bankrupt, and the fractious state of the 12 former Soviet republics is frustrating Western creditors and aid donors.

Deputy finance ministers of the Group of Seven (G-7) leading industrial nations sat down Nov. 18 for three days of talks with representatives of the republics to try to settle the Soviet debt crisis. According to various reports, the G-7 arrived with a proposal to defer payments on the debt and to offer some new credits. But the package depends on the Soviet republics implementing a memorandum signed last month to take joint responsibility for the estimated $70 billion Soviet debt.

According to the independent Soviet news agency Interfax, 10 of the republics signed a further agreement Nov. 19 on collective responsibility. The Ukrainian representative signed with the condition that his signature be confirmed in a week. During that time the republics must define their exact shares of the debt and of Soviet assets.

Uzbekistan refused to sign the document at all, insisting that it would not take responsibility for other republics' share of the debt. The Uzbeks, who produce about a quarter of Soviet gold, say only three or four republics are capable of earning money to pay the debt. They also accused the G-7 of imposing unreasonable conditions on the republics.

"They want to resolve the question in the form of an ultimatum—first sign the memorandum and then we'll talk about credits," Uzbek Vice President Shukurulla Mirsaidov told Interfax.

"There is no ultimatum at all," Canadian Deputy Finance Minister David Dodge responded, according to a Reuters report.

The insistence on republican unity "is unrealistic," says the head of the Moscow office of one leading Western bank. If they stick to that condition and do not offer some new loans, "the G-7 is going to go home empty handed," the banker says. He warns that the State Bank for Foreign Trade, the bank which is the agreed central manager for debt payments, is already freezing accounts of foreign clients, blocking the transfer of money overseas.

"They're obviously running out of money," Mr. Dodge says.

"Deferral [of debt payments] is in everyone's best interest," US Ambassador Robert Strauss told US reporters Nov. 18. "Failing to defer is not going to increase the chances of getting payment—it's going to decrease it," he argued.

The situation has been complicated by the recent actions of the Russian government of Boris Yeltsin. As part of a radical reform policy, the Russians over the weekend issued a series of decrees including what amounts to a nationalization of Soviet gold and currency reserves as well as Russian oil production, which is 90 percent of the Soviet total. The Russian decrees effectively dismiss the Soviet State Bank and Ministry of Finance.

The Russians are seeking to protect their reforms as well as bid for inheritance of the collapsing union. In turn, Russia has offered the West security by stating recently that it will be willing to guarantee the debt of other republics as well. "Yeltsin's policy seems to be of dual purpose now—to support Mikhail Gorbachev's efforts to create a union of sovereign states and at the same time to revive Russia's economic might as soon as possible," the daily Komsomolskaya Pravda wrote Nov. 19.

Mr. Strauss, who saw Mr. Yeltsin Nov. 16, said the Russian leader "had a very healthy realism about the problems ahead of him. He knows he's bet his future . . . on control of these economic problems. He thinks if he can get some support from the West, he can weather the next six to eight difficult months."

Strauss expressed concern about the growing political mood of opposition to foreign aid in the United States.

"I know it's hard for the American people to realize it's a good investment of a modest amount of taxpayers' money," Strauss said. "We can come out of here in a few years with a modestly stable government and society that has the values we believe in in our country," he said, opening the door to "the greatest period of peace and prosperity we have ever seen."

The ambassador warned that failing to give aid poses far greater dangers. A tough winter could easily bring people into the streets, Strauss predicted. "Out of that kind of climate demagogues are made . . . . I'd rather risk a couple of billion bucks . . . than fail to risk it and end up . . . with a fascist-type situation out here."

Independent Ukraine May Seal Soviet Fate

Daniel Sneider

12/03/91

The voters of the Ukraine dealt a decisive blow to the Soviet Union on Sunday. In a large turnout, the Ukraine voted overwhelmingly for independence, rejecting last-minute appeals by Soviet President Mikhail Gorbachev to avert what he called a "disaster."

"No one gave him the right to say that," retorted Ukrainian leader Leonid Kravchuk, speaking to reporters after he voted. "Only the Ukrainian people can speak for the Ukraine."

The Ukrainian parliament chairman, who won a clear victory in the presidential election held simultaneously, expressed the hope that the West would quickly recognize the results of the referendum.

"I am convinced that all democratic states of the world must, without fail, recognize an independent Ukraine," Mr. Kravchuk said.

Without the Ukraine, the end of a unified Soviet state is unavoidable, agreed a Western diplomat based here. "The Ukraine is gone," the diplomat said on Sunday.

Washington appears ready to grant diplomatic recognition, particularly after the Ukraine gives a clear guarantee of its readiness to observe arms-control agreements, including the treaty to reduce Conventional Forces in Europe (CFE) and the Strategic Nuclear Arms Reduction Talks (START) treaty with the Soviet Union (US reaction, left). The Ukraine has nuclear-armed Soviet intercontinental ballistic missiles, which it has pledged to eliminate. Ukrainian officials have also stated plans to form their own army of up to 400,000 men.

Preliminary results released yesterday were undeniable. About 83 percent voted to approve the act of independence passed by the Ukrainian parliament in late August after the failed hard-line coup in Moscow. Some 83.7 percent of the Ukraine, 37.6 million voters, cast their ballots. The pro-independence vote held up across the Ukraine varying from a high of 95 percent in the nationalist stronghold in the west to a lower but still impressive 76.4 percent in the Russian-populated industrial areas of Donetsk in the east. Even in the Russian-populated Crimea, a slim 54 percent majority voted for independence.

The depth of pro-independence sentiment was striking even in a random sampling of rural polling places south of Kiev and at locales within the capital city. Not a single person could be found, from the conservative chairman of a collective farm to a Russian computer specialist in the city, who voted against independence.

"The Russian people want the Ukraine to stay with them," says Nadizhda Kulbachna, a worker at the Pridnieprovski collective farm. "But look at Lithuania and other Baltic states becoming independent. The Ukraine should be independent, too."

Vote for 'Free Ukraine'

Inside the two-story House of Culture in the town of Tripolye [literally "three fields"] the community leaders were equally unanimous. Soviet council chairman Dmitri Petrovich Strogi, dressed nattily in a wool overcoat and felt hat, opined that his people were casting their votes for a "free Ukraine." Mr. Strogi echoed the common view that the Ukraine, the second richest Soviet republic, known for its rich black-earth agriculture, would prosper on its own. "The Ukraine is an extremely rich republic," he said. "We are capable of being well off."

Many Ukrainians share the nationalists' view that their wealth has been siphoned off by a voracious "center." A flier printed by Rukh, the umbrella coalition of democratic and nationalist groups, proclaims, "Each year the Ukraine gives 18 to 20 percent of its national product to the empire."

This is self-evident to the nearly 900 inhabitants of the Lenin's Testament Kolkhoz collective farm, a poor settlement of wood-frame houses and cow sheds amid a sea of early winter mud. Their produce disappears and they get "empty rubles" from Moscow, Rukh pollwatcher Alexei Kisilov complains.

"Everybody knows this; everybody sees this," said mathematics teacher Vasili Mayevski, the head of the collective farms' election commission. "People are sick and tired of the union."

Many Ukrainians were dismayed by the opposition to their independence from both Mr. Gorbachev and Russian President Boris Yeltsin. "How can they speak about democracy, about a voluntary union, on one hand, and on the other hand not want to let the Ukraine go?" asked Yuri Kramer, an engineering student at a Kiev polytechnic institute. "I just don't understand them."

While some voices could be found in favor of continued economic union with the former Soviet republics, most Ukrainians believe they can meet their needs through direct ties to Russia and the other republics. "Maybe we need them and maybe they need us," Pridnieprovski collective farm chairman Anastas Lukyanetz says simply.

The independence referendum, even though its outcome was hardly in doubt, seemed to generate far more interest than the hotly contested six-way race for president, the first free choice of a Ukrainian leader. All the presidential candidates favor independence, a separate Ukrainian currency and army, as well as market-based reforms.

"People are more excited by the referendum," commented Anna Solanik, head of the election commission at Polling Place 20 in Kiev's Moscow region. "The president doesn't matter," the computer expert added.

Stable alternative

Kravchuk seemed to benefit most from this, offering himself as a more stable alternative among a range of nationalist choices.

Sources at Kravchuk's headquarters say he won a 62 percent majority. The runner-up, Rukh candidate Vyacheslav Chernovil, is a longtime anti-Communist, dissident who spent some 15 years in jail for his nationalist and democratic beliefs. Kravchuk is a former ideology chief of the Communist Party, who has proved adept at getting in front of the popular mood.

In the countryside, Kravchuk's moderate image made him the clear favorite. "Most people support him, " said Ekaterina Ivan-ova, a teacher in Tripolye who wouldn't give her last name. "He is reasonable; he is thoughtful."

In Kiev, Kravchuk is viewed with suspicion for his Communist past. "Kravchuk doesn't tell the truth; you can't trust him," said Army Pvt. Igor Lysak, a draftee soccer player serving in a "sports" unit. "He is 30 years in the [Communist] Party."

Still, even among sophisticated Kiev city dwellers, Kravchuk won 56 percent, compared to Chernovil's 26 percent. "He knows the Communist system better and he knows ways out of it," said Kiev student Kramer.

For Ukrainians, the first and most important step, independence, has been taken. Now, said welding instructor Yuri Barvinko at his Kiev polling station on Sunday, "We are waiting for Bush to congratulate us tomorrow."

Independent Ukraine Finds Allies in Russia, Foes in Moscow

Daniel Sneider

12/04/91

Russian President Boris Yeltsin's quick recognition of Ukrainian independence after a landslide referendum Dec. 1 was welcomed here.

While the Ukraine is ready to wave goodbye to any political or even economic union with former Soviet republics, it is eager to pursue direct ties with Russia and other republics.

"I believe we already have a union with Russia, a bilateral agreement, as well as with other republics," said newly elected Ukrainian President Leonid Kravchuk.

From Soviet President Mikhail Gorbachev on down, officials of the remaining central government in Moscow have greeted the Ukrainian independence vote far differently than the Russian government. Mr. Gorbachev expressed the clearly outdated hope that the Ukraine might still decide to sign a new treaty on political union, which he has been touting of late.

Ivan Silayev, chairman of the Interstate Economic Committee and effectively the Soviet prime minister, had a more threatening tone. In an interview with the French daily Figaro published Dec. 2, he warned that "if the Ukraine decides to break off ties with the economic union, we shall be building relations with it as a foreign state." This means trade will be based on world prices and payable in convertible currencies such as dollars. If a Ukrainian currency is created, it will not be accepted, he added.

"The Ukrainian economy is not ready for all these measures," Mr. Silayev warned. "The Ukraine will suffer heavy losses if it decides to isolate itself from other republics."

But a Russian government spokesman in Moscow said such statements did not reflect their views. "There can be no question of payments in freely convertible currency in trade between Russia and the Ukraine, because neither has that currency," Cabinet spokesman Alex Ulyukaev told the Monitor. An agreement on payments will be worked out, he added, predicting a calming of economic tensions.

The Ukrainian government has signed the treaty to form an economic community, but it has since made it clear in numerous statements that it interprets this document very narrowly. Vladimir Nauminko, a young economist who heads the president-elect's team of economic advisers, sees no need for an economic union at this point. Ukrainian needs can be met through bilateral agreements.

The only role for central institutions should be strategic forces and maintenance of infrastructure such as railways, pipelines, and communications, he says.

New Ukrainian currency

The Ukraine plans to introduce its own currency, the grivna, by May or June of next year. But it is far from clear how the Ukrainian economy will interact with the rest of the Soviet republics in the interim or even after that point.

During the past year, the Ukrainian government has tried to protect its internal market, barring a flow of food and consumer goods to other republics. Ukrainian citizens were given coupons for up to 70 percent of their salaries in an attempt to restrict the purchases from non-Ukrainians. But such steps have failed, as evidenced by severe shortages of goods such as butter, which collective farms have been selling to Russia or even Poland to fetch higher prices.

This problem is likely to become more acute when the Russian government moves ahead this month with a decree freeing almost all prices from state control. The Ukrainians do not plan to free their prices until after introduction of their own currency, says Mr. Nauminko, giving incentive for more goods to flow illegally across the porous border.

Mr. Kravchuk has been slow to formulate economic-reform plans, says economist Greta Bull, who heads a Harvard University project on economic reform in the Ukraine. "The Ukraine isn't acting, it's reacting," she says. "Russia is going to be the thing that pushes them to reform. The choice is to close off or go forward . . . . I think it will be impossible to close these borders off."

So far, however, the policy pursued by Premier Vitold Fokin has been a combination of isolationism and support for economic union. Mr. Fokin is closely identified with the old Communist-controlled state bureaucracy and criticized for his decision to sign the economic union treaty. He opposes radical reforms.

The group of people around Kravchuk's adviser, Nauminko, favors more rapid steps to a market economy. The core team of 27 people includes younger managers of state-run enterprises whose principal model for reform, by Nauminko's own description, is the "shock therapy" approach carried out in Poland.

The advisory team has prepared a package of decrees that were to be announced on Dec. 5, the day of Kravchuk's inauguration as president, Nauminko says. The decrees focus on creating a mechanism for privatization, though not of land, which remains a touchy issue in the Ukraine. Price liberalization, freeing of trade, and the beginning of a three-to-four-year process toward internal convertibility will follow the currency introduction.

Spiraling inflation

The rapidly declining value of the ruble, as inflation spirals in Russia, is a major concern in both Russia and the Ukraine. For the Russians, the fear is that the introduction of separate currencies will bring a flood of rubles back into Russia, seeking goods and pushing inflation even higher. The Ukrainians want to get rid of the huge amount of rubles in their hands—about 180 billion to 190 billion according to Nauminko—fearing that when these are exchanged, the value of the new currency will be driven down.

The Ukraine, a country of 53 million with rich agricultural and mineral resources, will try to shift its trade away from the former Soviet republics to the West. This will be difficult, as evidenced by the problems faced by Poland and other Eastern European economies whose integration with the Soviet economy is even less than that of the Ukraine. But though the transition may be difficult, "they are better off outside of the union," says Ms. Bull. "If the Ukraine adopts the right economic policies . . . they could do very well in the long-run. In three to four years I would be pleased if the Ukraine is where Poland is now."

US, Europe Take Cautious Steps Toward the Ukraine

Linda Feldmann

12/05/91

The United States and Europe, each in their own way, are setting down markers for their acceptance of the Ukraine as Europe's newest independent nation.

All agree that the Ukraine must demonstrate its good faith on international arms control agreements, human rights, and reform toward a market economy. But the approaches part company over the timing of formal diplomatic recognition of the republic, whose population voted overwhelmingly Sunday to secede from the Soviet Union.

The US has dangled the carrot of imminent recognition in front of the Ukraine in an effort to shape events to the US's liking. European nations have also stated what they expect of the Ukraine, but are demonstrating much more reserve when it comes to recognition.

A ranking Bush administration official on European affairs suggests that the European Community's inability to help solve Yugoslavia's crisis has given the EC cold feet about getting involved in the breakup of another country, the Soviet Union.

In addition, the official says, "some of the thinking is based on historical worries about what happens when an empire breaks up," especially in close geographical proximity.

And where the EC is concerned, because 12 countries must come together on a policy, there's a tendency toward "least-common-denominator decisionmaking," which results in a fairly moderate position, he says.

Several countries, including Canada, Hungary, and Poland, have already recognized the Ukraine, as has the Russian Republic. Those that neighbor the Ukraine have explicitly recognized the current borders, addressing concerns that old territorial questions may be revisited now that the Ukraine has declared independence.

Meanwhile, the US-European military alliance, NATO, reasserted the need for assurances from the Ukraine that the Soviet nuclear weapons on its territory will remain under a unified Soviet command. The Ukraine has 176 ballistic missiles and one-third of the Soviet Union's tactical nuclear weapons.

After Tuesday's NATO meeting, Secretary-General Manfred Woerner stated four points NATO was asking the Ukraine to adhere to:

* Settle its relationship with the central Soviet government and with the Soviet republics peacefully.

* Comply with the Nuclear Nonproliferation Treaty.

* Comply with arms control treaties signed by the Soviet Union.

* Carry out other international accords to which the Soviet Union is a signatory, including the Conference on Security and Cooperation in Europe. That requires, among other things, a respect for the human rights of resident minorities.

The Ukraine's president-elect, Leonid Kravchuk, has stated that Soviet nuclear weapons will fall under the collective control of the four republics that house them: the Ukraine, Russia, Byelorussia, and Kazakhstan. He also promised that the Ukraine will comply with all international treaties signed by the Soviet Union, including the Strategic Arms Reduction Treaty and the Conventional Forces in Europe treaty.

But it remains unclear whether the West will ask the Ukraine to sign those accords.

This week a senior US diplomat, Assistant Secretary of State for European Affairs Thomas Niles, will visit the Ukraine for discussions with leaders about this and the other areas of US concern. Secretary of State James Baker III will follow in mid-December with visits to both Moscow and Kiev, with a stop afterwards in Brussels Dec. 19 for a meeting of the NATO foreign ministers.

In Kiev, Foreign Minister Anatoly Zlenko made special note of the fact that President Bush's congratulatory phone call to Mr. Kravchuk on Tuesday was the first from any Western leader.

Ukrainian-American leaders say Washington's leading role in welcoming the Ukraine into the free world is in part an attempt to make up for its delay in fully recognizing the three Baltic nations after the Soviet coup attempt in August.

But administration officials say the political dynamic in Moscow has changed greatly since then, and thus the two situations cannot be compared. Right after the coup, Moscow continued to function fully as the central government of the Soviet Union.

Now, with many of the republics taking their affairs into their own hands, and with the Russian Republic controlling the nation's purse strings, the notion of Moscow as a central coordinating point is vanishing.

Before, the Bush administration's impulse was to favor the center. Now, it realizes the old Soviet Union no longer exists, and the center is gone. Its aim is to shape developments as much to its liking as it can.

Slavic Leaders Will Present Gorbachev With Plan for Future

Daniel Sneider

12/09/91

The Soviet Union and its once-powerful central institutions are on the verge of disappearing. In their place a "commonwealth" of states is emerging, with an alliance of the three Slavic republics of Russia, the Ukraine, and Byelorussia at its core.

The leaders of those states met for two days over the weekend in a dacha outside of the Byelorussian city of Brest to work out a formula for their future ties. Today the Slavic leaders will present what amounts to a fait accompli to Soviet President Mikhail Gorbachev at a meeting in the Kremlin, also to be attended by the president of Kazakhstan. More than half of Kazakhstan is inhabited by people of Slavic origin.

These developments were precipitated by the 90 percent majority vote for independence Ukrainians cast in a referendum Dec. 1. That vote effectively ended the last hopes for a renewed political union among the 12 republics of the former Soviet Union. Nevertheless, Mr. Gorbachev renewed appeals for union last week, railing against "isolationists and separatists." He predicted war and economic chaos if those appeals are not met.

Gorbachev has been echoed by aides such as Foreign Minister Eduard Shevardnadze, as well as by St. Petersburg Mayor Anatoli Sobchak. They warn of an impending coup by military-led hard-liners, feeding off social tensions as the hard winter sets in. The coup rumors were further fed by the sudden dismissal over the weekend of Soviet Chief of the General Staff Vladimir Lobov, a move prompted, informed analysts say, by his increasingly open opposition to military reform.

While such ominous visions are not easily dismissed, many observers see such talk as the last attempts of a dying center to preserve its role. Some say the new commonwealth is likely to exclude any future for Gorbachev. Last week, the daily Izvestia accused the president of living in a "world of illusions" in resisting the new political realities.

"Everyone knows in their hearts that this union is already doomed," Ukrainian President Leonid Kravchuk said on arrival in the Byelorussian capital of Minsk.

"The republics have refused to voluntarily delegate to the center the powers which it has demanded of them," Russian President Boris Yeltsin told the Byelorussian parliament on Saturday. "Today we see the failure of the idea of a half-federation, half-confederation which would bind each state implicitly under a system of dual power."

In a clear warning to Gorbachev, Mr. Yeltsin added that "the main thing is not to demand the impossible from each other at this point. If we do otherwise, any treaty, however correct, may turn into just a piece of paper."

In the weekend talks, Yeltsin aimed to find common ground with the Ukraine, the second most wealthy and populous Soviet republic without whose participation, Yeltsin has said, any form of union is impossible.

From a variety of preliminary reports before conclusion of their talks yesterday, the new formula will throw out any form of political union. In its place will be a set of economic agreements under the broad umbrella of the treaty to form an economic community signed by 10 of the 12 republics (but still not ratified). It deals with common policies on prices, taxation, customs, debt, banking, and currencies.

"I can imagine a military-political agreement being added to the economic agreement, covering the Army, [and] strategic weapons," says Ivan Silayev, the head of the Inter-state Economic Committee. After several days of talks among senior republican officials, he announced agreement on a few key issues, including joint responsibility for the Soviet Union's foreign debt, management of pension and other social welfare funds, and ceilings on prices in inter-republican trade for some key basic goods such as food and energy products.

The first key test of economic cooperation is the Russian plan to free most prices from state control beginning Dec. 16. The price liberalization is a cornerstone of Russia's radical reform plans. But republics have urged the move be delayed, arguing it will trigger massive inflation and that too few bank notes will be available to meet the anticipated price rises.

While Yeltsin has shown some flexibility on the timing of price reforms, he also made it clear that Russia will not back off from its plans. "The practice of mending holes has outlived its usefulness," he said in his speech in Minsk. He argued against the idea that any republic "can fence itself off from these economic troubles."

"The crisis spares no one, and the sooner we go over to joint actions, the less painful the reform will be," he said.

The need to reform military ties among the republics was a factor behind the removal of General Lobov, who wrote a long article in the Army daily Red Star on Nov. 28 insisting on centralized armed forces and attacking "national egoism in the sphere of defense."

His ouster was "first of all a decision made by Yeltsin, and for Gorbachev it was easy to agree," says Sergei Blagovolin, president of the independent Institute of National Security and Strategic Studies.

The key military problem is joint control over the long- and short-range nuclear-armed missiles that are stationed in the three Slavic republics and Kazakhstan. Russian Deputy Defense Minister Alexander Tsalko said that in talks with Ukrainian officials in Moscow last week, the Ukraine said it wanted control of the weapons based on its territory.

"For them it is possible insurance against a threat from Russia," says Mr. Blagovolin. "It is nonsense. Russia is not in a position to threaten anybody except itself."

Soviet Breakup Sharpens Doubts Over Arms Control

Daniel Sneider/Peter Grier

12/10/91

In a deadpan declaration, apparently devoid of the emotions of the historic moment, the three Slavic republics of Russia, Byelorussia, and the Ukraine wiped away the Soviet Union on Sunday.

"We . . . state that the USSR is ceasing its existence as a subject of international law and a geopolitical reality," the leaders of the three states declared.

But the disappearance of the Soviet Union does not mean the end to its most powerful attribute as a superpower—the tens of thousands of nuclear warheads mounted on missiles, on artillery shells, and on aircraft across the vast territory of the former Union. Those nuclear weapons are now deployed on the territory of the three Slavic republics and the republic of Kazakhstan.

For both the leaders of the former Soviet Union and the world, the breakup of the country stirs terrifying visions of the emergence of multiple nuclear-armed states, and even potential use of those weapons in conflicts among them.

In Washington, US officials said that one of their main concerns regarding the new Slavic commonwealth was stable control of the former USSR's nuclear arsenal.

"We really do run the risk of seeing a situation created there not unlike what we've seen in Yugoslavia, with nukes—with nuclear weapons thrown in," US Secretary of State James Baker III said in a Sunday television interview. "That could be an extraordinarily dangerous situation for Europe and for the rest of the world and indeed for the United States," he added.

Thus Mr. Baker, when he travels to the former Soviet Union next Sunday, will urge that all Soviet nuclear arms be withdrawn to Russian soil for safekeeping. Many Soviet nuclear arms are to be dismantled under arms control agreements already signed with the US, and under the unilateral proposals exchanged by President Bush and Mikhail Gorbachev earlier this year. Baker is expected to urge breakaway Soviet republics to pledge adherence to all arms pacts reached by the former central government.

Both the Ukraine and Kazakhstan have stated their intention to become non-nuclear states. But both have also balked at the suggestion from Russia that nuclear weapons be sent back to their territory, arguing that the weapons should remain and be destroyed only on their own territory.

The joint declaration pledges that the members of the new "Commonwealth of Independent States" will "respect each other's desire to attain the status of a nuclear-free zone and a neutral state. They have decided to preserve the joint command over the common military-strategic space and the single nuclear arms controlling body."

The pledge is aimed at reassuring the West of continued control of the nuclear weapons. But Soviet military specialists question how a joint command can exist without central political institution.

"Without a central government it is impossible to have centralized control over nuclear weapons," says Sergei Blagovolin, president of the Moscow-based Institute of National Security and Strategic Studies. "It's a fairy tale and nothing more."

The bulk of Soviet nuclear weapons are currently on Russian soil but a considerable number are placed in the other three former republics.

Official data revealed on Nov. 2 in the Nezavisimaya Gazeta (Independent Newspaper) shows that intercontinental ballistic missiles (ICBMs) are widely dispersed: 4,278 warheads are located in Russia, 1,240 in the Ukraine, 1,040 in Kazakhstan and 54 (all mobile SS-25s) in Byelorussia. Air-launched cruise missiles are also widely distributed, with 367 warheads in Russia, 168 in Ukraine and 320 in Kazakhstan.

In addition to these strategic weapons, thousands of tactical nuclear warheads mounted on artillery shells, in short-range missiles, and on bombs to be dropped by aircraft are in the Ukraine. Mr. Gorbachev has pledged to unilaterally destroy all such weapons.

Ukrainian defense officials recently told their Russian counterparts that they will seek joint command over tactical as well as strategic weapons.

The former Soviet government, including the military, may no longer be able to control the process of dispersion of nuclear weapons, some in Moscow fear. Gorbachev government officials are looking to the West to link recognition of the independence of the Ukraine and Byelorussia, as well as prospects for economic aid and participation in international organizations, to their fulfillment of the strategic arms treaty and the pledge to destroy tactical weapons, preferably under international supervision.

At talks held in Washington recently between Soviet and US officials, the main topic was "to maintain strategic stability in a situation of disintegration of the union and fragmentation of our military structures," says Blagovolin, a participant in those discussions.

"Only a very strong and very definite pressure from the US, from NATO countries, from the European Community will help us escape from this situation," he said.

Slav Confederation Narrows Soviet Leadership's Options

Daniel Sneider

12/11/91

The dramatic declaration of the end of the Soviet Union by the leaders of its three Slavic republics and its replacement by a new commonwealth has provoked a deep political crisis here.

Opinions are sharply divided over the wisdom and legality of the statements issued after the Slavic summit on Dec. 8. For Soviet President Mikhail Gorbachev, the almost casual dismissal of the tattered remains of his central government is "illegal and dangerous" and "can only boost chaos and anarchy in society."

For the Russian leadership, the treaty between Russia, Byelorussia, and the Ukraine is "the only, and quite possibly the last, chance to avoid what has happened in Yugoslavia," as Russian Foreign Minister Andrei Kozyrev told reporters on Dec. 10.

The Russians argue that this was the only realistic basis for retaining links with the Ukraine, whose population voted overwhelmingly for independence Dec. 1 (Slavic confederation, Page 4).

Mr. Gorbachev, who has vowed to fight the new treaty, has persistently refused to accept the results of the Ukrainian referendum, just as he doggedly resisted the desire of the three Baltic states for independence. In a Ukrainian television interview on Dec. 8, he reiterated his argument that the voters had not rejected continued political union. In Gorbachev's mind, independence and union can coexist.

"Mikhail Sergeivich [Gorbachev] has lost his bearings as to what is going on in this country," said Byelorussian leader Stanislav Shushkevich. "His assessment of the outcome of the referendum in Ukraine was ridiculous. The change in public opinion in Byelorussia is the same as in Ukraine—it is impossible to ingore it."

In some respects, Gorbachev's insistence that union and sovereignty are the same thing has pushed the relatively moderate Ukrainian leadership of President Leonid Kravchuk to hold out for a structure in which there is virtually no trace of a central administration.

"We should not be blamed for breaking up the union," Mr. Kravchuk told reporters, clearly in response to Gorbachev's TV interview. "We were against only one factor—to have a state to govern us. Ukraine has always called for integration. Today, using their constitutional rights, the three states showed an example of integration, which is similar to the forms existing in Europe."

Gorbachev's resistance has angered some in the Russian camp; they accuse the Soviet leader of trying to maintain the old centralized state and his own personal role.

"Attempts to protect one's own interests at any cost are typical of the regime that ruled for 70 years," Mr. Kozyrev said.

Gorbachev's aide, Georgy Shakhnazarov, said Gorbachev would resign if the commonwealth treaty is allowed to stand. Russian leader Yeltsin tried to mollify Gorbachev in his meeting on Dec. 9 by hinting that he might retain some undefined role in the new commonwealth.

In a statement following this meeting, Gorbachev challenged the legal authority of the three Slavic leaders to dissolve the Soviet Union.

"The speed with which the document appeared is baffling," he said. "It was not discussed either by the citizens or the parliaments of the republics on behalf of which it was signed." The Soviet leader tried to treat the commonwealth treaty as an alternative draft to his own version of a political union treaty and called on republican legislatures to consider them both.

In somewhat more threatening terms, Gorbachev said it is necessary to convene a Congress of Soviet Peoples' Deputies, the supreme legislature of the former Union, or perhaps even call a nationwide plebiscite on the issue.

While the leaders of the Slavic republics are clearly trying to avoid a confrontation with Gorbachev, they have firmly rejected such ideas. As for another referendum, Ukrainian leader Kravchuk told reporters on Dec. 9 that "we are an independent country, and we wouldn't hold it."

"The Congress of Peoples' Deputies as a supreme governmental authority cannot be considered legal in these conditions," responded Sergei Shakrai, legal counsellor of the Russian government. "Attempts to convene this body and pass decisions would have to be considered unconstitutional. What we have is an attempt at confrontation."

Leaders from all three Slavic republics have made it clear that the majority of their representatives to this body, which ceased an active role after the failed coup last August, would refuse to attend any such session.

Mr. Shakrai argues that the three Slavic republics have a legal basis for dissolving the Soviet Union, as they are the original signatories of the 1922 Treaty of Union.

The only other signatory at that time, the Trans-Caucuses republic, no longer exists in that form, having been broken up into three separate republics.

The leaders of the three republics have the authority to do this, Kozyrev argued, by virtue of their own democratic elections. "The true will of the people was expressed in popular, democratic elections. They were relying on a clear mandate," he said.

Still, it is clear that Gorbachev and his close aides are preparing to launch an open political struggle against the pact. The meeting on Dec. 9 between Yeltsin, Gorbachev, and Kazakhstan President Nursultan Nazarbayev was apparently a tense one. Gorbachev and Mr. Nazarbayev spent 80 minutes listening to Yeltsin's explanation and arguing with him.

Nazarbayev made it clear in a press conference afterward that he was miffed that he was left out of the process.

His position is a difficult one. He is the head of a republic whose national population of Kazakhs is a minority, with Russians, Ukrainians, and other nationalities making up the majority. Nazarbayev, who is one of the more effective and popular republican leaders, has been a strong backer of continued union.

"It was a big mistake not to invite Nazarbayev," comments Russian parliamentarian Alexander Domrin, a member of the foreign relations committee.

"After all, Kazakhstan possesses nuclear weapons," he adds referring to the Soviet long-range nuclear missiles based in the vast territory of the republic.

There are fears that the Kazakhs could be pushed into the arms of the four Central Asian republics, whose lack of a role in the new commonwealth may be pushing them under the influence of neighboring Islamic states such as Iran.

"In the longer term, there could be the alienation of the Central Asian republics and this could be very dangerous for our security," says Mr. Domrin.

The leaders of the new commonwealth have stated, however, that the grouping is open to all participants—not only the former Soviet republics but possibly even former members of the Comecon economic pact, such as Bulgaria and Romania, as well as the now independent Baltic states.

New Slav Commonwealth Presses Economic Reform

Daniel Sneider

12/11/91

The formation of a new commonwealth by the three Slavic republics of the former Soviet Union has added a new element of uncertainty to an already highly unstable economic crisis.

The Russian government of Boris Yeltsin is on the verge of implementing sweeping radical reforms, originally set to begin Dec. 16 with a liberalization of almost all prices from state control. Until now, the Russian government has resisted all entreaties from other republics to delay or even indefinitely postpone this move, which will affect all of them.

But the agreement reached Dec. 8 in a dacha near the Byelorussian border with Poland commits Russia to coordinating its economic policies with the other members of the new Commonwealth of Independent States. That means postponing the price liberalization until Jan. 2, Russian Deputy Premier Yegor Gaidar told Russian television Dec. 9.

"It was a very difficult decision to make," Mr. Gaidar said, "but it will be compensated for by coordinated actions. That means we will be able to avoid conflicts that would arise if Russia alone had liberalized prices."

But Byelorussian leader Stanislav Shushkevich said on republican television that his republic would carry out price liberalization "step by step" and not necessarily at the same time as Russia, according to a Nega news agency report.

'Danger of public unrest'

Some observers worry that delays could endanger the success of price liberalization and other radical steps. "Yeltsin sacrificed his reform to preserve the political union," comments Russian Information Agency editor in chief Igor Sedykh. "This two-weeks' delay in liberalization of prices strengthens the danger of public unrest because prices are going up already, but it is not organized; it is wild liberalization."

Gaidar argues that the statement of Byelorussia, Russia, and the Ukraine on coordinating their economic policies contains some positive elements of compromise on a number of issues. It commits the three founding members of the commonwealth to pursue "coordinated radical economic reforms aimed at creating effective market mechanisms, transforming ownership relations, and ensuring free enterprises."

Most importantly, the ruble will continue to function as the common currency of the group, particularly for settling accounts between members. The agreement allows for introducing national currency "on the basis of special agreements, guaranteeing respect for the economic interests of the parties."

The Ukraine planned to introduce its own currency in mid-1992, but according to Mr. Shushkevich the three agreed not to take such a step until the end of the year. This is intended to allow time for the radical reforms to take effect and for the economy to stabilize after the expected inflationary surge of prices.

"The main reason the agreement was signed was because Russia had to take measures against the economic intervention of the Ukraine," says Russian parliamentarian Alexander Domrin, a member of the Committee on International Economic relations.

"The Ukraine has huge amounts of rubles, and they could be used against Russia," he explains, expressing a widespread fear that Ukrainians seeking goods would flood Russia with rubles, spurring hyperinflation.

Gaidar says the currency decision will be especially welcome to the Group of Seven leading industrial nations (G-7), whose economic assistance is considered crucial to the success of the Russian reforms. He expresses hope that it will "accelerate the financial aid of the G-7," perhaps leading to the creation of a stabilization fund to back the value of the ruble as it becomes freely convertible into other currencies, a key part of the reform package.

The Dec. 8 statement provides for joint steps to control inflation through monetary and budget austerity, including an inter-bank agreement to curtail the printing of money and policy coordination to limit budget deficits. It also moves toward a common approach to taxes, particularly regarding value-added tax rates. The Russian government has already decided to enact a high 28 percent value-added tax, intended as its main means of revenue, along with a new, graduated, personal income tax.

Trade at world prices

The commonwealth agreement seems to set up a common single market as well. It calls for coordinating signatories' external economic and customs policies and ensuring "freedom of transit" between member states. Trade between the states, although denominated in rubles, will switch to world market prices, Gaidar said.

The new pact eliminates virtually all the central economic institutions, including the huge industrial ministries. There will be no single budget among the countries in the commonwealth with the sole exception of a defense budget, explained Gaidar. Within 10 days, the three members are to decide on a 1992 budget for their combined armed forces, which are provided for in the political statement.

But what is far from clear is the fate of the broader economic community formed by a treaty in October, of which all the three Slavic states along with seven other former Soviet republics are signatories. That treaty formed an inter-state economic committee, currently headed by former Russian Premier Ivan Silayev, which is to coordinate economic policies and manage the economy.

"It is not clear what this stucture is and what it is doing," Russian Deputy Premier Gennady Burbulis told reporters Dec. 10. Some aspects of its operation, such as a banking union, may be preserved, he said, but a meeting of republican officials Dec. 13 will decide the fate of the broader structure.

Reformers Face Task of Overhauling Ruined Economy

Amy Kaslow

12/16/91

Despite the unending flux in the former Soviet republics, one constant remains—the pressing need for economic reform.

Goods and services must be restored to a deprived people on the brink of disaster.

But communism's demise has so far brought only increased hardship without any sudden rise of capitalism. Even as Mikhail Gorbachev's failure to halt the economic slide led to the shift in power to the republics, reformers there have also been reluctant to take the bold measures needed for fear of political consequences. They have yet to lift subsidies, close money-losing state industries, impose price hikes, and tighten fiscal policies to end free entitlements—from transportation to health care—that burden government budgets.

United States Central Intelligence Agency Director Robert Gates, a longtime Soviet watcher, worries that "the enormous economic and social challenges facing most of these new democratic forces may overwhelm them."

Indeed, public patience has snapped for reforms that, since perestroika's introduction in 1985, have done little more than disrupt daily life with food and fuel shortages, suspension of social services, and unemployment.

In the midst of instability, the question remains whether the republics can move quickly enough to stave off total economic collapse. While ethnic and nationalist conflicts flare up and the armed forces are restless, Soviet centrists such as President Gorbachev and Soviet Foreign Minister Eduard Schevardnadze say such a collapse might come in the difficult winter ahead.

Mr. Gates echoes an oft-expressed fear in Moscow that coming hardships "could produce a return to authoritarian government, whether led by reformers desperate to feed the people and stave off an explosion or by nationalists driven by a xenophobic, atavistic vision of Russia."

The reform challenge is complicated by breakup of the centralized state into independent republics and the new Commonwealth of Independent States.

The main hope for reform rests with Russian President Boris Yeltsin, the leader of the largest, richest, and most populous republic. The former boss of the industrial city of Sverdlovsk has long been accused of doing little on the economic front, falling back instead on populist rhetoric.

But Mr. Yeltsin has finally embarked on a radical reform program drawing praise from foreign analysts.

"They're working at an extraordinary pace now, but it's hard to see, because it's behind closed doors," says Anders Aslund, director of the Stockholm Institute for Soviet and East European Economics, who was in Moscow last week to discuss reform prospects and progress with Yeltsin and his chief economic advisor, Yegor Gaidar. "Clearly, the Russian reforms are all-out liberal," adds Mr. Aslund, who warned that Yeltsin's previous go-slow approach was perilous.

Mr. Gaidar acknowledges the program is full of political risks, as unemployment, soaring prices, and housing shortages set in. He has said publicly that it will be tough to sustain support for these "very unpopular" measures.

Plans to privatize huge state monopolies and to make the near-worthless ruble convertible—essential early steps in reform—are still on the back burner. Last week Russia postponed until Jan. 2 its first tough action on reforms—the plan to lift price controls.

Other republics have embarked on uneven reforms, and half-way measures have created more problems than they have cured. The most pervasive problem across the former Soviet empire is that, as privatization gets under way, former Communist bureaucrats are commercializing state property for their own gain.

In the Ukraine, for example, local leaders have emphasized privatization. Selling off state assets to the emerging private sector ideally releases the government of its costly obligation to shore up inefficient industry, reduces the budget deficit with proceeds from sales, and helps establish a market economy.

While over 1,500 such companies have been formed in the Ukraine, state assets—from machinery to plants—have been purchased by former Communist officials who are relatively well-off and, given their close connections to the state enterprises, well-poised to pay very low prices. Aslund says the line between what's fair and what's embezzlement has not been drawn. Prices are still fixed and far from being determined by the market.

Kazakhstan, the largest of the Central Asian republics, is busy establishing private property laws. It is among the richest of the republics in raw materials, with enormous potential for economic growth if local and foreign investments can be stimulated. While the republic's leaders clearly recognize that private property is the seed from which capitalism grows, they are at best "enlightened despots," says Aslund, an advisor to republican economic planners.

As the Central Asian republics now intend to join the new Commonwealth of Independent States, most republics will need to press for key reforms: price liberalization, a revamped distribution system, a new legal framework for a market economy, financial institutions that can help pay for reforms, and a social safety net to catch the millions of workers that will be displaced by plant and farm closures.

Conversion of the vast Soviet military-industrial complex—which has accounted for more than 25 percent of economic activity—is a top priority. Huge investments are needed from local and foreign investors to help shift defense production to the manufacture of consumer goods.

State resources are also needed for transportation and communication networks and to provide credit for a fledgling private sector to purchase plants and equipment.

Distribution

Under Gossnab, the centralized Soviet system that supplied farms and factories from a Moscow command center, state subsidies depressed prices and made everything affordable. Because the government had standing orders and set quotas for output and distribution, agricultural and industrial producers worried only about the quantity of their work, not about its efficiency or quality.

Now this system has virtually collapsed. Enterprises no longer enjoy a ready source of raw materials or parts, nor do they have a ready recipient for what they produce. Enterprises, farms, and families scramble for supplies. Aside from mostly barren state shops, people trade in black markets and in a form of barter based largely on access to "surplus" or pilfered supplies from state enterprises. The enterprises themselves are also resorting to barter, trading cars for tons of wheat, sometimes directly or through the network of exchanges that has sprung up around the former Union. Hoarding goods to trade has become a priority.

Kiev Train Station in Moscow, for example, is teeming with residents and travelers who have come to claim parcels sent from the Ukraine on the overnight train. Enterprising Russians try to capitalize on the relative availability of goods in the Ukraine by arranging for large train deliveries and then selling the goods at inflated prices in Moscow.

Economists say the best way to ensure a flow of goods to market is to free prices. Suppliers would then be confident of fetching competitive prices even as inflation climbs by almost three percent a week.

Until production and purchasing power increase, deregulation of prices is painful. The Russian plan to lift controls in early January would push up the cost of basic consumer goods by as much as 500 percent.

Legal framework

Laws must be enacted and enforced to nurture a market economy, and protect it from price gauging and bribery. Local and foreign investors lament that they operate in a very-high-risk environment, devoid of a court system in which judgments are steadfast. The sale of property is largely in limbo, because republican and central authorities have yet to decide who owns what—from land to industrial centers.

Ivan Silayev, chairman of the Interstate Economic Committee, reminds prospective foreign investors that "not long ago, it was a crime to even speak about ownership of private property."

Now, roughly 500,000 independent businesses and farms have begun operations in the former Soviet Union.

Local and foreign investors complain that paying off any number of officials on the central, republic and enterprise level is built into the cost of transacting business in the Soviet arena. "When deals go sour, it's usually because the Soviets have their palms extended," says the head of international investments for a large Italian engineering firm.

Laws supporting private ownership, sales and profits, taxes and customs, often have been passed on one level—central, republican, or municipal—but rescinded on another.

A Washington banker in the early stages of deals in several republics says, "You have to negotiate on many levels.... It's important to negotiate with leaders who are in and on the way up, not with those who are in and on the way out. And it's often hard to tell who's who."

The investors repeat a constant refrain when assessing prospects for large-scale investment in Russia and other republics. Until ownership rights are secured, price controls are completely lifted, and state enterprises are disbanded, they say, little foreign capital will flow.

Banking

A legal framework must also help regulate commercial banking, which is developing to service the private sector.

"Banking is a very important element in the economic reform process," says Jay Mitchell, an economist with PlanEcon, Inc., a Washington-based advisory firm specializing in Soviet and East European economies.

"Freeing prices and lifting subsidies are important, but if credit is not available, the reforms will stagnate because the private sector won't develop. Unless you provide new companies with needed financing, they will go under," he says.

"And because a legal framework has not been fully put into place, today's environment is dangerous for the banks that do exist. It encourages corruption, principally by those who have access to power and [state] accounts. The people who have access to power are operating in a vacuum, until laws are passed to regulate the banking system."

"Commercial banks are popping up," says Aslund, "but they are run by the nomenklatura, who know ways to put state money into private pockets."

Moscow Mayor Gavriil Popov's recent move to award Moscow residents ownership of their apartments without payment is a way of providing individuals with collateral. Measures like this could have a long-term impact on Moscow's coffers. When that collateral turns into the ability to invest in new businesses, the city will have a new tax base.

Local and republican budgets are bankrupt. Many, but not all, of the republics have agreed to repay the former Union's foreign debt. (Soviet estimates now put it near $100 billion.) Negotiations among the republics have apportioned debt according to the republics' respective contributions to the Soviet Gross National Product. But no matter how exact the debt allocation may be, it is unlikely that it will all be repayed. Domestic priorities prevail.

Pensioners, the poor, and those whose wages cannot keep up with raging inflation also will need state assistance. But there is nothing to sustain this "explosion of social expenditures," says Aslund. State revenues have collapsed. Enterprises are anxious to manage their own finances rather than submit to municipal accounts.

And a breakdown in export earnings—ranging from drastically reduced oil production to a virtual cutoff of trade with former Comecon partners—has dried up official coffers. Without money, the reform process is powerless.

The world's richest countries have been prepared to offer little more than stop-gap assistance to get the Soviets through the winter and prevent default on what they owe the West. The US has called an international conference to discuss what all countries can do to help.

Reforms will exact a high price from Soviets already under duress. St. Petersburg Mayor Anatoli Sobchak warns, "If we cannot feed the people, then as the Russian saying goes, 'We will lose our head if people are brought to the brink where they are not able to feed their family, no words about the necessity of reform will persuade them."

Politicians have trouble seeing past day-to-day worries to take steps to revitalize the economy. Until they do, moves toward a market economy will be haphazard, says Aslund. By now, he says, current social tensions should have demonstrated to republic leaders that they don't have the luxury of gradualism.

Grandson of Bolshevik Hero Masterminds Market-Style Economic Reforms in Russia

Daniel Sneider

12/16/91

Every Soviet schoolchild grew up with the inspiring tales of Arkady Gaidar, a hero of the Bolshevik Revolution at the age of 14, later a writer of children's books. His most famous work, "Timur and His Team," chronicles the exploits of a group of boys who perform heroic and selfless deeds for the sake of the revolution. The book was modeled on his own son, Timur, now an admiral in the Soviet Navy.

Today Arkady's grandson, Yegor Gaidar, is also engaged in a "heroic" task—the dismantling of the communist system. The young economist is the author of the radical reform plans of the Russian government of Boris Yeltsin, designed to rapidly shift Russia to a market economy. The smiling, round-faced former economics editor of the Communist Party newspaper Pravda was recently appointed deputy prime minister for economics and finance, in effect Mr. Yeltsin's economic czar.

Early in November Yeltsin unveiled the reform plans, which together constitute a Russian version of the "shock therapy" reform in neighboring Poland.

As in Poland, the Russians will free prices from state control, except for a handful of basic foods and fuels, allow enterprises to trade freely with other countries, let the ruble's value be determined solely by the market and take the first steps to make it freely convertible into other currencies. Price liberalization is now set to start on Jan. 2, in coordination with other former Soviet republics now grouped in the Commonwealth of Independent States.

The most widespread criticism of Mr. Gaidar's approach is the decision to begin by freeing prices, a move even he admits will usher in a huge wave of inflation. But the Russian economist hopes this will bring goods into the now empty stores, as it did in Poland. After doubling or tripling, he hopes prices will stabilize by next fall.

Critics say making this move in advance of privatizing farming and other sectors, will be ineffective. "It is clear no price reform will lead to a big influx of goods because we simply don't have them," argues St. Petersburg mayor and prominent liberal politician Anatoli Sobchak.

The key to controlling inflation is to bring the huge Soviet budget deficit under control. During the past several years the Soviet financial authorities—the Finance Ministry and the Soviet State Bank—have been printing money at an astounding rate to cover the budget gap and subsidize state-run enterprises.

This reality is the key behind Gaidar's Russia-first reform strategy, including moves to take over the Soviet central banking institutions and end funding of all central institutions with the exception of a seriously pared down military. Russia prefers a common banking union, modeled on the US Federal Reserve, and preservation of a single currency, the ruble.

"Each republic will have to pay heavily for separate currencies," Gaidar says. Inflation would surge in Russia as rubles rushed in from the Ukraine and elsewhere to buy Russian goods.

The new Commonwealth treaty provides for use of the ruble with national currencies to be introduced only later and by special agreement.

Gaidar is well aware of the political dangers surrounding this radical shift. He rejects, for example, an attempt to impose wage controls as an anti-inflation measure, arguing that this did not work in Poland. Wages will be constrained more by lack of money, by a strict monetary policy, than by attempting direct controls. "In this country, I don't believe any government can politically withstand the pressure for wage increases connected with price inflation," he says.

But politicians such as Mayor Sobchak accuse Gaidar and his team of having their heads in the clouds. "They are boys who very much want to do something but have never done anything in their lives. [Gaidar's] never been a leader. In my two years as a leader, I learned how complex it is. As a theoretician, I could write 10 programs like Gaidar, but when it comes to practice, that's a different matter."

Gaidar, perhaps recalling the courageous life and tales of his grandfather (who died fighting the Nazis in 1941) has his own reply:

"It is a very serious risk to do nothing. It is a serious risk to do anything unpopular. It is a serious risk to do anything popular because everybody understands that anything popular leads you nowhere."

Privatization Gets Off to a Rocky Start in Former Soviet Republics

Amy Kaslow

12/17/91

Yuri Burlinov sits erect, his clasped hands rest on top of his desk. Papers and files are neatly stacked, pencils perfectly arranged. He is one of the new Russian bureaucrats managing the shaky transition to a market economy, yet he is unflinching as he states the tasks before him.

"I am the vice chairman of the Russian State Committee for Antimonopoly and New Economic Ventures," he says. He is soon joined by his public relations assistant, whose title on her freshly printed card is "Chief Expert."

In simple terms, their office oversees the transfer of government-run, government-owned output to the nascent private sector.

Russia was once the bastion of the former Soviet empire's industrial production of goods and services; private ownership and trade in its economy is expected to carry this and other Soviet republics toward market reforms.

Sounding more like a functionary than a man helping to reshape his country's economic landscape, Mr. Burlinov refers a visitor to official reports rather than explaining what he is saying.

The 47-page "Program to Support Business Activity in Russia" reads like a communist manifesto: "The Program to support business activity provides not only the achievements of economic aims . . . it will also help to solve important social problems, to strengthen political stability in all the regions of the republic, to form positive public opinion with respect to business activity, to include parts of the population in this field, to oppose the unemployment, inflation, and other negative social phenomena."

While Burlinov's program covers procedure and goals, it does not address issues vital to private-sector development. The right to own land is assumed, but not addressed in the plan. The new republican governments have so far failed to work out the separation of their property from the Soviet central government.

Plans to broadly privatize the economy—that is, hold auctions, directly sell off, or give out free vouchers for, shares in state owned enterprises to individuals or groups—have been in the offing for years. But they have never taken off.

Vadim Plotnikov, chief executive officer at the Russian agency for the management of state property, says at least 10,000 state enterprises have filed applications to his agency. Among the firms trying to go private are automobile, truck, and tractor plants, oil producing and coal mining concerns, textile and finished-garment factories.

The privatization process has followed a two-steps-forward, one-step-back approach. Mr. Plotnikov cites legal frameworks that appear to be in place, 14 legally binding methods of assessing property values and procedures for selling it, for example. Yet businesses that have already been privatized under an earlier method must be re-registered under the current one.

Given the revolving door of economic advisors in republics and the center, the prospect always looms that what has been arranged will come unhinged.

The uneven course of privatization has much to do with political infighting among leaders, and the abuses that develop when rules are not applied consistently.

Former Communist Party apparatchiks, closely connected to state enterprises and well poised to assume control of them, are the main beneficiaries of unorthodox privatizations during the past year. In the Ukraine, young Communist officials formed 1,500 companies by selling themselves shares in state firms at very low prices.

"There's a tremendous amount of graft," concedes James Wilburn, dean of the Pepperdine University School of Business and Management and a consultant to the Russian State Committee on Privatization.

Soviet expert Anders Aslund, director of the Stockholm Institute of Soviet and East European Economics, calls this a "weird form of privatization, allowed to happen because the republic, under [Russian President Boris] Yeltsin, has been in total disarray."

Despite all the setbacks and pervasive embezzlement, Mr. Wilburn has been trying to encourage international investors to buy Soviet enterprises. He ferries back and forth from Malibu, Calif., to Moscow and says he would love to live here "because it's the most dynamic, changing economy in the world."

The 98 percent Soviet literacy rate provides a huge pool of some of the world's best educated, most highly skilled labor, he says. With the Soviet market hungry for consumer goods—both industrial and agricultural—the private sector can develop steadily to meet that demand as well as compete in international markets.

But lawlessness in Russia and other republics has provided a safe haven for organized crime, Mr. Aslund says. Every legal enterprise must pay at least 10 percent to 15 percent of its profits to the mafia as protection money, he says. Failure to do so puts the enterprise, and the people running it, at great financial and physical risk.

The system of extortion is so entrenched, it is an expected cost of doing business. Russians and citizens of other republics enjoy freedoms unknown for the past 74 years of oppressive rule. Crime has surged. Aslund notes the 23,000 murders committed in the Soviet Union last year (compared to 21,500 in the US).

Aslund, who makes frequent trips to various republics to confer with leading policymakers, says "privatization will only take off on a large scale after a change in the system. It will never take off if people can't say where to start. Yeltsin has avoided doing anything about the economy for the past two and a half years."

But the prospects for the future are brighter. Aslund says that Yegor Gaidar, Mr. Yeltsin's economic minister, is "a smooth politician who understands macroeconomics." In addition, he is well qualified for the job because he has served as the head of the privatization department at the Gaidar Institute, which he founded.

Mr. Gaidar was able to bring in a colleague from the institute with him, Anatoli Chubais, as Russia's new privatization director.

Russians Claim Soviet Mantle On Baker Visit

Daniel Sneider

12/18/91

From symbols to substance, United States Secretary of State James Baker III's two days in Moscow were filled with reminders that the Soviet Union is gone and that, increasingly, Russia has taken its place.

From the opening talks with Russian Foreign Minister Andrei Kozyrev on Dec. 15 to the four-hour meeting Dec. 16 with Russian President Boris Yeltsin in the glittering St. Catherine's Hall in the Kremlin, once reserved solely for Soviet leaders, the Russian government has repeatedly asserted its authority as the de facto replacement for the Soviet state.

Mr. Yeltsin is always careful to refer to the newly formed commonwealth as the new source of legitimacy supplanting the former Soviet Union. "We will, as equal partners, develop the Commonwealth of Independent States," he declared in a press conference after the Kremlin session.

The original three founders—Russia, the Ukraine, and Byelorussia—will be joined by six more at a meeting Dec. 21. Commonwealth members will conclude a collective security treaty that will put control of nuclear weapons in the hands of a single command but with political decisions made only through agreement among commonwealth leaders, he said.

But the Russian leader also said enough to send another message—that Russia sees itself as the inheritor of much of the Soviet state, in symbols as well as its huge and valuable machinery. The presence of Soviet Defense Minister Marshal Yevgeny Shaposhnikov and Soviet Interior Minister Viktor Barannikov at Yeltsin's side was calculated to communicate that Russia, not the lingering apparatus of Soviet President Mikhail Gorbachev, now commands their millions of troops.

"While the collective security treaty has not been signed yet, who is the military to lean upon now but the leadership of Russia?" says Maj. Gen. Geliy Batenin, military adviser to the Russian Ministry of Foreign Affairs.

Mr. Baker's meeting with Mr. Gorbachev later Dec. 16 seemed more a gesture of respect than a working session. The Soviet president, who has resisted the new commonwealth, acknowledged that the country "is in transition to a different authority, to a different state."

Baker paid homage to Gorbachev's historical role and his "political courage in beginning these transformations and carrying them through."

The US is already moving rapidly to accommodate itself to the new political realities here. The US was prepared to discuss diplomatic recognition with the Ukraine, whose leaders Baker was to meet Dec. 18, along with a stop in Byelorussia.

Kazakhstan, where Baker stopped Dec. 17 in a swing that included the Central Asian republic of Kirghizia, declared its independence Dec. 16.

But Baker admitted to being surprised by the Russian demand for recognition which he said he "heard for the first time" Dec. 15. Russia has never formally declared independence, in part because it seeks to retain the status of the former Union. Russia asks not only for recognition as a separate, independent state, Yeltsin said, but also the "possible succession of Russia to the seat of . . . the former Soviet Union in the [United Nations] Security Council that is becoming vacant."

In almost passing references, Yeltsin also laid claim to other assets of the Soviet state. The Interior Ministry will not exist on a commonwealth level, he explained, "so, the existing ministry will simply become a part of the Ministry of the Interior of the Russian Federation." On the same day, the Russian parliament placed all the assets of the Soviet parliament—its buildings and bank accounts—under its control. And Russian television news reported that central television and radio stations were being taken over as well.

The most sensitive issue is the control of the vast Soviet military, almost 4 million strong, armed with some 30,000 nuclear weapons, and long the only true manifestation of this country's claim to be a superpower. The commonwealth agreement compels Russia to share this awesome attribute of statehood, but the specifics of the division are far from clear. Baker's principal concern is the safety and control of the nuclear weapons based in Russia, the Ukraine, Byelorussia, and Kazakhstan, a subject he said was discussed in "quite a bit of specific detail" in the meeting with Yeltsin.

The commonwealth agreement provides for a unified command of the country's strategic forces, which according to Yeltsin and others in the Russian government includes a broad range of conventional forces as well. On Dec. 17, Yeltsin defined these as "the air force, the naval force, the air defense force, the nuclear weapons—both strategic and tactical—as well as the intelligence gathering operations." A commander in chief will be appointed who will not be able to use these forces without the decision of the heads of the four nuclear-capable republics.

In practice, this does not mean four "buttons" on the nuclear trigger, says General Batenin. "There will be one huge button with everyone holding part of it through a system of codes." But he admits they have yet to decide whether any one of the four may have what amounts to a veto or can simply opt out of a decision to use the forces.

To further complicate matters, Byelorussia and the Ukraine have stated their desire to become non-nuclear states (Kazakhstan is expected to follow suit), but Russia will remain a nuclear weapons state "for the time being," says Yeltsin. The weapons based on the other three are to be destroyed on their territory, but Batenin says only Russia has the facilities to store and destroy nuclear warheads.

"Politically it is a problem," Batenin admits, "especially taking into account that there will be certain difficulties in the nuclear disarmament process and that Russia will emerge as the only nuclear weapons state on the territory of the former Soviet Union. If Russia does not declare its own policy of nuclear disarmament at the highest level—and such a policy is being developed now—that will just give rise to certain apprehensions about what Russia will do with its nuclear potential."

A Rocky Start for Private Farming

Daniel Sneider

12/19/91

After 60 miles of deep birch forest, the road southeast from Moscow crosses the Oka river, rises over a crest and divides. The trucks laden with steel rods and machinery continue south toward Voronez and Rostov-on-Don.

The other fork turns east into a land of gentle rolling hills, of open wheat fields lightly crusted with snow or green with the first shoots of winter wheat, of empty roads broken occasionally by a sign marking a turnoff—the Karl Marx Collective Farm says one.

Here the vast agricultural heartland of Russia begins, the eastern continuation of the food producing belt that begins with the rich black soil of the Ukraine. Here Soviet regimes have launched countless agricultural reforms to revitalize the stagnant farm sector. All have failed.

"Today in Russia and in the Soviet Union, there is no other problem than . . . food . . . a normal supply of food so people won't be on the brink of hunger and of poverty," says reformer and St. Petersburg Mayor Anatoly Sobchak.

New radical plan

Now the Russian government of Boris Yeltsin has yet another plan in hand—this time to reverse more than 50 years of collectivized agriculture and restore private farming. With it they hope to harness wasted resources and finally end the food shortages that have long undermined Soviet life and now threaten the reformers' political future.

A visit to Skopin, about 180 miles from Moscow, provides a glimpse of how far the reformers are from their goal. The emergent market economy has almost no presence here, while the old state-run economy and its Communist Party bosses remain intact, albeit sometimes under new names.

The dramatic anti-Communist revolution that swept the big cities last August after the failed coup has not reached Skopin, a dreary kernel of industry amid the collective and state farms of the region. A lone traffic signal dangles at the intersection of Karl Marx Street and Lenin Street, where the grocery store "Gifts of Nature" offers a meager supply of cabbage, onions, potatoes, liver sausage, and fatty bones. A faded billboard of Lenin set against a flowing red flag stands next to the Skopin regional executive committee building and proclaims: "The Road to Revolution is the Road to Perestroika."

In the conference room a meeting of the Skopin agro-kombinat, the organization grouping collective and state farms in the region, is under way. Behind the collective farm leaders seated on the stage, stands a plaster relief of Lenin accompanied by the well-known slogan The Party is the wisdom, pride and conscience of our epoch testifying to the Communist Party functions that used to be standard fare here. The party offices are formally closed, as everywhere in Russia, but the party first secretary is still in place—now called the chairman of the regional soviet (council).

Alexander Yeroshin, the 34-year-old director of the agro-kombinat, still carries his party card as well as the ideas that went with it. Even as the central Soviet government is dismantled, the collective farms are awaiting their annual directives on how much to sell to the state, he explains.

"Some sort of plan should remain to guarantee minimum provisions to the state," he says. "We can't imagine ourselves without the state. The state is our source of fuel, of equipment. We don't have any other source. There has to be some central regulator. Maybe that's our mistake, but that's how we were taught."

Privatizing farmland

The Russian government law on farming passed last fall allows in principle for private land, provided it is resold only to the state. A more mild form of privatization, the long-term lease of collective farmland, is also encouraged. The Russian reforms are ahead of some more conservative republics such as in Central Asia but hardly comparable to the privatization carried out in the Baltic states, or in Armenia, where almost all the collective farms were disbanded earlier this year.

Private plot agriculture—small gardens and livestock kept by collective farm members—has long supplied a large part of the fresh vegetables, potatoes, and dairy products consumed in Russian cities. But full-scale private farming in Russia is negligible so far.

According to Mikhail Zaraev, a Russian journalist specializing in agriculture, private farmers number about 22,000 in Russia. Forecasts foresee some 50,000 to 100,000 in the next few years. But even that, he points out, amounts to about two to three farmers per collective farm. Skopin, for example, boasts 26 kolkhoz (collective farms) and five sovkhoz (state farms) with a total population of 29,000 people, but Mr. Yeroshin can only name five people who "expressed a wish to raise cattle."

The Skopin farm chairman points to a problem found everywhere in the Soviet Union—an aging population that fears the uncertainties of private farming and youth who prefer to leave. For example, the Druzhba (Friendship) Kolkhoz, a profitable producer of barley seed and beef cattle, has 650 members, some 300 of which are pensioners and only 180 are able workers.

"I offered people land but they don't want it," says Druzhba Kolkhoz director Viktor Guskov, sitting in an office decorated with red banners and prizes for surpassing their planned production levels. "Most of the people are over 40 years old and there are not many young people here. The youth all leave." Pressed, he remembers a few young men who rented some cattle a couple of years ago when land leasing began. After a year and half, they went back to being tractor drivers, he says with a shrug.

The combination of resistance from the collective farm managers and reluctance from a peasantry that has lost its taste for individual farming, makes privatization a distant proposition, Mr. Zaraev suggests.

Free market distribution

Instead, the farms themselves are entering the market as they are forced to seek independence from the collapsing state system.

Across the country, collective farm directors are refusing to meet state orders. By mid-October, according to published data, only 38.5 million tons of grain had been purchased by the state out of a planned 85 million tons. This boycott is creating more shortages this winter than the drop in the harvest, which dipped to 165 million tons, compared to an average of almost 200 million tons over the past five years.

The system of state orders still functions, in theory requiring collective farms to sell about 70 percent of their production to the state, 40 percent as product tax and 30 percent as state orders in exchange for supplies. In Skopin, the harvest this year amounts to 138,000 tons, down slightly from last year due to drought. Yeroshin denies withholding any grain, claiming to have given 45,000 tons to the state as grain and directing another 50,000 to produce 7,000 to 8,000 tons of beef, of which 5,000 tons will go to the state. An additional 4,000 tons of grain were sold to the state at three times the state-set price, he says.

Those state prices, though higher, are not even close to what the fledgling market economy can offer. The state offers an average price of 444 rubles a ton, but Yeroshin says a factory in Riga and brokers from the growing network of commodity exchanges came to region offering up to 6,000 rubles. He says the farms turned down the offers, preferring to keep their surplus as a reserve for their own use and for trading later.

Withholding grain from the state is triggered largely by the collapse of the state-run supply system which no longer can be trusted to provide fuel, equipment, consumer goods and construction materials to the farms. Without guaranteed supplies, and with the value of the ruble dropping daily, collective farms prefer to use their produce to barter for what they need directly from factories and others.

Over at the Druzhba farm, which boasts rarities such as indoor plumping and gas stoves in the homes of its members, the director explains how things work these days: "The director of a Chelyabinsk sovkhoz came here to this region and offered [gas] pipes in exchange for seed. We struck a deal: one ton of pipes for five tons of seed." Mr. Guskov received a shipment of lumber on a similar basis. He is getting some trucks, which used to come through the state distribution system, from the Bread Producers Association in exchange for grain.

Guskov is unprepared for the Russian price liberalization due to start in January, freeing prices from state control on all but a few basic goods. "We are used to being state people," he says. "We don't know how . . . they will plan these prices . . . . If the prices are very high, how will the working class live?"

Guskov, who proudly proclaims his allegiance to "Lenin's Communist Party," offers the kind of circular logic which drives reformers in Moscow crazy.

"We can't start practicing market relations when the market is empty. The market is good when there is a surplus of production. But we have a total deficit."

Russia Defines New Security Policy

Daniel Sneider

12/19/91

A draft security treaty for the new Commonwealth of Independent States will eventually leave Russia the sole nuclear power in the former Soviet Union, says a senior Russian defense official.

However the treaty seeks to reassure Russia's neighbors, and the world, by placing nuclear forces under a unified military command. In addition, the official reveals, the Russian government is now formulating its own disarmament policy which will aim at an 80 percent cut in the Soviet nuclear arsenal within this decade.

"Russia will still remain a nuclear power as long as there are still nuclear weapons in other countries, while there are still third countries with underground nuclear weapons or striving to acquire their own nuclear weapons," Maj. Gen. Geliy Batenin, the military adviser to Russia's Foreign Ministry, told the Monitor.

He unveiled details of the Russian defense policy discussed in private on Monday with visiting United States Secretary of State James Baker III. But a spokesman for Kazakhstan President Nursultan Nazarbayev told reporters that if Russia insisted on keeping nuclear arms, Kazakhstan would have to do the same.

Soviet nuclear forces are currently deployed in four of the former Soviet republics—Russia, the Ukraine, Byelorussia, and Kazakhstan. The Ukraine and Byelorussia have stated their desire to become non-nuclear states, pledging to destroy the weapons on their territories as part of the arms reductions called for by US-Soviet treaties.

Kazakhstan has called for "the complete destruction of nuclear weapons," but President Nazarbayev told reporters after his meeting with Mr. Baker on Wednesday that he talked to Russian President Boris Yeltsin about "having nuclear arms stay both in Russia and in Kazakhstan."

This potential dispute will be on the table on Saturday when the three original founders of the commonwealth (Russia, Byelorussia, and the Ukraine) meet with six new members including Kazakhstan and the four Central Asian republics. The security treaty, which has been drafted by representatives of the four nuclear republics plus the Soviet Ministry of Defense and General Staff, could be finalized there. This meeting is expected to lead to the formal end of the Soviet Union on New Years Eve.

While Russia has no intention to shed its nuclear superpower status, General Batenin says the Russian government has formulated an approach designed to clarify its intentions for its nuclear weapons.

The Russian forces will be reduced to a level for "minimal nuclear deterrence," he says. "In the course of the next five to seven years, we could come down to a level of 3,000 to 4,000 warheads, about seven to eight times less than now," the general explains.

Russia is ready to move beyond the Strategic Nuclear Arms Reduction Treaty (START) already signed with the US, says Batenin, who earlier served on the staff of the Communist Party Central Committee as an adviser to President Gorbachev. This might be better done through unilateral moves on the part of Russia than by negotiating a new treaty, he suggests.

The last element of the new Russian policy will be cooperation with the West on tight controls over the proliferation of "dangerous military technology" such as ballistic missiles and nuclear weapons. The draft treaty would create a single command for the nuclear forces, under the collective political control of the leaders of the four nuclear-weapons republics, according to Batenin, who worked on the draft from the Russian side.

The unified command will have under its wing all the nuclear forces, both the long-range "strategic" weapons such as inter-continental ballistic missiles and the short-range "tactical" weapons such as nuclear-armed artillery shells, short-range rockets, and plane-delivered bombs. This includes heavy bombers, missiles based in silos, and part of the naval forces, such as submarines and ships carrying long-range cruise missiles.

Strategic forces also include non-nuclear parts of the Soviet armed forces. The large air defense force made up of jet fighters and anti-aircraft missiles, as well as the complex communications and command systems, will all continue to be controlled by the central Ministry of Defense and the General Staff, Batenin says.

There will be a military commander in chief, although a civilian defense minister is also envisioned for the future. According to Reuters news agency, citing a senior US official accompanying Baker, the current Soviet Defense Minister Air Marshal Yevgeny Shaposhnikov, was named in the Monday meeting as the candidate for commander in chief.

But the bulk of the 3.7 million-man Soviet armed forces are infantry and armored units which will fall under the authority of republican armies and their own ministries of defense.

Batenin says there is also a proposal to create a second position of a chairman of a united General Staff, whose job it would be to coordinate among the republican armies for the common defense of the "military territory of the commonwealth."

The Ministry of Defense in Moscow will have the authority to put the unified forces on alert, says Batenin, but the ultimate political decision on their use will rest with the leaders of the four nuclear republics. Each of them will carry a version of the nuclear "button," namely codes to give approval for an attack.

It has yet to be decided whether all four must agree, giving any of them an effective veto.

In the other option under discussion, the Russian military official explains, "one president, for example [Ukrainian President Leonid] Kravchuk, says I don't want to participate with my nuclear weapons in the case of a retaliatory attack. In this case, the command line over Ukrainian nuclear weapons will be blocked but others will participate."

The Ukraine government, which has expressed concern over potential Russian domination, wants to end the joint command once the nuclear weapons are destroyed. Ukrainian defense officials and officials from the Soviet Ministry of Defense are holding talks in Kiev this week in an effort to come to a common view of the handling of nuclear weapons, including their disarmament.

The Russian government foresees the need for a unified command even if the nuclear weapons outside Russia are eliminated. "It is impossible and unwise to give exclusive powers only to Russia because nobody knows who will be in charge of Russia . . . tomorrow," says Batenin.

Commonwealth Creates New Political Regime

Daniel Sneider

12/23/91

Beneath the snow-capped peaks of the Tian Shan mountains, what began as a Slavic commonwealth expanded on Saturday to embrace almost all of the former Soviet Union.

The survivors of the collapse of the Soviet state managed to agree on who would constitute the new Commonwealth of Independent States—11 of the 12 former Soviet republics, with the three already independent Baltic nations and Georgia opting out for now. But they failed to concur on how to coordinate their defense and economic policies, leaving open the question of whether this loose commonwealth can handle the complex and divisive issues before it.

The leaders of the commonwealth who assembled in Alma Ata, the capital of Kazakhstan, invited Soviet President Mikhail Gorbachev "to resign with dignity," as Russian President Boris Yeltsin put it. They offered Mr. Gorbachev a pension and other post-presidential benefits, gently urging him to depart the

Kremlin stronghold he has held for more than six years.

Gorbachev is said to be preparing a final televised address to the nation, but the timing of his resignation remains a mystery, even to his close aides. "Nobody knows," longtime adviser Georgi Shaknazarov told the Monitor yesterday. "He will declare it himself. He says it's his own business when to do it."

The commonwealth leaders adopted five documents at their meeting, all of them negotiated in advance by teams of officials. Some thorny issues were dispatched:

* Russia won its demand to inherit the Soviet seat at the United Nations and its seat on the UN Security Council.
* Single control over nuclear weapons was confirmed.
* A coordinating structure was created.

* The existing borders were recognized.

However, the leaders failed to agree on the text of a new collective security treaty precisely defining their joint military system, including what forces will be under joint command and how the new unified defense structure will operate. Nor did they settle how the commonwealth will practically manage common economic policies such as currency.

The leaders will meet again in Minsk on Dec. 30 to settle these questions. Until then a "transitional period" is established during which the military will continue to operate under the command of present Soviet Defense Minister Air Marshal Yevgeny Shaposhnikov. A commonwealth council of heads of state will be the coordinating body until they can agree on a more defined structure.

Kazakhstan government spokesman Seitcazy Matayev explained that "There were many objections" to the military treaty, "including those from the Ukraine." He said the Ukraine had also objected to the appointment of Marshal Shaposhnikov as the permanent commander in chief.

"The main thing that satisfies me is that strategic [nuclear] weapons remain under single control," Shaposhnikov said. "Thus both the Soviet and world public will be calmed down." He said that he will be working on a revised plan for conventional forces and will submit it shortly to the Soviet General Staff.

A special agreement on nuclear arms was issued by the four states in which long-range nuclear weapons are based: Russia, Byelorussia, the Ukraine, and Kazakhstan. With the apprehensions of the West clearly in mind, the document states the weapons will be under unified command with decisions on their use made by the Russian president in agreement with the other three. Byelorussia and the Ukraine agree to join the Nuclear Non-Proliferation Treaty as nonnuclear weapons states. The three non-Russian states also agree to allow transfer of tactical nuclear warheads to Russia for dismantling under "joint supervision."

Some aspects, however, will trouble Western powers. The actual procedures for joint control remain to be determined in a separate document. And Kazakhstan has clearly decided to retain its weapons so long as Russia does, although Russian officials repeat their view that Russia will emerge as the sole nuclear weapons power out of the former Union.

Such ambiguity also surrounds economic cooperation. Mr. Yeltsin, according to a Tass news agency dispatch, told reporters upon his return to Moscow that the ruble will remain the common currency and that coordinating institutions will be created at the Dec. 30 meeting which will set the pace of reforms. But the Russian reforms are already set to begin with liberalization of all state-controlled price liberalization on Jan. 2. Uzbekistan President Islam Karimov told the news conference after the signing that prices should be freed only after the poorer regions had been adequately safeguarded.

The leaders also deferred for final approval a draft agreement on institutions for the commonwealth, including regular meetings of leaders and creation of ministerial level committees to coordinate policies on foreign affairs, defense, economics and finances, transport and communications, social security and law enforcement. Nor have they settled two controversial problems: the division of Soviet property, including its embassies abroad, and how to pay for joint projects such as the military.

The clearest document provides for Russia to inherit the Soviet UN seat and its permanent membership (and veto rights) in the Security Council. The Ukraine and Byelorussia are already members of the UN, and the other states are expected to follow. Aside from the three Slavic republics, the 11 members of the commonwealth include Azerbaijan, Armenia, Kazakhstan, Kirghizia, Moldavia, Tadzhikstan, and Uzbekistan. Georgia sent observers to the meeting.

Security Issues on Agenda For Commonwealth Talks

Daniel Sneider

12/24/91

Russian President Boris Yeltsin's finger will soon be on the nuclear button. But beyond that fact, little else is clear about the fate of the vast Soviet military machine as the Soviet Union turns into the loose Commonwealth of Independent States.

The meeting Saturday of the leaders of the 11 former Soviet republics now constituting the commonwealth ultimately failed to settle some of the most pressing issues surrounding the future of this former superpower.

"The most acute problems were the ones pertaining to the military issue, to the nuclear issue," Ukrainian President Leonid Kravchuk said in a television interview broadcast Sunday night.

The agenda for the commonwealth meeting included approval of a collective security treaty defining the common military structures of the members and the division of Soviet military apparatus among them. Commonwealth leaders also had to settle the handling of nuclear weapons, their control, safety, and disarmament.

Unanswered questions

But the gathering failed to agree on a security treaty, leaving that issue to be taken up again at another meeting of leaders in Minsk on Dec. 30. An agreement "On Joint Measures on Nuclear Arms" was signed by the four states with long-range nuclear weapons based on their territory—Russia, Kazakhstan, Byelorussia, and the Ukraine. But even that document leaves some significant questions unanswered.

The document states that nuclear weapons "are part of the unified strategic armed forces" and that until they are withdrawn from the Ukraine and Byelorussia, "decisions on the need to use them are taken, by agreement with the heads of the member states of the agreement, by the Russian president, on the basis of procedures drawn up jointly by the member states."

But neither those "procedures" nor a joint policy on nuclear issues, have been decided yet. The mechanisms of control remain vaguely defined.

"Until the nuclear weapons are destroyed, we pass over the control over the nuclear button to one president, Yeltsin," Mr. Kravchuk explained. "We don't run any risk because we are withdrawing nuclear weapons from our territory and the button will be blocked by me, [Byelorussian leader Stanislav] Shushkevich and [Kazakhstan President Nursultan] Nazarbayev."

The Ukrainians are almost rushing to rid themselves of their weapons, responding to the message from the United States that this is a condition for their entry into the West. This led them to reverse an earlier stance opposing transfer of tactical nuclear warheads to Russia where facilities exist for their dismantling. Both Byelorussia and the Ukraine are committed to destroying all their long-range as well as tactical (short-range) nuclear weapons, the latter by July 1, 1992.

"I talked to [US Secretary of State James] Baker about this," Kravchuk said. As for the intercontinental ballistic missiles (ICBMs) based in 176 silos in the Ukraine, 130 are to be destroyed under the US-Soviet Strategic Arms Reduction Treaty (START) and Kravchuk pledges to destroy the rest shortly.

Kazakhs stand apart

But the government of Kazakhstan has said it will retain nuclear weapons as long as Russia does. "I was astonished by Nazarbayev's statement," says Maj. Gen. Geliy Batenin, military advisor to the Russian Ministry of Foreign Affairs. "Taking into account our previous negotiations, it was unexpected."

General Batenin points to two factors he believes lie behind Nazarbayev's stance. "First, his Islamic political maneuvers, his attempt to gain support from the Islamic world," referring to the aspirations of the Muslim-minority Kazakhs to take a leadership role in the entire Muslim-populated Central Asian region of the former Union. "Second, it was a political game because he finally managed to distinguish himself from the other nuclear leaders, the Ukraine and Byelorussia.

But Batenin echoes other Russian officials in confidently predicting the Kazakhs will move shortly to a non-nuclear status. All the tactical weapons will be gone by 1992 and at least 50 percent of the silo-based ICBMs on Kazakh territory will be destroyed under START. "Besides," he adds, "those missiles are already 30 years old and outdated."

The desire to please the West makes the nuclear issue more tractable. But on the broader question of how to control and divide the 3.7 million-man Soviet armed forces, the differences emerge strongly, particularly between the Ukraine and Russia.

Three different drafts of a security treaty were prepared before the commonwealth conference—one drawn up by the Soviet Ministry of Defense under Air Marshal Yevgeny Shaposhnikov; one by the Russian government under Gen. Konstantin Kobets; and a third by the Ukraine government. According to Batenin, as well as other sources, the Shaposhnikov draft is the main one and the most ambitious in terms of maintaining a centralized Army. It calls for a supreme commander with a five-year term, a general staff, and two commanders, one in charge of nuclear forces and the other conventional forces.

The Shaposhnikov version seeks to keep most conventional troops under joint command to defend the entire territory of the commonwealth, limiting republics to small armies, with the Ukraine allowed a small navy.

The Russian alternative calls for one commander who controls the nuclear forces, including tactical weapons, air defense against bombers, anti-missile batteries, and anti-satellite weapons. This commander would also control mobile conventional forces from the Army, Air Force, and Navy dedicated to defend the borders of the former union. The draft, according to Batenin, calls for a political control system modeled on NATO with a nuclear planning group and a council of defense ministers.

Draft treaties considered

"The Ukraine draft clearly rejects any control over conventional armed forces," says Batenin. It agrees only to single command over strategic nuclear weapons.

All the republics are presently working on these drafts and experts may meet later in the week to try to come to a common view before the meeting next Monday. But agreement may be difficult to come by. "Even if we do not manage to sign the treaty itself [on the 30th], we will sign an agreement on the principles of joint defense," says Batenin.

As a compromise, they could agree to resubordinate units from republican armies to a joint command in the event of emergency or in response to aggression, he suggests. But even that could founder, he admits, because of the Ukraine's adamant stance "against any possibility of central control of its army."

Fare Well Reformer, Mikhail Sergeyevich...

Daniel Sneider

12/26/91

With sadness, anger, and flashes of defiance, Mikhail Sergeyevich Gorbachev ends a momentous six and a half years at the helm of his nation.

The West sees Mr. Gorbachev as a singular figure. But in his role as unrequited Russian reformer, Gorbachev has trod a well-worn path. From Czar Alexander II to Nikita Khrushchev, leaders before him have broken their swords battling to prod the vast country forward. They all met with what history has revealed to be the futility of trying to save a dying system through reform.

"During my tenure, I have been attacked by all those in Russian society who can scream and write . . . . The revolutionaries curse me because I have strongly and conscientiously favored the use of the most decisive measures . . . . As for the conservatives, they attack me because they have mistakenly blamed me for all the changes in our political system."

These words could have been written by Gorbachev—indeed he said as much many times. But they were penned by another great Russian reformer, Count Sergei Iulevich Witte, in his bitter resignation letter as prime minister in 1906. Witte had saved Nicholas II and his autocracy from war and revolution, only to be discarded.

Decaying system

Like Witte, Gorbachev was called in to save a society in collapse. The Russian empire was again weakened by foreign adventures, culminating in the disastrous war in Afghanistan. And underneath, the economic system was decaying, unable to meet basic needs.

"Gorbachev took this country like my wife takes cabbage. He thought that to get rid of the dirt, he could just peel off the top layer of leaves. But he had to keep going until there was nothing left." That is the assessment of Vitaly Korotich, who was Gorbachev's designated spearhead in the campaign to reclaim lost history as editor of the magazine Ogonyok.

Even before he took office as general secretary of the Communist Party of the Soviet Union (CPSU) in March 1985, Gorbachev described his goal as the renovation of the socialist system. In a speech on Dec. 10, 1984, he delivered his later famous watchwords deep transformations in the economy and the whole system of social relations, perestroika [restructuring] of economic management, democratization of our social and economic life," and "glasnost" (openness).

Gorbachev reduced fear in Soviet society and let a fresh wind blow through Eastern Europe. But when those reforms reached their limits—and they did so quickly—Gorbachev balked. The ultimate assault on the Leninist state and its state-run economy was always beyond his intent.

In much of this Gorbachev was following a path laid out by his political sponsor, Yuri Andropov, who advanced from chairman of the KGB to succeed Leonid Brezhnev as party leader in 1982. Andropov was described by those around him as a closet liberal, a lover of jazz who sought to bring socialist democracy to the Soviet Union. But Andropov died in early 1984. Gorbachev had to wait more than a year until the Brezhnev-prot, conservative stalwart Konstantin Chernenko, came and went in similar fashion.

Gorbachev began with familiar themes of Andropov: the need to restore discipline, to intensify production through technological progress and innovations such as giving state-run enterprises more freedom and workers salary incentives. These moves picked up the reformist thread of Khrushchev, lost during the long years under Brezhnev, which Gorbachev disdainfully referred to as "the era of stagnation."

"Gorbachev did not have a clear plan of what kind of political and social system must be created," says Fyodor Burlatsky, a former speechwriter for Khrushchev, close aide to Andropov, and sometime adviser to Gorbachev. "He came from our generation, from the 60s. He had in mind what Khrushchev wanted but maybe more than Khrushchev. He shared the . . . feeling that everything that came from the Stalinist system must be destroyed. It doesn't mean that the socialist system must disappear."

Perhaps Gorbachev's clearest goal, Mr. Burlatsky suggests, was to improve relations with the West. Alone among Soviet leaders, Gorbachev had traveled extensively in the West. "He saw the terrible distance between our country and the Western countries . . . . He understood the West is more successful, but he did not understand the reason."

Party resistance

Among the small number of reformers Gorbachev gathered around himself was Alexander Yakovlev, a party intellectual whom Gorbachev rescued in 1983 from a 10-year semi-exile as ambassador to Canada. Mr. Yakovlev become the theorist of perestroika. Earlier this month, in a little reported speech to the founding conference of the Movement for Democratic Reforms, Yakovlev reviewed the effort to reform Soviet communism.

"While the system completely rejected any attempt at sensible reform, Stalinist obstructions could be crushed only by a powerful ram. Khrushchev's direct and brave attack ended in defeat, although Brezhnev's refurbishing failed as well. A time of uncertainty settled in, but the outcome was already near and it came in the form of perestroika, elite revolution meant to develop in a peaceful way. Perhaps it couldn't have been otherwise. It was born within the politically active part of the CPSU and the society, and it was here that it encountered the most fierce resistance and rejection," he said.

In a rambling, nostalgic, two-hour farewell session with Soviet reporters on Dec. 12, Gorbachev still defended the attempt to bring reform via the party. "Under us everything was already boiling, starting with the 60s. All those attempts to begin the reforms were stifled. All those attempts mean that the problems had been knocking at the doors of our society for a long time already . . . . It was in the party where the forces were born that had the courage to decisively start the reforms. They took upon themselves the heaviest burden of responsibility."

Reform crossroads

For the first three years of his leadership, Gorbachev pursued his reforms in a series of thrusts, retreating slightly and advancing again on another front as each one met the opposition of Communist Party conservatives. By June 1988, when the 19th Party Conference dedicated to political reform was held, "the revolution from above . . . was at a crossroad," Yakovlev says.

At that moment, Gorbachev faced a choice: to turn perestroika into what Yakovlev calls "a truly, people's democratic revolution, going to the utmost, really bringing the society total freedom," or to remain a Communist reformer, operating in the familiar and controlled milieu of the party bureaucracy.

The path through the party was fraught with danger, Yakovlev says. Perestroika could "either be defeated by Stalinist reaction, Brezhnevist conservatism, or risk being stolen from itself by those forces who just shield themselves with its slogans, striving in the meantime to redistribute power in the framework of the former social system."

In early 1988, a major debate was under way over what kind of democratic system should be created. Burlatsky was a member of a small working group under the direction of Gorbachev's long-time associate Anatoly Lukyanov, which included close aide and politician-scientist Georgi Shakhnazarov. Two proposals came from this group, according to Burlatsky: one of his own and one from Mr. Lukyanov.

Lukyanov proposed removing the Stalin era system and going back to Lenin's 1924 Constitution. That structure was based on indirect, two-stage elections of a parliament, while concentrating legal authority in local soviets (councils), with a vague definition of the relation between the party and the soviets.

Some participants in this process claim the intent was always to introduce multiparty democracy, though carefully, with the party in control of the process. But Burlatsky says that when he proposed direct elections of parliament, president, and vice-president on a multiparty basis, he was strongly opposed by almost everybody except Yakovlev.

Gorbachev opted for the Lukyanov plan, carrying out a complex election in March 1989 in which some deputies were directly elected and others sent by official organizations. They in turn chose a relatively tame standing parliament. Even this opened the political process. The live broadcasts of the first session of the Congress, with the dramatic appearance of long-time dissident Andrei Sakharov, captivated the nation.

In the spring of 1990, Gorbachev again had an opportunity to overturn the political system. Article 6 of the Constitution giving the Communist Party a monopoly had been abolished and a presidential system was to be established. But he chose to be elected by the Congress instead of by the people. This was "his greatest political mistake," says Burlatsky. "Gorbachev is not like Khrushchev; he doesn't like risk."

"Perestroika didn't manage to overcome itself," Yakovlev explains. "Public, social, and political forces awakened by it remained unclaimed, while the old structures continued to exist and act against reforms."

But in a sense those forces were claimed, though not by Gorbachev. Perestroika brought another unforeseen, and for Gorbachev unhappy, result: the emergence of powerful nationalist movements in the 15 republics of the Soviet empire. From the Baltic republics to the heartland of Russia, democratic reformers won power by detaching themselves from the Communist Party.

Boris Yeltsin, the brash Urals party boss whom Gorbachev had brought to Moscow to lead reforms there, rode this wind. He was helped by the party conservatives who, with Gorbachev's consent, ousted Mr. Yeltsin from their leadership ranks in 1987. Yeltsin's comeback, culminating in his defeat of Gorbachev's choice for the post of chairman of the Russian parliament in June 1990, marked the second crossroad for Gorbachev.

Frustrated radical reformers quickly gathered around Yeltsin—men such as economist Grigory Yavlinsky whose plan for a quick 500-day march to a market economy had been buried by the plodding bureaucrats around Gorbachev. In August 1990, Gorbachev agreed to draft a new economic reform plan together with Yeltsin, based on the 500-day scheme, raising hopes that perestroika would finally breach the boundaries of the old system.

The party and state bureaucracy fought back, warning Gorbachev of collapse if such a radical course were pursued. Gorbachev cracked, coming out in October in favor of a deeply compromised, cautious approach.

"Since the autumn of 1990, the reactionaries and conservatives were launching open attacks," recounts Yakovlev. "I am convinced that the rejection of the 500-day plan served as an encouraging signal to them. It was a mistake with grave consequences. It demonstrated that perestroika was ready to retreat under pressure."

Missed moment

"I missed the moment," Gorbachev said in a newspaper interview this week. "I should have formed a strong alliance with democrats . . . . And in general I paid an enormous price."

In the months that followed, Gorbachev turned to the right, surrounding himself with foes of reform and losing the counsel of old friends such as Yakovlev and Foreign Minister Eduard Shevardnadze. "Thus the way was opened to bloodshed in Vilnius and to the putsch dress rehearsal held in Moscow on March 28, 1991," says Yakovlev referring to the military crackdown in Lithuania in January 1991 and the display of military force in the streets of Moscow, part of an effort to oust Yeltsin from power.

In the end, it was Yeltsin who saved Gorbachev from the hard-liners who finally moved to overthrow him in August. But in the bargain, Gorbachev lost power to the new nationalist movements.

"The main goal of my life has been accomplished," Gorbachev reflected in his Kremlin talk with reporters. "All the rest . . . well, maybe someone else will come and do it better. But you must understand, I wanted to succeed. What's special about me is that I can't accept defeat."

Daily Hardships Dim Assessment Of Gorbachev's Achievements

Daniel Sneider

12/27/91

Heavy metal chandeliers barely illuminate the cavernous hall of Moscow's Kazan train station, filled with people making their way from one part of the former Soviet empire to another. Central Asians heading home from selling their goods in the Moscow markets huddle along the peeling lime-green walls. Russians stand among their bags, waiting for trains to their hometowns deep in the Urals.

Here, on the morning after Mikhail Gorbachev bade goodbye to his nation, there is little sign of regret at his departure. "He's an indecisive person," pronounces Galina Vasilieva, her fur hat settled firmly in place. "What he did, he did. He performed his historic task. We thank him for what he started. But he should have resigned."

Ms. Vasilieva is returning to her Siberian hometown of Tara from what is politely called "business tourism" to Poland, a euphemism for the flow of Russians and others carrying cheaply bought goods to sell in Poland, where dollars and scarce commodities are easily had. Poland's relatively free economy looks good to Vasilieva, and she endorses Russian President Boris Yeltsin's version of Polish-style radical reform.

"I support Yeltsin," she says, smiling to reveal gold fillings. "He's the only person I still believe."

Mr. Gorbachev was himself right up until the end—proud and defiant. In his 12-minute address, the last leader of the now defunct Soviet Union defended the necessity of change and his record of achievements.

"When I found myself at the helm of this state it was already clear that something was wrong in this country," he said. "We were living much worse than people in the industrialized countries were living and we were increasingly lagging behind them.

"The reason was obvious even then. This country was suffocating in the shackles of the bureaucratic command system. Doomed to cater to ideology and suffer and carry the onerous burden of the arms race, it found itself at a breaking point . . . . We had to change everything radically."

Gorbachev ticked off his accomplishments—destroying the totalitarian system, initiating democratic reforms, turning to a market economy, ending the cold war.

Ludmilla Tsukanova managed to watch the speech as she made her way from Kursk in southeastern Russia, where she works, to her Urals hometown of Nizhni-Tagil for the holidays. When Gorbachev came to power, "there was hope for the future," the horse trainer agrees.

"But he didn't live up to the expectations people had," she concludes.

Such comments have been common for some time here, where Gorbachev's meandering and often hectoring speeches and television interviews were met with the ire of a people who saw little change in their daily lives.

For Ms. Tsukanova, like so many Russians, Mr. Yeltsin is the "right successor" to Gorbachev. "Yeltsin will be able to keep his promises. Even when he is answering questions in interviews, all his answers are to the point and without any blah, blah."

It is of course, an unfair view. "The current hardships of life make it difficult for people to sit down and think about what happened," Gorbachev told Cable News Network in an interview after his speech. "One day people will rid themselves of the burdens of everyday life and realize it was difficult . . . but we had to begin."

Right now Yeltsin enjoys the benefits of being freshly empowered. But the blame for those "burdens" will take little time to shift onto the broad shoulders of the Siberian bureaucrat. Indeed, some who are feeling the pain of change more than others are already pointing the finger in his direction.

"Yeltsin should be chased out, not Gorbachev," says Nina Prokofievna (she declines to give her family name), a Moscow pensioner waiting at the station for friends bringing a packet of meat sent by relatives for the holidays.

After 40 years of working in a factory making sewing needles, she is living on her 200-ruble-a-month pension. Under Yeltsin's reform plan, she will receive an additional 100 rubles, but given the rising prices, she exclaims, "How can I live on that?"

But weren't these prices going up already and wouldn't Gorbachev have had to do the same if he stayed in office, she is asked. "Only Yeltsin is behind those prices rises. As soon as he took office, prices began to rise."

Perhaps Yeltsin should worry then, since Gorbachev promised to remain in politics, ready to speak whenever he feels the democratic reformers are straying from their path. "I have no intention of hiding in the taiga [the Siberian woods]," Gorbachev said ominously. He did not yield in his resignation speech on his opposition to the new Commonwealth of Independent States, which has been formed from the rubble of the Soviet Union.

"The policy prevailed of dismembering this country and disuniting the state, which is something I cannot subscribe to," he declared. It is a view shared by many here, like the distraught aircraft assembly worker who phoned a Moscow friend after the speech. "Our motherland has been betrayed," he said in a voice heavy with grief.

Lt. Oleg Shatkovsky is on holiday leave from his paratroop unit in Transcaucasia to his home in the western Russian city of Bryansk. The men under his command are uncertain of their future. "They don't know what will happen tomorrow. They used to protect the Soviet Union and now they don't know what country we are to protect."

Lieutenant Shatkovsky conceals his youth behind a strawberry blond mustache, his military fur cap perched at a jaunty angle, proudly claiming a heritage that goes back centuries as a career Russian "military man." The lean paratrooper has no doubts about the man who now has his finger of the nuclear button.

"Yeltsin is a fantastic person. I admire him very much . . . . He showed his strong character when, in spite of pressure from the [Communist Party] Politburo, he survived and was victorious."

And Gorbachev? "He was applauded by people in the West and by many people in the Soviet Union. But he didn't understand that radical measures should be taken. He could have resigned with honor when Yeltsin was elected president."

Commodity Markets Reshape Distribution

Daniel Sneider

12/30/91

Yuri Sobolev sits quietly in a green plastic chair, studying a thick computer printout. Young men and women bustle around checking computer screens in the center of the large hall of the former central post office. A marble bust of Lenin perched in an archway on the second floor balcony surveys the scene.

Another day of trading is about to begin at the Russian Commodities and Raw Materials Exchange, the largest and most successful birzha of the almost 500 exchanges that have sprung up across the former Soviet Union. The exchanges bear a closer resemblance to oriental bazaars than to the pit of the Chicago Mercantile Exchange, trading in goods ranging from cassette tape recorders and used Mercedes sedans to tons of Siberian crude oil.

"This is a linguistic problem," says Russian Deputy Premier Yegor Gaidar. "We lead the world in the number of commodities exchanges, although trade in retail rather than wholesale goods is not what commodities exchanges do in the rest of the world."

Today, Mr. Sobolev hopes to buy 20,000 to 30,000 pieces of winter clothing for a state trading company in the far north. Sobolev was a computer programmer at a defense plant until a year ago when a friend organized the brokerage firm AvanBrok, whose main clients are state-run defense enterprises. "They've lost their supply outlets," he says of his clients. "They have to get it for themselves."

Exchange replaces state

The birzha is a unique product of the breakdown of the centralized Soviet distribution system, formerly run by Gossnab, the State Committee on Supplies. State-run enterprises received their supplies through Gossnab, and they returned most of their production to it. Alongside the official economy there emerged the "shadow economy," embracing everything from informal barter deals between factories to a black market in state goods.

In part, the birzha simply reflects the emergence of the shadow economy into the open. Some disdain birzhy as corrupt because of bribes regularly paid and deals often made outside the auction floor. But others see them as a bridge between the planned economy and the market, and as a place where young brokers are making fortunes that will be the seed capital for entrepreneurship.

The Russian Exchange was organized a year and a half ago by mathematics-professor-turned-entrepreneur Konstantin Borovoy. "It was clear economic decline was on the way," Mr. Borovoy recalls, sitting in an office decorated with pictures of himself with well known people such as the patriarch of the Russian Orthodox Church. "The ties between consumers and producers had been ruptured."

In the beginning, the exchange dealt with imports, because only they were free of state price controls. Then it expanded to include wood products, then metals. "It was like a whirlpool which sucked in everything," Borovoy says. Slowly state enterprises started dealing there, buying supplies and selling the small percentage of their production they were not forced to give up to the state. Officially about 12 percent of distribution is now conducted outside of the state system, but Borovoy estimates the number is at least twice that.

Even Gossnab created its own exchanges to act as a formal locale for state firms to carry out barter deals between themselves. Defense industries operate about 20 such exchanges.

Most of the exchanges result from the shortage economy. Experts believe that after the advent of free pricing on Jan. 2, the vast majority will fold or will convert into trading houses or brokerage firms. But as long as the state sets even a few prices, the exchanges serve a valuable role as the only place to determine something close to a market value.

Borovoy is proudly pursuing good old fashioned capitalist profits. "I hate Communists," he says with a broad smile. His open disdain for his enemies has made him one of the best known businessmen in the country. Borovoy claims the exchange prospered in part because it was not taken seriously by Gossnab. "We had no luck for 74 years while we were governed by fools. It turned out to be good luck for the exchange, because nobody understood how the exchange operated."

Immense volume traded

The Russian Exchange claims it accounts for about 70 percent of the total volume of all the exchanges, although that figure is hard to confirm. Its list of offerings has a combined value of 4 billion to 8 billion rubles every day ($720 billion to $960 billion at the market rate), but the deals struck amount to about 2 billion rubles a month, the exchange says. The exchange has spun off scores of subsidiaries, including the Russian Stock Exchange, a bank, and an economic information agency.

There are 1,120 officially registered brokers at the Russian Exchange, and the cost of a seat soared from an initial 60,000 rubles to 4.4 million rubles by the end of September. The exchange charges 0.175 percent commission, but individual brokers can reap up to 10 percent of a deal depending on its size.

In a pink sweater and black jeans, Irina Konyaeva looks more like a model than a member. She and her husband represent the "Wheel of Fortune" firm, which serves mostly small enterprises. in the provinces. Ms. Konyaeva is here with goods for sale—sugar, dried apricots, Israeli cloth, and artificial leather. The 60-70 tons of sugar comes from a state farm that wants the firm to buy it some audio and video equipment with the returns.

Konyaeva loves her work. "I get very tired, but I like dealing with people. And I have a quite good, steady income." Indeed, the 22-year-old graduate of a construction engineering institute makes about 30,000 rubles a month in a country where the average salary is only 300 rubles a month.

Budding capitalists

The young brokers are zealots for capitalism. "People say we are on the brink of hunger," says Sobolev. "But just look at the list—a huge amount of food is offered. All we need are structures to buy, sell, and store this food." Sobolev is saving up to start a bank with some friends.

The brokers vividly demonstrated their political leanings last August on the first morning of the attempted hard-line coup. They met at the exchange, decided to defy the putschists, and quickly gathered millions of rubles to aid the defense of the Russian parliament. Then they marched there together to join tens of thousands of others on the barricades.

But Borovoy does not hesitate to assail the Russian government for being filled with the same old bureaucrats. "The mentality remains the same: Everything should be controlled. Orders should be issued .... Progress is on the way but too slowly."

Byelorussia Eyes Commonwealth Agenda

Daniel Sneider

12/30/91

Byelorussian leader Stanislav Shushkevich hurries over to his broad desk to answer the telephone.

"Hello, Islam," he says, greeting Uzbekistan's President Islam Karimov. "The meeting is beginning at 11 a.m.; [Boris] Yeltsin is arriving at 9, [Leonid] Kravchuk at 9:20," he says, explaining when the Russian and Ukrainian presidents will arrive.

The gentlemanly former physics professor was speaking as host of the newly formed Commonwealth of Independent States. Just three weeks ago, Minsk was given the unlikely role as its "capital," chosen as relatively neutral ground for its coordinating sessions. At that meeting not far from this quiet republican capital, Mr. Shushkevich and his fellow Slavic leaders from neighboring Russia and the Ukraine surprisingly and quickly brought the Soviet Union to its end.

Today's gathering, the first since the commonwealth expanded to include 11 of the 15 former Soviet republics, promises to be tempestuous. Members are divided over complex defense and economic issues.

"We are working on the documents," Shushkevich tells Karimov. "I am optimistic."

But in an interview with the Monitor, Shushkevich freely concedes that "neither issue will be settled."

When it comes to defense problems, they will manage only to "outline ways to conclude an agreement," although he hopes that a final deal will come quickly. "As for economic problems," he says, I'll be happy if we resolve only a part of these issues."

Defense officials from the 11 commonwealth states met Thursday and Friday to try to finalize a collective security treaty that would create a joint military structure. Officials of the former Soviet Ministry of Defense, led by Defense Minister Marshal Yevgeny Shaposhnikov, propose creating not only a unified command over nuclear weapons—which all have agreed to—but also retaining some common conventional forces.

According to reports, the talks yielded only a set of documents on a broad defense policy, on the status of servicemen, on their enlistment and on a temporary coordinating body of commonwealth defense ministers, all of which will be discussed at today's meeting.

The Ukraine, along with Moldavia and Azerbaijan, balked at any form of common armies.

"The Ukraine is forming its own armed forces," explains Shushkevich. "Only strategic [nuclear] forces that are deployed on the territory of the Ukraine will be under common command." He worries that "the Ukrainian stance will prompt many republics to follow them."

The economic tension lines are also drawn most tautly between Russia and the Ukraine, the largest and richest of the former Soviet republics, respectively.

The three Slavic states originally agreed to coordinate economic-reform policies, including maintaining the ruble as a common currency as Russia wished. In turn, the Russians yielded on postponing the starting point of their more radical program, liberalization of state-controlled prices, until Jan. 2.

Now the tension is heightened. Both the Ukraine and Byelorussia are asking for further delay, which the Russian government is adamantly refusing. Other members such as the Communist-led conservative governments in Central Asia are opposing such reforms completely.

"We want liberalization of prices no less than Russia does," explains Shushkevich, who was elected chairman of the Byelorussian parliament in September after the failed hard-line coup.

But Russia will benefit unfairly from its control over the Soviet government mints, he argues, which allows it to print money at will.

Inflation will be higher in Russia so goods will be drawn there, he contends—particularly food, which is in relatively better supply here and in the Ukraine.

Byelorussia and the Ukraine want to protect their domestic markets by issuing coupons to their citizens for buying basic goods in state stores.

The Byelorussians intend to free prices on about 70 percent of goods, making the rest purchasable only with coupons, which will thus act as a de facto separate currency. Shushkevich calls the move "a bad measure but . . . necessary."

Shushkevich believes the commonwealth will hold up despite these strains and will last "for a long time." He dismisses former Soviet President Mikhail Gorbachev's assertion that the three Slavic leaders went behind his back in their Dec. 8 meeting.

"Gorbachev didn't want to know," Shushkevich says. "He wanted his own plan [for a new Union] to work. He didn't want to accept a structure in which he couldn't find a place for himself."

The decision to eliminate a central government is "very logical—we are afraid of totalitarianism," argues Shushkevich, the son of a Byelorussian poet sent to the Siberian prison camps by Stalin. "There is a need not to lose the simple communication between former members of the Union, but at the same time, not to have a center which dictates its conditions to everybody."

In talks with journalists later, Mr. Gorbachev was particularly angry that he learned about the commonwealth only after Mr. Yeltsin called US President Bush. Shushkevich, who was given the task of calling Gorbachev, says the call was delayed by a problem with the special secure line.

After Shushkevich told him the contents of the commonwealth declaration, "Gorbachev said, 'Do you realize what a negative reaction you'll face from the world community because your decision is unconstitutional?' I told him we had already informed the press and the reaction was quite calm. Even President Bush wasn't very disappointed and said he would carefully study the documents. At that point, the president [Gorbachev] got very indignant and asked me to hand the phone to Yeltsin. I said I would be very happy to do this."

Commercial Banking Is Off and Running

Daniel Sneider

12/31/91

A jazz band plays softly; men in black ties and ladies in long evening dresses swirl around tables laden with smoked sturgeon and champagne. Russian Vice President Alexander Rutskoi and other celebrities are on hand. Mercedes Benzes and BMWs fill every parking space outside the Moscow Commercial Club, while policemen block the street allowing only those with invitations to enter.

Menatep, one of the hottest and most controversial new firms to emerge in the wild world of finance in the former Soviet Union, is having a party. Begun by a group of men in their 20s, Menatep has grown from its beginnings in 1986 as an entrepreneurial offshoot of the Komsomol, the Communist youth organization, into an international financial group handling everything from overseas currency speculation to trade financing.

"Menatep is the most sophisticated [bank] in Moscow," says Daniele Nicylin of the Swiss investment firm Riggs Volmet, where Menatep has been a client for two years. "They are very young and really want to start a new business for their country."

Seeds of free market

Along with the emergence of hundreds of commodities exchanges, the growth of commercial banking is one of the most visible signs of the beginnings of a market economy in the former Soviet Union. Since the monopoly of the state-run banks was removed in 1988, registered commercial banks have increased from 41 in January 1989 to almost 1,500 today.

The banks' growth has outstripped the primitive legal structure. Now they lend money virtually without supervision or control of the central banking institutions, to the dismay of those authorities. "There is no legislation; there is no liquidity," says Viktor Pobedinsky, president of the private financial group Fininvest. "Everyone does whatever they like."

Among the commercial banks, Menatep has an unusually high profile. Its billboards decorate whole sides of Moscow buildings. People lined up last year to buy 1,000-ruble shares in the group. As one of a handful of banks allowed to deal in foreign currency, Menatep booths in Moscow post offices offer ordinary citizens the chance to exchange dollars for rubles or even to buy limited amounts of dollars.

But constant rumors dog Menatep about the origins of its funds and the legality of its dealings. It is widely believed that the firm is a front for the Communist Party and the KGB, that it laundered party money into foreign bank accounts. Such charges are by no means confined to Menatep—they beset almost any successful business here—and Menatep officials vigorously deny them.

Legal challenge

Many of the accusations of illegality come from central authorities, including the former Soviet State Bank, Gosbank, and the Russian Central Bank. The head of the Moscow office of one Western bank says State Bank officials warned him against doing business with Menatep. And the chairman of the Russian Bank called it a "dubious banking operation" in a September television interview. Menatep promptly sued, and won its case in a Russian court Dec. 16.

It might be more accurate to describe the entire banking system here as "dubious." Inevitably, many of the "commercial" banks formed in the last two years have their origins in the state-run economy. A 1986 banking reform divided the State Bank into a system of banks, largely as the mechanism to transfer money from the central ministries to enterprises. The Agroprom bank, for example, which is one of the largest in the country, services the collective farms and agro-industry. In some cases, existing state banks were just re-registered as commercial banks after 1988. In others, groups of enterprises created a bank based on their deposits.

But these banks also hold as assets the huge and largely uncollectable loans the government made to enterprises as subsidies for their losses. In turn the banks use these assets to lend money, the vast majority of it for short terms and at interest rates averaging 20 percent.

"Practically all Soviet banks are illiquid," admits Russian Deputy Premier Yegor Gaidar. "But we can't close them because it would leave the country without banking services."

But foreign bankers, who are critical of the lack of regulation, worry about the future. "What you're going to do here is foster a collapse which will set the system back decades," the Western banker says.

Menatep's core bank, the Commercial Innovation Bank, was formed in 1988 with two-thirds of its 3 million-ruble startup capital coming from the Zhilsotsbank, a state bank that financed housing and social services. It grew rapidly, spinning off other operations including insurance companies, trading houses, and 23 other banks.

But the group's ownership is murky. The firm claims 16,000 shareholders, but almost all the stock is owned by three investors—about half by Menatep, and the other half divided between an Armenian private enterprise and a Moscow joint venture with a European partner, both of whom company officials decline to identify further.

The dangers of financial crisis are acute when it comes to foreign currency dealings. The State Bank for Foreign Trade, Vneshekonombank, which used to enjoy a monopoly on foreign currency dealings, is effectively bankrupt. Indeed, the central banking authorities' dislike of Menatep is prompted partly by their desire to gain control over the hard currency needed to repay the more than $80 billion Soviet debt.

It is an open secret that Soviet state enterprises that earn hard currency from exports or other business have been doing everything they can to keep their money away from the central bank. Although it remains technically illegal for enterprises here to have foreign accounts, many including government-owned operations openly ask foreign clients to pay into such accounts.

"Many, many are engaged in this," says Menatep public relations director Vladislav Surkov. The independent news agency Interfax, for example, recently asked its foreign subscribers to pay their bills through Menatep's account in Bank of America.

All sorts of transactions take place, including offers to trade rubles for dollars at rates well above official ones. Mr. Surkov describes a typical Western banker buying rubles by creating a joint venture with a Soviet partner, having the rubles transferred to its account and placing dollars in a foreign account for the Soviet partner. The Westerner buys rubles at a favorable set rate, and the "Soviets acquired currency accounts not controlled by Gosbank," he says.

"A . . . lot of hot money has left this country and there are no rules," says the Western banker. He calls Menatep "the number one contributor to hot money in this country."

Menatep Financial Director Platon Lebedev says their banking operations are typical of any Western bank—financing trade contracts, buying and selling foreign currencies, offering investment services. They have correspondent ties to banks such as Bank of America, Citibank and Credit Lyonnais. He describes Riggs National Bank as "our teachers" and says, "their Swiss branch is our second home." Riggs Volmet is given as the locale of their Swiss office, although Volmet's Nicylin refers to them only as "clients."

Managing huge sums

Menatep is soliciting foreign clients for its services. For example, Surkov says they want to persuade Westerners holding rubles "to give us the right to manage these huge sums of money." With hyperinflation, "they are dangling over an abyss." Menatep will act as their trustee, investing the money in "real estate, gold, precious stones, art," which can maintain value.

Such a proposal sounds businesslike, but it is still illegal for foreigners to take such items out of the country or to directly own real estate. So Menatep offers a way around that problem: "The trust company will act as the legal person," says Mr. Lebedev. Surkov goes even further, saying that Menatep will keep the real contract in a Swiss bank to protect the confidentiality of a client. If asked in Moscow about the deal, he says, "we will produce a second contract which is different."

The square-jawed Lebedev is a graduate of the Communist Party's Marxism-Leninism University. But in his sleek, pin-striped suit he now happily grabs the title of "businessman." His model government these days is Switzerland. "I am for . . . a government . . . you cannot see," he says.

Regional Dispute Tests Unity Of Former Soviet Republics

Daniel Sneider

01/02/92

Less than a month after its formation, it is already reasonable to question whether the Commonwealth of Independent States formed on the rubble of the Soviet Union will survive.

The stormy eight-hour session of the leaders of the 11 commonwealth member states on Dec. 30 in Minsk, Byelorussia, yielded little agreement on the issues that really matter—common defense and economic policies. At most the heads of the former Soviet republics managed to postpone decisions, agreeing for example to try again to decide the future of the Soviet armed forces in two months.

But nothing captures the impotence of this new structure more starkly than its failure to take even the slightest step to halt a bloody and widening war between two of its members—Armenia and Azerbaijan.

The people of the two neighboring Caucuses states are already in combat, centering on the Azeri attempt to assert its control over the Armenian-populated autonomous region of Nagorno-Karabakh. As soon as Soviet Interior Ministry forces withdrew last week, Azeri troops escalated their attack, pouring hundreds of rocket and artillery rounds a day onto the regional capital of Stepanakert.

While the leaders were sitting around their table in Minsk, 18 Azeri battalions of 300 men each equipped with tanks and armored personnel carriers, were entering Nagorno-Karabakh near the city of Agadan, according to the independent Nega news agency. Armenian guerrillas with light automatic weapons and few pieces of heavy weaponry fought back fiercely in battles around the capital city.

"The Azeris will launch an offensive and there will be the total liquidation of the Armenian population," predicts Boris Gorev, a photographer for Literaturnaya Gazeta, just back from the battle zone. "The Azeris have more forces; they have a better system of supplies. They can ship in troops by rail and by air. Karabakh is an encircled island inside Azeri territory. Armenia can supply their forces only by two helicopters . . . . It is a nightmare."

Armenia calls for help

The Bolsheviks incorporated mountainous Nagorno-Karabakh into Azerbaijan in 1923, though it lies mere miles from Armenia. The most recent effort to negotiate a solution to the dispute, begun by Russia and Kazakhstan last October, has gone nowhere. The region's elected leadership issued an urgent appeal Dec. 30 for the commonwealth and the international community to stop the Azeri offensive.

The subject was on the agenda at the Minsk meeting, which both Armenian President Levon Ter-Petrosyan and Azeri President Ayaz Mutalibov attended. However, the discussion was postponed on the insistence of the Azeris, according to the Interfax news agency. Azerbaijan, along with Moldavia and the Ukraine, were also reportedly the major opponents of a proposed defense structure that would have placed most Soviet Army ground forces under a continued common command. (They did reaffirm a single command of nuclear forces.)

National sovereignty

The Azeri president and Ukrainian President Leonid Kravchuk have already declared themselves commanders in chief of all the armed forces based on their territories. For the Ukraine this is an issue of national sovereignty and an expression of its rivalry with Russia, the most powerful of the commonwealth members. But for Azerbaijan, it is clearly intended to give them a free hand in Nagorno-Karabakh.

"By forming its own army, Azerbaijan tries to solve the problem of Nagorno-Karabakh by liquidation and forced deportation of the Armenian population," stated a letter from 18 members of the Russian Academy of Sciences addressed to Russian President Boris Yeltsin and the commonwealth leadership.

"The policy of genocide conducted by one of the members of the commonwealth puts into question the prestige of this commonwealth and the confidence of the world public in it," they said, according to Nega.

The apparent abdication of shared responsibility is symptomatic of relations among members of the new commonwealth. They had agreed to form common economic policies, particularly when it comes to reforming the state-run Soviet economy into a market system and to maintaining a common currency and monetary system. But in practice, as the Minsk meeting demonstrated, each state is taking care of its own.

The Russians have decided that their only hope lies in rapid reform, and they are not ready to allow the more cautious approach of the Ukraine and others to slow them down.

Price liberalization begins as scheduled on Jan. 2, and with it the Russian government announced new decrees to escalate the pace of privatization of farm land, of retail shops and other services, and of industry.

"We move to the market by a somewhat different path," Mr. Kravchuk told reporters at the close of the Minsk meeting. Complaining that Russia has reneged on a promise to provide enough cash from the Russian-controlled printing presses to handle the effect of freeing prices and raising wages, the Ukrainians will try to close off their market by issuing part of salaries in the form of coupons. State stores will sell goods only for such coupons in an effort to stop non-Ukrainians from buying foodstuffs that are cheaper and more available there. Byelorussia is planning a similar approach.

Only one common bond

The only thing seemingly holding the commonwealth together is its members' inability to rid themselves of the legacy of the Soviet Union. "Russia must not be our big brother," a Kazakh spokesman said, "but there is no way around a single economy."

Eastern Europe Struggles to Shed Vestiges of Soviet Dominance

Peter Grier

01/07/92

They used to be dismissed as "puppet states," countries with no mind of their own. Now, in a great irony of history, it is the puppeteer that has exited the world stage, while the ex-Soviet "puppets" of Central and Eastern Europe struggle toward democracy and the promised prosperity of free-market economies.

So far, their road hasn't been an easy one. To varying degrees, all the remaining ex-East Bloc nations have been troubled by nagging political instability. Much of the region remains troubled by high unemployment and paralyzed industrial production.

The region's high hopes of 1989 and '90 have faded. "It will take a full generation before even the Central European nations can be considered secure, stable democracies," predicted J. Brian Atwood, head of the National Democratic Institute for International Affairs, in a recent speech.

Yet general dissatisfaction with the state of affairs hasn't translated into any nostalgia for the old days of communism. Public-opinion polls show multiparty politics and market economies still have strong support.

By large margins, the people of Eastern Europe "express their overwhelming desire to move forward," said Mr. Atwood.

That doesn't mean they're enjoying the transition. Poland, where political reform began earliest and prices were unfrozen two years ago, is an example.

Voters are apathetic in the country many credit with having sparked the collapse of communism in all its neighbors. Only 42 percent of those eligible cast ballots in last fall's general election.

The Polish parliament is a fractured body of many small parties. With stable coalitions all but impossible, power has been flowing inevitably to the executive—President Lech Walesa.

Even as he feuds with his latest nominee for prime minister, Jan Olszewski, Mr. Walesa is pressing for constitutional changes that would, in effect, allow him to go over a prime minister's head, pick a cabinet himself, and let it rule by decree. In a time of troubles Poland needs decisive government to stick with reforms, he argues.

"Poland may well be an indicator of what may happen in other countries," says Wolfgang Reinicke, a Brookings Institution European specialist.

Bulgaria, for instance, has progressed toward democracy faster than many Western analysts predicted it would. Yet the Bulgarian parliament is largely split between the old Communists, reborn as the Socialist Party, and Union of Democratic Forces reformers. The balance of power is held by a small party that represents ethnic Turks—not a happy situation in a country where anti-Turkish sentiment persists.

In Romania, a split along conservative and reformist lines threatens to divide the ruling National Salvation Front. Miners, fed up with skyrocketing prices and the turmoil of free market reforms, rioted in Bucharest last fall. General elections are still expected in the spring.

Even in Hungary and Czechoslovakia, executives are moving to increase their powers in the face of disillusion. Hungarian Prime Minister Jozsef Antall last month summarily dismissed a popular central bank president, whose sin apparently was to call for more open government. Czech President Vaclev Havel is trying to force through a referendum on Slovakian independence in the belief it will actually help keep his country from splitting in two.

All this turmoil is taking place in the context of perhaps greater turmoil over borders to the east.

The emergence of the Ukraine as an independent nation could reignite historic Polish-Ukrainian tensions. The former Soviet republic of Moldavia might ask for reunification with Romania.

"The changes in the former Soviet Union are far from being just a neutral question for these countries," says Mihaly Simai, a Hungarian economist studying at the United States Institute for Peace.

And while attention focuses on the dire economic plight of former Soviet citizens, things won't be much better in many parts of the old Soviet eastern empire this winter. Across the nations of the region, living standards have fallen by 20 to 50 percent, as production at big state-owned industries stops or stagnates and unemployment skyrockets.

Some Western analysts are pessimistic about further economic shocks. "I think it will get worse before it gets better," says Mr. Reinicke.

Others say the corner has been turned. In Poland, privately owned industry is growing at a 20 percent annual clip, according to the World Bank. Throughout the more-advanced nations of Central Europe lines have disappeared and goods have flooded shops, expensive as they are.

Continued integration of Central and Eastern European nations into Western economic institutions such as the European Community and the International Monetary Fund could be their best hope.

Russian Orthodox Devotees Celebrate First Christmas Since Bolshevik Revolution

Daniel Sneider

01/08/92

A brief but intense snow storm sweeps across Moscow the evening of Jan. 6, covering the quiet streets with a clean white blanket. Throughout the city, people in their winter coats and high boots walk carefully along the frozen sidewalks. It is Christmas Eve in Russia, celebrated by the Russian Orthodox Church on Jan. 7, according to the prerevolutionary Julian calender.

This is the first Christmas since the fall of the Soviet state, after the red flag was hauled down from the Kremlin ramparts.

Revolution Day, Nov. 7, the day to celebrate the Bolshevik seizure of power, is no longer on the official list of holidays in Russia. But Christmas is, by decree, once again a state holiday. The worship of Jesus, not Lenin, now has the imprimatur of the restored Russian state.

The archbishop of Moscow celebrates the Christmas liturgy at one of the most beautiful religious structures in Moscow, the Novodevichi Convent (New Convent of the Maidens).

The fairy tale cluster of churches, towers, and gate houses, surrounded by fortress walls, built in the 16th and 17th centuries and set above a duck pond and park along the Moscow River, is a favorite subject for Moscow painters.

The Christmas Eve service takes place in the Cathedral of Dormition, a rectangular hall which used to serve as the dining hall for the nuns. Icons, sacred paintings, are hung along its windowed walls, illuminated by the thin orange candles lit by devotees. The dimly lit, arched ceiling is covered with frescos of the life of Christ Jesus, leading to a set of three arched entries. Beyond, lies the iconostasis, the traditional Orthodox wall of icons, here richly framed by gold painted decorations and set in a sky blue background. At the center of the iconostasis stands the Czar's Gate, the doorway into the altar used only by the priest.

For Christmas, fresh cut fir trees and boughs surround the doors and archways. A carpet is rolled to the doorway of the cathedral hall, with a small circular carpet with a Russian eagle on it set at the entry. Priests in white cloaks hold long tapers and swing the kadila which spread vapors of sweet burning incense.

The parishioners stand along the length of the carpet. The stalwarts of Orthodoxy during the Communist era, the babushki (grandmothers), gather in their sturdy wool coats, kerchiefs wrapped tightly around their heads. But no longer are they the primary attendees at churches across Russia.

Here and elsewhere the young have made their appearance in large numbers: a young man in jeans and a jean jacket on one side of the carpet; opposite, a girl in beige slacks with a Mickey Mouse patch on her knee; and a military cadet in his long Army greatcoat.

At 10 p.m., Metropolitan Juvinali of Krytitskoye and Kolomna, as the head of the archdiocese of Moscow is traditionally titled, enters. The deacon sings out, answered by the twin choruses that stand at each corner of the iconostasis.

The chorus, joined by the parishoners, sing the traditional hymn of exhaltation "Velichaniye" ("Glory") as the Gospels in their brass decorative cover are carried from the altar to the center of the church.

The metropolitan reads from the Gospels in Church Slavonic, the bookish language of the church., created by two Greek-Bulgarian monks in the 8th and 9th centuries.

The service, which is performed by a bishop according to Orthodox tradition, is more elaborate than usual. It incorporates hymns and prayers in Greek, the language of the first bishops who brought Christianity to the Kievan Rus state from Constantinople in the 10th century.

The service goes through the night, accompanied constantly by the sometimes lilting, sometimes solemn voices of the chorus.

An old man and woman weave through the growing crowd with collection plates soon piled high with ruble notes bearing the face of Lenin.

Outside, the sky has cleared, bright stars leaping out of the night. The gold onion dome of the Smolensk Cathedral, turned into a museum by the Bolsheviks, nestles gleaming among smaller gray cupolas lightly dusted with snow.

Republics' Cash Reserves Run Dry

Daniel Sneider

01/16/92

The hard currency coffers of the former Soviet republics are essentially empty, a senior Russian official revealed here, making it practically necessary to postpone payments on the massive foreign debt of the former Soviet Union.

"The level of reserves is zero," said Pyotr Aven, chairman of the Russian Committee on Foreign Economic Relations.

On Tuesday officials from the Vneshekonombank, the former Soviet Bank for Foreign Economic Affairs which is jointly responsible for repaying the Soviet debt, met with representatives of Western banks in Frankfurt. Mr. Aven denied reports that they would seek a moratorium on interest payments on their debt, on top of the agreement already reached last December to delay repayment of the principal.

But, the senior official added, "there will be some delays on some interest payments in the next several weeks." In the meantime, he said, "we want the West to avoid any decisive actions."

Mr. Aven, one of the small group of young economists who are masterminding the radical Russian reform policies, cited two basic reasons behind what he called "an extremely sharp liquidity crisis." The first is the refusal of the other former Soviet republics to honor an agreement to collectively pay off the debt. Russia is now providing 85 percent of the Vneshekonombank's hard currency revenues, though under the agreement it is responsible for only 61 percent of the debt.

The second factor is massive capital flight out of the country and out of the bank that had previously held a monopoly over all foreign currency dealings in the Soviet Union. Both Soviet enterprises that earned hard currencies from exports and foreign firms doing business here were previously compelled to keep their accounts in that bank.

But now some 200 banks here have the right to deal in foreign currencies and enterprises are opening accounts overseas. Russian enterprises are moving their money rapidly out of the bank because their deposits are being used to service the former Soviet debt, Aven acknowledged. He says that $5.4 billion was taken to pay the debt from accounts of Soviet enterprises.

Nor are such measures confined to Russia. According to Reuters, the government of Belarus on Tuesday announced the "temporary confiscation" of 50 percent of the hard currency bank accounts of their republic's enterprises to pay for grain imports. The government promised to eventually return the money.

AVEN said the Russian government will repay the enterprises, but it could be in the form of state bonds or shares in a new bank to be created out of the division of the Vneshekonombank into several parts—one to continue managing the debt, another to be taken over by the Russian Bank for Foreign Trade, and a new commercial bank.

The government hopes to replenish its reserves by implementing a new system of taxes on earnings, replacing a more onerous policy followed by the former Soviet government. Under the new plan, raw materials exporters must sell 40 percent of their hard currency to the government for rubles at a rate which is half of the market rate. This covers oil, gas, and mineral exports that make up about 70 percent of Russia's exports. All the rest, including machinery exporters, will have to sell only 10 percent of hard currency revenues, and at full market rates.

Judging from past behavior, however, many Russian enterprises will try to evade such forced sales by keeping or sending their money overseas. At least $6 billion left the country during the past year in illegal capital flight, Aven said. Under new regulations, the government insists that all hard currency revenues must come back to the country within two to three months. A new agency is to be created to control those flows, Aven said.

Ultimately the best hope for stopping capital flight and ensuring that Russia and the other republics can repay the estimated $70 billion Soviet debt is the success of the current reform policies. Raging inflation following price liberalization at the start of this year makes holding the ruble an unattractive position. The government hopes its budget austerity and free-market policies will help to restore value to the ruble.

"If you stabilize, money will come back," Aven said.

Donor States Assess Needs Of Ex-Soviet Republics

Amy Kaslow

01/24/92

After promising fresh money and setting new priorities for assistance, delegates to this week's international conference on aid to the former Soviet republics pledged to reconvene in Europe this spring.

The conference in Washington considered the urgent, short-term needs of the beleaguered republics, including food, housing, medicine, and energy. When the donors meet again—in Lisbon this May—they will assess more formidable problems of transforming one lumbering communist bloc into 12 vibrant, market-driven economies.

By meeting in Lisbon, the international community recognizes the central role of the European Community (EC) in tackling the most pressing of world concerns. Part of the annual revolving leadership among the EC's 12 member-countries, Portugal assumed the presidency in January and made Lisbon the current capital of the 12-nation community.

Portuguese Foreign Minister Joao Deus Pinheiro, who serves as the president of the EC's ministerial council, will host the May meeting. Unlike the conference this week, the follow-up in Portugal will invite the 12 former Soviet republics to attend.

Mr. Pinheiro explains that the second conference is scheduled four months from now to give the World Bank, the International Monetary Fund (IMF), and the Organization for Economic Cooperation and Development time to prepare economic studies of the 12 republics. IMF director Michel Camdessus will provide assessments of Russia, Ukraine, Belarus, and Moldova by the end of April, says Pinheiro.

The donors' conference also looks to the World Bank and the IMF—the two most important financial organizations that will steer the republics toward macro-economic reforms—to coordinate global assistance in several failing sectors: health care, energy, and transportation.

According to one senior international banking official, the World Bank and the IMF, in turn, hope the international aid conference will "help shore up the reform process." He says that Russia's Jan. 1 move to liberalize prices, which sent them spiraling, also sent shock waves through Russian consumers.

"When you undertake a policy like price reforms, you want to put something on the shelves," says the banking official, who is helping to prepare the economic reports on the republics. Donors, he says, must address food shortages quickly, lest the nascent reforms lose all credibility. "If the reforms fail in the largest successor state, you will have autarky throughout the former Soviet republics," he warns.

The former Soviet Union's annual food import bill averages between $15 billion to $20 billion, he says. The 12 republics waste some 30 percent of their agricultural production due to poor farming, storage, and distribution. As the economy disintegrates further, import needs soar and the ability to pay for them plummets. "All 12 republics must develop the capacity to prioritize their needs for aid and their capacity to distribute it," says the banker.

By the end of 1992, the republics are expected to complete the steps necessary to apply for membership in the IMF and the World Bank. The bank is already setting aside between $2 billion and $3 billion to assist in the July 1992 through July 1993 period.

While that sum is a sizable portion of World Bank annual lending, it pales in comparison with the republics' needs. "No single institution can handle all the needs of the former Soviet Union," says Pinheiro. Indeed, Russia alone is asking for $6 billion in the near term.

Germany is one country that has felt the burden of assistance to the former Soviet empire. The single largest donor to the Soviet central government, Bonn has balked at US requests for more burden-sharing. Sensitive to Germany's resentment, the US placed Germany at the head of the conference table this week. Washington also pledged another $600 million in food credits to the republics.

"What matters is what we get done, not who gets the credit for it," conference host US Secretary of State James Baker III told scores of delegates on Wednesday.

Stressing that he speaks for 12 of the 47 foreign ministers who were at the table, Pinheiro smoothed over differences that threatened to overshadow cooperative efforts. Referring to the post-World War II Marshall Plan, US troops in Western Europe, and high US military spending, he says: "For the last 50 years the US has done a great deal in Europe. That sentiment prevails today."

The collapse of communism, Pinheiro says, "is the result of a victory of an effort after 50 years. Do not disqualify what the US has done. Think of the effort that's been made in financial and technical terms. And look at what the US is doing now, in working to disassemble nuclear capacities." The Portuguese foreign minister says he is not worried about US budgetary constraints and a lingering recession—although they promise to make it difficult for the Bush administration to initiate and gain congressional approval for large increases in US donations to the republics. "Those who can afford to, will pay more. Thank God Europe is in good shape, economically, to help. So is Japan. So are the [Persian] Gulf states."

Clearly proud of the West's achievements in curbing communism, and the ability of Europe, Japan, and the US to assist in the republics' economic recovery, Pinheiro adds a cautionary note: "They can count on us, so long as we can count on them, so long as they stop making nonsensical investments in their military sector."

The former Soviet military is still a threat, he says—especially if the West fails to provide financial help to house and resettle the now-displaced and disgruntled armed forces.

Index